Limited Classical Reprint Library

A COMMENTARY ON
THE PSALMS

BY

DAVID DICKSON

1583-1662

ONE TIME PROFESSOR OF
DIVINITY AT EDINBURGH

VOL. I

Klock & Klock Christian Publishers
2527 GIRARD AVE. N.
MINNEAPOLIS, MINNESOTA 55411

Originally published in London, 1655
Reprinted in 2 volumes, Glasgow, 1834

Copy from
Central Baptist Theological Seminary
Minneapolis, Minnesota

ISBN: Set — 0-86524-017-5

Published by Klock & Klock in the U.S.A.
1980 Reprint

FOREWORD

The republication of David Dickson's *Commentary on the Psalms* will be welcomed by those who have become acquainted with the writings of this stalwart Scott. Even though his life, ministry and writings are removed by centuries from us (c. 1583-1663), there exists a vibrancy of faith and an honesty of careful Biblical exposition refreshing to the twentieth century student of the Psalms. It is remarkable to find a man so shortly removed from the profound theological influence of the Roman Church who carefully maintains the Biblical distinction made between Israel and the Church. Similarly, Dickson discerned the error of those in his day who counted church membership or baptism as the basis for salvation. Dickson's comments on Psalm 15 clearly reveal his stand on faith as the means of salvation:

"Who shall ascend into the hill of the Lord? and who shall stand in his holy place?" He compareth the invisible church to a *hill* or *mountain*, and *the holy place*, because God's true church indeed for firmness, durableness, dignity above all other incorporations, and spiritual sublimity, is like a *hill* above the plain, lifted up above all the world, a holy society, wherein God delighteth to dwell. Not every one who is a member of the visible church, but only true converts, who make up the invisible church, have the honor and happiness of ascending unto the spiritual use, end, meaning, and profit of the ordinances of God in his church, and of keeping constant communion with God in heaven, represented by standing in the holy place. Therefore, for stirring up of outward professors of religion, to examine themselves, lest they be mistaken and so perish, the question is here made to God to show *who shall ascend to his hill, and who shall stand in his holy place.*

Dickson displays respect and appreciation for the messianic Psalms. His comments on Psalm 22:22 exemplify his understanding of the prophetic element and the difficult problem of its relationship to the historical setting of David the writer:

"I will declare thy name unto my brethren: In the midst of the congregation I will praise thee." After the conflict, the victory and the outgate by way of thanksgiving is set down, to the end of the psalm: wherein David's part is but a little shadow, and is swallowed up here in Christ's glory, shining in the fruits of his passion and resurrection. Learn from David's part, that delivery forseen by faith, worketh in some sort the effects of the delivery past in effect; to wit, quietness, peace, joy and thanksgiving as here is to be seen. From Christ's part promising and prophesying of the fruits of his death and resurrection, learn 1. Christ, though He be God Almighty, yet by reason of His incarnation for the redeemed's sake, He is not ashamed to call them brethren. 2. The preaching of the gospel of Christ's satisfaction for our sins by death, and of His resurrection for our justification, is matter of great praise to God and comfort to the redeemed: "I will declare," saith Christ, "thy name to my brethren."

David Dickson was a prominent Scottish theologian. He left the position of professor of philosophy at Glasgow University (where he had graduated) to assume the pastorate of the Ayrshire parish of Irvine. During his twenty-three years of ministry there, he played a significant part in the abolition of the episcopacy from Scotland. In his later years he returned to Glasgow University to fill the chair of divinity. After ten years he accepted the chair of divinity of Edinburgh University but was forced to leave this position after the restoration of Charles II to the throne.

Dickson's *Explications of the Psalms*, as he calls his commentary, is one of the earlier commentaries written on the text of the King James Version which had been published only a few decades earlier. His comments will give the student of doctrine a remarkable insight into the pulpit ministry of the Scottish church in the sixteenth and seventeenth centuries. Furthermore, it is a work that is rich in homiletical value to the man seeking help in arranging and preaching the truths of the book of Psalms for a contemporary congregation. The author arranges the lessons of the Psalms well. He demonstrates the noteworthy desire for the maturity of his reader, presenting lessons of his text so as to produce that end.

Bernard E. Northrup, Th.D.
Director of Graduate Studies
Central Baptist Seminary
Minneapolis, Minnesota

DEDICATION TO THE FIRST VOLUME.*

TO

THE TRULY HONOURABLE AND RELIGIOUS LADIES,

MY LADY MARCHIONESS OF ARGYLE,

AND

MY LADY ANN CAMPBELL,

HER ELDEST DAUGHTER,

GRACE AND PEACE THROUGH JESUS CHRIST.

IT is the good and wise way of God, in matters concerning this temporal life, to make manifest his bounty and kindness to all men, how unkind and wicked soever they be, and not leave himself without a witness against complainers; but in the matters of salvation, and things which belong to eternal life, he useth not to extend his special love so largely; for even the external means of saving knowledge are bestowed upon few nations and people, in comparison to the whole race of mankind. " He sheweth his word unto Jacob, and his statutes and his judgments unto Israel. He hath not dealt so with any nation, and *as for his* judgments they have not known them." And though the people be few to whom the offer of salvation is made, in comparison of the rest of the world; yet are they many in com-

---

* The following work was originally published, at different times, in three volumes, each containing a commentary on Fifty Psalms, with a Preface and Dedication—but as there does not appear any necessity for observing the same division, now that it is published collectively, all the Dedications and Prefaces are here printed together.

parison to those who find grace in the eyes of the Lord, to accept the offer of grace tendered unto them in Christ Jesus; " for many are called, but few chosen." And albeit it be true, that God's calling and election have place in all ranks and estates of persons, higher and lower, learned and unlearned, rich and poor; yet this grace stretcheth itself to many more of the meaner sort of the people, than of the wise, wealthy, and honourable in the world. " Ye see your calling, brethren, how that not many wise men after the flesh, not many mighty, not many noble are called." Therefore, so much the greater is the favour of God, which your souls have found, most honourable, that you are made some of those few, yea, after so comfortable a manner, that the daughter finding herself led by her mother's hand, in her tender youth unto Christ the Saviour, looketh on her as her mother twice; and the mother, having power and place to draw the veil of her daughter's virginal modesty, retiredness, and prudence, which concealeth much of the lustre of her accomplishments from the sight of others who stand at a greater distance, looketh upon her notable endowments and growing graces, as more than a recompense of all the pains sustained in bringing forth, and bestowed upon educating such a plant; a plant so well fitted for that which is most desirable in earth and heaven. And thus much I have reason to say, not only because it is my part, as I have occasion, to stir up parents to study to have their children timously engaged to the Lord, in hope to have the more early and abundant comfort by them in their own time; but also because I have been witness of the Christian behaviour of both your ladyships, in no small trial of your faith and patience by the troubles of the times, both public and private, for a number of years together; which experience hath now good use, to fit and prepare your honours for what further exercise true believers may be subject unto in this life, and for what this present time calleth unto all to be prepared for. As this condition is in all ages incident to the godly, it should not be looked upon, in our time, as some strange thing which has befallen us; for it is the Lord's ordinary way of dealing with his children, by changes of their condition, outward and inward, by vicissitudes, of straits and outgates, by interchange of crosses and comforts, and by much variety of several conditions, powerfully to train, advance, and settle their faith, and to increase the growth of all graces accompanying salvation in them; for what we cannot conceive at one lesson, because we are dull, he teacheth us by parts, in many and sundry instructions, all tending to bring us to a further measure of humiliation and self-denial, on the one hand, and of submission unto God and faith in Christ, on the other. And this way of God is made plain by the practice of the saints, and is laid open before us in the book of Psalms; whereof, at this time, I have only taken a third part to handle by way of essay, thereby to find the advice of judicious brethren, how to satisfy and edify the reader more in what remains to be handled, if God be pleased to give further employment and assistance in this service; and this which here is offered to the edification of the Lord's people, I have put forth under your honours' names, because of your constant affection to the study of the Scriptures, and respect to all the messengers of truth, and to me for the truth's cause, for which I will still remain,

Your honours' much obliged servant in the gospel,

DAVID DICKSON.

PREFACE TO THE FIRST VOLUME.

CHRISTIAN READER,

In this Essay on the Psalms, as in other like pieces, on some other books of Scripture, sent forth to the world from me, a part of my design is still the same, that hereby I may try, if it may be the Lord's will, to stir up some more able instruments to lay open briefly, in this mould, or any other they please better, the chief doctrines treasured up in the store-house of holy Scripture, whereby the Lord's people may be solidly informed in the knowledge, and established in the faith of true religion, by the most near and immediate way of drawing their light from the fountain of the Lord's own word : for this were a means, as I humbly conceive, to cut off many needless disputes wherewith the world is filled; a means to refute many errors which the ignorance of Scripture and of the power of God hath bred and fostered in the Christian church; a means to prevent many mistakes wherein well-meaning zeal ofttimes falleth, for lack of a brief introduction into the true sense and intent of places mistaken.   And I am not altogether out of hope, that the Lord shall hearken to my desire, and set some of his servants to work, ere it be long, to entertain this motion, and to take a share also in the task.   Meantime, I pray let my aim and endeavour be acceptable unto thee, and do not take exception that so much is left unsaid upon such preg- nant passages of Scripture as I go through briefly, and that so much good matter is hinted at, and past by so quickly, and sometimes so abruptly; nor that the deductions of sundry doctrines from the ground pointed at in the text, are ofttimes not so convincingly cleared as you would.   But take this consideration along with thee, that any longer insisting, either in explication of the grounds of the doctrines pointed at in the text, or in amplification of the doctrines deduced from the grounds, would have marred much the intended brevity of the mould, wherewith both the learned, and such as have less leisure to read longer discourses, possibly will be well pleased ; mainly for this cause, that they are not much taken off their studies, or their other necessary employments, by this manner of writing.   Remember also, that charitable censurers will perhaps be content when they perceive, that in this plainness and brevity, every reader shall quickly meet with good matter of meditation at least, whereby the smallest grains of sound truth, sown by this means among readers, may by God's blessing get root, watering, and increase in a good and honest heart : which blessing, that it may be very large, shall be the hearty prayer of,

Thy servant in the work of the gospel,

DAVID DICKSON.

DEDICATION TO THE SECOND VOLUME.

———

TO THE RIGHT HONOURABLE

THE EARL OF EGLINTON,

MERCY AND PEACE THROUGH JESUS CHRIST.

My Right Noble Lord,

THE reason of my sending forth this piece under your lordship's name, is, that by this means I may pay home, before I die, the old debt which I owe to your lordship, and to your whole noble family, for countenancing and encouraging me openly in my ministry, all the while that I was in Irvine, near your lordship, full twenty years.

And the reason why I confess my debt now, and go about to discharge some part of it, at this time of your lordship's restraint in England, is, because when I call to mind the time of my restraint about some thirty years ago, (when the high commission court of prelates procured my confinement within a little village in the north, beyond Aberdeen, because I could not give them satisfaction by receiving the yoke of some popish ceremonies, imposed then upon the ministry,) I cannot forget how comfortable your lordship was to me then, and what pains and travel you endured, summer and winter, without wearying, until they who at that time had power to loose me from my confinement, being made sensible, some of them of the iniquity, and all of them of the inexpedience of keeping me in bonds, restored me to the free and full use of my ministry. Wherefore I esteem it a part of due gratitude, to do what in me lieth, to be comfortable to your lordship in this your present condition; and heartily pray to God, that your exercise and trouble may prove a means of your happiness. It is true, indeed, that happiness without these means were to be wished, if so it were God's pleasure; but unto God only (in whose hands alone it is to make men blessed, and in whose friendship and favour only, through Christ, men are really blessed,) it belongeth, as to choose the man to whom, so also to choose the means whereby, and the manner how, he will communicate the right and possession of true blessedness. If happiness were at men's wish and carving, no man would choose God for his chief good, nor God's way to bring his felicity about; for the multitude of men are still saying, " Who will shew us any good ?"

The good which God doth show unto them, and the way how, by reconciliation with himself and walking humbly and uprightly before him, they may have God to be their rich reward, is not the thing they love to have ; but corn, and wine, and oil, and whatsoever may best please their fleshly fancy, are their desire.   And of this the Lord complaineth, " My people," saith he, " would not hearken to my voice, and Israel would none of me."   And what was it which they preferred unto God ?   They loved to have their own will in this world, whatsoever should befall them after death; they loved rather to have their own earthly desires satisfied, than to have the friendship of God : and their choice was given unto them to their own destruction.   " So," saith the Lord, " I gave them over to their own heart's lust, and they walked in the counsel of their own heart."   Few, when they look upon the course which the world runneth after, yea, very few, prefer the fellowship of God reconciled to them in Christ, before riches, honour, and sensual pleasure : for " Who will shew us any good ?" is that which many say.   But, " Lord, lift thou up the light of thy countenance upon us," is the petition of the few opposed to the multitude ; and even those few godly would wish to go to heaven with ease, and to be free from trouble in their journey, if it were the Lord's will, as we may see in the prayer of Jabez, " who called on the God of Israel, saying, Oh that thou wouldest bless me indeed, and enlarge my coast, and that thine hand might be with me, and that thou wouldest keep me from evil, that it might never grieve me."   But our loving and wise God, who knoweth perfectly what is fittest

for every man, crosseth and correcteth those natural desires
of his children. And howsoever he will now and then possibly grant the prayer of Jabez to some of his people, yet he
hath appointed this to be the ordinary road-way to heaven,
which the apostle pointeth thus forth to us; " we must
through much tribulation enter into the kingdom of God."

And this course of carrying God's children through many
afflictions, no ways hindereth their happiness; for how
many soever their crosses be, yet this holdeth always fast,
" Blessed is the man whom thou choosest, and causest to
approach unto thee." If, therefore, by plurality of chastisements, the Lord shall draw, and drive them to seek remission
of sins and reconciliation with himself, and the renewed
sense thereof through Christ, and shall by the rod hedge
them within the way of walking with him in a friendly
communion : they lose nothing except their lusts, and gain
eternal blessedness. And certainly, there are so many relics
of natural corruption, such strong inclinations unto sin, so
many actual outbreakings, and gross transgressions to be
found in the most precious saints, that there is no wonder
the Lord should visit their trespasses with the rod, and their
iniquity with stripes ; but all the wonder is, that he will not
take his loving-kindness utterly from them. There is also
so great need of loosing their affections from what seemeth
love-worthy in this world ; so great need of raising the hearts
of the heirs of salvation unto the seeking of a kingdom
which cannot be shaken, and of a crown incorruptible ; as
all reason doth call for the mixture of troubles with earthly
comforts, lest the sweetness of temporary vanities should
prove unto them poisonable. Moreover, the experience of
the saints set down in Scripture, and especially in the
Psalms, maketh it manifest, that by the variety of outward
and inward troubles, the faith of God's children hath
been tried, and trained to further strength. Their love,
hope, and patience, and all other spiritual graces in them
have been so fostered and augmented, that they have been
made, joyfully and thankfully, to subscribe this truth, " Blessed is the man whom thou chastenest, O Lord, and teachest
him out of thy law." This is the language of the Lord's

present dispensation towards his people, and the lesson which his providence recommendeth to us all, that we may learn it to our good : whereunto if this piece shall contribute any thing for the edifying of those who shall be pleased to read it, and in special, if it shall be acceptable to your Lordship, this shall do much more than recompense the labour of

Your lordship's obliged servant in the gospel,

DAVID DICKSON.

PREFACE TO THE SECOND VOLUME.

CHRISTIAN READER,

THE acceptance which the former fifty psalms have found, doth give me encouragement sufficient to offer these other fifty to thy view also, and to promise the last fifty so soon as the Lord shall enable me. I am still sparing of thy time, and do strive to point forth, not all the doctrines which may be deduced from the words; but so many only as, being joined together and compared with the text, may give unto thee both the sense and the use thereof. It is not possible to express grave purposes sufficiently without a volume, nor to open mysteries in few words unto thy satisfaction, who canst not choose but wish to have more of the purpose, where-of thou lovest to hear much, and findest but a little of it hinted at. No sort of writing, except that of the Scripture, hath all perfections : but this advantage thou hast by this mould, thou shalt not read long till thou meet with matter worthy of thy meditation ; and whensoever thou meetest with a word spoken in season, or fit for thy condition, thou mayst close thy reading for the time, without losing any long dis-course, and feed upon what thou hast found till it be digested, and then return when thou wilt, and seek for as much as may be another morsel. For the reading of many diverse doctrines without some interlaced meditation, is like eating of marrow without bread, and cannot but cloy thee for the

time, or give thee a surfeit of wholesome food : which evil,
if it befall thee, may be helped for after time by short ejacu-
lations of a word of prayer whilst thou are reading, according
as the purpose calleth thee to seek the Lord's blessing unto
that which thou readest; whose presence that thou mayst
find comfortable, is the prayer of

Thy servant in the gospel,
DAVID DICKSON.

DEDICATION TO THE THIRD VOLUME.

TO THE RIGHT HONOURABLE

THE EARL OF CASSILS,

GRACE AND PEACE THROUGH CHRIST JESUS.

My Right Noble Lord,

One of the special motives of my resolution to follow
this work in parcels, was the apparent hazard, that if, in this
time of trouble and of my old age, I should have delayed to
put forth some part of it till all had been ready, the whole
might have been miscarried or marred, by some passage of
providence which might have befallen me. But seeing it
hath pleased the Lord to spare my life, and my health, and
my liberty in his service, as I wanted not the example of
grave authors before me to divide the whole book of the
Psalms into three parts, and to dedicate every part to different persons; so I judged it good thrift, to take occasion
thereby to testify my bounden duty and respect, to so many
of the noble friends of Zion as I could overtake ; and that
with a mind to honour all the rest, who have put their
shoulder to the work of settling religion and the kingdom
of Christ among us : whose labours, albeit they should have

no other fruit in our time, than the right stating of the question between us and all adversaries of the true doctrine, worship, and discipline of Christ's house, as it is set down in the Confession of Faith, in the Directory for Public Worship, and in the Rules of Government of Christ's Church, drawn forth from scripture warrant; yet even that much is worth all the expense of whatsoever is bestowed, by any or all the Lord's worthies, upon religion. And howsoever the Lord claimeth, and calleth for, the whole glory of this work to himself alone, by staining the pride of the glory of all instruments whereof he hath made use about it, as now appeareth, lest the glory due to himself, in all and every one of the passages of promoting the same, should be eclipsed; yet will he never utterly reject this service, nor disallow the upright endeavours of his servants therein; but will in his own time and way, both advance it, and bear witness to his faithful servants in and about it, wheresoever he hath a mind to keep house, or to reign as king in Zion. Yea, he will also make it known to the world, that, as on the one hand he will not want a visible kingdom in the world, though not of this world; so, on the other hand, his kingdom shall be so far from hindering the civil government of magistrates, where it hath place, that, on the contrary, it shall be a chief prop and pillar of every kingdom where it is received.

In this number of upright promoters of the kingdom of Christ, your lordship hath been always looked upon, all the time of our late troubles, as one very eminent: and I, since my first admission into your lordship's acquaintance, have observed your constant care and endeavour, as to know what was the right in difficult questions, as also to hold it fast, according to your power, after you had discovered it. Which, as it may be your lordship's comfort, so is it your commendation, and all men's duty to do the like, especially in this dangerous time, wherein sins practised, and not repented of, are so severely and justly punished by God's giving over the impenitent to the open professing and defending of their unrepented faults: for God in justice and wisdom has suffered the hedges of his vineyard to be broken down, and the holy discipline of his house to be set at nought by all sorts of persons, that every spirit of error, having open way to come in at the breach, he might thereby try and exercise all his people, who stand in covenant with him by profession, and reclaim or punish such as live in error. And no wonder that he should do so : for when there is so little use made of the holy ordinances of religion ; when the Scriptures are either not read, or not esteemed ; when the form of godliness is separated from upright endeavour to feel and show forth the life and power of it ; when the grace of the gospel is turned into wantonness, and men are become so much the more bold to sin, as they hear much of the mercifulness of God ; when every divine truth is either not believed at all, or received only with human and temporary faith ; when Christ is looked upon by many only as a man, and not as God manifested in the flesh, nor as the eternal Son of God, who from everlasting was with God, and was God, co-worker in the creation with the Father and the Spirit ; when Christ is confessed to be Christ, but not employed as mediator, or, as if men had no need of him, not made use of in his offices ; when many cast open their souls unto, and seek after, another spirit than the Spirit of truth, the comforter, the Holy Ghost, who, according to the Scriptures, both wounds and heals the consciences of believers, and sanctifieth the heart and conversation of all them that come to God through Christ,—In this time, I say, when these and many other ungodly practices of men, walking after the imaginations of their own hearts, so abound ; what wonder is it that the Lord hath let loose so many unclean spirits, as no history can show more in so short a time, in any age, or in any place of the world ! By the ranging up and down of these spirits among us, God is about to make manifest the stability and sincerity of the faith of them who are approved, and to take trial of others, in whom such damnable practices, as by the doctrine of devils are now openly defended, will be found unrepented, whether, after they shall hear their ungodly pranks maintained and patronized by some sect-master, heretic, or schismatic, they will abhor such abominable doctrine, and repent their own former misdeeds, which have spoken the language of some of those vile errors ;

or whether they will justify their own faults, as their sect-masters teach them to do, either by despising all the ordinances, and lifting themselves above the same, or by rejecting the commands and cords of the moral law, will loose themselves from the obedience thereof, as if Christ had freed the believer from the command and authority of the law, no less than from the covenant and curse thereof; or by blaspheming the Scripture, will cry down the truth, and the use and power of it; or by calling every truth in question, will exempt themselves from the bonds of all religion; or will walk after the imagination of their own heart, and make their own conceits their oracle, their fancy their faith, and their lusts their God; or will, by opposing one or other of the persons of the Godhead, deny and separate the individual essence of one God in three persons; or by receiving the doctrine of some of those many lesser antichrists which are in the world, will incorporate themselves in the great mystical body of the one antichrist, spoken of in Scripture; or in a word, will, by rejecting the truth, and not receiving it in love, when it is offered, bring in upon themselves strong delusions, and give a powerful possession of themselves to the devil, whereby he may so rule in them, as to make them vent whatsoever hell can devise, to the dishonour of God, and the Christian religion, that all such may be damned, as for their not receiving the truth in love, so also for their taking pleasure in unrighteousness, according as the apostle prophesied should come to pass.

In such a time therefore as this is, wherein the Lord is manifesting who are of God, and who not, who know God, and who do not; who follow the Spirit of truth, and who are led by the spirit of error, and is deciphering them by this infallible mark which the apostle giveth, that the one give a believing and obediential ear to the penmen of holy Scripture, the other do not; what a mercy, yea, what an honour and happiness is it for the Lord's children, to make such use of a settled ministry, which is the great gift of Christ bestowed upon his church, as not to be carried about with every wind of doctrine, not to be led away with the error of the wicked, nor fall from their own steadfastness, but to grow in grace, and in the knowledge of our Lord and Saviour Jesus Christ! Which grace, and honour, and happiness, that it may not only continue with your lordship, but also be granted to all those that love our Lord Jesus Christ in sincerity, is the prayer of

Your lordship's ready servant in the gospel,

DAVID DICKSON.

PREFACE TO THE THIRD VOLUME.

CHRISTIAN READER,

In the two former parts of this work, I have spoken my mind to thee in relation to this Brief Explication of the Psalms: I will not here keep thee up in the entry of this last part, nor say any more unto thee save this, it is our bounden duty to bless Him that inhabiteth the praises of Israel, who will have all the mourners in Zion to be comforted, and who, as he hath prepared in this mountain to all people " a feast of fat things, a feast of wines on the lees, of fat things full of marrow, of wines on the lees well refined," by bestowing Christ and the unsearchable riches of his grace, upon every penitent who fleeth to him for delivery from sin and wrath ; so hath he also prepared to every such soul the excellent songs of Zion, to increase their festival gladness; and for evidencing of his purpose to give unto them everlasting joy, after this life is ended, hath put into their hands, for their comfort in every condition, wherein they can be in this present life and valley of tears, this sweet-smelling bundle of psalms; wherein he hath made his works of mercy and of judgment the pledges of his promises for complete happiness unto them, and also of the utter overthrow and perdition of all their enemies, and hath appointed both mercy and judgment to be the matter, as of their joy, so of his own glory in the church, to be lifted up, as a sacrifice upon the altar

Christ Jesus, by the voice of his people, singing with grace to him, both alone and in company, and making melody in their hearts. Therefore, as in the changes of our own particular private condition, we have liberty to choose for our use such parts of the psalms as speak closest to our present case: so let us be bound in public meetings of the church to join with the congregation in singing every truth uttered by God's Spirit in the psalms, as we are directed by the minister and mouth of the meeting, for glorifying Him who hath done, promised, threatened, and taught whatsoever is therein expressed; remembering that his praises are the pillars of our faith: and that his joy is our strength; and that those calves of our lips are acceptable sacrifices to God through Jesus Christ, in and for whom,

I am thy servant in the work of the gospel,

DAVID DICKSON.

SHORT ACCOUNT

THE LIFE OF THE AUTHOR.

Mr David Dick, or Dickson, was the only son of John Dick, or Dickson, merchant in Glasgow, whose father was an old feuar and possessor of some lands in the barony of Fintry, and parish of St Ninians, called the Kirk of the Muir. His parents were religious persons of considerable substance, and many years married before they had this child, and he was the only one ever they had, as I am informed. As he was a Samuel asked of the Lord, so he was early devoted to him and the ministry; yet afterwards the vow was forgot, till providence by a rod and sore sickness on their son, brought their sins to remembrance; and then he was put to resume his studies which he had left, and at the university of Glasgow he made very great progress in them.

Soon after he had received the degree of Master of Arts, he was admitted regent, or professor of philosophy in that college, where he was very useful in training up the youth in solid learning; and with the learned principal Boyd of Trochridge, the worthy Mr Robert Blair, and other pious members of that learned society, his pains were singularly blessed, in reviving decayed serious piety among the youth, in that declining and corrupted time, a little after the imposing of prelacy upon us.

By a recommendation of the General Assembly not long after our reformation from popery, the regents were only to continue eight years in their profession, after which such as were found qualified, were licensed, and upon calls after trials, admitted to the holy ministry. By this constitution, this church came to be filled with ministers well seen in all the branches of useful learning. Accordingly Mr Dickson was, in 1618, ordained minister to the town of Irvine, where he laboured about twenty-three years.

That very year, the corrupt assembly at Perth agreed to the five notorious articles, palmed upon this church by the king and prelates. Mr Dickson had not much studied these questions, till the articles were imposed by this meeting. Then he closely examined them, and the more he looked into them, the more aversion he found to them; and when some time after by a sore sickness he was brought within view of death and eternity, he gave open testimony of their sinfulness.

When this came to take air, Mr James Law, archbishop of Glasgow, summoned him to appear before the high commission, January 29, 1622. Mr Dickson at his entrance to his ministry at Irvine, had preached upon 2 Cor. v. 11, the first part, " Knowing the terrors of the Lord, we persuade men ;" when at this juncture he apprehended a separation, at least for a time, the Sabbath before his compearance, he chose the next words of that verse, " But we are made manifest unto God." Extraordinary power, and singular movings of affections, accompanied that parting sermon.

According to the summons, Mr Dickson appeared before the commission, the day named. His prudent carriage, the declinature he gave in, the railing of Archbishop Spottiswood thereupon, the sentence of deprivation and confinement to Turref passed upon him, with his Christian speech upon the intimation of it, are to be found in Mr Calderwood's history.

After much intercession with the bishops, and various turns in this affair, narrated by the last named historian, he got liberty to quit Turref, and returned to his longing flock, July, 1623, where his ministerial work was no more interrupted, until he was called to a more important station, as we shall hear.

At Irvine, Mr Dickson's ministry was singularly countenanced of God. Multitudes were convinced and converted ; and few that lived in his day were more honoured to be instruments of conversion, than he. People under exercise and soul concern, came from every place about Irvine and attended upon his sermons, and the most eminent and serious Christians from all corners of the church, came and joined with him at his communions, which were indeed times of refreshing from the presence of the Lord of these amiable institutions: yea, not a few came from distant places, and settled in Irvine, that they might be under the drop of his ministry. Yet he himself used to observe, that the vintage of Irvine was not equal to the gleanings, and not once to be compared to the harvest at Ayr in Mr John Welch's time, when indeed the gospel had wonderful success in conviction, conversion, and confirmation.

Mr Dickson had his week day's sermon upon the Mondays, the market days then at Irvine. Upon the Sabbath evenings, many persons under soul distress, used to resort to his house after sermon, when usually he spent an hour or two in answering their cases, and directing and comforting those who were cast down, in all which he had an extraordinary talent; indeed he had the tongue of the learned, and knew how to speak a word in season to the weary soul. In a large hall he had in his house at Irvine, there would have been, as I am informed by old Christians, several scores of serious Christians waiting for him, when he came from the church. Those, with the people round the town, who came in to the market at Irvine, made the church as throng, if not thronger, on the Mondays, as on the Lord's day, by these week-day sermons. The famous Stewarton sickness was begun about the year 1630, and spread from house to house for many miles in the strath where Stewarton water runs, on both sides of it. Satan indeed endeavoured to bring a reproach upon the serious persons who were at this time under the convincing work of the Spirit, by running some, seemingly under serious concern, to excesses both in time of sermon, and in families. But the Lord enabled Mr Dickson, and other ministers who dealt with them, to act so prudent a part, that Satan's design was much disappointed, and solid serious practical religion flourished mightily in the west of Scotland about this time, under the hardships of prelacy.

About the year 1632, some of our Scots ministers, Mr Robert Blair, Mr John Livingston, &c., settled among the Scots in the north of Ireland, were remarkably owned of the Lord, and their ministry and communions about the Six Mile water, were made useful for reviving religion in the power and practice of it. The Irish prelates, at the instigation of ours, got them removed for a season, much against excellent Bishop Usher's mind. When silenced and come over to Scotland about the year 1638, Mr Dickson employed Messrs Blair, Livingston, and Cunningham, at his communion; for this he was called before the high commission. He soon got rid of this trouble, the prelates' power being now on the decline.

I have some of Mr Dickson's sermons at Irvine taken from his mouth. They are full of solid substantial matter, very scriptural, and in a very familiar style, not low, but extremely strong, plain, and affecting. It is somewhat akin to Mr Rutherford's, in his admirable letters. I have been told by some old ministers, that scarce any body of that time came so near Mr Dickson's style and method in preaching, as the Rev. Mr William Guthrie, minister of Fenwick, who equalled, if not exceeded him here.

As Mr Dickson was singularly useful in his public ministrations, so I could give many instances of his usefulness more privately, both to Christians in answering their perplexing cases of conscience, and students who had their eye to the ministry, while he was at Irvine: his prudent directions, cautions, and encouragements, given them, were extremely useful and beneficial. I could also give examples of his usefulness to his very enemies, and the Lord's making what he spoke to one that robbed him on the road to Edinburgh of a considerable sum of money, the occasion of the poor youth's change of life, and at length of real conversion. The account of which I have from a worthy person, who had it from himself. But there is not room here to enlarge on these things.

It was Mr Dickson who brought the presbytery of Irvine to supplicate the council, 1637, for a suspension of a charge given to ministers to buy and use the service-book. At that time four supplications from different quarters, without any concert in the supplicants, met at the council-house door, to their mutual surprise and encouragement. These were the small beginnings of that happy turn of affairs, that and next years, of which it were to be wished we had fuller and better accounts than yet have been published.

In that great revolution, Mr Dickson bore no small share. He was sent to Aberdeen, with Messrs Henderson and Cant, by the Covenanters, to persuade that city and country about, to join in renewing the land's covenant with the Lord. This brought him to bear a great part in the debates with the learned doctors Forbes, Barron, Sibbald, &c. at Aberdeen, which being in print, I say no more of them.

When the king was prevailed with to allow a free General Assembly at Glasgow, November, 1638, Mr Dickson and Mr Bailey from the presbytery of Irvine, made a great figure there. In all the important matters before that grave meeting, he was very useful, but Mr Dickson signalized himself in a seasonable and prudent speech he had, when his majesty's commissioner threatened to leave the assembly. It is in mine eye, but too long to stand here, and too important and nervous to abridge. In the 11th session, December 5th, he had another most learned discourse against Arminianism, which I also omit.

The reports of the Lord's eminent countenancing Mr Dickson's ministry at Irvine, had, ere this time, spread through all this church; but his eminent prudence, learning, and holy zeal, came to be universally known, especially to ministers, from the part he bore in the assembly at Glasgow: so that he was almost unanimously chosen moderator to the next General Assembly at Edinburgh, August, 1639. Many of his speeches, and instances of his wise management at so critical a juncture, are before me in a MS. account of that assembly. In the 10th session, the city of Glasgow presented a call to him; but partly because of his own aversion, and the vigorous appearances of the earl of Eglinton and his loving people, and mostly from the remarkable usefulness of his ministry in that corner, the General Assembly continued him at Irvine.

But not long after, 1641, he was transported to be professor of divinity in the university of Glasgow, where he did
great services to the church and interests of real religion, by
training up many youths for the holy ministry. Notwithstanding his laborious work amongst them, he preached
every Lord's day forenoon in the high church there; and got
in, and I think, had for his colleague, the learned and
zealous Mr Patrick Gillespie.

In the year 1643, the church laid a very great work on
him, Mr Henderson, and Mr Calderwood, to form the
draught of a directory for public worship, as appears by the
acts of assembly. When the pestilence was raging at Glasgow, 1647, the masters and students of the university removed
to Irvine, upon Mr Dickson's motion. There the holy and
learned Mr Durham passed his trials, and was earnestly
recommended by the professor to the presbytery and magistrates of Glasgow, and in a little time ordained minister to
that city. Great was the friendship and familiarity between
these two eminent lights of this church there; and among
other effects of their familiar conversation, which still turned
upon profitable subjects and designs, we have the Sum of
Saving Knowledge, which hath been so often printed with
our Confession of Faith and Catechisms. This, after several
conversations, and thinking upon the subject and manner of
handling it, so as it might be most useful to vulgar capacities,
was by Messrs Dickson and Durham dictated to a reverend
minister, who informed me, about the year 1650. It was the
deed of these two great men, and though never judicially
approven of by this church, deserves to be much more read
and considered than I fear it is.

About this time, Mr Dickson had a great share in the
printed pamphlets upon the unhappy debates betwixt the
Resolutioners and Protesters. He was in his opinion for the
public resolutions, and most of the papers upon that side
were written by him, Mr Robert Bailey, and Mr Robert
Douglas; as those upon the other side were written by Mr
James Guthrie, Mr Patrick Gillespie, and a few others.

I have not inquired into the exact time when Mr Dickson
was transported from the profession of divinity at Glasgow,

to the same work at Edinburgh; but I take it to have been about this time. There he continued his laborious care of students of divinity, the growing hopes of a church; and either at Glasgow or Edinburgh most part of the presbyterian ministers, at least in the west, south, and east parts of Scotland, from the year 1640 to the happy revolution, were under his inspection. And from his Truth's Victory over Error, we may perceive his care to educate them in the form of sound words, and to ground them solidly in the excellent standards of doctrine agreed to by this church. May it still be the care and mercy of the church of Scotland, to preserve and hand down to posterity, the scriptural pure doctrine delivered by our first reformers to Mr Dickson and his contemporaries, and from him and the other great lights in his day handed down to us now upon the stage, without corruption and declining to right or left hand.

Mr Dickson continued at Edinburgh discharging his great trust with faithfulness and diligence, until the melancholy turn by the restoration of prelacy, upon king Charles's return; when, for refusing the oath of supremacy, he was with many other worthies turned out. His heart was broken with the heavy change on the beautiful face of this reformed church. He was now well stricken in years, his labour and work were over, and he was ripe for his glorious reward.

Accordingly in December, 1662, he fell extremely weak. Mr John Livingston, now suffering for the same cause with him, and under a sentence of banishment for refusing the foresaid oath, came to visit Mr Dickson on his death-bed. They had been intimate friends near fifty years, and now rejoiced together as fellow confessors. When Mr Livingston asked the professor how he found himself, his answer was, "I have taken all my good deeds and all my bad deeds, and cast them through each other in a heap before the Lord, and fled from both, and betaken myself to the Lord Jesus Christ, and in him I have sweet peace." Mr Dickson's youngest son gave my informer, a worthy minister yet alive, this account of his father's death. Having been very weak and low for some days, he called all his family together, and spoke in particular to each of them, and when he had gone through them all, he pronounced the words of the apostolical blessing, 2 Cor. xiii. 14, with much gravity and solemnity; and then put up his hand and closed his own eyes, and without any struggle or apparent pain, immediately expired in the arms of his son, my brother's informer.

Mr Dickson married Margaret Roberton, daughter to Archibald Roberton of Stonehall, a younger brother of the house of Ernock, in the shire of Lanark. By her he had three sons, John Dickson, clerk to the exchequer in Scotland; Mr Alexander Dickson, professor of the Hebrew tongue in the university of Edinburgh; and Mr Archibald Dickson, who lived with his family in the parish of Irvine. By these he hath left a numerous posterity.

It remains only now that I give some account of Mr Dickson's writings and works, he hath left behind him in print and MS., which speak when he is dead. He was concerned in, and I am ready to think one principal mover of, that concert among several worthy ministers of this Church, for publishing short, plain, and practical expositions upon the whole Bible. I cannot recover all their names who were engaged in this work, but I know Mr Robert Douglas, Mr Rutherford, Mr Robert Blair, Mr G. Hutcheson, Mr James Ferguson, Mr Alexander Nisbet, Mr James Durham, Mr John Smith, and some others, had particular books of holy Scripture allotted to them. The labours of the most of these are published, and the works of others of them yet remain in MS. Mr Dickson, with whom at present I am only concerned, published, his Commentary on the Hebrews, 8vo;— On Matthew, 4to;—On the Psalms, 8vo;—On the Epistles, Latin and English, 4to and folio;—Therapeutica Sacra, or Cases of Conscience Resolved, in Latin, 4to, in English, 8vo; —A Treatise of the Promises, 12mo, Dublin, 1630.—The work entitled Truth's Victory over Error, was translated from his Prælectiones in Confessionem Fidei, or heads of his lectures delivered in the Divinity chair, and first published after his death, Lond. 1688, 12mo.

Besides these, he wrote a great part of the Answers to the Demands, and Duplies to the Replies of the Doctors of Aberdeen, 4to, and some of the pamphlets in defence of the

public resolutions, as hath been observed; with some short
poems on pious and serious subjects, which I am told have
been very useful, when printed and spread among country
people and servants; such as, " The Christian Sacrifice," " O
Mother dear, Jerusalem !" and one somewhat larger, 8vo,
1649, entitled, " True Christian Love, to be sung with the
common tunes of the Psalms." This is all of his I have seen
in print.

Several of his MSS. remain unprinted. Besides some of
his original letters, I have his " Preparatio Tyronis Con-
cionaturi," which I suppose he dictated to his scholars at
Glasgow. " Summarium Libri Jesaiæ ;" his " Letter on the
Resolutions ;" his " First Paper upon the Public Resolutions ;" his " Reply to Mr P. Gillespie and Mr James
Guthrie ;" his " No Separation of the well-affected from the
Army." I am not sure but some of these may be in print,
they are generally pretty large papers, of several sheets in
writing. His sermons at Irvine upon 1 Tim. 1. 5, I have
mentioned already. I doubt not but many more of his
valuable papers are in the hands of others : such as his " Precepts for a Daily Direction of a Christian's Conversation."
" The Grounds of the true Christian Religion," by way of
catechism for his congregation of Irvine. " A Compend of
his Sermons upon Jeremiah and the Lamentations, and the
first Nine Chapters of the Epistle to the Romans." These I
have not seen, but I know they are in the hands of ministers.

ROBERT WODROW

Eastwood, *Jan.* 5, 1726.

A

BRIEF EXPLICATION

<small>OF THE</small>

PSALMS.

A BRIEF EXPOSITION

FIRST FIFTY PSALMS.

ALBEIT the Book of the Psalms be not composed after the manner of human writings, in some such method of parts as history or art could possibly prescribe; yet it is so digested in Divine Providence, as the order it hath is far better than human artifice could have given unto it : for the scope of this book being not only to teach us the grounds of divinity for our information, but also to direct us how to apply saving doctrines practically to ourselves, and to make use thereof for reformation of our affections and actions, and to help us by the example of the practice and exercise of God's dear children, to go after their footsteps, being led by this directory all along, as by the hand, unto the fruition of felicity, in higher and higher degrees thereof, till we be perfectly possessed of it in heaven.   The Psalms, in relation to this scope, are so placed, as the first psalm having divided all men into two ranks, in order to the way of seeking felicity, giveth directions to us to choose, not the counsel of the wicked, but the word of God, for the rule whereby to walk unto true blessedness.   And the second psalm giveth us God, in Christ, for a captain and leader to us, who is able to maintain his church, and all those who shall follow this rule, against all the opposition which can be made against them by the power and multitude of the wicked, who will not be bound by the bonds and cords (as they esteem) of this rule of the Lord's law.   And the rest of the Psalms hold forth the examples of Christ and his followers, yoked in conflict with their persecutors for righteousness' sake; in all assaults making use of their covenant with God, and prevailing by his power, which upholdeth, directeth, comforteth them in all their troubles, and giveth victory and delivery unto them out of them all ; to the intent that every one who shall choose to be truly blessed in the way prescribed of God, (who only can give and maintain felicity,) may resolve and prepare themselves for such a life as the saints have had in all generations before them ; that is, a life mixed with crosses and sweet comforts ; a life wherein they shall be put to make use of their faith in God by prayers, and shall not want for their answer in due time, matter of joy and praises to God ; a life composed of variety of godly exercises, and alternating vicissitudes of conditions, as the bulk of this book representeth ; but closing, as this bundle of psalms closeth, with six times pure praises, whereunto now and then the Lord frameth the heart of the believer with joy unspeakable and full of glory : that endless and uninterrupted thanksgiving and praise being reserved to the general assembly and full meeting of Christ, and all his redeemed ones, at the great day of our Lord's second coming.

BRIEF

EXPLICATION OF THE PSALMS.

PSALM I.

This Psalm teacheth, that no ungodly man is blessed, but the godly man only, v. 1, 2. Which is proved by three reasons: The first, because God blesseth the godly even in this life with grace to bring forth good works profitable to themselves and others, in every state of life, v. 3; but all that the wicked do for making themselves happy, shall be blasted, and found to be mere vanity, v. 4. Another reason is, because after this life the wicked shall be secluded from the presence of God and society of the godly, at the day of judgment, v. 5. The third reason, confirming both the former, is, because God approveth the way of the godly, and will make the end of the way of the ungodly destruction, v. 6.

1. *Blessed* is *the man that walketh not in the counsel of the ungodly, nor standeth in the way of sinners, nor sitteth in the seat of the scornful.*

2. *But his delight* is *in the law of the Lord, and in his law doth he meditate day and night.*

From the pronouncing of the godly man to be the blessed man, and not the ungodly, learn, 1. Though sin and misery abound among men, yet blessedness may be attained ; for God here pronounceth some to be blessed. 2. In relation to the seeking of blessedness, all men, within and without the visible church, are divided into godly men, that seek to be blessed in God's way ; and ungodly men, who seek blessedness, but not in God's way ; for so are they here all ranked. 3. To determine the question, who is the blessed man, is competent to God only, in whose hand alone it is to make a man blessed ; for here he taketh it upon him, to pronounce the godly man to *be the blessed man.* 4. The ungodly think themselves very wise in following the counsel of their own heart, and of others like themselves, that they may be blessed ; but this is not the way of the blessed man, *he walketh not in the counsel of the ungodly.* 5. The ungodly obstinately continue in the course of sinning, but the blessed man, if he be overtaken in a sin, doth not defend his sin, nor persist in it : *he standeth not in the way of sinners.*   6. The ungodly may come to that height at length, as to mock godliness, as mere folly, and to scorn admonitions and reproofs : but the blessed man never hardeneth his heart so, as to mock piety in others, or instruction offered to himself, *he sitteth not in the seat of the scornful.*   7. The blessed man maketh the word of God in holy Scripture, to be his counsellor concerning the remedy of sin and misery, and to be the rule to walk by, till his blessedness be perfected ; for the Scripture to him, for the obedience of faith, is a law, and that fenced with supreme authority : *it is the law of the Lord.*   8. In that measure that a man is godly and blessed, he maketh the word of God, which holdeth forth the way of reconciliation with God, through the Messiah, Christ, the way of growing in communion with God through him, the matter of his chief delight, and contentment ; *his delight is in the law of the Lord.*   9. In that measure that a man delighteth in the law of the Lord, he verseth himself therein upon all occasions : *in his law doth he meditate day and night.*

3. *And he shall be like a tree planted by the rivers of water, that bringeth forth his fruit in his season : his leaf also shall not wither ; and whatsoever he doeth shall prosper.*

4. *The ungodly are not so : but are like the chaff which the wind driveth away.*

This is the first reason proving the godly man to be the only blessed man, and not the ungodly : hence learn, 1. In that measure a man studieth holy communion with God, by delighting and meditating in his word, he shall be fixed and furnished with the influence of Grace from Christ, for the entertaining of spiritual life in him ; *he shall be like a tree planted by the rivers of water.*   2. The man that maketh the word of God his delight, shall be made fruitful in every good work, as opportunity is offered to him ; *he shall be like the tree that bringeth forth his fruit in his season.*   3. This man shall be enabled to bear out a holy profession of his faith in, and obedience to God, in adversity, as well as in prosperity : *his leaf also shall not wither.* 4. Whatsoever duty or service to God this man goeth about, shall not want the assistance of God, nor success, nor accep-

tance at his hands ; *whatsoever he doeth shall prosper.*
5. The ungodly man, whatsoever he may seem to be before the world, yet he is destitute of all spiritual life, and alien from the fellowship of God's grace, unfit for every good work, ready when tempted hard, to quit his counterfeit profession of religion, and is cursed in all that he doth ; for what the blessed godly man is here said to be, the wicked is the contrary ; *the ungodly are not so.* 6. Whatsoever appearance of godliness, or temporal prosperity, or hope of happiness the ungodly man seemeth to have, it shall be found but counterfeit, and shall stand him in no stead in his greatest need : *the ungodly are like the chaff which the wind bloweth away.*

5. *Therefore the ungodly shall not stand in the judgment, nor sinners in the congregation of the righteous.*

The second reason, proving the godly man to be the blessed man, and not the ungodly, is a consequence of the first : whence learn, 1. Not only shall all that the ungodly man soweth to his fleshly felicity, prove chaff ; but also for his pains he shall answer to God in the day of judgment, and there be condemned ; for it is said, *therefore the ungodly shall not stand in the judgment.* 2. Howsoever the godly cannot enjoy one another's fellowship in this life, for many reasons ; yet at last they shall meet in a general assembly of all saints, in the full fellowship of God ; for there is a day of judgment to be, wherein they shall stand, and not be cast or condemned, but shall be fully absolved, and remain in the *standing congregation of the righteous.* 3. Albeit now the ungodly and godly do live together, mixed in one kingdom, city, incorporation, visible church, family, and bed possibly, yet there shall be a perfect separation at last, of the one from the other ; for sinners or (servants of sin) *shall not stand in the congregation of the righteous.*

6. *For the Lord knoweth the way of the righteous : but the way of the ungodly shall perish.*

The third reason confirmeth the former two : Whence learn, 1. Albeit there be no man that liveth and sinneth not, yet the godly man, being justified by faith, and careful to bring forth the fruits of faith, is not a sinner in God's esteem ; for he is here called righteous. 2. However there be many imperfections and failings of the godly man's actions, yet the course he keepeth, and way which he endeavoureth to walk in, is holy and acceptable to God ; *for the Lord knoweth* or approveth *the way of the righteous.* 3. Let the men of this world please themselves, and applaud one another in their godless carriage ; yet the end of their course shall be everlasting destruction ; *for the way of the ungodly shall perish.*

PSALM II.

That this Psalm doth mainly, if not only, concern Christ, appeareth by this : That it hath not so much as *David's* name in the inscription, albeit he did write it : and by Acts iv. 25, 26, where it is appropriated to Christ. This Psalm hath two parts ; in the former is set down the stability of Christ's kingdom, against all the enemies thereof, v. 1, 2, 3. First, because God the Father taketh part with his Son, against all his enemies, and will establish Christ's kingdom, in spite of them all, v. 4, 5, 6. Secondly, because in the covenant of redemption, the Father hath promised to the Son enlargement of his kingdom, and victory over all his enemies, v. 7, 8, 9. In the latter part of the Psalm the prophet delivereth the use of this doctrine in an exhortation to great and small to repent of their sins, and to believe in Christ, v. 10, 11, 12.

1. *Why do the heathen rage, and the people imagine a vain thing?*

2. *The kings of the earth set themselves, and the rulers take counsel together, against the Lord, and against his Anointed,* saying,

3. *Let us break their bands asunder, and cast away their cords from us.*

The prophet showeth, that in vain shall Christ's enemies oppose his kingdom : whence learn, 1, That the ungodly world, being strangers from the life of God, are incensed in a mad mood against the church and kingdom of Christ in the world, *the heathen rage,* saith he, to wit, against the visible government of Christ in his visible church, as appeareth, v. 2, 3. 2. Their opposition is altogether unjust, without cause, and reasonless ; for being asked, they cannot render a reason *why.* 3. Though Christ's enemies promise to themselves success in their opposition to Christ, and that they shall surely overturn his kingdom, yet shall their imaginations prove folly ; they shall not prevail, *for they imagine a vain thing,* which is impossible to be effectuated. 4. The chief instruments that Satan stirreth up against Christ, to be heads and leaders to heathen and godless people in opposing and persecuting Christ's kingdom and church, are the magistrates, rulers, and statesmen, that he may colour his malice with the shadow of authority and law; *for the kings of the earth and rulers set themselves*, to wit, in opposition to him. In this attempt the great ones among men agree more easily together, than in any thing else; they fix their resolutions, communicate their counsels, and conjoin their power; *the kings of the earth set themselves, and the rulers take counsel together.* 6. Howsoever the persecutors of the church conceive themselves not to oppose God but men only, when they trouble his people and servants for righteousness, yet because the quarrel is the Lord's, therefore their opposition is declared here to be *against the Lord, and his Anointed*, or *his Christ*, who is distinguished here from the *Lord*, in regard of his incarnation, mediation, and offices, being otherwise, in respect of his Godhead, one in essence with the Father and the Holy Spirit. 7. Though the law and ordinances of God be most holy, most equitable, most harmless, yea, also most profitable : yet the wicked esteem of them, as they call them here, *bands and cords*, because they curb and cross their carnal wisdom and licentiousness of life. 8. It is not enough to the wicked to disobey and reject the law and ordinances of Christ for their own part, but they will also have them abolished, that God in Christ should not have a church at all, at least in their bounds, or where they have power. *Let us break their bands asunder and cast away their cords from us.*

4. *He that sitteth in the heavens shall laugh : the Lord shall have them in derision.*

5. *Then shall he speak unto them in his wrath, and vex them in his sore displeasure.*

6. *Yet have I set my King upon my holy hill of Zion.*

The first reason of the stability of Christ's kingdom is, because God scorneth men's opposing thereof, and will vex his enemies, and settle Christ's kingdom in his visible church, in the sight of his enemies: hence learn, 1. Though the church visible, and the ordinances of Christ be among the feet of potentates, and Christ's subjects want wisdom and power on earth, to defend themselves, yet their maintainer is *omnipotent* God, judge over all, *even he that sitteth*

2

in heaven.   2. All the devices and conspiracies of men against Christ's kingdom, (how terrible soever to God's people) are but ridiculous and foolish attempts in God's sight ; *the King that sitteth in heaven, shall laugh at them all,* and expose them to mockery before men : *he shall have them in derision.*   3. After the Lord hath made manifest the intent of his enemies, and brought their foolish and mad purposes to light, he will not fail to manifest his mind, and just indignation against them ; for *then shall he speak to them in his wrath.*   4. The Lord hath his appointed time wherein he will arise, and vex the enemies of his church, partly by disappointing them of their hopes, and partly by inflicting sore plagues upon them ; *then shall he vex them in his sore displeasure.*   5. When the Lord ariseth to judge the enemies of his church, then doth he give a further manifestation of his purpose to establish his church, and the visible kingdom of Christ, in the world, in spite of all opposition : *yet have I set my King upon my holy hill of Zion.*   6. Though all kings and kingdoms belong unto the Lord, yet he owneth the church (represented by the hill of Zion) and he owneth his Son Christ, the king thereof, in a special manner, as his peculiar property, wherein he glorieth more than in all his works ; therefore saith he, *I have set my King upon my holy hill ;* this is the speech of God the Father, speaking by his Spirit in the prophet concerning Christ his Son.

7. *I will declare the decree : the Lord hath said unto me, Thou* art *my Son, this day have I begotten thee.*

8. *Ask of me, and I shall give* thee *the heathen* for *thine inheritance, and the uttermost parts of the earth* for *thy possession.*

The second reason of the stability of Christ's kingdom is, the decreed agreement between God the Father and the Son in the covenant of redemption ; some articles whereof Christ by his prophet doth here reveal ; for this is the speech of Christ the Son of God, to be incarnate, speaking by his Spirit, concerning the stability of the church, and his kingdom over it : whence we learn, 1. The faith of the saints, in time of the persecution of the church, may, and should rest persuaded of the stability of the church, and of Christ's kingdom in it, because it is grounded upon the mysterious

and unchangeable decree of God, which here is brought to
light, *I will declare the decree*, saith Christ, not as yet incarnate. 2. It is Christ's office as Prophet, to reveal the
secret counsel of the Trinity, being the substantial Word of
the Father ; and who before the world was created, was
with God, and was God, John i. 1. 2. *I will declare the
decree*, saith the Son of God. 3. The Son of God as he
is a person, concurring in the decree of establishing of the
church, and kingdom of God in it, against all opposition ;
so is he party contractor in the covenant of redemption :
and as he is the promiser and undertaker, to pay the price
of the redemption of his people ; so also is he the receiver
of promises, made in favour of his church and kingdom.
It is he to whom the Father directeth his promise concerning his church, *first and immediately ;* for the Son, in declaring the decree, saith, *the Lord said to me.* 4. It is
one of the articles of the covenant of redemption, that the
promised *seed of the woman*, the Redeemer of his people
the promised seed of *Abraham*, the Messiah and Saviour
of the elect, the promised son of *David*, and true king of
Israel after his incarnation, shall not be disowned of the
Father.   But in and after his deepest humiliation and sufferings, as he shall be, and remain really the very Son of
God, so shall he really at the set day, be acknowledged by
the Father, to be the only begotten Son of God ; which
day, is the day of the resurrection of Jesus Christ from the
dead, as the apostle, Rom. i. 4, teacheth us, saying, *He
was declared to be the Son of God with power by the resurrection from the dead.*   For the resurrection of Jesus
Christ was a real speech, saying to Christ in the audience
of all the world, in effect as much as *I declare thee this
day to be my Son, my only begotten Son, one in substance
with me eternally.*   5. The declaration of the decree of the
manifesting of Christ to be the Son of God, is a sufficient
demonstration of the impregnable stability of the church,
in spite of all the opposition of all the power in the world ;
for to this very end is the decree of revealing Christ to be
the Son of God, here declared. *Thou art my Son whom
I have begotten*, is proof abundant ; for this is the rock
whereupon Christ undertaketh to build his church, against
which the gates of hell shall not prevail, Mat. xvi. 16, 18.
and *who is he that overcometh the world*, saith John, *save*

he that believeth that Christ is the Son of God. 1 John v. 5. 6. Another article of the covenant of redemption here declared is, that after Christ's resurrection, and declaration of his formerly over-clouded Godhead, he should continue in the office of his mediation and intercession ; and by virtue of his paid ransom of redemption, call for the enlargement of his purchased kingdom among the Gentiles : for this is the Father's compact with the Son, saying, *ask of me, and I will give thee the heathen.* 7. The opposition which the world shall make to the kingdom of Christ, shall not hinder the enlargement and spreading thereof ; but by the intercession of Jesus Christ, *the heathen shall be his inheritance, and the uttermost parts of the earth his possession ;* not his by a short tack, or lease for some few years, but a *lasting inheritance,* and constant *possession.* 8. The necessity of prayer is pointed out to all the Lord's people by this, that the possession of the purchase which our Lord hath made by his precious blood, is to be drawn forth by a sort of *prayer and intercession* suitable to Christ's person. *Ask of me,* saith the Father, *and I will give thee the heathen, &c.*

9. *Thou shalt break them with a rod of iron, thou shalt dash them in pieces like a potter's vessel.*

A third article of the covenant of redemption, is, a promise made to Christ, of full victory over all his, and his church's enemies, ver. 9 ; wherein observe, 1. That Christ shall not want enemies, who will not only for their own parts, refuse salvation offered by him, and subjection to be given to him ; but also will oppose him, and make head against him, till he destroy them ; for these kings and rulers spoken of ver. 2, 3, will not cease, *till he break them, and dash them in pieces,* and these are here understood, as repeated from ver. 1, 2, 3.

2. Though Christ's church be weak and unable to help itself against persecution, yet Christ will own the quarrel, and fight against all the enemies thereof himself, whereunto he is sufficiently furnished, for *he shall break them, in pieces with an iron rod.* 3. Though the enemies be numerous and strong, being compared with the godly, whom they do persecute, yet compared with Christ, or looked upon by him, they are but weak, brittle, and naughty things. *Thou shalt dash them in pieces as a potter's vessel.*

10. *Be wise now, therefore, O ye kings : be instructed, ye judges of the earth.*

11. *Serve the Lord with fear and rejoice with trembling.*

12. *Kiss the Son, lest he be angry, and ye perish*
from *the way, when his wrath is kindled but a little :
blessed* are *all they that put their trust in him.*

This is the latter part of the Psalm, wherein the uses of
the former doctrine are set down. Whence learn, 1. The
more clear advertisement is given concerning the sin and
danger of opposing Christ's kingdom, cause, work, or people ; the more wary should all men be, and namely potentates,
as they love their places or souls, to eschew this evil ; for he
hath said, *be wise now, therefore, O ye kings and judges
of the earth.* 2. Though it may seem wisdom to make
and execute laws in prejudice of Christ and his cause,
rather then vent their malice without a pretence ; yet it is
more wisdom to cease from opposition, and take laws from
Christ ; for so the Lord doth reckon, saying, *be wise now,
therefore, and instructed.* 3. If any be guilty of this sin
and not as yet smitten for it, the goodness of God offereth
to him mercy in time, and steppeth in timeously to take off
the snares of flatterers, who use to harden men, and especially great men, in this sin. *Be wise now,* saith the Lord,
O ye kings. 4. It is no disparagement to the greatest
monarchs (but a mean for them to eschew the wrath of
God) to be subject to Christ Jesus, to stand in awe of him,
to submit themselves to him, and promote his service
to their power ; for the command to all, and to them
in special, is *serve the Lord in fear.* 5. As there is matter
of fear to Christ's subjects, lest they provoke him ; for
there is matter of rejoicing for them to be under his
government, and these two affections may well consist in
his service : *rejoice in trembling :* yea there is no right
rejoicing in any thing without some mixture of fear to
offend him. 6. Because Christ Jesus the Son of God,
is a lovely king, bringing righteousness and eternal life to
all his true subjects, he should be submitted unto, and embraced (when he offereth grace) very heartily : to this
end, *kiss the Son,* or do him homage, is added ; for to
kiss is a sign of religious adoration, Hos. xiii. 2, and a sign
of homage and hearty subjection, Sam. x. 1. 7. Where

grace offered by Christ Jesus is refused, the refusing of mercy shall procure more anger than all former sins ; *kiss the Son lest he be angry.*   8. When Christ taketh a refusal off a man, to whom grace is offered, wrath will follow, to the cutting off of the refuser from all means of happiness, both temporal, which he hunteth after ; and eternal, which is offered in Christ unto him, and to the bringing upon him utter perdition ; for it is said, *kiss the Son, lest he be angry, and ye perish from the way of all possible salvation.* 9. Unspeakable must the wrath of God be, when it is kindled fully, since perdition may come upon the *kindling of it but a little.*   10. Remission of sin, delivery from wrath, communion with God, and life everlasting, are the fruits of embracing Christ, of closing in covenant with Christ, and resting on Christ ; for *blessed are all they that put their trust in him.*

PSALM III.

A Psalm of David when he fled from Absalom his son.

This Psalm holdeth forth a notable proof and benefit of faith in *David's* experience ; who, when his own son *Absalom* rebelled against him, and forced him to flee for fear of his life, first laid before the Lord his pitiful condition, v. 1, 2.   Secondly, he settled his faith on God, prayed, and obtained a comfortable answer, was quiet and refreshed in soul and body, and made confident against all fears possible, v. 3, 4, 5, 6. Thirdly, he continueth in prayer, confirming his faith from former experience, v. 7.   And lastly, he giveth forth the use of his experience to the church's edification in a general doctrine, v. 8.

From the inscription, learn, 1. How great calamity may befall the best of God's children, and that from those persons from whom they could least expect to be troubled : for David was deserted of his own subjects, and chased from his palace and royal state by his own son Absalom.   2. Although the Lord do not follow the sins of his children with vindictive justice, yet by the sharp rods of fatherly correction, he can make his own children, and all the beholders of their scandalous sins, see how bitter a thing it is to provoke him to wrath, as once David did.   3. Even when sin hath drawn on judgment, God must be dealt with for relief, no less than if it had been sent for trial only ; as David doth in the case of the correcting and purging of the pollution of his family, by the insurrection of his son against him.

1. *Lord, how are they increased that trouble me?
many* are *they that rise up against me.*

2. *Many* there be *which say of my soul,* There is
no help for him in God. Selah.

From his laying before God his pitiful condition : learn
1. The man who believeth in God, hath an advantage above
whatsoever any ungodly man can have in the time of
trouble : he hath the Lord to go unto for comfort and
relief, of whose kindness he may make use, as David did
here, laying out his trouble before him, and saying, *Lord,
how are they increased that trouble me! &c.* 2. The world
counteth a man's case desperate, when they see no worldly
help for him. *Many say, there is no help for him in God.*
3. Merciless beholders of the corrections of God's children
for their sins, think and say also oft times, that God is following them with vindictive justice, and is destroying them
both in regard of their souls and bodies, &c., without mind
of mercy to them. *Many say of my soul, there is no help
for him in God.* 4. Temptation to despair of relief, doth
accompany unexpected and sad troubles ; and this is more
grievous than the trouble itself : therefore David presenteth this temptation before God in the last place, as the
heaviest part of his exercise, with a note of uplifting the
mind and voice. *Selah.*

3. *But thou, O Lord,* art *a shield for me, my glory,
and the lifter up of mine head.*

In the second place he showeth how he made use of faith
in prayer ; and what fruit he received thereby : whence
learn, 1. The nature of true faith is to draw the more near
to God, the more it be driven from him, *many say, no help
in God; but thou art my shield.* 2. God is a counter-
comfort in all calamity, our shield in danger, our glory in
shame, *the lifter up of our head* in dejection. 3. As there
is relief in God out of all evil, so faith seeth in God sufficient help from all evil, and in special that the sword of the
enemy cannot be so near, but he can interpose himself, as
a *shield* to ward off the blow : *but thou, O Lord, art a
shield round about me, &c.;* yea, faith seeth in God matter
of rejoicing and gloriation in the midst of all the shame
and disgrace which men can cast upon the believer, and
can make a man say to God, *thou art my glory.* In a

word, faith seeth goodness and power in God to raise the believer out of the lowest condition wherein he can be. *Thou art the lifter up of my head.*

4. *I cried unto the Lord with my voice, and he heard me out of his holy hill.   Selah.*

5. *I laid me down and slept ; I awaked, for the Lord sustained me.*

6. *I will not be afraid of ten thousands of people that have set* themselves *against me round about.*

From the exercise of faith, and the fruits of it in these three verses, learn, 1. The conscience of seeking God by prayer is an ease to a man not only for the present time, while he is in prayer pouring out his heart, but refreshful also, when it is looked back upon : therefore by way of gratulation saith David here, *I cried to the Lord.*   2. Faith in a strait stirreth up affection and earnestness in prayer, and maketh the whole man to be taken up about it : *I cried to the Lord with my voice,* saith he.   3. The prayer of faith shall not want an answer, and the return thereof is worthy to be attended and marked, when it is obtained ; *I cried and he heard me.*   4. The prayer of faith trusteth God in Christ, as the propitiatory and mercy seat, and seeketh audience and answer only for Christ's cause, whose sacrifice, and mediation, and benefits were shadowed forth in the tabernacle : and the believer, as he should take heed that his prayer go up to God through Christ, so should he observe how it is answered and returned also through Christ, represented by the ark in the tabernacle, pitched on the holy hill of Zion : *he heard me also out of his holy hill.*   5. In the greatest extremity of danger, a believer may have his mind quieted, and his body refreshed also, after that in faith he hath had his recourse to God, and hath casten his care upon him : *I laid me down and slept ; I awaked.*   6. The quietness and settledness of a man's heart by faith in God, is another sort of work than the natural resolution of manly courage ; for it is the gracious operation of God's spirit upholding a man above nature, and therefore God ought to have all the glory of it : *the Lord sustained me.*   7. When the Lord will answer the believer to his comfort, he can not only satisfy him in the particular which he prayeth for, but also furnish him with confidence against whatsoever evil can be apprehended by him for time to come : *I will not be afraid of millions of people that have set themselves against me round about.* 8. When faith finds itself welcome to God, it is able to give a defiance to all adversaries ; more or fewer, weaker or stronger enemies, all are alike despised : *I will not be afraid of thousands of people.*

7. *Arise, O Lord, save me, O my God, for thou hast smitten all mine enemies* upon *the cheek bone : thou hast broken the teeth of the ungodly.*

In the third place, he continueth to pray against the evil which might thereafter follow : whence learn, 1. Faith in God is not a bragger, nor confident in the man's own strength or imagination; but humbly dependeth on God, and continueth in prayer, so long as the danger remaineth ; as David doth here, after delivery received. 2. The covenant of grace, wherein the believer is entered with God, furnisheth him with confident prayer and hope of salvation : *save me, O my God.* 3. When faith is fixed upon God covenanted, then by-gone experiences come up as pinnings in the building of a wall, to bolster it up, and confirm it ; *for thou hast smitten all mine enemies upon the cheek bone, thou hast broken the teeth of the ungodly.* 4. God smites the pride of persecutors with a shameful stroke, and their beastly cruelty, with breaking their power ; *thou hast smitten mine enemies on the cheek bone, thou hast broken the teeth of the ungodly.*

8. *Salvation* belongeth *unto the Lord : thy blessing* is *upon thy people. Selah.*

From the last part of the Psalm, wherein he giveth forth from his own experience a general doctrine, for the comfort of all the Lord's people, learn, 1. The use of the experience of the godly should be the confirmation of the faith of all others, as well as of their own ; as here is seen. 2. The fruit of the Lord's putting his own in straits, is to make them and all men see, that he hath ways of deliverance, more than they know of ; and that he will save his own when men count their case desperate : for, *salvation* belongeth *to the Lord.* 3. Whatsoever mixture his people find of crosses and comforts, or vicissitudes of danger and delivery, adversity or prosperity ; still the course of blessing of them standeth, which now and then they are forced to acknowledge to the Lord : *thy blessing is upon thy people.*

PSALM IV.

To the chief Musician on Neginoth. A Psalm of David.

Another experience of *David*, as an example of a Christian sufferer, unjustly persecuted and scorned for his piety, by his profane enemies; such as *Saul* and his courtiers were: wherein, first, he setteth down his prayer, v. 1.   Then being comforted in God, he insulteth over his enemies, and glorieth in God's favour, v. 2, 3.   Thirdly, he exhorteth his enemies to repentance and faith in God, v. 4, 5.   Fourthly, he preferreth the blessedness of his estate above whatsoever the worldly man can enjoy, v. 6, 7, 8.

From the inscription of this Psalm, which is the first wherein mention is made of the chief musicians, or musical instruments : learn 1. The praise of God and the joy of his Spirit, allowed on his people, surpass all expression which the voice of words can make; for this was signified by the plurality, and diversity of musical instruments (some of them sounding by being beaten, some of them by being blown,) superadded to the voice of singing in the prædagogy of Moses.   2. Albeit the ceremonial, figurative, and religious use of musical instruments be gone, with the rest of the Levitical shadows, (the natural use of them still remaining :) yet the vocal singing of Psalms in the church is not taken away, as the practice and doctrine of Christ and his apostles make evident; and so the voice of a musician in the public worship still is useful.   3. The Psalms are to be made use of with discretion, as the matter of the Psalm, and edification of the worshippers may require. And in the public, it is the called minister of the congregation's place, to order this part of the worship with the rest ; for this, the direction of the Psalms to the chief musician giveth ground.

1. *Hear me when I call, O God of my righteousness : thou hast enlarged me* when I was *in distress ; have mercy upon me, and hear my prayer.*

From his prayer, learn, 1. Though there be many and divers troubles of the godly, yet there is but one God to give comfort and relief, and one way to draw it from God ; to wit, by prayer in faith : *hear me when I call.* 2. Albeit the conscience of much sin be opposed to the prayer of the believer, yet the everlasting righteousness of faith, (whereof the Lord is God, author, and maintainer for ever,) doth open the way to the suppliant, especially when he cometh to God in a righteous cause : *hear me, O God of my righteousness.*   3. Acknowledgment of by-past mercies in former experience is a good preparation for a new mercy, and a mean to strengthen our faith to receive it : *thou hast enlarged me when I was in distress, have mercy upon me, and hear my prayer.*   4. Faith is a good orator, and a noble disputer in a strait. It can reason from God's readiness to hear, *hear me when I call, O God :* and from the everlasting righteousness given to the man, in the justification of his person ; *O God of my righteousness :* and from God's constant justice in defending the righteousness of his servant's cause, *O God of my righteousness :* and from both present distresses and those that are by-past, wherein he hath been : and from by-gone mercies received ; *thou hast enlarged me when I was in distress :* and from God's grace, which is able to answer all objections from the man's unworthiness, or ill-deserving ; *have mercy upon me, and hear my prayer.*

2. *O ye sons of men, how long* will ye turn *my glory into shame?* how long *will ye love vanity* and *seek after leasing? Selah.*

3. *But know that the Lord hath set apart him that is godly for himself: the Lord will hear when I call unto him.*

In the next place, after comfort received, he triumpheth in God's good will over all his enemies : whence learn, 1. Though a godly man, when he is both persecuted for righteousness, and mocked for his piety, may hang his head in his trouble for a little, till he goes to God with his complaint ; yet after that he is comforted, he will be able to speak a word to his mockers, and holily to insult over them, time about ; as after prayer, David here turneth him to speak to the *sons of men.* 2. Mockers of piety, when pious men are under affliction, bewray themselves to be still in the state of nature, and destitute for the present of the spirit of regeneration : for David calleth them, in relation to their sinful condition, *O ye sons of men.*

3. Though faith in God, and calling on him in trouble, and innocency of life under persecution, be the highest commendation and glory of a man ; yet the wicked, (though oft convinced of God's goodness to such persons,) do not stand to reproach piety, as a matter of scorn, so oft as God doth suffer the godly to fall into calamity : *how long will ye turn my glory into shame?* 4. Mere natural men cannot be made wise, neither by the word of God, nor by experience in their own and others' persons, to consider that things of this earth, as temporary riches, honour, and pleasure, are nothing but vanity and deceiving lies, which promise something, and pay nothing but vexation of spirit, because of guiltiness and misery following upon the abuse of them : *how long will ye love vanity, and seek after leasing ?* 5. The most satisfactory revenge, which the godly can desire of their persecutors and mockers, is, to have them made converts, to have them recalled from the vanity of their way, and brought to a right understanding of what concerneth their salvation, whereunto the godly are ready to offer themselves admonishers of them, and instructors, as here the prophet doth : *O ye sons of men, how long ? &c. But know, &c.* 6. The cause of the world's despising of piety in the persons of God's afflicted children, is the gross ignorance of the precious privileges of the Lord's sincere servants : the world cannot think that the godly, in the midst of their calamities, are God's peculiar jewels, chosen and called out of the world, for honouring of God ; admitted to fellowship with God in this life, and appointed to dwell with him for ever. Therefore, *know,* saith David, as speaking to ignorants, *that God hath set apart for himself him that is godly.* 7. This is one of the privileges of the godly, that how oft soever they are put to their prayers, by trouble or temptation, so oft they get audience, upholding, comfort, and delivery ; as their crosses abound, so do their consolations ; as the prophet testifieth, saying, *the Lord will hear me when I call upon him.* 8. The experience of one of the saints concerning the verity of God's promises, of the certainty of the written privileges of the Lord's people, is a sufficient proof of the right which all his children have unto, and ground of hope for their partaking in the same mercies in their need ; therefore, David, to prove his general doctrine, set down in the first

part of the verse, saith, *the Lord will hear me when I call unto him.*

4. *Stand in awe and sin not : commune with your own heart upon your bed, and be still.   Selah.*

5. *Offer the sacrifices of righteousness, and put your trust in the Lord.*

In the third place, he exhorteth his enemies to repentance and faith in God ; wherein as he laid down the course which they should keep, to wit, to have their judgment well informed in the principles of religion, in the former verse ; so here in this verse, he will have their heart and affections reformed : and in the following verse he will have their actions also reformed in relation to the duties of the first and second table, and their actions to flow from their faith in God.   Whence, learn, 1. Repentance is not real and sound, till the heart be affected with the sense of sin by-past, and fear of sinning hereafter, and be brought in subjection under the dreadful Majesty of God : therefore, after instruction, (v. 2, 3,) he saith here, *stand in awe and sin not.*   2. The means prescribed of God to make the heart sensible of its condition, is the serious and daily examination of the conscience, posing it to answer all interrogatories concerning the man's conformity to God's law, and that in secret in the night, without distraction: for a man had need to have all his wits about him, when he goeth to examine a deceitful thief: to this purpose, saith he, *commune with your hearts on your beds.*   3. The fruit of daily, serious examination of the conscience, concerning sin committed, is, to make a man humble, quiet, and submissive to the Lord.   This he insinuateth in foretelling them that thus they *shall be still, or silent,* not opening the mouth to excuse their sins, or to mock the godly.   As for reformation of their lives in relation to the law of God, (v. 5,) he teacheth, 1. That the formal discharge of the external ceremonies of religion will not prove a man to be a true convert, or a sincere penitent; but the true sacrifice of Christ's obedience unto the death, signified by the external sacrifices, must be looked unto; and the sacrifice of thanksgiving and well doing, and the dedication of the whole man, to the service of God, must testify the truth of repentance.   Therefore, in opposition to the external ceremonial sacrifice, he

commandeth to *offer the sacrifices of righteousness.* **2.** When a penitent hath for evidencing the sincerity of his turning to God, brought forth fruit suitable to repentance, he must not lay weight upon his works, but lay all his confidence upon God's free grace, who justifieth the true convert by faith only : therefore, after commanding them to offer the sacrifices of righteousness, he directeth them, saying, *put your trust in the Lord.*

6. There be *many that say, who will show us any good? Lord, lift thou up the light of thy countenance upon us.*

7. *Thou hast put gladness in my heart, more than in the time* that *their corn and their wine increased.*

8. *I will both lay me down in peace, and sleep : for thou, Lord, only makest me dwell in safety.*

In the last place he commendeth his own blessed estate, and to enforce the former exhortation, he compareth the happiness which the worldling seeketh after, with spiritual joy which is granted to the godly, and preferreth the last far before the other. Hence learn, 1. The blind worldlings, ignorant of what is truly good, are taken with insatiable wishing, and seeking for some earthly thing, whereby they conceive they may be happy. Of those speaketh he, saying, *there be many that say, Who will show us any good.* 2. The truly godly join one with another, in seeking their felicity in God's favour, and in the sense of his reconciliation, and not in seeking the worldly man's choice; for in the opposition to the worldling's wishes, David, with the rest of the godly, saith, *Lord, lift thou up the light of thy countenance upon us.* 3. The comfort of God's Spirit, and sense of a man's reconciliation with God in Christ, is greater than any worldly joy can be, and is able to supply the want of riches, honours, and pleasures worldly, and to season, yea and swallow up the sense of poverty, disgrace, and whatsoever other evil. This David testifieth by his own experience, saying, *thou hast put gladness in my heart, more than in the time that their corn and wine increased.* 4. Faith in God, as it bringeth joy, so also peace unspeakable, and passing understanding, in the midst of trouble. This David's experience teacheth also : *I will both lay me down in peace and sleep,* notwithstanding of all the opposition the sons of men made unto him. Whether God do give means of safety, or none at all which can be seen, preservation and safety is his gift, and the making a man observe the benefit of preservation is another gift also: wherefore, David giveth the glory of both unto God : *thou only makest me dwell in safety.*

PSALM V.

To the Chief Musician upon Nehiloth. A Psalm of David.

David, as a type of Christ, and one of the number of his afflicted followers, set forth in his affliction, as an example of exercise to others in after ages, doth pray for himself, and against his enemies, using sundry arguments to strengthen himself in his hope to be heard. First, from the grace of God bestowed on himself to use the means, v. 1, 2, 3. Secondly, from the justice of God against his wicked enemies, v. 4, 5, 6. Thirdly, from his own steadfast purpose and desire to continue in God's service, and to walk so uprightly, as the enemy shall not have advantange of him by his miscarriage, v. 7. 8. Fourthly, from the ripeness of sin in his adversaries, which prepared them for sudden destruction, v. 9, 10. Fifthly, from the certain hope of joy and defence, and spiritual blessing to be bestowed on himself and all believers, out of the free love and favour of God toward them, v. 11, 12.

1. *Give ear to my words, O Lord ; consider my meditation.*

2. *Hearken unto the voice of my cry, my King and my God : for unto thee will I pray.*

3. *My voice shalt thou hear in the morning, O Lord ; in the morning will I direct* my prayer *unto thee, and will look up.*

In his strengthening of his hope to be heard, from the grace of God bestowed on him, to use the means for obtaining a good answer, learn, 1. When the Lord giveth us a mouth to speak to him, there is ground of hope he will grant an ear to us ; for so reasoneth David, *give ear to my words, O Lord.* 2. In time of trouble, the heart hath more to say to God, than words can utter ; and what a man cannot express, the Lord will take knowledge of it, no less than of his words ; this the prophet hopeth for, saying, *consider my meditation.* 3. When extremity of danger forceth a way to the Lord, the believer's necessity hath a voice, louder than his expressed words, and whereunto the Lord will give ear ; *hearken to the voice of my cry.* 4. It is a point of spiritual wisdom for the help of our faith, to

take hold of those relations we have to God, whereby we
may expect what we pray for, as David doth here, when
we would have protection and delivery, saying ; *my King,
and my God.*   5. Faith knoweth no other to pray unto for
help, save God alone, nor any other way to be helped, save
by perseverance in prayer ; *for unto thee will I pray,* saith
he.   6. Resolved importunity in prayer must be joined
with taking hold of the first and fittest opportunity offered
for prayer : *my voice shalt thou hear in the morning, O
Lord,* saith he.   7. Calling on God in trouble, with dependence on him, giveth hope of audience, and delivery
by him, by way of a convincing syllogism, whereof the
promise of delivery made to such as call on the name of
the Lord in the day of trouble, is the first proposition ; the
conscience of resolved calling on him maketh the assump-
tion or second proposition ; and faith concludeth the expectation of deliverance ; for the prophet's reasoning is this in
effect—whosoever they be that pray to the Lord in their
trouble, thou wilt hear them : but I pray to thee, and
resolve to continue praying ; therefore thou, O Lord,
wilt hear me.

4. *For thou* art *not a God that hast pleasure in
wickedness : neither shall evil dwell with thee.*

5. *The foolish shall not stand in thy sight : thou
hatest all workers of iniquity.*

6. *Thou shalt destroy them that speak leasing : the
Lord will abhor the bloody and deceitful man.*

In the second place, he reasoneth from the justice of
God against his enemies : whence learn, 1. The worst
qualities in the adversaries of the godly, furnish good
matter of faith and hope to the believer to be rid of them :
for this use doth David make of the wickedness of his enemies in these three verses.   2. Such as take pleasure in
sin : *thou art not a God,* saith he, *that hast pleasure in
wickedness :* and such as will not part with sin, God shall
separate them from his company ; for it is said, *neither
shall evil dwell with thee.*   3. Let wicked men seem never
so wise politicians among men, yet shall they be found mad
fools before God, selling heaven for trifles of the earth,
holding war with the Almighty, and running upon their
own destruction in their self-pleasing dreams, to the loss of

their life and state, temporal and eternal ; for the *foolish*, saith he, *shall not stand in thy sight.* 4. Such as make iniquity their work, shall have the effects of God's hatred for their wages : for *thou hatest all the workers of iniquity.* 5. The enemies of God's people, while by slanders and lies they murder the innocent, draw upon themselves swift damnation from God : *thou shalt destroy them that speak leasing,* saith he. 6. Falsehood and cruelty, which are the characters of the foes of the godly, are abomination to the Lord, which he cannot endure : *thou wilt abhor the bloody and deceitful man.*

7. *But as for me I will come* into *thy house, in the multitude of thy mercy ;* and *in thy fear will I worship toward thy holy temple.*

8. *Lead me, O Lord, in thy righteousness, because of mine enemies : make thy way straight before my face.*

In the third place, he resolveth that whatever the enemy shall do, he will walk as God hath commanded him : with resolution to serve God in sincerity, as also a profession of hope to enjoy the society of his saints in God's public worship : and to this end he prayeth he may be kept straight in his walking, that the enemy might have nothing wherewith to reproach him. Hence learn, 1. Though the godly want not the conscience of their own sins, when they speak of the sins of their enemies, yet there is a difference between them and the wicked, in respect the godly are humbled in the sense of their sins, are brought to the acknowledgment of their need of mercy, and flee to God for having mercy, and to the *multitude of mercy,* as they see the multitude of their sins : and therefore saith he of himself, in opposition to the wicked, *but as for me, I will come into thy house, in the multitude of thy mercy.* 2. The faith which the godly have in the mercies of God, doth encourage them to follow the service of God ; and in some cases doth give them hope to be loosed from the restraints which hinder them from enjoying the public ordinances : *I will come into thy house, in the multitude of thy mercy.* 3. The right temper of the heart of a true worshipper, is fear before God : *in thy fear will I worship.* 4. Under the sense of sinfulness and unworthiness, faith must be supported by looking towards Jesus Christ, prefigured by the tabernacle and temple: *in thy fear*, saith he, *I will worship toward thy holy temple.* 5. When the godly are under trouble from their enemies, and under trial by other sorts of exercise, they are no less feared for their miscarriage and offending the Lord, than they are feared for what their enemies can do against them : therefore, *lead me, O Lord, in thy righteousness*, saith he. 6. So much the more as the godly are sensible of their own blindness, and weakness, and readiness, to go out of the right way ; so much the more do they call for, and depend upon God's directing of them. *Lead me*, saith he ; as one that seeth not, or as one who is not able to hold a right course, without a guide. 7. If the godly man take a sinful course, to be relieved from his trouble, the enemy is hardened in his wicked course, by this means to blaspheme the profession of piety, as mere hypocrisy, and so God is provoked to let the enemy prevail, because the miscarriage of the godly hath made way to him ; for avoiding of which inconvenience, he prayeth, *lead me in thy righteousness because of my enemies.* 8. The deceitfulness of sin, the ignorance of what is expedient and lawful in a particular case, the mist of private affections, and the example of ill counsel of the world, are ready to make a man mistake the right way, except the Lord make clear what is his duty: therefore, saith he, *make thy way straight before my face.*

9. *For* there is *no faithfulness in their mouth ; their inward part* is *very wickedness : their throat* is *an open sepulchre ; they flatter with their tongue.*

10. *Destroy thou them, O God: let them fall by their own counsels : cast them out in the multitude of their transgressions, for they have rebelled against thee.*

In the fourth place he strengtheneth his hope to be helped, because his enemies' sins were ripe for judgment. Whence learn, 1. Among other motives to make the godly take heed of their carriage in time of trial, this is one; they have to do with a false world, and hollow-hearted men, who will make false pretences of what is not their intentions, and will make promise of what they mind not to perform, and will give none but rotten and poisonable advice, gilded with false flattery, and all to deceive the godly, and draw them in a snare. This is it, he saith, *for there is no faith-*

fulness in their mouth ; their inward part is very wickedness ; their throat is an open sepulchre ; they flatter with their tongue ; and this is the nature of all carnal men, when it cometh to the point of defending God's cause in time of trial. 2. Though this prayer be not to be drawn in imitation against particular persons, by us who have not so infallible revelation of men's state before God ; yet is it a prophecy against all the irreconcilable enemies of God, and of his people, against whom the Spirit of God maketh imprecation here, saying, *destroy thou them, O God.* 3. There is no need of any other means to destroy the Lord's enemies, than their own devices : the very course they take to establish themselves will serve for their own ruin. *Let them fall,* saith he, *by their own counsel.* 4. The certain cause of the ruin of the persecutors of God's people, is the ripeness and full measure of their sins. *Cast them out,* saith he, *in the multitude of their transgressions.* 5. The opposing of truth, and of the ordinances of God, in the person of his servants who stand for the same, is not simply the opposing of mortal men, but the opposing of God, whose quarrel it is ; therefore saith he, *they have rebelled against thee.*

11. *But let all those that put their trust in thee rejoice : let them ever shout for joy, because thou defendest them : let them also that love thy name, be joyful in thee.*

12. *For thou, Lord, wilt bless the righteous ; with favour wilt thou compass him, as* with *a shield.*

In the last place, he maketh prayer for all the godly, militant in this warfare with himself, that they may share together in the Lord's favour. Hence learn, 1. Persecution for righteousness is a cause common to all believers, wherein they should all join, and pray one of them for another, and seek for a joyful out-gate to each other in their own time ; for this cause, after prayer against enemies, he saith, *but let all that trust in thee rejoice.* 2. The manifested care of God for his people, in protecting and delivering them from their enemies, is matter of exceeding joy to his people, because he is glorified herein, and his church is preserved : *let them ever shout for joy, because thou defendest them.* 3. Such believers as have gotten grace to love God's name, albeit it be not yet given unto them to suffer for his name, are allowed to share in the joy of victorious sufferers. *Let them also that love thy name*, saith he, *be joyful in thee.* 4. The person who is justified by faith, and studieth unto holiness, is an heir of God's blessing, whether he be less or more taken notice of by the world, whether entered in the conflict with persecutors or not : *For thou, O Lord, wilt bless the righteous.* 5. The favour and good will of God toward his own, is a strong and glorious defence to them ; it is a crowning shield,—a shield compassing a man round about like a glorious diadem,—a shield very handsome and strong which the believer ought to grip well, and hold fast, and manage warily, and oppose it to every assault of the adversary : a crowning shield, which circleth the man round about, and keepeth off the dint of the adversary's weapon, even when the pursued believer is not aware : *with favour wilt thou compass him as with a shield.*

PSALM VI.

To the Chief Musician on Neginoth upon Sheminith. A Psalm of David.

Another experience of David, useful to be known by all the children of God, who are subject to the like exercise ; wherein David, being under the sense of the Lord's heavy hand, upon his body and spirit, prayeth for the removal of self-wrath, v. 1, 2, 3. Next prayeth for the renewed feeling and experience of God's mercy towards him, laying forth his lamentable condition before the pitiful eye of God, v. 4, 5, 6, 7. After which, being heard and comforted, in the third place, he defieth and triumpheth over all his enemies, v. 8, 9.

1. *O Lord, rebuke me not in thine anger, neither chasten me in thy hot displeasure.*

2. *Have mercy upon me, O Lord, for I am weak ; O Lord, heal me for my bones are vexed.*

3. *My soul is also sore vexed : but thou, O Lord, how long ?*

From his prayer for removal of wrath, learn, 1. It is possible, that a true believer, who had been ofttimes refreshed with the sense of God's favour, may, by some sad exercise have his conscience so wakened to the sense of sin, as he can feel nothing but wrath, and fear of cutting off ; as this experience of David maketh manifest. 2. There is no relief in such case, save to set faith on work, whatsoever be felt or feared, and to seek mitigation and deliverance of God, as the prophet doth here. 3. Even the fatherly wrath of God, and far more the apprehension of hot displeasure of an angry judge, is insupportable to a soul that knoweth God, and hath ever tasted of his favour before: *rebuke me not in thy wrath*, saith he. 4. There is as much ground of faith holden forth in the Lord's name, *Jehovah*, (importing his unchangeable being, and his constancy in his promises,) as to ground a prayer upon it, for obtaining the change of a man's case to the better, in the hardest condition imaginable ; *O Lord*, or *O Jehovah*, saith he, *rebuke me not in thy wrath.* 5. Though sense feel wrath, and see nothing but hot displeasure, yet faith can pierce through clouds, and bespeak mercy : *have mercy on me, O Lord*, saith David, in the midst of this sad condition. 6. Though sin doth provoke anger, yet the misery and inability to subsist, presented unto God, is the object of mercy, and a motive to faith to expect compassion : *have mercy on me*, saith he, *for I am weak.* 7. When sin hath drawn on sickness, or any other danger, let pardon of sin be first sought, and after that, the removing of the stroke ; for first, he saith, *have mercy on me*, and then, *heal me.* 8. The Lord can make the strongest and most insensible part of a man's body, sensible of his wrath, when he pleaseth to touch him ; for here David's *bones are vexed.* 9. Anguish of spirit and torment of conscience, is heavier than any torture of body, as, *my soul is also vexed*, doth import. 10. The Lord's apprehended absence in trouble, and delaying to answer the supplicant, putteth a load above a burden, and surpasseth all expression of words; for here his speech is cut, *but thou O Lord, how long ?*

4. *Return, O Lord, deliver my soul : O save me for thy mercies' sake.*

5. *For in death* there is *no remembrance of thee : in the grave who shall give thee thanks ?*

6. *I am weary with my groaning ; all the night make I my bed to swim : I water my couch with my tears.*

7. *Mine eye is consumed because of grief; it waxeth old because of all mine enemies.*

In the next place, he prayeth for a renewed sensible experience of God's mercy to him, because of his pitiful condition. Wherein learn, 1. A renewed glimpse of the Lord's countenance will satisfy a soul in the greatest distress: therefore David craveth this for a remedy of all his sorrow: *return, O Lord.* 2. If desertion continue, fear of perishing utterly doth present itself; as this prayer insinuateth: *O Lord, deliver my soul.* 3. The only time to spread the praise of God, by making mention of him before them that know him not, is the time of this life: *for in death there is no remembrance of thee.* 4. The Christian's love of life, should proceed from the love of honouring God in this life, (where it may enlarge God's glory, before them who may be profited by preaching his praise,) and should be preferred to our own contentment for a time in heaven, so long as God pleaseth to take service of us here. For this is the force of the prophet's reasoning, *in the grave who shall give thee thanks?* 5. Our place waiteth for us, and no man can take it over our head, while we on earth are enduring toil and trouble, to bring more to heaven with us. 6. A true desire and purpose to glorify God in this life, to the edifying of others, may give hope of some prolonging of life, and assurance of not perishing for ever: for David's hope to be heard doth run here upon this ground. 7. The most lasting, pressing, and piercing sorrow that ever soul felt, is from the sense of sin, and of God's displeasure for it, as the prophet's expression here doth give evidence. 8. The exercise of the godly under the sense of God's displeasure, may be very heavy, and of long continuance; the prophet is *weary with his groaning, and his eyes consumed with grief.* 9. No delay of comfort, no sense of sin, no fear of God's utter displeasure can be a reason to the believer to cease from prayer, and dealing with God for grace; for the prophet is *weary*, but giveth not over; only his condition is the matter of fresh mourning to him night and day, and pouring out of tears in the Lord's bosom: *all the night maketh he his bed to swim, and watereth his couch with his tears.* 10. The insulting of enemies over the godly when the Lord's hand is heavy upon them, because it reflecteth upon religion and upon God's glory, is a main ingredient in the sorrow of the godly: *David's* eye had waxen *old and dim with grief because of all his enemies.*

8. *Depart from me all ye workers of iniquity; for the Lord hath heard the voice of my weeping.*

9. *The Lord hath heard my supplication; the Lord will receive my prayer.*

10. *Let all mine enemies be ashamed and sore vexed : let them return and be ashamed suddenly.*

In the third place David defieth all his enemies, being comforted by the light of God's countenance, and lifted up in his spirit. Whence learn, 1. The Lord can shortly change the cheer of an humble supplicant, and raise a soul trembling for fear of wrath, to a triumphing over all sort of adversaries, and over all temptations to sin arising from them, for the return of the prophet's prayer maketh him say, now, *depart from me all ye workers of iniquity.* 2. The sacrifice of a contrite spirit, offered by a believer, the Lord will not despise; *for the Lord heard the voice of the prophet's weeping.* 3. The hearing of our prayer should be thankfully observed and made use of, for strengthening our faith in prayer afterward : for after the prophet hath said, *the Lord hath heard my supplication,* he addeth, *the Lord will receive my prayer.* 4. The enemies of the godly shall all of them be disappointed of their hopes, and ashamed for their attempts against them, and filled with vexation for their pains ; for this prayer furnished by the Spirit, v. 10, to one of the godly against his wicked enemies, is a prophecy against all the rest of the enemies of the godly in all ages.

PSALM VII.

Shiggaion of David, which he sang unto the Lord, concerning the words of Cush, the Benjamite.

The prophet as a type of Christ mystical, and an example of Christians suffering, being slandered of treason against his prince, by one of the courtiers, first fleeth to God for delivery, v. 1, 2. Secondly, cleareth his innocence, v. 3, 4, 5. Thirdly, requesteth the Lord to judge between him and his enemies, v. 6, 7, 8, 9. And fourthly, in prayer is made confident, that the Lord will plead for him against his enemies, v. 10, 11, 12, 13, and will return their devised mischief against him, upon their own head, v. 14, 15, 16. Whereupon in the last place he promiseth praise to God for his righteous judgment, v. 17.

1. *O Lord my God, in thee do I put my trust : save me from all them that persecute me, and deliver me;*

2. *Lest he tear my soul like a lion, rending* it *in pieces while* there is *none to deliver ;*

As to the first part, wherein he fleeth to God to be delivered from the bloody tongues of calumniators; learn, 1. It is a part of the exercise of Christ's servants, to be slandered as traitors to their lawful magistrates, as David was by Cush, a flattering courtier. 2. God who is able to clear the innocent, and to defend them from malice, is in this case to be run unto, and use is to be made of faith in him, and our covenant with him, for relief from all adversaries, as the prophet doth here. 3. If God do not interpose himself, for defence of his unjustly slandered servants, there is nothing to be expected from wicked enemies enraged, but merciless beastly cruelty, as is shown in David's experience.

3. *O Lord my God, if I have done this; if there be iniquity in my hands;*

4. *If I have rewarded evil unto him that was at peace with me; (yea, I have delivered him that without cause is mine enemy;)*

5. *Let the enemy persecute my soul, and take* it*; yea, let him tread down my life upon the earth, and lay mine honour in the dust. Selah.*

In the second place, wherein he cleareth his own innocence, learn, 1. Though innocence cannot exempt a man from being unjustly slandered, yet it will furnish him with a good conscience, and much boldness in the particular, before God; as here is seen, v. 3, 4. 2. The more a man doth render good for evil, the more confidence shall he have when he cometh to God; for innocence served David for this good use, that he had delivered Saul, who without cause was his enemy, v. 4. 3. He that is conscious of doing, or intending injury to his neighbour, will have his own conscience against him, in the time when he meeteth with a greater injury done to him, and in that case will be forced to justify God's righteousness against himself, as David's conditional prayer here importeth, v. 5.

6. *Arise, O Lord, in thine anger, lift up thyself, because of the rage of mine enemies; and awake for me to the judgment* that *thou hast commanded.*

7. *So shall the congregation of the people compass*

thee about : for their sakes therefore return thou on high.

8. *The Lord shall judge the people : judge me, O Lord, according to my righteousness, and according to mine integrity* that is *in me.*

9. *Oh let the wickedness of the wicked come to an end ; but establish the just : for the righteous God trieth the hearts and reins.*

In the third place, he prayeth that God would judge between him and his enemies : whence learn, 1. Though the Lord for the trial and exercise of his children, sit still as it were for a time, when men are about to oppress them ; yet will he in due time manifest himself to be no idle spectator of wrong, but a just defender of the oppressed, and avenger of the injurious, *he will arise in anger and lift up himself* 2. When our enemies are desperately malicious, and nothing can mitigate their fury ; let the consideration of God's justice mitigate our passion : *for he will arise in anger against them.* 3. There is no less just zeal in God, to defend his own oppressed people, than there is malice in the wicked, to wrong them : *for his rising in anger*, is here opposed *to the rage of the enemies.* 4. Albeit judgment against the oppressor be not at the first executed, yet God in his word hath given out sentence against them, and in his active providence, hath prepared means and instruments for execution thereof in due time ; *when he shall awake to execute the judgment which he hath commanded*, or given order for. 5. When the Lord ariseth to judge his enemies, then the Lord's people will draw warmly unto him, and as it were, *compass him round about.* 6. In calling for justice upon the wicked enemies of God's people, we should not be led with private passion, or desire of revenge, but with desire of God's glory, and edification of his people : *for their sakes*, prayeth he, *return thou on high*, or ascend to thy tribunal seat. 7. Principles of religion, whereof we may have use in our exercises, should be solidly digested, that we may apply them readily to use, as need requireth, for strengthening of our faith, and prayer to God : for when the prophet hath settled his faith upon the doctrine of *God's judging and executing justice in favour of his people*, in the general, he applieth it to his own particular, saying, *judge me, O Lord.*   8. When a man hath made peace with God about all his sins, upon the terms of grace and mercy, through the sacrifice of the mediator, he may in comparison with his injurious enemies, in a particular cause, appeal to God's justice to decide the controversy ; as here the prophet doth, saying, *judge me according to my righteousness, O Lord, and mine integrity* that is *in me.*   9. When a process hath been lying long before God, and the controversy between the godly and their persecutors is not yet decided, the godly may put in a bill for passing the decree, and executing of the sentence, as here is done: *oh let the wickedness of the wicked come to an end, &c.*   10. The upright man needs not to fear that his enemies shall obtain a decree in their favour, or suspension, or reduction of the sentence pronounced: *for the righteous God trieth the heart and the reins.*

10. *My defence is of God, which saveth the upright in heart.*

11. *God judgeth the righteous, and God is angry* with the wicked *every day.*

12. *If he turn not, he will whet his sword; he hath bent his bow, and made it ready.*

13. *He hath also prepared for him the instruments of death; he ordaineth his arrows against the persecutors.*

14. *Behold, he travaileth with iniquity, and hath conceived mischief, and brought forth falsehood.*

15. *He made a pit, and digged it, and is fallen into the ditch* which *he made.*

16. *His mischief shall return upon his own head, and his violent dealing shall come down upon his own pate.*

In the fourth place, is the answer of his prayer, viz., assurance given of delivery to him, and of judgment on his enemies ; whereupon the supplicant giveth thanks to God. Whence learn, 1. The fruit of faith joined with a good conscience, is access to God in prayer, confidence, peace and tranquillity of mind, mitigation of trouble, protection and deliverance, as the prophet's experience here doth prove. 2. Victory granted unto faith, after wrestling with darkness, is satisfactory to the soul of the godly, as if all that the believer did hope for were perfected ; for he is now clear to say, *my defence is of God, &c.*   3. Whatsoever we think in the time of temptation, neither justice against the wicked, nor mercy toward the godly is idle ; for God's word and works speak mercy to the one, and wrath to the other, every day ; all things are working for the one's good ; and for the other's damage continually ; *for God judgeth the righteous and is angry with the wicked every day.* 4. God delayeth the execution of his judgment on the wicked, to lead them to repentance ; for here *God hath whetted his sword to strike, if the wicked turn not.* 5. If repentance intervene not, the destruction of the wicked is inevitable : *If he turn not, the instruments of death are prepared, and the arrows directed towards the persecutors.* 6. It is a matter of no small pains that the sinner is put unto, to serve the devil, and his own corrupt affections, *he travaileth* as with a child ; he digs a pit, one of the hardest pieces of work to slaves. 7. When once the wicked hath conceived mischief, he cannot rest till he bring his purpose to action, but his sinful thoughts may be wrought in effect : *he conceiveth mischief and travaileth with iniquity.* 8. The adversary of God's people shall have no profit of all his labour, but shall be met with disappointment, *he bringeth forth falsehood,* and the evil which is most contrary to his hope and intention shall befall him : *He is fallen in the ditch which he made and his mischief shall return upon his own head, &c.* as a stone thrown up against heaven, returneth upon the head of him who threw it.

17. *I will praise the Lord according to his righteousness ; and will sing praise to the name of the Lord most high.*

In the last place he promiseth praise, and closeth his song so. Whence learn, 1. The issue of the hardest exercise of the godly, is comfort to their souls, and praise to God, as here we see. 2. When faith is sensibly satisfied, and settled in assurance of what was promised, it will be glad and give thanks for what is to come, as if it were in possession already : so speaketh this conclusion, I will praise the Lord, and I will sing praise to the name of the Lord. 3. Let the party opposer of the godly be never so powerful and violent, and his place in the world never so high, faith may set to its seal, that God shall manifest himself a righteous judge in power and authority above the highest oppressing powers on earth : *I will sing praise to the name of the Lord most high.*

PSALM VIII.

To the chief Musician upon Gittith. A Psalm of David.

To the end the prophet may commend the glory of God's grace toward man, he first admireth his glory in the works of creation and providence, which are able to stop the mouths of all blasphemous atheists, ver. 1, 2 ; in the second place he admireth the Lord's love to man above all other, even the most glorious creatures, v. 3, 4 ; thirdly, he setteth out this grace of God to man, in the incarnation, humiliation, and exaltation of Christ for man's cause, and for restoring redeemed men in Christ, to their right unto, and over the visible creatures, ver. 5, 6, 7, 8 ; and closeth the psalm, with the admiration of God's glory in all the earth, ver. 9.

1. *O Lord our Lord, how excellent* is *thy name in all the earth ! who hast set thy glory above the heavens.*

2. *Out of the mouth of babes and sucklings hast thou ordained strength because of thine enemies, that thou mightest still the enemy and the avenger.*

From his admiration of God's glory in the works of creation and providence, learn 1. The godly are not always borne down with trouble ; sometimes they have liberty to go, and delight themselves in the beholding of God's glory and goodness towards themselves, as the whole psalm showeth. 2. The mystery of the glory of God, in his works of creation and redemption, is such, as none, save the eye spiritually illuminated by his Spirit, can see : and he that seeth it, cannot but be ravished therewith, when he discerneth it ; and none can sufficiently comprehend it, or take it up fully, save God himself. Therefore the prophet directeth his speech full of admiration, wholly to the Lord, throughout all the psalm. 3. The glory of the Lord is greatly sweetened unto the godly, in the time of their praising of his majesty, when they consider their own interest in him as in their own property. Therefore saith he, *O Lord our Lord, how excellent is thy name !* 4. No words are sufficient to set out the glory of the Lord, not only as it is in itself, but even as it is discovered to a spiritual understanding ; therefore by way of admiration, must he cry out, *how excellent is thy name !* 5. The heavens and celestial lights shining from above speak much of God's glory, but in effect his glory is greater than they can hold forth : for his glory is set above the heavens. 6. Albeit the glory of the Lord filleth the world, yet hath he enemies of his glory, to wit, profane and godless persons, atheists, epicures, and persecutors of his people and truth ; for here are enemies spoken of, and avengers, opening blasphemous mouths against him, and his people, as if God, and his people, had injured them. 7. Not only the providence of God in new-born babes, framing them in the belly, providing nourishment unto them when they are born, and making them to suck the breasts ; but also the giving of saving knowledge to some of them, in their tender years, is able to refute all atheists and profane despisers of the glory of the Lord ; *for out of the mouth of babes and sucklings he hath ordained strength*, or strong conviction, to *still the enemy and the avenger*, and put him to silence. Matthew 21. 26.

3. *When I consider thy heavens, the work of thy fingers, the moon and the stars, which thou hast ordained.*

4. *What* is *man, that thou art mindful of him ? and the son of man, that thou visitest him ?*

From his admiration in God's respect, and love to man above all other creatures, learn, 1. The weakness and unworthiness of man, considered both in himself, and compared with his glorious creatures made for his use, commend the bounty of God to man, and make it a matter of great admiration. For when the prophet considereth the glorious heavens, &c. he asketh *what is man, &c.* 2. Man of all the creatures is most esteemed and taken care of by God ; for he is mindful of man, and daily visiteth him.

5. *For thou hast made him a little lower than the angels, and hast crowned him with glory and honour.*

6. *Thou madest him to have dominion over the works of thy hands ; thou hast put all* things *under his feet ;*

7. *All sheep and oxen, yea, and the beasts of the field ;*

8. *The fowl of the air, and the fish of the sea,* and whatsoever *passeth through the paths of the seas.*

In the third place, he looketh on man considered in his creation before the fall, and as he is in his head, Christ (who is God incarnate, humbled and exalted for man's cause after the fall), restored to what he lost by the fall. Whence learn, 1. Look unto man in his creation, and God hath given him the place, in order of dignity, above all the creatures visible, next unto heavenly angels : *thou hast made him a little lower than the angels.* 2. Look unto man after his fall, restored by Christ unto his place, and in this respect he is established in that dignity to be next unto the glorious angels: *thou hast made him a little lower than the angels.* 3. Look unto man in our head Christ Jesus, God incarnate, and there man is wonderfully exalted in regard that for respect and love to man, the Man Christ being very God, is humbled unto the death of the cross. And in this sense doth the apostle, Heb. ii. 7, 9. take this place *thou madest him a little lower than the angels, for the suffering of death.* 4. Look unto man in Christ Jesus after his resurrection, and in his glorification ; *God hath crowned him with glory and majesty.* 5. It is no small point of dignifying man, that all believers have by Christ this title of heirship, with lawful use and possession of the creatures recovered and restored unto him : *thou madest him to have dominion over the works of thine hands.* 6. As there is nothing which may do man good service, which God hath not granted man dominion over, in and through Christ, so there is nothing can harm him, but he hath put under Christ's feet and under believers' feet in and through Christ, to wit, sin and Satan, and all our enemies, and death the last enemy ; *he hath put things under his feet,* as the apostle gathereth, 1 Cor. xv. 26. 7. Christ shall not lay down his kingdom which he hath in his church, and over all her enemies, till he hath put down all rule and authority, and power against him and his church, and have subdued all enemies under himself. *For he must reign till he hath put all things under his feet,* as the apostle collecteth, 1 Cor. xv. 25. 8. Nothing is excepted or exempted from being subject to Christ, as man ; no, not the holy angels (who are made ministering spirits, to serve believers) but only God, essentially considered, he only is excepted. *For he hath put all things under his feet ; but when he saith, all things are put under* him, it is *manifest that he is excepted who did put all things under* him, as the apostle proveth from this place, 1 Cor. xv. 27.

9. *O Lord our Lord, how excellent* is *thy name in all the earth !*

He closeth the psalm as he began it with admiration

whence learn, 1. The praises of our Lord, and the excellency of our covenant right, and interest in him, are worthy again and again to be considered; and that God should be proclaimed Lord of us whom he hath lifted up to so high a dominion : therefore is this verse repeated again. 2. When a man hath begun to declare some reason of his wondering at the glory of God, manifested in the whole world, and specially in his church, he must give over the full explication of this glory, and close, as he began, with wondering still; as here the same exclamation of wondering at the excellency of God's glory concludeth the psalm as it began, *O Lord our Lord, how excellent is thy name in all the earth!*

PSALM IX.

To the chief Musician upon Muth-Labben. A Psalm of David.

Here is David's song of praise to God, first, for his own experience of God's goodness towards himself, and God's righteous judgment against his enemies, v. 1, 2 3, 4. Secondly, for the Lord's readiness to do the like work, in favour of all the godly, v. 5, 6, 7, 8, 9, 10. Thirdly he exhorteth the godly to praise God with him, v. 11, 12. Fourthly, he prayeth for his own delivery out of his present distress, v. 13, 14. Fifthly, he hath assurance of the overthrow of all his enemies, v. 15, 16, 17, 18. And last of all, for the execution of this overthrow, he heartily prayeth, v. 19, 20.

1. *I will praise thee, O Lord, with my whole heart; I will shew forth all thy marvellous works.*

2. *I will be glad and rejoice in thee: I will sing praise to thy name, O thou most High.*

3. *When mine enemies are turned back, they shall fall and perish at thy presence.*

4. *For thou hast maintained my right and my cause: thou sittest in the throne judging right.*

From the first part of this song of praise, learn, 1. The exercise of the saints in variety of troubles occasioneth the setting forth of the glory of God in all his attributes as in this psalm is shown. 2. When the heart is enlarged with the sense of God's goodness, the work of praising God will be more heartily undertaken, and a large heart will make a loosed tongue and an open mouth, to set forth his glory. David *will* now *praise the Lord with his whole heart.* 3. One work of God's wonderful goodness useth to call for another that they may go forth together in each other's hands to set forth his excellency; as here David *will show forth all his wonderful works.*   4. A lover of the glory of God cannot rest till he communicate with others what he knoweth of the Lord's wonders: *he will show forth* (for others' upstirring) *all the Lord's marvellous works.*   5. Not any benefit or gift received of God, but God himself, and his free favour is the matter of the believer's joy: David *will be glad and rejoice in God himself.*   6. It is not enough to have joy in our heart in the Lord, but it is his glory, that the joy which we have in him, be openly known as occasion offereth : therefore *will* David *sing praises to the name of the Lord most high.*   7. The way of giving God the glory in every action, and in special of our victories over our enemies, is to acknowledge him to be the chief worker thereof, and the creatures to be but instruments by whom he turneth the enemy back : for *the enemy falleth and perisheth at his presence.*   8. As for time by-gone God should have the glory of what is done, so must we consecrate the glory of what shall be done, and of what we would have done altogether to the Lord : therefore also for time to come David speaketh, *when mine enemies are turned back,* (to wit, by thy power,) *they shall fall at thy presence.* 9. Were a cause never so right and just, it requireth God's power for keeping it on foot : the justness of the cause must not be relied on, but God must have the trust of the cause, and the glory of maintaining it : David acknowledgeth *God the maintainer of his right and cause.*   10. What judge soever shall condemn us unrighteously, there is a higher judge to judge the cause over again, and the parties also : who when he showeth himself, should be glorified in his justice by us ; *thou sittest in the throne judging right,* saith David, after he was condemned of the judges of the land.

5. *Thou hast rebuked the heathen, thou hast destroyed the wicked, thou hast put out their name for ever and ever.*

6. *O thou enemy, destructions are come to a perpetual end ; and thou hast destroyed cities ; their memorial is perished with them.*

7. *But the Lord shall endure for ever : he hath prepared his throne for judgment.*

8. *And he shall judge the world in righteousness, he shall minister judgment to the people in uprightness.*

9. *The Lord also will be a refuge for the oppressed, a refuge in times of trouble.*

10. *And they that know thy name will put their trust in thee: for thou, Lord, hast not forsaken them that seek thee.*

In the second place, he foreseeth in the Spirit what shall become of all God's enemies, and adversaries of his people, and prophesieth concerning them, to the praise of God, and comfort of the godly, who were to live after his time: whence learn, 1. Although the conscience of the persecutors of God's people be silent in their security, yet shall God's judgment against them awake their conscience at last, whether they be enemies without the church, or within it; yea, the Lord shall destroy them: *for thou, O Lord, hast rebuked the heathen, thou hast destroyed the wicked.* 2. Although the enemies have a great name in the world, yet shall their glory be blasted, and their renown vanish, as if it had never been heard of: for *thou, Lord, hast put out their name for ever and ever.* 3. The destructions of the Lord's people, and of their dwellings, intended by the wicked, shall be charged upon their enemies, though they have not executed and brought their malice to pass, even when the enemies themselves know and think, they have not attained their purpose: their intended *destructions shall come to a perpetual end.* 4. The time shall come, when the godly shall triumph over all their oppressors: yea, in the midst of the enemies' insolencies, the godly by faith may triumph over them, and say as here, *O thou enemy, destructions are come to a perpetual end.* 5. As the enemies of God's church have destroyed the earthly dwellings of the Lord's people ; so the Lord hath destroyed, and will *destroy their cities and their dwellings, and make their memorial cease with them.* 6. The reign of the wicked adversaries of God's people is very short, and in a few days they are cut off; but *the Lord shall endure for ever*, to defend his people from age to age. 7. Courts of justice among men are not always ready to hear plaintiffs ; but the Lord holdeth court continually; the taking in of no man's complaint is delayed so much as one hour, though thousands should come at once, all of them with sundry petitions : *he hath prepared his throne for judgment.* 8. Albeit in the courts of men justice be not always found, and very rarely in any matter concerning Christ; yet *the Lord shall judge the world in righteousness, and minister judgment to the people in uprightness :* the injuries done to his people shall be all of them righted by him. 9. Although the Lord's children have no residence, but be chased from place to place, and know not whither to go in the earth ; yet there is an open city of refuge unto them, where they shall find shelter : *for the Lord also will be a refuge to the oppressed.* 10. The Lord's relief which he giveth to his people, is reserved, till other inferior reliefs fail, till the godly man be humbled and emptied, and then will he help: *unto the oppressed he will be a refuge in time of trouble.* 11. The way of the Lord's helping and comforting his own people, is by lifting up the believer above any thing which can overtake him ; above the reach of all creatures ; *the Lord will be a high tower,* a high place as the word importeth, whence the believer may look down and despise what flesh can do unto him. 12. The ignorance of the Lord's goodness, mercy, truth, and other his attributes, is the cause of making so little use of God in prosperity, and so little believing in him in the time of trouble; for, *they who know his name, will trust in him.* 13. They to whom the spiritual knowledge of God is revealed, will certainly trust in him : and they that trust in him will *seek* him : and they that seek him, will find him to be what he is called: for the man *knowing God, trusting in God, and seeking God,* is the same here. 14. The Lord may for a time hide himself, or delay to manifest himself to a believer that seeketh him, (which he doth sometimes for the believer's trial, exercise, and profiting,) yet no age can give an instance of his rejecting such a supplicant : *for thou, Lord, hast not forsaken them that seek thee.* 15. As many experiences as are past of God's grace to believing supplicants before this day, so many confirmations of faith are given, and so many encouragements to all believers to seek his face in Christ : *for he never forsook them that sought him.*

11. *Sing praises to the Lord, which dwelleth in Zion : declare among the people his doings.*

12. *When he maketh inquisition for blood, he re-*

membereth them: he forgetteth not the cry of the humble.

In the third place, he exhorteth the rest of the godly to praise God with him ; whence learn, 1. It is the duty of all believers to join themselves cheerfully in the setting forth the Lord's care over them, and whatsoever may make his lovely Majesty known to the world: for so he requireth the present precept and example,—*sing praises to the Lord.* 2. The only true God, and the right object of our joy and praises, is he who manifested himself to the church of the Jews of old; who gave his Scriptures and his ordinances to them ; and among whom he took up his residence in Jerusalem, *in Zion,* in the temple, in the mercy seat, betwixt the cherubims, (which was a figure of the incarnation of the Son of God; in whom, as the only Mediator, is the trysting place between God and believers, for accepting their persons and worship,) for so doth the description of the true God here teach us : *sing praises to the Lord who dwelleth in Zion.* 3. The acts of the Lord for his people are so stamped with the impression of his divinity, that they are able to purchase glory to God even among the nations that are without the church, and to draw them to him : and so it is not a needless, fruitless, or hopeless work, to *declare his doings among the nations.* 4. If the Lord be pleased to honour himself with the martyrdom of any of his servants, it is not for disrespect to their persons, for they remain, even when dead, honourable in his estimation, and high in his affection ; for *he remembereth them* in a special manner. 5. There is a time appointed of God for bringing to judgment every sin, and especially murder ; and of all murders, to avenge most severely the slaughter of his servants, concerning whom it is here said, *when he maketh inquisition for blood, he remembereth them* : precious in his eyes is the death of his saints. 6. There is not a lost word in the earnest prayers of the humble believer, poured forth in the day of his necessity : every petition shall have a full answer, partly in this life, and partly in the life to come : for *God forgetteth not the cry of the humble.*

13. *Have mercy upon me, O Lord; consider my trouble which I suffer of them that hate me, thou that liftest me up from the gates of death!*

14. *That I may show forth all thy praise in the gates of the daughter of Zion: I will rejoice in thy salvation.*

In the fourth place, he cometh to his own particular and present case, and prayeth for a new experience of the truth formerly set down, believed, and sealed by him. Whence learn, 1. When new troubles befall experienced believers, they must betake them to their old refuge, and to the formerly blessed means of prayer; as here David doeth : *have mercy, O Lord, upon me.* 2. Never a word of merit should be in the mouth of a true believer ; for, *have mercy on me, O Lord,* is David's only plea : any good in us, is but a sandy ground to build on. 3. It sufficeth a believer acquainted with God, to present before God the trouble he suffereth unjustly from his enemies, and to expect deliverance from the Lord's grace towards himself, and from his justice in relation to the adversary : for this is the argument here used, *consider my trouble which I suffer of them that hate me.* 4. Extreme danger of present death, should not dash nor discourage the believer to pray for deliverance, because experience hath proven, that the Lord *can lift a believer up from the gates of death.* 5. Life should not be loved so much for itself, as that we may glorify God in our life, and edify others in the knowledge of God ; for deliverance from death is here asked of God, that he *may set forth all the praises of God in the gates* and most open places *of the daughter of Zion :* that is, in the audience of the people of God. 6. He gets a satisfactory answer : which teacheth us, that in a moment the Lord can persuade the supplicant of the grant of his prayer, and fill him with joy ; as here in one breath, ere the prophet could close his prayer, he is made to joy in the salvation or deliverance which he was persuaded God was to give to him ; *I will rejoice in thy salvation.*

15. *The heathen are sunk down in the pit* that *they made: in the net which they hid is their own foot taken.*

16. *The Lord is known* by *the judgment* which *he executeth : the wicked is snared in the work of his own hands. Higgaion. Selah.*

17. *The wicked shall be turned into hell,* and *all the nations that forget God.*

18. *For the needy shall not always be forgotten: the expectation of the poor shall* not *perish for ever.*

In the fifth place is set down, how with confidence of his own delivery, he is made sure of the overthrow of the enemy : whence learn, 1. Ordinarily, the delivery of the persecuted people of God is joined with the overthrow of their oppressors : and certainly, the wicked cannot take a readier way to ruin themselves, than to seek the overthrow of the Lord's church and people ; for here, *the heathen are sunk down in the pit that they made ;* andtheir crafty counsel against the godly, is the trap to take themselves in : *in the net which they hid, their own feet are taken.* 2. None of God's judgments, and specially none of those judgments whereby he pleads the cause of his church against her enemies, should be lightly looked upon ; *for the Lord is known by the judgments which he executeth.* His judgments bear the impression of his wisdom and justice : so as the sin may be read written on the rod. 3. Amongst other manifestations of God's wisdom and justice in punishing his adversaries, this is one, the Lord makes the works of the wicked, and specially what they do against his people, to be the very means to undo them : *the wicked is snared in the work of his own hands.* 4. As the devices of the wicked come from hell, so they return thither, and draw the devisers with them : though they cry, Peace, peace, and put the fear of hell far from them, yet *all the wicked shall be turned into hell.* 5. As they who give themselves to sin, and specially enemies to peace, cast away the knowledge of God out of their mind and affection ; so shall God cast them away far from his presence : *all the nations that forget God, shall be turned into hell.* 6. Albeit the Lord does not presently execute judgment on the godless oppressors of his people, yet for respect the Lord doth bear to his people, their destruction shall certainly come : *they shall go down to hell ; for the needy shall not always be forgotten.* The cry of the needy and oppressed shall bring judgment upon the oppressors. 7. The Lord's people are an humbled people, afflicted, emptied, sensible of their need, driven to a daily attendance on God, daily begging of him, and living only upon the hope of what is promised: for so are they here described needy, poor supplicants, and expectants of the performance of what is promised. 8. Albeit the Lord seems to lay aside the prayers of the oppressed godly, and forget them: and albeit the godly man's hope doth seem for a time vain, *yet shall he not always be forgotten, nor his expectation perish for ever,* and specially the expectation he hath of things everlasting, shall not be disappointed, but shall be satisfied *for ever.*

19. *Arise, O Lord; let not man prevail; let the heathen be judged in thy sight.*

20. *Put them in fear, O Lord;* that *the nations may know themselves* to be but *men. Selah.*

In the last place he followeth his condemnatory sentence of the wicked with prayer, that the Lord would put it in execution, even in his own time. Whence learn, 1. The Lord doth not so delay to execute judgment on the oppressors of his people, but he may be entreated to make speedy despatch, and as need requireth *to arise* and fall to work. 2. The time of God's arising is, when the cause of God which the godly maintain is like to be lost: *arise, O Lord, let not man prevail.* There is his reason, why he would have God to arise. 3. When God ariseth for the godly, he maketh it appear, that they are his people, and that their adversaries are in effect before him but heathen and strangers for the inward covenant and commonwealth of his people, whether they be within the visible church or not ; for he prayeth, *let the heathen be judged in thy sight.* 4. So long as the Lord doth spare his adversaries, they misknow themselves, and God also. Sin doth so besot ignorant and graceless people, that they forget that they are mortal, and that God is their judge. Therefore David desireth, *that the nations may know themselves to be but men.* 5. Where there is any hope or possibility of the salvation of enemies, the godly man's desire is they should be brought in subjection to God, and humbled before him ; and that judgments might be so tempered as the enemy might profit thereby, and God be glorified : *put them in fear, that they may know themselves to be but men.*

PSALM X.

This Psalm wanteth an inscription, and that is God's wisdom, that being less restricted to a particular man's case, it may be of more general use, whensoever the godly find themselves in a condition whereunto this prayer may be suitable: and specially in time of general persecution. The prophet here complaineth to God and craveth justice against the persecutors of his people, because of the intolerable wickedness of the oppressor, ver. 1—11. Secondly, he prayeth for hastening of the delivery of the Lord's people, and for hastening of judgment upon the persecutors, for vindication of the glory of God's justice against his enemies, and of his mercy to his people, ver. 12—15. Thirdly, he professeth his confidence that he shall be heard, and so glorifieth God, ver. 16—18.

1. *Why standest thou afar off, O Lord?* why *hidest thou* thyself *in times of trouble?*

2. *The wicked in* his *pride doth persecute the poor : let them be taken in the devices that they have imagined.*

3. *For the wicked boasteth of his heart's desire, and blesseth the covetous,* whom *the Lord abhorreth.*

4. *The wicked, through the pride of his countenance will not seek* after *God : God is not in all his thoughts.*

5. *His ways are always grievous ; thy judgments* are *far above out of his sight :* as for *all his enemies, he puffeth at them.*

6. *He hath said in his heart, I shall not be moved : for* I shall *never* be *in adversity.*

7. *His mouth is full of cursing, and deceit, and fraud : under his tongue* is *mischief and vanity.*

8. *He sitteth in the lurking places of the villages : in the secret places doth he murder the innocent*: *his eyes are privily set against the poor.*

9. *He lieth in wait secretly as a lion in his den : he lieth in wait to catch the poor : he doth catch the poor, when he draweth him into his net.*

10. *He croucheth,* and *humbleth himself, that the poor may fall by his strong ones.*

11. *He hath said in his heart, God hath forgotten : he hideth his face ; he will never see* it.

In this complaint he speaketh to God after the manner of men, in the terms of sense, and as matters did seem to

him in outward appearance. Whence learn, 1. How far
contrary to the word of promise, may God's word and dispensation seem to speak : the word saith, *he will ever be
with his own, and not forsake them ;* and here his dealing
with them seemeth to say, *that he standeth afar off, and
hideth himself in times of trouble.* Sense may sometime
speak contrary to faith. 2. In this case the speech of sense
is not to be subscribed, but the truth of the word should
be relied upon ; and the objection made by sense, or suggestion against the word, is to be brought before the Lord
in prayer, that it may be discussed : as here the prophet
doth : *why standest thou afar off, &c.* 3. Observe how
homely an humbled soul may be with God, and how far the
Lord will be from mistaking of his people, when faith borroweth sense's tongue. The Lord will suffer such speeches
and not take them in ill part, knowing that they proceed
from faith and love, wrestling with sense ; yea, and he will
suffer them to be registered in his book, as here we see,
for prudent use-making of them, though they appear to
challenge him, *for standing aloof, and hiding himself.* 4.
Ofttimes it cometh to pass, that the godly are in a mean
condition in the world, when their adversaries are in high
places and power, and so be able to oppress them as their
underlings : *the wicked in his pride doth persecute the
poor.* 5. In respect that pride disdaineth what is apparently good in a mean person, and overvalueth its own worth,
therefore pride is easily coupled with oppression, and pride
is able to raise persecution : *the wicked in his pride doth
persecute the poor.* 6. What persecutors devise against
God's people, may with good grounds be expected to
turn to be a snare unto themselves. *Let them be taken in
the devices they have imagined.* 7. All the politicians on
earth cannot describe the vileness of the wicked, so well as
the Spirit of the Lord doth point it out, for he setteth him
forth. 1. He is an arrogant, self-confident man, threatening to bring to pass what he would have done, as if he were
able in despite of God to effectuate it : *he boasts of his
heart's desire.* 2. He accounts of no man, but such a one
as by hook and crook is able to enhance honour and riches ;
he blesseth the covetous man. 3. He valueth not what
God judgeth of a man, whether he be a man whom God
oveth and respects, or not ; he setteth his opinion in op-

position to God's judgment of men, *he blesseth the man whom
God abhorreth.* 4. The wicked man hath such a conceit of
his own ability and perfection, as his countenance and carriage doth testify that he scorneth to employ God by prayer
for any thing : *through the pride of his countenance he will
not seek God.* 5. For the rule of his life, he consulteth not
what may please or displease God, what may honour or dishonour God ; he troubles not himself with such thoughts :
God is not in all his thoughts ; that is, as the Hebrew phrase
doth mean, all his thoughts are, that there is no God : or
none of his thoughts are upon God. 6. His ways are ever
noisome, tending especially to hurt the godly : *his ways are
always grievous* ; or as his ways prosper, they vex others.
7. He feareth not God's judgments, he believeth not that they
shall ever come ; he putteth them far away in his conceit :
yea, and what the Lord hath set down in his word, as his
judgment, he apprehendeth it not ; he is not capable of
spiritual wisdom : *the Lord's judgments are far above
out of his sight.* 8. He neither feareth God nor man : *all
his enemies he puffeth at them ;* as disdaining what they can
do against him. 9. The wicked promise to themselves
perpetuity of prosperity, and do not fear evil, to see a
change to the worse ; *he assureth himself never to be moved,
nor to be in adversity.* 10. For his words, he standeth
not to blaspheme God, to lie, swear, and curse, if it may
purchase him credit, and may help him to deceive others.
His mouth is full of cursing. 11. His fair promises are
but vanity ; and when he minds a mischief, he hides it with
pretences of best intentions, *under his tongue is mischief
and vanity.* 12. As thieves and cut-throats lie in wait
about villages, to catch the straggling passengers, where
there are few to help them, so do the wicked watch where
they may oppress those who have few to do for them : *he
sitteth in the lurking places of the villages, in secret places
doth he murder the innocent.* 13. As an archer in the
hunting of his prey, so doth the wicked mark and spy out
a poor man, to take advantage of him : *his eyes are
privily set against the poor.* 14. As a lion in his den,
or some lurking place, lieth still till the prey come by, and
then he leapeth out upon it, when he is able to take it : so
doth the wicked dissemble his malice, till he be master over
a man, and then doeth what he can against him : *he lieth*

secretly in wait, as a lion. 15. As a crafty hunter spreadeth his net for a prey, and miskenneth it, till the prey be
entangled ; so doth the wicked lay some device to catch the
poor, and taketh him: *he doth catch the poor, when he
draws him in his net.* 16. As the lion lieth low in the
dust, as if he minded to do no harm at all; so do the wicked men pretend themselves the most reasonable men that
can be, and most observant of law and equity, till by their
power they may have their intent of the poor: *he
croucheth and humbleth himself, that the poor may fall by
him, or his associates.* 17. Present prosperity joined with
impurity maketh him persuade himself that God will never
take notice of him hereafter, or call him to account, or
punish him: *he hath said in his heart, God hath forgotten, he hideth his face, he will never see it.*

12. *Arise, O Lord; O God, lift up thine hand:
forget not the humble.*

13. *Wherefore doth the wicked contemn God? he
hath said in his heart, Thou wilt not require it.*

14. *Thou hast seen it; for thou beholdest mischief
and spite, to requite it with thy hand: the poor committeth himself unto thee; thou art the helper of the
fatherless.*

15. *Break thou the arm of the wicked and the evil*
man: *seek out his wickedness* till *thou find none.*

Thus he hath given the character of the enemies of
God's people, and so made a ditty for them.   Now in the
second place, he prayeth against them, that their doom
may be given out, and may be executed.   Whence learn,
1. The more we see atheism in the wicked, the more we
should draw near to God : and albeit the godly conceive
God to lie off, and sit still from executing justice, the
godly being tempted with the temptations which overcome
the wicked, yet they must not yield to the temptation, but
pray against it, as is here done; *arise, O Lord, lift up thy
hand.*   2. The merciful respect and love which the Lord
hath to his afflicted people, will not suffer his justice
against these persecutors to be long quiet, *for he will not
forget the humble.*   3. As the interest which God hath in
his own people, engageth him to fall on their enemies; so
the vindication also of his own glory from the contempt

which they do to his name engageth him against them; for *wherefore doth the wicked contemn God, &c.?* 4. The godless enemies of God's people deny God's providence, and deny God's justice; yet his people are comforted under their saddest sufferings by the Lord's seeing and marking thereof; for the godly say here, *thou hast seen it, and beholdest mischief.* 5. God's judgments on the wicked shall really refute the atheism of the wicked, and requite their opposition made to the godly. *He beholds mischief and spite to requite it with his hand.* 6. When a man hath laid forth his desires, and poured out his heart before God, he should quiet himself, and cast himself with his burden upon the Lord; for here *the poor committeth himself to God.* And when an humble believer hath cast his burden on the Lord, the Lord will not fail to take care of what he is trusted with, it is an engaging of God, that the poor hath committed himself to him. 7. As the Lord's office, custom, and nature is, so is his real work to do for them who employ him, and are not able to do for themselves; *he is the helper of the fatherless.* 8. The power of persecutors cannot be so great, but God shall weaken and break it, so as they shall not be able to trouble his people. *Break thou the arm of the wicked.* 9. Though the Lord reckons not with his enemies for their sins at first, yet he reckons for all at last; for less and for greater, for one and for all, and doth not pass a farthing of the debt of punishment unexacted: *but seeketh out their sins till he find none.* O how fearful a reckoning must it be, which the Lord maketh with the impenitent, who die unpardoned, and unreconciled with God, through the Mediator Christ Jesus!

16. *The Lord is King for ever and ever: the heathen are perished out of his land.*

17. *Lord, thou hast heard the desire of the humble: thou wilt prepare their heart, thou wilt cause thine ear to hear.*

18. *To judge the fatherless and the oppressed, that the man of the earth may no more oppress.*

In the last place, the answer of the petition followeth, in a comfortable persuasion of the supplicant, concerning the grant thereof: whence learn, 1. That the prayer of the persecuted shall not be rejected, because the kingdom of

Christ in his church is perpetual : earthly kings cannot
live still to help their friends, followers, or flatterers, or to
persecute and molest God's church : but *Christ is the
Lord and King for ever and ever*, to defend his people, and
punish his foes.   2. The wicked within the visible church,
howsoever they have the external privileges of God's people,
yet if they continue unreconciled, and oppose piety, they
shall be in God's estimation, and in the day of his judging
them, counted as they are here called, heathen, and shall
be separated from the fellowship of God and God's people,
the heathen shall perish out of his land.   3. It is the Lord's
way to exercise his children with trouble, till he humble
them and make them sensible of the need of his help, till he
turn their sense of need into a desire of his relief, and
their desire into a prayer, and then he will in due time give
answer : *Lord, thou hast heard the desire of the humble.*
4. Grace to pray, and the fixing of the heart in prayer on
the Lord, is his gift, no less than the answer of the prayer :
and where the Lord giveth the one grace, he will also give
the other : *thou wilt prepare their heart, thou wilt cause
thine ear to hear.*   5. When God beginneth to show his
respect to the prayers of his people against their oppressors,
then the helpless and weak servants of God shall have deliverance from the power of oppressors, and their oppressors
shall not be able to do any more harm, when the Lord
causeth his ear to hear their prayer: *the fatherless shall be
judged,* yea declared righteous, absolved and delivered ;
and the oppressor shall no more oppress.   6. If there were
no more comfort to the godly oppressed, yet this may
suffice, that their life, inheritance, and happiness is in
heaven ; and that their oppressors, in opposition to them,
are declared here, to be *but men of this earth*, whose portion is no better than what they have here in this world.

PSALM XI.

To the Chief Musician.   A Psalm of David.

David, as an example of a Christian under the trial of his faith in time
  of trouble, and tempted to desperation, resisted the temptation, how
  desperate soever his condition seemed, v. 1, 2; and disputeth for the
  confirmation of his own faith, v. 3—7.

1. *In the Lord put I my trust: how say ye to my soul,
Flee* as a *bird to your mountain?*

2. *For, lo, the wicked bend* their *bow, they make ready their arrow upon the string, that they may privily shoot at the upright in heart.*

Before the prophet dispute, and produce his reasons against the temptations unto unbelief, he asserteth and avoweth his faith, and presenteth the danger he is in, before God. Whence learn, 1. It is the surest method in our spiritual combat against Satan, and his fiery darts, to hold up the shield of faith, and to fix ourselves in resolution never to loose our hold of the Lord; as David doth here: *in the Lord put I my trust.* 2. Having once fixed our foot on the rock, we may the more effectually rebuke our adversaries, for mocking of our confidence: as David doth here, saying, *how say you to my soul, flee?* 3. God is a strong refuge to his own, whereunto they should fly like birds, chased to their strength, in all necessities, for he is our *rock* or *mountain*. 4. The wicked world scorn the godly man's confidence, and the avowing of his faith in God, when they see no visible help for him on earth. Take up your faith now, say they, when they see the man beset by apparently inextricable troubles, as here they say to David, *flee now as a bird to thy mountain.* 5. The believer is not stupid in time of danger, nor senseless of difficulties, when he asserteth his faith: *for lo,* saith he, *the wicked bend their bow,* they have me, as it were, under the aim of their shot. 6. The Lord for the exercise of the faith of his own, and for discovery of the plots of the wicked against them, and for showing his own glory in protecting them more clearly, suffereth the wicked to make all ready, even unto present execution of their cruelty, as here, *they make ready their arrow upon the string to shoot, &c.*

3. *If the foundations be destroyed, what can the righteous do?*

4. *The Lord* is *in his holy temple, the Lord's throne* is *in heaven: his eyes behold, his eyelids try, the children of men.*

5. *The Lord trieth the righteous; but the wicked, and him that loveth violence, his soul hateth.*

6. *Upon the wicked he shall rain snares, fire and brimstone, and an horrible tempest:* this shall be *the portion of their cup.*

7. *For the righteous Lord loveth righteousness; his countenance doth behold the upright.*

In the next place, he disputeth for the confirmation of his own faith by sundry reasons or several considerations.

The first reason to confirm his faith, is from the absurdity of the temptation, tending to the overturning of the very foundation of religion, whereunto, if the believer should yield, he is lost and gone. Whence learn, 1. Faith in God, and flying to him in all straits for relief, is the *foundation* of all religious and righteous persons, whereupon they build their hope and happiness solidly; for David had laid it for a foundation, that God was *a rock*, or mountain of refuge for men to flee unto in straits. 2. A temptation to mistrust God, and not to flee to him in all hazards, is most dangerous, and destructive of all true religion, for it is the destroying of the very foundations of righteousness and happiness; and the resisting of this temptation is so necessary, as in what measure it is yielded unto in that measure the righteous man is put to a stand, and to a comfortless perplexity, and should despair certainly if he went from it: for, *if the foundations be destroyed, what shall the righteous man do?* If it be in vain to fly to God, righteous men are lost men, which is absurd.

The next reason to confirm his faith is the establishment of a Mediator, set forth in the word of God, and other holy ordinances, concerning the covenant of grace, and the benefits of it, and duties required in it, all to be found in the Lord's holy temple, or tabernacle, representing Christ Jesus and his church, and the mutual relations between God and his people. Whence learn, 3. The way to refresh and strengthen faith, is to look to God in Christ the Mediator, reconciling the world to himself, according as he was shadowed forth in the temple of Jerusalem, and as he is still holden forth in the church, in his word and other ordinances. First and last, Christ is the trysting place, where God is constantly to be found on his mercy seat; for *the Lord in his holy temple* did speak so much to the church in typical terms.

4. The third reason is, because God is a perfect judge to take order in due time, both with them who oppose his work and people, and with those who will not make use of his mercy: *the Lord's throne is in heaven.* 5. The

Lord's knowledge of all men's carriage is perfect: *his eyes behold.*   6. When the Lord doth not make manifest by his work that he seeth men's carriage, but seemeth, as is were, to wink and close his eyes, he is then about to try the hearts of men, and to bring their thoughts to light: *his eye-lids* (when his eyes seem closed) *try the children of men.*   7. The troubles whereunto the Lord doth put his children in times of temptation, are not to be exposed as acts of displeasure, or mere justice, but as acts of wisdom and love, to try, exercise, and frame them to obedience. *The Lord trieth the righteous;* at such time as he sendeth trouble specially.   8. However he giveth the wicked and violent persecutor to have a seeming prosperity, while the godly are in trouble, yet that is no act of love to them: for *the wicked, and him that loveth violence, his soul hateth.*   9. All the seeming advantages which the wicked have in their own prosperity, are but means of hardening them in their ill course, and holding them fast in the bonds of their own iniquities, till God execute judgment on them: *upon the wicked he shall rain snares.*   10. Whatsoever be the condition of the wicked for a time, yet at length sudden, terrible, irresistible, and remediless destruction they shall not escape: *fire and brimstone, and an horrible tempest is the portion of their cup.*

The fourth reason for confirmation of his faith is from the Lord's love, settled upon his upright servants, in the midst of their troubles, while they suffer for righteousness' sake. Whence learn, 11. The respect that the Lord hath to the cause for which his servants suffer, hasteneth on, and fasteneth wrath upon their adversaries: for *the righteous Lord loveth righteousness,* is given as a reason of the sentence in the preceding verse.   12. Though clouds sometimes hide the expressions of the Lord's respect and love towards his people, yet still his love is set upon them; for *continually his countenance doth behold the upright.*

PSALM XII.

To the chief Musician upon Sheminith.   A Psalm of David.

The prophet having observed, as is set down, v. 8, how wickedness lifteth up the head in all the land, when the places of power and trust come into the hands of naughty and vile men, giveth direction by his own example unto the godly; first, to have their recourse to God by prayer, while they are borne down by the wicked in such an ill time, v. 1, 2; and next how to comfort themselves by the word of God, pronouncing the sentence of justice upon all loose-tongued men, v. 3, 4; and promising delivery to the oppressed godly, and preservation of his church in all generations, v. 5—7.   Howsoever, he suffers wicked men to bear rule sometimes, and wickedness to abound by that means, v. 8.

1. *Help, Lord; for the godly man ceaseth: for the faithful fail from among the children of men.*

2. *They speak vanity every one with his neighbour:* with *flattering lips,* and *with a double heart, do they speak.*

David finding no friend at court, nor any place or power, who either would speak a word in his favour, or give him any friendly counsel, turneth himself to God.   Whence learn, 1. The face of the visible church may sometimes be so far defaced, that there cannot be a man found to show himself openly, for a good cause, as here is noted: *the godly man ceaseth, the faithful fail from among the children of men.*   2. In such a case God can and will supply the lack of friends and counsellors to his own, when they say to him, *help Lord; the Lord will help.*   3. At such a time, a godly person may not think upon seditious practices against those that are in lawful authority, but take himself to prayer; for David who had a fairer pretence for such a practice than any private man or men can have, because he **was** designed successor to the kingdom, goeth to God in this case, and crieth, *help Lord.*

He proveth the lack of godliness and faithfulness, because there was no upright, nor honest dealing among the people, but falsehood and flattery.   Whence learn, 4. Where true godliness is out of request, the common bonds of neighbourhood, (including bonds of blood, alliance, and acquaintance,) will fail also, and every one will go about to deceive his neighbour; so that a man cannot trust what another saith: for *they speak vanity every one with his neighbour.*   5. When ungodly men intend most to deceive, then they are sure to speak fairest, giving pleasant words, with insinuation of respects in abundant compliments.   They *speak vanity to their neighbour with flattering lips.*   6. Vain talk, cozening speeches, flattering words are unbeseeming honest men, and argue in so far as men affect them, ungodliness, unfaithfulness, and deceitfulness in a man; for when *with flattering lips they speak, with a double heart they speak.*

3. *The Lord shall cut off all flattering lips,* and *the tongue that speaketh proud things;*

4. *Who have said, With our tongue will we prevail; our lips* are *our own: who* is *Lord over us?*

He setteth down in the next place the comforts of the godly, which are three. The first is from God's justice in punishing calumniators of the godly, and proud boasters. Whence learn, 1. Although pickthanks, and flatterers of great men, in prejudice of the godly, hope to stand by their flattery, yet *the Lord shall cut off all flattering lips.* 2. Albeit men in power and place threaten to bring about great things against God's people, yet they shall not be able to do what they have said: *for God shall cut off also the tongue that speaketh proud things.* 3. Wicked men are confident, and assure themselves to double out their course by their falsehood, flattery, and calumnies against the godly; *they have said, With our tongue will we prevail.* 4. Wicked men make no conscience to use well the gifts which they have gotten of God; such as wit or language, or any other thing; for they say, *our lips are our own.* 5. Wicked men stand not in awe of God; they fear not punishment from him, for in effect they say, *who is Lord over us?* But we must learn from their faults three contrary lessons; to wit, 1. That nothing which we have is our own. But, 2. Whatsoever is given to us of God is for service to be done to him. 3. That whatsoever we do, or say, we have a Lord over us, to whom we must be answerable, when he calleth us to account.

5. *For the oppression of the poor, for the sighing of the needy, now will I arise, saith the Lord; I will set* him *in safety* from him that *puffeth at him.*

6. *The words of the Lord* are *pure words :* as *silver tried in a furnace of earth, purified seven times.*

7. *Thou shalt keep them, O Lord, thou shalt preserve them from this generation for ever.*

The second comfort of the godly in an ill time, is from the promise of God, to deliver the godly out of the hand of the wicked. Whence learn, 1. When the Lord hath exercised the godly for a while, with the oppression of the wicked, he will not fail to make manifest, that he hath heard their sad supplications, and seen their oppression ; *for the oppression of the poor, for the sighing of the needy, now will I arise, saith the Lord.* 2. The proud persecutor thinketh little of the godly, or any power that can defend him, but doth mock the hope he hath to be helped ; yet *God will set the godly in safety from him that puffeth at him.* This promise the prophet commendeth to the church, as a precious truth which will be found forth-coming to the full, in experience. Whence learn, 3. To the end that the word of promise may be comfortable to us, till new experience comes, we must consider whose word it is, and that there is no vanity in promises, but all contained in them, shall be found very solid, like the refined silver, or gold, which is purged from all dross, and the oftener it is put in the fire, it is the more fair, and of greater value ; for *the words are the Lord's words, and pure words,* tryed, true in his experience, *as silver tried in a furnace of earth seven times,* and clear from all dross.

The third comfort of the godly is from assurance given of the perpetuation of the church, and custody of it by God in all ages. Whence learn, 4. Let men persecute the godly as much as God pleaseth to suffer them, yet shall God preserve a church of godly persons at all times to the end of the world : *for God shall preserve the godly from this generation for ever.* 5. Albeit the discomforted godly, under persecutors, are not always able to draw presently comfort from this promise ; yet it is a truth which God will own, which God will keep in his hand to us, when we come to him, and which every believer must own, though no man should take it off his hand. Therefore doth David turn himself to God, in delivering this charter of the church's safety ; *thou,* saith he, *shalt keep them.*

8. *The wicked walk on every side, when the vilest men are exalted.*

In the close of the psalm, upon his own experience, he draweth up a general observation of what may be expected, when the most wicked are most advanced. Whence learn, 1. God sometimes so disposeth in his wisdom and justice, for punishing of wicked people, and exercising of the godly, that the places of government in a kingdom, are filled not with the best men, but with the *vilest of the sons of men ;* for in David's experience it was so, and he presupposeth it might fall to be so, that the vilest of men should be exalted. 2. The wickedness of the ungodly, in this case, breaketh forth most, and spreadeth itself among the subjects, being heartened thereunto by the ruler's toleration, connivance, or instigation, or example, and countenance ; *for when the vilest men are exalted, then the wicked walk on every side.* Turn you where you will, you shall meet with them, at such a time *as the vilest are exalted.*

PSALM XIII.

To the chief Musician.   A Psalm of David.

Another Christian experience, wherein David under the sense of desertion, laying forth his lamentable case before the Lord, ver. 1, 2 ; prayeth for relief, ver. 3, 4 ; and by faith is refreshed and comforted, ver. 5. 6.

1. *How long wilt thou forget me, O Lord? for ever? how long wilt thou hide thy face from me?*

2. *How long shall I take counsel in my soul,* having *sorrow in my heart daily? how long shall mine enemy be exalted over me?*

In laying forth his grief, he beginneth at his apparent desertion ; then speaking of the perplexity of mind, arising herefrom ; and last of all, he mentioneth the continuance of his outward trouble from his enemies. Whence learn, 1. Trouble outward and inward, of body and spirit, fightings without, and terrors within, vexations from heaven and earth, from God deserting and men pursuing, may fall upon a child of God at one time, and continue for a time long enough, as here ; *how long wilt thou forget me? how long shall mine enemy be exalted over me?* 2. When trouble is continued, and an appearance of means of delivery is not, and God both witholdeth inward and outward help, sense calleth this the Lord's *forgetting* and *hiding of his face*: *how long wilt thou forget me, and hide thy face?* 3. The Lord's children in their resolution for faith and patience, set to themselves a shorter period usually than the Lord doth, for making them have their perfect work ; therefore, when their hope is deferred, it makes their heart sick, and cry out, *How long? how long?* 4. When comfort trysteth not with our time, fear of eternal off-casting may readily slide in : and this fear, a soul acquainted with God, or that loveth him in any measure, cannot endure : *wilt thou forget me for ever?* saith he. 5. Whatsoever sense speaketh, or suggested temptations speak, faith will relate the business to the Lord, and expect a better speech from him : for in this condition the prophet goeth to God, saying, *How long, O Lord?* 6. A soul finding desertion, multiplieth consultations, falleth into perplexity, changeth conclusions, as a sick man doth his bed, falleth in grief, and cannot endure to live by its own finding, but runneth upon God for direction, as here we see it ; *how long shall I take counsel in my soul, having sorrow in my heart daily?* 7. The enemies taking advantage, (by the continuance of trouble upon the godly,) against his cause and religion, and against God, augmenteth both the grief and temptation of the godly ; *how long shall mine enemies be exalted over me?*

3. *Consider* and *hear me, O Lord my God : lighten mine eyes, lest I sleep the* sleep of *death ;*

4. *Lest mine enemy say, I have prevailed against him ;* and *those that trouble me rejoice when I am moved.*

Now followeth his prayer for some comfortable answer, lest both he should perish, and God be dishonoured : whence learn, 1. The edge of temptations is blunted, and grief assuaged, when the swelling of the soul venteth itself to God : and certainly complaints are then best eased, when they are dissolved in humble supplications, as here, *consider and hear me, O Lord my God.* 2. Albeit faith believeth that God considereth and heareth always, yet it cannot rest till it feel by some effect that he doth hear and consider, by his giving some real support, or help in need, according to covenant ; this is imported in his praying, and words of prayer, *consider, hear me.* 3. If the Lord think it not good to give an outward delivery, faith will be content of a glimpse of God's countenance for the present ; *lighten mine eyes,* saith he ; that is, let me have some immediate comfort to uphold me in the hope of my delivery. 4. It is a death to the godly man who hath seen him that is invisible, to be long without the sense of God's love :

sense of succumbing and perishing in trouble, doth in this case usually set upon the godly, as here, *lighten mine eyes lest I sleep the sleep of death.*   5. The enemies of the godly feed themselves with the trouble of the godly, and rejoice the more they see them in distress and discouragement; which two inconveniences the Lord useth to prevent, for he cannot endure long to see the pride and rejoicing of the enemy to feed itself on the miseries of his children; and this the prophet insinuateth, when he seeketh relief, *lest the enemy glory that he hath prevailed, &c.*

5. *But I have trusted in thy mercy; my heart shall rejoice in thy salvation.*

6. *I will sing unto the Lord, because he hath dealt bountifully with me.*

Here the prophet is raised up unto comfort by degrees : first he settleth himself upon the tried grounds of faith, then promiseth to himself deliverance, and thirdly, findeth comfort: whence learn, 1. Albeit we find not present relief or comfort when we pray, yet we must resolve to adhere to God by faith: when we have poured out our soul in his bosom by prayer, we must resolve to settle our feet on the ground of faith, before we can expect to be comforted : for here David relied on *God's mercy*, and ratifieth his former resolution and practice of resting on his mercy: *I have trusted on thy mercy.* 2. So soon as faith is fixed, and resolute to adhere to covenanted mercy, hope lifteth up the head, and this anchor of the tossed ship stayeth the soul from being driven ; the believer looketh out for God's salvation, by some way of delivery, which God thinks good to give, and assureth himself it shall come, and that he shall find joy in God's way of deliverance : *my heart*, saith he, *shall rejoice in thy salvation.* 3. When the believer is resolved to rest on God's mercy by faith, then followeth peace, at least, and readily more comfort of God's Spirit, than for the present he expected to have : yea, as much as shall satisfy him, and make him count himself richly dealt with, as here David acknowledgeth, saying, *he hath dealt bountifully with me.* 4. Fresh experience of favour from God, in the renewed sense of his good-will to a soul, is a matter of great joy in the midst of trouble ; and the right fruit of it is a renewed resolution cheerfully to praise God, as here we have the example, *I will sing unto the Lord, because he hath dealt bountifully with me.*

PSALM XIV.

To the Chief Musician.   A Psalm of David.

David, looking on the constitution of the visible Church, and seeing the great body of the people lying in their natural state, working iniquity and hating the truly godly amongst them, even to the death, verse, 1—3, comforteth the godly, first by the care the Lord hath of them, in pleading their cause against the ungodly, vers. 4—6, and next by giving hope of better days for the godly, when, after sore plagues come on that people, Christ should manifest himself unto them, vers. 7.

1. *The fool hath said in his heart,* There is *no God. They are corrupt; they have done abominable works; there is none that doeth good.*

2. *The Lord looked down from heaven upon the children of men, to see if there were any that did understand, and seek God.*

3. *They are all gone aside, they are* all *together become filthy; there is none that doeth good, no, not one.*

The prophet divideth all those who were in the visible church, into unregenerate men on the one hand, and God's true people converted inwardly unto him, on the other hand; and argueth all the unregenerate to be practically atheists, without God in the world, by the same proof whereby the apostle convinceth all men in nature, to be in the state of sin, Rom. iii. 13. Whence learn, 1. Every man so long as he lieth unrenewed and unreconciled unto God (how wise soever, or of how great parts soever he may seem to be to himself or the world), is nothing in effect but a madman, running to his own destruction in losing his soul and eternal life, when he seemeth most to gain the world, therefore he is called *the fool.* 2. It is not heeded by God what a man's mouth saith of God, or of himself, but what his heart saith: *the fool hath said in his heart, There is no God.* 3. It is not the word, or outward profession, which truly exposeth the heart, but the current of a man's life and actions; for here it is proved, that the heart is full of atheism, by this that *they* are *corrupt* in their conversation, *and do abominable works.* 4. God is the only right judge of regeneration and unregeneration, and the only true searcher of the heart: it is *he who looketh down from heaven, to see if any of the sons of men*, or any in the state of nature, have any wisdom in them, or affection after God ; *if any of them have understanding, or seek after God;* for he that doth not seek God, hath no understanding, nor principle of spiritual life in him. 5. Whatsoever may be the odds among unrenewed men, some more, some less gross in their outbreaking, yet God pronounceth of them all *that they are all of them gone out of the way*, to wit, of holiness and happiness, *they are altogether become filthy ;* that is, all their actions, flowing forth from their corrupt hearts, are vile and loathsome in God's sight, and they are all in one rank in this, *there is none of them that doeth good ;* none of them, being unreconciled to God, do, or can do, any thing at all commanded of God, as commanded from right principles, and for right ends.

4. *Have all the workers of iniquity no knowledge ? who eat up my people* as *they eat bread, and call not upon the Lord.*

5. *There were they in great fear : for God* is *in the generation of the righteous.*

6. *Ye have shamed the counsel of the poor, because the Lord* is *his refuge.*

In the next place he comforteth the people of God, living in society of the visible church, with the unrenewed multitude. First, by this, that the Lord doth plead their cause against the ungodly. Whence learn, 1. That the nature of all unrenewed men, is to bear deadly enmity against those that are really God's people, and delight to undo the godly, as contemners of all that live not as they do : *they eat up my people as they eat bread,* saith the Lord. 2. The Lord owns the quarrel, and wrongs done to the godly, as done to him, in whomsoever his image is hated or persecuted : *they eat up my people,* saith he.   3. The causeless hatred of the godly is a most unreasonable thing, and argueth admirable stupidity in wicked men, who malign the innocent, by whose life they are admonished of their duty, and taught the way to felicity: *have all the workers of iniquity no knowledge?*   4. The miskenning of God, and working of iniquity, and persecuting of the godly, are three conjunct properties of a man in nature, not reconciled to God: *for to be workers of iniquity, and eaters up of God's people as bread, and not calling on God,* are put for the marks and properties of the same sort of ungodly men.

Upon the challenge of the ungodly, the prophet inferreth the consequence of certain and sad judgments to follow on the wicked, because God is nearly concerned in the quarrel of his people. Whence learn, 5. The persecution of piety in the godly, provoketh God to inflict the most fearful and most sudden judgments: *for therein specially were the ungodly put to fear, where they had no fear at all.* 6. The near conjunction which God hath with the godly, is the reason of the greatness of the sin of persecution of them for godliness: for here it is given for a reason why *there* they were in fear, why they were to tremble when God came to avenge the oppression of the godly, which the wicked never feared to be questioned: *because God is in the generation of the righteous.* 7. Persecuting a man for piety, were it but in jesting at a man, or mocking of him for piety, is the turning of piety, which is a man's glory, into a matter of reproach to him; and a means to drive him and others from seeking of God: *you have shamed the counsel,* or resolution, *of the poor,* when you scorn, because he hath made God his refuge.

7. *Oh that the salvation of Israel were come out of Zion ! When the Lord bringeth back the captivity of his people, Jacob shall rejoice,* and *Israel shall be glad.*

The next comfort of the godly, is from the hope of Christ's coming, in whom the redressing of this evil, and of all other, is to be found, for whose coming he wisheth. It is true, the sending of deliverance unto the distressed people of God in Saul's time, by bringing David to the kingdom, was worthy to be wished for : but this could not fill up the measure of the wish here stirred up by the Spirit. Therefore we must look to the substance in Christ, in whom this wish and prayer hath full accomplishment, which in effect is, *O that Christ the Saviour of Israel were come out of Zion.* And this same wish closeth the fifty-third psalm also ; where salvations of Israel in the plural number is set down, to note the perfection of salvation which cometh only by Christ, at whom the very form of the Hebrew wishing doth look, as pointing at the person which shall give all sort of salvation to Israel, *who shall give;* now there was a coming of Christ in the flesh *unto Zion,* foretold by the Spirit, Zech. ix. 9, and this is presupposed in this wish; for Christ must be in Zion before he come out of it. But not by this coming were so many Israelites saved as here is wished for; not by this coming was the body of Israel brought back from the captivity here prophesied. There is also, Isaiah ii. 3, a coming of Christ *out of Zion* to the *Gentiles;* and this coming is presupposed here, before that Israel's captivity be loosed. There is, Isaiah lix. 20, compared with Rom. xi. 26, a coming out of *Zion* for the bringing salvation to the body of the now misbelieving nation of the captive Israelites, lying in captivity, scattered among the Gentiles, and this is directly prayed for, and longed after in this place: *O that the salvation of Israel were come out of Zion,* even the time when the Lord shall bring back the captivity of his people. Paul, Rom. xi. 26, calleth this the Redeemer's coming *out of Zion,* in regard of the time when, and the condition wherein Christ is to find the Israelites, to wit, *out of Zion,* out among the Gentiles, scattered among the Gentiles, to whom Christ came when he left Judea. And Isaiah calleth it a coming *to Zion,* in respect to the benefit to be given to the Jews, who are designed oft by Zion. Whence learn, 1. Christ is the salvation of *Zion,* both figuratively and properly called so, as well before he came as after; for here he is looked on as the *salvation of Israel,* in whom all our salvation, Jews or Gentiles, is founded. 2. Whosoever seeth him, (from how far off soever,) cannot choose but long for a further manifestation of him, for perfecting of the blessedness of his people: *O that the salvation of Israel were come out of Zion!* 3. It was revealed to the prophets, that Christ was to come to the church of the Jews, and from thence to manifest himself to the Gentiles, casting off the Israelites for a time, scattering them among the Gentiles, and then to come about again towards the Jews in their scattering and captivity, without casting off the Gentiles; and this last turn is in the prophet's eye, and aimed at by the Spirit, when he wisheth that *the salvation of Israel were come out of Zion.* 4. It was revealed also to the prophets, and to David, that before the constitution of the church of Israel should be freed from the persecution of domestic enemies, vexing the hearts of the

godly, or delivered from such men's power, as are described,
v. 1—3, that sore plagues were to be poured out upon
that people, and that the Israelites were to be driven out
of their own land, and led in captivities, as the words here,
and Psalm liii. 6, import ; for they who were to be brought
back from captivity after Christ's coming out of Zion unto
the Gentiles, are presupposed to be in captivity, when
Christ cometh to give salvation unto them.   5. Because of
the large pouring out of the Spirit upon the body of the
converted Jews or Israelites, when the time shall come of
their turning Christians, prophesied of here, and Isaiah lix.
20, and Rom. xi. 25, 26, as their mourning in repentance
for the injuries done by them and their progenitors, to
Jesus Christ, shall be as the mourning of Hadadrimmon,
in the valley of Megiddon, Zech. xii. 10, 11 ; so here,
joy in Jesus Christ reconciled unto them, shall be greater
than any that ever that nation saw, whether in David's
time, or Solomon's: for then *the Lord shall bring back the
captivity of his people*, here prophesied of, to be under the
time of the gospel, (whether by loosing their captivity
bodily as well as spiritual, whether they shall return to
their own land or not, or what the Scripture speaketh to
this purpose, this place is not for the determining of it.)
*Then Jacob shall rejoice, and Israel shall be glad, when the
Saviour of Israel shall come out of Zion to them.*

PSALM XV.

A Psalm of David.

The prophet, for distinguishing of the true members of the church from
those who were only outwardly professors, asketh of the Lord how the
one may be known from the other, ver. 1, and receiveth answer to the
question, ver. 2—5.

1. *Lord, who shall abide in thy tabernacle ? who
shall dwell in thy holy hill ?*

The question is proposed about the marks of the sincere
believers, the true covenanters with God, the true professors
of true religion ; they who shall not be cast out from the
society of God's true church.   Whence learn, 1. The tabernacle pitched by Moses, and the hill of Zion, where the
tabernacle and the temple were at last settled, was a type of
the true church, and of communion with God in Christ the

Mediator, a type of God incarnate, dwelling, and exercising all his offices in his church, and of the heavenly condition of his people called out of the world, and lifted up toward him, designed under the name of God's tabernacle, and God's holy hill. 2. Some of those who profess to be of this fellowship may be thrust out from it again, and debarred from all communion with God, when other some shall remain in this state, and not be removed. For the question is moved, What are the marks of the members of the church invisible? and who they are *who shall abide in God's tabernacle, and dwell in his holy hill?* 3. Only the Lord who searcheth the heart, can put the difference between the true and the false; for this cause the question is proposed to God, *Lord, who shall abide in thy tabernacle?*

2. *He that walketh uprightly, and worketh righteousness, and speaketh the truth in his heart.*

3. *He that backbiteth not with his tongue, nor doeth evil to his neighbour, nor taketh up a reproach against his neighbour.*

4. *In whose eyes a vile person is contemned; but he honoureth them that fear the Lord: he that sweareth to his own hurt, and changeth not.*

5. *He that putteth not out his money to usury, nor taketh reward against the innocent. He that doeth these* things *shall never be moved.*

The Lord answereth in the rest of the Psalm, by showing the fruits of faith manifested in obedience to God's commands, both moral and judicial, in the sight of all men : the sincerity of which faith and truth was to be certainly known to God only, and to the conscience of every man's self; which was sufficient to satisfy the question, quieting and comforting of the upright ones. Whence learn, 1. The sincere endeavour of universal obedience in a man's conversation, is a fruit and evidence of true faith, and a mark of a true member of the church invisible; *he walketh uprightly and doth righteousness.* 2. Another fruit of true faith is conscience-making of what a man speaketh, ruling his tongue so, as his heart and his tongue agree in the truth : *he speaketh the truth from the heart.* 3. A third fruit of unfeigned faith, is making conscience in all his dealings, that he harm not his neighbour, neither in his

name, nor in his person, nor his goods : and making conscience not to receive readily a false report of his neighbour, when it is devised by another; *he backbiteth not with
his tongue, nor doeth evil to his neighbour, nor taketh up a
reproach against his neighbour.* 4. A fourth fruit of sound
faith, is the low estimation of any worldly excellency wherewith a wicked man can be busked; to whom, although the
godly, according to duty, will give civil honour, as his
place requireth, yet he counteth him a poor miserable man
for all his honour and wealth, because he walketh in a godless way : but where he seeth one that feareth God, he esteemeth highly of him in his heart, whatsoever external expressions thereof he find fit to give, because of the honourable way of holiness, wherein the godly walketh; *for in his
eyes a vile person is contemned, but he honoureth him that
feareth the Lord.* 5. A fifth fruit of sound faith, is tender
respect to the name of God, and care to keep lawful promises, covenants, and oaths, whatsoever civil inconveniences
may follow upon the strict keeping of them; *though he
swear to his own damage, he changeth not.* 6. A sixth
fruit and evidence of faith, is dispensing with commodity,
when God, by a special reason, calleth for so doing, albeit
otherwise a man might take reasonably more gain. Many
of such sort of cases occur in merchandise, and in exacting
rents and debts, as circumstances may teach, when and
where God calleth for most moderation. Such was the
judicial dispensing with commodity, put upon the Jews, for
loosing the yoke of a bought servant, being a Jew, at the
end of six years; and quitting of houses and lands bought
from a Jew at the year of jubilee, how dear soever it cost
the buyer; and not taking usury of a Jew; wherein the
Jew was privileged above men of another country : for in
all these three particulars, it was lawful for the Jew to do
otherwise with other countrymen, to wit, in buying a servant from a stranger, and not letting him loose all his days,
and buying land from a stranger of another country, and
transmitting it to his own posterity, and taking usury of a
stranger, according to the rate which was acknowledged on
all hands to stand with equity; which commodity, if an
Israelite did not dispense with towards an Israelite, it made
him short of this commendation of the true Israelite, *who
putteth not his money to usury.* 7. The seventh fruit and

evidence of faith, is freedom from bribery, with love of justice, which the believer will not pervert, to the detriment of the man who hath a good cause, for whatsoever bud or reward man can give him. This is the upright man's last property, *he taketh not a reward against the innocent.*

Having numbered out the evidences of a sound convert and true believer, who shall never be thrust out of God's fellowship, he concludeth, *that whosoever doeth these things,* or studieth to do them, *shall never be moved;* that is, he that shall evidence his faith in God, by a sincere endeavour to do the duties of the first and second tables of God's law, shall not be removed from God's house, but shall abide in his tabernacle, and dwell in Zion, in the fellowship of God and his saints for ever.

PSALM XVI.

Michtam of David.

David, in this Psalm, finding himself in the state of grace, prayeth for preservation in general, in relation to all dangers and evils of body and soul, and whatsoever other evil, from which a godly man, with allowance of God's word, might pray to be preserved. His only reason to assure himself to be heard, is, because he had gotten grace to trust in God ; the sincerity of which trust in God, he proveth by sundry evidences, ver. 1—4. In the second place, he climbeth up to the comfort and joy of believing ; and all the grounds of joy whereupon he goeth, serve both to confirm his faith and to give him assurance of the granting of his prayer, ver. 6—11.

1. *Preserve me, O God: for in thee do I put my trust.*

He findeth himself in a good condition, and all the prayers he prayeth, are, in one word, for preservation. Whence learn, 1. As our being, living, and moving natural, and our bringing into the spiritual and blessed estate of grace, is of the Lord, so is our keeping therein of the Lord also, and our duty is to acknowledge God in both, and to live unto, and pray for, his upholding of us, and not to lean upon our own wisdom, strength, or holiness ; for David teacheth so to do ; *preserve me, O God.* 2. The grace of God having granted to us lively faith, settled on God, is a sufficient ground of our hope, and assurance to persevere, and to be still preserved, for this is the reason whereby David confirmeth his prayer, *for in thee do I put my trust.*

2. O my soul, *thou hast said unto the Lord, Thou* art *my Lord: my goodness* extendeth *not to thee;*

3. But *to the saints that* are *in the earth, and* to *the excellent, in whom* is *all my delight.*

Because he hath made his faith in God, the reason of his hope of perseverance, and of his having his prayer granted, he proveth the sincerity of his faith by five evidences or fruits thereof. Whence learn, 1. The first solid evidence of the sincerity of saving faith, is the testimony of the conscience, bearing witness to a man, that he hath laid hold on the covenant of grace, and hath chosen God for his protector and master, and that he is resolved to depend upon God, and to serve him, as David did, saying, *O my soul, thou hast said unto the Lord, Thou art my Lord.* 2. Another evidence of the sincerity of faith, is renunciation of all confidence in a man's own works, and the rejecting of all conceit of any possibility of merit at God's hand, who cannot be profited by our goodness; for we have what we have of him, and can never put an obligation on him by any thing which we can do: *my goodness doth not extend to thee.* 3. A third fruit and evidence of faith, is love and kindness to the godly, and bestowing of our own goods for supplying their need, joined with a high estimation of their preciousness, above the godless world, and with pleasure-taking in their fellowship; so reckoneth the prophet, saying, *my goodness extendeth not to thee, but to the saints that are on the earth, and to the excellent, in whom is all my delight:* where, by the way, let us observe, he knew no saints to whom he could be profitable, save only the saints who are *upon the earth.*

4. *Their sorrows shall be multiplied* that *hasten* after *another* god: *their drink-offerings of blood will I not offer, nor take up their names into my lips.*

A fourth fruit and evidence of faith, is, the hating of false religion, and counting all followers of idolatry, or worship of another god, than the true God, to be accursed; such a hating of false religion as is accompanied with the discountenancing, open discrediting, and abhorring of all idol service, as David expresseth here in the whole verse. Whence learn, 1. Men, as they are naturally averse from following the true God and the true religion, so are they naturally bent to all idolatry, and zealous in following idols, and any false religion ; *they hasten after another god.* 2. The more men hasten after felicity in the way of idolatry, they have the worse speed ; for *their sorrows shall be multiplied that hasten after another God.* 3. The more madly the world run after idolatry, the more shall the faithful man testify his abomination thereof, as David doth. *Their drink-offerings of blood will I not offer, nor take up their names into my lips.* He cannot speak of them without disdain.

5. *The Lord is the portion of mine inheritance and of my cup : thou maintainest my lot.*

A fifth fruit and evidence of faith in God, is delight and satisfaction in, and resting on God, as all-sufficient for the believer's complete happiness, as the whole verse holdeth forth. Whence learn, 1. The believer hath as sure right unto God, as any man hath to the patrimony whereunto he is born ; or any tribe ever had to his share in the land of Canaan. *The Lord is the portion of his inheritance.* 2. The Lord is the believer's lot and share, when the world are seeking, some one, some another temporal good ; *the Lord, and the light of his countenance,* is the believer's complete good ; whatsoever measure of earthly things is given to the godly beside, Levi's portion is his portion : *the Lord is the portion of his inheritance.* 3. The Lord is the believer's livelihood, and the furnisher of his daily bread ; *he is the portion of his cup.* 4. The Lord giveth himself to the believer for his felicity, as he also maintaineth the believer in the right unto, and possession of himself : *he maintaineth his lot ;* and so, as the believer cometh to his right he hath unto God, not by his own purchase, but by spiritual birth-right, as a child of Christ by faith, or by free donation of this inheritance, received of God by faith ; so he may lay claim to God, and enjoy the possession of God, as firmly as his inheritance ; as fully as if God were his particular property and portion ; as sweetly as his daily food, and the portion of his domestic cup : and with as great quietness and security, as the immediate vassal of the mightiest monarch, being willing, able, and engaged most deeply to maintain his lot.

6. *The lines are fallen unto me in pleasant* places; *yea, I have a goodly heritage.*

In the second place he climbeth up to the joy of faith, arising from the certain persuasion, and present sense of his being in the state of grace. The reasons or grounds of his joy are six. The first reason of his joy, is founded upon the properties and self-sufficiency of God, compared to a *goodly* and pleasant *heritage*, which wanteth no commodity within itself. Whence learn, 1. Pleasure and profit, and all commodities of life, are abundantly to be found in God ; and whatsoever can be represented by any goodly heritage, lying in most pleasant places, is but a shadow of what is to be found in him, as the comparison taken from lower things here importeth. 2. The more the believer considereth what the Lord is, and what are his perfections, and what is the believer's own interest in God, the more is he satisfied, and ravished in the beholding of God, and his own felicity in him. No wonder, therefore, if David say, for the measuring out of this share to him, *that his lines are fallen out to him in pleasant places, &c.* 3. The believer hath liberty to appropriate God in a manner to himself, and in comparison with the share of the worldlings, to prefer his own portion above all others. This doth David, when he calleth God his *own pleasant places, and his own heritage.*

7. *I will bless the Lord, who hath given me counsel ; my reins also instruct me in the night-seasons.*

The second reason and ground of joy, is because God hath persuaded him to believe in the Messiah, or Christ to come, as is clear by the next verse, and that God hath taken the directing of him. Whence learn, 1. As it is the work of God only, to give effectual counsel to any man to believe in Christ ; so also the way of persuasion of a soul to trust in God, is a way of working, proper only to God ; for it maketh the man so free an agent, in the act of believing, as if God's work were counsel only, and the work of active persuasion so invincible, as the work is effectually wrought and infallibly : for he calleth the bestowing of saving faith, or grace to consent to the covenant of grace, a giving counsel : *he hath given me counsel.* 2. The glory of trusting in God, is not a matter of gloriation of the believer, in his own disposing of himself, but a matter of thanksgiving to God, and glorifying of him, who giveth the counsel to believe, and maketh the counsel to him effectual ; for David saith, *I will bless the Lord who hath given me counsel :* to wit, effectually ; for faith is not of ourselves, it is the gift of God, wherein flexanimous power and voluntary consent are sweetly joined together. 3. This mercy of powerfully persuading a soul to make choice of God, to close in covenant with him, and to trust in him, putteth a perpetual obligation of thanksgiving unto God upon the believer, to make him say in all time coming, and for ever, *I will bless the Lord, who hath given me counsel.* 4. With the gift of saving faith, or persuasive counsel to believe in God, is joined the sweet guiding and directing of the Lord's spirit, how to order the ways of the believer ; for here instruction of him in the night-season, is joined with the former mercy, and is made a reason of thanksgiving and blessing of God : for he addeth, *my reins also shall instruct me in the night-seasons.* 5. The framing of the will, desire, appetite, affections, inclinations, thoughts, and secret meditations, is so inward, secret, and deep a work, as the Spirit of God thinks good to express this his giving discretion secretly to David, in the terms of the teaching of the reins, because they are the most hidden parts of the body, and nearest to the back of any of the inward noble parts ; and because of the nature of the reins, which have much affinity with the affections, and have for their office the discretive purging of the blood, the natural furniture of life, *my reins also instruct me in the night-seasons.*

8. *I have set the Lord always before me : because he is at my right hand, I shall not be moved.*

The third reason and ground of joy, is the gift of the grace of God, making him always keep his eye (for getting assistance, direction, and comfort,) to good purpose upon Jesus Christ, the Lord, of whom this place is exposed, Acts ii. 25. Whence learn, 1. The duty of the believer, and the way for him to have and retain joy in the Lord, is to fix the eye of faith, always, in all estates, on the Mediator, the promised Messiah, the Lord Jesus, for direction, assistance, comfort, and delivery. For this was David's way, *I have set the Lord always before my face.* 2. Such as implore Jesus Christ for all things in all estates, shall be sure to have his effectual presence near hand to help him in time of need ; for *he is at such a man's right hand, at all times.* 3. Faith, kept in exercise by employing of Jesus Christ, may have

4

assurance of perseverance, and enjoying constantly the state of grace : whatever alterations and commotions come, their state shall stand fixed ; they shall stand in grace; for upon this ground the prophet saith, *I shall never be moved.*

9. *Therefore my heart is glad, and my glory rejoiceth ; my flesh also shall rest in hope:*

A fourth reason of joy abounding in his heart, and breaking forth in his words, is his victory over death and the grave, by faith in Jesus Christ. Whence learn, 1. Faith in Christ is able not only to give peace that passeth understanding, but also to fill the heart with joy, and to make the tongue, which is a man's glory, above all other creatures, sometime to break forth in expressions of joy ; for *therefore,* saith he, *my heart is glad, and my glory rejoiceth.* 2. So great victory over death and the grave is gotten by faith in Jesus Christ, that a believer can lay down his body in the grave, as in a bed, to rest it there, in hope of the resurrection ; and here an instance and example of it, *my flesh also shall rest in hope.*

10. *For thou wilt not leave my soul in hell ; neither wilt thou suffer thine Holy One to see corruption.*

The first reason of his joy is the assurance of the resurrection of Jesus Christ, his head, through whom he hopeth to be raised in his own order and time. Whence learn, 1. A believer is so nearly joined with Christ, that he may give to him the styles of what is nearest and dearest to him, and call him his very life and soul, as here David saith of Christ, who behoved to rise again, Acts ii. 25, *thou wilt not leave my soul* (or my life) *in the grave :* and by this means he also is assured of his own resurrection in due time ; for our life and soul is bound up in Christ, our life is hid with God in Christ, specially in respect of that wherein he standeth in our room, such as his suffering, rising, reigning, as our surety and attorney. 3. The body of Christ not only was to rise from the dead, but also could not so much as putrefy in the grave : for of Christ he saith, *thou wilt not suffer thy Holy One to see corruption.*

11. *Thou wilt show me the path of life : in thy presence is fulness of joy ; at thy right hand* there are *pleasures for evermore.*

The last ground and reason of his joy, is the assurance

he hath of blessedness and of eternal life ; whence learn, 1. The believer who is fixed by faith on Christ, may be assured of his perseverance in the way leading to life : *thou wilt show me the way to life ;* that is, thou wilt point out the way that I should walk in, thou wilt go alongst with me, and make me effectually find thy help, to walk in it. 2. The fruition of God's immediate presence is not like the joys of this world, which neither feed nor fill a man : but when we shall enjoy God's presence fully, we shall have full contentment, and complete felicity, for *in his presence is fulness of joy.* And the felicity of believers is not like the pleasures of this world, which pass away suddenly as a dream : but it endureth for ever. *At his right hand are pleasures for evermore.*

PSALM XVII.

A Prayer of David.

This psalm, according to the inscription thereof, is a *prayer of David*, mixed with sundry reasons for helping; wherein, first, he craveth, in general, justice in the controversy between him and his oppressors, ver. 1—4. Secondly, more specially he requesteth for a wise carriage of himself under this exercise, ver. 5, 6. Thirdly, prayeth for protection and preservation from his enemies, ver. 7—12. Fourthly, for disappointment to his enemies, and for delivery of himself from them, ver. 13, 14 ; and closeth comfortably in confidence of a good answer, and hope of satisfactory happiness, ver. 15.

1. *Hear the right, O Lord, attend unto my cry ; give ear unto my prayer,* that goeth *not out of feigned lips.*

2. *Let my sentence come forth from thy presence ; let thine eyes behold the things that are equal.*

3. *Thou hast proved mine heart ; thou hast visited me in the night ; thou hast tried me,* and *shalt find nothing : I am purposed* that *my mouth shall not transgress.*

4. *Concerning the works of men, by the word of thy lips I have kept* me from *the paths of the destroyer.*

The first part of the prayer is unto God, as a righteous judge, to hear his plaint, and to decide in his favour, according to his just cause, and righteous carriage in relation to his enemies : whence learn, 1. As righteous men are

subject unto injuries and oppressions, as well as others are,
and are driven by trouble to seek relief of God, as in this
case ; it is a special comfort to have God, a righteous judge,
to hear them, and a righteous cause to bring before him,
that the man may say, *Hear the right, O Lord.*   2. The
conscience of earnest and honest dealing with God, in the
singleness of our heart, in prayer, is a good reason to help
our faith in prayer, when we may say, We *cry* and *pray
not with feigned lips.*   3. When we are unjustly condemned
by men, we may appeal to God, and call the appellation,
and seek and expect a more just sentence pronounced and
executed by God ; we may say, *Let my sentence come forth
from thy presence.*   4. Although men cast out our true
defences, which we make against false libels, and do not
respect equity ; yet God will take notice of the whole process, *his eyes will behold things that are equal.*   2. Sincerity
of heart giveth boldness to a man to present himself to God,
to be examined, after that the conscience, in its private
trial of the man's carriage toward the adversary, hath, in
the sight of God, absolved him ; as here the prophet, in relation to his carriage toward the oppressor, speaketh to
God, *thou hast tried me in the night, and hast found nothing.*   6. Sincerity of carriage for time by-past, must be
joined with a purpose of sincerity in time coming, that he
may say with David, in relation to his part, *I am purposed
that my mouth shall not transgress :* that is, not to speak a
wrong word against him.   Natural men's manner of dealing, when they are injured, is to recompense evil for evil ;
for *the works of men* are to follow *the paths of the destroyer.*   8. There is no way to keep the children of God from
these paths of the destroyer, when they are provoked to
injuries, except in the fear of God, they look to what God's
word directeth them to do.   Thus did David escape an ill
course, when his nature might have tempted him to it.   *By
the words of thy lips have I kept me from the paths of the
destroyer.*

5. *Hold up my goings in thy paths,* that *my footsteps slip not.*

6. *I have called upon thee ; for thou wilt hear me, O
God : incline thine ear unto me,* and *hear my speech.*

The second part of the prayer, wherein he requesteth for
grace to be kept still in a righteous and holy way ; whence

learn, 1. The most holy man, though he have stood fast formerly, is most feared to offend, and most suspicious of himself, and most earnest with God to be holden up, that he fall not in time to come; and giveth all the glory of his standing in a good cause unto God, as is evidently holden forth in this petition of David, *Hold up my goings in thy paths, that my footsteps slip not.* 2. The best way to have deliverance from, and victory over adversaries, is to keep a straight course of carriage in the fear of God; *going in God's paths;* that is, as God hath prescribed our way in his word. 3. Our prayer should be such, and so put up, as we may be sure to be heard; and when we have prayed unto God, according to his will, we may be confident of a good answer with David, *that he will incline his ear, and hear our speech.* 4. Confidence to be heard, must not slacken our hands in prayer, but hearten us to pray, as this example teacheth us.

7. *Show thy marvellous loving-kindness, O thou that savest by thy right hand them which put their trust in thee, from those that rise up* against them.

8. *Keep me as the apple of the eye; hide me under the shadow of thy wings.*

The third part of his prayer, is, for a merciful protection, and preservation from his enemies. Whence learn, 1. The believer must hold his eye in time of dangers and straits, especially upon God's good-will and kindness, as a counter-balance to all the malice of men: and here, though his straits were never so great, he shall read a possibility of wonders for his delivery, as here is seen: *show thy marvellous loving-kindness, O Lord.* Beside common favours, God hath other mercies in keeping for his own, and those are marked even with some wonderfulness, either in the time, or manner, or measure, or mean, or some other respect. 2. The Lord's power and his office of Saviourship, and his constant manner of dealing for believers, are the pillars of the persuasion of help to be had in God; so reasons David, saying, *O thou that savest with thy right hand them which put their trust in thee:* for God's nature, Christ's office, and his manner of dealing, are equivalent to promises, when they are looked unto by a believer. 3. Such as trouble unjustly them, of whom the Lord hath taken the maintenance, do in a sort engage God to be their party, and to defend his servants, *for they rise up against* not only God's servants, but against *God who saveth by his right hand.* 4. The care God hath of his poor children, that depend upon him, is unspeakable ; and the tender love he beareth unto them, no one similitude can express, as plurality of similitudes, joined here, give evidence ; for God's care of them is comparable to man's care *of the apple of his eye ;* God's love to them is comparable to the love of the bird-mother toward her young ones, whom she warmeth, and *hideth under the shadow of her wings.* O wonderful goodness, and wisdom of God, who admitteth himself to be compared to such low similitudes, that he might lift up our faith above all objections of misbelief.

9. *From the wicked that oppress me,* from *my deadly enemies,* who *compass me about.*

10. *They are enclosed in their own fat: with their mouth they speak proudly.*

11. *They have now compassed us in our steps ; they have set their eyes bowing down to the earth ;*

12. *Like as a lion that is greedy of his prey, and as it were a young lion lurking in secret places.*

The reason of his prayer, is taken from the deadly malice of his enemies, v. 9 ; from their pride, v. 10 ; from their confidence, v. 11 ; from their beastly cruelty, v. 12. Whence learn, 1. The enemies of God's people are ordinarily wicked, oppressors, deadly enemies to them, proud of their wealth and power, boasters, crafty foxes, cruel lions : and the more of these evils break forth against God's people, the more should the dangers be laid before God ; not for information of him, but for the exoneration of our griefs, temptations, fears, and dangers before God, and laying of our care upon him : and so much the more also is vengeance on the enemy, and the delivery of the godly near hand ; and hopes of answering the prayers put up against them, are the more made certain, as the use of the wickedness of the enemy made by the prophet here teacheth.

13. *Arise, O Lord ; disappoint him, cast him down : deliver my soul from the wicked,* which is *thy sword :*

14. *From men* which are *thy hand, O Lord, from men of the world* which have *their portion in* this *life, and whose belly thou fillest with thy hid* treasure : *they*

are full of children, and leave the rest of their substance *to their babes.*

The fourth part of the prayer is, for frustrating the intention of the enemy, and setting the supplicant free from
the danger. Whence learn, 1. When danger is most nigh,
God is more nigh, and he can shortly interpose himself, to
the overturning of the design of the enemy, and to the ruin
of the enemy himself: he can quickly *arise, and disappoint him, and cast him down.* 2. The power of the enemy
standeth in the Lord's employing him; he cannot strike,
except God strike by him; therefore he is called *God's
sword.* 3. The shortest way to be safe from what the
wicked can do, is prayer to God, to overrule him. Therefore saith David, *deliver my soul from the wicked, which is
thy sword.* 4. The Lord ordinarily for execution of wrath,
and for hard trials, and troubles of the godly, doth in his
providence make use of the wicked; *deliver me,* saith he,
from men which are thy hand. 5. The wicked neither
have, nor seek any felicity, but what may be had in this
life, *they are men of this world, and have their portion in
this life,* they need look for no more good than they find
in the world, and that is, *a poor,* and sorry happiness. 6.
The belly full of sensual lust, and rarest dishes, and best
meats which God's store-house can afford, is the height of
the happiness of a poor rich worldling. In his own person, it is all that God giveth him for his portion, and which
the fool hath chosen, even the *filling of his belly with
God's hid treasure,* or of some rare meat, which meaner
people cannot have, and therefore it is called *God's hid
treasure.* 7. All the felicity which the worldling can have,
in the point of honour and riches to himself, and his posterity, is worldly wealth while he liveth, and a number of
children to enjoy his wealth after him; whether they shall
live and inherit it, whether they shall prove wise men or
fools, he knoweth not; this is his all; for in God's favour
he hath no interest; heaven he hath nothing to do with;
and at the best, *they are full of children, and leave the rest
of their substance to their babes.*

15. *As for me, I will behold thy face in righteousness: I shall be satisfied, when I awake, with thy
likeness.*

He closeth his prayer comfortably, with the hope of true
fe'icity in fellowship with God. Whence learn, 1. In the
midst of whatsoever worldly trouble the godly can be,
his hope is far better than the worldly man's possession;
and the prophet here, for this cause, doth prefer his present
condition being in danger daily of his life, to all his enemies'
prosperity, saying, by way of opposition, *as for me, I will
behold thy face.* 2. The enjoying of the presence, and
sense of the loving-kindness of the Lord, is the felicity of
the godly, in that measure they attain it; the hope whereof upholds the believer's heart in the darkest times of
trouble. *As for me,* saith he, *I will behold thy face.* 3.
The enjoying of God is proper only unto the man justified
by faith, and endeavouring to live righteously; and it is
righteousness with God, that such a man be brought to the
enjoying of his hope, *I will behold thy face in righteousness,*
saith he. 4. There is a sleep of deadness of spirit, out of
which the shining of God's loving countenance awaketh a
believer and reviveth the spirit of the contrite ones ; and
there is a sleep of death bodily, out of which the loving-
kindness of the Lord shall awake all his own, in the day of
the resurrection, when he shall so change them into the
similitude of his own holiness and glorious felicity as they
shall be fully contented for ever; and this first and second
delivery out of all trouble, may every believer expect and
promise to himself: *I shall be satisfied, when I awake, with
thy likeness.*

PSALM XVIII.

*To the chief Musician. A Psalm of David, the servant of the Lord,
who spake unto the Lord the words of this Song, in the day that
the Lord delivered him from the hand of all his enemies, and from
the hand of Saul. And he said :*

David in this psalm, as a type of Christ, and fellow partaker of the
sufferings of Christ in his mystical members, and of deliveries and
victories over his and their enemies, being now settled in the kingdom,
praiseth God for his marvellous mercies ; and as a type of Christ, he
prophesieth of the enlargement and stability of his own kingdom, and
of Christ's kingdom, represented thereby ; and first obligeth himself
thankfully to depend upon God, whatsoever enemies he shall have to
deal with, v. 1—3. Secondly, he giveth a reason of his resolution,
from the experience of the Lord's delivering of him out of his deepest
distresses, v. 4—19. Thirdly, he amplifieth this mercy, acknowledging that this was a fruit of his faith, and righteous dealing with his
party adversary ; the like whereof every believer might expect, as well

as he, for the time coming, by reason of this his by-gone large experience, from v. 20—30. Fourthly, he praiseth God in particular, for the experience he hath had in time by-gone in warfare, and victories in battle, to v. 43. Fifthly, as a type of Christ, he promiseth to himself the enlargement of his own kingdom, and prophesieth of the enlargement of Christ's kingdom among the Gentiles, for which he praiseth God unto the end of the psalm, v. 43—50.

In the inscription, he telleth the time, and occasion of his writing of this song, whence learn, 1. That after long trouble, the Lord will give his children rest at last, one way or other, and delivery from all their enemies, as here is given to David from Saul and all his enemies. 2. When the believer getteth relaxation from trouble, he should set himself to glorify God for his delivery, and give evidence of his thankfulness, as David doth in penning this song, when God delivered him. 3. It is a greater honour to be a real servant of the Lord in any calling, than to have the honour of being a king, not being his servant: so esteemed David when he made this inscription, *a psalm of David, the servant of the Lord.*

1. *I will love thee, O Lord, my strength.*

2. *The Lord is my rock, and my fortress, and my deliverer ; my God, my strength, in whom I will trust ; my buckler, and the horn of my salvation,* and *my high tower.*

3. *I will call upon the Lord,* who is *worthy to be praised : so shall I be saved from mine enemies.*

In the first part of the psalm, he settleth his resolution yet more to love God, to believe in him, and to worship him still in all difficulties, knowing by experience, this to be the way to be saved from all his enemies. Whence learn, 1. The chief fruit of faith, and end of God's mercies to us, is to grow in estimation of, and affection towards God: for so doth David, saying, *I will love thee, O Lord.* 2. Whatsoever a believer hath need of, that will the Lord supply; that will the Lord be himself unto him according to his need, as here he is David's strength in weakness; his rock of refuge, when he is pursued ; his fortress, when besieged ; and his deliverer when in extreme danger. 3. Experience of the Lord's faithfulness, and kindness to us, should confirm us in the covenant of grace, and strengthen our resolution to believe in him : for upon this account David calleth the Lord, *my God, my strength, in*

whom I will trust.   4. When the believer is yoked in fight
with whatsoever adversary, he shall be sure to have defence
in it, delivery out of it, and preservation after it.   Therefore doth David glory in God, as a buckler to be opposed
to all blows, and throws of darts from adversaries, as the
horn of his salvation, powerfully fighting for his delivery
and victory: and as his high tower, whence he might look
down, and despise all the wit, malice, and power of his
enemies.   5. Prayer and invocation of God, should be
always joined with praises and thanksgiving, and used as a
means, whereby faith may extract the good which it
knoweth is in God, and of which he hath made promise, *I
will call upon the Lord who is worthy to be praised.*
6. Delivery, safety, and peace may the believer expect, as
the answer of his invocation upon God: *so shall I be safe
from mine enemy.*

   4. *The sorrows of death compassed me, and the
floods of ungodly men made me afraid.*
   5. *The sorrows of hell compassed me about; the
snares of death prevented me.*

   In the second part, he bringeth forth his experience,
whereby he was encouraged unto the foresaid duties:
whence learn, 1. Although the word of God be infinitely
sure, and true in itself, yet experience of the truth thereof,
helpeth much to strengthen our gripping thereof, and to
cherish hope, as here is declared.   2. The believer in his
exercise, may be put hard to it, and brought in sight of
apparent perishing of soul and body; while men seek his
life, God for a time hideth his face: for David felt deadly
fears, and extreme torment of soul, even *the sorrows of
death, the sorrows of hell, and the snares of death preventing him,* that he could not get free from them.

   6. *In my distress I called upon the Lord, and cried
unto my God: he heard my voice out of his temple, and
my cry came before him, even into his ears.*

   He hath set down the strait he was in; now he setteth
down the mean he used to be relieved, to wit, prayer to
God, as in covenant with him; and how he was mercifully
heard through Christ: whence learn, 1. No strait is such
but God can deliver out of it, no case is so desperate, as to
make prayer needless or useless: for David saith in his

deepest distress, *I called on the Lord.* 2. It is necessary not to give over, when help is delayed; yea, it is necessary to grow more fervent, and for this end to lay hold on the covenant of reconciliation, and upon God in covenant with us: for he addeth, *I cried to my God.* 3. By virtue of Christ's sacrifice, and his intercession, notice is taken of prayer graciously, and answer cometh to the believer; for he addeth, *he heard my voice out of his temple, and my cry came before him* even *into his ears*; he pointeth at the temple, in regard of the ark, and other figures representing Christ in his intercession for us in heaven.

7. *Then the earth shook and trembled; the foundations also of the hills moved and were shaken, because he was wroth.*

8. *There went up a smoke out of his nostrils, and fire out of his mouth devoured: coals were kindled by it.*

9. *He bowed the heavens also, and came down: and darkness was under his feet.*

10. *And he rode upon a cherub, and did fly; yea, he did fly upon the wings of the wind.*

11. *He made darkness his secret place; his pavilion round about him* were *dark waters* and *thick clouds of the skies.*

12. *At the brightness* that was *before him, his thick clouds passed; hail-*stones *and coals of fire.*

13. *The Lord also thundered in the heavens, and the Highest gave his voice; hail-*stones *and coals of fire.*

14. *Yea, he sent out his arrows, and scattered them; and he shot out lightnings, and discomfited them.*

15. *Then the channels of waters were seen, and the foundations of the world were discovered at thy rebuke, O Lord, at the blast of the breath of thy nostrils.*

The manner of his delivery is set down in comparative speeches, alluding to the most glorious manifestations which ever God gave of himself, in mount Sinai, or in the days of Joshua, or in the days of the Judges, or Samuel, all which glorious manifestations of God to his people, David esteemeth to be reacted in the wonderfulness of his delivery; so as he thinks he may justly compare the wonders shown in his preservation from his enemies, to any of, or to all

God's former wonders, in saving his people: Whence learn, 1. Although our natural stupidity, unbelief, and enmity against God, extenuate the works of God's providence about his children; yet the believer should look upon them with a spiritual and discerning eye, and should so set them forth to others, as David doth here. 2. The most sensible mutations in heaven and earth, are not so observed by the blind world, as a soul illuminate with spiritual light will observe God's spiritual providence in his works towards his people, and towards himself, as here David's example showeth. 3. The history of the Lord's redeeming his church, set down in Scripture, and by David alluded unto, may be seen in God's particular dealing with his children, as very like to the same, and as appendicles of the same work repeated. This is imported in David's re-calling to memory what is said, Exod. ix. 23, 24, and ix. 18; Josh. x. 11; Judg. v. 4; 1 Sam. xii. 18, concerning the Lord's manifesting of himself. 4. The terribleness of God coming to judge his enemies, is a matter of consolation to the believer, and of praise to God, as here is set down.

16. *He sent from above, he took me, he drew me out of many waters.*

17. *He delivered me from my strong enemy, and from them which hated me: for they were too strong for me.*

18. *They prevented me in the day of my calamity: but the Lord was my stay.*

19. *He brought me forth also into a large place; he delivered me, because he delighted in me.*

Now he draweth forth his delivery in lower comparisons, and more proper words, for the more clear capacity of the church; to wit, that God delivered him as one in peril of drowning, v. 16; as helping a weak man from a strong party, v. 17; as upholding a man circumvented, and ready to fall and fail, v. 18; and setting a man free from all danger, v. 19. Whence learn, 1. Our weakness in the time of our delivery, commendeth God's power, as David's delivery is magnified, because it was as a *drawing of him out of many waters, where he was like to drown.* Whether God use means or not in our deliveries, the work must ever be ascribed to him alone: *he sent from above and took me out.* 3. Power of adversaries will not hinder God's helping hand; he can, and doth usually *deliver his own from them that are too strong for them.* 4. A soul sensible of God's merciful work, cannot satisfy itself with expressions about it. And as many new considerations as a believer hath of the circumstances of a mercy, so many new mercies doth he see; therefore is it that David repeateth the same work of deliverance in more and more new expressions, and cannot express himself in one word, with satisfaction to himself. 5. When a man is enclosed, and prevented from escaping out of trouble, faith would fail, and then despair should follow, if God did not interpose himself, and did not furnish strength in this difficulty. David being thus circumvented, saith, *but the Lord was my stay.* 6. The Lord doth not leave his work about his own, till he perfect it, but he completeth their delivery ere he cease, and crowneth his mercy with joy: to express this, David saith, *he brought me forth also into a large place.*

19. *He brought me forth also into a large place; he delivered me, because he delighted in me.*

20. *The Lord rewarded me according to my righteousness; according to the cleanness of my hands hath he recompensed me.*

21. *For I have kept the ways of the Lord, and have not wickedly departed from my God.*

22. *For all his judgments were before me, and I did not put away his statutes from me.*

23. *I was also upright before him, and I kept myself from mine iniquity.*

24. *Therefore hath the Lord recompensed me according to my righteousness, according to the cleanness of my hands in his eye-sight.*

The third part of the psalm, wherein he goeth on to amplify mercy sundry ways; and first, from the cause of it, which is the mere good- will and love of God. Whence learn, 1. That the cause of any mercy shown to us, is not to be found in us, but in God's free love; *he delivered me, because he delighted in me.* 2. The belief of God's love sweeteneth and commendeth the mercy exceedingly: the delivery here is great, but this word, *because he delighted in me,* is far more sweet, verse 20. There is another point of amplifying the mercy of his preservation and delivery, in

the clearing of his innocency, and freeing him from the
slanders of ingratitude, rebellion, treachery against his
father-in-law, and his prince, which was the fruit of another
grace of God, given unto him; to wit, righteousness and
innocence, in relation to his enemies, ver. 20; and a study
to keep God's commands, ver. 21; and the fear of God
fastening him to God's statutes, ver. 22; and sincere and
tender walking with God, and watching over the sin which
did most beset him, ver. 23; where his delivery from his
enemies, and clearing his innocence from calumnies, was a
gracious reward, ver. 24.   Whence learn, 1. In a good
cause it is necessary we have a good carriage, lest we mar
our cause, and our comfort also; for David studied *righteousness and cleanness of hands*, in relation to his enemies,
when he was most unjustly persecuted.   2. A godly behaviour in a good cause shall not want fruit, for the free love
of God rewarded David according to his righteousness.   3.
The conscience of a godly behaviour in time of persecution is
twice profitable: once under the trial and trouble it sup-
porteth: again, after the delivery, the looking back upon
it comforteth, as here 's shown.   4. As we should at all
times take heed to our conversation, so in special, when by
persecution we are troubled for a good cause, for now we are
upon the trial of our faith, patience, wisdom, and other
graces, as David was, and should do as he doth here.   5.
We have special rules of good behaviour set down in David's example.   First, we must be sure to follow such ways
as God's word alloweth, that we may say, *I have kept the
ways of the Lord.*   Secondly, if in our infirmity we be miscarried at any time, we must not persist in a wrong course,
but return to the way of God's obedience, that we may say,
I have not wickedly departed from my God, neither in the
point of belief, nor practical obedience.   Thirdly, we must
set all the commands of God, and his written judgments before us, to be observed, one as well as another, and must
have respect to God's threatened and executed judgments
also, that we may say with David, *all his judgments were
before me, and I did not put away his statutes from me.*
Fourthly, we must study sincerity in our carriage, doing
good actions well from right principles, and for the right
end, that we may say, I was also upright before him.
Fifthly, we must keep strict watch over our wicked nature,

and most raging passions and affections, lest they break out ;
that our conscience may not contradict us, when we say, I
have kept myself from mine iniquity.   6. It is wisdom to
join one mercy with another, in our reckoning, that we may
say that we have gotten grace for grace, as David acknowledgeth ; that as God had given him grace to study righteousness and innocence, *so had he recompensed* him *according to his righteousness.*   7. When the world would
bury our innocence with slanders, it is lawful and expedient to defend our own good name, and to speak and write
in defence of it, as David doth here.

25. *With the merciful thou wilt shew thyself merciful ; with an upright man thou wilt shew thyself upright ;*
26. *With the pure thou wilt shew thyself pure ; and
with the froward thou wilt shew thyself froward.*
27. *For thou wilt save the afflicted people ; but wilt
bring down high looks.*

From his own experience he draweth up a general doctrine, concerning the Lord's holy, just, and wise manner of
dealing with all men, according to their carriage towards
him.   Whence learn, 1. The experiences which any of the
saints have, of the effects of God's word, are proofs of the
certainty of God's promises and threatenings, and pawns of
the like effects to follow unto others ; for here David draweth a general doctrine from his particular experience.   2.
As a man would have a meeting from God, so must he study
to behave himself toward God and man, for God's cause ;
for with the bountiful, merciful, upright, and pure, he will
deal accordingly.   3. Whoever shall walk contrary to God,
and strive with him, or will not submit themselves unto him,
he shall walk contrary unto them, and punish them seven
times more, because of their stubbornness ; for *toward the
froward, he will shew himself froward.*   4. Albeit the godly
be for a while afflicted, and the wicked prosper, yet after
the affliction of the godly, salvation shall come to them ;
and after the prosperity, vain and proud gloriation of the
wicked, their destruction shall follow, for he *will save the
afflicted people, but will bring down high looks.*

28. *For thou wilt light my candle : the Lord my
God will enlighten my darkness.*

From bygone experience he strengthens his own hope of further experience thereafter, as need should require. Whence learn, 1. Believers being delivered out of many bygone troubles, must not promise to themselves exemption from new troubles hereafter, but rather make themselves ready for new exercise, and more sad passages of God's dispensations towards them. For David presupposeth here, that he may, yea, and that he shall be thereafter in darkness, and want, for a while, the candle light of consolation. 2. As the godly man may expect crosses, so may he be sure also of as many consolations, and sweet seasonings of his troubles, and deliverances out of them ; so that he may say, both before trouble come, and in the midst of it, *the Lord will light my candle, and my God will enlighten my darkness.*

29. *For by thee I have run through a troop ; and by my God have I leaped over a wall.*

Here is another part of his experience, concerning his victories and good success in battle, the glory whereof he ascribes altogether to God. Whence learn, 1. Although the courage, valour, and success of all soldiers is from the Lord, yet only the believer giveth God the glory thereof, as David here. 2. Natural courage, and whatsoever measure a man may have of it, now and then may faint and fail altogether, when it meeteth with very strong opposition ; but the spiritual courage which is from faith, is from a more sure ground, and will not fail, when faith setteth it on, whatsoever be the apparent difficulty : for by faith in God David was made to *run through a troop*, or *leap over a wall*, into a town full of his enemies, with assurance of victory.

30. As for *God, his way* is *perfect : the word of the Lord is tried ; he* is *a buckler to all those that trust in him.*

31. *For who* is *God save the Lord ? or who* is *a rock save our God ?*

The fourth part of the psalm, wherein he praiseth the Lord expressly for what he had found in him, and in this he is a special type of Christ, in his conquest and victories. The reasons of his praising are four, set down in order. Whence learn, 1. The constant, equable, and old way of God's dealing with those that believe in him, is a matter of God's praise, and a reason why the experience of one believer may be a ground of hope for another, to find the like, because it is said here, *as for God, his way is perfect.* This is one reason of his praise, and of the believer's hope. 2. In all times bygone, experience hath proved the word of the Lord to be most solidly true; which serveth for the second reason of praising God, and grounding of our hope : *the word of the Lord is tried.* 3. There is none of the believers excepted from the benefit of his promises, which is a third reason of God's praise, and our hope, for *he is a buckler to all those that trust in him.* He is a defence which we may constantly carry along with us wherever we go, and make use of his power and love as of a buckler, in all conflicts. 4. A fourth reason of God's praise, and ground of our hope, is, that as there is no true religion, nor true faith, save one, so there is no true God save only one, whose true and tried word is with his true church and saints, who believe in him : *for who is God save the Lord ? or who is a rock save our God ?* 5. There is no fountain of comfort, or of strength, or delivery, save the Lord, of whom only all things have their being : *for who is God save the Lord ?* 6. There is no ground to build our confidence and felicity upon, save God alone, who is in covenant through Christ with us : *Who is a rock save our God ?*

32. It is *God that girdeth me with strength, and maketh my way perfect.*

33. *He maketh my feet like hinds' feet, and setteth me upon my high places.*

34. *He teacheth my hands to war, so that a bow of steel is broken by mine arms.*

35. *Thou hast also given me the shield of thy salvation; and thy right hand hath holden me up, and thy gentleness hath made me great.*

36. *Thou hast enlarged my steps under me, that my feet did not slip.*

He goeth on to reckon the furniture and ability for war, which the Lord gave to him. Whence learn, 1. The man of God must resolve to be a man of war, and to yoke with adversaries of one sort or other ; such as was David, and Christ, and his followers, represented by him. 2. The man whom the Lord sendeth out to fight his battles, he will arm him completely from head to foot, he will gird him with strength, and make his way plain and perfect ; he will make his feet swift, he will furnish him with a retiring place on high, he will furnish him with a bow of steel, and with all arms offensive, and will enable him with more skill and strength then to make use of them ; he will furnish him also with *a shield of salvation,* which shall save him in effect : and with all arms defensive, and uphold him by his right hand, when he is like to be overcome ; and by his tender care of him, will make him a great man, a valiant man of war, and hold him on his feet, that he fall not in his service ; whereof David here hath experience in his warfare, bodily and spiritual. 3. What God hath done for a man will be better seen after the trouble is ended, than in the mean time. The back-look upon the Lord's assistance is most clear, as here David giveth the clearest count of God's assistance, when his experience is reviewed. 4. All the furniture of spiritual armour, in our spiritual warfare, which here is chiefly aimed at, is only from the Lord ; for he, even he only, is here declared the furnisher thereof, and without him the man is altogether weak, witless, and naked.

37. *I have pursued mine enemies, and overtaken them ; neither did I turn again till they were consumed.*

38. *I have wounded them, that they were not able to rise : they are fallen under my feet.*

39. *For thou hast girded me with strength unto the battle : thou hast subdued under me those that rose up against me.*

40. *Thou hast also given me the necks of mine enemies, that I might destroy them that hate me.*

Here he maketh mention of the victories which God gave to him, as a type of Christ, over all his enemies. Whence learn, 1. It was revealed to David, that as he himself had, so also should Christ have many enemies, and should fight against them, and prevail over them, and make all his followers victorious over them all; that he should pursue his and their enemies, in every age, and *not turn again till they shall be consumed,* as is ver. 37; *till he cast them down, that they be not able to rise,* ver. 38; *till he hath subdued them all under his feet, and ours,* ver. 39; *till he have taken them captives, and destroyed them,* ver. 40. For

Christ's victories are common to him and his followers, in as far as their warfare is from him, and he is engaged to fight our battles for us, or by us, as he sees fit.

41. *They cried, but* there was *none to save* them ; even *unto the Lord, but he answered them not.*

42. *Then did I beat them small as the dust before the wind; I did cast them out as the dirt in the streets.*

In the type of some passages of some severe justice which David executed against his enemies, he setteth forth the certain destruction of Christ's enemies, in judgment merciless. Whence learn, 1. That whosoever look for release out of their trouble, and that not through Christ, shall have no release at all: *though they cry, there shall be none to save them.* 2. It may be some may think themselves friends to God, and God a friend to them, and pray to him, albeit they be enemies to Christ; but that prayer which is put up to God, without reconciliation made through Christ, shall be rejected. *Though they cry to the Lord, he shall not answer them.* 3. If men, pursued by Christ for their enmity against him, shall, not under the rod at least, turn to him, there remaineth nothing for them, but that they be utterly destroyed, and, as it were, *beaten as small as the dust.* 4. The obstinate enemies of Christ's kingdom shall perish shamefully, and as they have despised the blood of Christ, and of his servants, so shall the Lord despise them; he shall *cast them out as the dirt in the streets.*

43. *Thou hast delivered me from the strivings of the people; and thou hast made me the head of the heathen: a people whom I have not known shall serve me.*

44. *As soon as they hear of me they shall obey me: the strangers shall submit themselves unto me.*

In the fifth and last part of the psalm, he promiseth to himself the settling and enlargement of his own kingdom, and prophesieth also of Christ's kingdom represented thereby. Whence learn, 1. As was David's, so is Christ's kingdom, subject to intestine commotions, tumults, and dissensions; as in the one there were, so in the other have been, and will be contentions, and *strivings of the people,* raised by Satan, fostered by wicked hypocrites, and by the corruption of the Lord's children. 2. Such striving and dissension put our Lord's kingdom in a sort of hazard, if we look to second causes, so as there will be need of God's help for a delivery from it. But the kingdom of Christ shall stand for all that, notwithstanding these contentions, that it may still be said of his kingdom, as it is said here of the typical kingdom, and is prophesied of Christ's kingdom, *thou hast delivered me from the strivings of the people.* 3. To the prophet it was revealed, that Christ's kingdom was not to remain straitened within the bounds of Judea, but to be extended to the Gentiles, over whom Christ was to reign, and now hath a long time reigned: *the Father*, as he made David the type, so *hath he made Christ head of the heathen.* 4. The wickedness of a person or people, whose works have been most loathsome to the Lord, cannot hinder him to show mercy to them through Christ, when he pleaseth to convert them; for he hath said, *a people whom I have not known, shall serve me:* which hath ofttimes come to pass, and will yet more be seen effectually. 5. The word of the Lord is the sceptre of his kingdom, the sword whereby he subdueth his people to himself; *as soon as they hear of me,* saith the Lord, in the mouth of his type, and prophet, *they shall obey me.* 6. The more room the word gets in a man's heart, and the sooner it be believed and obeyed, after signification of God's will to him by his word, the more kindly is the conversion, and the more of the Lord's power is evidenced: as here is imported in, *as soon as they hear of me.* 7. When Christ subdueth nations to himself by his word, and converteth the elect, or his own redeemed ones: strangers in heart will come also outwardly unto the society of his church and kingdom, though feignedly: *the strangers shall submit themselves to me: feignedly*, as the word importeth. 8. Even this outward offer of submission to Christ's kingdom, made by strangers coming to the visible church, is not refused, but received *pro tanto*, and made a matter of glorifying of Christ: *the strangers shall feignedly submit themselves to me.* For it is no small glory to Christ that the majesty of his word and ordinances, maketh many stoop before him, who are not turned truly unto him. Meantime, albeit by entering into, and submitting to the external covenant, a man be admitted into the visible church, and outer court of God's house, yet not without real conversion is a man made a member of the invisible church, and admitted into the inner court of heaven.

45. *The strangers shall fade away, and be afraid out of their close places.*

He prophesieth what shall become of Christ's enemies at length. Whence learn, 1. As some strangers shall come into the outward fellowship of Christ's kingdom, so others of them shall remain professed strangers, and disaffected to his kingdom, and whether strangers within or without, shall continue to be strangers still, both of them shall perish : *for strangers shall fade away.* 2. Albeit Christ at first, may have many enemies and unfriends where he cometh to set up his kingdom, yet where and when he pleaseth to stay and keep up his kingdom, his open enemies shall grow fewer : *the strangers shall fade away :* to wit, where he minds to stay, and for that end thinks good to diminish them. 3. Whether the Lord be pleased to convert strangers or not, their strong holds (whether their high imaginations, or their earthly power) shall not be able to stand before him ; let him come to convert them outwardly or inwardly also, or destroy them as he shall be pleased, his terror shall affright them; *for the strangers, before him, shall be afraid out of their close places.*

46. *The Lord liveth; and blessed* be *my Rock; and let the God of my salvation be exalted.*

47. It is *God that avengeth me, and subdueth the people under me.*

48. *He delivereth me from mine enemies; yea, thou liftest me up above those that rise up against me : thou hast delivered me from the violent man.*

49. *Therefore will I give thanks unto thee, O Lord, among the heathen, and sing praises unto thy name.*

50. *Great deliverance giveth he to his king ; and sheweth mercy to his anointed, to David, and to his seed for evermore.*

He concludeth the psalm with' thanksgiving, and praiseth the Lord for his personal preservation unto eternal life, v. 46, for overthrowing of his enemies, v. 47, for delivery of him from them, v. 47, 48, and in Christ's name he setteth forth the Lord's glory before the Gentiles, for the mercies following the kingdom of Christ, and his own kingdom, the type thereof, v. 49, 50. Whence learn, 1. The end of all our speeches, concerning what we have been employed into, and have done, or have had success in, should be to show forth the glory of God to others, and to offer praise and thanks to him : for this, *blessed be my rock, &c.*, is the end whereunto *David's* example driveth. 2. *Life,* and *blessed life, quickening life,* the only *fountain* of life, is the proper style of God, of whom most properly and deservedly we may say, *the Lord liveth.* 3. Because God is the fountain of all blessedness to angels and men ; therefore should we acknowledge him, and proclaim him *blessed,* that the hearer may seek blessedness in him alone. 4. The perfection of God in himself, the out-letting of his goodness to the creature, his immutability in his love to his own, his making himself to be as it were the proper good of the believer by covenant, and his giving the certainty of salvation to the believer, established by covenant : these and other perfections should exalt the Lord highly in the estimation and affection of the believer, and make the believer heartily wish the Lord may be known to his praise : for this cause, saith the prophet, *the Lord liveth,* and *blessed be my Rock, and let the God of my salvation be exalted.* 4. David, as a type of Christ, in name and behalf of Christ, giveth unto God the glory of taking order with his enemies, for preserving and propagating his kingdom, and for the delivering his people from cruel persecutors. *It is God,* saith he, *that avengeth me, and subdueth the people under me. He delivereth me from mine enemies ; yea, thou liftest me up above those that rise up against me ; thou hast delivered me from the violent man.*

49. *Therefore will I give thanks unto thee, O Lord, among the heathen ; and sing praises unto thy name.*

Besides present praising of God, he promiseth to insist in praise and thanksgiving. This the apostle, Rom. xv. 9, showeth to be the speech of Christ, and a prophecy of the conversion of the Gentiles. Whence learn, 1. Beside all the victories given to the church in David's time, as a pledge of promises, it was foretold that the Gentiles should see many victories over the enemies of the church of Christ, after his coming, and that they should join with the Jews in thanksgiving to God for the same ; for upon account of the Lord's lifting up Christ above his adversaries and cruel persecutors, *thanks shall be given unto the Lord among the hea-*

then. 2. The sacrifice of praise offered up in the church, as it is the work of the saints in one respect, so it is the work of Christ in another respect; because he raiseth by his Spirit the song in their hearts, and offereth up the sacrifice of thanks unto the Father. For it is Christ who here saith, *I will give thanks unto thee, O Lord, among the heathen; and sing praises to thy name.*

50. *Great deliverance giveth he to his King: and sheweth mercy unto his anointed: to David and to his seed for evermore.*

David, as a type of Christ, giveth a reason of perpetual praising of God; to wit, the constant course of God's mercies shown to him and his house, and to be shown to Christ, and his children and house, for evermore. Whence learn, 1. As difficulties, enemies, and dangers of the church, are many and great; so shall their victories over these evils be great also; *for great deliverance giveth he,* in a continual tract and course, as it were, one after another, as need is. 2. All the deliverances are given to Christ principally, and in him to his church, and particular souls through him; for it is said, *great deliverance giveth he to his King.* 3. The choosing of a man for a service, shall, by the calling of him to it, and qualifying him for it, and sustaining him in it, be confirmed to him, and by the course of mercy following him in all his difficulties, which he shall meet with in his calling. Therefore significantly doth he say, *Great deliverance giveth he to his King,* to *David,* a chosen type, and to his anointed Christ, represented by him: *he sheweth mercy to his anointed,* Christ his seed. 4. It is mere mercy whereof Christ's followers, Christ's children and seed, stand in need: and mercy by course constantly shall follow them, not for a short time, but world without end; for *the Lord sheweth mercy to David and his seed for evermore.*

PSALM XIX.

To the Chief Musician. A Psalm of David.

This psalm is a sweet contemplation of the glory of God's wisdom, power, and goodness, shining in the works of creation, v. 1—6, and of the glory of his holiness and rich grace, shining through his word and ordinances in his church, v. 7—10, whereof the prophet having proof, prayeth to have the right use and benefit, v. 11—14.

1. *The heavens declare the glory of God: and the firmament sheweth his handy work.*

Albeit the whole earth be full of the glory of the Lord, yet the prophet contenteth himself to pitch his meditations on the heavens alone, and the vicissitude of day and night, and upon the course of the sun's light: whence learn, 1. Albeit the glory of the Lord shine in all his works, yet any portion thereof will take up a man's meditation, when he beginneth to think upon it, as here the heavens are the prophet's theme and subject matter of meditation. 2. The invisible things of God, even his eternal power and Godhead, and glorious attributes of wisdom, and goodness, and majesty, are to be seen in the works of creation, from the beginning of the world: *the heavens declare the glory of God, and the firmament sheweth his handy work.* 3. Though his glory be shown to all men, yet it is the illuminate child of God that can observe it; for he that setteth it forth to others, doth it by the inspiration of the Lord's own Spirit: he is a prophet who here is stirred up to point unto us this lesson, most worthy of our observation. For in substance the heavens declare that they are not their own maker, but that they are made by one infinite, incomprehensible, omnipotent, everlasting, good, kind, and glorious God. And the firmament (taking it for the region of the air, and place of the stars) declares how curiously he can adorn the work of his hands, and how powerfully he can put glory abundant on the creature, though it have no matter in it to make it glorious.

2. *Day unto day uttereth speech, and night unto night sheweth knowledge.*

3. There is *no speech nor language* where *their voice is not heard.*

4. *Their line is gone out through all the earth, and their words to the end of the world. In them hath he set a tabernacle for the sun;*

He looketh next upon the vicissitude of night and day, and as he saw what the heavens gave him to read, so he hearkeneth and heareth what the day and the night did speak; and he compriseth all their speech in the doctrine of knowledge: whence learn, 1. The right observation of the vicissitude of the night and day, may give instruction unto us to be wise; *for day unto day,* in their revolution, *uttereth speech* to the observing ear; *and night unto night,* in their vicissitude *sheweth* to the understanding man *knowledge.* For in substance, the vicissitude of day after day, serveth to teach man that he liveth in time, and that his days are numbered, that his days go quickly away, and that time is precious, and cannot return when it is gone; and that so long as it shall last, it shall serve man to view the works of the Lord, and to go about his own necessary labours; and such like other speeches doth it speak : also the night saith, that man in himself is weak, and cannot endure long toiling in labour; that as some little short rest and recreation of the labourer is necessary, so it is prepared for him, that he may lie under a curtain, and sleep a while, and so be fitted for more work, if more time be lent unto him; and that he may now quietly examine, what he hath been doing, may commune with his heart and be still ; and that if he do not what he hath to do in time, *the night cometh when no man can work :* by which and such like speeches men may learn knowledge. 2. There is no people nor country, but as much of the speech of the creature is spoken convincingly unto them, as may make them inexcusable ; and albeit all do not learn wisdom, yet *the voice* of the works of creation and providence, *is every where* in some measure *heard : their line* and ction *is gone out through the earth.*

5. *Which* is *as a bridegroom coming out of his chamber,* and *rejoiceth as a strong man to run a race.*

6. *His going forth* is *from the end of the heaven, and his circuit unto the ends of it: and there is nothing hid from the heat thereof.*

He contracteth his thoughts from the highness of the heavens, and pitcheth upon the sun, and beholdeth God's glory in it. Whence learn, 1. All the glory to be seen in the sun belongeth unto the Lord ; for he made it, and set it in its place, *as in a tabernacle,* for a time, so long as he hath use and service for it. 2. The beauty of the sun when it ariseth in the morning; the wonderful swift and regular motion of it, so tempered by the huge distance thereof from the earth, that it cannot be seen moving, when it is running in a circle in the heaven most swiftly : the constancy of the motion of it from day to day, from year to year, without wearying or failing; the vast circle which it maketh every twenty-four hours; the heat and virtue, and powerful operation upon all inferior creatures,—are all admirable, and matter of manifesting the glorious perfection of God, who made it, and moveth it; *as the bridegroom he riseth, compasseth the circle of heaven and earth, and nothing is hid from the heat thereof.*

7. *The law of the Lord is perfect, converting the soul: the testimony of the Lord is sure, making wise the simple:*

8. *The statutes of the Lord are right, rejoicing the heart: the commandment of the Lord is pure, enlightening the eyes:*

9. *The fear of the Lord is clean, enduring for ever: the judgments of the Lord are true and righteous altogether.*

10. *More to be desired are they than gold, yea, than much fine gold; sweeter also than honey, and the honeycomb.*

The next part of his contemplation, is concerning the glory of the Lord declared in his word and Scripture; which light, as it is more necessary for our blessedness than the sun's light for our bodies, so he commendeth this point of God's glory far above that which shineth in the work of creation, from the perfection, efficacy, infallibility, and sundry other properties of it.   Whence learn, 1. The doctrine of life and salvation, set down to us in God's word, as a law to us, and a rule of faith and obedience, needeth no deck of human traditions; it is sufficient in itself, and wanteth nothing necessary unto salvation; *for the law of the Lord is perfect.*   2. No doctrine, no word save this divine truth, set down in Scripture, is able to discover the sin and misery of man, or the remedy and relief from it; no doctrine save this alone, can effectually humble a soul, and convert it to God; or make a soul sensible of the loss it hath by sin, and restore it to a better condition than is lost by sin; for it is the property of this law or *doctrine, to be converting of souls.*   3. Whosoever hearkeneth to this word, shall be satisfied about what is the Lord's mind and will in all matters of religion, concerning God's service, and man's salvation; *for it is the testimony of the Lord*, wherein he giveth forth his will, concerning what he approveth, and what he disalloweth. 4. This word being understood rightly, as it may be understood when it is compared with itself, one part of it with another, and other means also used, which God hath appointed, may be safely relied upon: it will not disappoint a man; *for the testimony of the Lord is sure.* 5. Albeit there be many deep mysteries in this word, which may exercise the greatest wits, yet for the points necessary for the salvation of every soul, it is so plain and clear, that it may be understood by persons of mean wits, and may make those who are otherwise dull of understanding, wise to salvation; for it is a *testimony making wise the simple.* 6. Nothing is commanded by God in his word, but that which the illuminate soul must subscribe unto, as equitable in itself, and profitable to us; *for the statutes of the Lord are right.* 7. The approving and following of the Lord's directions given to us in his word, is a sure mean to get comfort and joy raised in our conscience: *for the statutes of the Lord rejoice the heart.* 8. There is no mixture of error, no dross nor refuse doctrine, no deceit in the Lord's word; for *the commandment of the Lord is pure.* 9. By the word of God a man may clearly see himself in himself blind and naked, and wretched, and miserable, and by coming into the grace and mercy offered in the Messiah, Christ, may see himself entered in the only safe way of salvation. By the word of God a man may see every thing in its own colours; virtue to be virtue, and vice to be vice and vanity: *for the word illuminates the eyes.* 10. The way of worshipping, fearing, and serving God, set down in his word, is holy, and in substance the same in all generations, and always unalterable by man for ever. *The fear of the Lord is clean, enduring for ever.* 11. The doctrines set down in the word of God, are all of them decrees of the Almighty Lawgiver, given forth in his own court with authority uncontrollable; all of them are true and worthy to be obeyed; for the *judgments of the Lord are true, and righteous altogether.* 12. The word of God is able to enrich a man more than all the riches in the world, because it is able to bring him to an everlasting kingdom; for God's judgments being as judicial sentences, to determine all necessary truths and controversies about saving truth, *are more to be desired than gold, yea, than much*

fine gold. **13.** There is more sweet comfort and true pleasure to be found in the Lord's word, than in any pleasant
thing in this world : *they are sweeter than honey, and the
honey-comb.*

11. *Moreover, by them is thy servant warned:* and
in keeping of them there is *great reward.*

The prophet subscribeth this commendation of God's
word, by his own experience, and seeketh to make good
use of it. Whence learn, 1. That man, of all other, is
most meet to commend the word of the Lord, who in himself hath felt the experience of the effects and good use
thereof, as the prophet's example showeth. 2. As the
word of God is able to make a man wise to salvation, so
also to make him prudent in his carriage, to eschew not
only sin, but also inconveniences, and to warn him of
snares, wherein he may fall by imprudence. For beside
all the former commendation, he addeth, *moreover by them
is thy servant warned.* 3. When a man hath said all he
can, in commendation of the word of God, he shall not be
able to say all, but must close in some general, because the
benefit of observing the Lord's statutes and commands,
passeth his reach ; for thus the prophet closeth, *in keeping of them* there is *great reward.*

12. *Who can understand* his *errors? cleanse thou
me from secret* faults.

Lest he should seem to speak like one who seeks to be
justified by his works, he acknowledgeth himself a man
that cleaveth not to his own righteousness, but to the fountain of free grace, and to the expiation of sin made by
Christ, signified under the shadow of ceremonial cleansing.
Whence learn, 1. The most holy man, after conversion,
must make still use of the law for his humiliation, and for
driving of him to Christ continually : and when he compareth himself with the law of God, he will be forced to
blush and acknowledge himself and every other man unable
to condescend upon the particulars, and the multitude even
of his actual sins. Therefore saith he, *who can understand
his errors?* 2. Sins of ignorance, sins passed out of memory, leave guiltiness upon the man, and must be counted for in heap at least : and mercy through the blood of
cleansing must be requested for, as here ; *cleanse thou me
from secret sins.*

13. *Keep back thy servant also from presumptuous* sins; *let them not have dominion over me : then shall I be upright, and I shall be innocent from the great transgression.*

He puts up another petition, to wit, That he may be preserved from presumptuous sins. Hence learn, 1. Holiest men are most sensible of their by-gone sins, and so also of their natural sinfulness and readiness to fall, whereof the prophet here is in fear, saying, *Keep back also thy servant from presumptuous sins.* 2. Even the regenerate, if the Lord do not keep them from temptation, or if he leave them in temptation, unto their own will and strength, they may fall into most scandalous sins, against the light of their conscience, and be slaves thereunto ; therefore prayeth he *to be kept back from presumptuous sins, and that God would not suffer such sins to have dominion over him ;* insinuating his own weakness, if God did not prevent, did not assist and help him to prevail against them. 3. Uprightness and integrity in God's obedience may stand with sins of infirmity and sins of ignorance, but cannot stand with presumptuous sins, against the light of conscience ; for if the Lord shall save him from presumptuous sins, *then,* he saith, *he shall be upright.* 4. Presumptuous sins, and letting sin reign in a man's mortal body, is the highway to the sin unto death, or sinning maliciously, with despite against God ; and he that makes conscience of secret sins, and is feared to fall into presumptuous sins, and fleeth to God to be cleansed from the one, and preserved from falling into the other, may be sure not to fall into the sin against the Holy Ghost. For the prophet having prayed to be cleansed from his secret sins, and kept back from presumptuous and reigning sins, assureth himself, *that so he shall be innocent from the great transgression.*

14. *Let the words of my mouth, and the meditation of my heart, be acceptable in thy sight, O Lord, my strength, and my redeemer.*

The third petition, is, for the acceptance of his service in his prayer, and purpose of heart. Whence learn, 1. As pardoning grace, and preventing grace, and restraining grace, must be prayed for ; so also powerful, sanctifying, or enabling grace, both for inward and outward service ;

yea, and grace accepting the service when it is offered, must be fought for by prayer from God. For as the prophet hath prayed for the former acts of grace, so also he prayeth here for the latter sort, saying, *let the words of my mouth and the meditation of my heart be acceptable.* 2. As all our prayers, and all our holy endeavours, and abilities to serve God, must be furnished unto us by our Redeemer, who is Jesus Christ; so also every other grace, and the acceptance of our persons and services, must come through him; and we may look for all these by virtue of the covenant of grace, whereby Christ is made our strength and Redeemer in all respects: therefore layeth he all the weight on this, *O Lord, my strength, and my Redeemer.*

PSALM XX.

To the chief Musician. A Psalm of David.

This Psalm was dited to the church in form of a prayer for the kings of Israel, but with a special eye upon, and relation unto Christ, the King of Israel; in respect of whom this prayer is a prophecy, and a form of blessing of Christ, and praying for his kingdom, whereof the kingdom of Israel was a type, and the kings thereof are types of Christ. Not that the kingdom in every condition was figurative, or every king a type of him; but as the priests being taken not severally, one by one, but together, shadowed forth, in something, Christ in the office of his priesthood; so the kings, not every one, but taken together, shadowed forth in something, Christ in his royal office, and their kingdom resembled his kingdom in his visible church in some things, and in his invisible church in other some things, leaving room to some persons, both among the priests and kings, to be more specially types than any of the rest in common, v. 1—5. After which the church's confidence to be heard is set down, and their gloriation in God over their enemies, with dependence on God for salvation in all difficulties and straits, v. 6—9.

1. *The Lord hear thee in the day of trouble; the name of the God of Jacob defend thee.*

2. *Send thee help from the sanctuary, and strengthen thee out of Zion.*

3. *Remember all thy offerings, and accept thy burnt-sacrifice. Selah.*

4. *Grant thee according to thine own heart, and fulfil all thy counsel.*

5. *We will rejoice in thy salvation, and in the name*

of our God we will set up our *banners : the Lord fulfil all thy petitions.*

From this prayer of the church for the king of Israel, learn, 1. It is the duty of all the godly, wherever they live, to pray for the welfare of their kings, rulers, and magistrates, as this example teacheth. 2. Greatest men, though they be also gracious, are subject to trouble : for even the best of the kings of Israel, and Christ typified by them, were not exempted therefrom : *the Lord hear thee in the day of trouble.* 3. It is the part of such as desire the prayers of others to be made for them, to pray also themselves, were they never so great kings; and prayer must be counted their best weapons in trouble ; *the Lord hear thee,* saith he, *in the day of thy trouble.* 4. No defence to be expected from God, but when he is looked upon and believed in as he is manifested to us in his word ; therefore he saith, *the name of the God of Jacob defend thee.* Or, God, who in his word hath revealed himself to Israel, and entered in covenant to be his God, *defend thee.* 5. It is by virtue of God's dwelling amongst men, and his taking on man's nature in the person of Christ (represented by God's presence in *Zion* and the sanctuary), that help must be expected from God. Therefore, saith he, *the Lord send thee help out of the sanctuary, and strengthen thee out of Zion.* 6. Kings, and all for whom the godly may pray with confidence, must be worshippers of God, believers in Christ, reliers upon the mercy of this only once offered sacrifice, represented by often repeated typical burnt-offerings ; for this is imported in, *the Lord remember all thy offerings, and accept thy burnt sacrifices.* For it is for Christ's sacrifice that we are accepted, and that any grace is granted to us. 7. A believer in Christ, praying according to the revealed will of God, ask what he will, it shall be granted ; he who studieth to walk sincerely before God, studying to do what is pleasant to God's heart, shall receive satisfactory answers according to his own heart's wish. Upon this ground the prayer goeth here, *the Lord grant thee according to thine own heart, and fulfil all thy counsel.* 8. Whosoever partaketh with Christ's subjects in trouble, shall share with them also in the joy of their deliverance ; therefore it is said, *we will rejoice in thy salvation.* 9. When it goeth well with the king, and chief magistrates, it goeth

the better with all the subjects ; and the praise of delivery
and welfare redoundeth to the glory of God, who is the fountain of all felicity ; for, *in the name of our God, we shall
set up our banners,* saith the church, if God shall be the
king.

6. *Now know I that the Lord saveth his anointed :
he will hear him from his holy heaven with the saving
strength of his right hand.*

7. *Some trust in chariots, and some in horses ; but
we will remember the name of the Lord our God.*

8. *They are brought down and fallen ; but we are
risen, and stand upright.*

9. *Save, Lord : let the King hear us when we call.*

This is the church's confidence to be heard, and her
gloriation in God, and dependence on God for salvation ;
whence learn, 1. A believer may be sure he hath his request granted, when he hath prayed according to God's
will ; in special when he prayeth for the safety of the church
and kingdom of Christ. *I know,* saith he, *that the Lord
saveth his anointed.* 2. He that seeketh God by the means
appointed ; in special, he who seeketh God, and help from
him, through Christ, in whom the fulness of the Godhead
dwelleth, shall have the grant of his prayer from heaven ;
for *help sought to come from the sanctuary,* ver. 2, *is granted
from his holy heaven,* ver. 6. 3. Whatsoever be the straits
of God's church, or any member thereof, faith seeth suffi-
ciency in God to relieve out of it, and doth lay hold on it,
for *he heareth with the saving strength of his right hand.*
4. Weak man cannot choose but have some confidence, without himself, in case of apparent difficulties ; and natural men
do look first to some earthly thing wherein they confide :
some trust in chariots, and some in horses, some in one
creature, some in another. 5. The believer must quit his
confidence in these things, whether he have them, or want
them, and must rely on what God hath promised in his word
to do unto us : *but we will remember the name of the Lord
our God.* 6. That which terrifieth the believer in the first
assault of a temptation, before he go to his refuge, is contemned by the believer when he looks to the Lord, his true
defence ; chariots and horses when they are invading God's
people are terrible ; but now when the Lord is remembered,

they are here set at nought in comparison. 7. The condition of the worldly man and of the enemies of God's people seems to be the better, at the first, and the condition of the church the worse ; but a short resolution cometh, which determineth the question in the end ; the standing of the ungodly is followed with a fall ; and the low condition of the godly hath a better condition following upon it. The worldly man and enemy, is brought down, and falleth ; but the godly are made to say, *we are risen and stand upright.* 8. True confidence strengthens itself by prayer : *Save, Lord.* 9. That which is prayed for in the type, is perfected in Christ, who is the truth ; salvation is granted to all his subjects, whensoever they call; *let the King hear us when we call.* 10. And when the Lord is relied upon for safety, the means shall have the promised blessing. The kings of Israel were to be the more useful to the people when safety was sought from the Lord. First, they pray, *Save us,* and then, *let the King hear us when we call,* or implore him.

PSALM XXI.

To the chief Musician. A Psalm of David.

As the former psalm was a prayer for the preservation of the kingdom of Israel, in relation to the kingdom of Christ, represented by it, so this psalm is a form of thanksgiving unto God by the church, for blessing the kingdom of Israel, representing the blessing, and cause of thanksgiving, to be found in Christ and his kingdom ; wherein a number of good things are set forth, heaped upon the King, ver. 1—7; and a number of miseries set forth, heaped on the head of his enemies, ver. 8—12; for both which the Lord is glorified, ver. 13. The reason why the former psalm and this are referred in so many particulars to Christ, is, because the verity of these things here spoken of is to be sought in Christ and his kingdom : for but in some few only of the kings, and in some few times of the kingdom only, was the shadow of what is here spoken of to be found, when the whole history is consulted.

1. *The king shall joy in thy strength, O Lord ; and in thy salvation how greatly shall he rejoice !*

2. *Thou hast given him his heart's desire, and hast not withholden the request of his lips. Selah.*

3. *For thou preventest him with the blessings of goodness : thou settest a crown of pure gold on his head.*

5

4. *He asked life of thee,* and *thou gavest* it *him,* even *length of days for ever and ever.*

5. *His glory* is *great in thy salvation : honour and majesty hast thou laid upon him.*

6. *For thou hast made him most blessed for ever : thou hast made him exceeding glad with thy countenance.*

7. *For the king trusteth in the Lord ; and through the mercy of the most High he shall not be moved.*

The benefits bestowed on the king and his kingdom, are seven or eight, which are so many reasons of thanksgiving. The first is, joy in the king's heart, for strength and salvation given unto him.   Whence learn, 1. As prayer is necessary, so also is thanksgiving ; and the offering of both to God, as it is our duty, so it is his due ; and as we should seek the concurrence of others in prayer, so should we seek their concurrence in praise ; and he that offereth prayer one day, shall have matter of praise to offer another day, as here we are taught.   2. Christ, and all his true subjects, are sure to be furnished with furniture of strength from God, for every employment, and to be delivered out of every danger by God, and to have joy and rejoicing in the experimental feeling thereof : for, *the king shall joy in thy strength, O Lord, and in thy salvation how greatly shall he rejoice !*   This is the first reason of praise and thanks, for this first benefit.   The second benefit bestowed on Christ, to be forth-coming to his true subjects, is this : satisfactory answers shall be given to all the articles of Christ's intercession, and all the articles of the saint's warrantable supplications.   *Thou hast given him his heart's desire, and hast not withholden the request of his lips.*   The third benefit is this : there shall be a ready out-giving of liberal gifts for Christ's subjects, and fruits of God's love, before the need thereof be felt, or observed ; *thou preventest him with the blessing of goodness.*   The fourth benefit is right, and title, and possession given to Christ ; a name of glory, or the gift of a glorious kingdom, wherein Christ shall give all his subjects crowns of glory : *thou settest a crown of pure gold upon his head.*   The fifth benefit is right to eternal life, as the fruit of Christ's intercession ; *he asked life of thee, and thou gavest it him, even length of days for ever and ever.* The sixth benefit given to Christ and his subjects, is growing honour, and growing weight of glory, a load of it, even before men ; for nothing can make men more glorious, even before the world, than God's owning them before the world, and putting respect upon them ; yea, and the world shall more and more see and admire the glory which God shall put upon Christ and his kingdom ; *his glory is great in thy salvation; honour and majesty hast thou laid upon him.* The seventh benefit is a begun possession of everlasting blessedness and joy unspeakable; partly from the feeling of the first fruits, partly from the hope of a full harvest; for God will never make an end of blessing whom he will bless. *Thou hast made him* and his followers *most blessed for ever; thou hast made him exceeding glad with thy countenance.* The eighth reason of thanksgiving, and the last benefit, in relation to the giving of what is good to Christ, and to his subjects, (among whom David and every one of the godly come in to share,) is the unchangeableness of God's mercy, and powerful love toward the believer, who hath closed in covenant with him, and trusteth in him. *He shall not be moved.* And why so ? *The king trusteth in the Lord.* What then ? The covenanted mercy of the most High is unchangeable, and maketh all blessedness fast to Christ and to every believer ; *through the mercy of the most High he shall not be moved.* Christ's kingdom in his person, and his subjects with him, shall stand when all the kingdoms of the earth shall stagger and fall.

8. *Thine hand shall find out all thine enemies ; thy right hand shall find out those that hate thee.*

9. *Thou shalt make them as a fiery oven in the time of thine anger ; the Lord shall swallow them up in his wrath, and the fire shall devour them.*

10. *Their fruit shalt thou destroy from the earth, and their seed from among the children of men.*

In the second place, there is a prophecy of God's vengeance on the enemies of Christ and his church, under the type of the enemies of David's kingdom. Whence learn, 1. All the enemies of Christ and his church shall be pursued by God, and overtaken, and none of them shall escape his hand, neither open enemies nor close lurking traitors. The Lord's hand shall find out all the King's enemies, and his right hand shall find out all those that hate him. 2. A ll the enemies of Christ and his kingdom, howsoever they may possibly be spared and forborn for a while, yet there is a set time for punishing them, here called the time of God's anger. 3. When the time is come, their judgment is inevitable, horrible, and completely full: *thou shalt make them as a fiery oven,* when the burning is extremely hot, the heat striking upon what is in it, from all hands, above, below, and about, on all hands, and the door closed from going out, or suffering any cool refreshment to come in. 4. There is no possibility to apprehend the horrible punishment of Christ's enemies: for after their casting into a fiery oven, they are set down here as fuel, to suffer what God's being incensed in anger, as a consuming fire swallowing them up, and devouring them in his incomprehensible wrath, importeth. 5. After the Lord's vengeance is come upon the enemies of Christ's kingdom, his curse shall follow the works of their hands, and upon whatsoever they sought to make themselves happy by in their life : and his vengeance shall follow upon their posterity, till he have rooted out their memorial from among men. *Their fruit shall he destroy from the earth, and their seed from amongst the children of men.*

11. *For they intended evil against thee ; they imagined a mischievous device,* which *they were not able* to perform :

For evidencing the Lord's justice, he giveth a reason of this from the design which the enemies have to root out the Lord's anointed, and his seed, ver. 11. Whence learn, 1. The malicious enemies of Christ's kingdom, (beside all the hatred they have shown, and evil which they have done) are still upon plots and designs to overturn Christ's kingdom and work: *they intended evil against thee.* The enemies of Christ's kingdom may possibly conceive they only oppose such as trouble men's interests, and not as they are the Lord's children ; yet it is found, that what they do against them, they do it against the Lord, because they do it against his children and subjects, for his cause and service. 2. Plot what the wicked please against Christ and his church, they shall not be able to accomplish their design or desire ; *they have imagined a mischievous device, which they are not able to perform.* 3. The evil which the wicked would do, and set themselves to do, shall be made their ditty, and the reason of their doom and destruction, as well as the evil which they have done, if they repent not. For *they intended*, is here given as the reason of the judgment.

12. *Therefore shalt thou make them turn their back,* when *thou shalt make ready* thine arrows *upon thy strings against the face of them.*

He cleareth their ditty and judgment yet more, vers. 12, teaching us, 1. That the Lord will suffer his enemies to manifest themselves in open opposition ofttimes, before he fall upon them : for here they are found in the posture of pursuers and opposers of God, setting their face against him when he cometh to execute judgment on them : *thou shalt make them turn their back.* 2. When God falleth upon his enemies to be avenged upon them, he useth to make them and the beholders see, that he hath set them up as a mark to shoot at : for *he will make ready his arrows*, one after another, *against the face of them.* 3. The Lord's wrath shall so meet his enemies in the teeth, wheresoever they turn, that they shall be forced to forsake their pursuing of the church: *thou shalt make them turn their back.*

13. *Be thou exalted, Lord, in thine own strength :* so *will we sing and praise thy power.*

He closeth the psalm with giving glory to God, including also a prayer. Whence learn, 1. When the Lord's church is preserved from persecutors, then the Lord is exalted: *be thou exalted*, saith he. 2. When the church is delivered, it is not by her own strength, but by the power of the Lord : *be thou exalted in thine own strength.* 3. Albeit the godly be put to mourn for a time, yet when the Lord appeareth for them, they get matter of joy to themselves, and praise to God. *So will we sing and praise thy power.*

PSALM XXII.

To the Chief Musician upon Aijeleth Shahar. A Psalm of David.

This psalm is a prophecy of Christ's deepest sufferings, whereof David's exercise is a type. The agony of spirit in Christ, and wrestling of David's faith as the type, is set down to ver. 22, and the victory and the outgate, to the end of the psalm. In the exercise there are three conflicts between sense and faith. The first conflict, wherein the sense of trouble is set down, ver. 1, 2, and faith's wrestling against it, ver. 3—5. The second conflict, wherein is the second assault of sense, ver. 6—8, and faith's wrestling against it,ver. 9—11. The third conflict, wherein the third assault of sense is, ver. 12—18, and faith's wrestling with it, ver. 19—21.¶Then follows the victory, set forth, first in a promise of praise, ver. 22; secondly, in an exhortation to all the godly to praise the Lord, with a reason from his experience, ver. 23, 24; thirdly, in a renewed promise of praise and thanks, to the edification of the church, ver. 25; fourthly, in a prophecy of the increase of God's glory in the earth, as a fruit of Christ's suffering and victory, ver. 26 —31.

1. *My God, my God, why hast thou forsaken me?* why art thou so *far from helping me* and from *the words of my roaring?*

2. *O my God, I cry in the day time, but thou hearest not, and in the night* season, *and am not silent.*

In this exercise of David the type, and of Christ represented here, both agree in these four things. 1. Both are under the sense of wrath, and of oppressing trouble; 2. both are tempted to doubting and desperation; 3. both wrestle against the temptation, and against trouble, the occasion thereof; and 4. both get the victory. But they differ in these four things. First, in the measure of the trouble; David's trouble was little in comparison of Christ's trouble; David laid not down his life under trouble; but Christ's trouble was incomparably more, and his soul made heavy unto death, and the trouble took his life from him. Secondly, in the manner of the trouble they differ; for David's trouble was only a probatory exercise, without vindictive wrath; not a curse, but a cross for trying of him, and training of him to believe against sense; which trouble of his paid no debt, neither his own nor any others; but Christ's trouble was a vindictive and avengeful punishment; for real wrath was against him, as he was bearing our sins, and the bitter curse of the law was cast upon him: for he was made a curse for us; and his punishment paid our debt; and was expiatory and satisfactory to justice. Thirdly, though both David and Christ were tempted to doubting and desperation, yet David's temptation could not be sinless because of his sinful imperfections, common to him and all the rest of the godly; the temptation got some advantage of him, because of the imperfection of his knowledge, faith, love, and abilities; and because of the power of the body of original sin in him. But Christ's passive temptation was altogether sinless, and could not have any sin at all on his part ; for albeit he was tempted in all things like unto us, yet it is said, *without sin*. Because, when the prince of this world, Satan, came and took essay of him, he found none of his own stuff in Christ : he had *nothing in him* to work upon ; and it was impossible that sin could be in him, being the *Holy One of Israel our sanctifier, Holy Lord God almighty* and man also, in one person, Isaiah vi. 3. Job xii. 41. Fourthly, they differ in their wrestling and victory ; for David wrestled not in his own strength, got not the victory in his own strength, but in and through Christ's strength, who gave David a taste only, or a smell rather, of the cup which he was to drink out unto the dregs, and with the dregs, and who helped him to wrestle by faith. But Christ wrestled and got the victory in his own strength, which is one with the strength of the Father ; for he is Jehovah our righteousness. In all the psalm we shall look upon every passage, not so much as it concerneth David the type, as wherein it concerneth Christ the truth. In the first conflict of the sense of trouble with faith, learn from the words as they are Christ's words, 1. God is Christ's God ; he being considered as God and man, in one person, entered in the covenant of redemption with the Father as Mediator and surety for men ; that he shall satisfy justice, and do all the Father's will in behalf of the elect, and that God shall be his God, and the God of all the elect redeemed by him. Therefore doth he here say, *My God, my God.* 2. Faith, as it is a virtue giving perfect trust and credit unto God's promises made to his Son the Redeemer, is a part of that original holiness in the man Christ, and a point of his personal perfection, suitable to his employment. This faith he professeth while he saith, *My God, my God.* 3. Christ, as man lying under the curse of the law for us, was really deserted and forsaken for a time, in regard of all sensible consolation : for it behoved him to bear the wrath, or effects of wrath, due to our sins really, so far as might satisfy for us, and relieve us from wrath. It is true, the man Christ could no more be forsaken, in regard of the divine presence supporting him, than the personal union of the two natures could be dissolved. But in regard of sensible consolation, he was, by way of punishment for our sins, and by way of cursing our sin in him, really in our stead for a while deprived, as man, of the sense of the comfort of his own Godhead. The sense of wrath filling now the soul of the man to the brim, and running over; therefore speaks he of his forsaking, *Why hast thou forsaken me?* 4. As sense and reason can express themselves in seeming contradictory terms, and yet without contradiction can very well agree in their seeming opposite and inconsistent expressions: so can faith and sense express themselves in seeming contradictory terms, and yet very well agree; for as sense, and pain, and sickness, in the patient can, in its own language and style of natural feeling, say to the chirurgeon cutting and lancing the flesh, and to the physician who hath given a bitter potion, *You have hurt me, you have made me sick:* when indeed in the style of reason and wit, he hath been healing the man, and recovering him from sickness;—so sense of sorrow, grief, pain, and affliction, desertion, and wrath, can speak in the terms of natural feeling, that which may seem to cross, but doth not indeed cross, faith speaking in the terms and language of supernatural theological truth. Therefore, *My God, my God,* spoken in the perfection of faith's language, can very well agree with *Why hast thou forsaken me? why art thou so far from helping me, and from the words of my roaring?* spoken here in the language of perfect natural sense; for perfect faith, and perfect natural sense were in our Lord Christ: very God and very man, completely holy. 5. Bitter was the cup of divine wrath which Christ did drink; great was the price our Redeemer paid to ransom us, when the sense thereof drew forth of his Majesty such expressions. Thus faith and feeling may both speak, each of them their own language to God in one breath, as here they do. Now as these words are David's who had in him sinful corruption of nature, learn, 1. Sense, and temptation, and corrupt nature, may represent God in his dispensations to his own children, as if he had forsaken altogether, and regarded not their hard condition, and would not help, as here is shown in David's experience. 2. Faith should correct sense, and refute temptations, and bridle affections, and not suffer their words to go forth, expressing sense or appearance of doubting God's favour, till first faith speak, and go before, and fasten its gripes on the covenant;

as here faith goes foremost, and calleth the Lord, *My God, my God,* before that sense utter a word. 3. At one time, and in one exercise, these three may concur. 1. Desertion in the point of comfort. 2. Growing trouble without help seen. And, 3. Apparent rejecting of prayer : and these three joined together, set sore upon the faith of a child of God ; for continuance of trouble is a sore temptation, albeit comfort be now and then mixed. Want of sensible comfort, mixed with trouble, doubleth the burden, and disquieteth the mind much ; but to seem to lose labour in prayer made for either help or comfort, is the heaviest part of the exercise : *I cry day and night, and thou hearest not,* is a sad condition. 4. In this case it is the best remedy to lay the worst of our thoughts single before the Lord, and to tell him whatsoever is suggested to us, and not to be secretaries to Satan, but to reveal ourselves fully to God, and fix ourselves on the covenant of grace, wherein we have closed with him, yea, and to double and treble our gripes of *My God.*

3. *But thou* art *holy,* O thou *that inhabitest the praises of Israel.*

4. *Our fathers trusted in thee: they trusted, and thou didst deliver them.*

5. *They cried unto thee, and were delivered: they trusted in thee, and were not confounded.*

Now faith having spoken with sense, and grappled with the temptation, speaketh alone, that it may prevail. Whence learn, 1. Were temptations ever so black, faith will not hearken to an ill word spoken against God, but will justify God always; this should be our part in time of greatest perplexity, to say, *But thou art holy.* 2. It is wisdom for a soul in a sad exercise, to take side and part with faith, to gather arguments to strengthen it, to divert the mind from thinking still on its calamity, and to set it upon the contemplation of God's perfections in himself, and toward us in his Gospel, and of the passages of his providence toward his people, whereby he hath purchased constant praises at their hands : in the right of which praises and possession whereof, God is resolved to keep himself and to dwell therein as in a habitation wherein he delights to remain. *O thou that inhabitest the praises of Israel.* 3. It is wisdom to look to the carriage of the godly in former times; *our fathers trusted in thee*; to their trusting, and trusting in God constantly in their trouble; *they trusted in thee, they trusted*, and the third time *they trusted*: and to look upon their patient depending on God, doubling their diligence in calling on him; as their straits did grow, *they cried, they trusted*: and to remember that they did never seek God in vain, but every one of them were delivered, and not confounded ; for this direction is holden forth to us in this example, which our Lord Jesus could well make use of for our consolation, and whereof David made use for his own upholding.

6. *But I* am *a worm and no man; a reproach of men, and despised of the people.*

7. *All they that see me, laugh me to scorn: they shoot out the lip, they shake the head,* saying,

8. *He trusted on the Lord, that he would deliver him: let him deliver him, seeing he delighted in him.*

The second conflict, wherein the sense of trouble is set forth as a new assaulting of faith. Whence learn, 1. Never was any child of God before Christ under so much misery as Christ was himself: his own heavens, his own Father, his own Godhead, did hide their face and consolation from him: our sins willingly taken on him, and God's wrath pressed the weight of punishment with the full power of justice, both upon his soul and body: those for whom he died despised him; he himself being emptied of all things which make men respected to the world, and depressed lower than ever any man was, as a worm to be trod upon, he was made a matter of common talk and reproach in all men's mouths; set at nanght by the basest of the people; derided and scorned in his most holy behaviour; sport and matter of laughter was made of his sufferings; malice feeding itself with pleasure upon his pain and misery, and expressing itself with the basest signs of disgrace which disdain could devise, for flouting of him, mocking of his saving doctrine, and faithful testimony given unto it ; insulting over him, as if he had been neither God's Son, nor an honest man ; and all this was counted little enough for satisfaction to justice, exacting of him, as the due punishment of our sins, whatsoever is imported in the sad expression set down in the text. 2. As the more

misery the children of God are under, the more doth temptation make their misery seem weighty, for bearing down
their confidence in God : so the more that misery seemeth
to grow, and the world to turn their back on God's children in their trials, the more should they draw near to
God, and lay out their case before him, as here we are
taught by this example. 3. Let no man wonder to be despised of men, and mocked for religion, for so was the man
according to God's own heart ; and Christ our Lord was
mocked more than any in his sad sufferings. *Let God deliver him, seeing he delighted in him,* said his enemies.

9. *But thou* art *he that took me out of the womb;
thou didst make me hope* when I was *upon my mother's
breasts.*

10. *I was cast upon thee from the womb: thou* art
my God from my mother's belly.

11. *Be not far from me, for trouble* is *near; for*
there is *none to help.*

Here faith opposeth whatsoever the complaint could import to the prejudice of confidence, and laboureth to
strengthen itself by all arguments. Whence learn, 1. As
Satan maketh assault after assault against faith, upon new
representations of calamity and misery, so we should raise
bulwark after bulwark for defence; and after we have
looked upon other men's experiences before us, we should
recount our own experiences of God's care towards us, and
should make use of all that the Lord hath done unto us for
our strengthening ; for so doth this example teach us.
2. Albeit men in a fit of misbelief, will admit no proof of
God's respect unto them, except singularities, and will
question also special grace when it is given, yet the humbled believer is so wise as to make use of the most common
benefit which the man hath received from God for confirmation of his own faith ; even the ordinary work of our
conception, frame of body, birth, and education, may suffice us to draw in to God who made us, and hath done so
much for us (ere we could implore him, or do any thing for
ourselves,) as may encourage us to come to him, and seek
his favour, whatsoever objection can be made to the contrary, for this example teacheth us so to do. 3. Seeing the
Lord doeth many things for us, which in the time he doeth

them for us we do not observe, it is our duty to look upon
them afterwards, that they may furnish us with matter of
praise to God and faith in him ; for so doth this example
teach us.   4. Whatsoever instruments and means the Lord
maketh use of, the spiritual eye pierceth through them,
and looketh on God as worker of all things, for and upon
them from their cradle: *thou lookest me out of my mother's
womb.* 5. Children born within the covenant have God
for their God from their nativity, and may lay their reckoning so ; and whensoever they would draw near to God to
make use of the covenant, they may say, *Thou art my God
from my mother's belly.* 6. The approaching of trouble,
and nearness of danger, should draw us near to God : who
in an instant can interpose himself between us and the evil :
and the less help we have beside the Lord himself, the more
hope may we have to be helped by God.   This is the prophet's plea, *be not far from me, for trouble is near, &c.*

12. *Many bulls have compassed me: strong* bulls *of
Bashan have beset me round.*

13. *They gaped upon me* with *their mouths, as a
ravening and a roaring lion.*

From v. 12—22, is the third conflict of sense with faith,
upon the consideration of the multitude, power, and cruelty
of his enemies, compared with his own infirmity, now
emptied of all strength to resist them ; and these are mixed
one with another.   The enemy's terribleness is first set
forth, then his emptiness and weakness by turns, to v. 19 ;
unto all which faith opposeth itself, by prayer to God, to
v. 22.   He compareth, v. 12, 13, his persecutors to *bulls,
many bulls,* strong, cruel, gaping, roaring, devouring lions.
Whence learn, 1. The persecutors of Christ and his people
are but beastly sensual bodies, sold to this present world,
and destitute of grace and humility : more like in their
rage to savage beasts than to rational men ; commonly also
they are men of riches and worldly power, fed and fat bulls,
and many in number, all of them ready for an ill turn, and
so cruel, that nothing less will satisfy them than blood and
slaughter, as they are here described.   And no wonder
that Christ's servants shall find it so in their case, seeing
Christ himself and his servants before us have had experience of such enemies.

14. *I am poured out like water, and all my bones are out of joint: my heart is like wax; it is melted in the midst of my bowels.*

15. *My strength is dried up like a potsherd; and my tongue cleaveth to my jaws; and thou hast brought me into the dust of death.*

What the Lord wrought upon his body, and natural spirits, and strength. is here set down. Whence learn, 1. It was determined by God, that with outward persecution of Christ, by his cruel adversaries, the Father should bruise him and break him inwardly also, and punish him with all severity : for here his suffering is in body and mind, in flesh and bones, in his natural spirit and natural courage, in heart and whole strength, that in nothing he should be unpunished, wherein we sinners are found polluted : to the intent, that he being fully emptied, the ransom might be full ; he is *poured like water*, and emptied of all that the created human nature could furnish. The terror of divine justice and wrath did in a manner loose *all the joints of his body*, so that natural courage, before the dreadful avenger of sin, did fail, *his heart was made soft like wax* to receive and keep the impression of divine terror, till justice should be satisfied, and was dissolved like wax, in the point of resolution to withstand it. It is *melted in the midst of his bowels*, his natural strength is dried, burnt up like a *potsherd*, baken in the fire ; his mouth was stopped from all defence and apology, for he was content to be holden as guilty, standing in our room, *therefore his tongue cleaved to his jaws*. And in a word, the hand of God exacteth the full price of him, and brings him down so, as there is not a bit of him free of the punishment ; *thou*, saith he, *hast brought me into the dust of death*. This, David had but a taste of in his deepest trouble. The verity and weight of this are to be found only in Christ, of whom this was prophesied, that it should come, and indeed is come, done and ended, and so it behoved to be.

16. *For dogs have compassed me; the assembly of the wicked have inclosed me; they pierced my hands and my feet.*

Again he bringeth forth his enemies' part, to show us that Christ's enemies were to prove but bloody dogs, when they should be let loose upon him, whom nothing but *Crucify him, crucify him,* could satisfy: and such will they be still who persecute his church. Next, to show, that although his enemies were to be the assembly of the visible church, for open profession, yet by rejecting his grace, and opposing him in God's sight and estimation, they were holden for the *assembly of the wicked.* Thirdly, to foreshow the death of the cross to be appointed for Christ, it is said, *they pierced my hands and my feet.*

17. *I may tell all my bones: they look* and *stare upon me.*

18. *They part my garments among them, and cast lots upon my vesture.*

Another, and further point of Christ's fore-prophesied suffering, is his nakedness on the cross, and the discovery of his lean body, being wasted with decreed sorrows, and the gazing of his enemies upon him hanging on the cross, and the parting of his garments among the soldiers, and the casting of lots for his upper garment, because it was woven, and could not be divided. Whence learn, 1. All that our Lord Jesus suffered, was before decreed and agreed upon, betwixt the Father and the Son, and foretold by Christ himself long before his incarnation, speaking by his Spirit in his prophets, as here appeareth by the description of our Lord's death and passion, so plainly and particularly as if it were a history, and not a prophecy. 2. Beside pain of body, leanness of flesh, with daily sorrows and trouble of spirit, the least disgrace done to our Lord, the least wrong, a look unto him, the least injury in the matter of his clothing, are all reckoned up in his sufferings, all counted up in the price of redemption, that there may be nothing inlacking in the punishment of our cautioner, whereby God's justice might be satisfied, or our consciences quieted, for the expiation of our sin, by his suffering in body, soul, fame, apparel, and every other thing else, wherein justice could overtake the guilty.

19. *But be not thou far from me, O Lord, O my strength, haste thee to help me.*

Unto this last assault, faith opposeth prayer for divine assistance, for strength to bear out, and for delivery, in all which he was heard. Whence learn, 1. Faith is made vic-

torious over all assaults, by opening of its temptations to
God, and putting up prayer to him for help, as here is seen.
2. If God shall not withdraw his sweet presence for supporting a soul, albeit it should not find his presence for
comforting of it, supporting presence may suffice in a time
of sad exercise: for this much did satisfy our God in his
agony: *be not thou far from me, O Lord.* 3. Faith findeth
God to be its strength when the believer is emptied of his
own strength; *O my strength,* saith David, the type, and
Christ as man by him represented. 4. As the haste of our
necessity doth require, we may without limitation request
the Lord to haste: *haste thee to help me.*

20. *Deliver my soul from the sword: my darling
from the power of the dog.*

21. *Save me from the lion's mouth: for thou hast
heard me from the horns of the unicorns.*

He prayeth to be delivered from the violent blood-shedder,
and bloody doggish persecutor, and from the cruel lion-like
oppressor, and then saith presently, that he is heard and
delivered from the power of the enemies which were setting
upon him as unicorns. Now concerning David, the matter
is clear; for he was delivered so from his enemies, that they
got not his life: but of Christ the question may be, how he
was delivered, seeing his life is taken: for answer, Christ
here doth say, that he was delivered; and so it was indeed;
for when he had paid the price, he was not holden by the
bonds of death, and the grave, but rose again the third day.
Whence learn, 1. Christ was no less delivered from dogs,
lions, unicorns, his persecuting enemies, by his resurrection after death, than if he had been taken out of their
hands, when they came to apprehend him in the garden;
yea, this delivery out of the grave, was a far greater delivery than if he had not been slain at all: for then he had
delivered himself only, and not us: but now by the laying
down of his life, he hath discharged himself of his suretyship
for us, and delivered us with himself, and so hath saved
both himself and us; yea, by his rising out of the grave,
he is demonstrated more fully to be the Son of God, than by
any of his miraculous escapings out from the hands of the
multitude, when they were about to apprehend him: *thou
hast heard me,* that is, delivered me. 2. To get victory

over trouble, is a no less glorious delivery from trouble, than to be preserved from falling into trouble; yea, it is a more glorious delivery. For the troubles are broken, by falling on the believer, like waves of the sea on the rock, and the believer remaineth victor, and settled as a rock. 3. It is a notable argument of confidence to be heard by way of delivery, when a man can say he hath in extremity of danger prayed, and hath been heard as a supplicant: *save me, for thou hast heard me from the horns of the unicorns.*

22. *I will declare thy name unto my brethren: in the midst of the congregation will I praise thee.*

After the conflict, the victory and outgate by way of thanksgiving is set down, to the end of the psalm: wherein David's part is but a little shadow, and is swallowed up here in Christ's glory, shining in the fruits of his passion and resurrection. Learn from David's part, that delivery foreseen by faith, worketh in some sort the effects of the delivery past in effect; to wit, quietness, peace, joy, and thanksgiving; as here is to be seen. From Christ's part promising and prophesying of the fruits of his death and resurrection, learn 1. Christ, though he be God Almighty; yet by reason of his incarnation, for the redeemed's sake, he is not ashamed to call them *brethren.* 2. The preaching of the gospel of Christ's satisfaction for our sins by death, and of his resurrection for our justification, is matter of great praise to God and comfort to the redeemed: *I will declare,* saith Christ, *thy name to my brethren.* 3. In the right preaching of the gospel, the ministers are in effect but Christ's voice. Christ himself is the principal prophet and preacher: *for I,* saith he, *will declare thy name in the midst of the* great *congregation;* to wit, of the whole catholic church on earth.

23. *Ye that fear the Lord, praise him: all ye the seed of Jacob, glorify him; and fear him all ye the seed of Israel.*

24. *For he hath not despised nor abhorred the affliction of the afflicted; neither hath he hid his face from him; but when he cried unto him he heard.*

He exhorteth all that fear God, to praise and glorify God, because of Christ's victory, and God's hearkening un-

to his intercession made for the redeemed. Whence learn,
1. Such as are made partakers of the benefit of Christ's passion and resurrection, are chiefly called, and bound to praise
God for their redemption, and to fear God more and more,
that they may be more and more fitted to praise and glorify
him ; for of a sanctified mouth only will God accept praise.
*Ye that fear the Lord, praise him : all ye seed of Jacob,
glorify him; and fear him, all ye the seed of Israel.* 2. The
Father's hearkening untoChrist's intercession, and delivering
of him from our sin, and our deserved punishment laid upon
him, is the common benefit of all the redeemed, the matter
of their common thanksgiving and praise, and the matter
of their assurance of their delivery from sin and death ; of
the certainty of which delivery Christ's deliverance is both
a cause and a pawn : *for he hath not hid his face from
him, but when he cried, he heard him.* 3. Neither the
sense of a man's own meanness and despicableness, nor the
mean estimation that the world hath of him, will prejudge
him when he is a supplicant at the Lord's hand ; *for he
hath not despised, nor abhorred the afflictions of the afflicted.*

25. *My praise* shall be *of thee in the great congregation : I will pay my vows before them that fear him.*

He reneweth the promise of thanksgiving, which, as it
concerneth David, teacheth, 1. That the purpose of praising God, is no light motion in the hearts of his children,
when the Lord hath given them experience of his respect
to them ; but a fixed and solid resolution to set forth
the goodness of God before others. For here he receiveth his promise to praise. 2. The Lord, and the Lord
only, is the theme which the believer handleth in point
of praise ; no other subject of praise acknowledgeth he ;
my praise shall be of thee, &c. 3. The opportunity of
time, place, and persons, offered for praising of God,
ought to be taken, and made use of by every one, according
to their calling : *my praise shall be of thee in the great congregation.* 4. Duties, specially when lying upon us by vows
or oaths, ought to be the more heeded, and made conscience
of : *I will pay my vows before them that fear him.* As this
concerns Christ's undertaking, it teacheth, 1. The Son of
God, and promised Son of David, Christ Jesus, by all the
work of redemption, studieth, as to bring salvation to his

elect, so to honour the Father; saying here, *My praise shall be of thee in the great congregation.* 2. Albeit our Lord hath finished all his undertaking for the payment of the price and ransom of redemption, yet hath he not yet performed all which he hath undertaken for making use of his purchased salvation, unto the enlarging of the glory of his Father, and gathering into the great congregation all his redeemed ones to be worshippers of the Father in spirit and truth: but as he is still upon this work from generation to generation, so is he willing still to lie under this engagement and these vows, till he perform them to the full: *I will pay my vows before them that fear him.*

26. *The meek shall eat and be satisfied: they shall praise the Lord that seek him: your heart shall live for ever.*

He alludeth to the manner of offering peace-offerings, where the godly friends concurring in the thanksgiving, had a share in the feast of what was sacrificed. Whence learn, 1. The mercy bestowed upon one of the godly, serveth to refresh the souls of the rest: and in special there is a banquet prepared for the souls of the redeemed by the purchase of Christ's sacrifice, whereof the humbled believer is made partaker: *the meek shall eat, and be satisfied.* 2. Albeit the believer at all times do not find the sweetness of this feast, but be put to work after a meal received, put to fight after a feast, and made hungry after a new meal, and be made to pray for it, and to seek after the Lord in the use of the means, yet shall he eat again in due time, and be satisfied: *for they shall praise the Lord that seek him,* is as much as they that seek him, shall find so much as shall make them both to have cause of praising, and also in effect to praise him. 3. Whatsoever alterations or vicissitudes of things be in the condition of humble believers, seeking more and more communion with God, they may be sure of eternal life, beside what they get by way of earnest in this life; for the Spirit of the Lord, directing his speech to them, hath said, *Your heart shall live for ever.*

27. *All the ends of the world shall remember, and turn unto the Lord: and all the kindreds of the nations shall worship before thee.*

28. *For the kingdom* is *the Lord's; and he* is *the governor among the nations.*

Now followeth special prophecies of the enlargement of Christ's kingdom, wherein the prophet by the Spirit of prophecy doth speak, and teach us, 1. That the calling of the Gentiles after Christ's resurrection, was a concluded matter with God, whereof he gave warning long before it came, which though it be come to pass, yet not in so ample a measure as may be yet further expected ; because, for the making of these words yet more clearly seen to be fulfilled, it shall come to pass, that *all the ends of the world shall remember.* 2. So long as men shall lie unconverted, they know not what they are doing, they are as men sleeping or distracted, not making use of so much as the very principles of truth, which, by the light of common reason from inspection of the creatures, may be learned, concerning the invisible things of God ; but when the light of Christ's gospel shineth in upon their heart, they are made *to remember and turn to the Lord.* 3. Such as are converted, make God the object of their worship, embrace his ordinances, and subject themselves to his laws and discipline ; *for they worship before him,* become subjects to him, and that by the powerful subduing of them to himself: *for the kingdom is the Lord's, and he is governor among the nations.*

29. *All* they that be *fat upon earth shall eat and worship : all they that go down to the dust shall bow before him ; and none can keep alive his own soul.*

30. *A seed shall serve him ; it shall be accounted to the Lord for a generation.*

31. *They shall come, and shall declare his righteousness unto a people that shall be born, that he hath done* this.

A further clearing of this prophecy of Christ's kingdom enlarged among the Gentiles. Whence learn, 1. That kings, rulers, and magistrates shall have no cause of jealousy from Christ's kingdom, and his governing over nations ; for so many of them as shall embrace Jesus Christ, not only may brook their places, honours, riches, and all lawful benefits, wherein their fatness and worldly welfare seem to consist ; but also shall be made partakers of the delicates of the Lord's house, which shall so satisfy their souls, as they shall count his gospel their choice cheer, and shall bless God for his consolations ; for it is promised to all

Christ's true subjects, who are in high place: *all they that be fat upon earth shall eat and worship.*   2. As the highest condition worldly shall not be hurt by obedience to Christ, but helped, for the benefit of the true believer; so believers in the meanest condition they can be in on earth, shall find relief, comfort, and making up of all their inlacks in Jesus Christ, and shall fall down and worship their rich and bountiful Lord: *all that go down to the dust shall bow before him.*   3. Whosoever shall not come to Christ to be saved by him, shall perish; and they that come unto him, shall be forced to hold their salvation of him: *for none can keep alive his own soul:* this is the proper work of the only Saviour Jesus.   4. Albeit every particular person, in every nation and kingdom, be not converted unto Christ: yet so many persons of all ranks, out of all nations, shall be converted, as shall make evident Christ's power and sovereignty to conquer subjects to himself at his pleasure, even as many as may perpetuate his kingdom, and the succession of worshippers of him from one generation to another; *for a seed shall serve him, it shall be accounted to the Lord for a generation:* he will make little reckoning of the rest, whom he converteth not.   5. Albeit there be little appearance of accomplishing prophecies and promises of the propagation of Christ's kingdom from age to age, yet the promise and prophecy shall be fulfilled: *they shall come,* who shall receive the doctrine of Christ's righteousness by faith in him, and *shall declare this righteousness* of faith, and God's faithfulness in promise-keeping, *to another generation, unto a people that shall be born.*   6. The whole work of redemption, converting of souls, comforting of souls, propagation of the doctrine of righteousness, and manifestation of God's glory thereby, shall from age to age be declared to be the work of God himself, which he doth by his instruments and means; *they shall declare to their children* and successors, that *God hath done this;* to wit, all that is spoken of here, or elsewhere in his word: *unto a people that shall be born, that he hath done this.*

PSALM XXIII.

A Psalm of David.

This Psalm is the expression of the prophet's confidence in God's grace, wherein, from the settling himself in the belief of our covenanted relation between God and him, he draweth sundry comfortable conclusions and confirmations of faith from it, concerning the Lord's furnishing every necessary good thing to him, v. 1, 2; for recovery of him from every evil condition, wherein he may fall, v. 3; and for assisting and comforting him in the greatest danger he could fall into, v. 4; and for making him blessed in despite of his enemies, v. 5; and for his continuing in God's grace and fellowship for ever, v. 6. ~

1. *The Lord is my shepherd, I shall not want.*

He layeth down for a ground his relation to God, and thence confirmeth his assurance to have the fruits thereof. Whence learn, 1. The Lord is content to demit himself to be compared unto any thing which may import his love, and respect, and care of his own : as here for our comfort he is pleased to be called a *shepherd*. 2. The grounds of our faith in God, making us to have right unto him by covenant, should be solidly laid ; and these being firmly laid, then comfortable conclusions may, and should be, drawn from thence, as here the prophet doeth. 3. In special, whatsoever sweet relation the believer standeth in with God, he may assure himself of all the fruits, and good, which that relation can import. As here having said, *the Lord is my shepherd*, he assureth himself then, *he shall not want :* to wit, what such a shepherd seeth necessary for such a sheep.

2. *He maketh me to lie down in green pastures : he leadeth me beside the still waters.*

3. *He restoreth my soul : he leadeth me in the paths of righteousness for his name's sake.*

He goeth on numbering the benefits following from the foresaid relation, partly showing what experience he hath had, partly assuring himself what further to find. Whence learn, 1. As the shepherd provideth good and wholesome pasture for his sheep, and a place of safety and rest, with the commodity of all needful refreshment of calm running waters : so doth the Lord furnish the food of life to the believer with quiet rest, and satisfaction of timous consolation, by his Word and Spirit: *he maketh me lie down in green pastures, &c.* 2. It is possible through the evil that is in us, we may fall into decay of graces, into sicknesses of divers

sorts ; yea, and that we may wander away from the shepherd,
and the society of the flock sometime.   In which case we
should perish, if our careful Lord did not apply himself to
our necessities, to relieve us; for it is *he that restoreth
our soul* ; it is he that reclaimeth us from our wanderings;
it is he that directeth us, and keepeth us from going on
still in by-paths : *he leadeth me*, saith he, *in the paths of
righteousness.*   3. It is not for any good we deserve, or
have done, or can do, for which he taketh such care of his
weak and foolish children.   It is for the glory of his free
grace, constant love, and sworn covenant, even *for his own
name's sake.*

4 *Yea, though I walk through the valley of the shadow of death, I will fear no evil: for thou* art *with
me ; thy rod and thy staff they comfort me.*

He presupposeth he may fall into new and harder troubles
than ever he fell into before, and yet hopes to be delivered
therefrom.   Whence learn, 1. The believer in his best condition may not promise to himself immunity from trouble
or perils; but must prepare for the worst, even to be put
to extreme danger of perishing, and in such darkness as
were most like, and near (unto death) *to walk through the
valley of the shadow of death*, where sheep may fall into the
pit, or be fallen upon by every devouring beast in the dark.
2. The fruit of former delivery out of trouble, should encourage us to hope for deliverance out of whatsoever new
trouble we may fall into, as the prophet's example doth
teach.   3. Faith after a victory is very stout, and hath
warrant indeed to be so, and may and should resolve to be
stout by God's grace ; howsoever, when trouble cometh,
which is the touchstone of the strength of faith, it may
discover weakness for a time : for here David saith, *I will
fear no evil, though I walk through the valley of the shadow of death.*   4. The consideration of God's covenanted
presence with his own in trouble, and of his power to protect and deliver them, and of his wisdom and goodness to
make his own profit by troubles, may and should comfort
the believer against the fear of perishing, in whatsoever
trouble ; for David giveth this as a reason of not fearing
evil, *Thou art with me, thy rod and thy staff they comfort
me.*

5. *Thou preparest a table before me in the presence of mine enemies; thou anointest my head with oil; my cup runneth over.*

From the grounds of his faith, confirmed by experience, he seeth still satisfaction from God, who giveth the banquet to him, as it were, in his enemies' sight. Whence learn. 1. Albeit sometimes the believer may be put to hardship and hazard, for trying and training of his faith; yet sometimes also the Lord will give him rich evidence of his love and kindness unto him, if not in both outward and inward benefits, yet at least in spiritual consolations comparable to a royal feast; as here, *thou preparest a table before me.* 2. Although the enemies of the godly are not few, both bodily and spiritual, all concurring to mar the felicity of the Lord's children, yet shall they not be able to hinder their sense, now and then, of satisfactory blessedness maugre them all; for as oft as God seeth fit, he giveth his own the banquet *in the presence of his enemies.* 3. When it pleaseth the Lord to comfort a believer, and to give him the banquet, there is nothing wanting, during the time of the Lord's comfortable entertaining of him, which may strengthen him or rejoice him; but as much given unto him sensibly, as may make him say, *thou anointest my head with oil, and my cup runneth over,* Psal. xcii. 10, and civ. 15.

6. *Surely goodness and mercy shall follow me all the days of my life; and I will dwell in the house of the Lord for ever.*

He showeth that in his former speeches, he meant not of earthly benefits, although these also be worthy of acknowledgment and of thanksgiving for them; but of spiritual mercies, by this, that he is assured of the continuance thereof, in this life and in the life to come. Whence learn. 1. The delight and satisfaction of the believer is not in any earthly portion, but in God's good-will and pity toward him; God's goodness and mercy is the matter of his contentment. 2. An humble believer, who in his own eyes is like a weak, witless sheep, and yet doth follow the shepherd, may assure himself, from the covenant relation between God and him, of the constancy of God's good-will and actual outletting of liberal gifts of good things unto him, and of removing of evils, both of sin and of the fruits of it, and be persuaded of his own perseverance in the way to salvation, all the days of his life; for here is an instance of it, *surely goodness and mercy shall follow me all the days of my life.* 3. As a believer may be assured of the constant course of God's love to follow him, and of his own preserving in the way of life, so may he be persuaded of eternal life, and everlasting communion with God in heaven. And this perfecteth the felicity of the believer; and no less can do it than this; *I will dwell in the house of the Lord for ever.*

PSALM XXIV.

A Psalm of David.

The psalmist having in the first place set down God's Lordship in the world, that he may thereby commend the special prerogative of the true church, v. 1, 2, describeth, in the next place, the true citizens of this spiritual kingdom. v. 3—6; and exhorteth, in the third place, all incorporations, and in special the visible church, to accept the offer of a more entire communion with God in Christ, that they may enjoy the spiritual privileges of the subjects of the invisible and spiritual kingdom, v. 7—10.

1. *The earth is the Lord's, and the fulness thereof; the world, and they that dwell therein:*

2. *For he hath founded it upon the seas, and established it upon the floods.*

From the lordship and sovereignty of God over all the world, learn, 1. The Lord's power and authority over the saints, considered in their natural condition, is no less than over the rest of the world, and the Lord is no more bound to one than to another, laying aside the decree of his own good-will and pleasure; *the earth is the Lord's and the fulness thereof; the world, and they that dwell therein.* 2. The earth is as full of the riches of God's bounty towards man as it can hold; and the standing miracle of the dry land, lifted up contrary to the nature of that element, which is to be under and not above, and much higher than the element of water, is a standing evidence of God's power and care employed to make a habitation for man : *for he hath founded the earth upon the seas, and established it upon the floods,* commanding the element of water to go down below the earth, as if it were the foundation thereof.

3. *Who shall ascend into the hill of the Lord? and who shall stand in his holy place?*

4. *He that hath clean hands, and a pure heart; who hath not lifted up his soul unto vanity, nor sworn deceitfully.*

5. *He shall receive the blessing from the Lord, and righteousness from the God of his salvation.*

6. *This* is *the generation of them that seek him, that seek thy face, O Jacob. Selah.*

In the second place, he cometh to the special dominion of God and Christ in the church, and asketh for the marks and privileges of the true subjects of this kingdom. Whence learn, 1. God hath chosen a church out of all the earth, to be his peculiar people, with whom he may converse, and to whom he may give privilege of communion for ever with himself; he hath his own *holy and high hill*, he hath his own *holy place*, to wit, a holy universal church, represented by the *hill of Zion*, lifted up above the inferior valleys; he hath his holy tabernacle, where he giveth the signs of his presence, separate from the common multitude, and worldly affairs; *who shall ascend into the hill of the Lord? and who shall stand in his holy place?* He compareth the invisible church to a *hill* or *mountain*, and *the holy place*, because God's true church indeed for firmness, durableness, dignity above all other incorporations, and spiritual sublimity, is like a *hill* above the plain, lifted up above all the world, a holy society, wherein God delighteth to dwell. 2. Not every one who is a member of the visible church, but only true converts, who make up the invisible church, have the honour and happiness of ascending unto the spiritual use, end, meaning, and profit of the ordinances of God in his church, and of keeping constant communion with God in heaven, represented by standing in the *holy place*. Therefore, for stirring up of outward professors of religion, to examine themselves, lest they be mistaken and so perish, the question is here made to God to show *who shall ascend to his hill, and who shall stand in his holy place*. 3. The marks of a citizen of the invisible church and kingdom of God, are only such as God and a man's own conscience can soundly judge of; to wit, faith in God, manifested by endeavoured sanctity of thoughts, words, and

deeds, by way of obedience to the first and second table in
sincerity: for he must, after covenanting with God by faith
which makes him a subject, study also cleanness of hands,
or innocency of life, and that out of a pure heart, cleansed
by the blood of sprinkling for justification, and by the clean
water of begun sanctification; and therefore he must not any
more look upon the deceitful baits of sin, with a longing
desire to have them; for that were to *lift up his soul unto vanity.*   Neither must he misregard an oath, whether in
or after the taking of it; for that were to *swear deceitfully,*
seeming to stand in awe of God when he doth not fear him
at all.   4. Every believer who setteth himself to bring
forth the fruits of his faith in obedience to God's law, shall
have a gracious reward; *he shall receive the blessing from
the Lord.*   5. The holy life of the true believer, is not the
cause of his justification before God, by reason of the im-
perfection thereof, and impossibility to satisfy the law thereby; but he shall receive justification and eternal life, as a
free gift from God, by virtue of the covenant of grace:
therefore it is said here, that *he shall receive righteousness
from the God of his salvation.*   6. Whosoever they be within the visible church, who have the marks of true covenanters, such as are here described, yea, whosoever are seeking
God, to make them such; whosoever are seeking reconciliation with God, and communion with him, whether they be
Jews or Gentiles, bond or free, male or female; they are
the generation that shall ascend and dwell in God's holy
place; for *this is the generation of them that seek him.*   The
generation that seek thy face, saith he to God.   This is
the true Jacob, the true heir of the promises.

7. *Lift up your heads, O ye gates; and be ye lift up,
ye everlasting doors; and the King of glory shall come
in.*

8. *Who* is *this King of glory? The Lord strong and
mighty, the Lord mighty in battle.*

9. *Lift up your heads, O ye gates; even lift* them
*up, ye everlasting doors; and the King of glory shall
come in.*

10. *Who* is *this King of glory? The Lord of hosts,
he* is *the King of glory.   Selah.*

In the third place, having described those persons who

shall surely dwell in heaven with God, he exhorteth all the
members of the visible church, to the intent they may receive
righteousness and salvation from God (who is in covenant
with his church), heartily to welcome Christ Jesus, the
King of glory and Lord of hosts, dwelling in the midst of
them in the tabernacle, shadowing forth and signifying his
coming in the flesh, by his giving oracles from the ark of
the covenant, defending them, feeding them, and fighting
their battles, and at length in David's time ascending on
mount Zion, he and the ark of the covenant triumphantly,
to let them see in a shadow, how, after his great battles,
foughten for our redemption, he should ascend to heaven,
and make way for his subjects to come up after him, to
dwell with him: he exhorteth, I say, patent doors to be
made unto him, wherever he offereth himself to kingdoms,
cities, incorporations, visible churches, families, and hearts
of men in special.   Whence learn, 1. The way to make
men true converts, true believers, true saints, and inheri-
tors of heaven, is to receive Christ heartily and honourably,
to cast up doors in hearty consent of faith and love, like
triumphant arches, for welcoming so glorious a conqueror
to be their guest; *lift up your heads, O ye gates, &c.*
2. Whosoever shall receive the offer, and open the heart to
him, he shall close covenant with him: *be ye lift up, ye
everlasting doors, and the King of glory shall come in.*
3. He is an unknown king till he be manifested to us; and
such as are wise, when they hear of him, will seek to know
him: *who is this King of glory?* will be their question.
4. Such as seek to know Christ, shall indeed have experimental knowledge of him: that he is able to save them to
the uttermost, to work all their work for them, to defend
them from their adversaries, and to give them complete victory; *he is the Lord strong and mighty, the Lord mighty
in battle.*   5. We have need again and again to hear the
offer of Christ's grace, and to be wakened up to observe
Christ and his glory; need to be exhorted again and again
to open our hearts wide to him: *lift up your heads, ye
gates,* the second time.   6. Christ is indeed glorious, and a
glorious king, in all the passages of redemption, and salvation of his people; albeit the ignorance and unbelief, and
the crosses and troubles following his kingdom in this
world, do obscure his glory to the carnal eye: and there-

fore no wonder, that men do often move the question about his kingdom and glory, asking, *who is the King of glory?*   7. Christ Jesus (whose ascension was prefigured by the ascending of the ark upon mount Zion, convoyed with David, and all Israel,) as he is true man, so he is also very God Almighty, one with the Father, and Holy Spirit, in his Godhead: for *the Lord of hosts he is the King of glory.*

PSALM XXV.

A Psalm of David.

In this psalm the prophet being in danger of his life by his enemies without, and troubled with the sense of sin within, maketh his prayer for relief from both, mixing meditation with prayer, along the psalm, for strengthening of his faith: so first he prayeth from v. 1 to 8, then meditateth, v. 8—10.   In the third room he prayeth again, v. 11.   In the fourth is a new meditation, v. 12—15.   In the last room is a prayer from v. 16 to the end.

1. *Unto thee, O Lord, do I lift up my soul.*

2. *O my God, I trust in thee: let me not be ashamed; let not mine enemies triumph over me.*

3. *Yea, let none that wait on thee be ashamed: let them be ashamed which transgress without cause.*

In the entry of his prayer, he draweth his eye off all relief save God alone, and fixeth his trust upon him, and then prayeth.   Whence learn, 1. It is necessary for a supplicant, if he would have help from God, to loose his confidence off all creature help, and set his eye and heart on God, as David here *lifteth up his soul to God.*   2. Faith in God, fixed on the covenant, giveth wings to the soul, as misbelief causeth it to sink: *O my God,* saith he, *I lift up my soul, I trust in thee.*   3. It is not enough to act faith in time of a strait; but it is profitable to observe also the least measure of faith bestowed on us, and to entertain it, were it never so little, and to avow it that it may be fixed when we go to pray: for, before David put up any petition, he prefixeth, *I lift my soul to thee, I trust in thee;* for otherwise the prayer of the supplicant can find no footing.   4. The believing supplicant shall never be disappointed of promised help; nor shall the hope and expectation of the enemies of God be satisfied: *he will not suffer the believer to be ashamed, nor the enemy long to triumph.*   5. The godly in their prayers are not selfish, nor suitors for singularities to be granted unto them, but are content, yea and desirous, that all other believers may share in their mercies : *yea, let none that wait for thee be ashamed,* saith he. 6. The godly shall not want enemies, albeit they give no offence to the world : for carnal hope and expectation to obtain worldly gain by opposing of the godly, may, and usually doth, set the wicked on work against them ; but they that look to have advantage that way, shall be close disappointed ; for the godly shall escape their snare, and they shall lose their hoped advantage, and shall gain to themselves nothing save shame and a mischief : for *let them be ashamed that transgress without a cause,* is an enduring petition, and a granted petition against them.

4. *Shew me thy ways, O Lord; teach me thy paths.*

5. *Lead me in thy truth, and teach me: for thou art the God of my salvation; on thee do I wait all the day.*

6. *Remember, O Lord, thy tender mercies and thy loving-kindnesses; for they have been ever of old.*

Here he prayeth for grace to behave himself holily under his exercise, and to have renewed experiences of mercies, such as he had felt formerly. Whence learn, 1. The understanding of the way how the Lord useth to deal with his children, serveth greatly for patient bearing of affliction ; and the best way to eschew the snare of adversaries, is to carry ourselves holily. Therefore prayeth David four times to be instructed, and effectually taught and guided in the ways and paths of God's truth or faithful word. 2. Because the Lord in covenanting with us, taketh the work of our salvation in hand, not to lay it down till he hath perfected it ; he alloweth his children, in all particular difficulties, to hold this ground, and constantly to expect the accomplishment thereof, whatsoever strait they fall into : and to wait for direction how to behave themselves, till it be perfected : for David giveth this for a reason of his prayer, *thou art the God of my salvation ; on thee do I wait all the day long.* 3. Though the course of kindness and mercy seem to be interrupted by affliction and temporal desertion, and to be forgotten on God's part ; yet faith must make use of experiences, and read them over unto God out of the register of a sanctified memory, as a recorder to him that cannot forget: *remember thy tender mercies, O Lord, and thy loving-kindnesses.* 4. Mercies and kindnesses some-times felt, may be, and should be, followed up unto the very fountain of eternal love and election from which they came ; so shall the channel be opened and run clear with fresh consolation so much the sooner ; *remember thy mercies to me, for they have been ever of old.*

7. *Remember not the sins of my youth, nor my transgressions : according to thy mercy remember thou me for thy goodness' sake, O Lord.*

He laboureth to have his sins removed, as the chief impediment of the granting of his prayer. Whence learn, 1. New afflictions may easily renew the sense of old sins, even from the time of youth, albeit forgiven of God, and forgotten by the believer, and the tempter can make use thereof against faith in the day of trouble ; in which case the believer without loss may read over blotted accounts, and renew petitions for pardon : *remember not,* saith David, *the sins of my youth, nor my transgressions.* 2. As God holdeth two courts in a man's conscience, concerning sin ; one of justice according to the law, or covenant of works ; another of mercy, according to the gospel, and covenant of grace offered in the Mediator, which is posterior to the other court ; wherein the man who hath glorified justice, and acknowledged his sin, and deserved perdition, is pardoned, for the ransom paid by the Messiah Christ Jesus the Mediator, to whom the sinner is fled for refuge. So the believer hath two reckonings with God, about his sins ; one according to justice, and another according to mercy ; and albeit the believer will never refuse to read, acknowledge, and subscribe again and again, the first reckoning to be just, yet he will not stand to that reckoning for payment, but will hold him to the last bargain of grace, and mercy, and goodness, which cleareth the claim of the first account : for this is David's practice here that the first account may be forgotten : *remember not the sins of my youth,* and that the last account and reckoning may stand, and be held in memory, saying, *according to thy mercy, remember thou me.* 3. For evidencing the stability of the account of mercy for pardoning of sin, the glory of God's goodness is laid in pawn in the covenant ; and that holdeth all fast unto the

believer: therefore, saith he, *remember, for thy goodness'
sake, O Lord.*

8. *Good and upright* is *the Lord; therefore will he
teach sinners in the way.*

9. *The meek will he guide in judgment; and the
meek will he teach his way.*

10. *All the paths of the Lord* are *mercy and truth
unto such as keep his covenant and his testimonies.*

In the second place, after praying, he falleth upon a meditation of the grace and good will of God to a believer,
and of his merciful dealing with him in every condition.
Whence learn, 1. In the secret exercise of the saints, a pause
may be usefully made in prayer, and a meditation, or soliloquy may be fallen upon, when the Lord doth fit matter for
fostering faith, and furthering of prayer, as here we may
in David's practice observe. 2. The goodness and faithfulness of God in his promises, and his readiness without respect of persons, to be gracious to every one who cometh
unto him, are the fountain of the believer's strength, hope,
and consolation; *good and upright is the Lord,* is here a
well of comfort to the supplicant. 3. The conscience of
sin must not keep the believer back from confidence to be
heard in his prayer, when he cometh to seek direction: for
from this ground, *that the Lord is good,* the prophet draweth
this consequence, *therefore will he teach sinners in the way.*
4. God's justice will not hinder his mercy to be bountiful,
nor will former breaking of commands prejudice the sinner, who, being weary of his wandering, doth seek to be
directed hereafter in the Lord's way; *he will teach sinners
in the way.* 5. When by affliction a man is humbled, and
brought to submit himself to God, he shall not want a guide
to lead him out of his trouble, to direct his paths, till the
delivery come; for *God will guide the meek in judgment,*
most wisely and discreetly, as his good requireth, *and teach
him his way.* 6. The property of the believer, is to cleave
to the covenant and to what the Lord hath set down in his
word; *they keep his covenant and his testimonies,* and will
not part with them whatsoever cometh. 7. Whosoever
hold fast the covenant of grace, and make conscience of
obeying God's word, they may be sure that all their troubles
and variety of exercise is nothing but God's way, to make

them partake of God's promises; for unto such *all the paths of the Lord are mercy and truth.*

11. *For thy name's sake, O Lord, pardon mine iniquity; for it* is *great.*

In the third place, having laboured to strengthen his faith, he falleth to prayer again, for remission of sin. Whence learn, 1. The conscience of sin will oftener assault our faith than once, and so oft as it assaulteth, it is to be answered with renewed prayer to God ; *O God,* saith he, *pardon my iniquity.*   2. The honour of the Lord is engaged by covenant for remission of sin to the penitent believer, and the Lord counts it a glory to be merciful ; therefore, saith he, *for thy name's sake pardon.*   3. Faith can make advantage of misbelief's arguments to retort them against it, and can plead for pardon from the very multitude and grievousness of sin; as here, *pardon my iniquity, for it is great.*   For the greater sin is acknowledged to be, the more is the object of pardon made clear, because it cannot be paid for by the sinner ; and the more is the Lord's pity letten forth, that the believer be sensible of the weight.

12. *What man* is *he that feareth the Lord? him shall he teach in the way* that *he shall choose.*

13. *His soul shall dwell at ease ; and his seed shall inherit the earth.*

14. *The secret of the Lord* is *with them that fear him ; and he will shew them his covenant.*

In the fourth place, there is another meditation of God's goodness to a believer, for strengthening of his faith yet further, wherein he layeth down three general promises, made to them that believe in God, and stand in awe to offend, ver. 12—14 ; and by way of syllogism he assumeth of himself, that he is a believer, whereupon he inferreth the conclusion, ver. 15. Whence learn, 1. The fear of God (importing care to serve God according to his word, and to stand in awe to offend him) is the necessary property of a true and lively believer ; therefore it is made the believer's cognizance, and mark to discern him by : *what man is he that feareth the Lord?*   2. The believer walking in the fear of God, may expect from the Lord direction and light how to carry himself in all perplexities, so oft as he in his need shall seek it of God ; for, in dubious cases, *God shall teach him in the way that he shall choose.* 3. Albeit the believer be put to trouble, and hard exercise, yet shall he have place always with God, as a man reconciled to him, and peace in his conscience also, as his good doth require, and he shall have contentment in his lot; for, *his soul shall dwell at ease.* 4. The surest way to transmit inheritances to a man's children, and to make houses to stand, and, however matters go, for a man to be sure of the kingdom of heaven, (signified by an inheritance in the land of Canaan) is, that the parents fear God, and that the children do follow their footsteps, and fear God also; *for the seed of the man fearing God shall inherit the land.* 5. The man that feareth God, shall know more of God's mind than others shall; he shall know the good and acceptable will of God for his direction in dangerous controversies, and for his satisfaction about God's dispensations, both toward himself and others, and for his consolation in all afflictions; *for the secret of the Lord is with them that fear him.* 6. Albeit the Lord's covenant with the visible church be open, and plain in itself to all men, in all the articles thereof, yea, it is a mystery to know the inward sweet fellowship which a soul may have with God, by virtue of this covenant; and a man fearing God shall know this mystery, when such as are covenanters only in the letter, do remain ignorant thereof; for *to the fearers of God only* is this promise made, *that to them the Lord will shew his covenant.*

15. *Mine eyes* are *ever toward the Lord; for he shall pluck my feet out of the net.*

Having laid the ground of his reason in the former verses, which is in sum this, to every believer God will be gracious, as his need is, now he assumeth I am a believer; *for mine eyes are ever toward the Lord.* Therefore to me God will be gracious in my need, and so *pluck my feet out of the net,* as my need now requireth. Whence learn, 1. The believer can read his own name, and his own blessedness in the promises made to believers, and can draw out the extract of God's decree of absolution, direction, consolation, and salvation, in his own favour; for where the general is written, there all the particulars are also written in effect: and so the believer may read his name written in the book of life, as here David doth read

6

his own deliverance, in the charter of believers ; *mine eyes are ever toward the Lord, therefore he will pluck my feet out of the net.* 2. The believer is not a little helped to believe, and to draw sweet conclusions from inspired scripture, to strengthen himself by avowing himself to be a believer, or to have the true property of a believer, as here David doth, saying, *mine eyes are ever toward the Lord;* first, he avoweth his faith, and then draweth this conclusion from it, *he shall pluck my feet out of the net.* 3. To depend on God for the supply of all necessities, and for deliverance out of all straits, is the property of true faith: for the prophet, to prove himself a believer, and to have an interest in the mercies formerly set down, v. 12—14, saith, v. 15, *mine eyes are ever toward the Lord.* 4. Though the godly walk among snares, and nets, set by their enemies, bodily and spiritual, to entrap them, yet God will either direct their way, to eschew these snares and nets, or will pluck their feet out of them; for this is the prophet's comfort, *thou shalt pluck my feet out of the net.*

16. *Turn thee unto me, and have mercy upon me; for I am desolate and afflicted.*

17. *The troubles of my heart are enlarged : O bring thou me out of my distresses.*

After meditation, he concludeth his exercise with petitions for himself and for the church. The petitions for himself are six, in so many verses. In the first learn, 1. Natural sense and suggestion of Satan saith, that God doth turn his back on us, when he doth not sensibly, by outward works, show himself for us as we could wish; but faith maketh advantage of the temptation by adhering to God in time of a seeming desertion, and prayeth for his manifesting of himself unto us; *turn thee unto me, and have mercy upon me.* 2. A felt and acknowledged miserable, helpless, and desperate condition, is, to the believer, half a promise, and a whole reason to expect relief from God; *turn thee unto me, and have mercy on me, for I am desolate and afflicted*; and so also in his second petition, *the troubles of my heart are enlarged, O bring me out of my distresses.* As his troubles were multiplied and enlarged, his heart was straitened and his distresses multiplied, and this he bringeth for a reason of his hope to be brought out of these straits.

18. *Look upon mine affliction and my pain, and forgive all my sins.*

From the third petition learn, 1. How sad and fearful troubles a believing and beloved soul may be brought into, no words can sufficiently express: he is *desolate, afflicted, the troubles of his heart are enlarged;* he is in more distresses than one; he is in *affliction and pain,* which no eye can see, nor any beholder judge of, save God only; therefore saith he to God, *Look on my affliction and my pain.* 2. Sore trouble will waken up the conscience of sin afresh, and call to mind forgiven and buried sin; which new challenge cannot be answered but by prayer for a new application and intimation of remission of sins, as here; *forgive all my sins.*

19. *Consider mine enemies, for they are many; and they hate me with cruel hatred.*

20. *O keep my soul, and deliver me: let me not be ashamed; for I put my trust in thee.*

From the fourth and fifth petitions, relating to the hazard of his life from his bodily enemies, learn, 1. The multitude, power, rage and cruelty of the enemies of the Lord's people, are a ground of hope to the believer to be delivered from them; *consider my enemies, for they are many, &c.* 2. There is no surer evidence of deliverance, than faith in God, settled on a promise; *let me not be ashamed, for I put my trust in thee.*

21. *Let integrity and uprightness preserve me; for I wait on thee.*

The sixth petition is for the fruit of his innocent behaviour toward his enemies. Whence learn, 1. Albeit a man be burdened with the sense of many sins against God, yet he may have the conscience of innocency toward his enemies; and here a good conscience giveth great boldness before God to hope for delivery; *let integrity and uprightness preserve me.* 2. Integrity of life, or a good behaviour after prayer, is as needful as before it; yet neither integrity before nor after must be leaned upon, but God's goodness and mercy only; *let uprightness preserve me,* so David reasoneth, *for I wait on thee.*

22. *Redeem Israel, O God, out of all his troubles.*

He closeth his exercise with a prayer for the church. Whence learn, 1. It is the common lot of all the saints to

be exercised with plurality of troubles; and as the troubles
of each particular member should not swallow up the sense
of the troubles of the church, but rather private troubles
should make every one sensible of the like or greater troubles
of the rest of the body; so should the delivery of the whole
church be sought after, as our own, yea, and more than our
own, and as our last petition; and, however the matter shall
go with ourselves, let us pray, *redeem Israel, O Lord, out
of all his troubles.*

PSALM XXVI.

David being oppressed by the judges of the land, his powerful adversaries,
and being exiled from the house of God, he appealeth to God, the supreme judge, in the testimony of a good conscience, bearing him witness, first, of his endeavour to walk uprightly, as became a believer, ver.
1—3; and secondly, of his keeping himself from the contagion of the
evil counsel, sinful courses, and example of the wicked, ver. 4, 5;
thirdly, of his purpose still to behave himself holily and righteously,
out of love to be partaker of the public privileges of the Lord's people
in the congregation, ver. 6—8. Whereupon he prayeth to be free of
the judgment coming on the wicked, ver. 9, 10. According as he was
purposed to eschew their sins, ver. 11. And he closeth his prayer with
comfort and assurance to be heard, ver. 12.

1. *Judge me, O Lord; for I have walked in mine
integrity: I have trusted also in the Lord;* therefore
I shall not slide.

2. *Examine me, O Lord, and prove me; try my
reins and my heart.*

3. *For thy loving-kindness* is *before mine eyes; and
I have walked in thy truth.*

From David's appellation from the unjust sentence of
men against him in their courts and elsewhere, calumniating him, and burying him under slanders, from which God
and his own conscience knew he was free; learn, 1. God's
children may be, for a time unjustly in their cause and name,
so borne down with calumnies by judges and others, that
they must content themselves with the approbation of God,
and of their own conscience, as David doth here. 2. When
no remedy is seen on earth for God's oppressed children,
remedy may be had from God, the supreme judge, who can
redress all matters abundantly. This did David, when he
said, *judge me, O Lord:* that is, do the part of a just
judge to me, in this controversy between my adversaries

and me.　3. He who appealeth to God, had need of a good cause and a good conscience for his carriage in it, that he may say with David, *I have walked in mine integrity*. 4. A good carriage in any controversy is then only comfortable and commendable when it is the fruit of faith in God: therefore David addeth, *I have trusted also in the Lord*. 5. He that in obedience to God doth carry himself righteously, may be assured he shall stand and prevail; for this conclusion doth the prophet draw from these grounds, saying, *I shall not slide*.　6. Not only must a man's hand be free from injuring his party, but his affections also: in which case the upright man is content the Lord should try him, and tell him what is wrong, that it may be amended hereafter; for here sincerity saith, *examine me and try my reins*. 7. Sincerity of behaviour may abide the trial of the conscience, and expect the approbation of God, when the word of God is the man's rule, and fear of interrupting the sense of sweet communion with God, is the awband to keep him to his rule, for so doth David prove his sincerity here : *for thy loving-kindness is before mine eyes, and I have walked in thy truth*, to wit, looking to thy precepts, threatenings, and promises.

4. *I have not sat with vain persons, neither will I go in with dissemblers.*

5. *I have hated the congregation of evil-doers; and will not sit with the wicked.*

The second part of the testimony of his conscience, that he hath rejected the course of wicked men, and their ill counsel, and that he would neither follow the way against his enemies which they followed against him, nor hearken to the evil advice which wicked men, under whatsoever pretence of good-will to him, did offer to him, for a sinful transaction or private revenge.　Whence learn, 1. Though innocency may seem to make the godly a prey to their enemy, yet it will promote their cause more before God, and give greater contentment to the conscience than witty wicked plotting against witty and wicked enemies; for this doth David's example teach us.　2. A godly man may take the service of many in a case of law-businesses and civil matters, whose counsel he must refuse in a moral duty ; as when David's followers counselled him to slay the king when he had him in his power in the cave.　In such a consultation or debate, he will not *sit* nor *go in with the wicked*.　3. He

that giveth ill counsel, whatsoever pretence of friendship
or advantage be made to commend the counsel which he
offereth, yet in that point he is a vain man and a dissembler.
So doth the prophet style him here.   4. It is necessary to
hate and abhor every wicked course, lest, if we do not hate
it but hearken unto it, we be drawn over to embrace it; *I
hate*, saith he, *the congregation of* the *evil-doers*.

6. *I will wash my hands in innocency: so will I
compass thine altar, O Lord;*

7. *That I may publish with the voice of thanksgiving, and tell of all thy wondrous works.*

8. *Lord, I have loved the habitation of thy house,
and the place where thine honour dwelleth.*

The third part of the testimony of his conscience, is concerning his resolution to behave himself righteously and
godlily, out of love to honour God and to be the fitter for
worshipping God and serving him, as he should be employed.   Whence learn, 1. The man whose hands are not clean
from injuries done to men, his conscience should tell him that
he is not meet to offer worship to God : and where guiltiness is, it should be taken away, lest the worship be refused; so resolveth David, *I will wash my hands in innocency, and so compass thine altar*.   2. Whatsoever was
the ceremony of the godly with their friends, in compassing
the altar with songs of praise when they offered their
peace-offerings, it yieldeth a fit direction for every worshipper, and offerer of prayer or praise to God, to do it with
an eye to Jesus Christ, the true altar that sanctifieth our offerings, and maketh our persons and services acceptable ; for
the compassing of the altar, with an eye on it, signified this
duty. 3. The Lord's mercies to his own are marvellous in effect, when all circumstances are well considered ; therefore
are they here called *wondrous works*.   4. To love the fellowship of the saints in the public worship of God, is a token
of our interest in God ; and the conscience of this love is
refreshful, as here ; *Lord, I have loved the habitation of
thy house.*   5. The meetings of the church should be to
proclaim the Lord's glory in the exercise of all his ordinances; and where this is endeavoured, there will God
dwell, for such holy assemblies are the places where his
honour dwelleth, albeit many of the members of the church

be such before God as they were in Saul's time, whereunto
this psalm relateth.

9. *Gather not my soul with sinners, nor my life with
bloody men;*

10. *In whose hands* is *mischief, and their right
hand is full of bribes.*

11. *But as for me, I will walk in mine integrity :
redeem me, and be merciful unto me.*

Now he prayeth to be exempted from the company of the
wicked in their punishment, seeing he hath gotten grace to
resolve not to walk in their sin. Whence learn, 1. The
Lord hath a harvest and a gleaning time also set, for cutting
down and binding together, in the fellowship of judgments,
God's enemies, who have followed the same course of sinning ; for here we are given to understand, that God will
gather their souls, and so will let none escape. 2. Such as
separate themselves, not from the lawful society, but from
the sinful ways, of the world, shall also be separate from the
society of their punishment ; the soul of the one and the
other shall not be gathered together; *gather not my soul
with sinners.* 3. Ungodly men will never stand to consent
to the taking the life of the godly. If, by a fit of temptation, they be put to it, a bribe, or fear, which is all one, will
do the turn ; for sinners here are declared bloody men, *in
whose hands* a *mischief is, and their right hand is full of
bribes.* 4. It is the mark of a wise and godly soul, not to
be diverted from his God or godliness by the temptation of
loss or gain, which overturneth the worldly man ; for David resolveth, go others where they will, *as for me, I will
walk in my integrity.* 5. A man so resolved, that is, who
hath chosen God for his redeemer, and God's ways for his
rule, may be sure to be borne through all difficulties, all
troubles and temptations, and to meet with mercy in the
course and close of his life ; for David, after resolution of
faith in God, and resolution honestly to endeavour obedience
to God in his course, prayeth (which is as good as a
promise to us), *redeem me, and be merciful to me.*

12. *My foot standeth in an even place; in the congregations will I bless the Lord.*

He closes the Psalm comfortably. Whence learn, 1. The
believer, resolving obedience to God, and wrestling in prayer

with God, shall not want a comfortable answer; his conscience shall speak good to him, and God shall ratify the
testimony of it with his testimony : thus shall the man be
established in that sweet course of faith and obedience,
and have cause to say, *my foot stands in an even place.* 2.
Such a man may be assured to bless God effectually, for
the performance of promises, and that in good company,
either in this life, or in the next, or in both ; and in this
life with assurance, he may say with David, *in the congregation will I bless the Lord.*

PSALM XXVII.

In this psalm David setteth down what use he had of his faith in God,
in the time of his trouble: and first, how he strengthened his faith,
v. 1—6, and next, how he prayed, upon the foresaid grounds, v. 7—
12 ; and thirdly, what advantage he had by believing in God, in the
time of his exercise, v. 13. Whereupon he exhorts all the godly to
follow his example, under hope to be helped, as he was helped, v. 14.

1. *The Lord is my light, and my salvation; whom
shall I fear? the Lord is the strength of my life; of
whom shall I be afraid?*

The grounds of strengthening of his faith are three.
The first is, that God by virtue of the covenant hath obliged himself to give direction and comfort in trouble, and deliverance out of it ; from which he inferreth, that he needeth not fear his enemies. Whence learn, 1. When we are
to wrestle in prayer, against the doubts which trouble and
temptation may raise in our hearts to mar our confidence
in prayer, it is wisdom to arm ourselves by faith against
these doubts, before we pray, for so doth the prophet's example teach us. 2. He who is in covenant with God,
hath solid ground to expect from God direction and comfort in every trouble, and deliverance out of it ; for by virtue of the covenant of grace David saith, *the Lord is my
light and my salvation.* 3. When we have fastened our
faith on God, we may then with reason defy our enemies,
and say with the prophet, *of whom shall I be afraid?* 4.
When our enemies appear strong, and we know ourselves
to be but weak, we should oppose the Lord's strength to
our temptation, that we may resist all fear ; for so teacheth
David, *the Lord is the strength of my life, of whom shall I
be afraid?*

2. *When the wicked,* even *mine enemies and my foes, came upon me to eat up my flesh, they stumbled and fell.*

The next ground of confidence is, that he had proof and experience of the fruit of the covenant, when he was in greatest danger of being overtaken by his enemies. Whence learn, 1. When the rage of the wicked against the godly doth break forth, then no less than the precious life of the godly can satisfy their beastly cruelty ; they hunger even to *eat their flesh.* 2. God can easily make the wicked, in their hottest pursuit of the godly, to come short of their purpose, as here, *to stumble and fall.* 3. Experience of God's power is very forcible to confirm our faith, and to erect our hope, as it did David's faith.

3. *Though an host should encamp against me, my heart shall not fear; though war should rise against me, in this will I be confident.*

After settling of his faith, he puts on a resolution to stand to his point, in resisting assaults of fears, from whatsoever temptation. Whence learn, 1. It is a mean to strengthen faith, to resolve by the grace of God to put faith in act, in whatsoever difficulty, and in a manner to lay hands on ourselves, to hold up this shield against whatsoever fiery darts, albeit possibly when it cometh to push of pike, we be not found so strong as we are stout, as here David doth. 2. The Lord being ours by covenant, and the Lord proved to be ours in experience, is warrant and reason sufficient for us to put on such a resolution; *though war be raised, in this* (that is, upon the foresaid ground) *will I be confident,* saith he.

4. *One thing have I desired of the Lord, that will I seek after; that I may dwell in the house of the Lord, all the days of my life, to behold the beauty of the Lord and to enquire in his temple.*

A third ground of confidence, is the conscience of his purpose to study to have constant communion with God, in the use of the means, and the conscience of his very earnest desire to have the benefit of all the public ordinances, in the fellowship of the church. Whence learn, 1. Hearty resolution to subject ourselves to all God's ordinances, and to follow the appointed means of communion-keeping with God, is a sound mark of solid faith; and the conscience of this resolution, serveth much to confirm our confidence in God, if we can say with the prophet, *this one thing have I desired, &c.* 2. In the using of the means and ordinances of God's house, the glory of the Lord may be seen, counsel and direction in all things may be had, with comfort and spiritual delight to our souls; for in the ordinances David was to *behold the beauty of the Lord,* with delight, *and to enquire in his holy temple.* 3. The desire of communion with God, and love to his ordinances, where it is sincere, should have the chief place in the heart, above all earthly desires and delights whatsoever: *one thing have I desired.* 4. A sincere desire must not be suffered to go away, but should be pursued resolutely, and recommended to God daily; *this I will still seek after,* saith he: and the means of communion with God in the public fellowship of the church must be constantly continued in, *even all the days of our life.*

5. *For in the time of trouble he shall hide me in his pavilion: in the secret of his tabernacle shall he hide me; he shall set me up upon a rock.*

He giveth a reason of his so earnest a desire to have fellowship with God entertained by the use of all God's ordinances, because in this way he was sure that faith should draw all necessary comfort and protection from God, as need should require. Whence learn, 1. Faith keeping communion with God, findeth him all-sufficient in all necessities, to supply every inlack of the creature, where the believer standeth in need; *he will be a pavilion in warfare, and a hiding-place and rock of refuge,* that is, God will make a man as quiet by faith, in himself, as if there were no hazard; *in the time of trouble he shall hide me in his pavilion: in the secret of his tabernacle, shall he hide me; he shall set me up upon a rock.* 2. The godly cannot promise to themselves the influence of God's grace in time of need, otherwise than by following divine ordinances, both private and public, so far as they may be had; for the prophet promiseth to himself this protection, as a fruit of his faith, fostered by the use of the ordinances, *I desire,* saith he, *to dwell in thy house, and to enquire in thy holy temple; for in the time of trouble he shall hide me, &c.*

6. *And now shall mine head be lifted up above mine enemies round about me : therefore will I offer in his tabernacle sacrifices of joy ; I will sing, yea, I will sing praises unto the Lord.*

After this wrestling of faith, he obtaineth victory, and assurance of satisfaction to his desire, and the grant of all that he was to seek in his prayer. Whence learn, The Lord can give a believer assurance of what he would have, and make him so clear of the possession of the promise, as if it were in his hand ; as here the psalmist is sure to prevail over his enemies, sure to come to the temple even as he wished : *and now shall mine head be lifted up above mine enemies, I will offer sacrifices of joy in his tabernacle.*

7. *Hear, O Lord, when I cry with my voice : have mercy also upon me, and answer me.*

8. *When thou saidst, Seek ye my face ; my heart said unto thee, Thy face, Lord, will I seek.*

In the second place, having thus strengthened his faith, he entereth the lists with his present trouble and temptations, and encountereth them by prayer to God upon the foresaid grounds, in three petitions. In the first he prayeth for the sensible experience of God's favour, as his present condition required ; wherein he strengthens his faith by three considerations. The first is, because he had gotten grace to close with the word of God, inviting him to seek what he sought, v. 8. Whence learn, 1. Confidence in God is diligent in prayer, and despiseth not the means whereby the mercy hoped for may be brought about ; but by prayer it maketh particular application of the Lord's good-will, offered to all, unto itself, that it may be helped in the present need, as here David doth : *hear me when I cry, have mercy on me, answer me.* 2. As the Lord's word encourageth us to seek things of God which, without a warrant, we durst not seek ; so, when we have gotten grace to embrace God's warrant given to us by precept or promise, we may ask with confidence to obtain: *hear me, answer me ;* why ? *when thou saidst, seek ye my face ; my heart answered, I will seek thy face, O Lord.*

9. *Hide not thy face far from me ; put not thy servant away in anger: thou hast been my help ; leave me not, neither forsake me, O God of my salvation.*

He meets here with an objection from his sins and mis-deservings, and prayeth it down, adding another consideration to confirm his faith from bygone experience of mercy, notwithstanding his unworthiness. Whence learn, 1. Though, when we would draw near to the Lord, sense of sin and unworthiness, and fear of wrath, fly in our throat, yet faith cleaving to God's goodness, and to the promises of mercy, and to our relation unto our God, may cry down the temptation : *hide not thy face, put not away thy servant in anger.* 2. The former experiences which we have had of God's being gracious to us, according to the tenor of the covenant of salvation, should confirm our faith, that God will never cast us off, nor any man that cannot endure to be separate from him : thus David reasons, *thou hast been my help, leave me not, neither forsake me, O God of my salvation.*

10. *When my father and my mother forsake me, then the Lord will take me up.*

A third consideration to confirm David's faith, is a nearer relation between God and David, than between David and his parents.   Whence learn, that the bands between God and a believing soul are more strait and intimate, and more strong than any band, civil or natural, between him and any creature ; and they are appointed to hold fast when natural bands fail, as here is asserted : *when my father and my mother forsake me, then the Lord will take me up.* This is for the first petition.

11. *Teach me thy way, O Lord, and lead me in a plain path, because of mine enemies.*

The second petition is for direction in a holy and wise carriage, that his enemies get no advantage against his behaviour or person.   Whence learn, 1. There is danger of desertion, or of God's leaving us to the will of our enemies, if we carry not a good cause in a lawful, holy, tender way ; and therefore we had need to seek our direction from God, *to be taught in his way, and led in a plain path.*   2. Because the enemies of the godly are ready to calumniate their cause, and their intentions, and to take advantage to calumniate them upon the least occasion of a questionable practice, we had the more need to be circumspect, and to pray to be directed *in a plain path, because of our enemies.*

12. *Deliver me not over unto the will of mine ene-*

mies : for false witnesses are risen up against me, and such as breathe out cruelty.

The third petition is, to be delivered from the power of the enemy, prosecuting their false calumnies, and raging in cruelty. Whence learn, 1. The godly have reason to pray with submission, that they may not fall into the hands of men because of their cruelty, and to say to God, *deliver me not over unto the will of mine enemies.* 2. Because it is easy for the Lord to mitigate the enemies' fury, or to break their power, or to elude their craft and power; let us pray, *deliver,* and let God choose the way of delivery. 3. When the good cause of the godly and the persons also, are left to suffer both together, there is ground that God in that case will interpose himself in due time : for this is David's reason of hope to be helped, because false witnesses resolved to oppress him in name, and *breathers out of cruelty* were set to have his life, ever *rising against him :* and here he is a clear type and example of the suffering of Christ and his followers.

13. I had fainted, *unless I had believed to see the goodness of the Lord in the land of the living.*

14. *Wait on the Lord; be of good courage, and he shall strengthen thine heart: wait, I say, on the Lord.*

In the third place, he cometh to show and to make use of the benefit he had by believing, that he may encourage others to follow his example in their trials. Whence learn, 1. Discouragement under trouble is a sort of quitting of our cause, and of all comfort in it; but faith keepeth a man close to his cause, and from being overcome with troubles; it holds up his heart in his duty till the Lord send an outgate, wherein he were not able to subsist otherwise : *unless I had believed I had fainted.* 2. Our experiences of the good of believing in the time of straits, should be communicated to others, as our calling may suffer, to encourage them; for so doth the prophet, saying, *wait on the Lord, and be of good courage.* 3. The striving to take courage from the ground of faith, shall be followed with strength from God to go under the trouble, and to find comfort now and then, and full delivery at last : *he shall comfort thy heart.* 3. Albeit the Lord let the trouble lie on, and strong temptations to increase, and grief of heart to grow, yet must we still wait; for at the due time the outgate shall come: *wait, I say, on the Lord.*

PSALM XXVIII.

In the first part of this psalm we have the prophet's conflict against his
enemies, such as in the former psalm is to be seen, wherein he prayeth
for audience, ver. 1, 2, and delivery to himself, ver. 3, and that God
would vindicate his own justice against his disdainful enemies, ver. 4, 5.
In the latter part, the prophet having gotten comfort in his prayer,
doth glorify God, ver. 6, and strengthens his own and the rest of the
godly's faith, ver. 7, 8, and prayeth for a blessing to the church, ver. 9.

1. *Unto thee will I cry, O Lord my rock ; be not*
silent to me : lest, if thou be silent to me, I become like
them that go down into the pit.

2. *Hear the voice of my supplications, when I cry*
unto thee, when I lift up my hands toward thy holy
oracle.

In his conflict with trouble he runneth to God for a comfortable answer, with reasons to help his hope to be heard.
Whence learn, 1. It is good to pray in time of trouble, and
to be instant, and resolved to be instant ; for *unto thee will*
I cry, doth import these three. 2. A soul in great straits
is not able to suspend and want comfort long ; it must have
some comfortable answer, because of what God is unto it
by covenant,—*my rock, be not silent unto me.* 3. It bringeth
deadness of soul on a supplicant, when his prayer is not
taken off his hand, which albeit it be by no reason but a
consequence ill inferred from the Lord's not answering of
us, yet we are subject to this evil, and should pray to have
it prevented : *be not silent,* saith he, *lest I become like them*
that go down into the pit. 4. Though the heart be in
bonds in time of prayer under trouble, yet the Lord will
not despise the voice, nor the knees bowed, nor the hands
lifted up, nor the least expressions of a supplicant's desire
to be helped by him : *hear my voice when I cry, and the*
lifting up of my hands, saith he. 5. Seeking of God in
Christ, and trysting the fulness of the Godhead in the person of the Mediator, represented by the tabernacle and
oracle, answer all objections from the supplicant's unworthiness, and give encouragement to expect a good answer
from God ; for to this purpose doth he mention *his lifting*
up of his hands towards the Lord's holy oracle.

3. *Draw me not away with the wicked, and with*
the workers of iniquity, which speak peace to their
neighbours, but mischief is in their hearts.

Now he prayeth God would deliver him, and not deal with him as with an enemy. Whence learn, albeit there be sin in the godly, yet are they not workers of iniquity, nor treacherously disposed toward their neighbours, when they pretend to have friendship with them ; and therefore may the godly expect from God not to be dealt with as obstinately wicked and impenitent sinners ; for this he meaneth, saying, *draw me not away with the workers of iniquity, &c.*

4. *Give them according to their deeds, and according to the wickedness of their endeavours: give them after the work of their hands; render to them their desert.*

5. *Because they regard not the works of the Lord, nor the operation of his hands, he shall destroy them, and not build them up.*

He prayeth now against his enemies, not out of private revenge, but being led with the infallible spirit of prophecy, looking through these men to the enemies of Christ and of his people in all ages. Whence learn, 1. Albeit imprecations must not be used against our own enemies, nor for any injury done to us, nor against any in hatred of their persons, nor against every enemy of God, but only against desperate sinners, and that in general, rather than with an eye to this man or that man in special, about whom we may be mistaken : yet the imprecation of the Spirit of God standing in the scripture, crieth still against obstinate sinners, although we cannot condescend particularly upon their names ; *God shall give them according to their deserts.* In the controversy between the godly and their enemies, not only doth God show by his word which party he alloweth, but also by the works of his providence, in favour of the godly and against their enemies, he doth give forth his mind, according to what he hath said in his word to be observed ; but when both these are misregarded, he will destroy the wicked, and not suffer them to carry on their purpose ; for, *because they regard not the works of the Lord, nor the operation of his hands, he shall destroy them, and not build them up.*

6. *Blessed* be *the Lord, because he hath heard the voice of my supplications.*

7. *The Lord* is *my strength and my shield: my heart trusted in him, and I am helped; therefore my heart greatly rejoiceth, and with my song will I praise him.*

8. *The Lord* is *their strength, and he* is *the saving strength of his anointed.*

The other part of the psalm, wherein he maketh use of the good answer given to him; first, honouring God for it; then strengthening his own faith by it; and thirdly, strengthening the faith of others also. Whence learn, 1. The believing supplicant shall not seek God in vain; he shall not fail in due time to find such fruit, as shall make him bless and praise God for the answer; for in the entry of the psalm it was, *be not silent to me, O Lord, lest I become like them that go down to the pit,*—and here, *blessed be the Lord, because he hath heard the voice of my supplication.* 2. What faith saith to God in wrestling, it shall be made to subscribe it victoriously and experimentally thereafter; *my rock,* said he, *hear me,* v. 1; and here, *the Lord is my strength and my shield;* to furnish me within and without. 3. It is a good use made of experience, to confirm our faith thereby, and to commend the course of believing in God, as here David doth; *my heart trusted in him, and I am helped.* 4. The joy of faith and of sense also, will be given sometime together to the godly, for the increasing of their joy, as here he showeth; *therefore my heart greatly rejoiced.* 5. Albeit we must praise God in whatsoever condition we can be in; yet spiritual rejoicing doth specially call for singing a psalm unto God; *therefore with my song will I praise him,* saith he. 6. What the Lord is to one of the godly calling on him in the sense of need, he is unto them all the same: as he was David's *strength,* v. 7, so *is he their strength,* to wit, all his people's strength, v. 8. 7. All the blessings which believers get belong unto Christ, first as to the anointed of the Lord in chief, and to his servants as partakers of his anointing; for the Lord *is the saving strength, or the strength of salvation to his anointed,* or to his Christ, and those that are true Christians, partakers *of his unction,* or holy Spirit: what concerneth David is but a shadow, and as one who is a partaker of the holy unction through Christ.

9. *Save thy people, and bless thine inheritance: feed them also, and lift them up for ever.*

He closeth his prayer with intercession for the church. Whence learn, 1. Such as find access in prayer to God for themselves, should speak also a word for his church, and pray, *Lord, save thy people.* 2. The privileges which the godly have are common to them all. The godly are all God's *people, his inheritance, his flock:* and as the benefits imported under these titles are common, so are the duties due from us to God, imported thereby, common also; and to be so studied, that we may discharge them, as we would find from God the benefits of protection and deliverance, as subjects whom he will save; of being watered and warmed, as *his inheritance; fed and led on,* as his flock, and exalted over all our enemies, or being lifted up for ever.

PSALM XXIX.

David exhorteth princes and great men to humble themselves before God, and to worship him, as he hath commanded, in his public ordinances, v. 1, 2. First, because he is infinitely higher than they, and more terrible to all men, than they can be to their subjects or inferiors, as the uttering of his majesty and power by thunder maketh evident, v. 3—9. Secondly, because he offereth the means of saving knowledge, even all his ordinances, whereby men may heartily glorify him in their assemblies, v. 9. Thirdly, because he is an everlasting king and ruler of all the creatures, v. 10. And fourthly, because such as do humbly submit themselves to him, and worship him as his people should do, shall be furnished with abilities for every good work, and shall be abundantly blessed.

1. *Give unto the Lord, O ye mighty, give unto the Lord glory and strength.*

2. *Give unto the Lord the glory due unto his name; worship the Lord in the beauty of holiness.*

He directeth his speech and exhortation to the potentates of the earth, that they may humble themselves before God, and give him the glory of all power, and authority, and excellency above themselves, and above all other creatures. Hence learn, 1. Of all men princes should be most careful to glorify God, and yet it is most rare to see them humble themselves before him: for natural corruption is as strong in them as in others: their education breedeth them to high and stately thoughts of themselves, their riches and power puff them up, and flatterers, ordinarily following them,

make them forget themselves and God also; therefore **are**
they here thrice exhorted to give glory to God.   2. It is
most necessary that potentates humble themselves before
God, and be particularly dealt with to that purpose, because
their example and authority move many outwardly to submit to God, or stand out from his service: therefore he
speaketh to them in their grandeur, *give glory to God, O*
ye mighty.   3. As men are great in the world, so they are
ready to think much of their own strength, of what their
power is able to reach to, and what honour is due to them;
but if they reckon right, *strength and glory belong to*
God.   And according as he is above them in power and
excellency, so should he proportionably be magnified; *give*
unto the Lord glory and strength, and *give unto the Lord*
the glory due unto his name.   4. He will have no glory of
men, but as he hath prescribed to men in his own ordinances,
given forth in his word to his church: *worship him in the*
beauty of holiness, that is, in the glorious sanctuary, the
place of public meeting; beautiful indeed, not for timber or
stones so much, as because the holy and beautiful means of
grace to men, and God's worship showing forth his glory,
was there to be found.

3. *The voice of the Lord* is *upon the waters: the*
God of glory thundereth; the Lord is *upon many*
waters.

4. *The voice of the Lord* is *powerful; the voice of*
the Lord is *full of majesty.*

He proveth that strength and glory belong to the
Lord, by one only work of thundering, and kindling fire in
the midst of watery clouds, that he may make thunder in
the conflict of water closing in the fire, and fire breaking
through the clouds, how oft soever he pleaseth to show his
power to the children of men.   Whence learn, 1. Though
the standing works of creation speak most of God, yet such
is our foolishness, that we are least apprehensive of that
which is daily seen, and a less work more rarely occurring
will move more; as for example, the thunder or the eclipse
of the sun or moon, will move more than the making of
heaven and earth.   2. No work of the Lord is rightly taken
up till he himself **be looked** unto, as the immediate worker
of it: therefore **he points** out the sound of the thunder, as

the voice of the Lord upon many waters. 3. Though the Lord should be observed as the worker of every work, yet not at first is he seen in his work to any purpose, till we by oftener reviewing his operation about it, be some-what affected with his glory and power therein; therefore he repeateth the second time, *the God of glory thundereth;* and the third time, *the Lord is upon many waters.* 4. When the thunder or any work of God is well considered, some invisible thing of God will appear therein; as for example, his power and majesty will be evidenced in the thunder, for *the voice of the Lord is powerful and full of majesty.*

5. *The voice of the Lord breaketh the cedars; yea, the Lord breaketh the cedars of Lebanon.*

6. *He maketh them also to skip like a calf; Lebanon and Sirion like a young unicorn.*

7. *The voice of the Lord divideth the flames of fire.*

8. *The voice of the Lord shaketh the wilderness; the Lord shaketh the wilderness of Kadesh.*

9. *The voice of the Lord maketh the hinds to calve, and discovereth the forests; and in his temple doth every one speak of* his *glory.*

He insisteth in his subject, and showeth the effects there-of, on trees, v. 5; on mountains, v. 6; on the fire of the thunder, parting it in lightning, v. 7; on the waste wil-derness, v. 8; on the beasts and woods where they haunt, v. 9. Whence learn, 1. That the stupidity and senseless-ness of man is greater than that of the brute creatures, which are all more moved with the thunder, than the hearts of men for the most part, as here may be seen in the comparison. 2. One work of God dwelt upon, shall show more of God than many of his works being slightly looked on, and passed over: as for example, this one of the thunder, considered with the effects, saith more than many; yea, one sensible and understanding man, will discover more of God in one work of God, than many in their ordinary mood, either in that work, or in any other, or in all his works.

9. *The voice of the Lord maketh the hinds to calve, and discovereth the forests; and in his temple doth every one speak of* his *glory.*

He giveth a second reason of his exhortation to the

mighty, *to worship God in the beauty of holiness*, **because in** his temple every one doth speak of his glory. Whence learn, 1. The glory of the Lord is shown forth in all the earth, and in all his works; but in his temple, in his church, his works are holden forth expressly and fully, for there by his word, his counsel is opened, his holiness, his goodness, justice, mercy, and all his attributes are declared. Without the church, men are compelled to acknowledge glory now and then, but in his church men do declare his glory distinctly and willingly: *in his temple doth every one speak of his glory*; all men there confess his praise, and every thing in the temple holdeth forth something of Christ and his benefits, to the glory of God's mercy; and this is more than the world understandeth.

10. *The Lord sitteth upon the flood; yea, the Lord sitteth King for ever.*

A third reason to move princes to give to God glory and strength, is, because his kingdom reacheth to the ruling of the waters, and because he is a king immortal. Whence learn, 1. As the strength of the Lord appeareth in all his works, so especially that he ruleth the raging sea, whereby once he did drown the world, and now bindeth it up, that it should do no more so again: *the Lord sitteth upon the floods.* No king is king over every kingdom and king, but God is King above all kings; no king is of long continuance, but the Lord is the everlasting King, *he sitteth King for ever;* and therefore every mighty man should do him homage, as his King, his Lord, and supreme superior.

11. *The Lord will give strength unto his people; the Lord will bless his people with peace.*

The last reason to move potentates to give all glory to God, and to join with his people in glorifying him, is, because of the blessedness of his people, who worship him in his holy temple. Whence learn, 1. The power of the Lord is not against his people; but for his people, against his and their enemies, *he giveth strength to his people*, to wit, against their enemies, and for furnishing them to every part of his service whereunto he calleth them. The Lord's people do give the glory of power and strength to the Lord; *and the Lord will give strength to his people.* 2. The true worshippers of God, whatsoever may be their exercise in the world, may be sure of reconciliation with him, and of true blessedness, *for the Lord will bless his people with peace.*

PSALM XXX.

A psalm and song at the dedication of the house of David.

David praiseth God for his late deliverance from the hand of Absalom, v. 1—3. And secondly, he exhorteth others to praise God also for his mercies, v. 4, 5. Thirdly, he confesseth his carnal security, and how he was corrected for it, v. 6, 7. Fourthly, he showeth how he prayed for mercy, v. 8—10. And fifthly, he praiseth the Lord for his gracious answer, v. 11, 12.

The inscription of the psalm showeth, that it was indited at the dedication of David's house, after it was polluted by Absalom's vileness with his father's concubines, as David's security and trouble after that herein described, giveth us to understand. Whence learn, 1. That no benefit or creature-comfort is lawful and pure to us, except it be sanctified by the word and prayer, except we dedicate ourselves and the creatures also to God's service; and more specially the dedication of a man's house with the ceremonies of the law, used about the dedication thereof, teacheth us to consider and to acknowledge before God, that we are the Lord's tenants at will, received by him in his lodgings, to be entertained by him during our abode on earth; it teacheth us also that our houses should be holy, both for the persons in our company, and for the exercise of religion therein daily, before and after our lawful daily refreshments and employments therein; and that the Lord only is the preserver of us, and of our houses, against what evil might otherwise befall us, by men, or devils, or any other accident; and that the house is polluted, especially when God is openly dishonoured therein : in which case we are to seek mercy to ourselves, and to our families, and to pray to God for the continuance of his guard about us, and his grace, to make a right use of our house hereafter, which is the substance of the old ceremonies used in dedication of a man's house.

1. *I will extol thee, O Lord; for thou hast lifted me up, and hast not made my foes to rejoice over me.*

2. *O Lord my God, I cried unto thee, and thou hast healed me.*

3. *O Lord, thou hast brought up my soul from the grave: thou hast kept me alive, that I should not go down to the pit.*

He praiseth God for a number of mercies concurring together in his deliverance out of the hazard of losing both his life and his kingdom. Whence learn, 1. The more the Lord exalts us, we should humble ourselves the more before him, and magnify his bounty : for David *will extol the Lord* here, *because the Lord had lifted him up.* 2. The disappointment of our enemies is a new mercy, beside our delivery from their cruelty, and a reason of thanksgiving to God, when he makes our foes not to rejoice over us. 3. When God seemeth to desert us, and expose us to hazards, readily our spirits grow sick, and deadness of spirit (with inability to go about any point in our calling, or of his service) seize on us; but when, after the prayer of faith grounded on the covenant, the Lord sendeth relief, it is a reviving of us again, as we see in David's case: *O my God, I cried unto thee, and thou hast healed me.* 4. Preservation from evil, and delivery out of evil, are mercies equivalent; rescuing a man from instant death, should be looked upon as resurrection from death, and acknowledged so to be in our thanksgiving to God; for David here saith, *The Lord hath brought up his soul from the grave, because he had kept him alive, that he should not go down into the pit.*

4. *Sing unto the Lord, O ye saints of his, and give thanks at the remembrance of his holiness.*

5. *For his anger* endureth but *a moment; in his favour* is *life; weeping may endure for a night, but joy* cometh *in the morning.*

The second part of the psalm, wherein he stirreth up others to praise God for his mercies. Whence learn, 1. Dwelling a while upon the consideration of mercies shown unto us, bringeth with it rejoicing in God, and a singing disposition, whereunto when we are once wakened and warned, we will think that one mouth to praise God is too little, as here we see in David, who not only praiseth God himself, but also setteth all the saints on work to the same purpose, saying, *sing to the Lord, all ye saints of his.* 2. Albeit we have no present sense of lately received remark-

able mercies, yet bygone experiences of the Lord's faithfulness and holiness, should give matter of thanks and praise
on all occasions, specially in the congregation, where his
works are called to mind : *give thanks,* saith he, *at the remembrance of his holiness.* 3. Albeit we were not upon
the thoughts of any particular experience, yet the known
perfections of God should furnish matter, and in special,
because howsoever we be sinful, and do provoke the Lord
often, yet he, *as he is slow to anger,* so is he soon pacified,
his anger endureth but for a moment. 4. When reckoning
is rightly made, the tokens of God's displeasure are but for
a moment. But the evidence of his favours to believers is a
life-time, for in the midst of wrath he remembereth mercy ;
and the tokens of his favour are far more than of his displeasure, and wrath soon goeth, and favour shineth latest,
and is of longest continuance ; wrath is but temporary at
the longest, but favour endureth for ever : *his anger is but
for a moment, but in his favour is life, yea life everlasting.*
5. When the Lord showeth himself angry at a soul, it is
dark and cold night with it, and what can it do but weep
or walk heavily in this case, when the bridegroom is as
absent : *weeping may abide for a night.* 6. Unto the believer the longest winter night hath a change to the better
following it : consolation is certain after a mournful condition ; *weeping may endure for a night, but joy cometh in
the morning.*

6. *And in my prosperity I said, I shall never be
moved.*

7. *Lord, by thy favour thou hast made my mountain
to stand strong: thou didst hide thy face, and I was
troubled.*

In the third place, he cometh to his late experience,
which gave occasion and matter of this psalm ; he abused
his prosperity, not remembering that because his standing
was by grace, therefore he should have stood in awe, and
feared to forget himself, and therefore he was chastised for
it. Whence learn, 1. A child of God, after long trouble
may have a time of outward rest and prosperity ; for example, David, whose troubles were many, acknowledgeth
here that he was in prosperity. 2. As men in trouble
do fear they shall never be rid of it, so when God granteth
a change to the better, they think never to be so troubled

again ; this fleshly security is a soul-sickness, attending prosperity, and the most holy men may easily be overtaken
with it ; for David confesseth, *I said in my prosperity, I
shall never be moved.*   3. The consideration that our standing in any good condition, is of God's mere favour and
grace, should keep us in fear and trembling to offend, and
prevent our falling in carnal security.   This David acknowledgeth for aggravating of his fault, *Lord, by thy favour
thou hast made my mountain strong.*   4 .The Lord will
not suffer his own to lie still in carnal security, but will
withdraw the bolster and pillow of those benefits whereon
they sleep, and together with that, will withdraw also the
sweet sense of reconciliation, and put his own in trouble
to waken them : David's experience teacheth so much,
thou didst hide thy face, and I was troubled.   5. Men
understand the folly of their sinful way, and of their careless entertaining of God's favour, not so well in the time of
prosperity, as after they have smarted for their folly, and
have found the fruit of their forgetfulness of God, and of
their too much embracing and resting on prosperity, to be
nothing save sore and sad troubles, both bodily and spiritual ; for this is taught us by the reckoning that David
now maketh, as a pilot discovering a rock, to forewarn
others to beware of security ; and this reckoning is all after
his trouble, and after his victory also over it.

8. *I cried to thee, O Lord; and unto the Lord I
made supplication.*

9. *What profit* is there *in my blood, when I go
down to the pit?   Shall the dust praise thee?   shall it
declare thy truth?*

10. *Hear, O Lord, and have mercy upon me: Lord,
be thou my helper.*

In the fourth part of this psalm he showeth his recovery
out of his trouble, and out of his sinful security which
drew it on ; he prayed, disputed, and dealt with God, till
the Lord delivered him.   Whence learn, 1. As the fire
and the hammer, and the files serve to put off the rust
of iron, so doth affliction to rouse a godly soul out of security, and drive him to earnest prayer ; for after trouble
is come, David crieth to the Lord.   2. Albeit a man hath
miscarried, and proved ungrateful to God in his prosperity,

and unmindful of his resolutions and promises made to God in his low estate, when he should come to prosperity ; yet when trouble cometh to waken him up, and call him to a reckoning, he must not despair, nor sit down in discouragement in the conscience of huge guiltiness.　But because the Lord is angry, and no remedy but God's grace, he must lay himself at God's feet a supplicant : *unto the Lord David made supplication.*　3. Faith in God is very argumentative, and will dispute well for the man's life, having the covenant of grace as a ground to go upon.　It will take a reason to strengthen itself from God's nature, who doth not delight in the death of a penitent sinner, and a reason from no advantage unto justice, by the man's destruction, when justice may have satisfaction in the Redeemer, and the man may be saved also.　*What profit is there in my blood, when I go down to the pit ?* and a reason from the man's purpose to glorify God, to the edifying of others in his life, if he should be spared : from which mercy if he should be cut off, it would be better to him than death: *shall the dust praise thee? shall it declare thy truth ?*　4. When faith hath said to God what it hath to say, it will wait for a good answer; will rely on his mercy, and expect relief from the Lord, as here David doth ; *hear, O Lord, have mercy on me, be thou my helper.*

11. *Thou hast turned for me my mourning into dancing: thou hast put off my sackcloth, and girded me with gladness.*

12. *To the end that* my *glory may sing praise to thee, and not be silent.　O Lord my God, I will give thanks unto thee for ever.*

In the last part of the psalm he thankfully praiseth God, for granting unto him all he desired, and obligeth himself to a more careful carriage, and setting forth of God's glory. Whence learn, 1. It becometh the child of God to weep when he is beaten, and to humble himself in the exercise of prayer and fasting ; for David's *mourning* and *sackcloth,* showeth his exercise in his former trouble.　2. As security turneth all our joy into trouble, so sincere seeking of God in trouble, is the way to turn all our trouble into joy ; *thou hast turned for me all my mourning into dancing, &c.,* and great is that joy which a reconciled soul findeth in God, after renewed feeling of the interrupted sense of mercy.

3. A well-ordered tongue, watching all opportunities to glorify God, and edify others, is a main point of a man's excellency, not only above beasts,. but also above all men, who do not use their tongue for God, and for good to others. Therefore David calleth his tongue his glory. 4. The very intent of God's showing mercy to men, is to oblige them to give praise and glory to himself before the world ; *thou hast girded me with gladness,* saith he, *to the end my glory may sing praise to thee, and not be silent.* 5. The right use of our experiences of God's mercy to us, is first to fasten our faith in God, and to stand fast to the Lord's covenant made with us in Christ; next, after acknowledging that this is our duty, to be thankful to God to engage our hearts to the discharge thereof constantly. The first of these the prophet doth here by calling God, *the Lord my God ;* the next he doth in these words, *I will give thanks to thee for ever.*

PSALM XXXI.

To the chief musician.   A psalm of David.

Another exercise of David, wherein he being in great danger to be taken by his enemies, prayeth for delivery, ver. 1—6.   Secondly, he strengtheneth his faith by his by-gone experience, ver. 7, 8.   Thirdly, in prayer he layeth out his lamentable condition before God, ver. 9—13.   Fourthly, he wrestleth on in prayer for comfort and safety to himself, and confusion to his enemies, ver. 14—18.   Fifthly, being delivered and comforted by a new experience of God's merciful preservation of him, he maketh good use of it, by praising God for it, and exhorteth the godly to love God and rely on him, ver. 19—24.

1. *In thee, O Lord, do I put my trust ; let me never be ashamed : deliver me in thy righteousness.*

2. *Bow down thine ear to me ; deliver me speedily : be thou my strong rock, for an house of defence to save me.*

3. *For thou* art *my rock and my fortress : therefore, for thy name's sake, lead me, and guide me.*

From his interest in God, by covenant, he strengthens himself in prayer for delivery. Whence learn, 1. Faith avowed and maintained, furnisheth prayer, and giveth hope to be heard ; for David having first said, *In thee, O Lord, do I put my trust ;* he subjoineth, *let me never be ashamed ;* for this much may a believer expect, that albeit he be put to hang down the head for a little, yet he shall not at last be ashamed. 2. As the Lord sendeth, in his wisdom, trouble after trouble upon a believer, so he sendeth, in his justice and faithfulness, promised delivery after delivery from oppressors: *deliver me in thy righteousness.* 3. Where the danger is pressing, and the affection is ardent, the petition may be repeated without babbling, and speedy help may be craved without limitation of God; and hearkening to a poor supplicant, as it were, with a bowed down ear, may be prayed for without abasing of God's majesty, as here, *bow down thine ear to me, deliver me speedily.* 4. Were there but a moment betwixt us and perishing, and our enemies, stronger than we, were ready to lay hands on us, faith seeth that God can interpose himself speedily, and lift us up above our enemies' reach: *be thou my strong rock, for a house of defence to save me.* 5. What the Lord is engaged to be unto us by covenant, we may pray and expect to find him in effect; *be thou my strong rock,* saith he, *for thou art my rock.* 6. When trouble and uncouth passages discover our ignorance, our blindness and weakness unto us, we have God engaged for his glory's cause to take care of us, and to bring us through; for the prayer of the believer is, *for thy name's sake lead me and guide me.*

4. *Pull me out of the net that they have laid privily for me; for thou* art *my strength.*

5. *Into thine hand I commit my spirit: thou hast redeemed me, O Lord God of truth.*

6. *I have hated them that regard lying vanities: but I trust in the Lord.*

He cometh more particularly to his danger, and prayeth for delivery, and strengthening his faith by sundry reasons. Whence learn, 1. As the children of this world are more wise in their generation, than the children of the light: so do they hunt and overtake the godly, by their crafty devices against him; *they laid their nets privily against* David, *and ensnared him.* 2. Though the godly be both weak and simple-witted, yet they have a wise and strong God to call upon, who is able to break the snare, and set his own free, whose help David imploreth here; *pull me out of the net,* for thou art my strength. 3. The way to quiet our minds, in the hazard of our mortal life, (which is soon and easily taken away, and we cannot ourselves preserve,) is to put our soul over on God's care and custody, *into his hands committing our spirits.* 4. The word of God, giving assurance to the believer of his redemption, is a ground sufficient to make him confidently commit his soul to God's keeping; for he may say with warrant, *thou hast redeemed me, O God of truth.* 5. Worldly men that believe not in God, have some other thing wherein they trust beside, as riches, friendship, their own wit, &c., which carnal confidences are but lying vanities, whereof the true believer must be aware, and hate the way of such as follow them; for David hated them that *regarded lying vanities, because he trusted in God.*

7. *I will be glad and rejoice in thy mercy : for thou hast considered my trouble ; thou hast known my soul in adversities ;*

8. *And hast not shut me up into the hand of the enemy : thou hast set my feet in a large room.*

In the next place, he strengtheneth his faith by his former experience, and promiseth himself after this present sorrow, joy and gladness, whereof he hath some present sense, stirred up by calling its memory his experience. Whence learn, 1. In the midst of trouble faith will furnish matter of joy, and promise to itself gladness, especially from the memory of by-past experiences of God's mercy; as here, *I will rejoice and be glad in thy mercy.* 2. When a believer is in adversity, the Lord will not misken him, he will make him know, that even then he hath an eye upon him, and friendly affections to him : *thou hast known my soul in adversity.* 3. Adversary powers shall not get their will of a fixed believer, but he shall have delivery from them, and victory over them, either temporally or spiritually, or both ways; for here is the experience of it, *thou hast not shut me up in the hand of the enemy, thou hast set my feet in a large room.* 4. The ground of our gladness, when we have found a proof of God's kindness to us, should not be in the benefit so much, as in the fountain of the benefit; for this giveth us hope to drink again of the like experience, from the fountain which did send forth that benefit. Therefore David says, *I will be glad and rejoice in thy mercy for ever.*

9. *Have mercy upon me, O Lord, for I am in*

trouble: mine eye is consumed with grief, yea, *my soul and my belly.*

10. *For my life is spent with grief, and my years with sighing: my strength faileth because of mine iniquity, and my bones are consumed.*

11. *I was a reproach among all mine enemies, but especially among my neighbours, and a fear to mine acquaintance: they that did see me without fled from me.*

12. *I am forgotten as a dead man out of mind: I am like a broken vessel.*

13. *For I have heard the slander of many; fear* was *on every side: while they took counsel together against me, they devised to take away my life.*

In the third place, he layeth out his lamentable condition in regard of perplexity of mind and decay of natural strength, by grief and sorrow of heart, and in regard of the contempt of his adversaries, and neglect of his friends, and hazard of his life, joined with the sense of God's displeasure for his sins, wherein he is a type of Christ suffering for our sins imputed to him, and an example of the hard exercise of the saints. Whence learn, 1. Great and of long continuance may the troubles of the godly be, great may their grief and heaviness of heart be, before they get comfort, as the example of this meek man—so holy in his way, so subdued in his affections—showeth by sundry expressions. 2. Albeit the Lord needs no words to inform him of our condition, or to move his affection to his children in trouble, yet he hath appointed us, for evidencing our faith in him, and dependence upon him for relief, to come and tell him what aileth us; and indeed it is an ease to the godly heart to have the Lord to speak unto, and lay out their case before him, as here we see. 3. The conscience of sin joined with trouble is a load above a burden, and able to break a man's strength more than any trouble; for here he saith, *my strength faileth because of mine iniquity, and my bones are consumed.* 4. When the godly have many and powerful enemies, then their acquaintance and neighbours, and the multitude of the people will readily believe that all the misreports of them are true, and this maketh the grief of the godly the greater; as here, *I was a reproach among all mine enemies, but especially among my neighbours.* 5. When the godly fall under persecution and trouble, their worldly friends, for fear of danger or burden by them, will turn their back on them, and forget acquaintance, yea, and natural bands with them also ; and then must the godly lean to God, and expect comfort from him.   This is holden forth in this type of Christ, and example of believers under trials : *I am a fear to my acquaintance*, &c. 6. Long lying in trouble will make a man to be forgotten of his friends, as if he were dead, and make him to lose all estimation at their hands, as if there were no worth in him at all ; *I am forgotten as a dead man out of mind, I am like a broken vessel.* 7. It is Satan's policy to draw great men and councillors of state into a disgust of the godly, because commonly what great men esteem of the godly, that passeth for current ; and it is Satan's policy first to load the godly with slanders, and then to persecute them to death ; *I heard the slanders of many, they took counsel together to take away my life.* 8. In a sharp trial, a soul may be assaulted with terrible temptations on all hands, and feel terror and fighting within and without : *fear*, saith he, *was on every side.*

14. *But I trusted in thee, O Lord : I said, Thou art my God.*

15. *My times are in thy hand : deliver me from the hand of mine enemies, and from them that persecute me.*

16. *Make thy face to shine upon thy servant : save me for thy mercies' sake.*

17. *Let me not be ashamed, O Lord; for I have called upon thee : let the wicked be ashamed, and let them be silent in the grave.*

18. *Let the lying lips be put to silence ; which speak grievous things proudly and contemptuously against the righteous.*

In the fourth place, he wrestles by faith for delivery and comfort in the mean time, till delivery come to himself and disappointment to his enemies. Whence learn, 1. It is the nature of faith, and it is the believer's duty, to oppose help from God unto all temptations, were they ever so many, as here David did : *but I trusted in thee, O Lord.* 2. Except we hold fast the grip of our covenant with God, and avow it before him, trust will fail and temptations readily prevail. Much use made David of the covenant in his strait : *I said, thou art my God.*   3. Faith can make good cheer of the general grounds of God's providence, by making application thereof to its present use.   The dispensations of all men's comforts and troubles, life and death, are in God's hand, and not in men's power : *my times are in thy hand,* saith David.   4. Because all power is in God's hand, prayer to him will prevail more for delivery from enemies than any means besides : *deliver me from the hand of mine enemies, and them that persecute me.*   5. When the cloud of trouble hideth the Lord's favour, faith knoweth it may shine again, and therefore prayeth through the cloud for dissolving of it : *make thy face to shine upon me.*   6. As we must study to approve ourselves to be the Lord's servants, by studying obedience to him ; so must we make grace, and nothing else save grace, the ground of our hope to be helped, comforted, or saved : *shine upon thy servant,* saith he, *save me for thy mercy's sake.*   7. As the humble prayer of the persecuted godly shall be granted and have effect ; so the proud brags, coloured calumnies, and threatenings of slanderous and cruel adversaries, shall be shamefully refuted and disappointed ; and if the enemies shall not timously cease to persecute, they shall be made to cease in their graves : *let me not be ashamed, for I have called upon thee ; let the wicked be ashamed, and let them be silent in the grave : let the lying lips be put to silence, which speak grievous things proudly and contemptuously against the righteous.*

19. Oh *how great* is *thy goodness, which thou hast laid up for them that fear thee ;* which *thou hast wrought for them that trust in thee before the sons of men !*

20. *Thou shalt hide them in the secret of thy presence from the pride of man ; thou shalt keep them secretly in a pavilion from the strife of tongues.*

21. *Blessed* be *the Lord ; for he hath shewed me his marvellous kindness in a strong city.*

Comfort and deliverance being the answer of his prayer, he praiseth God, and stirreth up the godly to set their hearts on God, and trust in him at all times.   Whence learn, 1. The bounty of the Lord to his own people, seen in the world, observed in the Lord's ordinary dispensations towards them, and felt in a man's own experience, is able to ravish the heart with admiration of the blessedness of God's people ; as here, *Oh how great is thy goodness !*   2. Beside what consolation of spirit the Lord giveth to his own, the Lord sometimes will manifest so much respect in his providence to his servants, that not only the godly, but also they who are but children of men, will be forced to acknowledge the Lord's singular respect to them ; and beside what the Lord bestoweth, either inwardly or outwardly, upon his own, in this life, there is yet more laid up for afterwards, for completing the blessedness in the life to come : *how great is thy goodness which thou hast laid up for them that fear thee, which thou hast wrought for them that trust in thee before the sons of men!*   3. How great peace of conscience before God, and comfort in the Holy Ghost, the Lord can give a believer, when he hath to do with proud, open persecutors, and privily whispering slanderers! it is a secret and hid mystery to the worldly man: this David describeth in a similitude taken from warfare: *thou shalt hide them in the secret of thy presence from the pride of man, thou shalt keep them secretly in a pavilion, from the strife of tongues.*   4. As every believer, having gotten any experience of God's goodness, should read it as a particular proof of some general promise made to the godly ; so should he subscribe the truth of that promise, in favour of all believers, and bless God for his own particular experience of it ; for so doth the prophet here, saying, *he hath showed his kindness to me,* that is, how kind a God he is to his own, *as in a strong city;* that is, preserved me in the wilderness, as if I had been in the best fenced city in the world, furnished with men, victual, and ammunition in abundance.

22. *For I said in my haste, I am cut off from before thine eyes : nevertheless thou heardest the voice of my supplications when I cried unto thee.*

He confesseth the great distress he was in, and how weak his faith was under the temptation; this he to his own shame acknowledgeth, also, that he may give the greater glory to God.   Whence learn, 1. The faith of the godly may be shaken, and the strongest faith may sometimes show its infirmity : *I said in my haste, I am cut off from before thine eyes.*   2. Though faith be shaken, yet it is fixed in the root, as a tree beaten by the wind, keeping strong gripe of good ground ; though faith seem to yield, yet it faileth not, and even when it is at the weakest it is uttering itself in some act as a wrestler ; for here the expression of David's infirmity in faith is directed to God, and his earnest prayer joined with it : *I am cut off from before thine eyes, yet thou heardest the voice of my supplications.* 3. Praying faith, how weak soever, shall not be misregarded of God ; for *nevertheless,* saith he, *thou heardest the voice of my supplications.* 4. There may be in a soul at one time both grief oppressing and hope upholding ; both darkness of trouble and the light of faith : both desperate doubting and strong griping of God's truth and goodness ; both a fainting and a fighting ; a seeming yielding in the fight and yet a striving of faith against all opposition ; both a foolish haste and a settled stayedness of faith ; as here, *I said in my haste, &c.*

23. *O love the Lord, all ye his saints ; for the Lord preserveth the faithful, and plentifully rewardeth the proud doer.*

24. *Be of good courage, and he shall strengthen your heart, all ye that hope in the Lord.*

Now he maketh farther use of his experience, in exhorting all the godly to follow his example, encouraging them yet with hope of like success. Whence learn, 1. The gracious dealing of God with believers should glue their own hearts, and all other saints' hearts that hear of it, unto God, in faith and love : *O love the Lord, all ye his saints.* He putteth love for faith, because it is inseparable from faith ; and faith worketh by love, and love proveth the sincerity of faith. 2. The faithful man shall not want an upholder, albeit he had no friends : *for the Lord preserveth the faithful.* 3. The proud man shall not want a pursuer, and one to be avenged on him for his pride and oppression, though all the world should let him alone: *for the Lord plentifully rewardeth the proud doer.* 4. Albeit opposition be made unto a believer, yet must he resist every thing which might put him back from trusting in God ; for it becometh a believer to be stout: *be of good courage.* 5. Whoso aimeth at courage in the Lord shall be furnished with strength to double out his undertaking of faith : *be of good courage, and he shall strengthen your heart.* 6. Hope, grounded on the promise, must be fixed, that our courage may be founded, not on ourselves but on the word of God : *be of good courage, all ye that hope in the Lord.*

7

PSALM XXXII.

A psalm of David.   Maschil.

David, in this psalm, describeth the blessedness of the man justified by
faith, by way of general doctrine; set down, ver. 1, 2: which he cleareth by his own experience, ver. 3—5. Then he showeth the uses, both
of the general doctrine and of his own experience; first, for inducing
the godly to go to God by prayer, in trouble, ver. 6; secondly, for confirming of his own faith, ver. 7; thirdly, for teaching all men submission to God, and not to strive with him when he doth correct or exercise
them, ver. 8, 9; fourthly, for believing in God in all conditions, ver.
10; and, fifthly, for making the Lord the joy and delight of the justified man.

Maschil is put in the inscription of the psalm, signifying
instruction; to teach us, that the doctrine of justification
by faith is a lesson which all men have need to learn, and
to learn more and more solidly; because salvation and daily
consolation, in all the exercises of a man's soul, dependeth
on it.

1. *Blessed* is he whose *transgression* is *forgiven,*
whose *sin* is *covered.*

2. *Blessed* is *the man unto whom the Lord imputeth
not iniquity, and in whose spirit* there is *no guile.*

In the doctrine set down in these two verses, Learn, 1.
That sin draweth on a debt which no man can satisfy;
such a debt as a man must perish, if it be *not forgiven.* 2.
Sin is a filthiness which neither God can behold, without
abominating the sinner, nor the guilty conscience can look
upon without horror, except it *be covered.* 3. Sin draweth
on a guiltiness which may draw men to damnation, if it
shall be *imputed.* 4. There is no justification of a sinner,
by his good works, before God; but only by the forgiveness
of his evil works, as the apostle, Rom. iv. 6—8, citing this
place, proveth : *blessed is he whose transgression is forgiven.*
5. Justification by faith, or remission of sins, is accompanied
with right unto salvation, because it is written, *blessed is the
man whose transgression is forgiven.* 6. Justification by
faith, or absolution from sin, is accompanied also with the
upright endeavour of sanctification; for of the justified man
it is said, *blessed is the man in whose spirit there is no guile.*
7. Albeit no man liveth and sinneth not, yet God hath a way
to cleanse the conscience of the upright man, who honestly,
and without guile, endeavoureth to walk before God, by
bringing him to give account of his debt, and to acknow-

ledge his filthiness and his guiltiness before God, and then, for Christ's sake, *forgiving him*, and with Christ's righteousness *covering him*, and for Christ's mediation *not imputing iniquity unto him*.

3. *When I kept silence, my bones waxed old, through my roaring all the day long :*

4. *For day and night thy hand was heavy upon me : my moisture is turned into the drought of summer. Selah.*

He declareth this doctrine by his own experience, how God's wrath never left pursuing of him, till he came to make use of this doctrine, acknowledging his sin and fleeing to the benefit of remission of sin, for the blood of the Messiah, the Lamb slain from the beginning of the world, in the symbol of the expiatory sacrifice then daily offered for sin. Whence learn, 1 That man is fittest to speak of the doctrine of man's sin and misery, and of God's free grace and mercy, who hath felt the bitterness of sin and wrath, and the sweetness of God's grace by experience of God's pardon ; therefore is this doctrine recommended to the church by David, who had felt both. 2. A justified man who knoweth the doctrine of justification by faith in Christ, possibly, yea readily, may forget to make use of this precious truth, when he hath most need of it, being under guiltiness and the pressure also of God's fatherly wrath for it ; for David for a while being in this condition, was silent, and did not come to the acknowledgment of his sin, but was taken up only with the sense of the rod. 3. When the Lord is about to make his child sensible of his sins, and of the necessity of a free remission of them through the Mediator, he can awake the conscience of sin, by the sense of sad affliction, and can increase the heat of the furnace, and make his child roar for sorrow and pain, and thereby weaken his natural strength, and waste his spirits and his flesh, and his bones, and drive him to death's door, till he make use of the doctrine of justification, or remission of sin by faith in God the Redeemer. This was David's case ; *when he kept silence, his bones waxed old. God's hand was heavy upon him night and day, and the sap of his body* was dried up as a piece of moist earth is dried *in the drought of summer.*

5. *I acknowledged my sin unto thee, and mine ini-quity have I not hid. I said, I will confess my trans-gressions unto the Lord; and thou forgavest the ini-quity of my sin. Selah.*

At last the Lord led him to the right remedy, pointed out the way unto him of humiliation, and confession of sin, and seeking of mercy, as it is prescribed in the word, and so he was relieved. Whence learn, 1. Before the Lord let his child go from under the rod, after he hath given him an essay of himself, and of his own way how unprofitable it is, he will bring him about to the right way of relief, as here we see. 2. The only way to quiet the conscience, to pacify wrath, and remove judgment, is ingenuously to con-fess sin, and to aggravate it sincerely, (laying aside extenu-ations, excuses, and subterfuges, for justifying of God's dealing with us, and for humiliation of our ownselves be-fore him,) and to fly to God's mercy, laying out all before him, as before a gracious God, who doth pursue controver-sies with his own, only to the intent that they may make peace with him in the Mediator, and so be reconciled. So did David ; *he acknowledged his sin, and that unto God, he hid not his iniquity.* 3. Reconciliation with God, and re-newing our peace is ready at hand, when we take the right way as is said, to be delivered ; for so soon as David re-solved upon this course, and said *he would confess*, it fol-loweth, *thou forgavest the iniquity of my sin.*

6. *For this shall every one that is godly pray unto thee in a time when thou mayest be found; surely in the floods of great waters they shall not come nigh unto him.*

The first use of this doctrine and of David's experience, is to teach others how to behave themselves in their trouble. Whence learn, 1. The doctrine of justification by gracious forgiving iniquity, is the ground of all the godly's approaches to God, and right worshipping of him ; for, to show the use of this doctrine, thus tried by experience, he saith, *every godly one shall pray unto thee.* 2. There is a time when God may be found, to wit, so long as God is offering grace and sparing extremity of wrath, which time men ought to lay hold on, not knowing how short while it may last : they shall pray *in a time when thou mayest be found.* 3. It is possible, that a godly man may be in the midst of the waters of sore troubles, and yet these troubles not come near unto him, because God can furnish the man an ark in Christ, whereby he shall swim above the deluge; and when God keepeth off trouble, that it proveth not hurtful, (much more when he maketh trouble a means of spiritual good to a man, and giveth the man true peace and contentment in himself,) it is verified what is promised here : *surely in the floods of great waters, they shall not come near him.*

7. *Thou* art *my hiding-place; thou shalt preserve me from trouble; thou shalt compass me about with songs of deliverance. Selah.*

From the second use wherein David confirmeth his own faith for time to come, learn 1. Experience of God's mercies bygone should fasten resolution to make use of faith hereafter in all troubles, as here. 2. The godly after one trouble, should prepare for another, after one delivery expect another, as here. 3. What God hath proved himself to be to us before, we may promise he shall be the same to us in effect hereafter, because he is that by covenant and promise to us, what in practice we have found him to be; for David reasoneth thus, *thou* art *my hiding place; thou shalt preserve me from trouble;* that is, I shall have no damage by trouble, as is said. A justified soul resolving to make use of God in every condition that can come unto him, according to the covenant, may promise to himself a comfortable outgate of all his troubles, and matter of praise and joy from God on all hands; yea, he may confidently say with David, *thou shalt compass me about with songs of deliverance.*

8. *I will instruct thee, and teach thee in the way which thou shalt go: I will guide thee with mine eye.*

9. *Be ye not as the horse,* or *as the mule,* which *have no understanding; whose mouth must be held in with bit and bridle, lest they come near unto thee.*

From the third use of teaching others to be wise by his example, learn 1. The right use of experience is to edify others as our calling requireth; when we are converted, we should strengthen our brethren; for this David doth, *I will instruct thee, &c.* 2. When we have heard how others have been afflicted, we should be wiser, and take instruction by their example, that we strive not with God, but submit ourselves under his hand, acknowledge our sins, and seek mercy of him: *be not as the horse or the mule.*   3. Whosoever will not submit unto God, and seek unto his favour, shall find themselves so much the more hardly dealt with, as horses and mules *are bound in with bit and bridle.*

10. *Many sorrows* shall be *to the wicked: but he that trusteth in the Lord, mercy shall compass him about.*

From the fourth use of maintaining a course of adhering to God in all conditions, because it shall be better with the believer than with the wicked; learn, 1. There is no advantage to be had by repining against God, only the multiplication of sorrows shall follow thereupon, sin upon sin, wrath upon wrath, judgment upon judgment; and after temporal evils, everlasting shall follow, *for many sorrows shall be to the wicked.*   2. Not repining against God, taking with our chastisements, acknowledging of our sins in our affliction; seeking God's mercy, and leaning unto him,—putteth difference between the wicked and the godly ; for here the believer is set in opposition to the wicked, and to the man that is like a horse or mule; for he is called *the man that trusteth in the Lord.*   3. Whatsoever temptation, trouble, or opposition shall make assault against the believer; mercy shall make the defence, and shall give the deliverance on all hands, *for mercy shall compass him about.*

11. *Be glad in the Lord, and rejoice, ye righteous: and shout for joy, all* ye that are *upright in heart.*

From the last use of making God our joy and delight, learn, 1. Such as understand the way of justification by grace, and have fled to God for pardon of sin, and so are justified, have great matter of rejoicing, and should make conscience to rejoice in God; for to them it is said, *rejoice, ye righteous.*   2. The justified man is no counterfeit in the matter of religion, nor hypocrite in the matter of outward obedience to the Lord's law: *he is a righteous man, he is upright in heart.*   3. The matter of his joy and triumphing is the Lord himself, his grace, his good-will, his covenant, his promise, and constant kindness and mercy, for it is said to them, *be glad in the Lord.*

PSALM XXXIII.

This psalm in God's providence hath no inscription, as also many others have none; that we may look upon holy Scriptures as altogether inspired of God, and not put price upon it for the writers thereof, whether their name be expressed or not.　In it there is first an exhortation to praise God, v. 1—3, for his powerful, wise, and righteous government of all things in general, v. 4, 5 ; and more specially for his powerful guiding the works of creation, v. 6, 7.　Secondly, an exhortation, as to praise God, so also to fear him, for his omnipotency and his powerful over-ruling and disappointing all the devices of men against his church, and his powerful executing all his own will, v. 8—11.　Thirdly, a proclaiming the blessedness of the Lord's church and people, and of God's praises in reaching his providence over all the world, in favour of his people, v. 12—15.　In special, for disappointing and evacuating all vain confidences of men, great and small, who do not trust in him, v. 16, 17, and taking care of such as fear him and trust in him, to deliver them from all evil, v. 18, 19.　Fourthly, the use is set down which the godly make of this doctrine and song of praise.

1. *Rejoice in the Lord, O ye righteous; for praise is comely for the upright.*

2. *Praise the Lord with harp; sing unto him with the psaltery* and *an instrument of ten strings.*

3. *Sing unto him a new song, play skilfully with a loud noise ;*

From the exhortation made to the godly to praise God, learn, 1. That to rejoice in God is a point of praising of him, for it is here expounded to be praise ; *rejoice in the Lord,* saith he, *for praise is comely.*　2. Albeit all be bound to praise God, yet none will do it cheerfully and acceptably, save only the godly ; *rejoice, ye righteous.*　3. There is no exercise more becoming the godly, than praising of God, whether we look to the object of the praise, which is God ; or whether we look to their obligation above all people in the world ; *for praise is comely to the upright.*　4. There is no exercise whereunto we have more need to be stirred up, than to praise ; such is our dulness, and such is the excellency and necessity of the work, as the ceremonial use of musical instruments in the pedagogy of Moses did signify and import ; the religious use whereof, albeit it be taken away with the rest of the ceremonial law, (the natural or civil use thereof remaining still the same, both before the ceremonial law and after it;) yet the thing signified, which is the bending all the powers of our soul and body to praise God, is not taken away : and this necessity of our up-stirring is imported in a threefold exhortation. 5. The praises of the Lord, being well considered, will yield continually new matter, and fresh delight in the work. *Sing unto him*, saith he, *a new song.*

4. *For the word of the Lord is right; and all his works are done in truth.*

5. *He loveth righteousness and judgment: the earth is full of the goodness of the Lord.*

From the arguments of praise taken from his good governing of all things in general, learn, 1. The powerful appointment of what is done in the world, and the execution thereof in effect, is most holy, just, and equitable, that the creatures are so ranked as they are, some of them superior, some inferior; some of them ruling, some of them serving; some of them stronger, some weaker; some of them agreeing to other, some of them disagreeing one from another; some of them feeding upon, and others of them made food and prey to others: all making up a harmony of well-ruled concords and discords, all is done well and equitable: for, *the word of the Lord is right, and all his works are done in truth.* 2. The Lord cannot but do justly, because his nature is such, *he loveth righteousness and judgment.* 3. There is no part of the world we can set our eyes upon, but speaketh praise to God for his bounty to his creatures, and specially to man; *the earth is full of the goodness of the Lord.*

6. *By the word of the Lord were the heavens made; and all the host of them by the breath of his mouth.*

7. *He gathereth the waters of the sea together as an heap; he layeth up the depth in storehouses.*

From the works of creation, learn, 1. The omnipotence and wisdom of God in creating heaven and earth, and all things of nothing; as they praise God, so also do they prove the power and righteousness of his governing them; *by the word of the Lord the heavens were made.* 2. How easy a thing it is to God to govern and guide the world well, appeareth by his making of all things at a word; *he made all the host of them by the breath of his mouth,* and it can cost him no more to uphold and rule them at his pleasure. 3. He is able to ward off whatsoever evil can befall us: *for he gathers the waters of the sea as an heap,* which would naturally overflow the earth.   4. He hath more bands over our heads to keep us in fear and awe before him, and amongst the rest, *he layeth up the deep in store-houses,* to let them loose when, and where, and how far he pleaseth.

8. *Let all the earth fear the Lord : let all the inhabitants of the world stand in awe of him :*

9. *For he spake and it was* done; *he commanded, and it stood fast.*

10. *The Lord bringeth the counsel of the heathen to nought : he maketh the devices of the people of none effect.*

11. *The counsel of the Lord standeth for ever, the thoughts of his heart to all generations.*

In the second place, he exhorteth us to praise, so also to fear him.   Whence learn, 1. The right use of the works of creation, is, to take up how glorious and how dreadful the Creator of them is, and to beware to offend him : *let all the earth fear before the Lord.*   2. No man on earth is exempted from God's judgment, when he transgresseth God's law, albeit he be without the church : *let all the inhabitants of the world stand in awe of him.*   3. His omnipotence, manifested in framing and settling the frame of the world at a word, should move men to fear him ; for it is given for a reason to fear him, *because he spake, and it was done; he commanded, and it stood fast.*   4. Such as fear not God, have many devices of their own how to make themselves blessed, and how to overturn his church and people ; but God disappointeth them of their design, both in the one and in the other ; *he bringeth the counsel of the heathen to nought, and he maketh the devices of the people of none effect,* and therefore all should fear him.   5. The whole work of the Lord's providence, from the beginning of the world to the end thereof, is all at once before his eyes, and all the Lord's work is deliberately fixed by him ; *the counsel of the Lord standeth for ever.*   6. The Lord goeth on in executing of his determinate resolution, from one generation to another, without being frustrated of his purpose in any thing, less or more at any time : *the counsel of the Lord standeth for ever, the thoughts of his heart to all generations.*   7. Such as follow God's direction, obey his revealed will, take the course set down by him in his word for their reconciliation with him, through the Messiah Christ, and set his word before them, to be the rule of their faith and obedience, cannot be disappointed of what is promised by God in his revealed will; *for the counsel of the Lord standeth for ever, and the thoughts of his heart to all generations.*

12. *Blessed* is *the nation whose God* is *the Lord;* and *the people* whom *he hath chosen for his own inheritance.*

13. *The Lord looketh from heaven; he beholdeth all the sons of men.*

14. *From the place of his habitation he looketh upon all the inhabitants of the earth.*

15. *He fashioneth their hearts alike; he considereth all their works.*

In the third place, he showeth the blessedness of God's people, in order to his praise who hath chosen them, and who disposeth of all things to their behoof. Whence learn, 1. Of all the people on the earth, the Lord hath only entered into covenant with his church, to be their God in a peculiar way; for here, *there is a nation whose God is the Lord.* 2. Such as do lay hold on God as their God, are the only blessed people in the world; for it is said, *blessed is that nation whose God is the Lord.* 3. Such as, in the sense of their own sin and misery, and consideration of the vanity of all things beside God, have chosen God for their God, to live in communion with him, have evidence of their election; for they are here called, *the people whom he hath chosen.* 4. Such people, as is said, are that peculiar portion of the world which God hath set apart for himself, to draw the rent of his glory in the world by them, and from them in a special way; and whom he will keep in his possession for ever, and not suffer himself to be bereft of them: *for they are the people whom he hath chosen for his inheritance.* 5. Though the church be the only inheritance of God, yet the rest of the world is the object of his wise, holy, and powerful providence, no less than the church: *the Lord looketh down from heaven, and beholds all the sons of men.* 6. There cannot be a plot on earth against God's church, but God is privy to it, and knoweth it perfectly; *for from the place of his habitation, he looketh on all the inhabitants of the earth.* 7. The Lord cannot be ignorant

of the most secret devices of men, better or worse, because
he is the Maker of the hearts of all men : *he fashioneth their
hearts alike* (that is, the heart of one as well as of another),
he considereth all their works, that he may make of them
what he will. 8. Men had need to consider whereupon
their heart is set, and what course they are upon, and what
work they are about, for he knoweth the heart, *and considereth every man's work.*

16. *There is no king saved by the multitude of an
host: a mighty man is not delivered by much strength.*

17. *An horse is a vain thing for safety: neither
shall he deliver* any *by his great strength.*

18. *Behold, the eye of the Lord* is *upon them that
fear him, upon them that hope in his mercy;*

19. *To deliver their soul from death, and to keep
them alive in famine.*

Here he sets at nought all carnal confidence of men, that
his people may neither fear their enemies, nor trust in their
own furniture, and preferreth trusting in God to all carnal
confidence whatsoever. Whence learn, 1. Trusting in
means, (such as a man's strength, and the assistance of
other men, or other creatures,) is an error so natural and
fixed, as it hath need to be refuted by God, who hath said,
that they are a vain confidence to lean unto, which cannot
deliver a man ; *there is no king saved by the multitude of an
host ; a mighty man is not delivered by much strength ; and
a horse is a vain thing for safety.* And the actual frustrating of men's hopes, to be helped by authority, strength, or
external helps, should teach men not to lean to them, when
they are making use of them. 2. The man that believeth
in God, and feareth him, is in a more safe condition than
the wicked in all their power and riches : *behold the eye of
the Lord is upon them that fear him, and hope in his mercy,
to deliver them.* 3. The whole perfection of a Christian life
is comprised in these two,—trusting in God's mercy, and
fearing him : for this is the description here of the elect
and blessed man. 4. The godly cannot secure themselves
from being brought into straits and necessities, but may be
sure that God shall have a care of them in their necessities,
and give them a blessed outgate out of them all ; *for his eye
is on them, to deliver them from death, and to keep them
alive in famine.*

20. *Our soul waiteth for the Lord: he is our help and our shield.*

21. *For our heart shall rejoice in him; because we have trusted in his holy name.*

22. *Let thy mercy, O Lord, be upon us, according as we hope in thee.*

In the last place is set down the use of this doctrine which the godly should make of it. Whence learn, 1. All the points of the Lord's praise, are props of the saints' faith and grounds of their hope, as this conclusion drawn from this song of praise doth show: *our soul waiteth for the Lord, &c.* 2. Every believer may rejoice, and promise to himself cause of rejoicing, through faith in his name; *our hearts shall rejoice in him, because we have trusted in him.* 3. Faith always differenceth itself from presumption, by praying for what is promised; *let thy mercy be upon us,* say the believers. 4. Because the hope of the godly is grounded upon God's promises, therefore it shall not be disappointed, *but God's mercy shall be on them, according as they hope in him.*

PSALM XXXIV.

A psalm of David, when he changed his behaviour before Abimelech; who drove him away, and he departed.

In this psalm David praiseth God for his delivery from the king of Gath, and exhorteth others to praise God with him, for his experience of God's mercy, ver. 1—6. Then for making farther use of this mercy, he gives out general doctrines concerning God's protection and care of his children, with the uses thereof, ver. 7—10. Thirdly, he giveth counsel how to lead a blessed life, ver. 11—14. Fourthly, he enforceth his council by promises to the godly who obey God's counsel, and threatenings to the wicked man who obeyeth not, ver. 15—22.

From the inscription we learn, 1. That it is to good purpose to observe special mercies in a special manner, and to note the circumstances thereof as here is done. 2. And that men in a preposterous fear, flying from one danger may fall into another worse, as David did, when he fled into an unhallowed place, amongst God's enemies, for fear of Saul, he falleth into Abimelech or Achish's hands. 3. And that God pitieth the infirmity of his children, and gives success some whiles to weak and unthrifty shifts, as here when David changed his behaviour, he escaped. 4. That God can and doth dispose of men's hearts, as he hath a mind to work by them: for he did move the heart of Achish not to take notice of David, otherwise than of a distracted man.

1. *I will bless the Lord at all times: his praise* shall *continually* be *in my mouth.*

2. *My soul shall make her boast in the Lord: the humble shall hear* thereof, *and be glad.*

He promiseth here for his own part to praise God for the mercy received. Whence learn, 1. As no mercy should be misregarded; so, notable mercies should be specially remembered, and God blessed for the same. 2. It is a point of thankfulness, to take all occasions to speak of God to others; *his praise shall be continually in my mouth.* 3. Whatsoever be our condition in ourselves, matter of gloriation in God shall never be wanting to the believer, and this gloriation is a duty and a point of praising God; *my soul shall make her boast in the Lor d* Only humble souls sensible of their own weakness are the people who reap benefit by God's mercies, bestowed on others and themselves: *the humble shall hear and be glad.*

3. *O magnify the Lord with me, and let us exalt his name together.*

4. *I sought the Lord, and he heard me and delivered me from all my fears.*

He exhorteth others to praise God with him, magnifying him for his greatness, and exalting him for his highness. Whence learn, 1. The saints are obliged to help one another in praises as well as in prayer, albeit it cometh to pass that many do crave aid of others' prayers, who call not for their help to praise: for here it is, *let us exalt his name together.* 2. By prayer the Lord is sought and found, and it is no small matter of comfort to us, and glory to God, that our prayer is regarded: *I sought the Lord,* saith he, *and he heard me.* 3. The fear of what is like to be, should not hinder prayer; for the fears of the godly are not certain prophecies; for God can deliver out of them all: *he delivered me out of all my fears.*

5. *They looked unto him, and were lightened; and their faces were not ashamed.*

6. *This poor man cried, and the Lord heard* him, *and saved him out of all his troubles.*

He is glad, and commendeth God's goodness to him for the fruit of this mercy to other believers. Whence learn, 1. One man's experience may be an encouragement to many to run to God for the like alms. This David foreseeth shall be the fruit of God's mercy to him, when men, seeing him delivered, shall look to God, and take comfort and confidence by this means; *they looked on him,* that is, on David, and so may we on Christ, (represented by him,) and at the fulness of the Godhead dwelling in Christ : so they were lightened, and thus comforted in the midst of the darkness of their troubles : *and their faces were not ashamed,* because of confidence raised by this experience, that they should find the like mercy when they stood in need. 2. The way to make the best use of the example of God's mercy to any persons set down in Scripture, or which fall forth in our time, or are made certainly known to us any way, is to look upon them, not as they differ from us or our condition, but as they draw nearest in similitude to us, and unto the mean condition we are in, for so do the saints look on David, saying, not this rare saint David, or this great prophet David, or this holy man David, who was according to God's heart —but *this poor man* David *cried, and the Lord heard him, and saved him out of all his troubles.*

7. *The angel of the Lord encampeth round about them that fear him, and delivereth them.*

8. *O taste and see that the Lord* is *good : blessed* is *the man* that *trusteth in him.*

In the next place, are set down general doctrines concerning God's care of believers, to protect and feed them, and the uses thereof, to trust and fear God. Whence learn, 1. A right sight of God's dealing with a man's ownself will give him great light about the Lord's manner of dealing with others, his children, as here. 2. Though the godly walk among foes, and be in a continual warfare, yet they are well looked to and guarded : *the angel of the Lord encampeth round about them.* 2. The sense of God's mercy and goodness is the sweetest thing that ever was felt, and is able to season the bitterest cup that ever believer drank of : *taste and see that the Lord is good.* 4. By faith is the taste of this sweetness gotten, *for blessed is the man that trusts in him.* 5. All that the believer can attain to in this life of spiritual consolation, whether by faith or experience, sweetened with lively comforts of the holy Ghost, is but a taste in comparison of what is to be had hereafter, and yet that taste, O how sweet a joy unspeakable, and full of glory is it ! *O taste and see that the Lord is good.* 6. Affliction purgeth the taste of the believer, and a soul driven from all worldly helps, is fitted for exercising spiritual senses, as here we see David's taste is purged well after trouble. 7. As God is very communicative of his goodness, and offereth himself to men to be taken a proof of, so also gracious souls do wish and invite others to share with them in whatsoever grace the Lord doth bestow on them, as David doth here, saying to all, *O taste and see.* 8. Albeit this sweetness be not found at the first out-putting of faith, yet let faith rest on God and it shall feel in due time, for blessed is he that putteth his trust in God ; yea, faith itself is a taste of that grace that is in God.

9. *O fear the Lord, ye his saints: for* there is *no want to them that fear him.*

10. *The young lions do lack, and suffer hunger : but they that seek the Lord shall not want any good* thing.

Another doctrine concerning God's care to feed and provide for all necessary furniture unto the believer, with the use thereof, which is to fear God. Whence learn, 1. True believers in God must study holiness for evidencing of their faith, for therefore are they called saints, and *his* saints. 2. The fear of the Lord is the property of the saints, whereby they are set on work to do what the Lord commandeth, and to forbear what he forbiddeth, and no bonds of inclination, counsel, example, laws, fear of shame, or punishment from men, are able to keep a man in order when he meeteth with a fit temptation to sin ; but the fear of God restraineth the man both outwardly and inwardly, in secret and open, always, and everywhere ; and whatsoever measure of holy fear the saints have attained unto, yet may they be exhorted, and must hearken unto exhortation, to grow in this grace ; *O fear the Lord, ye his saints.* 3. Such as fear God need not to want any necessary furniture in God's service; *for there is no want to them that fear him.* 4. Proud oppressors, wealthy and potent princes, that trust in their own power, shall not be so sure of their

own standing and furniture, as the meanest of true believers are; *the lions do lack, and suffer hunger, but
they that seek the Lord shall not want;* though the godly
may want many earthly things, yet shall they have food and
raiment, *and shall not want any good thing.*   6. The
right sort of fearing God, and labouring for more and
more near communion with him, are inseparable properties
of the saints, for they that are called saints are called here
fearers of him and seekers of him also.

11. *Come, ye children, hearken unto me; I will
teach you the fear of the Lord.*

12. *What man is he that desireth life, and loveth
many days, that he may see good?*

13. *Keep thy tongue from evil, and thy lips from
speaking guile.*

14. *Depart from evil, and do good; seek peace, and
pursue it.*

In the third place, he giveth direction how a man shall
live blessedly; by evidencing the sincerity of the fear of
God in him, which is a grace inseparable from faith in
God, manifesting itself in obedience to his commands.
Whence learn, 1. There should be such mutual love and
respect between the teacher and the people taught, as is
between parents and children, yea, God in his servants offereth himself as a father, ready to instruct his visible
church as his children; *come, ye children,* saith he, *and
hearken unto me.*   2. The true fear of God is the way to
live blessedly in this life, where misery most aboundeth; and
this should be a motive to seek after this grace, for it is asked
here, *what man is he that desireth life?* &c., and then the
way to attain to it is set down in some particulars of the
fear of God, as the inseparable companions of faith in God.
3. The true fear of God must evidence itself by the fruits
thereof, such as are the ruling of man's tongue, and of the
rest of the outward man, eschewing whatsoever the Lord
forbids, and endeavouring every good duty which God
commandeth, and the keeping peace with all men so far as
in us lieth, for so doth the prophet's words bear; ver. 13,
14.   This is the evidence of the fear of God in effect, when
such outward works proceed from inward principles of
saving grace.

15. *The eyes of the Lord* are *upon the righteous, and his ears* are open *unto their cry.*

16. *The face of the Lord* is *against them that do evil, to cut off the remembrance of them from the earth.*

In the last place, he presseth this doctrine by showing the privileges of the righteous, and the miserable state of the wicked, setting the one against the other thrice. In the first learn, 1. It is a good means to keep our hearts in the fear of God to consider the gain of godliness, and the damage and danger of wickedness, as here they are set in opposition. 2. Such as have their eye upon God and his word for righteousness and life, may be sure of the watchful eye of God on them for their direction in their way, their consolation in their grief, and deliverance out of trouble ; for *the eyes of the Lord are upon the righteous.* 3. As the righteous lend their ears to God's word, to his promises and precepts, so the Lord lendeth his ear to their supplications and desires : *his ears are open to their cry.* 4. On the other hand, as the wicked who fear not God, set their face to do evil, and to transgress God's commands, so God shall set his face against them, to be avenged on them : *the face of the Lord is against them that do evil.* 5. The only happiness which the wicked man seeketh, is to have riches, honour, and pleasure in the earth, and to have his own name in estimation among men hereafter, and these things also, beside the loss of heaven, shall be taken from him, and his temporal life withal : for *the face of the Lord is set against them, to cut off their remembrance from the earth.*

17. The righteous *cry, and the Lord heareth, and delivereth them out of all their troubles.*

18. *The Lord* is *nigh unto them that are of a broken heart ; and saveth such as be of a contrite spirit.*

19. *Many* are *the afflictions of the righteous : but the Lord delivereth him out of them all.*

20. *He keepeth all his bones : not one of them is broken.*

21. *Evil shall slay the wicked ; and they that hate the righteous shall be desolate.*

Another opposition of the good appointed for the godly, and the evil appointed for the wicked. Whence learn, 1.

The Lord putteth the godly to trouble, and by trouble putteth them to their prayers, and delays answer till the need be great; and then they cry to the Lord, and he giveth evidence of his hearing, and sendeth deliverance: for *the righteous cry, and the Lord heareth, and delivereth them out of all their troubles.* 2. It is as true as it may seem strange, that the Lord will press his own so long with trouble till he break their heart, and kill their natural courage and confidence; for here are the godly described to be men of *a broken heart and contrite spirit.* 3. Though the Lord so break the natural confidence of his own, and so empty them, by trouble, of all conceit of their own worth, wisdom, or ability to deliver themselves out of trouble, that they may rely on God only; yet will he not withdraw himself from them, nor suffer them to perish in discouragement: *the Lord is near to them that are of broken heart, and saveth such as be of a contrite spirit.* 4. Though the righteous be the only men in the world whom God loveth best, yet will he not only not exempt them from trouble, but also will exercise them with multitudes and varieties of troubles from his own hand immediately, from Satan's temptations, from the malice of the wicked of the world, &c.: *many are the troubles of the righteous;* for thus will the Lord conform the redeemed to their Head—try, and train them up in faith, and patient submission to God's will; teach them to pray and wait on, and give proof of the sincerity of the grace given to them. 5. The godly are as oft delivered as they are troubled, either by removing the trouble, or by giving strength and patience to bear it, or comfort under it and certain hope of outgate from it, or by ending all troubles to them at once: *many are the afflictions of the righteous, but the Lord delivereth him out of them all.* 6. The Lord moderateth, weigheth, and measureth all the troubles of his own—what they shall suffer in their life and death—and leaveth it not to the will of the instruments of their trouble: *he keepeth all his bones: not one of them is broken.* This was true of Christ our Lord, of whom many things were prefigured and prophesied in the psalms, and in this among the rest: which showeth, that in the psalms, as the matter will suffer, Christ is much to be eyed, and more than David, of whom, at first, the same seem to speak chiefly. 7. As to the opposite state of the wicked, we learn, that the wickedness of the wicked is both the meritorious cause and the means of the wicked man's destruction: *for evil shall slay the wicked.* 8. It is the mark of a wicked man *to hate the righteous* for his righteousness; and so is it set down here. 9. He that hateth the righteous, or the image of God in his neighbour, shall be guilty of all the consequences of the enmity, and be destitute of comfort when he hath most need: *he that hateth the righteous shall be desolate.*

22. *The Lord redeemeth the soul of his servants; and none of them that trust in him shall be desolate.*

The third opposition between the righteous and the wicked, is in relation to what is said in the former verse. Whence learn, 1. The wicked shall perish in their sin, and for their sin, but the righteous shall not perish in their sins, nor for them: for *evil shall slay the wicked, but the Lord shall redeem the soul of his servants;* to wit, out of sin and misery. 2. As the wicked are servants of sin, and serve an ill master, and get an ill reward; so the godly are servants of righteousness, and have God for their master, and shall have delivery and salvation for their reward; as the comparison here set down showeth. 3. As the wicked, who are destitute of faith in God, when they fall into trouble, want consolation; so all the righteous, who are no other than sincere believers in God, shall have good company and consolation in all their trouble, and never be left alone: for *the haters of the righteous shall be desolate, but none of them that trust in God shall be desolate.*

PSALM XXXV.

A psalm of David.

This psalm is a representation of Christ's hottest contest with his adversaries, wherein they are about to do their worst against him, and his kingdom; and he denounceth the hottest wrath of God against them, for their everlasting overthrow, set forth under the shadow of David's contest with his irreconcilable enemies: wherein he prayeth God to arise for him, ver. 1—3, and take order with his despiteful enemies, ver. 4—8; which, as it may comfort the supplicant, so shall it serve also for God's glory, ver. 9, 10. A main reason for which petition is the unjust and ungrateful dealing of his enemies with him, ver. 11—16; whereupon he reneweth his petition the second time, ver. 17—19, pressing his former reason from the enemy's unjust and insolent disposition, ver. 20, 21; and then reneweth his petition the third time for himself, ver. 22—26, and for all the favourers of his cause, ver. 27, 28.

1. *Plead* my cause, O Lord, *with them that strive with me: fight against them that fight against me.*

2. *Take hold of shield and buckler, and stand up for mine help.*

3. *Draw out also the spear, and stop* the way *against them that persecute me; say unto my soul, I am thy salvation.*

From his petition for himself, learn, 1. Such as take part with God against his enemies, the Lord will take part with against their enemies: if any plead against the believer by verbal calumnies and slanders, the Lord will be their party: if any will oppose the godly with violence, the Lord will oppose them; for this prayer of one of the godly is as good as a promise to all: *plead my cause, O Lord, with them that strive with me: fight against them that fight against me.* 2. There is defence in abundance to be found in God against whatsoever the enemy can do; a shield and buckler in God's hand, when he pleaseth to stand up and help. 3. The Lord can terrify the enemy so that he dare not assault the man whom God pleaseth to defend, and hold him off with long weapons, giving the enemy some other thing to do than pursue his people: he can *draw out the spear, and stop the way against them that persecute the godly.* 4. He can quiet the hearts of his own in the midst of persecution, and make them fearless in persuading them of their salvation, everlasting at least; and this may fully satisfy, if the Lord *say unto their soul, I am thy salvation.*

4. *Let them be confounded and put to shame that seek after my soul: let them be turned back and brought to confusion that devise my hurt.*

5. *Let them be as chaff before the wind: and let the angel of the Lord chase them.*

6. *Let their way be dark and slippery: and let the angel of the Lord persecute them.*

7. *For without cause have they hid for me their net in a pit,* which *without cause they have digged for my soul.*

8. *Let destruction come upon him at unawares; and let his net that he hath hid catch himself: into that very destruction let him fall.*

From his petition against his enemies, learn, 1. Shameful disappointment shall they find at length who intend to destroy the godly: *let them be confounded and put to shame*

that seek after my soul.   2. Though the enemies of Christ
and the godly advance in the prosecution of their hurtful
devices; yet shall they be forced to retire with shame: *they
shall be turned back and brought to confusion who devise
their hurt.*   3. As the enemy hath pursued, so shall God's
wrath pursue, chase, and drive him to perdition: *they shall
be as the chaff before the wind.*   4. Albeit there were no
earthly man to pursue Christ's enemies, yet avenging angels,
or evil spirits, shall be let forth upon them and their families,
to trouble them: *let the angel of the Lord chase them.*   5.
The Lord shall put them to such straits as they shall not
know what hand to turn to, what way to take, and in the
way which they take they shall fall: *let their way be dark
and slippery.*   6. When they fall into mischief, the hand of
the Lord shall be stretched out against them: *let the angel
of the Lord pursue them.*   7. Though the godly, by behav-
ing themselves innocently, cannot eschew the persecution of
the wicked; yet innocent behaviour is a great ease to the
conscience of the godly, a matter of encouragement to them
in their addresses to God, and a great aggreging of the
ditty of the enemy; as here twice he saith, *without cause
they hid their net.*   8. Though the enemies of the godly do
plot secret devices against them, yet not so secret but God
can give warning of it, and make it an errand for the godly
to pray to him to disappoint the plot; as is here imported:
they have hid for me their net in a pit.   9. The wicked know
not how to be sure of their prey when they hunt for the life
of the godly: *they prepare the net and set it; they hide it,
and they hide it in a pit.*   10. When the enemies of God's
people least expect harm, then shall mischief surprise them:
destruction shall come upon them unawares.   11. The very
course which the enemy taketh against God's church and
people, shall be the nearest course to destroy themselves:
*let his net that he hath hid catch himself: into that very
destruction let him fall.*

9. *And my soul shall be joyful in the Lord: it shall
rejoice in his salvation.*

10. *All my bones shall say, Lord, who* is *like unto
thee, which deliverest the poor from him that is too strong
for him, yea, the poor and the needy from him that
spoileth him?*

He brings a reason of his prayer from the comfort which

he should have, and the glory which God should have, by
its answer.   Whence learn, 1. It is a good reason to
strengthen our hope to be heard, when our comfort and
God's glory may both be promoted by the granting of our
desire, as here we find it.   2. The destruction of the enemies of the church is not a matter of rejoicing in men's
destruction, but of rejoicing in the Lord, and in his wise
manner of delivering his people : *my soul shall be joyful in
the Lord : it shall rejoice in his salvation.*   3. In the estimation of the godly, the tongue is too little to magnify the
Lord for his mercies ; for their desire is, that all the powers
of the soul, and all the parts of the body, even the bones,
which are least sensible in their own kind, might praise
him : *all my bones shall say, &c.*   4. The Lord hath wonderful ways, other and more than ever man conceived, whereby he can deliver his own, in their lowest condition, from
their oppressors, when they are in the height of their power
and pride : *Lord, who is like unto thee, which deliverest the
poor from him that is too strong for him, &c.*   5. Though,
before deliverance come, faith hath cause to say all that
sense can say of God's praises after deliverance is come ;
yet, when sensible experience of a hoped delivery is come,
there is a more hearty and cheerful manner of expressing
the Lord's praises than can be before it come ; as the pre-
mise of the prophet to say so and so, as is in the text, after
the delivery is come, doth import.   6. It is a sort of, as it
were, engaging of God to deliver, when the heart of the
believer engageth itself to glorify God after the delivery ;
for here the prophet maketh use of this, promising praise
towards this end.

11. *False witnesses did rise up : they laid to my
charge* things *that I knew not.*

12. *They rewarded me evil for good,* to *the spoiling
of my soul.*

13. *But as for me, when they were sick, my clothing
was sackcloth : I humbled my soul with fasting ; and
my prayer returned into mine own bosom.*

14. *I behaved myself as though* he had been *my
friend* or *brother : I bowed down heavily, as one that
mourneth* for his *mother.*

15. *But in mine adversity they rejoiced, and gathered*

themselves together; yea, the abjects gathered themselves together against me, and I knew it *not; they did tear* me, *and ceased not:*

16. *With hypocritical mockers in feasts, they gnashed upon me with their teeth.*

He amplifieth that reason of his petition, taken from his enemies' carriage, by laying before God their falsehood and ingratitude. Whence learn, 1. The godly are subject, not only to be backbitten, and reduced privily, and slandered more openly; but also to be charged unjustly before judges, and pursued criminally for their life without a cause, and to have false witness led against them, that they may be condemned under colour of law; this was found in effect by David, and Christ represented by him. *False witnesses did rise up; they laid to my charge things that I knew not.* 2. No bonds of nature or humanity will bind up the wicked from persecuting the godly, even to death, how well soever the godly have deserved of them; *they rewarded me evil for good, to the depriving me of my life.* 3. True love is best known, as by rejoicing at another's welfare, so by grieving for his grief; *when they were sick, my clothing was sackcloth.* 4. Hearty prayer also for any man, is a token of unfeigned love to a man, specially when prayer and fasting are joined together for them: *I humbled my soul by fasting.* 5. When the expressions of grief, by words or tears in prayer for any, waken up the affection yet more to pray ardently for them; it is yet a farther token of unfeigned love of them for whom we pray. *My prayer,* saith he, *returned into my bosom;* which is as much as my expressions in prayer, in sighs, affectionate words and tears, affected my heart, Lament. iii. 49—51, with new motions of earnest dealing for them. 6. True Christians' affection to their enemies, is able to affect the soul as much to the seeking their welfare, and commiserating their misery, as the natural affection of a natural man can affect him toward friends and kinsfolk, in nearest natural relations unto him; for David saith, *I behaved myself as though he had been my friend or brother; I bowed down heavily as one that mourneth for his mother.*

From the evil meeting which he received of his enemies, v. 15, 16, learn, 1. Many of those that pretend great friendship to the godly in time of prosperity, may not only

turn their back upon them in time of adversity, but also
turn to be their open enemies, and rejoice in their calamity ;
but in my adversity, saith he, *they rejoiced.* 2. The
troubles of the godly draw the wicked into a more near
union amongst themselves, as it were congratulating one
another in their sinful courses, and strengthening one another ; *they gather themselves together.* 3. Base rascals,
who have nothing to commend them save merely their
hatred of God's people and of their piety, will get respect
amongst the enemies of Christ and of his people, for that
very reason, because they hate the godly, and will be admitted into the fellowship of ringleading enemies ; *yea, the
abjects gathered themselves together against me.* 4. In the
meeting of the wicked among themselves, Christ and his
followers have their name torn and rent in pieces continually, with calumnies and slanders, which possibly come not
to their ears, half of them : *they gathered together, and I
knew it not : they did tear me in pieces and ceased not.* 5.
Sad taunts and scoffs of pretended holy men jeering at true
piety, is no small part of the persecution of Christ, and of
his followers ; for here amongst the rest are *hypocritical
mockers.* 6. When the wicked without fear fill and stuff their
belly in their feasting, in the time of the church's trouble:
their scoffs and their jests, yea and their bloody expressions
of cruelty against the godly, are the most relishing sauce of
their banquets : *with hypocritical mockers in their feasts,
they gnash upon me with their teeth.*

17. *Lord, how long wilt thou look on? rescue my
soul from their destructions, my darling from the lions.*

18. *I will give thee thanks in the great congregation : I will praise thee among much people.*

19. *Let not them that are mine enemies wrongfully
rejoice over me;* neither *let them wink with the eye that
hate me without a cause.*

20. *For they speak not peace ; but they devise deceitful matters against* them that are *quiet in the land.*

21. *Yea, they opened their mouth wide against me,*
and *said, Aha, aha! our eye hath seen* it.

He repeateth his petition for delivery from his enemies
the second time, and presseth the same reason taken from
the insolent and cruel disposition of the enemy. Whence

learn, 1. The time of trouble and persecution of the godly may continue much longer than the godly expected, in which case, as they must wait on patiently till the Lord put to his hand to relieve his church and punish their enemies; so they may ease their heart, in laying their earnest longing to be delivered before the Lord, and say, *Lord, how long wilt thou look on?* 2. As it is lawful to lament the Lord's seeming long delay to help us, so we must not complain too soon; for, before David uttereth this, *how long*, he is long in trouble, and in danger of his life, by unreasonable and beastly cruel men, and is altogether destitute of all means of relief, as his prayer testifieth; *rescue my soul from their destructions, my darling from the lions.* 3. The godly, by faith in the deepest danger, may see their delivery in their saddest and darkest sorrow; yea, may behold the light of consolation coming; in their banishment, may behold their liberty, and see their fellowship with the saints; and, in the midst of complaints, may promise to themselves reasons of praise, and the payment of their vows made to God, as here we see in the midst of this sad condition the prophet saith, *I will give thee thanks in the great congregation: I will praise thee among much people.* 4. It augmenteth the grief of the godly, to see the wicked take advantage of their trouble, and mockers of religion rejoice over their sufferings in a good cause; and they may heartily deprecate this evil, that it may not at least last long; *let not those that are my enemies rejoice over me.* 5. The less cause of provocation of our enemies be given to them by us, the greater is the hope of delivery, and the readier shall be our help from God, and the less cause shall be to the enemy to wink with the eye, as witty well-pleased scoffers do, when they get their will; *neither let them wink with the eye*, saith he, *that hate me without a cause.* 6. Albeit godly men's quiet carriage in the land where they live, will not save them from the hostile speeches, and malicious plottings of their adversaries against them, yet shall their quiet behaviour speak to God for them, and against their enemies, and make a speedy mischief come upon them from the Lord; for, to this purpose he saith, *they speak not peace, but they devise deceitful matters against them that are quiet in the land.* 7. The enemies of the church are a base generation, taking pleasure and sport in the miseries of the godly, who do not injure them, yea, are a vain and insolent generation, triumphing over the weakness of the innocent when they are in low condition, and in the case of suffering, which common humanity and ordinary generosity abhorreth : *they opened their mouth wide against me, and said, Aha, aha, our eye hath seen it.*

22. This *thou hast seen, O Lord : keep not silence : O Lord, be not far from me.*

23. *Stir up thyself, and awake to my judgment,* even *unto my cause, my God and my Lord.*

24. *Judge me, O Lord my God, according to thy righteousness; and let them not rejoice over me.*

25. *Let them not say in their hearts, Ah, so would we have it : let them not say, We have swallowed him up.*

26. *Let them be ashamed, and brought to confusion together, that rejoice at mine hurt : let them be clothed with shame and dishonour that magnify* themselves *against me.*

He reneweth his petition for himself and against his enemies the third time. Whence learn, 1. Such as feed their eyes upon the miseries of the godly, the Lord shall not wink at their wickedness, but make it appear, that he hath marked their cruelty, that he may punish it exemplarily ; for after the enemies' crying out, *our eye hath seen,* the prophet addeth, *this thou hast seen, O Lord, be not silent.* 2. The hardest condition that can befall a believer, is a tolerable case and condition, if God draw near to his soul : for all the remedy that David craveth, till the outgate come, is, *O Lord, be not far from me.* 3. Though the Lord for a time suffer his own to lie under foot oppressed, yet for his justice' sake, and for his covenant's sake, he will justly determine the controversy, and clear his own servants ; *he will stir up himself to do judgment, and decide their cause.* 4. In the decision of the controversy between the godly and their enemies, the cause of the godly shall get no wrong, but be declared to be righteous, and the enemies shall have no matter to rejoice in. *He shall judge the godly according to their righteousness, and shall not suffer the wicked to rejoice over them.* 5. When the enemies of the church have laid the last reckoning of the issue of their bloody course against the godly, they shall see the matter go otherwise than they would, or expected, on both hands. They shall not have cause to say, *so would we have it,* or *we have swallowed them up.* They are too precious a morsel for them to devour. 6. Shame and confusion, dishonour and disgrace, on all hands shall be upon one, and upon all Christ's enemies, who seek the detriment of his cause, and to have gain to themselves, by opposing him and his cause in his people's hand; for this prayer against them shall still speak effectually, *let them be ashamed and brought to confusion together, and let them be clothed with shame and dishonour, &c.*

27. *Let them shout for joy, and be glad, that favour my righteous cause; yea, let them say continually, Let the Lord be magnified, which hath pleasure in the prosperity of his servant.*

28. *And my tongue shall speak of thy righteousness, and of thy praise, all the day long.*

As David prayeth for himself, so he prayeth for all the favourers of his righteous cause, as the type of Christ, whose Spirit spake by him, for the edification of the church in all times coming. Whence learn, 1. It is one mark of godliness amongst many others, to befriend the cause of Christ, and to further it in the person of his saints, suffering for righteousness, with their best affection; for here they are described by being *the favourers of their righteous cause.* 2. In the persecution of the godly for the cause of God's truth and true religion, all the godly are concerned; and as they partake of the sufferings with others under Christ the Head, so shall they partake of the joy of the victory and outgate, which shall be exceedingly joyful at last : *let them shout for joy, and be glad,* saith the type of Christ, *that do favour my righteous cause.* 3. The troubles of the godly are not so many but room is left sometimes for prosperity; for God *loveth the prosperity of his servants;* to wit, as it may conduce to his purpose and their good. 4. When any of the godly are delivered from their persecutors, all the rest of the godly are bound, as they understand it, to set forth the power of God, and his love and bounty, manifested and forthcoming to his people: *let them say continually, Let the Lord be magnified, which hath pleasure in the prosperity of his servants.* 5. Whatsoever opposition the enemies of

Christ and of the godly shall make, Christ shall keep up the open profession of true doctrine, which manifesteth the righteousness of God—leading men to eternal life, and bringing glory to God ; for this is the undertaking of the type, and of Christ represented by him, after the hottest contest between him and his wicked enemies : *my tongue shall speak of thy righteousness, and of thy praise all the day long.*

PSALM XXXVI.

To the chief musician.   A psalm of David, the servant of the Lord.

This psalm hath three parts. In the first, David sets down the perverseness of the wicked in their sinful course and devices against the godly and himself, ver. 1—4.   In the second, he comforts himself, and doth settle his faith on the praises and properties of God, ver. 5—9.   In the third, he prayeth in the behalf of God's children, and for himself, to be delivered from the wicked, ver. 10—12.

From the inscription, learn, that to be a servant of the Lord is an honour, and a privilege above all earthly privileges ; and by giving a sweet testimony to the conscience, it doth season every condition of life, more than any earthly advantage can do.

1. *The transgression of the wicked saith within my heart,* that there is *no fear of God before his eyes.*

2. *For he flattereth himself in his own eyes, until his iniquity be found to be hateful.*

3. *The words of his mouth* are *iniquity and deceit: he hath left off to be wise,* and *to do good.*

4. *He deviseth mischief upon his bed; he setteth himself in a way* that is *not good; he abhorreth not evil.*

From his observation of the carriage of the wicked ; learn, 1.   Albeit all the world cannot be discerned to be graceless and unconverted, yet the lewd life of some may speak their being in the state of corrupt nature unconverted, to the conscience of a discerning man ; *for the transgression of the wicked saith in my heart, that there is no fear of God before his eyes.*   2. It is not the imperfection or shortcoming in the fear of God, but the being destitute of it altogether, that proveth a wicked man : *there is no fear of God before his eyes.*   3. As a man that feareth God is watchful over his own ways, and censorious of himself ; so the man that feareth not God is secure, and well-pleased

with his own doings ; *he flattereth himself in his own eyes*
4. As the man that feareth God laboureth to inform his
conscience well, that he may not commit iniquity ; so the
man that feareth not God, gulleth and deceiveth his own
conscience, till he have gotten the iniquity accomplished,
and it be now made open in its own colours ; *he flattereth*
himself in his own eyes, till his iniquity worthy to be hated
be found, or his iniquity be found to be hateful.   5. As the
man that feareth God will discern the sin in himself, whereof he is in danger, before any man perceive it ; so the man
that feareth not God, will not see his own sin, no not when
any that looks upon his way may see it ; *he flattereth him-*
self in his own eyes, till his iniquity be found to be hateful.
6. As the man that feareth God makes conscience of his
speeches, and will be loth to cover sin with vain pretences
and excuses, but rather will confess it ; so the man that
feareth not God will not stand, whatever pretence he
useth for doing iniquity, nor what excuse he maketh
for the iniquity, when it is done, for deceiving both
others and himself : *the words of his mouth are ini-*
quity and deceit.   7. As the man that feareth God, by all
means striveth that he may grow wiser and holier, so the
man that fears not God, will misregard and cast off the
means of wisdom and holiness ; *he hath left off to be wise,*
and to do good ; whatsoever he seemed to have before, he
goeth back even from that more and more.   8. As the
man that feareth God, communeth with his heart upon his
bed, that he may not sin, no not in his heart ; so the man
that feareth not God, deviseth how he may plot and perform
sin willingly ; *he deviseth mischief on his bed.*   9. As the
man that feareth God abhorreth that which is evil, and laboureth to be sure that the way he is upon is good ; so the
man that feareth not God, taketh no farther notice of what
he doth, than what is most for his purpose ; and neither
abhorreth what he would be at, because it is evil, nor af-
fecteth it, because it is good ; but having digested his purpose by meditation and resolution, he goeth on obstinately ;
he setteth himself in a way that is not good ; he abhorreth
not evil : and such were David's enemies, and such will be
the enemies of Christ and his people.

5. *Thy mercy, O Lord,* is *in the heavens ;* and *thy*
faithfulness reacheth *unto the clouds.*

6. *Thy righteousness* is *like the great mountains ;*

thy judgments are *a great deep : O Lord, thou preservest man and beast.*

7. *How excellent* is *thy loving-kindness, O God ! therefore the children of men put their trust under the shadow of thy wings.*

8. *They shall be abundantly satisfied with the fatness of thy house ; and thou shalt make them drink of the river of thy pleasures.*

9. *For with thee* is *the fountain of life : in thy light shall we see light.*

The second part of the psalm, wherein David comforteth himself in God, and settleth his faith on the praiseworthy properties of God. Whence learn, 1. The turning of the believer's eye off the wickedness of adversaries, and looking to God's goodness and wise dispensation, will comfort his heart against all that the enemy can do, and set him on work toward godliness, so much the more as he perceiveth atheism in them ; for when David had pointed out his enemy, he falleth to the praising of God, saying, *thy mercy, O Lord, is in the heavens.* 2. Albeit the carriage of the wicked toward God and the godly doth tend to obscure God's glory in the point of justice toward the one, and point of mercy toward the other, yet the works of creation, and the constant government thereof, shall bear witness of the constancy of God's mercy, and faithfulness, and righteousness, and judgment, as here is shown. 3. Though the effects of God's mercy should not appear to the believer on earth, yet faith will see them in their fountain and cause ; *thy mercy, O Lord,* saith the believer, *is in heaven.* 4. Let God's works and his word be compared together, and the truth of his promises and threatenings shall be so traced, and seem to be true, as shall satisfy us, and let us see so far till our eye can follow no farther ; *thy faithfulness reacheth unto the clouds.* 5. Whatsoever carnal reason may judge of God's dispensations towards the godly and the wicked, yet his holiness and justice is firm and unchangeable ; *thy righteousness is like the great mountains.* 6. Albeit we cannot see through matters, nor reconcile cross cogitations, sometimes offered from the grounds of faith on the one hand, and from the effects of providence offered by sense on the other hand, yet must we remember that God is wiser than we, and his deep draughts are past finding out by us; *thy judgments are a great deep.* 7. This one consideration of God's course of kindness to his own creatures, making his sun to shine and his rain to fall on his enemies as on his friends, may quiet our mind concerning God's sparing for a time the wicked, and liberal dealing with them; *O Lord, thou preservest man and beast.* There is a course of common preservation and kindness running unto all. 8. Over and above common kindness, there is a more entire, special, and precious love and kindness toward believers in God, which is inexpressible and wanteth comparison; *how excellent,* or precious, *is thy loving-kindness, O God!* saith David, speaking of this. 9. The belief of God's readiness to let forth this love, may, and should, and doth animate men to draw near unto him, albeit they have as yet no experience of the fruits of it; *therefore the children of men that put trust under the shadow of thy wings.* 10. The Lord, without exception of any to whom he sendeth the gospel, and without exception of any within the visible church, doth offer to be reconciled through Christ Jesus to every man who shall fly into the propitiatory and mercy-seat erected in Jesus Christ, who is God incarnate, according as he was holden forth in the figure of the golden ark of the covenant, and the stretched forth wings of the cherubim, as is here said, *therefore the children of men put their trust under the shadow of thy wings.* 11. Such as do not give the lie to God when they find not at first what they hoped for, but indeed believe in his word, and wait on till he make his word good to them; such as do not tempt or take essay of God, as if they would see what believing may do, and then quit their gripes if their expectation be not answered—but indeed trust God upon his word, and resolve to die with the gripe in their hand of his freely offered covenant of grace in Christ, and of his promises made to them that fly to him for refuge,—shall be sure to be in more respect with God than common subjects. They shall be domestics of his house, of the household of faith, to whom God shall keep a table furnished for spiritual life unto them; he shall make them now and then, when it is meet time for the hungry, to feed abundantly and to be satisfied; *they that put their trust under the shadow of thy wings, shall be abundantly satisfied with the goodness of thy house.* 12. In the use of the means and holy ordinances of God given to his church, God shall make the man that indeed giveth him credit upon the word of his grace, sensibly feel the joy of the holy Spirit to be unspeakable and full of glory, and that there are greater contentments to be found for a man's soul in God, reconciled through Christ, than the world can yield beside ; for, *thou shalt make them drink of the rivers of thy pleasures.* 13. Whatsoever can be found in the creature, even when God blesseth the use thereof to his own children, is but a drop from the ocean, is but a little water out of the well, in comparison of what a believer will see and feel to be in God reconciled through Christ ; for, *with thee is the fountain of life.* 14. No light save the light of God's revealed word in the holy Scriptures for the mirror, no light but the light of God's Spirit illuminating the mirror, can make a man understand, or believe, or sensibly discern, the wisdom, comfort, and felicity which are held forth to his church in his ordinances, and felt in himself by experience ; *in thy light*, saith he, *shall we see light.*

10. *O continue thy loving-kindness unto them that know thee; and thy righteousness to the upright in heart.*

11. *Let not the foot of pride come against me, and let not the hand of the wicked remove me.*

12. *There are the workers of iniquity fallen: they are cast down, and shall not be able to rise.*

The last part of the psalm, wherein he prayeth for all believers, himself being included, and then for himself in particular. Whence learn, 1. The true mark of a godly man standeth in the conjunction of faith in God with sincere study of obedience to him, for he is the man that knoweth God, and is upright in heart. 2. Albeit what the believer hath found in God by experience, he may expect it shall be continued unto him, both for his entertainment by God, and defence and deliverance in his righteous cause from his enemies ; yet must he follow his confidence with prayer: *O continue thy loving-kindness unto them that know thee, and thy righteousness to the upright in heart.* 3. As we have no right to any benefit, but in so far as we are of the number of upright-hearted believers, so should we seek every benefit we would have, as being of this number, and as seeking that others may be sharers with us, as David doth before. 4. It is the Lord only who can divert proud persecutors, that they hurt not his children, and it is the Lord only who can keep his children in the course of faith and obedience, when the wicked employ their power against them. Therefore David prayeth, *let not the foot of pride come against me, and let not the hand of the wicked remove me.* 5. The ruin of the enemies of the godly is as certain as if it were already past, yea, faith may look upon it through the prospect of the word of God as if it were to be seen and pointed out to others to behold with their eyes; *there are the workers of iniquity fallen.* 6. The fall of the wicked is not like the fall of the godly, for though the godly fall sundry times, yet they recover their feet again; but a fall is prepared for the wicked, after which they shall not recover themselves; *they are cast down, and shall not be able to rise.*

PSALM XXXVII.
A Psalm of David.

This psalm tendeth to guard the godly against the ordinary temptations unto envy, emulation, fretting, and discouragement in the way of godliness, arising from the temporal prosperity of the wicked, and that by eight directions or counsels from the Lord; each of them is confirmed by reasons, most of which are comparisons of the blessed estate of the godly at the worst, with the estate of the wicked at their best. The first direction or counsel, v. 1, 2; the second, v. 3; the third, v. 4; the fourth, v. 5, 6; the fifth, v. 7; the sixth, v. 8—26; the seventh v. 27—33; the eighth direction, v. 34 to the end.

1. *Fret not thyself because of evil-doers, neither be thou envious against the workers of iniquity:*

2. *For they shall soon be cut down like the grass, and wither as the green herb.*

The first direction is to beware of fretting at, or envying of, the prosperity of the wicked, because their prosperity is but temporal. Whence learn, 1. Wicked men may be in a more prosperous condition in the world than the godly, and oftentimes, yea, and for the most part are; for this is presupposed here, as an ordinary temptation in all ages and places. 2. Albeit carnal reason, and suggestions of Satan and corrupt nature, from the prosperity of the wicked, and the ordinary troubles of the godly, furnish temptations unto the godly to be malcontents with God's dispensation, yet should

8

the godly take heed that they be not overcome by, or yield in any sort to, this temptation : *fret not thyself because of evil-doers.* 3. As temptation to malcontentment maketh assaults, on the one hand, to render the godly weary of well-doing, so temptation to emulate the course of the wicked, and following their way, assault, on the other hand, but should no way get place : *neither be thou envious against the workers of iniquity.* 4. If it were well considered that all the prosperity of the wicked is but in things concerning the outward man, and that this prosperity is but temporal, and often of shorter continuance than a man's own brittle life, there should be no ground of envy found therein ; *for they shall soon be cut down like the grass, and wither as the green herb.*

3. *Trust in the Lord, and do good :* so *shalt thou dwell in the land, and verily thou shalt be fed.*

From the second point of God's counsel and direction, learn, 1. Holding fast the covenant of grace made with God, through Christ, and studying to bring out the fruits of faith, in obedience to God's command, is a sovereign remedy against malcontentment with a man's own condition, and against envying the wicked : *trust in the Lord, and do good.* 2. Continuance in the faith and obedience of God, whatsoever temptation we meet with, is the surest way to have God's blessing in this life, and to have heaven, represented by Canaan, after this life: *trust in the Lord, and do good, so shalt thou dwell in the land.* 3. The upright believer in God is the only man that gets the right use of the creature, and into whose cup the true juice of God's benefits, being pressed out, is poured ; whose bread is dipped in oil, and in whom spiritual life is constantly entertained : *verily thou,* that art such a man, *shalt be fed.*

4. *Delight thyself also in the Lord; and he shall give thee the desires of thine heart.*

From the third direction to ward off the temptation, learn, 1. The godly man hath warrant to make God the object of his delight, who, being reconciled to the believer through the Mediator, is become the believer's own, in whom he may continually rejoice ; but the object of the ungodly prosperous man's delight is but some creature, or temporal trifle ; for to the believer it is said, *delight thyself in the Lord.*   2. Though the believer be rich in his rights, yet he is slow to make use thereof, and hath need to be stirred up to take possession : *delight thyself.*   3. If the believer shall make use of his covenant right and interest in God, and set his affections upon him, he shall find such solid contentment and satisfaction in God, as he shall not envy the condition of the most prosperous wicked man in the world ; for it is said, *delight thyself in the Lord, and he will give thee the desires of thy heart.*   And certainly the forgetting, or not hearkening to this direction, is the cause of our being malcontented with our lot, and of our envying the wicked.

5. *Commit thy way unto the Lord; trust also in him, and he shall bring* it *to pass :*

6. *And he shall bring forth thy righteousness as the light, and thy judgment as the noon-day.*

From the fourth direction, learn, 1. When we bear the burden of our own affairs ourselves, and are chastened with anxiety and want of success, and with envying the ungodly who prosper better than we do ; the best remedy is, first, to do our duty, as we are enabled, in the use of the means ; then cast the care of the success over on God, as the plough-man doth when he hath harrowed his land, and let the burden of it rest on God, and let us not take it off him again, but put our mind to rest, resolved to take the harvest in good part, as he shall send it : *commit thy way unto the Lord, trust also in him.*   2. The man who followeth this direction shall come to speed best in his affairs, because God shall do that wherewith the man shall have reason to be satisfied, for that which he would have done, or what is better, shall be effected : *commit thy cause unto the Lord, and he shall bring it to pass.*   3. It is possible that the godly, following this counsel, may be misreported of, and both lose his labour and estimation among men, yet it shall not be long so ; for *God shall bring forth thy righteousness as the light.*   4. Albeit the godly and his cause may be obscured by a shorter or longer winter-night of trouble, as shall please God to appoint, yet shall he, and his cause and integrity, be found absolved by God in due time : *he shall bring forth thy judgment,* or decree of absolution, *as the noon-day.*

7. *Rest in the Lord, and wait patiently for him : fret*

*not thyself because of him who prospereth in his way,
because of the man who bringeth wicked devices to pass.*

From the fifth direction, learn, 1. The victory over the
temptation to envy the wicked is not gotten at first, nor by
carnal reason, but by faith in God, and patient waiting on
him : *rest on the Lord, and wait patiently for him.*   2. As
the temptation to fretting is very pressing, when we see the
wicked get so much of their will, so much of their purpose
brought to pass ; so we have need to be pressed again and
again to resist this temptation : therefore is it said again,
*fret not thyself because of him who prospereth in his way,
because of the man who bringeth wicked devices to pass.*

8. *Cease from anger, and forsake wrath : fret not
thyself in anywise to do evil.*

The sixth direction is to curb this temptation, in case it
hath already defiled and fired a man's spirit, lest it break
out, and make the believer put forth his hand to iniquity.
Whence learn, 1. The insolence of the wicked is such, and
their provocation of the godly ofttimes so great, that their
spirits are much stirred and kindled with indignation and
thoughts of private revenge ; yet must not this passion prevail with the godly, but should be striven against : *cease from
anger, and forsake wrath ;* vengeance is the Lord's, he will
repay.   2. The godly should eschew the motions of fretting,
anger, or envy against the wicked ; and if anger enter, he
must cease from it : if it urge itself on him with pretences of
reason or violent impulse, he must *forsake it ;* but by any
means he must keep this temptation within doors, that it
drive him not to break forth to a completed sin in action
and doing wrong : *fret not thyself in anywise to do evil.*

9. *For evil-doers shall be cut off : but those that wait
upon the Lord, they shall inherit the earth.*

The prophet presseth this direction by sundry reasons ;
and in special, by six comparisons of the Lord's way and
purpose about the wicked and the godly, how prosperous
soever the wicked may be for a time, and howsoever the
godly may be afflicted and exercised for a time.   The first
comparison is in this verse.   Whence learn, 1. If any who
pretend to be godly shall, by the foresaid temptation, forsake the way of godliness and follow the way of the wicked,
they shall have the reward of the wicked for changing their

way : *for evil-doers shall be cut off.*   2. It is not the present condition wherein men are which is to be looked to, but what shall become of them at length ; for all the prosperity of the wicked is blasted with this one sentence of the supreme Judge : *evil-doers shall be cut off.*   3. Albeit the godly be kept in some hardships for a time, as young heirs in their minority ; yet shall their inheritance in heaven (represented by the land of Canaan) be reserved unto them ; and, in the meantime, by their heirship in Christ, they have solid right to what portion in this world God alloweth them ; they have the use thereof with a good conscience, and remain on the earth as long as God hath service for them, however the wicked would thrust them out of the world as unworthy of it : and if they be banished out of one country, they know that *the earth is the Lord's, and the fulness thereof,* and they live more contentedly in that condition, than the wicked in their nest : for *those that wait upon the Lord, they shall inherit the earth.*

10. *For yet a little while, and the wicked* shall *not* be : *yea, thou shalt diligently consider his place, and it* shall *not* be.

11. *But the meek shall inherit the earth ; and shall delight themselves in the abundance of peace.*

From the second comparison of the wicked and the godly, learn, 1. We must not pass sentence suddenly, to absolve their way who are prosperous, or condemn their way who are crossed ; but we should wait upon God's word till God, from heaven, manifest his judgment about both, which shall not long be delayed in regard of the wicked ; *for yet a little while, and the wicked shall not be : yea, thou shalt diligently consider his place, and it shall not be.*   2. Submission unto God's dispensation allayeth all troubles, and enlargeth the good of every benefit ; and a good construction of God's dealing with us bringeth much peace and quietness of mind with it, and enricheth our portion : *the meek shall inherit the earth ; and shall delight themselves in the abundance of peace.*

12. *The wicked plotteth against the just, and gnasheth upon him with his teeth.*

13. *The Lord shall laugh at him ; for he seeth that his day is coming.*

14. *The wicked have drawn out the sword, and have bent their bow, to cast down the poor and needy,* and *slay such as be of upright conversation.*

15. *Their sword shall enter into their own heart, and their bows shall be broken.*

The third comparison of the wicked and godly looseth a doubt, when the godly cannot get living in their mean condition, in presence of the wicked, but their life is also in peril by their plotting, for the effectuating the destruction of the godly. Whence learn, 1. The godly have not only to wrestle against the thriving condition of the wicked, but also with their deadly hatred ; *the wicked plot against the righteous, and gnasheth upon him with his teeth.* 2. The godly must make the Lord to be party against the wicked, and must oppose his justice, power, and wisdom to the enmity of the wicked ; for albeit the godly be forced to mourn at their threatening, yet their plotting and prattling against the godly, as if they could do any thing of themselves, is ridiculous ; *the Lord shall laugh at them.* 3. If the godly did consider of the wicked, as the word of the Lord speaketh of them, they might look upon their boasts, as on the brags of a man upon the scaffold, ready to be executed ; *for, God seeth his day is coming.* 4. The godly must resolve to bear the open violence also of the wicked, and to be made as butts for their arrows, and sheaths for their swords, which is more than their words ; for, *the wicked have drawn out the sword, and bent their bow.* 5. Before deliverance come unto the godly, they shall find themselves in a weak condition, for any thing they can do for themselves ; for here they are poor and needy, and the wicked thinks *to cast them down.* 6. Those are the truly godly, and the objects of the wicked's malice, who for their inward condition depend on God in the sense of their poverty and neediness, and withal are of *an upright conversation,* as they are here described. 7. When the wicked are most near to do a mischief to the Lord's people, then is a mischief most near unto them ; *their sword shall enter into their own heart, and their bows shall be broken.*

16. *A little that a righteous man hath is better than the riches of many wicked.*

17. *For the arms of the wicked shall be broken : but the Lord upholdeth the righteous.*

The fourth comparison of the godly and wicked, looseth another doubt about the wealth and power of the wicked. Whence learn, 1. The odds between men's living and means of livelihood stands not in more or less abundance of worldly goods, but in God's blessing, which because it accompanieth the provision of the godly, have they less or have they more ; therefore, *a little that one righteous man hath, is better than the riches of many wicked.*   2. The little something of the godly's provision is made to subsist for the poor man's standing, while the power and wealth of the wicked comes to nothing ; *for the arms of the wicked shall be broken : but the Lord upholdeth the righteous.*

18. *The Lord knoweth the days of the upright ; and their inheritance shall be for ever.*

19. *They shall not be ashamed in the evil time ; and in the days of famine they shall be satisfied.*

20. *But the wicked shall perish, and the enemies of the Lord* shall be *as the fat of lambs : they shall consume ; into smoke shall they consume away.*

From the fifth comparison of the godly and wicked, learn 1. The godly have two advantages above the wicked ; one in this life, another in the life to come.   For the first, all the vicissitudes of dangers and daily necessities of the godly are taken notice of in a special way by God choosing and weighing to them exercises for their condition, moderating them in their measure and time, seasoning them with mixture of consolation, turning them to their best, furnishing all necessaries to bear out their exercises, and sending particular deliverances, one after another ; *for the Lord knows the days of the upright.*   As for the next life, he hath reserved for them an inheritance of constant blessedness, never to be taken from them ; *their inheritance shall be for ever.* 2. Albeit the Lord will not exempt the godly from sharing in common calamities with the wicked, yet shall they have the evidences of God's favour to them in the time of trouble, and shall not be disappointed of the kindness promised by God and expected by them ; *they shall not be ashamed in the evil time.* 3. Whatsoever scant or inlack be of creature-comfort, the godly shall be supplied to their reasonable satisfaction ; *in the days of famine they shall be satisfied.* 4. When the wicked are most liberally dealt with, it is but a feeding

of them like beasts to the slaughter; all their glory shall vanish, and they themselves shall be destroyed in God's wrath :
*but the wicked shall perish, the enemies of the Lord shall be
as fat of lambs, they shall consume into smoke, they shall
consume away.*

21. *The wicked borroweth, and payeth not again :
but the righteous sheweth mercy, and giveth.*

22. *For* such as be *blessed of him shall inherit the
earth ; and* they that be *cursed of him shall be cut off.*

From the sixth comparison, learn, 1. In the midst of the
wicked man's wealth he is ofttimes wanting, as if he were a
poor man ; if he have much wealth, he hath much to do
with it, and many times is unable to defray his charges
without borrowing ; and when he has borrowed, he is either
unable or unwilling to pay again, and so is but a miserable
wretch with all he hath ; or he is a profuse prodigal and
deceiver of his creditors : *the wicked borroweth, and payeth
not again.* 2. On the contrary, the righteous man, by his
godly behaviour, manageth the little which God giveth him
so well, as he needeth not to borrow ; he wanteth not for
any good work which God calleth him unto, and is able to
supply others' necessities : *the righteous showeth mercy, and
giveth.* 3. The blessing of God on the godly maketh the
odds betwixt them and the wicked, for it is to him as good
as the inheritance of the whole earth; but God's curse
rooteth the wicked man out of the earth ; for, *such,* saith
he, *as be blessed of him, shall inherit the earth ; and they
that be cursed, shall be cut off.*

23. *The steps of* a good *man are ordered by the
Lord ; and he delighteth in his way.*

24. *Though he fall, he shall not be utterly cast down:
for the Lord upholdeth* him with *his hand.*

25. *I have been young, and* now *am old ; yet have I
not seen the righteous forsaken, nor his seed begging
bread.*

26. He is *ever merciful, and lendeth ; and his seed*
is *blessed.*

He closeth the confirmation of the sixth direction with
enumerating sundry privileges of the godly, of some whereof
he made observation in his own time. Whence learn, 1. The
privileges of the godly are so great as should content him,

albeit his outward prosperity and wealth be not such as he conceiveth the wicked to have; for God teacheth the godly how to behave himself in his particular actions, prudently and holily; *the steps of a good man are ordered of the Lord*, he approveth the course the godly man keepeth: *he delights in his way.* Though the godly man through infirmity fall into a sin, or by his sin draw a calamity on himself, yet the Lord recovereth him again: *though he fall, he shall not be utterly cast down;* and that he perish not when he falleth, the Lord shall preserve him by holding a grip of him: *the Lord upholdeth him with his hand.* 2. Albeit the Lord will not exempt the godly from poverty, nor yet their seed; albeit we presuppose the children be godly also, if he think it good to exercise them so, yet the Lord hath made the examples of such misery so rare, as a man of good years could observe few or none of them beggars; especially in the prophet's time, when God by external benefits was training his people to the hope of spiritual things, as David here testifieth. 3. It is a gift of God to use whatsoever a man receiveth of God, so as others be helped thereby: *the godly is ever merciful, and lendeth.* 4. The readiest way to bring a blessing to a man's house and posterity, is to be godly himself; for, *the godly man's seed is blessed.*

27. *Depart from evil, and do good; and dwell for evermore.*

28. *For the Lord loveth judgment, and forsaketh not his saints; they are preserved for ever: but the seed of the wicked shall be cut off.*

29. *The righteous shall inherit the land, and dwell therein for ever.*

From the seventh direction and the reasons thereof, teaching how to guard against fretting at, and envying of, the prosperity of the wicked, learn, 1. To meet an injury with another injury, or to recompense evil for evil, or to forbear to do good where it is not deserved, is not the way to be blessed; but, on the contrary, the way of possessing settled felicity is *to depart from evil, and to do good; so shall a man dwell for ever.* 2. The love that the Lord beareth to righteousness, is the cause why it cannot but be well with the righteous; for, *the Lord loveth judgment.* 3. The Lord may well exercise his children with trouble, yet he will not withdraw himself from them in trouble, but will stay with

them, and bear them company, and save them to the uttermost: *he forsaketh not his saints; they are preserved for
ever.*   4. As wickedness is the ready way to root out a man
and his family from off the earth, so is righteousness the way
to establish a man's family, and to bring himself to a solid
habitation with God for ever ; for, *the seed of the wicked
shall be cut off.   The righteous shall inherit the land, and
dwell therein for ever ;* that is, in heaven, signified by that
land.

30. *The mouth of the righteous speaketh wisdom,
and his tongue talketh of judgment.*

31. *The law of his God is in his heart ; none of his
steps shall slide.*

Because so much is spoken of the righteous man, he describeth him by three properties ; one in his words, another
in his affections, a third in his deliberate actions and course
of his ways and life.   Whence learn, 1. The righteous man
studieth in his speeches to glorify God, and edify those he
speaketh to, and in all things he is truth's friend ; *the mouth
of the righteous speaketh wisdom, and his tongue talketh of
judgment.*   2. For his affections, he loveth that which is
commanded of God, and hateth that which is forbidden him,
because God hath taken him into covenant with himself to be
his man ; *the law of God is in his heart.*   3. For his course
of life, whatsoever temptation he meeteth with, to divert
him from the faith and obedience of God, he will not choose
another way than the law of his God ; *none of his steps shall
slide.*

32. *The wicked watcheth the righteous, and seeketh
to slay him.*

33. *The Lord will not leave him in his hand nor
condemn him when he is judged.*

For clearing of the seventh direction, he answereth an
objection from the persecutions which the righteous are subject unto from the wicked.   Whence learn, 1. Temporal
blessings or benefits are not so promised to the godly, as
that they shall be free from troubles, crosses, and persecutions ; for the Lord, for his own glory, for edification of
his church, for conviction of his enemies, and for perfecting his children in holiness, useth to suffer the wicked to
hunt and persecute them, even to death ; *the wicked watch-*

eth the righteous, and seeketh to slay him. 2. The wicked
may apprehend the righteous man's person, lay false accu-
sations to his charge, and bring him before judges, and not
get his will of him, to drive him from a righteous cause ;
for, *the Lord will not leave him in his hand.* 3. Albeit the
righteous man by persecutions may be judged and condemned to death unjustly, yet may he be more than a conqueror through God that loveth him, and careth for him ;
for God will not condemn him when he is judged ; and that
may suffice him against whatsoever flesh can do to him.

34. *Wait on the Lord, and keep his way, and he
shall exalt thee to inherit the land : when the wicked
are cut off, thou shalt see it.*

35. *I have seen the wicked in great power, and
spreading himself like a green bay-tree :*

36. *Yet he passed away, and, lo, he was not ; yea,
I sought him, but he could not be found.*

The eighth direction is to wait on God, and to keep his
way ; serving, with the former direction, to guard the godly
man's heart against all the temptations of fretting, envy,
anger, and emulation, because of the wicked man's seemingly more prosperous condition in the world than his own ;
and this direction is confirmed with five reasons.   Whence
learn, 1. He that believeth on God must not make haste,
nor judge rashly of matters as they seem for the present,
but must attend till God make his word good ; *wait on the
Lord.* 2. True patient hope and waiting on God, must be
joined with the study of obedience to God's directions ; *wait
on the Lord, and keep his way.* 3. Though the godly be
kept under for a while and humbled, yet God shall lift them
up to a satisfactory estate ; *he shall exalt thee to inherit the
land.*   This promise is the first reason to move us to wait
on the Lord.   In every age some of the wicked shall be
made spectacles of God's threatened judgment, before the
eyes of the godly, to give assurance of his judgment ; that
he shall overthrow all the rest in due time, and avenge on
them all the wrongs done by them unto the godly : *when
the wicked are cut off, thou shalt see it.*   And this is the
second argument to confirm the exhortation. 4. How the
wicked have seemed very glorious in the world for a while,
and shortly both they and their glory vanished, every man
in his own time should make his own remarks and obser-

vations, as the prophet showeth here, that he had his observations in his time, v. 35, 36. And this is the third reason to confirm the direction taken from experience concerning the wicked.

37. *Mark the perfect* man, *and behold the upright : for the end of* that *man* is *peace.*

38. *But the transgressors shall be destroyed together ; the end of the wicked shall be cut off.*

The fourth reason of the direction, is from the happy close of the course of the godly, and the certain perdition of the wicked. Whence learn, 1. The Lord gives so many remarkable instances of the comfortable departure of the godly out of this life, as may give assurance of the dying of all the upright in God's favour ; *mark the upright man, for the end of that man is peace.* 2. Whether men be witnesses or not of the departure of the wicked, one and all of them die in a desperate condition ; they are deprived of heaven and earth, and perish, soul and body, at the expiring of their breath ; *transgressors shall be destroyed together; the end of the wicked shall be cut off.*

39. *But the salvation of the righteous* is *of the Lord ; he* is *their strength in the time of trouble.*

40. *And the Lord shall help them, and deliver them : he shall deliver them from the wicked, and save them, because they trust in him.*

The last reason to move men to wait on God, is from his care of the godly. Whence learn, 1. How hard soever the condition of the godly be, the Lord hath ways of his own to preserve and save them ; yea, the Lord is resolved and hath passed his word that he will save them ; *the salvation of the righteous is of the Lord.* 2. So long as God is pleased to let righteous men's trouble continue, he will now and then comfort them, and will enable them to bear their trouble, when comfort is suspended ; *he is their strength in time of trouble.* 3. When the godly in their trouble feel their own wants and weakness, he will furnish what in them is lacking, till the delivery come ; *the Lord shall help them, and deliver them.* 4. Albeit many be the troubles of the godly, especially from their wicked persecutors, yet by faith in God they shall keep their conscience clean ; their cause they maintain whole, and shall have their souls safe, do what their persecutors can ; *he shall deliver them from the wicked, and save them because they trust in him.*

PSALM XXXVIII.

A psalm of David, to bring to remembrance.

In this psalm, David, in trouble both of soul and body, as an example of the hardest exercises that Christ's followers can fall into, first, prayeth for the mitigation of his trouble, and removal of wrath, v. 1 ; and secondly, layeth out this sense of the trouble which he felt immediately from God, v. 2—8 ; thirdly, having put up his confused desires to God for prayers, in the sense of his inability to express himself, v. 9, 10, he lays out his sense of the grief and troubles which he felt from men, and endured with great patience, v. 11—14 ; fourthly, he sets down the wrestlings he had in prayer to God, because of his persecution by his adversaries, v. 15—20 ; and closeth the psalm, not having gotten comfort for the time, v. 21, 22.

From the inscription, learn, that exercises of conscience, the more heavy they have been, the more should they be remembered, and the passages thereof more carefully marked when the sense is most fresh, lest they pass without the fruit which may be had of them after delivery : for thus much are we taught by the inscription of this psalm, wherein it is entitled, *a psalm of David, to bring to remembrance.*

1. *O Lord, rebuke me not in thy wrath : neither chasten me in thy hot displeasure.*

From his prayer for mitigation of trouble and removal of wrath, learn, 1. It is consistent with God's fatherly love, and our sonship, to taste of fatherly wrath against our sins, as this place proveth. 2. Albeit it is not lawful for us to follow our natural desires in prayer, or to seek to be free of chastisement, yet we may seek mitigation of trouble, and tempering of our cup, so as we may digest it, and we may pray for the removal of fatherly wrath also ; *rebuke me not in thy wrath, nor chasten me in thy hot displeasure.*

2. *For thine arrows stick fast in me, and thy hand presseth me sore.*

3. There is *no soundness in my flesh because of thine anger ; neither* is there any *rest in my bones because of my sin.*

4. *For mine iniquities are gone over mine head; as an heavy burden they are too heavy for me.*

5. *My wounds stink,* and *are corrupt, because of my foolishness.*

6. *I am troubled; I am bowed down greatly; I go mourning all the day long.*

7. *For my loins are filled with a loathsome* disease; and there is *no soundness in my flesh.*

8. *I am feeble and sore broken: I have roared by reason of the disquietness of my heart.*

He giveth reason of his prayer from his pitiful case both in soul and body. Whence learn, 1. When it pleaseth the Lord to make his children sensible of their sins, and of his dreadful justice, he can make the tokens of his displeasure against sin piercing sharp, and pressing heavy; *thy arrows stick fast in me, and thy hand presseth me sore.* 2. Although the Lord should set us as a mark to shoot at, and lay the heaviest load of judgments on us for our sins; yet we must not seek the ease thereof, nor can we have ease from them, save by coming to God himself, to bemoan our misery, as this example teacheth us. 3. As the sense of trouble on our body, or any way else, will waken the conscience of sin; so the conscience of sin and feeling of wrath due for our sin, will make no small alteration on our very bodies; *there is no soundness in my flesh, because of thine anger, nor rest in my bones because of my sin.* 4. One sin will waken the memory of more sins, till they present themselves as an innumerable army; *my iniquities are gone over my head.* 5. How light soever sin may seem when it is committed, it will be found insupportably heavy, when God pursues for it; *as an heavy burden, they are too heavy for me.* 6. When the Lord smiteth the conscience for sin, the rod will not fail to make a wound, which shall have need of the cure of the physician, according to the bruise made by his hand, or deep piercing of his arrows; for after arrows and pressing hand, he mentions wounds more than one. 7. When a wounded spirit is not timously, by a right cure, bound up and healed, the wounds grow the longer the worse; the longer, the more guiltiness, filthiness, and perplexity of spirit grow; *my wounds stink and are corrupt.* 8. As through our inconsideration of our duty, and danger of sinning, we fall actually into sin, and draw upon ourselves wrath ; so by our inconsideration of the right remedy, we augment that measure of both ; *my wounds stink, and are corrupt ; because of my foolishness.* 9. So long as the conscience of sin and sense of wrath kept on thereby last, the man's wit and his courage, and his countenance and his joy are smitten, both before God and men ; *I am troubled, I am bowed down greatly, I go mourning all the day long.* 10. To add to the pace, and to make the sense of sin more bitter, the Lord can lay his hand on the body, and make the loathsomeness of the sickness resemble the loathsomeness of the sin which drew it on, and to speak unto the conscience in its own language, the cause why it is sent unto him ; *for my loins are filled with a loathsome disease ; and there is no soundness in my flesh.* 11. A wounded spirit will dash and beat down the stoutest heart it can meet with ; *I am feeble and sore broken.* 12. If the Lord pursue a man's conscience for sin, and intimate his displeasure against him, and continue this exercise for any time ; it will pass the man's power to hide or smother his grief, or hold in the expressions thereof ; *I have roared by reason of the disquietness of my heart.*

9. *Lord, all my desire is before thee ; and my groaning is not hid from thee.*

10. *My heart panteth, my strength faileth me : as for the light of mine eyes, it also is gone from me.*

In the third place, that he may bring forth the trouble which he suffered from men, and his patience towards them, he presenteth his heart to God, as if it was full of confused desires, instead of explicit prayers, being now unable to express himself more largely. · Whence learn, 1. As sin causeth wrath, and wrath sore strokes and sorrow ; so these evils looked upon, should waken desires to have them removed, and send us to seek the true remedy thereof in God, as here the psalmist doth. 2. As desires and groans, if they be presented to God, have their own speech, which we cannot express in time of confusion ; so should we account them, not as vanishing expressions of nature, but as prayers stirred up by God, and standing before him till they receive their answer ; *Lord, all my desire is before thee.* 3. It is not wrestling with trouble within ourselves, nor vent-

ing our grief as natural men, which can give us ease, but
pouring out our heart before the Lord which must do it ;
all my desire is before thee. 4. The strength of faith in the
godly is not so great as to swallow up all infirmities ; but
so great as to wrestle with them, and confess them to God,
who useth to supply his own with his strength and wise direction, when their own strength is evacuated, and the man
is before God humbled ; for here even *David's heart panteth
and his strength faileth him, and the light of his eyes is gone
from him ;* not so much in regard of the body's decay, as in
his spiritual condition, expressed in bodily terms ; and thus
much for the troubles, which he felt immediately from God's
hand.

11. *My lovers and my friends stand aloof from my
sore, and my kinsmen stand afar off.*

12. *They also that seek after my life lay snares* for
me ; *and they that seek my hurt speak mischievous things,
and imagine deceits all the day long.*

13. *But I, as a deaf* man, *heard not ; and* I was *as
a dumb man* that *openeth not his mouth.*

14. *Thus I was as a man that heareth not, and in
whose mouth* are *no reproofs.*

From the troubles which he felt from men, learn, 1. A
wounded spirit is a disease which the natural man hath no
skill of, nor will to meddle with, but flieth from it, as from a
plague or pest ; *my lovers and my friends stand aloof from
my sore.* 2. In time of sad affliction and narrow trial of
our faith, natural bonds between us and our kinsfolk will
shrink and fail us, so as we shall have little comfort in the
earth ; *my kinsmen stand afar off.* 3. In time of sad exercises and hard trials, as friends may fail, so enemies may
make head ; and, by craft and cruelty, by slander and cun-
ning policy, open enmity and secret plotting, may conspire
against a man's fame, good cause, and life ; *they also that
seek after my life, lay snares for me ; and they that seek my
hurt, speak mischievous things, and imagine deceits all the
day long.* 4. The more emptied, afflicted, disconsolate, forsaken of friends, and pursued by foes, a man be ; if he go to
God for reconciliation and relief, he hath ground of hope to be
helped, and to have God engaged to him so much the more ;
for here David maketh this use of all his troubles, he layeth

all out before God.   5. It is possible, yea and ofttimes cometh to pass, that the godly have so many lies made of them, calumnies and slanders devised and vented against them by so many mouths, that they are not able to follow them, or to answer and refute them, but are forced to mis- ken them, and in patience hold themselves quiet till God make matters clear for them ; *but I as a deaf man heard not, and as a dumb man opened not my mouth.*   6. When the godly, overloaden with a multitude of calumnies and a multitude of enemies backing them, sit down in patient si- lence, not seeing to what purpose they speak, they are taken readily as guilty, or as such who cannot refute the thing which is alleged of them, nor maintain the truth which they profess ; and this is an addition unto all the rest of their trouble, as David importeth, saying : *thus was I as a man that heareth not, and in whose mouth are no reproofs.*

15. *For in thee, O Lord, do I hope : thou wilt hear, O Lord my God.*

16. *For I said,* Hear me, *lest* otherwise *they should rejoice over me : when my foot slippeth, they magnify* themselves *against me.*

17. *For I* am *ready to halt, and my sorrow* is *con- tinually before me.*

18. *For I will declare mine iniquity ; I will be sorry for my sin.*

19. *But* mine enemies are *lively,* and *they are strong ; and they that hate me wrongfully are multiplied.*

20. *They also that render evil for good are mine ad- versaries ; because I follow* the thing that *good* is.

In the fourth place, he setteth down his wrestling against his persecutors, seeking to destroy both him and his righteous cause.   Hence learn, 1. It is a sore and high degree of the trial of the godly, when at one time God pursueth for sin, and friends withdraw from them in the duties of humanity, and persecutors are likely to destroy their lives, and withal suppress religion in their person by this means ; and yet this hath been the case of many of God's children, and may be also, as this example teaches us ; yea, also our Lord Jesus' condition was like this, when he suffered for our sins.   2. Sore trials cannot be borne without holding fast the grip of the covenant of grace ; for this fixeth faith, and strengtheneth hope, and furnisheth patience in greatest troubles ; for David rendereth this reason for his bearing patiently his foresaid hard condition ; *in thee, O Lord, do I hope ; thou wilt hear, O Lord, my God.* 3. If the covenant be holden fast, whereby we may warrantably call God our God, we may be, as it were, surety to ourselves for a good answer from God ; *thou wilt hear me, O Lord my God.* 4. When the enemies of the godly in their righteous cause, are ready to triumph over the godly and their cause, and the godly are like to be discouraged, if the Lord help not, then the godly may be sure the Lord will hear and help : for David giveth this as a reason of his persuasion, that God would hear him, v. 15, because the enemies otherwise would triumph, and he be made to halt, and turn off the way, v. 16, 17 ; for in this the Lord's glory is interested. 5. When the outward prosperous condition of the godly is changed, and their feet slip, and the hand of the Lord lieth on sore without relaxation, even they of strong faith are ready to be discouraged and faint ; so weak are we in faith when a hard trial cometh ; for, *when the enemy magnified himself against David ; when his feet slipped, when his sorrow was continually before him,* he confesseth he was ready to halt, to warn the godly, that they might guard against this tentation. 6. To keep ourselves from fretting under trouble, it is expedient that we compare our sins with God's fatherly chastisements of us, and that we take course for remission of our sin, and turn the sorrow raised by affliction into godly sorrow for sin ; for this David resolved in his distress ; *I will declare mine iniquity, I will be sorry for my sin.* 7. The Lord so disposeth of the outward condition of the godly and the wicked in this life, that the godly ofttimes have the mourning part, and the wicked the rejoicing part, and that so much the more as they see the head of the godly is borne down ; *I will be sorry for my sin, but mine enemies are lively and strong.* 8. As it is a matter of grief to see the affliction of the godly growing, and the enemies growing in joy, and strength, and number ; so it is a matter of comfort, that the enemies of the godly are enemies without a just cause given to them ; *they that hate me wrongfully, are multiplied.* 9. We must not leave off the doing of what God requireth at our hands, albeit we should have the hatred of the world ; for *David followed that which was good*, albeit his adversaries for that very cause did render to him evil for good.

21. *Forsake me not, O Lord: O my God, be not far from me.*

22. *Make haste to help me, O Lord my salvation.*

He closeth the psalm with prayer, laying all his weight on the covenant, not having gotten comfort for the time. Whence learn, 1. We must not limit the Lord to give us comfort and deliverance when we think we have greatest need of it, but must leave our prayer at his feet, as the prophet doth. 2. The believer must be so wary of leaning to sense, that he must hold the grip of faith not only when he misseth sense of comfort, but also when God's dispensation towards him, and his sense thereof, seem to speak most contrary to faith: *forsake me not, O Lord: be not far from me. Make haste to help me*, saith David's faith, when his sense speaketh what his prayer here importeth; that is, present perdition. 3. The bond of the covenant of grace is able to bear the weight of the believer's heaviest burden, and by virtue of it he may lay claim to God, as his own God, and lay claim also to salvation in him; for, notwithstanding all the troubles and temptations set forth in this psalm, the believer sustaineth all on this ground—*O my God, O Lord my salvation:* and here is the victory of faith.

PSALM XXXIX.

To the chief musician, even to Jeduthun. A psalm of David.

Another such like hard exercise as in the former psalm, wherein David acknowledgeth his infirmity in a passionate expression, when he was in trouble, ver. 1—4; secondly, he recovered and comforted himself, ver. 5—7; thirdly, what was his prayer in this exercise, ver. 8—13.

1. *I said, I will take heed to my ways, that I sin not with my tongue; I will keep my mouth with a bridle, while the wicked is before me.*

2. *I was dumb with silence; I held my peace, even from good; and my sorrow was stirred.*

3. *My heart was hot within me; while I was musing the fire burned:* then *spake I with my tongue.*

4. *Lord, make me to know mine end, and the measure of my days, what it* is; *that I may know how frail I am.*

The prophet, for fear of impatient expression in his trouble, resolved to keep silence in the audience of the wicked, but was not able to keep in his passionate wishing for death. Whence learn, 1. As it is the Lord's will that we should have the infirmities of the saints registered unto us, for our edification, as well as their virtues; so it is his will, that, when the confession of our infirmity may profit others, we should not spare to let it be known, as this passage teacheth us. 2. Consciousness of our weakness, and of the unruliness of our tongues, ready to break forth in the time of temptation, should make us take better heed to ourselves, and to watch over our speech: *I said, I will take heed to my ways, that I sin not with my tongue.* 3. Because the wicked may take advantage of the godly's miscarrying in time of their trouble, it is the more needful to watch over our behaviour and words in their presence : *I will keep my mouth with a bridle, while the wicked is before me.* 4. When we are about to keep in our corruptions, and amend our faults by our own way of it, by our wisdom, strength, or resolutions, we do not eschew the evil we would eschew, and we also fall into a fault we were not aware of ; as here, instead of praying to God to direct one part of his speech after another, that he might speak prudently in the audience of the wicked, he did not speak at all; he did not speak that which he might and should have spoken : *I was dumb with silence ; I held my peace, even from good.* 5. When grief is not rightly vented but suppressed, it is not thereby assuaged but rather increased : *I held my peace, and my sorrow was stirred.* 6. The power of sinful nature and enraged passion is such, that even when they are opposed by reason of strength of grace in us, they may easily overpower us, except God put to his hand to help us in the conflict: *my heart was hot within me : while I was musing the fire burned : then spake I with my tongue.* 7. It is a natural evil in man, when he is overcome by trouble in this life, to wish for death, expecting to be in a better condition by the change ; as the sick man expecteth ease by changing his bed ; and here, v. 4, we have the example of it. 8. The shortness of this life is a mitigation of the troubles thereof unto the godly, and the fear that life should continue longer than the afflicted man wisheth, augmenteth his trouble ; and this is the fountain of this passionate and curious wish :

Lord, make me to know mine end, and the measure of my days, what it is; that I may know how frail I am.

5. *Behold, thou hast made my days as an hand-breadth, and mine age is as nothing before thee: verily every man at his best estate is altogether vanity. Selah.*

6. *Surely every man walketh in a vain shew; surely they are disquieted in vain: he heapeth up riches, and knoweth not who shall gather them.*

7. *And now, Lord, what wait I for? my hope is in thee.*

In the second place, not being answered in this curious question, but secretly checked for his impatient wish, he contents himself with the known truth, that this present life is but short, how long soever it shall last, and resolveth to wait on God's time patiently. Whence learn, 1. For tempering our condition, whatsoever it be, it should suffice us to know that, whether we be in prosperity or adversity, our time in this life is but short: *thou hast made my days as an hand-breadth, and mine age is as nothing before thee.* 2. Not in prosperity, but in adversity, is the uncertainty, weakness, emptiness, and vanity, of prosperity and things temporal, well seen; for in trouble, says David, *verily every man at his best estate is altogether vanity.* 3. Whatsoever seemeth excellent in the eyes of natural men in this world, is but the shadow of what it seemeth: health, strength, prosperity, riches, pleasure, honour, dominion, power, authority, are but the shadows of things so named: *every man walketh in a vain shew.* 4. Too much care and anxiety about things of this life, is a sickness and folly: *surely they are disquieted in vain.* 5. Experience putteth a deep stamp of the truth upon a man's mind, and causes him to set his subscription unto it without hesitation: *verily, surely, surely,* is the seal of this truth here delivered after his experience. 6. The excessive care which men take to gather riches, this toiling and travailing, this spending of body, of wit and time, this frowning on some and fawning to others, this pleading and fighting with some and flattering of others, with other shifts by which men use to gather riches, (which they must leave behind them, and do not know to whom,) is a point of great folly and vanity in men: *he heapeth up riches, and knoweth not who shall gather them.* 7. The right use of the per-

ceived vanity of all things under the sun, is, that we should
be sent by that consideration unto God, to rest on him : *and
now, Lord, what wait I for?*   8. That which God hath
promised in the life to come is only satisfactory and able to
quiet a man's mind, and make him patiently wait on God
in all his trouble: *what wait I for? my hope is in thee.*

8. *Deliver me from all my transgressions ; make me
not the reproach of the foolish.*

9. *I was dumb, I opened not my mouth ; because thou
didst* it.

10. *Remove thy stroke away from me : I am consumed by the blow of thine hand.*

11. *When thou with rebukes dost correct man for
iniquity, thou makest his beauty to consume away like
a moth : surely every man* is *vanity.   Selah.*

12. *Hear my prayer, O Lord, and give ear unto my
cry ; hold not thy peace at my tears: for I* am *a
stranger with thee,* and *a sojourner, as all my fathers*
were.

13. *O spare me, that I may recover strength, before
I go hence, and be no more.*

In the third place, he prayeth to be freed from his sins
and the sense of God's wrath, using sundry reasons to help
his faith.   Whence learn, 1. Seeing sin plungeth us into
all perplexities, and bringeth trouble after trouble upon us,
the best cure of our trouble is to seek pardon for our sins :
deliver me from all my transgressions. 2. The ungodly are
fools, let them seem to themselves and others what they
please ; for all their way and work is to make themselves
miserable ; therefore the scripture calleth them *foolish.*   3.
That the wicked get no advantage of us, so as by troubling
us to drive us from the profession of righteousness, for
which they persecute us, should be the main care of every
believer under persecution ; for this is David's prayer : *make
me not the reproach of the foolish.*   4. It is usual for us to
see our duty, after we have sinned, better than before ; for,
after experience of his falling, he resolveth it to be his duty
not to speak an impatient word, but *to be silent, and not
open his mouth ;* to wit, impatiently.   5. The consideration
of God for our party, with whom we have to do in trouble,
should humble us and make us quiet : David saith, he should

not have openedh is mouth, *because thou, Lord, didst it.*
6. Prayer for removing the tokens of God's displeasure, especially after prayer for remission of sins, is not contrary to patience and silent submission under God's hand ; for he prayeth also, *remove away thy stroke from me.*　7. When we feel the Lord's hand heavy upon us, we may bemoan ourselves to him, with submission to his will ; for he pitieth us, and will lay no more on us than we are able to bear : *I am consumed by the blow of thy hand.*　8. The stoutest and strongest courage will soon be brought down by trouble of conscience ; when God entereth into judgment with him, man falls down : *when thou with rebukes dost correct man for iniquity, thou makest his beauty to consume away like a moth : surely every man is vanity.*　9. When God seemeth to refuse to hear prayer, true faith will follow God with more fervent prayer, and crying, and tears, and not leave God without a good answer : *hear my prayer, O Lord, and give ear unto my cry ; hold not thy peace at my tears.*
10. The more our hearts are alienated from this world and conversant with God by faith, the more we miss our country, our parents, our kinsmen on earth, and have our conversation in heaven ; the more we may be assured that God shall avow himself to be our God : *I am a stranger with thee, and a sojourner.*　11. Entering ourselves heirs unto the godly, who lived before us in their estrangements from the world, and seeking after heaven, entitleth us unto their comforts also ; *I am a sojourner, as all my fathers were.*
12. It is a usual temptation unto the godly in their trouble, that they shall never be relieved out of it in this life : *O spare me, before I go hence.*　13. The godly may pray for a little breathing before death, with submission, that they may the more quietly render up their spirits to God : *spare me, that I may recover strength, before I go hence, and be no more.*　14. If the Lord hearkeneth not to us when we would, let us leave our petition beside him till he answer it, as here the prophet doth.

PSALM XL.

To the chief musician.　A psalm of David.

David, as a type of Christ in the whole psalm, and as an example of the exercise of the godly, giveth thanks for the experience of God's delivering him out of a notable trouble, v. 1—4.　In the second place,

he is led on in his thanksgiving to praise God for the great work of
redemption by Christ the Son of God coming into the world, which is
the fountain of all other mercies to the saints, v. 5—8. In the third
place, David in type, and Christ in the accomplishment, giving account of his prophetical office, intercedeth and prayeth for the evidence
of God's favour to himself personally and mystically considered, v. 9—
13: and for disappointment of his enemies, v. 14, 15, and for the
comfort of all the godly beholding his exercise and his delivery which
he confidently doth expect, v. 16, 17.

1. *I waited patiently for the Lord, and he inclined
unto me, and heard my cry.*

2. *He brought me up also out of an horrible pit, out
of the miry clay, and set my feet upon a rock,* and es-
tablished my goings.

3. *And he hath put a new song in my mouth,* even
praise unto our God: many shall see it, *and fear, and
shall trust in the Lord.*

4. *Blessed* is *that man that maketh the Lord his
trust, and respecteth not the proud, nor such as turn
aside to lies.*

In his thanksgiving, learn, 1. As the Lord of set purpose delayeth to answer the prayer of his own, and sus-
pendeth to help them out of trouble for a time, that he may
try and train their faith to a better measure; so the believer must resolve to wait on patiently; *I waited patiently
for the Lord.* 2. Albeit waiting for the time is joined with
languor and grief, yet the remembrance of it is sweet, and
it wants not a blessing following it; *I waited, and he inclined to me, and heard my cry.* 3. The godly may be
brought in their trouble to as desperate-like condition, as
a man fallen into a horrible, deep, and dark pit, sinking in
miry clay, out of which there is no appearance of relief: in
which case, as the greatness of the danger commendeth the
faith of him that calleth upon God, and waiteth for him;
so doth it commend God's wisdom, power, goodness, and
faithfulness in delivering the patient waiter. To this end
saith the psalmist, *he brought me out of an horrible pit, and
out of the miry clay.* 4. The man who dependeth on the
Lord, when he is delivered out of trouble, is not left to himself; but the Lord's care attendeth him to guide him after
his delivery; *he brought me out of the miry clay, and set
my feet upon a rock, and established my goings.* 5. As it
is a part of our duty to glorify God after every mercy, and

in a special manner when the mercy is very notable : so it
is a new gift of God to enable a man to give thanks and
praise for the mercy received ; therefore it is put for a
point of thanksgiving ; *he hath put a new song in my mouth.*
6. As the experience of God's mercy to one who is in covenant with God, is the encouragement of all believers: so
should it be the common matter of praise unto God from
them all, therefore he calleth the praises which he did sing
the praises of our God. 7. The right observation of God's
mercy to his children, especially when he will show himself
eminently, is able to strike a man with much awe and reverence of God, who is fearful even in his praises ; *many shall
hear and fear.* 8. Then do we make right observation of
God's mercy to his children, when thereby we encourage
ourselves to look for the like mercy, when we call for it in
our need ; *many shall hear and fear, and trust in the Lord.*
9. As the preciousness of faith is not seen in the time of
trial so well as after the victory; so the fruit of it when it
is seen is no less than true blessedness ; *blessed is the man
who maketh the Lord his trust.* 10. All true believers are
humble toward God, and of a high spirit against whatsoever
cometh in competition with him, and will despise every
man's way who regardeth not him: so the misbeliever is
proud towards God and his truth, but a base subject of his
own spirit and to lying vanities ; for the believer here is
opposed to the *proud*, and to such *as turn aside to lies.*

5. *Many, O Lord my God,* are *thy wonderful works*
which *thou hast done, and thy thoughts* which are *to
us ward ; they cannot be reckoned up in order unto
thee :* if *I would declare and speak* of them, *they are
more than can be numbered.*

In the second place he is led up to the consideration of
God's wonderful care and providence about men, and in
special to the work of redemption by Christ's coming into
the world. Whence learn, 1. One of the Lord's wonderful works of providence well meditated upon, may and should
lead us to the consideration of many other of his works of that
kind ; *many, O Lord my God, are thy wonderful works,
which thou hast done.* 2. The works of God's providence
about us should lead us up to the counsel of God, to behold
his care of us, his mind and purpose to us ward, who are

brought into covenant with him, for confirming of our faith in him ; *many, O Lord my God, are thy thoughts which are to us ward.*   3. Albeit the Lord's deep thoughts and works of wonder about his own people, be unspeakable, unsearchable, and innumerable, yet must we not cease to look upon them, and speak of them in heap when we cannot attain to them in tale ; *they cannot be reckoned up in order to thee : if I should declare and speak of them, they are more than can be numbered.*

6. *Sacrifice and offering thou didst not desire; mine ears hast thou opened : burnt-offering and sin-offering hast thou not required.*

7. *Then said I, Lo, I come : in the volume of the book* it is *written of me.*

8. *I delight to do thy will, O my God : yea, thy law* is *within my heart.*

He condescends upon a particular which did not overcome his declaration and searching, to wit, the covenant of redemption between the Father and the Son coming into the world, some articles whereof he toucheth, as they are rehearsed by the Son speaking here by his Spirit.   Whence learn, 1. The work of redemption by Christ, the covenant betwixt the Father and the Son about our redemption, the incarnation of the Son of God, and the course of the salvation of the redeemed, is one of the most wonderful things that ever was heard tell of, wherein so many wonderful works of God, so many wonderful thoughts of God about us concur, that they can neither be declared, nor numbered, nor set in order ; for this work here touched is set down for an instance of what was said in the former verse : now that this is spoken by Christ, the apostle, Heb. x. 5, 6, &c., showeth unto us.   2. Albeit sacrifices and oblations were appointed to be offered before Christ came, yet were they not acceptable in themselves, but in respect of the sacrifice of Christ signified by them ; not they, but Christ signified by them, could take away sin ; *sacrifices and offerings thou didst not desire, burnt-offerings and sin-offerings thou didst not require,* to wit, for any worth in themselves, or as real satisfactions for sin.   3. The ceremonial law was not to remain, but to be taken away when Christ came to offer himself, who was foreshadowed by the sacrifices and

Levitical ordinances; for, *sacrifices and oblations thou didst not desire, but mine ears thou hast opened;* which presupposeth *thou hast formed a body unto me,* as the apostle, Heb. x. 5. showeth; and so the rejecting of the ceremonies, is at the incarnation, or at the forming of the body of Christ, and bringing the Son into the world.   4. The Son of God incarnate becomes voluntarily. a very capable, discreet, ready, and obedient servant to the Father for us : *mine ears hast thou opened,* to wit, for receiving of every command ; *or mine ears hast thou* bored, as the servant's ears were bored under the law, when he chose to stay still with his master in service, Exod. xxi. 5.   5. By offering of burnt-offering God was not satisfied for sin, but only by Christ's coming and offering himself a sacrifice once for all : *burnt-offering and sin-offering hast thou not required; then said I, lo I come,* saith Christ.   6. Both in the book of God's eternal decrees and in the book of holy scripture, this way of taking away the sins of men was established, as the only way to effect it ; for, that the seed of the woman by his suffering should bruise the head of the serpent was foretold by God, Gen. iii. 15. and Christ was the lamb slain in the representative sacrifices from the beginning of the world: *in the volume of the Book it is written of me.*   7. Jesus Christ, God incarnate, is in covenant with God the Father, that believers may be in covenant with God by this means also, therefore doth he call him, *O my God* : as our Lord, John, xx. 17, saith, I ascend to my Father and your Father, to my God and your God.   8. All Christ's sufferings and service done in our name for us, were most willingly and heartily undertaken and discharged by Christ ; *I delight to do thy will,* that is, as the apostle, Heb. x. 10, doth expound it, to perform whatever might sanctify us throughout for ever. 9. The way of our redemption by Christ's doing and suffering for us, is God's own device, his very will and pleasure ; and the obedience of Christ unto the very death of the ross done in our name unto the Father, hath pleased the Father fully ; *I delight to do thy will, O my God.*   10. The Son of God incarnate was perfectly holy, so as he could answer to the law completely, and give account of it to the Father ; *yea thy law is within my heart.*   That these words may be applied to David, and made use of by every believer in their own degree and measure, there is no question : but that they are principally and in the main intention to be applied to Christ speaking of himself, the matter itself doth evidence ; for who but he can ascribe to himself the accomplishing of what the typical sacrifices foreshadowed ? who but he could satisfy for sin, which the sacrifices could not ? Again the apostle Paul, Heb. x. 5, 6, &c., cleareth the matter so, as no ground of doubting is left.   In all the psalm, let David be as the shadow, but let Christ be the substance.

9. *I have preached righteousness in the great congregation: lo, I have not refrained my lips, O Lord thou knowest.*

10. *I have not hid thy righteousness within my heart ; I have declared thy faithfulness and thy salvation : I have not concealed thy loving-kindness and thy truth from the great congregation.*

In the third place, as Christ hath given an account of the execution of his priestly office, in expiation of sin, so here he giveth account of his prophetical office, to make way for his intercession.   Whence learn, 1. Christ did not only undertake to suffer for expiation of our sins, but also he undertook to apply to his people, by preaching, the fruits of his sufferings, for their righteousness and salvation, for justifying, sanctifying, and saving the redeemed ; *I have preached righteousness in the great congregation.* 2. The way appointed for application of the grace purchased to the redeemed, is preaching ; *I have preached righteousness in the great congregation,* in the visible church, and in all confluences of the redeemed where opportunity is offered. 3. As Christ did not conceal what might save souls, but communicated it carefully, so should they who are trusted by him to preach without fear sincerely, as they will be able to answer God, proclaim it: *I have not refrained my lips, O Lord, thou knowest.* 4. The true way of justification of sinners by faith, is a jewel so precious and necessary for poor souls, that it should not be concealed ; *I have not hid thy righteousness within my heart.* 5. One sermon on this subject is not sufficient, it is necessary to make this mystery plain, how by faith in Christ the man that flieth to him is justified from his sins, and saved according to the covenant passed between the suffering Mediator and God the faithful promiser, to justify and save by his own way ; *I have de-clared thy faithfulness and thy salvation.* 6. The way of righteousness and salvation purchased unto believers by Jesus Christ, is very solid and complete ; for, first, this way of forgiving sins unto us, because of the satisfaction made by Christ for us in his obedience unto the Father, even unto the death of the cross, is of God's own devising, and his free gift; therefore, as it is called the righteousness of God, Rom. iii. 21, 22 ; so here it is called God's righteousness ; *O Lord, I have not hid thy righteousness.* And the salva-tion or eternal life annexed to this imputed and gifted righteousness bestowed upon the embracer of it, is also of God's devising, and his free gift, therefore it is also called his salvation ; *I have declared thy salvation.* Next, the cer-tainty and ground of the believer's assurance that this right-eousness and salvation are made fast unto him, are the truth and faithfulness of God, obliging himself to make good this way of justification and salvation by the covenant of redemption made between the Father and the Son our Mediator, as in the promises of the covenant of grace, is set down in scripture; which can no more disappoint the believer, than the truth and faithfulness of God can fail ; *I have declared thy faithfulness and thy salvation.* And, last of all, the fountain, spring, and rise, and unchangeable ground of righteousness and salvation, purchased by the re-demption made by Jesus Christ, and applied to us by faith in him, is the mere good-will and pleasure of God : the free grace, the free love and bounty of God, without any de-serving of the redeemed ; *I have not concealed thy loving-kindness and thy truth from the great congregation.* This indeed is a solid ground. 7. The plain preaching, de-claration, and manifestation of this gospel, with the grounds thereof, are able, by the blessing of God, to persuade a trembling soul to lay itself over upon Jesus Christ, and to rest upon the unchangeable truth and kindness of God of-fered to every poor humble sinner, without exception, for the preaching of these things, not refraining the lips, not hiding this precious and saving truth, the declara-tion and not concealing of it, is given up here for the suffi-ciency of means to apply the purchased righteousness and sal-vation by Christ to the redeemed ; and this execution of Christ's prophetical office hath been faithfully performed by him, not only in his personal preaching in the days of his flesh, but also in his ministers, both befoe his incarnation and since, which also shall be continued from generation to generation, to the end of the world, maugre all opposition : for Christ shall be able to make no less perfect account of his other offices than of the kingly office, when he shall give up the kingdom to his Father. 8. What may concern David here as the type of Christ, or as one of the servants of Christ, we take up in one word, which is this :— the more faithful preachers are to declare the gospel to the salvation of souls, the more confidence and comfort shall the testimony of their conscience afford to them in the day of their trouble, when they come before God : as the prophet here by experience findeth.

11. *Withhold not thou thy tender mercies from me, O Lord: let thy loving-kindness and thy truth continually preserve me.*

12. *For innumerable evils have compassed me about ; mine iniquities have taken hold upon me, so that I am not able to look up: they are more than the hairs of mine head : therefore my heart faileth me.*

13. *Be pleased, O Lord, to deliver me : O Lord, make haste to help me.*

Christ having given account of his performance of what was undertaken, intercedeth for the promised mercies to his mystical body and to himself, as standing in the room of the ransomed, wherein David, as the type of Christ, and as a member of Christ's mystical body, hath his own place. Whence learn, 1. Because the price of redemption is holden here as fully paid, and nothing is left unpaid by Christ, therefore the application of the purchased mercy must be granted ; for Christ, here speaking, having declared his performance of his part of the covenant, from v. 6, to v. 11, doth now require the performance of promised kindness and mercy to him and his mystical body : saying, *withhold not thy tender mercies from me, O Lord: let thy loving-kindness and thy truth continually preserve me ;* and this is a standing petition of the Mediator, in favour of his afflicted mystical body in all generations. 2. The unchangeableness of God's loving-kindness, and truth of promises made in his covenant, are solid grounds of assurance that the Lord will not withhold his tender mercies from the afflicted believer ; for, upon this ground do the parts of his petition run : *withhold not thy tender mercies from me, and let kindness and truth continually preserve me.*　3. Albeit the troubles which are inflicted be drawn on by sin, and be the effects of just wrath for sin, yet are they also the object of tender mercies, when the afflicted present both their troubles and their sins, which deserved them, before God's merciful eye ; for here a reason of hoping for tender mercy, is brought from both trouble and sin lying on ; *for innumerable evils have compassed me about, and mine iniquities have taken hold on me.*　4. By virtue of the intercession of Christ, every believer may take up the same supplication in Christ's name, and present it in his own behalf unto God, in the time of trouble and necessity ; for, since David might make this use of it, as one of the members of the mystical body, so may all the rest of believers also ; because Christ the Mediator owneth all the sins of all his redeemed ones as his own, as made his by consent to have them imputed unto him, and hath borne the punishment thereof so much as may and doth satisfy justice for them.　Therefore Christ in behalf of his redeemed ones, and every believer in Christ for that respect may expect continual preservation by the loving-kindness and truth of God laid in pawn for it by the covenant, when they have recourse to God in the time when trouble and guiltiness both set on at once ; for the reason of the prayer is so conceived, as it may fit both the Mediator interceding for his mystical body, and every wearied soul also who is fled to God through Christ by faith in him, that he may find his outgate and deliverance in, with, and for Christ : *let thy loving-kindness and thy truth continually preserve me ; for innumerable evils have compassed me about, mine iniquities have taken hold on me.*　5. Nothing can so empty a man, and lay him low, and fill him with confusion of face, as his sin pursuing him : *mine iniquities have taken hold upon me, so that I am not able to look up.*　6. When all that is a man's own, as natural strength, wit, or courage, faileth, yet God doth not fail, and faith doth not fail : *for here when it is come to this, my heart faileth me,* faith stands up, and in prayer pleadeth for mercy and kindness for this very reason, because the heart faileth.　7. As the strait is great, and the burden heavy, and the creature weak, so are the delivery and help near at hand : *be pleased, O Lord, to deliver me : O Lord, make haste to help me.*

14. *Let them be ashamed and confounded together that seek after my soul to destroy it ; let them be driven backward, and put to shame, that wish me evil.*

15. *Let them be desolate for a reward of their shame that say unto me, Aha, aha !*

From this part of his prayer, which is against his enemies, learn, 1. As the Lord, for the intercession of Christ, will not fail to help his people in trouble, so will he not miss to disappoint and bring mischief upon the enemies of his people, how many and how strong soever they be : *let them be confounded together and ashamed that seek after my soul to destroy it.* 2. Not only the open persecutors of the godly, but all their ill-willers and unfriends, who could be content to see evil come upon God's church, shall be punished with the open adversaries: *they shall be driven backward, and put to shame, that wish them evil.* 3. The mocking of the godly, and putting them to shame, is the shame indeed of the mockers, and not of the godly, upon whom, in their sufferings, the spirit of glory resteth, and therefore shall the wicked scorners bear their own shame and their punishment : *let them be desolate for a reward of their shame, that say unto me, Aha, aha !*

16. *Let all those that seek thee rejoice and be glad in thee : let such as love thy salvation say continually, The Lord be magnified.*

17. *But I am poor and needy ; yet the Lord thinketh upon me : thou art my help and my deliverer ; make no tarrying, O my God.*

From this prayer, that the rest of the godly may have comfort by his delivery, which delivery he confidently expecteth, learn, 1. As every mercy to every believer giveth a proof of God's readiness to show the like mercy to all believers when they stand in need, so should every mercy shown to any of the number, being known to the rest, be made the matter and occasion of magnifying the Lord ; *let all those that seek thee rejoice and be glad in thee.* 2. The godly, whose property it is to be partakers of the affliction of Christ with others, and to seek God, and to wait for the Lord's way of delivery, and to love the safety of his people, shall have reason to rejoice and praise God continually for new evidences of his mercy to his own : *let all those that seek thee rejoice and be glad in thee : let such as love thy salvation say continually, the Lord be magnified.* **3.** It is a usual condition of the godly, before they be delivered out of any difficulties, to be made once sensible of their own weakness, emptiness, and necessities, as here ; *I am poor and needy.* **4.** It is an ordinary exercise of the afflicted, to be despised of the world, and contemned ; and this also is a temptation to move them to mistake their own condition before God ; for so doth the psalmist propound the matter before God ; *but,* saith he, *I am poor and needy.* **5.** Whatsoever the world, or sense and false suggestions say of the afflicted, yet faith gives ground of assurance that our base and mean condition is so far from making us loathsome to God, that, on the contrary, the lower we are brought the more we are in his heart and estimation ; *yet the Lord thinketh upon me ;* and God's respecting us may easily make up our loss of respect among men. **6.** When the believer hath fastened his faith, he may expect shortly his relief; *thou art my help and my deliverer,* saith he, and then, *make no tarrying, O my God.*

PSALM XLI.

To the chief musician.　A psalm of David.

David as a type of Christ, and one of his afflicted followers, after prayer comforteth himself against the uncharitable judgment, which the wicked had of him in his affliction, v. 1—4.　In the second place, he complaineth of his enemies' cursed disposition against him, and prayeth to be delivered out of his trouble, v. 5—10.　In the third place, he is answered comfortably, and praiseth God for it, v. 11—13.

1. *Blessed* is *he that considereth the poor: the Lord will deliver him in time of trouble.*

2. *The Lord will preserve him, and keep him alive; and* he shall be *blessed upon the earth : and thou wilt not deliver him unto the will of his enemies.*

3. *The Lord will strengthen him upon the bed of languishing: thou wilt make all his bed in his sickness.*

4. *I said, Lord, be merciful unto me : heal my soul · for I have sinned against thee.*

9

That he may comfort the godly in their afflictions, and correct the common judgment of the world concerning afflicted people, he giveth a reason for which it is safe to judge charitably of every man who humbleth himself before God in his affliction. Whence learn, 1. Albeit it be usual for the world to judge all them that are afflicted to be plagued of God in wrath, yet it is a blessed course to study to frame our hearts to a wise and discreet judging of other men's estates, by looking to a man's behaviour in his trouble, and to judge charitably of the man who is contrite, and humbleth himself before God in his afflictions ; *blessed is he that considereth the poor*, or giveth comfort and instruction to the weak. 2. It is a blessed thing for a man afflicted and humbling himself before God to judge charitably of his own condition, as well as of another's condition in the like case ; for, *blessed is he that considereth the poor*, is so set down as it is applicable to the patient in affliction judging of himself; no less than to the beholder of another in affliction : and, for confirmation of this, he giveth six reasons of comforting the afflicted and humbled man, and confirming the charitable beholder and judger of him as a fellow sufferer with him. 3. The afflicted and humble man shall be delivered out of his trouble, be what it may be ; *the Lord will deliver him in time of trouble.* This is the first reason of the comfort, and withal a reason of confirmation and encouragement of him that judgeth wisely of the afflicted. 4. The Lord hath a way of delivery, not only from trouble, that a man fall not into it, and not only of delivering from trouble by removing of the trouble, but also a way of delivery, when the trouble is yet remaining ; to wit, by sustaining the man, comforting him, saving him from any harm by the trouble, giving him good by the trouble, quieting his mind by patient submission unto God under the trouble, &c. *The Lord will deliver him in time of trouble* : and this is branched out in particulars in the verses following, as so many reasons of comfort, and charitable judging of his own condition and others. 5. Albeit the godly be brought very low, yet shall he not perish, *the Lord will preserve him and keep him alive ;* and this is the second reason of comfort; albeit he faint, and have soul-faintings now and then, yet shall spiritual life be kept in him. 6. None of the godly man's afflictions shall hinder or take away his begun blessedness, even in this world ; *he shall be blessed on the earth :* and this is the third reason of comfort ; if it may be for God's glory and the man's good, this temporal life shall be preserved, and evidences of God's blessing shall be seen upon him. 7. No persecutor shall drive the godly man from his point, and make him forsake God, or the way of godliness ; if he slip in a step, God shall raise him up again ; *thou wilt not deliver him to the will of his enemies :* and this is the fourth reason of his comfort. 8. The Lord will strengthen the godly to bear whatsoever trouble he putteth on him : *the Lord will strengthen him on the bed of languishing :* and this is the fifth reason of his comfort. 9. The Lord shall mitigate and moderate all the afflictions of the godly, and ease him under his trouble, as tenderly as when a sick person's bed is made the best way that can be for his ease ; *thou shalt make all his bed in his sickness :* and this is the sixth reason of his comfort. 10. The man who may look for all these consolations, and may be judged of charitably, whether it be himself, or another, is the man who in the sense of his sins, humbleth himself before the Lord, especially when he is afflicted and flieth to God's mercy ; first, to have sins pardoned, and next to have his trouble removed, as God seeth it fit for his salvation. This is pointed out in David's behaviour under his trouble, of set purpose, that he may give the character of the Lord's poor man, to whom the foresaid comforts belong, and of whose estate a good construction is to be made ; *I said, Lord be merciful to me, heal my soul, for I have sinned against thee.*

5. *Mine enemies speak evil of me ; when shall he die, and his name perish?*

6. *And if he come to see* me, *he speaketh vanity : his heart gathereth iniquity to itself ;* when *he goeth abroad, he telleth* it.

7. *All that hate* me *whisper together against* me : *against* me *do they devise my hurt.*

8. *An evil disease,* say they, *cleaveth fast unto him : and* now *that he lieth, he shall rise up no more.*

6. *Yea, mine own familiar friend, in whom I trusted, which did eat of my bread, hath lifted up* his *heel against me.*

10. *But thou, O Lord, be merciful unto me, and raise me up, that I may requite them.*

From his complaint against his enemies, set down in the second place, learn, 1. Evil speeches against the godly will be taken notice of by God, and made a part of the wicked's duty ; *mine enemies speak evil of me.*   2. The malice of the enemies of godliness is such against the godly, as nothing but their utter overthrow and rooting out from the earth of such a sort of people can satisfy them ; *when shall he die, and his name perish,* say they.   3. The godly have to do, not only with open enemies, but with secret false dissemblers also, who will profess friendship with fair words, when they are following the way of malice, from whose falsehood there is no refuge more than from the force of the open enemy, save to fly to God, the Judge of all oppressed people ; *if he come to see me, he speaketh vanity ;* many fair words, but none of them true.   4. The end of the wicked man's pretended kindness to the godly, and of his insinuating himself into their fellowship, is, that he may make observation of something in their behaviour, or condition, or speeches, whereof he may make advantage against them ; *if he cometh to see me, his heart gathereth iniquity to itself ; when he goeth abroad he telleth it.*   5. Albeit the wicked can do no more against the godly than God will permit to be done for the godly man's exercise and good, yet many are the consultations which the wicked have, that they may hurt and destroy the godly ; *all that hate me whisper together against me, against me do they devise my hurt.*   6. When the godly fall into straits, the wicked judge that the godly shall never get out of their trouble, and in this hope refresh themselves ; *an evil disease cleaveth fast unto him, and now that he lieth, he shall rise no more.*   7. The lot appointed to Christ, and to all the true members of his mystical body as well as to David, is to find in the time of their trials a hard meeting in the world from the wicked, how many bonds soever of nature, friendship, familiarity, or obligations of the wicked unto the godly intervene, which otherwise might require better offices ; *yea, mine own familiar friend in whom I trusted, which did eat of my bread, hath lifted up his heel against me.*   8. We must not dwell upon our miseries in time of trouble, as if we had nothing to do, save to weep and mourn, but we should turn ourselves to God, and pray to him for mercy, and expect a delivery, as the psalmist doth here; *but thou, O Lord, be merciful to me, and raise me up.* 9. Albeit it be not fit for every believer to resolve requiting their persecutors and enemies, as it was fit to David as a magistrate, and to Christ who is King of kings, here represented by him, to resolve vengeance, and to execute the same also against their enemies; yet every believer may be assured of this, that what injuries are done to Christ in his person, Christ shall requite his persecutors; for he, in his mystical members, shall never be so borne down, but he shall be raised up again as he was raised up personally after his personal suffering. *Raise me up, that I may requite them.*

11. *By this I know that thou favoures tme, because mine enemy doth not triumph over me.*

12. *And as for me, thou upholdest me in mine integrity, and settest me before thy face for ever.*

13. *Blessed* be *the Lord God of Israel from everlasting, and to everlasting. Amen, and Amen.*

In the last part of the psalm is his thanksgiving, presupposing that the psalm was drawn up after the delivery from the trouble which is set forth in the former part. Whence learn, 1. Albeit external deliveries from enemies, and success external do not always serve for marks of God's favour, (for an ill man in an ill cause may have success for a time;) yet when the man is reconciled to God, and the cause which the reconciled man defendeth against his persecutors, is the Lord's cause, in this case; if God shall give to his servant either spiritual victory, that the enemy prevail not so over him as to drive him from his righteous cause, or external victory, and deliverance also from the power of the adversary, together with the spiritual victory; in this case, I say, the word and work of God concurring, give evidence not only of God's favouring the man's person, but also of his favouring the man's cause and carriage in the cause, so as he may say, *by this I know that thou favourest me, because mine enemy triumpheth not over me.* 2. Uprightness is a special means to bring a man through difficulties, and whatsoever infirmities the believer be subject unto, he shall not want comfort, if he keep conscience of integrity, uprightness, and sincerity; for this is the psalmist's rejoicing, when he looks back upon his former exercise under trouble; *as for me, thou upholdest me in mine integrity.* 3. The wise wrestler with temptations is made at length to see and acknowledge by the experience he hath of himself and of God's help in time of temptation, that all the glory of his standing and bearing out in trouble for righteousness, belongeth to the Lord ; *thou upholdest me in mine integrity.* 4. Experience of God's gracious bearing out of a believer in time of trial, serveth for a good argument to make him confident of the continuance of God's favour to him for ever ; yea, after experiences and victory, God useth to give some measure of persuasion of his everlasting love toward them that have overcome ; as here, *thou settest me before thy face for ever.* 5. He that gets a sight of God's love to him, may knit God's felt favour in effect with God's everlasting love decreeing to show favour, and his everlasting love communicating itself to him, and performing the decrees of love touching him, and may behold the course of everlasting blessings running from eternity before the world, to everlasting after the world ; and the believer having seen it, should acknowledge this with praise and thanksgiving ; as here, *blessed be the Lord God of Israel, from everlasting to everlasting.* 6. He that seeth the course of God's love to himself, seeth God's love in conjunction with the rest of the Lord's people also, who are joined in the same covenant with him unto God in Christ ; *blessed be the Lord God of Israel,* says the psalmist, now when he will bless God for his own particular mercy. 7. Fresh experiences of God's love in a particular trial, especially when the soul is lifted up to the eternal original and everlasting endurance of it, will make a soul heartily, with all his strength, give everlasting praise to God, and seal it affectionately again and again ; *blessed be the Lord God of Israel from everlasting to everlasting, amen, and amen.*

PSALM XLII.

To the chief musician, Maschil, for the sons of Korah.

In this psalm David showeth what was his longing after the fellowship of the saints in their public worship and service of God, in the time of his banishment, by the persecution of Saul, v. 1—4, and how he wrestled with discouragements, by checking himself for it, and by praying to God, whereby he was erected unto hope and confidence to be answered, v. 5—11.

1. *As the heart panteth after the water-brooks, so panteth my soul after thee, O God.*

2. *My soul thirsteth for God, for the living God: when shall I come and appear before God?*

3. *My tears have been my meat day and night, while they continually say unto me, Where is thy God?*

4. *When I remember these* things, *I pour out my soul in me: for I had gone with the multitude; I went with them to the house of God, with the voice of joy and praise, with a multitude that kept holy-day.*

He setteth down his sad condition in his banishment, especially when he remembered the solemn assembly of God's people at the temple, and saw himself, either in the wilderness or among the heathen, deprived of the use of public ordinances. Whence learn, 1. It is not a bare formal use of the ordinances, but communion with God himself, which the lively believer seeketh after, in the use of public ordinances: *my soul panteth after thee, O God.* 2. Spiritual affections, when they are raised, and, by delay or by outward restraint, are kept off from satisfaction, are comparable, in measure or in point of sincerity, to the kindly appetite of natural food: *as the hart panteth after the water-brooks, so panteth my soul after thee, O God.* 3. Worshippers of the true God find, and may more and more find, lively refreshments to their souls in him; the experience whereof kindleth their desire for renewing them by such means as they have found satisfying before; *my soul thirsteth for God, for the living God.* 4. Because the assemblies of the church, for the exercises of religion, are the trysting-places, where God showeth himself to his people; therefore, lovers of God are hearty lovers of the public ordinances, and most desirous to frequent them for that cause: *when shall I come and appear before God?* 5. It is not enough for the wicked to see the godly in affliction, except they impute the misery of the godly unto their religion, and insult them, either as atheists, false worshippers, or hypocritical people, forsaken of God: *they continually say unto me, Where is thy God?* 6. To find Satan, wicked men, and God's dispensations, seeming to speak rejection from God, and to see the glory of the true religion, and a man's own interest in God, called in question, and thrust through with fiery darts of insulting enemies; is a matter indeed of great grief, and sufficient to render all creature comforts tasteless to a godly soul: *my tears have been my meat day and night, while they continually say unto me, Where is thy God?* 7. As they who have had most of the means of grace may have scarcity of them ere all be done ; so no one will take the inlack of them more heavily than they who have reaped most spiritual benefit by them : *when I remember these things, I pour out my soul in me.* 8. The saints should be so far from separation from the fellowship of the visible church, in the public exercises of holy ordinances, albeit they know certainly that all are not sound professors who are to join with them, that it should be their joy to have multitudes partaking in the use, at least of some, of the public means, and such as were not publicly scandalous, joining in all the ordinances whereby God might be openly honoured, and his elect among them might, in his own time, be converted ; for David *went with the multitude, and that to the house of God, with the voice of joy and praise, and with a multitude that kept holy-day.*   And this was at the time when king Saul and his courtiers were joined in the public ordinances with him, and with Jonathan, and other such godly persons.   Now, what the constitution of the church visible was in Saul's days, in regard to the hypocrisy of professors, known to David, sundry of his psalms make evident ; and yet, for all that, he wisheth to have the like occasion of worshipping God again, and accounteth highly of what he sometimes enjoyed.

5. *Why art thou cast down, O my soul? and why art thou disquieted in me? hope thou in God; for I shall yet praise him* for *the help of his countenance.*

In the second part of the psalm, he wrestleth with discouragements ; and the conflicts are four.   In the first he laboureth to comfort himself three ways ; first, by checking himself for his dejection of spirit and disquietude ; next, by stirring up the grace of God in himself, namely, faith and hope ; thirdly, by application of the word of promise made unto him for strengthening both, to bear him out till the Lord should manifest his promised kindness.   Whence learn, 1. When sore troubles, instead of humbling a man, press him down unto dejection and discouragement of mind ; it is a gracious man's part to check himself for this reasonless fit of unbelief, and to put his conscience to answer for yielding so far to the temptation : *why are thou cast down, O my soul?* 2. Misbelief, in a child of God, is followed by restlessness of spirit, as a chastisement drawn on by that sin, for which disquieting of himself the man may justly be challenged also, and will not be able to give a reason for it: *why art thou disquieted within me?* 3. The only means of remedying discouragements and unquietness of mind, is to set faith on work to go to God and take hold on him, and to cast anchor within the vail, hoping for, and expecting, relief from him: *hope thou in God.*   4. The believer, in the midst of trouble, may promise to himself new experience of God's kindness and consolation, by delivery out of it; and to God he may promise praises: *I shall yet praise him for the help of his countenance.*

6. *O my God, my soul is cast down within me : therefore will I remember thee from the land of Jordan, and of the Hermonites, from the hill Mizar.*

In the second conflict he turneth him to God, and layeth the case of his discouraged heart before him, labouring to make use of old experience.   Whence learn, 1. Albeit a dejected and disconsolate soul may and should deal with itself rationally, to recover itself, yet can it not do it effectually; but, as a man sick and weak, and fallen from his bed, calleth for help, so must it call to God, and lay out its case before him, that he may recover it: *O my God, my soul is cast down within me.* 2. Albeit the power of making the means effectual be not in us but in the Lord's hands, yet must we not cease to use the means rationally still, whereby the Lord useth to convey his efficacious power, and to call to mind experiences, as a good means for recovering ourselves: *O my God, my soul is cast down within me ; therefore will I remember thee from the land of Jordan :* that is, I will aim at comforting myself by remembering what I have found by experience, in several places of Judea, of thy goodness to me; and I will look to the Holy Land and to the temple, the place where thy gracious presence is vouchsafed, and where thine honour dwelleth.

7. *Deep calleth unto deep at the noise of thy waterspouts : all thy waves and thy billows are gone over me.*

In the third conflict, wherein the very remembrance of bygone experience, which even now was made use of to comfort him, kindleth afresh his grief, learn, 1. Though using the right and appointed means to comfort us should seem to us to have a contrary effect to what we intended, and to increase our grief by our using them, yet still must we wrestle,

using one mean after another, mixing prayer with all other
means, as David doth here, saying, *deep calleth unto deep
at the noise of thy water-spouts.* 2. As the noise of rain
from the clouds causeth a noise in the inferior waters and
floods ; as the raising of brooks raiseth the rivers, and all
shut themselves into a sea; and as the waves of the sea
call one upon another to follow the former at the back ; so,
one grief wakeneth another, one temptation strengtheneth
another, one affliction augmenteth another, till a sea of
troubles, raised by a storm, be like to overwhelm the man:
all thy waves and thy billows are gone over me.

8. Yet *the Lord will command his loving-kindness
in the day-time, and in the night his song* shall be *with
me,* and *my prayer unto the God of my life.*

9. *I will say unto God my rock, Why hast thou forgotten me? why go I mourning because of the oppression of the enemy?*

To oppose this new assault, faith puts forth itself the
third time, promising to the wrestler what God hath promised to the believer; whereupon he resolveth to plead his
cause more hardly, and ply God yet again with prayer more
earnestly, that he may prevail.   Whence learn, 1. Faith seeth
in God's word, and in bygone evidence of his truth manifested in his word, as it were a written order and commission,
ready to be given forth in acts of providence, for satisfying
the believer with so much fresh experience as may fill him
day and night with a sense of God's love and songs of praise :
*yet the Lord will command his loving-kindness in the day-
time, and in the night his song shall be with me.*   2. The
care of our life, bodily, spiritual, and everlasting, lieth upon
God, by virtue of his covenant with us to keep it, to feed
it and renew it in all the decays thereof, till it be possessed
of unchangeable blessedness; the belief whereof is a ground
of perseverance in prayer : *my prayer shall be unto the God
of my life.*   3. Faith may improve its right before God, and
plead that the believer be not rejected, and may regret any
appearance, which is offered to sense, of rejection : *I will
say unto God, Why hast thou forgotten me?*   4. The believer, in his complaints, must not weaken his own faith,
but weaken his unbelief rather, and to this end should fasten
his faith ere he complain : *I will say unto God, My rock*—
there faith is fastened ; then followeth the complaint—*why*

hast thou forgotten me? why go I mourning because of the oppression of the enemy?

10. As *with a sword in my bones, mine enemies reproach me; while they say daily unto me, Where is thy God?*

11. *Why art thou cast down, O my soul? and why art thou disquieted within me? hope thou in God; for I shall yet praise him,* who is *the health of my countenance, and my God.*

In the fourth conflict, which he hath chiefly with the mockers of his religion, his cause, and his trust in God, learn, 1. The sharpest part of a believer's trial and affliction is, when, in his person, religion and God's glory is mocked; this cruel sort of persecution pierceth deepest in his heart, because it tends to drive the man to desperation, and to make religion and faith in God out of request: *as with a sword in my bones, mine enemies reproach me.* 2. Continuance of the reproach of godliness, and of the insolence of mockers scorning religion in the afflicted man's face, in the time when it seemeth that his affliction speaketh desperation of relief, greatly increaseth the power of the temptation and the godly man's grief: *a sword in my bones, while they say daily unto me, Where is thy God?* 3. As the battle against discouragements and unbelief useth to be oftener renewed even after the believer hath gotten the victory once and again, and as the wrestler's weakness useth oftener to be made evident; so the same means and weapons must be oftener used, and we must not be weary to fight on; for, *why art thou cast down, O my soul,* is now repeated as before; the misbelief, and disquietness drawn on by misbelief, must be yet again rebuked: *why art thou disquieted within me?* faith and hope must be set on work against all the disappearances of help: *hope thou in God;* we must, as it were, be surety to ourselves for God's promises made to us, that they shall be performed: *I shall yet praise him.* 4. As when the Lord withdraweth both the outward tokens of his favour and his inward consolation for a time, the countenance of the godly cannot but be heavy, cast down, and look sad, like a man that is sick; so, when God returneth to comfort and to own his own, either both inwardly and outwardly, or inwardly only, the man's face looketh cheerful: *he is the health of my countenance.* 5.

Although the Lord, for a time, shall neither remove the outward affliction nor inwardly give comfort, yet faith will sustain itself upon the covenant, and lay its whole weight upon it, and may do it confidently ; for it will not sink under the man nor under his burden : *he is my God.*

PSALM XLIII.

This psalm tendeth to the same purpose with the former ; for David in exile complaineth of his persecutors, and prayeth for delivery, and regretteth his sad condition, ver. 1, 2 ; prayeth for restitution unto the liberty of the public ordinances, promising to praise God at his returning cheerfully, ver. 3, 4 ; and wrestleth with his discouragements, as he did in the former psalm, ver. 5.

1. *Judge me, O God, and plead my cause against an ungodly nation : O deliver me from the deceitful and unjust man.*

2. *For thou* art *the God of my strength : why dost thou cast me off? why go I mourning because of the oppression of the enemy?*

From his complaint and prayer against his enemies learn, 1. As the godly have usually enemies powerful, many, crafty and cruel, oppressing them for righteousness, so they want not an impartial judge, who is sufficient to take order with their adversaries, to whom they may and should address themselves in their affliction, as David doth here : *judge me, O Lord, and plead my cause against an ungodly nation.* 2. The cruelties and falsehood, and fair pretences, whereby the enemies palliate their cruel purposes, are more dangerous than their professed cruelty ; from which no wisdom, except divine direction, can save a man ; *O! deliver me from the deceitful and unjust man.* 3. What the oppressed church, or particular believer wanteth, God hath and will be forthcoming for the believer's use and benefit, as his need shall be, to uphold him by it, and comfort him, and deliver him, and bless him ; *for, thou art the God of my strength.* 4. Although the Lord be all in all to us by covenant, yet for our good and his own glory he may so exercise us, as we may want possession for a time of what we have in promise ; and seem also to be thrust out of our right ; in which case if we shall once fix our faith, we shall have liberty to dispute our right against all temptations, and to express the sense of our condition unto God without being mistaken, as here David doth, saying (not before, but after the fixing of his faith ;) *why dost thou cast me off? why go I mourning for the oppression of the enemy?*

3. *O send out thy light and thy truth : let them lead me, let them bring me unto thy holy hill, and to thy tabernacles.*

4. *Then will I go unto the altar of God, unto God my exceeding joy : yea upon the harp will I praise thee, O God, my God.*

From this prayer and promise of thanksgiving, learn, 1. No temptation unto discouragement, nor seeming desertion should divert the believer from pursuing his desire of relief, but rather kindle his affection in prayer; *O send out thy light.* 2. Comfort, deliverances from troubles, and performance of promises, when they most disappear, are kept in store for us, and fast locked up, to be let forth to us in due time; *O send out thy light and thy truth.* 3. Direction how to conduct ourselves till we obtain our desires, and observation of the steps of God's providence, bringing us to the possession of promised mercies, are necessary preparations for the mercy which we seek, and should be prayed for as mercies in order preceding that particular which we should have ; *let them lead me; let them bring me unto thy holy hill.* 4. Spiritual grief must have spiritual comfort ; godly sorrow for distance from God and want of the comfortable use of his ordinances, admits of no comfort, save a comfort of that kind ; for David longeth more to have the free use of the public ordinances, than to have the kingdom ; therefore saith he, *let them bring me to thy holy hill and to thy tabernacles.* 5. The first thing a soul is to attend to in his address to God, is the means of expiation of his sin, and that is Christ represented by the altar, offering himself a ransom for the sinner, and sanctifying the person of the offerer, and the worship and service of the man that comes to God through him ; *then will I go to the altar of God.* 6. This way of making address to God by Christ, gives present access to God, and peace to the soul of him who draws near this way ; *thus I will go to God.* 7. God laid hold upon through Christ, furnishes not only peace, but unspeakable joy also to the believer ; yea, God reconciled through Christ, is the life of the believer's gladness ; *I*

will go to God, my exceeding joy. 8. As is the longing of the soul after God, when it is at a distance from
him : so are the consolation and satisfaction which it findeth
after renewed access ; and as the supplicant is earnest for
renewed sense of fellowship, so he purposeth that the
praises of God shall be hearty, at the receiving of that which
he longed for, and also that his faith shall be stronger by
the fastening of the bond of the covenant between him and
God more strongly : *I will praise thee with the harp, O my
God.*

5. *Why art thou cast down, O my soul ? and why
art thou disquieted within me ? hope in God : for I
shall yet praise him,* who is *the health of my countenance, and my God.*

He closeth this psalm as the former one, setting faith and
hope on work to wrestle with discouragement. Whence
learn, 1. The strongest believer may be overtaken with fits
of dejection and discouragement ; for this champion findeth
his soul cast down. 2. A praying soul, believing in God
through Christ, hath no reason of dejection and discouragement, whatever reason of humiliation he may have ; *why
art thou cast down, O my soul?* 3. It is a sanctifying means
for wrestling out of discouragement, to dispute misbelief to
the door, or to dispute ourselves out of melancholy by reason taken from the Lord's word ; and it is wisdom to get
the conscience to be our friend, when the mind and the
heart are in a wrong temper in this case ; it is necessary to
take God's part against misbelief, and unwarrantable unquietness, and to dispute both his cause and our own against
temptations ; *why art thou disquieted within me?* 4. No
rest to a troubled and disquieted spirit, but by casting anchor on the Rock, and hoping in God ; *hope thou in God.*
5. Hope cannot raise itself in trouble, but by the grip of
a promise ; *hope in God, for I shall yet praise him.* 6.
Though faith be in darkness, yet it will see afar off ; as soon
as it puts the prospect of the covenant of grace to its eye,
it discerneth the proper remedy of present evils to be in
God, and the good it would be at, coming along unto it,
and is as sure of it, as if it were in possession : *he is the
health of my countenance, and my God.*

PSALM XLIV.

To the chief musician, for the sons of Korah.   Maschil.

The Church, under heavy persecution, first strengtheneth her faith in
God before she enter upon her lamentation, ver.1—8.   In the second
place, she layeth forth her sad sufferings under the hands of cruel persecutors, v. 9—16.   In the third, she professeth her constant adherence
unto God, and avoweth his truth for time by-past, and her purpose
to continue for time to come, v. 17—22.   In the last place, they pray
unto the Lord to arise and relieve them from their cruel persecutors,
for the glory both of his justice and mercy, v. 23—25.

From the inscription, learn, seeing the canon of the whole
Hebrew bible is commended to us by Christ and his Apostles,
as the undoubted word of God, and the undoubted Scriptures
given by inspiration of the Holy Spirit to the holy men of
God, the writers thereof, as kept entire and not vitiated by
the Jews, (whose honour for preserving faithfully the oracles
of God committed unto them, is unstained, Rom. 4, 2.) We
are not to trouble ourselves about the name of the writer, or
time of writing of any part thereof; especially because God
of set purpose concealeth the name, sundry times, of the
writer, and the time when it was written, that we look in
every book, more to the inditer of it, than to the writer of
it; and that the use of any exercise of any of the saints set
down therein, might be so much the more large, as the consideration of particular circumstances of time and persons,
(whereunto it might seem only to be applied) were laid aside;
for this psalm, wanting the name of the writer, and time of
the writing of it also, is looked upon by the Apostle,
Rom. 8, 36, not only as an experience of the church before
us, but also as a prophecy of the martyrdom of Christians
under the gospel, and as encouragement to stand constant in
the faith in hottest persecutions.

1. *We have heard with our ears, O God, our fathers
have told us,* what *work thou didst in their days, in the
times of old.*

2. How *thou didst drive out the heathen with thy
hand, and plantedst them;* how *thou didst afflict the
people, and cast them out.*

3. *For they got not the land in possession by their
own sword, neither did their own arm save them; but
thy right hand, and thine arm, and the light of thy countenance, because thou hadst a favour unto them.*

For the confirmation of their faith, they lay forth three
arguments. The first is from the Lord's mighty work in
driving out the Canaanites and planting their fathers in
Canaan, made mention of in holy Scripture. Whence learn,
1. The information which the Scripture giveth us of God's
working for his people, is as sure, and should be so looked
upon by us, as if the people of God who lived in the days
when these works were done, and who were eye witnesses
thereof, should also rise up from the dead, when the Scriptures are read, and testify unto us, saying, of these things
we were eye witnesses, and we tell them unto you for un-
questionable truths ; for thus much do these words import :
*we have heard with our ears, O God, our fathers have told
us what thou didst in their days.* 2. The Scripture keepeth the declarations of God's work and will so fresh, and
clean, and pure from the mixture, and superfluity, and im-
perfection of human tradition, that God will own it as his
own proper testimony, when we bring it before him : *our
ears have heard, O God, what thou didst in the times of old.*
3. God's old works have new use in all ages, for the further-
ance of believers' faith, patience and comfort : *we have heard
what thou didst in times of old,* say the saints now in trouble,
and standing in need of experience of the like works of God
for them. 4. Albeit comparison of by-gone better times with
ours, augmenteth grief and temptation at first ; yet when
they are well looked upon in their end and use, they serve
to comfort us, and confirm our faith, as here the persecuted
Kirk's use-making of the like condition of the Lord's people
before them teacheth us. 5. Although families and nations
were rooted in a land, like old oak trees, and were very long
possessors of it ; yet God can drive them out of it, by what
instruments soever he pleaseth to do it ; the work of van-
quishing nations, and subduing them, and casting them out,
is the Lord's work : *thou didst drive out the heathen with thy
hand.* And so is the planting of a people in a land, or continuing families in succession ; *thou plantedst our fathers,
and castedst out the people.* 6. The Lord's part in a work
is best seen, when man's part and all that he, as an instrument, hath done, or could have done, is all declared null ;
being considered as separate from God, who moved the instruments, and wrought by them what he pleased ; *they got
not the land in possession by their own sword, &c.* 7. The

fountain of all good which is done to, or by the church, is only the mere favour of God and his good pleasure ; that they are an incorporation, a church planted, fostered, defended so long, watered, spared so long, all is free favour ; *neither did their own arm save them, but thy right hand, &c., because thou hadst a favour unto them.* 8. When God showeth the light of his countenance to a people or person, he will also show his power for them ; *thy arm and the light of thy countenance, gave them the land in possession.* These two go together.

4. *Thou art my King, O God : command deliverances for Jacob.*

The second argument for confirmation of the church, is from the relation between God and her ; *thou art my King, O God, &c.* Whence learn, 1. Trouble maketh faith thirsty, and teacheth the believer to make use of his right and interest, and relations between God and him, which otherwise possibly might have lien idle in his coffer ; yea, and faith by trouble is made wise to choose out the relation which serveth most for its present use ; *thou art my king, O God.* 2. Relations between God and his people, stand constantly in adversity, as well as in prosperity. The godly in persecution have God for a king to come unto, from whom they may expect all the benefits which subjects can expect from a potent king ; as here the church saith to God, however thou thinkest it fit to put us under the feet of persecutors, yet *thou art my king, O God.* 3. Whatsoever be the particular condition of any member of the church, his prayer should be put forth for the whole body ; specially when the persecution is of the whole ; *command deliverance for Jacob.* 4. It will cost the Lord but a word to deliver his people : let him give out order, and it shall be effected ; the church craveth no more, but *command deliverance.*

5. *Through thee will we push down our enemies ; through thy name will we tread them under that rise up against us.*

6. *For I will not trust in my bow, neither shall my sword save me.*

7. *But thou hast saved us from our enemies, and hast put them to shame that hated us.*

8. *In God we boast all the day long, and praise thy name for ever. Selah.*

The third argument to confirm their faith, is the conscience of their sincere purpose to give God the glory of enabling them unto all duties, whereunto he has promised to enable them. Whence learn, 1. The believer may promise to himself whatsoever God hath promised unto him. Hath God promised to give his own people the victory over their enemies ? then the believer may promise to himself he shall overcome his persecutors, and through God's strength be more than a conqueror over them : *through thee will we push down our enemies.* If the enemy make head against them after a defeat, the believer may say, *through thy name will we tread them under that rise up against us.* 2. The less confidence we have in ourselves, or in any thing besides God, the more evidence have we of the sincerity of our faith in God : *for I will not trust in my bow, neither shall my sword save me.* 3. It is a proof of sincerity of faith, to give God as much credit for time to come, as he hath gained to himself by the evidencing of his truth in time by-gone : *my sword shall not save me : but thou hast saved us, and therefore through thee will we push down our enemies.* 4. Whosoever hateth the Lord's people, shall be forced to think shame of their enmity one day : *thou hast put them to shame that hated us.* 5. The glory which we give to God in prosperity, we should give him the same in our adversity ; change of times and dispensations should not change his glory, nor our confidence in him. Though the church be under foot of men, the church's God is above all : *in God will we boast all the day long, and praise thy name for ever.*

9. *But thou hast cast off, and put us to shame ; and goest not forth with our armies.*

10. *Thou makest us to turn back from the enemy ; and they which hate us spoil for themselves.*

11. *Thou hast given us like sheep* appointed *for meat ; and hast scattered us among the heathen.*

12. *Thou sellest thy people for nought, and dost not increase* thy wealth *by their price.*

13. *Thou makest us a reproach to our neighbours, a scorn and a derision to them that are round about us.*

14. *Thou makest us a by-word among the heathen, a shaking of the head among the people.*

15. *My confusion* is *continually before me, and the shame of my face hath covered me,*

16. *For the voice of him that reproacheth and blasphemeth; by reason of the enemy and avenger.*

Having thus fastened a resolution to believe constantly in God, the psalmist layeth forth the lamentable condition of the church before God, with the temptation that assaulteth his people in their sufferings. Whence learn, 1 It can stand with the constant love of God to his people, to put them to so hard exercises by variety of troubles, as he may seem not only to break off his former course of kindness towards them, but also to cast them off, and turn against them, by sending sore judgments on them, which ordinarily speak unto human sense wrath, and utter wrath : *thou hast cast off ;* yea, and they may seem disappointed of their hoped for protection and assistance from God : *thou hast put us to shame :* and may lose heart and hand when they go to battle against their enemies in a good cause : *thou goest not forth with our armies*; v. 9, and be put to flight in battles, and made a spoil to their despiteful enemies ; *thou makest us turn back from our enemies, and they that hate us spoil for themselves,* v. 10; and, being destitute of human help for recovery, may seem to be left in the hand of the enemy, to dispose of them as it may seem to his pleasure : *thou hast given us like sheep for meat.* And albeit all believers cannot be cut off, yet we may lose the face of a church or congregation : *thou hast scattered us among the heathen,* v. 11, and may be made underlings and slaves to oppressors with no apparent advantage to the Lord's glory, but seeming loss rather : *thou sellest thy people for nought, and dost not increase thy wealth with their price,* v. 12 ; and may be deprived, not only of the common duties of humanity, which may be expected of neighbours, but also be disdained by them, mocked and reproached by them : *thou makest us a reproach to our neighbours, a scorn and derision to them that are about us,* v. 13 ; and, in a word, may be the most despised people under heaven ; which, as it is the just punishment of the scandalous carriage of the visible church, when they make God's name to be reproached among idolaters and heathen people ; is also the sharpest trial and temptation of the truly godly that can be : *thou makest us a byword among the heathen, a shaking of the head among the people,* v. 14.   Learn also, 2. As God's presence, manifested among his people, and for them in the sight of the world, makes them the most famous, wise, courageous, prosperous, and blessed people in the world : so when God, being provoked by the wicked behaviour of his professed people, leaveth them, withdraweth his protection from them, and showeth himself angry at them, they become foolish and feeble sheep, a despicable and a disdained people above all others : *we turn back from the enemy.   Thou hast given us as sheep appointed for meat, a reproach, a scorn, a by-word.* 3. Whatsoever calamity cometh upon us, howsoever, and for whatsoever cause, we may safely take God for the worker of all our woe ; albeit the meritorious cause be in ourselves, the inflicting of the calamity is of the Lord ; for there is no trouble in the city which the Lord will not avow himself to be the inflicter of ; for here the prophet puts all upon God : *thou hast done it,* five or six times.   4. When the visible church hath drawn misery on herself, and God hath inflicted calamities justly on her, it is safer to go to God, and lay before him all his work of justice, and the misery which lieth on us, than to keep it within our breasts, or tell it of him to others ; he that hath wounded us is only able to heal us, so this example teacheth us to do. 5. When the visible church is visited with sad calamities, the true members thereof are partakers of the trouble, and sorrow, and shame of that condition : *my confusion is continually before me,* saith the psalmist. 6. It is not very soon that the church is delivered out of her trouble, when once she falleth into it ; there is a time wherein it is continued : *my confusion is continually before me, and the shame of my face hath covered me,* v. 15.   7. When the enemy reproacheth religion and righteousness, because of the calamity of the godly, the more is spoken of God's respect to the godly and their cause, the more the enemy reproacheth and putteth the godly to shame ; and so, while God's dispensation seemeth to speak the contrary, it seemeth to be but their own confusion for the godly to speak of God, or godliness and the righteousness of their cause. This is a sad case ; *the shame of my face hath covered me, for the voice of him that reproacheth and blasphemeth ; by reason of the enemy and the avenger,* v. 16.

17. *All this is come upon us ; yet have we not for-*

gotten thee ; neither have we dealt falsely in thy covenant.

18. *Our heart is not turned back ; neither have our steps declined from thy way.*

19. *Though thou hast sore broken us in the place of dragons, and covered us with the shadow of death.*

20. *If we have forgotten the name of our God, or stretched out our hands to a strange god ;*

21. *Shall not God search this out? for he knoweth the secrets of the heart.*

22. *Yea, for thy sake are we killed all the day long ; we are counted as sheep for the slaughter.*

In the third place, the godly profess, for all that is said, their steadfastness in the profession of their faith for which they were persecuted. Whence learn, 1. It is the duty of the Lord's people, whatsoever trouble or persecution they shall fall into, to be steadfast in the profession of the true religion, and in every point of controverted truth : *all this is come upon us, yet have we not forgotten thee.* 2. As the maintaining of controverted truth must flow from faith in God and love to him, entertaining the affectionate remembrance of God's kindness, whatsoever change of dispensation they shall feel ; so the passing from a point of truth in time of trouble, is a forgetting of God, who is but hiding himself for a while, till the trial be perfected : therefore say the faithful, *all this is come upon us, yet have we not forgotten thee.* 3. As the Lord hath been pleased to enter into covenant with his church, and to make the covenant a sanctified means for keeping his people more steadfast in their duty ; so should his people make conscience of keeping covenant made with God, and of remaining steadfast in the maintenance of every duty whereunto they stand bound therein, that, when they give account thereof, they may say with comfort, *we have not dealt falsely in thy covenant.* 4. Covenants which people make for adhering to the true religion, and to moral duties commanded in God's word, are not of the nature of human covenants, wherein man and man are the parties, and God only judge and witness, but are such covenants as God is also a party therein, to whom a people is so much the more engaged, as they are sworn to keep his law, and therefore such covenants are called God's covenant : *we have not dealt falsely in thy covenant.* 5. No excuse from hazard of trouble, or persecution, can guard the conscience, to shift or pass from the covenant of God ; nothing can make us give a comfortable account of our carriage in relation to the covenant, save upright and straight dealing before God : *we have not dealt falsely in thy covenant,* v. 17. 6. The Lord can procure more honour to himself in the time of the persecution of his scattered people, by the constancy of his martyrs and suffering saints, in their open profession and maintenance of his truth before their persecutors, than when the visible church lived in prosperity, and scandalized their neighbours by their ill behaviour, as this experience of scattered Israel maketh evident. 7. A good conscience much sweeteneth affliction in the time of trial, as here appeareth. 8. It is necessary for making a man constant in the outward profession of truth in the time of persecution, that his heart be established by grace, that his heart be fixed, trusting in the Lord: these shall be borne through who may say, *our heart is not turned back.* 9. It is necessary to watch over our several actions, lest by little and little in particular passages we be drawn aside from our walking with a straight foot toward the gospel ; and lest the heart be stolen away by little and little from the truth ; therefore these two must be joined together in our endeavour ; *that neither our heart be turned back, neither our steps decline from the Lord's way,* v. 18. 10. Albeit the Lord, for perfecting the full trial of the faith of his people, should put them in the power of most cruel tyrants, and in daily danger of losing their life; yet should they choose to suffer all extremity of torments, and death itself, rather than to depart from the truth ; for so did the Lord's approved witnesses before us: *though God did break them sore in the place of dragons, and cover them with the shadow of death,* v. 19. 11. In the time of trial concerning religion, two sorts of sins are to be eschewed. The one is the passing from any point of the truth of doctrine or divine ordinances ; the other is the practising of any point of false worship of another institution than what is the Lord's ; whether under pretence of offering it to the true God, or with profession unto another God; for both these are to be eschewed, because the first sort of sin is a forgetting of the name of God, the other is *a stretching out of our hands to a strange god.*

12. The Lord, who searcheth the depth of a man's heart, will make special search for corrupters of religion, and depravers of divine doctrine, worship, or ordinances, and all sorts of idolatry, whatsoever excuses or pretences be used for the colouring or covering of the same : *if we have forgotten the name of our God, or stretched out our hands to another god, shall not God search this out ?* v. 20.   13. In time of persecution for religion, nothing can counterbalance the terrors and allurements of the persecutors, and make a man steadfast in the cause of God, save the fear of God, and love to God settled in the heart ; for the reason of the saints' steadfastness in this psalm is, *because God would have searched out their sin*, if they had done otherwise ; for *he knoweth the secrets of the hearts*, v. 21.   14. Such as resolve to bear out the profession of the truth, must resolve to give their life for the maintenance of it : *we are killed all the day long.*   15. It is ordinary for the world to hate the servants of God and true saints, more for their faithfulness to God, and uprightness in his service, than for any other cause : *for thy sake are we killed.*   16. It is mercy to us, that when God might punish us for our sins, he maketh our correction honourable, and our troubles to be for a good cause : *for thy sake are we killed.*   17. Although all the hours of the day the persecutors were taking and killing some of our brethren, the saints, for their faith in God and fidelity in his service ; yet that must not divert the rest from following the truth, and professing true religion ; how long soever the Lord continue the persecution and our trouble for his cause, we should resolve constantly to endure to the end : *yea, for thy sake are we killed all the day long,* v. 22.

23. *Awake, why sleepest thou, O Lord? arise, cast us not off for ever.*

24. *Wherefore hidest thou thy face,* and *forgettest our affliction, and our oppression ?*

25. *For our soul is bowed down to the dust ; our belly cleaveth unto the earth.*

26. *Arise for our help, and redeem us, for thy mercies' sake.*

In the last part of the psalm, the psalmist in behalf of the church prayeth to be delivered from the cruelty of persecutors ;

and, being in bitterness of spirit for anguish and grief, venteth his present sense of God's dispensation, yet corrected by
faith.   Whence learn, 1. Albeit the Lord who watcheth over
Israel be most vigilant for every one of his children, and
never slumbereth nor sleepeth, but is still upon his work, his
glorious work of preparing his jewels for eternal life, even
when he putteth his people in the furnace of affliction by
hottest persecution, (for then in special he is about to glorify
himself and his saints also in the trial of their precious faith,
and is bringing to the view of men and angels, that he hath
a people who love him better than their own lives, and who
will endure any misery rather than deny any point of his
truth committed unto them ;) yet such is the strength of natural senses and affections, such is the partiality of self-love
in carnal disputation about God's providence, when he putteth his people to so sad sufferings for no fault done to their
persecutors ; and such is the power of Satan's temptations,
helped on by human infirmity and perturbation of passions,
that God is looked on as if he misregarded the case of his own
people, and took no more care of them than a sleeping man
doth of his business ; and this is imported in this expression,
awake, why sleepest thou, O Lord ?   2. Faith doth not allow
nor subscribe unto carnal sense, but in presenting the objections thereof unto God, really refuteth them ; first, in
that by prayer it goeth to God, who is the hearer of the most
secret sighs of supplicants, at whatsoever time, night or day,
or in whatsoever place opened up unto him ; secondly, by
intreating him to refute the slander and calumny which carnal sense and suggested temptations put upon him: *awake,
arise ;* that is, let it be seen by the manifesting of thy justice
and mercy, as thou usest to do by thy open working for us,
that thou takest notice of our sufferings, and of our persecutor's violence ; thirdly, by avowing that such misregarding of his own cause and servants, as sense and temptation
vented, is inconsistent with his nature, covenant, promises, and
practices towards his people ; for, *why sleepest thou*, is as
much as, it is not possible that thou sleepest ; and why here
is not a word of quarrelling, but a word of denying, that any
reason can be given for such a thought, as God sleepeth ;
fourthly, by avowing faith and hope of God manifesting himself in due time, for deciding of the controversy between them
and their persecutors ; for what he prayeth for, he believeth

to obtain.　His prayer being according to the revealed will
of God : and *awake, why sleepest thou, O Lord,* is as much
as I believe, Lord, that thou wilt indeed let us and the world
see that thou art not sleeping in all this our hard sufferings
for thy sake, and therefore I pray thee show thyself early.
3. As temptation, if it cannot fasten upon us any thought of
God's careless misregarding of us in our sad sufferings, yet
will it suggest suspicions of God's wrath, indignation, hatred,
rejection, and reprobation of us ; so faith will study to dispel this mist, and quench this fiery dart by prayer also ; *cast
us not off for ever ;* giving assurance, that albeit there were
wrath in their exercise, yet it shall be but for a short time,
and shall not be perpetual.　4. As temptation, if it cannot
fasten upon us suspicion of God's hatred of us, and of his
purpose to cast us off for ever ; yet it will suggest that God
is pursuing us for some sin which we know not of, that he is
wroth with us in suffering persecutors to prevail and to oppress us, (when in the mean time he is glorifying himself, and
his truth in us, edifying others by our constancy in such a
point of truth, and by our patience in bearing the cross, to
the advantage both of the present age and posterity :) so
faith must study to dispel this mist also, and to quench this
fiery dart as well as the former, by rejecting this to be the
cause ; for it is no token of God's pursuing sin in wrath,
when God giveth us grace, not only to believe in him, but
also to suffer for his name's sake, and the gospel's ; when he
maketh us to be his public martyrs and witnesses for his truth,
some in one degree of martyrdom, some in another ; when
he maketh the Spirit of glory and of God to rest upon us,
and so blesseth us, that when on the persecutor's part he is
evil spoken of, he is on our part glorified.　This, I say, is
no token of wrath, no token of pursuing us for our sins.
Therefore albeit sense calls this a hiding of his face, yet faith
will not admit these causes which might import wrath : for,
wherefore hidest thou thy face, is in the terms of faith, as
much as, albeit it be true that we have sinned, and *thou
seemest to hide thy face,* yet I cannot admit this thought, that
this thy dealing with us is in wrath ; I see no reason why
I should expound thy dispensation so ; yea, the very question
wherefore, importeth that the psalmist cannot condescend
upon any suggested reason of this sort, to prove the hiding
of God's face, as sense would say ; and therefore he expect-

eth the Lord will show forth tokens of his love and good-will to them in due time. 5. As when these temptations are refuted by faith, long-lasting trouble meeting with infirm flesh holdeth up the complaint of poor frail man, not being able to endure trouble long, weak nature is ready to think that it is forgotten or laid aside, and striketh still upon its own string of lamentation, whatsoever faith speaketh to the contrary, whether it have reason or not ; so faith must do its office, and that is, when it cannot stop complaining, it must lay forth before God in prayer the lamenter and his lamentation, to find pity ; *why forgetteth thou our affliction, and our oppression ?* 6. All the reason that a poor perse-cuted and afflicted person can bring from himself, to plead pity when he lamenteth his case to the Lord, is his own weak-ness, emptiness, low condition, near-drawing to discourage-ment, fainting, and dying ; for, *our soul is bowed down to the dust.* 7. The godly soul under persecution, resolveth never to yield to the will of the persecutors, nor quit the Lord's cause, but to lie supplicant at God's feet from day to day, and there to die, if it be his will to delay or deny outward re-lief. Thus much the gesture of the supplicant speaks ; *our belly cleaveth to the earth.* 8. Though the believer find no reason in himself of his prayer for relief, yet he findeth rea-sons sufficient to give him hope in God : as, first, the Lord's sovereign power and place to help such weak creatures as come to him in their need ; *arise for our help, arise a help for us ;* secondly, the office of a redeemer, wherewith he clothed himself in the Messiah Christ Jesus; in the paction of whose redemption, and payment of the price of it, and be-gun and perfected accomplishment of it, every believer hath undoubted interest and right unto all particular deliveries out of all straits, as branches and appendices of the great re-demption of their souls unto eternal life. And this is hinted at in these words; *arise for our help, and redeem us ;* thirdly, the purchased, promised, and constantly running forth, and offered mercy of God to believers, looseth all objections and doubts arising from our sins, unworthiness, and ill-deserving; for, *redeem us for thy mercies' sake,* importeth so much.

PSALM XLV.

To the chief musician upon Shoshannim, for the sons of Korah, Maschil. A song of loves.

Laying aside what useth to be spoken here of Solomon's marrying Pharaoh's daughter, and of some typical things therein, (tending to the extenuation of Solomon's fault,) as conjectural and serving nothing to the advantage of that marriage, presuppose the conjecture held, both concerning the occasion, and also what might seem typical in it; because similitudes taken from, and types made of, what thing soever God pleaseth, serve to make clear what the Spirit will have taken up about Christ, or about any spiritual antitype; but doth not serve to make clear the thing resembled by the antitype, from being sinful, as, by the type of Agar, and of the brazen serpent, and of Jonah's punishment, and sundry other similitudes and parables set down in Scripture appeareth. But we are sure this psalm is a song, describing the mystical marriage of the Messiah, Christ Jesus our Lord, and his church, wherein Christ the bridegroom is praised, ver. 1—9;—and the church his spouse is instructed in her duty to him, ver. 10—15;—and the end of the song declared to be the everlasting praise of Christ, ver. 16, 17.

Concerning the inscription, that this psalm is altogether spiritual and holy, appeareth, first, by this, that it is directed to the public minister of God's worship, to be made publicly use of in God's public praises: *to the chief musician, for the sons of Korah;* secondly, it is entitled Maschil, a song to give instruction to the church of God, concerning the majesty and the grace of the kingdom of Christ, and the duty of the church, and the spiritual blessings of the believers; thirdly, it is a part of divine scripture, ranked among the psalms, and acknowleged by the church of the Old Testament for such; fourthly, the testimony of the apostle, applying it directly as the word and speech of the Father to the Son of God, Christ Jesus, Heb. i. 8; fifthly, the matter and words of the psalm, which cannot be verified in any person save in Jesus Christ alone; sixthly, the plurality of loves here spoken of, to show unto the reader the excellency of the love of Christ, or the love of God to us in Christ Jesus; wherein the perfection of all loves that ever were heard tell of, is surpassed; *it is a song of loves.*

1. *My heart is inditing a good matter; I speak of the things which I have made touching the king; my tongue is the pen of a ready writer.*

This verse is a commendation given to this song by the Spirit of God, by way of preface. 1. It is a good matter. 2. It is inspired; the Spirit of the Lord making the heart filled with his presence, to be boiling in the inditing of it.

3. It is of Christ the King. 4. It is the poem of the inspired prophet, made ready to express what is furnished by the Spirit, for the edification of the church in all ages. Whence learn, 1. The knowledge of the love of Christ to his church, and of his espousing her, is the sweetest subject, the matter of the most glad tidings that ever sinners heard of, and worthy indeed to be called a good matter. 2. The heart, acquainted with this sweet and saving knowledge, will be more ready to communicate what it knoweth, than able to express itself; the heart will be as a spring well, a boiling pot, according to the measure of the Lord's presence in it. 3. The theme of the praises of the believing soul is Christ's person, clothed with offices for the salvation of souls; for the main subject of the song is touching the king. 4. When the heart is full of gracious affection, the tongue will be loosed to praise God, so as others may be edified: out of the abundance of the heart, the mouth will speak heartily; *my tongue is the pen of a ready writer.*

2. *Thou art fairer than the children of men; grace is poured into thy lips: therefore God hath blessed thee for ever.*

3. *Gird thy sword upon* thy *thigh, O* most *Mighty, with thy glory and thy majesty.*

4. *And in thy majesty ride prosperously, because of truth, and meekness,* and *righteousness; and thy right hand shall teach thee terrible things.*

5. *Thine arrows* are *sharp in the heart of the King's enemies;* whereby *the people fall under thee.*

6. *Thy throne, O God,* is *for ever and ever: the sceptre of thy kingdom* is *a right sceptre.*

7. *Thou lovest righteousness, and hatest wickedness: therefore God, thy God, hath anointed thee with the oil of gladness above thy fellows.*

8 *All thy garments* smell *of myrrh, and aloes,* and *cassia, out of the ivory palaces, whereby they have made thee glad.*

9. *Kings' daughters* were *among thy honourable women: upon thy right hand did stand the queen in gold of Ophir.*

In the description of the excellency of Christ, the very true Son of God, there are set down sundry points of glory.

1. No beauty among men is comparable to the beauty of Christ, who is not only the fairest of ten thousand for wisdom and holiness, and whatsoever virtue can be named, as he is man; but also, as he is God, he is the resplendency of his Father's glory, the Holy One of Israel, of whose glory the whole earth is full, by whose beautiful righteousness and power the deformity of sin and misery of his own is taken away in part, and shall be removed fully; therefore justly is it said of him, *thou art fairer than the children of men.* 2. Christ, by the doctrine which he delivereth, is able not only to discover sin and misery, and the true way of delivery from the same by grace, and to direct a man in the way of salvation by grace, but also graciously and powerfully to persuade a man to embrace it: *grace is poured into thy lips.* 3. Christ, as man, is furnished, abundantly and above measure, for communicating the blessing to his hearers invincibly and infallibly, and for making his doctrine effectually powerful to salvation to whomsoever he will; for *therefore,* or to this purpose, *God hath blessed him forever.* 4. Christ is furnished to subdue and conquer and bring in so many as he pleaseth under subjection unto his kingdom; he hath his *sword,* even the rod of his mouth, his word, which is sharper than any two-edged sword, which no man can withstand. 5. He goeth not abroad to conquer or subdue without this his sword, which is his word; it is always with him ready to be drawn forth, and to be thrust into the soul and conscience of the hearer with whom he mindeth to deal: *his sword is girded upon his thigh.* 6. Christ is almighty, and so able to make good all that he speaketh, and to make his word of precept, promise, and threatening effectual unto the errand for which it is sent: *he is most mighty.* 7. Where he is pleased to open his word and to discover himself what he is, they that sit in darkness see a great light of his own glory as God; a shining light, a glorious light, making open the deep counsel of God and mystery of men's salvation: *gird thy sword upon thy thigh, O most mighty, with thy glory.* 8. Where he pleaseth to show himself, there the stateliness of a mighty monarch is seen, the sovereignty of the rule of heaven and earth is seen, able to shake with fear and awe of his greatness; with his *glory* there is *majesty,* or stately magnificence. 9. The wheels of Christ's chariot, whereupon he rideth when

he goeth to conquer and subdue new converts to his kingdom, are *majesty, truth, meekness, righteousness*, manifested in the preaching of his gospel ; *majesty,* when the stately magnificence of his person and offices is declared ; *truth*, when certainty of all that he teacheth in Scripture is known ; *meekness*, when his grace and mercy are offered to rebels ; and *righteousness*, when justification by faith in his name is clearly set forth. 10. Christ goeth no voyage in vain, he cometh not short of his intent and purpose, but doth the work for which he cometh, preaching the gospel : *in his majesty, truth, meekness, and righteousness he rideth prosperously.* 11. Christ can do what he will ; he can do terrible things, to make his enemies tremble and his friends reverence him with holy fear, having omnipotency in him to work by, as ready as a man hath his right hand to employ ; let him but will to have any thing done, and it shall be done ; he hath not long to advise what he is able to do, as men consult with their ability whether they be so powerful as to effect what they intend or would have done : *thy right hand shall teach thee terrible things.* 12. Albeit he needeth no admonition to do what he is doing or will do, yet loveth he to have his children furthering the advancement of his kingdom, showing unto him what they would have done, and praying unto him that his kingdom may more and more come, as the form of speech indited by the Holy Spirit importeth : *gird thy sword, ride thou prosperously, &c.* 13. Christ in his conquest is to meet with his enemies, of whom some will openly oppose him, some will feignedly profess subjection, but will not heartily submit themselves unto him, but stand aloof and at a distance, being far from him in their hearts when with their lips they draw near hand unto him ; both these are here called *the King's enemies.* 14. Such as do not draw near unto him in their heart, he can and will send messengers of wrath unto their heart, *threatenings* which shall be executed, *terrors* which shall be followed with judgments, and *judgments* which shall end in their destruction, sudden and unexpected ; how many or how strong soever they seem to be, they shall not stand before him nor be able to hinder his conquest : *thine arrows are sharp in the heart of the King's enemies,* whereby *the people fall under thee.* 15. Christ Jesus, the promised Messiah, was revealed to the church of Israel to be the very true eternal God, that their faith and ours might have satisfaction, and a solid ground to rest upon, in the all-sufficiency and infinite worthiness of the promised Redeemer; as the apostle, Heb. i. 8, confirmeth unto us, citing to this purpose this very text, *thy throne, O God, is for ever and ever.*   16. Christ shall not want a church, from generation to generation; let persecutors do their worst, he shall reign as King, and sit on his throne in his church, giving forth his laws, and executing them, oppose him who will: *thy throne, O God, is for ever and ever.*   17. The sceptre of Christ's kingdom, which is the gospel, or the word of God in Scripture, whereby he gathereth his subjects and ruleth them, and the manner of his governing his people by the rules of his law and discipline, are most just and equitable; a righteous sceptre, whereby the subjects may be instructed in all righteousness, and may be justified and made righteous: *the sceptre of thy kingdom is a right sceptre.*   18. The holiness and righteousness of Jesus Christ, both as he is God and as he is God incarnate, are so essential to his person and employment, that his rule of government and administration of his affairs in his kingdom cannot be but right, as for direction, so also for rewards to them who obey his direction, and punishments of the disobedient: *thou lovest righteousness and hatest iniquity.*   19. As Christ is very God, so is he very man in all things, except sin, like unto us whom he calleth, Psal. xxii. 22, and Heb. ii. 12, *his brethren*, and here his *fellows*, sharemen and partakers of all that is given to him, and joint-heirs with him, Rom. viii. 17, and by reason of making covenant in our name with the Father, and by assuming our nature, according to the tenor of the covenant, God becometh his God and our God, and he, in our name, as man, receiveth the gifts of the Holy Spirit without measure, for fitting him, as he is man, to manage his kingdom in righteousness effectually ; for it is said, *therefore*, or to that intent, *God, thy God, hath anointed thee with the oil of gladness.*   20. The gifts and graces of the Holy Spirit, spoken of here in terms of oil, (employed for figuring men's furnishing unto their calling, and enabling of kings and priests unto their offices, and employed also in the entertainment of honourable guests invited to a feast,) are so bestowed on believers, joint-heirs with Christ, as Christ is not degraded from his sovereignty by his partners' exaltation ; for of Christ it is said, *thy God hath anointed thee with the oil of gladness above thy fellows.* 21. As the attendants of great persons are refreshed by the smell of their ointments and perfumed garments, so are Christ's attendants refreshed with the consolations of Christ's Spirit perfuming all his outward ordinances, wherein, as in his garments, he showeth forth himself to his church more comfortably than any perfume or odoriferous spice can set forth : *all thy garments smell of myrrh and aloes and cassia.* 22. Not only the heavens, where God showeth forth his glory to souls of just men made perfect, but also all the places where his honour dwelleth, all the meetings of his church where he showeth himself in his ordinances to a spiritual eye, are all of them most glorious and stately palaces ; for there is the temple of the Holy Ghost, and there is the beauty of holiness, whence cometh forth the smell of his graces in his ordinances, as *out of ivory palaces.* 23. It is savoury and well-pleasing to Christ when his people find pleasure in him and are refreshed by his blessing upon the public ordinances ; for *thereby they have made thee glad,* saith the psalmist to Christ.   24. Albeit the catholic church, consisting of true converts or real saints, be but the one and only true spouse of Christ, yet particular visible churches, consisting of saints by calling, by obligation, by profession, and common estimation, their own or others ; some of them being true saints indeed in the spirit, some of them but counterfeits and saints in the letter only, are in number many, as they are dispersed for time and place wherein they live, and make up sundry incorporations and ecclesiastic consociations in parishes, towns, countries, and kingdoms, as the Lord giveth them occasion, opportunity, or possibility, to make use of one another for communion of saints ; in this respect, I say, they are many, and therefore the true spouse, the true church, consisting of true converts, (whose praise is of God, to whom only they are certainly known, and not of men,) being but one, is compared to the queen ; but the particular churches, whose collections and consociations are known to men, being many, are compared to ladies of honour which serve the queen; of this sort it is here prophesied, that the most renowned cities, countries, provinces, and kingdoms, should be professed attendants of Christ the bridegroom's honour, and professed servants of

his church, and promoters of the honour, estate, and welfare of his spouse: *kings' daughters among thy honourable
women.*   25. Albeit our Lord will allow a place of honour
and room in his own court unto visible churches, in their
several consociations, greater and smaller, for that service
which they may do in order to the gathering in of the elect
into the inner court of nearest spiritual communion with
him, yet it is the universal invisible church which he counteth his spouse; she is the queen who hath access unto him,
to be in highest honour beside him: *upon thy right hand
did stand the queen.*   26. As the whole society of true
saints reverently attend the will of the Lord, that every one
of them in their place may honour the Lord; so are they
all highly honoured of the Lord, and adorned with whatsoever may make them glorious; for the ornaments put on
by Christ, such as adoption, justification, sanctification,
with all other relations tending to their felicity, are here
compared to the finest gold: *the queen doth stand at his
right in gold of Ophir.*

10. *Hearken, O daughter, and consider, and incline
thine ear; forget also thine own people, and thy father's house;*

11. *So shall the King greatly desire thy beauty; for
he* is *thy Lord, and worship thou him.*

12. *And the daughter of Tyre* shall be there *with
a gift;* even *the rich among the people shall entreat
thy favour.*

13. *The King's daughter* is *all-glorious within; her
clothing* is *of wrought gold.*

14. *She shall be brought unto the King in raiment
of needle-work: the virgins her companions that follow
her shall be brought unto thee.*

15. *With gladness and rejoicing* shall *they* be
brought: they shall enter into the King's palace.

This is the other part of the psalm wherein the Spirit
of the Lord speaketh to the true church militant, and directeth her in her duty; and encourageth her by sundry in-
ducements to follow the Lord's direction.   Whence learn,
1. As because there is spiritual love and respect between
God and his church, therefore the covenant and the spiri-

10

tual communion between Christ and his church are compared to a marriage; so, because the derivation of all spiritual life, grace, and motion which the church hath, is from
God, and dependeth on him; therefore the church is compared to a daughter; *hearken, O daughter*, and ver. 13,
she is called *the King's daughter*.   2. The way and order
of bringing the church to her duty, is by hearing of
his word, consideration of what is taught, and subjection
of her spirit to the obedience of faith; *hearken, O daughter, and consider, and incline thine ear.*   3. Because even
the true members of the church, whose praise is not of men
but of God, are in this life entangled in affection to their
old ways and corruption of manners; therefore every one
hath need to renounce and forget more and more his old
lusts and enticements of the world, which is a very true
fruit, and necessary evidence of their hearing in faith; *forget also*, saith he, *thine own people, and thy father's house.*
4. The more we renounce and abandon our lusts and sinful inclinations in obedience to God, the more are we beautified with holiness, and are acceptable to God in our endeavours; *forsake thy father's house, so shall the King
greatly desire thy beauty.*   5. Christ hath all right unto
our service, and by creation, redemption, and covenant, we
are absolutely bound to serve and honour him in all things;
he is thy Lord, and worship thou him.   6. When the church
honoureth Christ he will honour her, and make the noble
and potent in the world submit themselves to her and seek
communion with her, and to esteem the meanest true member of the church, more blessed than riches or honour can
make any man; *the daughter of Tyre shall be there with a
gift: the rich among the people shall entreat thy favour.*   7.
The glory of the true kirk, and of every true member
thereof is in things spiritual, not discernible by the uptaking of the natural man; for what is outwardly professed,
is inwardly studied unto sincerity by them who worship God
in spirit and in truth; and the graces wherewith she is
adorned, as knowledge, faith, love, hope, zeal, courage,
sobriety, patience, are not the object of outward beholders,
but most beautiful in the eyes of a spiritual discerner, and
in the eyes of Him that seeth in secret: *the King's daughter
is all-glorious within.*   8. Whatsoever inherent graces the
saints have, and how beautiful soever they be; yet they

have need of a garment which may hide their imperfections, and beautify them before God; to wit, the imputed right-eousness of Christ, the husband of the church, who only hath this garment to sell, Rev. iii. 18; and though it be bought without money and without price, yet it is very rich, for whatsoever either nature or art can furnish to set it forth, is but a shadowing similitude of it; *her clothing is of wrought gold.* 9. Though the marriage of Christ and his church be bound up, and the hand-fastening be past, and tokens of love be given to the bride, yet the full solem-nity of the complete marriage is delayed till a set time, that the particular members and the whole church may be per-fected. The time of the bride's being brought to a constant habitation with Christ, is at the Lord's appointed time; to wit, at the death of every particular saint, and of the whole church together at the day of our Lord's second coming; the day is coming, wherein *she shall be brought unto the King.* 10. Albeit now there be many imperfections of the saints, which Christ's imputed righteousness hideth, yet in the day of the church's being brought into the pre-sence of God, to be with him for ever, she shall have no im-perfection, spot or wrinkle, or want of any thing which may perfect her glory in all respects. She shall put on immor-tality and incorruption, and her very body of flesh shall be made conformable to the glorious body of our Lord Jesus; *she shall be brought unto the King in raiment of needle work:* wherein the height of artifice and of nature's ma-terials are joined, as the fittest similitude which can express this inexpressible glory. 11. The same shall be the glori-ous state of particular saints, and particular congregations, which shall be of the whole church universal; whereof as every true congregation and particular saint therein is a part, and have contributed their service in their time to the good of the whole church, as handmaids to their mistress: so shall they share in the glorious reward; *the virgins, her companions shall be brought unto thee,* saith the psalmist unto Christ. 12. Great shall be the joy of men and angels in the general meeting of the whole church, all being gathered together by the angels, who have lived from the beginning of the world to the ending thereof, and all re-ceived into the fellowship of God in blessedness to endure for

*ever; with gladness and rejoicing shall they be brought,
they shall enter into the King's palace.*

16. *Instead of thy fathers shall be thy children,
whom thou mayest make princes in all the earth.*

17. *I will make thy name to be remembered in all
generations: therefore shall the people praise thee for
ever and ever.*

The two last verses may be applied both to the bride the
true militant church, and to the bridegroom Christ Jesus,
the King of saints. As it is applied to the church, learn,
1. The saints have no ground of gloriation in their progenitors according to the flesh, of whom they draw nothing
but what is polluted with sin; but all the glory of the
church is rather in her children which she bringeth forth by
the gospel unto God: *instead of thy fathers shall be thy
children.* 2. What any member of the church seemeth to
lose in the world by forsaking thereof and coming to Christ,
it is made up to them by Christ in spiritual respects, if not
also in temporal blessings when God seeth fit; *instead of
thy fathers shall be thy children.* 3. The true children of
the church are indeed the excellent ones of the earth, and
princes indeed, wherever they live, in comparison of all
other men who are but the beastly slaves of Satan; *thy children are princes in all the earth.* 4. The true church shall
be honourable, and honoured by her kindly children in all
generations, because of the estimation which God putteth
upon her in his holy Scripture; *I will make thy name to be
remembered in all generations: therefore the people shall
praise thee.*

These verses may also be applied more pertinently to the
bridegroom Christ Jesus, for whose praise the whole psalm
is composed, ver. 1. Of whom only the words can be verified fully, as only capable of what is ascribed directly to the
person spoken unto here, and cannot be well ascribed to
Solomon and Pharaoh's daughter in their marriage; because partly Solomon's marriage with outlandish women is
marked among his faults, and so can hardly be esteemed to
be honoured with this song delivered to the church for her
perpetual instruction; partly because in the inscription there
is not so much as mention of Solomon's name, either as

type or resemblance of this marriage of Christ and his church; and partly also because what is here spoken, hath little typical verity answering to it in the history of Scripture concerning Solomon's marriage, or children of Pharaoh's daughter. And lastly, this song is set down not in a typical manner, but in a simple similitude of the marriage of a king and queen indefinitely, whose marriage useth to be the most glorious of all earthly marriages, and fittest to lead us up to that incomparably glorious spiritual marriage of Christ and his church. In which consideration, from these words, learn, 1. Christ draweth not glory from his progenitors according to his flesh, but giveth being, and gracious being, to such as he regenerateth by his word and Spirit, to be his children; and so it may be said to Christ, *instead of thy fathers shall be thy children.* 2. The excellency of Christ's children, and their princely disposition above the rest of mankind unregenerate, is of Christ's making; he only it is, of whom properly it may be said, *thou shalt make thy children princes in all the earth;* for, *he hath made us kings and priests to God and his Father.* 3. By the Spirit that indited this psalm, and all other Scriptures, Christ's name shall be holden forth and remembered from age to age, while the world lasteth : *I will make thy name,* saith the Spirit, *to be remembered to all generations.* 4. Christ's espousing unto himself a church, and gathering more and more from age to age by his word and Spirit unto it, his converting souls, and bringing them into the fellowship of his family, and giving unto them princely minds and affections wherever they live, are large matters of growing and everlasting glory unto his majesty; for in regard of this point, and what is said before in this psalm, he addeth as the close of all, *therefore shall the people praise thee.*

PSALM XLVI.

To the chief musician, for the sons of Korah. A song upon Alamoth.

After some notable delivery of the church from her enemies, the Lord's people confirm themselves in their resolution to trust in God, and not to be afraid of trouble, because of his comfortable presence among them, which is like unto a river of continual refreshment, as late experience gave evidence, v. 1—6 ; and exhort all men in the world to observe this his late work, and make use of it for their humiliation, v. 7—10, as the church maketh use of it for confirmation, v. 11.

1. *God* is *our refuge and strength, a very present help in trouble :*

2. *Therefore will not we fear, though the earth be removed, and though the mountains be carried into the midst of the sea ;*

3. Though *the waters thereof roar* and *be troubled,* though *the mountains shake with the swelling thereof. Selah.*

From bygone experience of God's defending his church, the Lord's people strengthen themselves in the faith of God's word, concerning the care of his people; and from this ground guard their heart against the fear of all possible trouble in time coming. Whence learn, 1. Faith in God's word and profession of it, are made much more vigorous and lively after experience of the verity thereof; for the church believed this truth before this late delivery, but now after this fresh experience they are animated to set to their seal to it more confidently, saying, *God is our refuge.* 2. Albeit the church were destitute of all human strength within herself, and were forsaken, yea and pursued by all kings and princes, yet hath she God for a retiring place, and for furnishing of what is sufficient for her subsistence; *God is our refuge and strength.* 3. Albeit the Lord will not exempt his people from trouble, yet he will be near them in time of trouble; and when their weakness is discovered to them, then he will help them, and will not delay his help too long, but will give help in time of need effectually; for God is to his people *a very present help in trouble.* 4. Nothing can guard the heart of God's people against the terror of possible, or imminent troubles, save faith in God; for here the Lord's people, having fixed their faith, make this inference, *therefore will we not fear.* 5. The terror of apparent trouble, is the touchstone of confidence in God, and then is faith fixed, when it doth look upon the greatest dangers and troubles that can be imagined, with resolution to adhere to God, and to that truth which persecutors oppose, whatsoever may come: *we will not fear, though the earth be removed.* 6. Albeit the whole frame of the world were changed, and the work of creation were either dissolved or confounded, which shall be in effect at the last day; yet faith findeth footing and ground to stand upon in God himself; *we will not fear, though the mountains be carried into the midst of the sea, though the waters thereof roar and be troubled, though the mountains shake with the swelling thereof. Selah.*

4. There is *a river, the streams whereof shall make glad the city of God, the holy* place *of the tabernacles of the most High.*

5. *God* is *in the midst of her; she shall not be moved : God shall help her,* and that *right early.*

The church looketh upon the Lord's word and ordinances, joined with the blessing of his Spirit among them, as upon a sufficient consolation against whatsoever trouble can be imagined. Whence learn, 1. Although there be many particular persons in the Lord's church militant, and many particular congregations as there were many habitations in Jerusalem, and many tabernacles at the time of the solemn feast, when all the Lord's people were gathered to- gether to the keeping thereof; yet they are all one church universal, one kingdom of God, one city, compact together in the union of one sealed covenant, one true faith, and one Spirit ; the plurality *of the tabernacles of God* doth make but *one city of God* here. 2. Albeit trouble without com- fort may fall on men who know not God ; yet to believers within the church there can no trouble come, wherein the true citizens may not find consolation and joy to uphold them against all causes of sorrow ; *there is a river, the streams whereof make glad the city of God.* 3. The con- solations which God furnishes to all who will make use of them within the church, are not like the consolations which the world can afford, which are in all respects insufficient to overcome trouble ; but the consolations of God are abun- dant, constantly running, ready at hand, and able to make a man a conqueror over trouble effectually, and to make him rejoice in the Lord in the midst of trouble; for this is im- ported in the similitude of refreshing water ; *there is a river, the streams whereof shall make glad the city of God.* 4. God will never forsake his people who seek after him, but where they are following his ordinances in any measure of sincerity, there will he be : *God is in the midst of her.* 5. As the consolation of the church, so also the stability of the church, and continuance of it from generation to genera- tion, dependeth upon God's settled residence therein : *God is in the midst of her, she shall not be moved.* 6. God's presence among his people will not exempt them from trouble, but from perdition in trouble : he will not exempt the bush from burning, but from being consumed ; *for God shall help her.* 7. Albeit the Lord does not appear at the point of time when we would, yet shall he come and help in time of need most timously ; *God shall help her, and that right early.*

6. *The heathen raged, the kingdoms were moved ; he uttered his voice, the earth melted.*

7. *The Lord of hosts* is *with us ; the God of Jacob* is *our refuge.   Selah.*

He cleareth the doctrine delivered, by a late experience of God's taking order with the enemies of the church, at the time when they in great confluence and power made assault against her.   Whence learn, 1. It is no small indignation which the world beareth against the Lord's kingdom, his people, and work among them : nor is it any mean power, from which the church is in danger to suffer hardship; but fury in the height of it, and force in the farthest extent of it, may she expect to encounter with : *the heathen raged, the kingdoms were moved.*   2. It is not the worldly power of the Lord's people which can sustain the assault of their raging enemies, but God must prove party to her oppressors ; therefore here the Lord interposeth himself for his people ; *the Lord uttered his voice.*   3. It shall not cost the Lord any business to despatch the enemies of his people ; let him show himself a little, let him but say the word, and they are gone ; as snow before the sun, or fat cast into the fire, so are they consumed ; *he uttered his voice, the earth melted.*   4. Any one experience of the Lord's working for his church, may suffice to confirm the faith of his people concerning his perpetual presence in his church, for assistance of his people in their difficulties ; for, from this one experience he draweth the inference ; *the Lord of hosts is with us.*   5. What the Lord is in wisdom, power, and other attributes, that may the church apply to herself, and be sure to have the fruit of it as her need requireth ; if hosts of heathen and huge great armies of whole kingdoms be against his church, yet still we may be sure that God the Lord of armies will stand up against them, and for his church : *the Lord of hosts is with us.*   6. The covenant of

God made with the church in former ages is good enough
security for the church in after ages, for obtaining whatsoever benefit his covenant includeth; *the God of Jacob is our
refuge*; yea, the right made to the incorporation of the
church, is as good security for the use of every particular believer, as if it were made personally to every member by
name; and therefore, as wise citizens reckon whatsoever they
can claim by their town charter, no less to belong to them
than their own private possessions : so whatsoever the believer can claim by virtue of the great charter made to the
church, he should reckon it as sure to be his, as if his proper
name had been specified in the promises; for, *the God of
Jacob is our refuge*, is thus much; because God is undoubtedly the God of Jacob, and his children's refuge, he must
undoubtedly be our God, who are members of that incorporation, and our refuge.

8. *Come, behold the works of the Lord, what desolations he hath made on the earth.*

9. *He maketh wars to cease unto the end of the earth;
he breaketh the bow, and cutteth the spear in sunder;
he burneth the chariot in the fire.*

10. *Be still, and know that I* am *God : I will be
exalted among the heathen, I will be exalted in the
earth.*

11. *The Lord of hosts* is *with us : the God of Jacob is our refuge.   Selah.*

In the latter part of this psalm, he exhorts all men to
make use of this deliverance given to the church for their
humiliation, confidence in God, and consolation.   Whence
learn, 1. When God worketh works of wonder in favour of
his church, most men mark not the Lord's doing; such is
the dulness and stupidity, ingratitude, misbelief, and perverseness of men, either thinking little of his work, or ascribing the praise to instruments, or some other thing besides
God; so that there is need to call unto men, and set them to
their duty; *come and behold the works of the Lord.   2.*
Wonderful calamities doth God pour out upon the enemies
of his people, when he entereth into judgment with them;
for what they intended to do to his people, he doth unto
them; *behold what desolations he hath made in the earth.*
3. When it seemeth good to the Lord, he can give peace

universally to his church, and awhile's breathing from the
troubles of outward enemies: *he maketh wars to cease to
the ends of the earth.* 4. Long preparations for war, arms
and ammunition which have been made with great labour
and expenses against his church, the Lord can soon give a
short account of them, and make them useless when he
pleaseth; *he breaketh the bow, and cutteth the spear in sunder, he burneth the chariot in the fire.* 5. Because men
cannot understand what they are doing, or what is their
duty, so long as their passions are aloft, so long as their
minds are tumultuous, busied about many things, and distracted from what is most necessary; it is good for people,
from time to time, to gather in their straying thoughts, to
silence their passions and perturbations, and humbly com-
pose themselves for observation of whatsoever God requireth of them: *be still, and know that I am God.* 6. It is
better for men to be wise and acknowledge the Lord by the
words of his instruction, than to leave their lesson to be
learned by doleful experience and danger of destruction; *be
still, and know that I am God.* 7. There is not so ready
a way for the Lord's people to quiet their mind against the
fear of trouble and persecution of men, as to settle their
faith about God's taking care of his people and of his own
cause, and of his mind declared against his and their enemies; *be still, and know that I am God.* 8. The Lord will
not be at a loss by the opposition of his enemies; he will not
fail to enlarge his glory, the more that men go about to suppress it; he will make an inroad upon his adversaries' lands,
and make them know himself to be God, either to their
conversion, or confusion and destruction; *I will,* saith he,
be exalted among the heathen. 9. How little notice soever
be taken of the majesty of God ofttimes in the visible church,
and always without the church he be misregarded, yet will
he see to his glory, not only in the church, but also among
the enemies of the church; and not only among such as have
actually invaded his people, but also among them far and
near that have taken no notice either of him or of his people:
I will be exalted in the earth. 10. Whatsoever manifestation of God's power be made in the world by his judgment
against his enemies who know him not; yet he is ever doing
for his church, and not against her: *the Lord of hosts is
with us.* 11. The church of God, or believers, need not

care how many be against them, seeing they have more for them than can be against them; to wit, God and all the creatures at his command : *the Lord of hosts is with us.* 12. The strength of the church stands in her renouncing her own and fleeing unto God's strength, and not in opposing their enemy by strong hand, but by betaking themselves to God : *the God of Jacob is our refuge.* 13. We have need to make God the ground of our confidence, and to make our communion with God the ground of our comfort; for God is sufficient for us against every evil, and God is sufficient unto us for furnishing every good; and we have need to fix and settle our grounds, by oftener subscription of this truth, and oftener avowing of it : *the Lord of hosts is with us, the God of Jacob is our refuge,* is repeated.

PSALM XLVII.

To the chief musician.   A psalm for the sons of Korah.

This psalm is a prophecy of the enlargement of Christ's kingdom, and of the conjunction of Jews and Gentiles in one body under Christ their Head and Lord, delivered by way of exhortation to Jews and Gentiles, joyfully to praise the God and Saviour of his people, Jesus Christ, on whom the psalmist looketh as now ascended into heaven triumphantly, after the full payment made of the price of redemption, and as going about the gathering in of the redeemed Gentiles, till he bring in the fulness of them into one church with the Jews. The exhortation is prefixed, ver. 1, and repeated, ver. 6, 7. The reasons of the exhortation to a joyful praising of him are seven. The first, ver. 2; the second, ver. 3; the third, ver. 4; the fourth, ver. 5; the fifth, ver. 7; the sixth, ver. 8; the seventh, ver. 9.

1. *O clap your hands, all ye people ; shout unto God with the voice of triumph:*

From the exhortation to Jews and Gentiles, joyfully to praise the Redeemer, learn, 1. Christ's kingdom and the benefits thereof belong to more nations than one, for in him the redeemed in all the nations of the earth are blessed : *clap your hands, all ye people*, or, *all ye nations*, saith the Lord. 2. The kingdom of Christ coming to a people, or family, or person, is matter of chief joy to them, because thereby delivery cometh from sin, Satan, and misery, and sure mercies of righteousness, peace, and joy in the Holy Ghost, with eternal life, brought to them, and therefore just reason to say to them to whom Christ cometh, *O clap your hands, shout unto God with the voice of triumph.* 3.

Our joy and our victory over all our enemies, which Christ hath purchased and bringeth to all believers in every nation, are the matter of Christ's praise, and declare that he is God, who, having in his manhood suffered, wrestled against sin, Satan, death, hell, and the curse of the law, did, by the power of his Godhead, prevail before he brought joy to the Gentiles. Thus much the words of the exhortation import; for his triumph presupposeth his victory, and his victory presupposeth his battle before he overcame, and the commanding of the Gentiles *to clap their hands and shout*, and to shout *with the voice of triumph*, presuppose their interest in the victory; and, while they are bidden shout to *God*, the triumpher, who, in all this psalm, is the Redeemer, Christ (as shall appear hereafter), it imports that the Redeemer is God, and howsoever he is God inseparably from the Father and the Holy Spirit, yet here he is distinctly to be looked on in his person; and howsoever he is inseparably to be praised with the Father and Holy Spirit, yet here he is distinctly to be praised for this his work of victorious redemption of sinners; therefore it is said with distinct relation to his person, *shout unto God with the voice of triumph.*

2. *For the Lord most High* is *terrible :* he is *a great King over all the earth.*

From the first reason of the joyful praising of Christ, taken from his sovereign majesty over all the world, learn, 1. That the Redeemer, the victorious triumpher, is the Lord very God, essentially *Jehovah, the Lord most high.* 2. Christ is able both to keep his subjects in subjection by his rod and corrections, and to take order with his enemies also, how high soever they be: *the Lord most high is terrible.* 3. Christ hath right and just title to erect a church in what country and kingdom he pleaseth, without asking any man's license, and to set up among his subjects the profession of his name, and practice of all his ordinances pertaining to the exercise of religion, in doctrine, worship, and ecclesiastic government of his subjects : *he is a great King over all the earth.*

3. *He shall subdue the people under us, and the nations under our feet.*

From the second reason for joyfully praising Christ, taken from the increasing of his own kingdom, and the exalting of all his subjects above the rest of the world, learn, 1. The true church of Christ may, from age to age, promise to herself addition of new subjects, or bringing down of their enemies under their feet; for, as the true church in the prophet's time might say, so may also every true church say after them, *he shall subdue the people under us, and the nations under our feet.* 2. If it will not please the Lord at such a time as men would wish, to execute judgment on their enemies, nor yet to convert them, and make them additional subjects to his kingdom, yet shall he not fail to make his own people victorious over their opposition, power, and persecution, and more than conquerors in this respect : *he shall subdue the people under us, and the nations under our feet.*

4. *He shall choose our inheritance for us, the excellency of Jacob, whom he loved.   Selah.*

From the third reason of Christ's praise, taken from the care he hath for sustentation and welfare of his subjects, learn, 1. As God, by allotting earthly Canaan for the inheritance of his people, testified his care to provide for them both earthly sustenance and an enduring substance for their spiritual subsistence represented thereby; so will he provide for the sustenance of all his subjects in all ages, both bodily and spiritual: *he shall choose our inheritance for us.*   2. As he is most loving of us, and more wise to make choice of what is good for us than we ourselves are; so will he employ his wisdom and love in carrying out unto us our lot, measure, portion, and inheritance : *he shall choose our inheritance for us*, and not leave it to our carving.   3. The main part of the inheritance of Christ's subjects is no earthly thing, but his very best blessing, such as he gave to Jacob above Esau : *their inheritance shall be the excellency of Jacob.*   4. The fountain of Christ's care for all his subjects, is common to them and to Jacob, and that is his love : *the excellency of Jacob whom he loved, shall be their inheritance. Selah.*

5. *God is gone up with a shout, the Lord with the sound of a trumpet.*

From the fourth reason of Christ's praise, taken from his glorious triumphing over all his enemies and ours when he ascended to heaven, learn, 1. " He that ascended, what is it but that he also descended first into the lower parts of the earth? he that descended is the same also that ascended up far above all heavens, that he might fill all things," Eph. iv. 9. That is, Christ, being very God, descended, in humbling himself to take on him the shape of a servant, and when he had perfected the work of redemption, ascended in our nature, the same very person still, very God, which descended; for *God is gone up with a shout.*   2. As the ark of the covenant, the figure of Christ, after the victory gotten over the chief enemies of the church, ascended up to Zion and God's presence; so Christ, after victory obtained over his chief enemies on the cross, ascended triumphantly into heaven: *God is gone up with a shout, Jehovah with the sound of a trumpet.*

6. *Sing praises to God, sing praises ; sing praises unto our King, sing praises.*

7. *For God is the King of all the earth ; sing ye praises with understanding.*

The exhortation given to all people to praise Christ for the work of redemption, is repeated, and directed to the church of the Jews more particularly, with a fifth reason of praise, taken from a nearer conjunction between Christ and them, than between him and any other nation.   Whence learn, 1. Albeit the Lord showeth his glory in the works of creation, and is shining daily in the works of providence also; yet in the work of redemption, conversion, and salvation of souls, his glory is manifested far more; for here, *praise, praise, praise,* and the fourth time *praise* is called for.   2. When believers in Jesus Christ consider how he abased himself to assume our nature, how he paid the ransom for us as surety, how he encountered and fought with all our enemies, and, being victorious in our name, ascended in our nature with the shout of victory and sound of the trumpet of the triumpher, they cannot choose but see reasons for praising joyfully the glorious Godhead of Jesus Christ, and of singing praises to him as God again and again.   3. Of all nations of the earth the Jews have the first place, privilege, and prerogative, most bonds with and interests in Jesus Christ; for he delivered them out of Egypt, settled them in Canaan, held house among them in a tabernacle, answered them by oracle out of the ark of the covenant, the type of his incarnation, took upon him to be their king and sanctifier, the Holy One of Israel, their Redeemer, took of them his human nature, and was born a Jew, therefore had the prophet good reason to say to the church of the Jews, *sing praises to our King, sing praises ;* and in this song may all they join with the Jews who have embraced Jesus for their king.　4. Christ is so king over the Jews, as he also extendeth his kingdom over all the earth, not only in regard of his power in a common manner, but in regard of his special grace gathering in subjects out of all parts of the world, till he have the full number brought in and saved; he, he only, is the true catholic king : *for God is the King of all the earth.* 5. As none can praise God, or praise Christ sincerely, who do not understand the reasons for which they should praise; so he that praiseth understandingly, cannot choose but praise affectionately, therefore, saith he, *sing ye praises with understanding.*

8. *God reigneth over the heathen : God sitteth upon the throne of his holiness.*

From the sixth reason of Christ's praise, taken from the keeping a church among the Gentiles for gathering the redeemed out of all tongues and languages, and reigning among them as king of saints, and author of holiness, learn, 1. To the end that faith may find footing and a rock to rest upon, we must, in all the promises, works, and praises of Christ, still remember that as he is now very man, so is he also eternally God, and that no man reasonably or with understanding can praise him as the redeemer and perfecter of what is spoken of him in Scripture, except he acknowledge him to be God; therefore is Christ eight times in this psalm called God, beside the ascribing unto him works proper to God only; and twice he is called by the incommunicable name of Jehovah the Lord; and in this verse Godhead is twice acknowledged in him, as King of the church among the Gentiles : *God reigneth over the heathen, God sitteth upon the throne of his holiness.* 2. Because the sum of Christ's kingdom is holiness, and his work is to teach, prescribe, and command holiness, to take away sin, and powerfully to apply and work in his own redeemed ones holiness, and to continue in his actual governing of his subjects, till he have made all and every one of the redeemed perfectly holy; therefore is his throne in a special manner called the throne of holiness : *God sitteth upon the throne of his holiness.*

9. *The princes of the people are gathered together,*

even *the people of the God of Abraham ; for the shields of the earth* belong *unto God : he is greatly exalted.*

From the seventh reason of Christ's praise, taken from his converting great men of the earth (as kings and princes), and bringing them to the obedience of the faith and union with the true church, learn, 1. Albeit ofttimes it is seen, that not many rich, noble, or potent are called; yet God for his own glory is, from time to time, bringing in some of them, and when it may glorify his name, shall bring in and perfect what is promised and prophesied here : *the princes of the people are gathered together.* 2. It is a point of Christ's praise in the conversion of men, that his omnipotency maketh men voluntary subjects, and to come in to him as by invincible power on his part, so also deliberately with a free election, and hearty consent of will on the converted man's part : the princes of the people and excellent ones in the earth, of whatsoever rank, converted unto Christ, are voluntary people; for the original suffereth also this reading : *the voluntary of the people are gathered together.* 3. The church of the Jews is the mother church, whereof Abraham and the godly Jews, yea, and Christ himself were members; the church of the Jews is the olive-tree, whereinto all the converts of the Gentiles are ingraffed, gathered, and made one people with Abraham and the faithful among the Jews : *the princes of the people are gathered together, the people of the God of Abraham.* 4. The unity of the church standeth in the union of the Spirit, under the service of the only true God and in conjunction with his people; for the union of Jew and Gentile *is the gathering together of the princes of the people to the God of Abraham.* 5. As there is a necessity of the union of Jews and Gentiles in one visible Christian church, because it is promised and prophesied that it shall be so; so there is reason to wish for the more evident union of them, that they may be as eminently consociate as ever the Christian churches were, either in the Apostles' time, or in the Christian emperors' time, in a general assembly or œcumenical council; because there is at least a possibility of an œcumenical council, or a general assembly of Jews and Gentiles in this world under Christ their King. This place makes it plain, because after it is foretold that there shall be such a union of all the people of the God of Abraham, Jews and Gentiles, as *their princes shall be gathered together*, he takes away the chief ground of a great objection which may be made from the discord and disagreement of the princes of the world; some of them being averse altogether from the Christian religion, some of them from the true religion of Christ, and all of them almost dissenting one from another, and warring one against another; whereby now for many years the gathering of an œcumenical council hath not been possible. He meeteth this objection in the text, saying, *for the shields of the earth belong unto God*, that is, the hearts and power of all the kings of the earth are in the Lord's hand, and he hath the disposing of shields, armies, and ammunition, with all their commanders and rulers in the world, and therefore can make them serviceable for the nearest conjunction and union of his visible church, which can be for his glory in this world, as he sees fit, how and when he will. 6. When all is said of Christ's praise that man can express of him, there is no possibility to attain the full or satisfactory setting forth of his glory as it deserveth; but men must content themselves to set sail, and to rest in the general, that Christ is and shall be very highly glorified; for so the psalmist closeth, saying after all, *he is greatly exalted.*

PSALM XLVIII.

A song and psalm for the sons of Korah.

In this psalm the Lord is magnified for all his mercies bestowed on his church, resembled by Jerusalem, v. 1—3. And in special for a late mercy manifested in a passage of his care to preserve Jerusalem, a type of the church universal, against the assault of mighty kings, ver. 4—6. The uses of which mercies are set down, in number seven; the first, v. 7; the second, v. 8; the third, v. 9; the fourth, v. 10; the fifth, v. 11; the sixth, v. 12, 13; the seventh, v. 14.

1. *Great* is *the Lord, and greatly to be praised in the city of our God,* in *the mountain of his holiness.*

2. *Beautiful for situation, the joy of the whole earth,* is *mount Zion,* on *the sides of the north, the city of the great King.*

3. *God is known in her palaces for a refuge.*

In the first place, he declareth his purpose to give God the praise of whatsoever is commendable in Jerusalem, or done unto it, or wrought for it. Whence learn, 1. As God shows his greatness and glory in all his works, and specially

in his care for, respect unto, and operation in his church;
so should he have glory and praise from his church, for and
from all his works, but specially for his care of her : *great
is the Lord, and greatly to be praised in the city of our God.*
2. As it is the benefit of Jerusalem, and of his church represented thereby, to be united and governed in a regular
incorporation; so it is a matter of God's praise that he
maketh his visible church above all other incorporations and
societies of men in the world to be his city, with which he
will be in covenant, and wherein he will manifest his holy
name; therefore Jerusalem, and the church represented by
her, is here called, *the city of our God, and the mountain of
his holiness.*   3. Whatsoever could commend Jerusalem for
situation in point of pleasantness, commodity, strength, or
stateliness; all is but a shadow of the glory of the Lord's
church, and in particular, as the joy of the whole land depended on Jerusalem's welfare, and this city did adorn all
Judea, and the great King's palace adorned her; so the
church is the joy of the whole earth, by holding out to all
the light of saving doctrine, and showing the authority,
power, wisdom, and grace of Christ; who is her great King,
and who beautifieth her, for the illumination of the blind,
dark world : *beautiful for situation, the joy of the whole
earth is mount Zion, on the sides of the north, the city of the
great King.* 4. As the walls, houses, and palaces of Jerusalem were not the strength of the citizens, but God was
her strength, as they had learned by experience; so worldly
strength is not the confidence of God's church, but God
only, who defendeth her by his power : *God is known in her
palaces for a refuge.*

4. *For, lo, the kings were assembled, they passed by
together.*

5. *They saw* it, and *so they marvelled ; they were
troubled,* and *hasted away.*

6. *Fear took hold upon them there,* and *pain, as of
a woman in travail.*

He confirmeth what he hath spoken, by a late experience
of deliverance from the invasion of mighty kings, gathered
to besiege and destroy Jerusalem.   Whence learn, 1. The
Lord by experience, from time to time, maketh manifest his
care to defend his church against most mighty oppressors,

who use to combine themselves together, when they mind to overthrow the church : *for, lo, the kings were assembled.* 2. Many imaginations are in the heads of adversaries when they are plotting the ruin of God's church, which, when they are about to execute, vanish and prove presumptuous and vain apprehensions of their own ability, and of the church's weakness : *when the kings were assembled, they passed by together.* They found themselves unable to effect what they intended and hoped to bring to pass. 3. When the strait cometh, and the church is in danger, then the Lord showeth himself for her, and against her enemies, and makes men see his interest in his church; now, when the kings were assembled, they perceived themselves mistaken wonderfully : *they saw it, so they marvelled.* 4. Such as come to bring trouble to God's church, come to catch trouble to themselves : when kings assembled to trouble God's people, *they saw, and marvelled, and were troubled.* 5. If the enemies of the church could foresee their own foul retreat, they would not advance, or make assault against the church; for now when they saw matters as they were indeed, *they were troubled, and hasted away.* 6. Besides the mischief which God bringeth upon the church's enemies, when he begins to plead by way of judgment against them, he sendeth terror on them also, a messenger of the ill tidings to forewarn them that worse shall yet befall them : *fear took hold upon them there.* 7. Heart and hand, courage and strength, counsel and resolution fail a man, when he seeth God to be his party, and to be prevailing against him : *fear took hold on them, and pain as a woman in travail ;* sudden, unexpected, sore, and inevitable, is their destruction when it cometh.

7. *Thou breakest the ships of Tarshish with an east wind.*

The first use they make of this experience is this, they are led up by it to see and acknowledge God's power in all the world, to take order with, and destroy whomsoever he will. Whence learn, 1. No power can stand before God, and none can escape his hand; go whither they will, he can arm some of his creatures against them, both by land and sea : *thou breakest the ships of Tarshish with an east wind.* 2. One work of the Lord's justice or power against his enemies, and one experience of his merciful defending his church, should lead his people to acknowledge his sovereign power and omnipotence over all, whereby he, having all creatures at his disposal, can secure his people from all quarters, and destroy all that shall rise against them; for this speech saith this in substance : thou, who hast scattered the armies of kings who had invaded us, hast power in all the world by sea and land to overtake thy enemies; for, *thou breakest the ships of Tarshish with an east wind.*

8. *As we have heard, so have we seen in the city of the Lord of hosts, in the city of our God : God will establish it for ever.   Selah.*

The second use is this : by this experience we perceive that the Lord will keep his promise to his church, and preserve her for ever.   Whence learn, 1. They that believe the word of God, and mark his works foretold in the word, shall see and find by experience the event thereof to answer to the prediction; and, having their faith so confirmed, they should say, *as we have heard, so have we seen in the city of the Lord.*   2. The mercies of the Lord bestowed on his church for her defence and continuance, flow from his covenanting with his church; for the reason of the mercy now bestowed is, *because the city of the Lord of hosts is the city of our God.* 3. Albeit all kingdoms and commonwealths be subject to destruction, and have their certain limits and periods; yet the church, the kingdom of Christ, the city of God, shall endure throughout all generations, and the gates of hell shall not prevail over it : *God shall establish it for ever.*

9. *We have thought of thy loving-kindness, O God, in the midst of thy temple.*

A third use is the acknowledgment of the sweet fruit of their former patient depending upon God's kindness in the use of public ordinances, and now they perceive by this late experience it was not vain.   Whence learn, 1. They that believe God's loving-kindness in the time when there are apparent signs of his wrath, and patiently depend on him in the use of holy ordinances, shall not be frustrate of their expectation, as here the psalmist acknowledgeth. 2. As it is a good thing patiently to wait on God's loving-kindness in the use of the means, when troubles and dangers come; so it is a good thing for the godly, after receiving the fruit of their faith, hope, and patience, to observe the grace gotten of God, which made them to meditate upon and look unto his loving-kindness, and so to strengthen themselves in their resolutions to follow this blessed course hereafter, as the faithful do here : *we have thought of thy loving-kindness, O God, in the midst of thy temple.*

10. *According to thy name, O God, so* is *thy praise unto the ends of the earth : thy right hand is full of righteousness.*

A fourth use is their gladness because of the increase of God's glory by this his late mercy towards them, wherever it should be mentioned. Whence learn, 1. Whatsoever God giveth himself out for, that will he be found to be answerable unto in effect, even to all his holy and magnificent attributes: *according to thy name, O God, so is thy praise.* 2. The manifestation of God's name by preaching of his word cometh to many, who will not subscribe all to be true that is said of him; but afterward, when he maketh his word good, to the comfort of his people and overthrow of his enemies, men will be forced to say of him, that he is as good as his word, and that his works loose his word laid in pawn for performance of it : *according to thy name, O God, so is thy praise unto the ends of the earth.* 3. The Lord's power is not idle, but constantly working in equity and justice for performance of promises and threatenings, for defending his people, and punishing his enemies: *thy right hand is full of righteousness.*

11. *Let mount Zion rejoice, let the daughters of Judah be glad, because of thy judgments.*

A fourth use is to stir up all good people to rejoice, because God hath pleaded their cause against their enemies. Whence learn, 1. It becometh all men to be glad to see God glorify himself in deciding controversies equitably; but most of all the people of God, who have the present benefit thereof, and in whose favour controversies between them and their enemies are decided : *let mount Zion rejoice, and let the daughters of Judah be glad.* 2. Albeit it be lawful for God's people to rejoice when the enemies are punished; yet had they need to take heed to their spirit, that their joy be not fleshly, for satisfaction gotten to their vindictive passions; but spiritual, for the declaration of God's kindness to his people, and just indignation at the wickedness of their malicious persecutors: *let them be glad, because of thy judgments.*

12. *Walk about Zion, and go round about her : tell the towers thereof.*

13. *Mark ye well her bulwarks, consider her palaces ; that ye may tell* it *to the generation following.*

The sixth use of this late experience of the church's delivery, is to observe the impregnable defence of the church, shadowed forth by the walls of Jerusalem, for the encouraging of God's people in all ages, and cautioning all men to beware of attempting to do her wrong in time coming. Whence learn, 1. The church of God is so well guarded by God's wisdom, power, good-will, and justice, as with a wall of fire, that all the strength to be observed in the walls and towers of earthly Jerusalem are but shadows; for, *walk about Zion, and go round about her, and tell the towers thereof*, is no other thing than look through the type, and consider God's protection represented thereby.   2. When a type is to be studied, observation particularly may and should be made of whatsoever in it may lead us further in upon the right uptaking of the antitype resembled thereby: *walk about, go round about ; mark ye well her bulwarks, consider her palaces ;* for in God, or in God's attributes, something answerable to all these will be found.   3. What light the Lord furnisheth concerning himself and his church, which may glorify God, and serve posterity for their edification, should be transmitted to them : *mark ye well, that ye may tell it to the generation following.*

14. *For this God* is *our God for ever and ever : he will be our guide even unto death.*

The seventh and last use of this experience of the church, is consolation in God to God's people in every hard case, and encouragement to them against all future fears, because God is the same constantly to his people in all ages as the late experience of the church had given proof.   Whence learn, 1. The great Maker of heaven and earth, and Redeemer of his people is one and the same for ever, both in himself and towards those that believe in him; *this God is our God.*   2. God is still in covenant with his church, and with all the members thereof, as well in one age as in another; now, as of old; for, *this God is our God for ever and ever.*   3. God will guide them whose God he is, when they seek his counsel out of desire to follow it, and he will not lay down the conducting and governing of those who have committed themselves unto him, but will guide them constantly all the days of their life; *he will be our guide, even unto death.*

PSALM XLIX.

To the chief musician.   A psalm for the sons of Korah.

This psalm sets forth the gloriation of a believer in the grace of God, and in his blessed condition, wherein he is lifted up above all the wealthy and honourable men in the world who are not reconciled unto God: and this the psalmist delivereth out of his own feeling and experience. And, first, because it is a main matter and worthy of all acceptation, he maketh a preface to his gloriation, v. 1—4.   Then he cometh out with it, making his boast in God, that by faith in God he was so secured against sin and misery that they should not be able to mar his happiness, v. 5.   Thirdly, he preferreth his blessedness above whatsoever wealth or riches could yield to man, v. 6—10, and above whatsoever dominion over fair lands, or honour among men could yield to any man, either living or after his death, either to himself or to any of his posterity, v. 11—14.   Fourthly, he giveth reason of his gloriation, because, being justified by faith, and at peace with God, he was sure of delivery from every evil, and to be received out of his grave into glory and fellowship with God, v. 15.   Fifthly, he guards every true believer against every temptation which might disquiet him, when he seeth himself and other godly persons in outward trouble, and the wicked in prosperity, v. 16—20.

1. *Hear this, all* ye *people ; give ear, all* ye *inhabitants of the world :*

2. *Both low and high, rich and poor, together.*

3. *My mouth shall speak of wisdom ; and the meditation of my heart* shall be *of understanding.*

4. *I will incline mine ear to a parable ; I will open my dark saying upon the harp.*

The preface calleth to the hearer for attention, faith, and affection to this excellent mystery which he is to deliver unto all men, concerning the blessedness of the believer above all other men in the world.   Whence learn, 1. A prepared and sanctified ear is necessary for heavenly doctrine, and people had great need to be stirred up to take knowledge of the excellency of it; *hear this, all ye people, give ear.* 2. The doctrine of salvation, of faith, and of consolation against sin and misery, concerneth all people in the world to know;

give ear, all ye inhabitants of the world, both low and high, rich and poor, together. 3. That is true wisdom and understanding, which maketh men wise unto salvation, and which maketh them truly blessed in this life; and this wisdom is not the birth of man's brain, but is revealed in the word of the Lord, delivered to his church by the holy men of God in holy scripture; *my mouth shall speak of wisdom, and the meditation of my heart shall be of understanding.* 4. As it is necessary for the preacher's encouragement to believe what he preacheth; so is it a great inducement to the people to hear God's word from him who speaketh God's word, because he believeth and subjecteth his spirit to the Lord's word, as the prophet doth here; *I will incline my ears to a parable.* 5. The doctrine of true blessedness, and the mystery of man's salvation manifested in the Scripture, far transcendeth the carnal wisdom of the world; the excellency of the gospel unto the natural man, is a *parable and dark saying: I will declare my dark saying on the harp.* 6. How dark and difficult soever the mystery of the gospel be to the carnal world; yet to the man of experience it is plain, sweet, and comfortable; and a man of experience as he is best seen in that matter, so is he most willing, heartily to communicate it to others : *I will open,* saith he, *my dark saying upon the harp*; intimating his delight in the doctrine.

5. *Wherefore should I fear in the days of evil,* when *the iniquity of my heels shall compass me about?*

After this preface he uttereth his parable and dark saying, the substance whereof is this : I am so persuaded of the favour of God now reconciled to me by the blood of the covenant, that neither do I need to fear by-past sins, nor any trouble which can come on me hereafter : and this I say, to let all men know that this blessedness may be attained by every man, who shall acknowledge his sins and embrace the offers of grace made by God with his directions unto life, as I have done. Whence learn, 1. What God has spoken in his word of the blessedness of the man that is justified by faith, every true believer may find, and may attain to be fully assured of his perseverance unto eternal life; for here is a proof and example of it in the psalmist's person. 2. This doctrine of the unspeakable peace of the believer reconciled to God through the blood of the covenant, is a point of truth which the world is ignorant of, and hardly will believe: no wonder therefore he before called it, and here uttereth it, as *a parable and dark saying.* 3. A believer after reconciliation, must neither exempt himself from danger of sinning, nor from giving daily account of his carriage unto God, not from challenges for sin, nor from ordinary chastisements for sin, nor from heavy troubles and ill days which he may meet with; whether by God's immediate hand for his correction, or by the persecutors of godliness for his further trial, exercise, and training of faith; for here the psalmist presupposes that evil days will come : he presupposeth that every sin or iniquity of every action and passage of his life, shall leave behind it an impression of guiltiness to be taken notice of thereafter, like the print of a man's foot when he lifts his heel and walketh forward; he presupposeth after remission of sin, after the daily exercise of repentance, after frequent intimation made of remission of sin, and that oftener from day to day repeated, a man may be brought back in the day of trouble to an account for altogether, and old reckonings may be raked up again by the troubled conscience, and by the accuser of the brethren, and that God will be ruling the business for the further glory of the riches of his grace, and the further good of his exercised child; for here the psalmist foreseeth, and speaketh of his looking for days of evil, and of the iniquity of his heels compassing him about, as what shall or may befall him. 4. Faith in the Messiah Jesus Christ, is able to make a man, not only at length triumph over sin and misery, over the curse of the law, and condemnation, or trouble and persecution, but also before trouble come in humble and solid confidence to be fearless for what can come, and to look all possible evils out of countenance; *wherefore should I fear in the days of evil, &c.* 5. Albeit it be possible when it cometh to push of pike, and when the man is yoked in the conflict with troubles from without, and challenges for his sins within, that the strongest in faith may find himself not a little afraid; yet when he considereth the ground laid down for settling his faith, to wit, the truth of the covenant, the merit of the Mediator's sacrifice, and the freedom, riches, and immutability of God's love and grace, with the psalmist he may confidently profess and acknowledge, that he has no reason to be feared for what Satan or conscience may threaten him with;

for this also is imported in *wherefore should I fear in the days
of evil, when the iniquity of my heels shall compass me about?*
which is as much as if he had said, Whatsoever may be my
weakness, and exercise in trial; yet I know there is no just
reason why I should fear condemnation, or be debarred
from the possession of full blessedness, by whatsoever possibly can come unto me.

6. *They that trust in their wealth, and boast themselves in the multitude of their riches ;*

7. *None* of them *can by any means redeem his brother, nor give to God a ransom for him :*

8. *(For the redemption of their soul* is *precious, and
it ceaseth for ever ;)*

9. *That he should still live for ever, and not see corruption.*

10. *For he seeth* that *wise men die, likewise the fool
and the brutish person perish, and leave their wealth to
others.*

In the third place, the believer preferreth this his blessed
condition to whatsoever either riches or honour or any earthly thing can yield to any man. Whence learn, 1. The blessedness of the believer and the glory of faith are best seen,
when the vanity of all earthly happiness and worldly gloriation in any thing beside God is discovered and compared with
the condition of the believer, therefore are *they that trust in
their wealth* brought in comparison with the believer here.
2. In whatsoever men count their felicity to stand, in that
they put their confidence, and do glory in it, as here is presupposed : they that count riches their happiness *trust in
their wealth, and boast themselves in the multitude of their
riches.* 3. The weakness of all worldly things to make a
man blessed best appears when death cometh; for when the
time thereof is come, no rich man can help himself, nor yet,
joining his with his brother's riches, can help his brother,
either by lengthening his life and suspending death temporal, or by recovering him from death when he dies : *none
can by any means redeem his brother.* 4. All men are God's
prisoners of war, his captives, and liable by justice to death
temporal and eternal ; and there is no delivery from death,
whether temporal or eternal, but by paying a ransom
unto God, which is impossible for a mere man to pay :

none can give to God a ransom for his brother. 5. We are not redeemed with silver or gold, or any perishing thing; our ransom must be of greater value than a mere man can pay, that is a man, and no more : *the redemption of a man's soul is precious,* and it ceaseth for ever. 6. Not so much as this worldly life can be perpetuated, by whatsoever wealth, or riches, or human ability can do; far less can the life of God, and that blessedness in heaven be purchased by any mere man : *none can redeem his brother, that he should still live for ever and not see corruption.*

11. *Their inward thought* is, that *their houses* shall continue *for ever,* and *their dwelling-places to all gene- rations : they call* their *lands after their own names.*

12. *Nevertheless, man* being *in honour abideth not : he is like the beasts* that *perish.*

13. *This their way* is *their folly ; yet their posterity approve their sayings. Selah.*

14. *Like sheep they are laid in the grave ; death shall feed on them ; and the upright shall have dominion over them in the morning ; and their beauty shall con- sume in the grave from their dwelling.*

He compareth the gloriation of the believer with the con- dition of those who are not only rich, but also honourable, and lords of great rents, fair lands, houses and heritages ; and he preferreth the blessedness of the believer to their con- dition also. Whence learn, 1. Albeit experience teaches that death is common to men of all ranks, wise and foolish, rich and poor; yet men are so besotted, as when they see this, they do not consider that they should not place their happi- ness in any thing, wherefrom they may be separated by death : *the worldly man seeth the wise man die, and also the foolish.* He sees also that many rich men leave their goods, they know not to whom : *they leave their wealth to others :* and yet for all this their seeing the mortality and the folly of mortal men dying before them, they that survive a little do not draw wisdom from this observation, but dream they shall deceive death, and make themselves some way eternal; they think to perpetuate their name in their posterity by their heritages, and the honours of their great families : *their inward thought is, that their houses shall continue for ever, and their dwell- ing-places to all generations. They call their lands after their own names.* 2. The cause of this folly are his deceived heart, and vain conceits and imaginations, which by death are blown away : *their inward thought is to eternize themselves. Nevertheless, man being in honour abideth not,* or attains not his fancied eternity. 3. The blessedness of the wealthy, potent, and honourable man, as it is not permanent; so it leaves him in the dirt at length, and in no better case (if he hath no faith or saving knowledge) than a beast ! *nevertheless, man being in honour abideth not, he is like the beasts that perish.* 4. Though the men who are most able to purchase lands, and to transmit them to their posterity, are counted ordinarily the most wise men; yet when men spend their wit and care mainly about things of this present earth, the Lord pronounceth them to be fools : *their way is their folly.* 5. Though the observation of the folly of predecessors should make the posterity wise; yet few are found father-better, or father-wiser; but fools follow fools in a race, and folly will not want a patron so long as fools are gone before : *this their way is their folly, yet their posterity approve their sayings.* 6. A worldly man not reconciled to God, dieth as a foolish, sensual, and secure beast as he lived : *like sheep they are laid in the grave,* for they are death's prey, both soul and body : *death shall feed on them.* 7. The righteous man justified by faith, and studying to live righteously, albeit you look on him in the worst estate he can be in in the world, under poverty and persecution; yet he is in better condition than the richest and most honourable ungodly man in all the earth; and albeit this doth not appear in this dark world, to blind men that have not the light of God's word in them; yet at the resurrection it shall be seen, that the poor and mean just man shall be in a glorious condition above the worldling : *the upright shall have dominion over them in the morning.* 8. The whole glory of the worldly-minded man is shortly consumed so soon as he dieth, and then he changeth his lodging for the worse, the best days that ever he shall see are gone : *their beauty shall consume in their grave from their dwelling.*

15. *But God will redeem my soul from the power of the grave ; for he shall receive me. Selah.*

In the fourth place, he perfects the comparison, and gives a reason of his gloriation, whereof we heard, v. 5, the sum whereof is this: wealth and riches, nobility, honour and do-

minion among men can follow an ungodly man no farther
than the grave, there all welfare doth forsake him for evermore : but as for me who am reconciled to God, justified,
and in some measure sanctified, though I die, yet do I live in
my soul, being kept by God till the day of complete redemption; and then my soul, being deprived only for a while of the
body, shall have it restored again in the resurrection, and then
soul and body both shall be fully redeemed and delivered from
the power of the grave : for, as God hath received me into
favour in this life, and shall receive my soul at death; so, at
the time of the delivering of my body from the grave, he shall
receive me, both soul and body, into his fellowship, and
therefore my condition is better, how many days of evil soever I shall see in this life, than the condition of an ungodly
man in the world, how wealthy, how honourable and apparently happy soever he be in this world ; yea, I may
justly glory over all ungodly men, and say yet again, *wherefore should I fear in the days of evil, when the iniquity of
my heels shall compass me about ; for God will redeem my
soul from the power of the grave?* Whence learn, 1. Albeit
the godly may be subject to mortality and the outward misery
of this mortal life, common to him and the ungodly, yet
here is the difference, he is sure of a deliverance from all
misery; *but God shall redeem my soul,* saith he; which God
will not do to the ungodly. 2. Hope of the resurrection is
the godly man's chief consolation, and this was the hope of
the saints before Christ came, as well as since : *God shall
redeem my soul from the power of the grave.* 3. A believer
hath good warrant to be persuaded, not only of his reconciliation with God in this life, but also of the receiving of
his soul after this life into the fellowship of the glory of
God, both in soul and body, at the resurrection : *God shall
redeem my soul from the power of the grave; for he shall
receive me. Selah.*

16. *Be not thou afraid when one is made rich, when
the glory of his house is increased;*

17. *For when he dieth he shall carry nothing away;
his glory shall not descend after him :*

18. *Though while he lived he blessed his soul ; and*
men *will praise thee, when thou doest well to thyself.*

19. *He shall go to the generation of his fathers; they shall never see light.*

20. *Man* that is *in honour, and understandeth not, is like the beasts* that *perish.*

In the last part, by way of exhortation to make use of this doctrine, he guardeth every believer against every temptation which may arise from the prosperity of the wicked, and the hardship of the godly in this life. Whence learn, 1. It is a temptation which shaketh the faith of the godly sometimes, when they see the flourishing prosperity of the wicked, and their own daily affliction; but this should not move the godly, nor make them suspect themselves to be in a wrong course, and the ungodly in a better way : *be not thou afraid when one is made rich.* 2. The consideration of the shortness both of our temporal calamity and of the ungodly man's prosperity, both which end at death, is the way to overcome the foresaid temptation; for, *when he dieth, he shall carry nothing away, his glory shall not descend after him.* It is not so with the godly, whose glory and happiness meet him at death. 3. A man's own self-deceiving heart, measuring all happiness by a man's present outward condition in the world, and hearkening to the flattery of fools about him, who use to curry the favour of the wealthy, and love to have the like condition themselves, is the cause why the miserable man is kept still in a golden dream, as if he were happy : *though while he lived he blessed his soul ; and men will praise thee when thou dost well to thyself;* that is, when thou takest a life of it while thou mayest have it; yet he and they are altogether deceived. 4. The ungodly at their death shall go the way the ungodly went before them, to the place of darkness and disconsolation, being separate from God and his saints, and from all blessedness, and shall never have comfort in their miserable estate for ever: *he shall go to the generation of his fathers :* and what shall become of such wretches? *they shall never see light ;* that is, they shall never see the meanest appearance of any joy or comfort. 5. It is not honour, but want of understanding, want of saving faith and wisdom to provide for eternal life, that puts man down from his excellence, and debarreth him from blessedness : *man that is in honour, and understandeth not,* is the man here set at nought, and declared to be far from true blessedness. 6. Whatsoever natural excellence be in man above the beasts; yet sin hath put him so far down, that, except he get saving knowledge of God, and be reconciled to him, he is in no better condition, at least when he dieth, than a beast: *man that is in honour, and understandeth not, is like the beast that perisheth.*

PSALM L.
A psalm of Asaph.

This psalm is a citing of the visible church before God, the Judge of all the earth, (who at last shall judge all flesh in the day of judgment, and take vengeance on the wicked,) to compear before the tribunal of God, now in time while mercy may be had, timously to consider the Lord's controversy against the sinners in his church, that they may repent and be saved. And, first, the dreadfulness of the judgment is set down, v. 1—3. Secondly, the citation of the party, that is, the visible church, with the witnesses, v. 4—6. Thirdly, there is a challenge of self-work-justiciaries, legalists, and formal ceremonialists, who rested upon outward good behaviour, and upon the outward discharge of the ordinances, as if the sacrifices of the law, or any performance of external duties, had been sufficient to expiate sin, and justify a man, v. 7—13. Fourthly, there is a direction unto them how to come off their legal righteousness and carnal way of worship, and to turn themselves to the right way of worshipping God in spirit and truth, v. 14, 15. Fifthly, there is a challenge of those who were grossly wicked, v. 16—21. And lastly, there is a direction also to them to repent, and to give God glory in time, with an encouragement to the upright believers to go on their way, v. 22, 23.

1. *The mighty God, even the Lord, hath spoken, and called the earth, from the rising of the sun unto the going down thereof.*

2. *Out of Zion, the perfection of beauty, God hath shined.*

3. *Our God shall come, and shall not keep silence : a fire shall devour before him, and it shall be very tempestuous round about him.*

From the description of the terror of the Lord coming to judge his visible church, for the slighting of the means of salvation, and looseness of life and conversation, learn, 1. As the Lord is to judge the whole world one day, so in a special and most exact manner will he judge those that draw near to him in the profession of true religion, as this whole psalm holdeth forth. 2. This advantage have they who live in the visible church, they are warned of the judgment ere it come; for, as many other places of Scripture, so this psalm is an express warning piece to the church to prepare for judgment. 3. The terrible process of the day of God's severe judgment being well meditated upon, is a special means to waken men's consciences to take course about their sins in time, that they may be pardoned, and their ersons reconciled, which is the scope of the whole doctrine delivered in this psalm. 4. The mystery of the great and terrible day of general judgment is to be learned from the Scriptures, and express predictions thereof in God's word, the authority, weight, certainty, and efficacy whereof flows from, and depends upon God Almighty only: *the mighty God*, even *the Lord hath spoken.* 5. God Almighty, the sovereign Judge of all the earth, hath appointed that all who ever took life, in whatsoever time or place they have lived in the world, shall compear before his majesty in the appointed time: *the Lord hath spoken, and called the earth, from the rising of the sun unto the going down thereof.* 6. The true visible church, where God's ordinances are set up as he hath appointed, where his word is purely preached, is the most beautiful thing under heaven, and there is God's glory set forth and manifested more clearly than in all the Lord's handiwork beside in heaven or earth; therefore is the place of the Lord's temple here so highly commended, and *Zion called the perfection of beauty*, because of the glory of God sundry ways revealed there: *out of Zion God hath shined*, saith he, in regard to the clear manifestation of his will, specially in the matter now in hand about the day of judgment. 7. Men will take no heed unto what the word of the Lord declareth, till the authority, supremacy, omnipotency, and justice of God the Judge be apprehended by them, and the great day of his terrible judgment be looked upon as a thing which shall most certainly come to pass at the time appointed; therefore is it said, *our God shall come, and shall not keep silence.* 8. So many as are reconciled with God, and have closed uprightly with him in the covenant of grace, may look upon the day of judgment without terror or perplexity; yea, and with comfort and confident hope to find the Judge gracious to them, according to the tenor of the covenant, even their God: *our God*, saith the prophet, *shall come.* 9. Look how fearful and terrible the Lord showed himself at the giving out of the law, no less terrible shall he be in the execution thereof, in the day of judging

all those whose sins shall be found not pardoned before: *a
fire shall devour before him, and it shall be very tempestuous
about him.*

4. *He shall call to the heavens from above, and to
the earth, that he may judge his people.*

5. *Gather my saints together unto me; those that
have made a covenant with me by sacrifice.*

6. *And the heavens shall declare his righteousness:
for God* is *judge himself. Selah.*

In the second place, he sets down the citation, and sum-
moning of officers, parties, and witnesses, to make all ready
for the judging of all the world, but in special of the people who have given up their name to God and have made
a covenant with him, and professed themselves to be his
people; all of them shall find at last, that they have had to do
with a righteous judge. Whence learn, 1. In the great
day of the last judgment, heaven and earth, and all the
elements shall be moved to render up all they have received
in custody unto that day; *the Lord shall call to the heavens
from above, and to the earth.* 2. We need not question
how all the dead shall be raised, how souls shall be reunited
to their bodies, how they shall all be gathered together, and
how such great things shall come to pass; one word re-
solves all; *he shall call to the heavens and to the earth.*
For as at a word all were made: so at a word when he
shall call and give out the order for compearance, the dead
shall be raised, and all shall compear; good angels and
wicked spirits, all men, good and evil, young and old, every
reasonable and understanding creature in heaven and earth,
by his almighty power, shall be made quickly to present
themselves; *he shall call,* is sufficient to effect whatsoever
he will. 3. What will be the course the Judge shall follow
regarding those who have not heard of him, or who have
heard of him and lived without the church, is not the main
matter which the Lord's people should inquire about; but
this is their part to know, to wit, what concerneth themselves; therefore doth the Lord say no more here, but, *he
shall call to the heavens and to the earth, that he may
judge his people.* 4. All who are in covenant with God,
every member of the visible church are saints by calling;
God alloweth this stile upon them because they are dedicat-

ed and consecrated to him, since they are all by special vow
obliged to be saints; all make profession of their purpose
to be such; all claim for themselves, and will have allowed
unto them by others, the estimation of God's people, whatsoever be their deserving; therefore, saith he, *gather my
saints together unto me.*   5. At how great a distance soever, whether of time or place, God's people by profession
have lived in this world, all of them shall be assembled at
length to the judgment of that great day; some to the
judgment of absolution, some to the judgment of condemnation, good and bad, all shall be gathered before the Judge
at once; *gather my saints together unto me.*   6. The Lord
shall not want officers, sergeants, and servants sufficient for
this work; he hath angels innumerable, who shall effect
what he giveth order unto them for; *gather ye my saints
together.*   7. The external covenant with God, is the
ground of the title and honour of saintship, and church
membership; whosoever are in visible covenant with God,
are called, by his allowance, *his saints*; for so here he ex-
poundeth whom he calleth *his saints,* even all those *who
have made a covenant with him by sacrifice.*   8. No covenant can be made with God without the interposing of, or
professed respect unto a sacrifice, according as the Lord
did teach his people in the type and shadow of the ceremonial sacrificing; for, as God by appointing a sacrifice to be
offered by his people would have every covenanter to acknowledge and profess that he was worthy to die for his sins,
and that it behoved him to fly to a surety to die for him,
(even to the promised Messiah Jesus Christ, that Lamb of
God which was slain from the beginning of the world, to
take away the sins of the world;) and to consecrate himself
wholly to God's service; so the Lord requireth still the
same things of every covenanter, from every one of his people; and whosoever profess their accepting of the conditions of the covenant, are called those that have made *a
covenant with God by sacrifice.*   9. In that general judgment, the wise framing of the world, the constant course of
governing it, the appointing of the seasons of summer and
winter, spring and harvest, the making of the sun to shine
and the rain to fall upon all, and the furnishing all with
food and good things, shall be witnesses for God's part toward all men, and so *the heavens shall declare his right-*

cousness. 10. No man shall be injured or suffer wrongfully that day; yea, all men shall have wrongs done to them repaired, all rewards shall be given according as the word of the Lord hath said; *for God is judge himself. Selah.*

7. *Hear, O my people, and I will speak ; O Israel, and I will testify against thee : I am God, even thy God.*

Having now foretold his people, that there shall be certainly a great day of judging all men, and specially his covenanted people; he entereth here into a friendly manner of controversy with his visible church or professed people, that they might repent and find mercy in time, before they were brought to a tribunal of severe justice.   And first, he useth a preface, directing his speech to such as were of a better outward behaviour than the worst, to wit, such as trusted in their own works, and specially in the external sacrifices and ceremonies of the law, without looking to the end and intent thereof; as if by those external sacrifices their sins had been expiated, and God fully satisfied for them.   Whence learn, 1. A people settled upon the dregs of their carnal customs, in security and presumption, cannot be moved to enter into consideration of their ways, or into suspicion of their dangerous condition, except the Lord show himself to them, and rip up their conscience; therefore saith he to them, *hear, O my people, and I will speak.*   2. Albeit the Lord suffereth such as are without the church, strangers to the covenant and commonwealth of Israel, to lie still in their sins; yet will he debate his quarrel against his own people, which is no small mercy : *O Israel, I will testify against thee.*   3. The covenant made with God, joined with his absolute sovereignty, lays double bonds upon God's people for the obedience of faith, obliging them not to seek salvation otherwise than he teacheth us, but to worship and serve him as he appointeth; for, *I am God, even thy God,* saith the Lord.   4. Whatsoever quarrel the Lord has against his people for not keeping covenant made with him; yet so long as there is hope of repentance, he will not dissolve the covenant, but will offer the benefit thereof unto them; for when the Lord hath said, *I will testify against thee,* he addeth, *I am God, even thy God,* v. 11.

8. *I will not reprove thee for thy sacrifices, or thy burnt-offerings,* to have been *continually before me.*

9. *I will take no bullock out of thy house*, nor *he-goats out of thy folds:*

10. *For every beast of the forest* is *mine*, and *the cattle upon a thousand hills.*

11. *I know all the fowls of the mountains ; and the wild beasts of the field* are *mine.*

12. *If I were hungry, I would not tell thee : for the world* is *mine, and the fulness thereof.*

13. *Will I eat the flesh of bulls, or drink the blood of goats ?*

After the preface, the Lord passeth by the reproof for much neglect, even in the external performances of outward ordinances, and challengeth only their relying upon the outward work, and their putting a sort of merit upon their work, as if they minded to render God obliged to them by their outward performances. Whence learn, 1. Albeit there be just reason to challenge men for coming short of their duty in the discharge of outward ordinances; yet when that is not the main fault, or when the mending of that fault will not satisfy God, he will waive that challenge for the present, and fasten upon their chief sins : *I will not reprove thee for thy sacrifices, or thy burnt-offerings which should have been continually before me.* 2. As men are ordinarily little sensible of their omissions of duties, so are they ready to overvalue their outward performances, and to think that what they do in this kind shall be very acceptable to God, as the carnal Israelites, here challenged, conceived their bullocks *and goats out of their houses or folds* should have been esteemed by God, as of as much worth as they who offered them put upon them. 3. That which is most esteemed by men, without allowance of God, is abomination to God : such were the external sacrifices of carnal Israelites, who rested upon the offering of external sacrifices, without looking to that only true sacrifice of the Mediator represented thereby : *I will take no bullock out of thy house, nor he-goat out of thy fold.* 4. It is a disease of foolish man to think with himself that God is obliged to him when he offereth unto God any part of his goods, although in the mean time a man hath nothing but what God hath given him, and which is the Lord's by primitive right: *every beast of the forest is mine, and the cattle upon a thousand hills.* 5. Albeit all men profess that they acknowledge God to be owner of all the creatures, because he hath made them all; yet their practice many ways bewrayeth their heart-ignorance on this point, and that they have need to be taught this lesson from God: *I know all the fowls of the mountains, and the wild beasts of the field are mine.* 6. Unrenewed men cannot choose but have gross conceptions of God, and to think of him after their own fancy, as the carnal Israelites conceived that a fat sacrifice was as acceptable to God as a fat dinner was to themselves; but God is not like man, and standeth in no need of supply from man or from any of his creatures; all of them have their being and dependence on God, to dispose of them, and bestow them on whom he will, at his pleasure: *he is not hungry;* and put the case he had a mind to serve himself of any of the creatures, yet he needs not employ man for that effect; for, *the earth is the Lord's and the fulness thereof.* 7. The Lord disdaineth the fleshly conceits which men have, to satisfy his justice for their sins by any thing that man can offer unto him, as imaginations unbeseeming a reasonable man: *will I eat the flesh of bulls, or drink the blood of goats?*

14. *Offer unto God thanksgiving; and pay thy vows unto the most High:*

15. *And call upon me in the day of trouble; I will deliver thee, and thou shalt glorify me.*

In the third place, he exhorteth them to forsake this carnal way of seeking salvation, and setteth them upon the right course of true blessedness and spiritual service. Whence learn, 1. The way of salvation and of God's worship is spiritual, and may possibly be resembled and furthered by external bodily exercises, but does not stand on things external; and to speak it more particularly, God will have the man whose person and service he will accept, to be sensible of his own want of every good thing, and inability to furnish to himself any thing which he lacketh, to acknowledge God only to be the all-sufficient fountain of grace and of every good donation, to seek what he hath need of from God, to depend upon his grace when he hath sought it, and to return the praise of God's free and gracious gift unto him when he hath received it; for all this is presupposed and imported in this offering of thanks: *offer unto God thanksgiving;* to wit, for every point and passage of his undeserved favour: and this he calleth for, because this offering of the sacrifice of praise and thanks was more acceptable to God than their ceremonial sacrifices of slain beasts. 2. God will have the man whose person and service he will accept, to make conscience of all his lawful vows made unto God, in special of his covenant vow, made for giving God the obedience of faith all the days of his life, which vow true worshippers are wont upon sundry occasions solemnly to renew: *offer unto God thanksgiving, and pay thy vows unto the most high God.* 3. Were a man ever so faithful and upright in the Lord's service, yet he is not exempted from trouble, for reasons concerning God's glory, good of the person troubled, and benefit of others; this the Lord holdeth forth in preparing their minds, by making mention unto believers *of a day of trouble.* 4. Among other ends of the Lord's sending trouble, this is one; to cause the believer, in the sense of his need, to make use of his covenant with God, and by faith to draw near to him in prayer for help and relief in due time: *call upon me in the day of thy trouble.* 5. The true believer and depender upon the sure and rich grace of God, cannot possibly fall into any trouble out of which he shall not be delivered, but, whatsoever evil come, he may, by praying to God, yea, he shall be delivered: *call upon me in the day of trouble, I will deliver thee.* What more absolute promise can be made to a believing supplicant? 6. A believing supplicant shall not only be graciously answered, and so have cause of praising God, but shall also have grace in effect to praise God: *and thou shalt glorify me.*

16. *But unto the wicked God saith, What hast thou to do to declare my statutes, or that thou shouldest take my covenant in thy mouth?*

17. *Seeing thou hatest instruction, and castest my words behind thee.*

18. *When thou sawest a thief, then thou consentedst with him, and hast been partaker with adulterers.*

19. *Thou givest thy mouth to evil, and thy tongue frameth deceit.*

20. *Thou sittest and speakest against thy brother; thou slanderest thine own mother's son.*

21. *These things hast thou done, and I kept silence; thou thoughtest that I was altogether such an one as*

thyself: but *I will reprove thee, and set* them *in order before thine eyes.*

In the fourth place, the Lord mercifully remonstrateth with the gross sinner and scandalous liver, for abusing this privilege of the covenant by his lewd conversation and secure atheism, that he, being convinced of his sin, might repent, and eschew the wrath which is to come.　Whence learn, 1. To such as profess religion, and observe the outward ordinances thereof, and do not live scandalously, the Lord, howsoever he lets them know he is not well pleased with their way, yet speaketh unto them more mildly, because it is possible some beloved Laodiceans, young and unskilful true converts, may be guilty of no small measure of dead formality; but to such as live in gross scandalous sins, the Lord speaketh more roughly, calling them by the name of *wicked : but unto the wicked God saith.*　2. Such is the deceivableness of sin, and the deceit of the heart, and the power of Satan upon secure sinners, that they can without remorse of conscience profess the true religion, pretend to a covenant with God, and yet live loosely as pagans or atheists : *they take God's covenant in their mouth,* and meantime *hate instruction, and cast God's words behind them.*　3. Such as by their lewd conversation give an open affront to their religion, are so detestable to God, that he accounteth them wicked haters of reformation, contemners of Scripture, disgracers of their holy profession, and such as he will take no religious service from : *unto the wicked God saith, what hast thou to do to declare my statutes, or that thou shouldest take my covenant in thy mouth, seeing thou hatest instruction, and castest my words behind thee ?*　4. Albeit men profane the covenant, and deserve to be thrust out of it as unworthy to have the benefit of it, or to be suffered any more to profess it; yet God will not give them up hastily, but will, after a friendly manner, declare to them their sin and misdeserving, that their conscience may be moved towards repentance : *what hast thou to do to take my covenant in thy mouth, seeing thou hatest instruction ?* 5. The man who casteth God's word behind him, cannot choose but serve a worse master, and be made slave to his lusts, and be led away to every sin, as temptation leadeth him; he will not stand to be a greedy thief and a filthy adulterer, v. 18, and to loose his tongue to all the evils whereunto the tongue can serve, v. 19, yea and to become unnatural to those to whom he is bound in nearest bonds of blood, v. 20. 6. Such is the Lord's patience, that he doth ofttimes endure very long horrible provocations of those that are in outward covenant with him, so that by his long-suffering he may lead them to repentance : *these things thou didst, and I kept silence.* 7. When men profit not by the means which should lead them to repentance, they grow worse for the means, more secure and hardened in their ill ways, and more godless in all respects : *thou thoughtest I was altogether such a one as thyself.* 8. Such as live a loose life with a profession of religion under the shining light of God's word, keep not their consciences quiet, otherwise than by transforming God into an idol after their own fancy, and by feigning him to be what he is not, and not to be what he declareth himself to be : *thou thoughtest that I was altogether such a one as thyself ;* that is to say, *no more displeased with thy ways than thou thyself wast.* 9. Although the Lord keep silence for a time, yet he will at length let the sinner know by his word and rods, how displeased he is at sin ; *but I will reprove thee*, saith the Lord. 10. Sins forgotten, cast behind back, and cast together in confusion by the secure sinner, shall, in the day of God's reckoning, be brought to remembrance with time, place, and other circumstances, and so presented to the consci nce, as the sinner shall not be able to look aside from his fearful accusation and ditty : *I will set them in order before thine eyes.*

22. *Now consider this, ye that forget God, lest I tear* you *in pieces, and* there be *none to deliver.*

23. *Whoso offereth praise glorifieth me : and to him that ordereth* his *conversation* aright *will I shew the salvation of God.*

In the last place, the Lord being loath to dissolve the covenant, or to destroy those that are in the visible church, how wicked soever, exhorteth them to repentance while it is time, before he cast them off utterly, and so showeth them the way of returning home to him, as he also encourageth such as are sincere worshippers of him to go on. Whence learn, 1. The Lord's controversy with his people and threatening of wrath upon them, carry much love and mercy in their bosom ; it is admirable that such offers of grace and reconciliation are made by God after so just and fearful challenges, as here we read.　2. As the affectionate remembrance of God is an awband to keep from sin, and a spur to all duties; and as consideration of God's word is a means to waken the conscience and affect the heart with high and right thoughts of God : so the forgetting of God, and consideration of what is necessary, casts a man open to all sin, and makes way for his destruction : *consider this, ye that forget God, lest I tear you in pieces.*　3. If they who have gone far away from God, haste not home unto him, they are likely to meet with merciless judgment, and to find no opportunity or time granted as they could wish to repent : *consider, lest I tear you in pieces, and there be none to deliver you.*　4. To set men on work to promote the honour of God by worshipping him in spirit, and to conform the outward actions of the body to the rule of God's word, is the scope of all God's pleading with his own people; for his controversy is closed with a direction to all, *to glorify God, and to order their conversation aright.* 5. That man worshippeth God in spirit, who giveth him the praise of his justice, in acknowledging his sins against God's law and his ill deservings in the course of daily renewed repentance; and who giveth unto God the praise of his grace and mercy, in flying to the refuge set before him in the gospel, in the course of daily renewed acts of faith in Christ; and who giveth God the praise of his holiness, in studying daily to mortify the lusts of the flesh by his Spirit, and to be renewed in his mind and affections; and in a word, who, in his heart and affections studieth to give God the honour of all his attributes, titles, or name, by whatsoever occasion manifested to him.　This is the worshipper of God in spirit and truth, whom the Lord by all his dealing with his people is seeking to form and gain to himself : *whoso offereth praise, glorifieth me.*　6. Sincere endeavour to worship God in spirit, is best seen in a man's care to conform his life and bodily actions to the rule of God's word; for with *glorifying God* he joineth-here, *ordering his conversation aright.*　7. Whosoever shall set himself to be God's servant in spirit and truth, shall find God to be his Saviour to the uttermost, how godless soever, how vile soever he hath been.　If he shall prepare himself against the dreadful day of judgment, by receiving the offer of grace in Jesus Christ, with all the fulness of the salvation of God in him, and in Christ's strength shall study to bring forth the fruits of his faith in a blameless conversation, he shall undoubtedly be saved : for God hath said, *whoso offereth the sacrifice of praise, glorifies me, and to him who ordereth his conversation aright, will I shew the salvation of God.* Amen, Amen.

PSALM LI.

To the chief musician.   A psalm of David, when Nathan the prophet came unto him, after he had gone in to Bathsheba.

The psalmist, in the sad sense of his guiltiness, prayeth for remission of sin, with an eye to the Lord's large mercy, v. 1, 2, and followeth his petition with a deep and hearty confession of his sinfulness, v. 3—6. He prayeth the second time for remission of sin, with an eye toward the blood of the Messiah, v. 7, and followeth it with another petition for comfort to his afflicted spirit, v. 8.   He prayeth for remission of sins the third time, v. 9, and followeth it with another petition for renewed comfort of the Holy Spirit, and for removal of felt wrath, with a promise of making use thereof, to the edification of God's people, v. 10—13.   He prayeth for remission of sin the fourth time, namely of that particular sin wherewith for the present his conscience was most troubled, v. 14 ; and he followeth it with another petition to fit him for a more spiritual and sincere manner of serving God hereafter, renouncing all confidence in the external ceremonies of the law, v. 15—17.   And last of all, he prayeth for mercy to the church, v. 18, 19.

From the inscription, learn, 1. How soon the most mortified lust may be kindled, and break forth like fire in the embers when it meeteth with powder; how frail the strongest of the saints are in themselves, when they are tempted to sin; and what need he who standeth hath to take heed lest he fall; for the holy prophet, the sweet singer of Israel, is here foully defiled by *his going in to Bathsheba.*   2. How fast asleep in sin even the most watchful watchman may fall, and that he cannot at all awake of himself, till God of his grace (who in love pursueth fugitives) by some means of his own choosing, stir up his conscience, as here is evidenced in the case of the psalmist, who lay still secure in his sin till Nathan the prophet came to him.   3. How faithful ministers ought to be in their proper charges, reproving sin, even in the greatest personages, when God calleth them unto it, and how acceptable their reproof should be to the honest heart : as David's seer, Nathan the prophet's coming unto David and rebuking him after the open knowledge of his sin, and David's acceptance of this office at his hands, and the honourable mention made of his fidelity here, teach us. 4. How little a true penitent hesitateth to shame himself,

when his sin hath dishonoured God, and he seeth that the
confession of it may glorify God; and how far the penmen
of holy Scripture differ in this point from the writers of
human histories, as David, in the inscription of this psalm,
giveth proof.

1. *Have mercy upon me, O God, according to thy
loving-kindness ; according to the multitude of thy tender mercies blot out my transgressions.*

2. *Wash me thoroughly from mine iniquity, and cleanse
me from my sin.*

In this first affectionate prayer for remission of sins, learn,
1. As the conscience, till it be awakened by God, cannot apprehend how displeasant sin is to God; how it meriteth
wrath, and how insupportable a burden it is to the sinner,
when he is charged with it; so, after it is wakened, it can
see no refuge till it consider that mercy may be had in God,
and then the more it is pressed by the law, or fear of wrath,
the more it seeketh after God's mercy, as here we see: *have
mercy on me, O God.*   2. The consideration of the Lord's
loving-kindness and readiness to forgive the sinner that
cometh unto him, should keep the sinner (how grievous
soever his offence hath been) from running away from him,
yea should give him hope to meet with mercy, whatsoever
may be his demerits: *have mercy upon me, O God, according
to thy loving-kindness.*   3. Sin is a debt obliging a man to a
penalty which he cannot pay; but it must be forgiven, otherwise he perisheth : as *blot out my transgressions* importeth.
4. All doubts arising from the multitude of sins forgiven
before, and from the abuse of many mercies already received,
and from the deep deservings of many heinous sins, are
solved, when God's loving-kindness and the multitude of the
mercies of God are opposed to these doubts and fears, and
are put in the balance over against them ; *according to thy
loving-kindness, according to the multitude of thy tender mercies blot out my transgressions.*   5. When a saint now justified doth any thing against the law of God, his sin is so far
from being extenuated or made less, that, on the contrary, it
is multiplied so much the more, and found to have in it a
plurality of sins, when rightly considered : *blot out,* saith he
in the plural number, *my transgressions.*   6. Sin, as it
bindeth a man over to punishment, till he be forgiven; so

it defileth a man, and puts an abominable deformity on him, which his enlightened conscience cannot look upon without loathing, till it be, by pardon and purging, washed away : *wash me, and cleanse me from mine iniquity and my sin.* 7. The pollution of sin goes through the whole powers of the soul and body, which have been serviceable to it; through mind, will, affections, senses, bodily and all; and nothing can quiet the soul here, except it find pardoning mercy, and sanctifying mercy following all the foul footsteps of sin, and doing away the filthiness thereof : *wash me thoroughly, and cleanse me.*

3. *For I acknowledge my transgressions : and my sin* is *ever before me.*

4. *Against thee, thee only, have I sinned, and done* this *evil in thy sight ; that thou mightest be justified when thou speakest,* and *be clear when thou judgest.*

5. *Behold, I was shapen in iniquity ; and in sin did my mother conceive me.*

6. *Behold, thou desirest truth in the inward parts ; and in the hidden* part *thou shalt make me to know wisdom.*

Here he maketh confession of his sin and sinfulness, and aggravateth his guiltiness from the very root of original sin, and subscribeth whatsoever God hath spoken in the Scripture, of man's sinful nature and deserved punishment, approving himself unto God for the sincerity of his confession. Whence learn, 1. Whosoever would have mercy and pardon of his sin from God, must acknowledge his sin and debt, and must take part with God, and with justice against himself, because the psalmist here giveth this for a reason of his hope of pardon : *for I acknowledge my transgression.* 2. Albeit God hath pardoned sin to a penitent soul, and albeit his ministers have made declaration of the pardon to him; yet the conscience will not pronounce the sentence of absolution, but still present the sin as unpardoned, till God quieteth it by his immediate intimation; for David, after Nathan had told him from the Lord that his iniquity was pardoned, still findeth the conscience pursuing for the guilt : *my sin is ever before me.* 3. The dividing of the grant of pardon from the effectual intimation thereof unto the conscience, is done in God's wisdom and mercy towards his child for good;

for here it ripeneth repentance, and bringeth forth this deep confession : *I acknowledge mine iniquity, and my sin is ever before me.* 4. It is most suitable for true repentance, to pitch upon some particular sin, in the vileness whereof the evil of other sin may be taken up and lamented: *against thee have I done this evil*: he meaneth the particular whereof Nathan charged him in the matter of Uriah. 5. The material injury and hurt of a sinful action may resolve upon a creature; but the formal obliquity of the action resolveth upon the law or command of God, and upon his sovereign authority which gave the law: *against thee, thee have I sinned.* 6. If the injury done to the creature, could be severed from the offence done to God, the conscience would not be so much troubled for the first, as for the last; or if the injury done to God against so many obligations, be compared with the injury done to the creature; the injury done to God is so high as it comprehendeth all the challenge which the creature could make for its part, and leaveth nothing to the creature to say besides : therefore, saith he, *against thee, thee only, have I sinned, and done this evil in thy sight.* 7. Albeit no man should challenge for a wrong done by one man to another, and in particular for a wrong done to a subject by a prince or ruler, yet will the Lord challenge for it, and bring the man to an account for it : *against thee, thee only, have I sinned.* 8. How closely soever the circumstances of a sinful action be conveyed, that men should not see the vileness thereof, yet before God all the matter is plain : *I have done this evil in thy sight*, saith he. 9. The conscience rightly wakened to the sense of sin, cannot but justify what God hath spoken in his word of man's sinfulness, and of the demerit of sin, and of whatsoever God hath done, or shall do in punishing : for David maketh this deep confession of sin against himself, *that God may be justified when he speaketh, and clear when he judgeth.* 10. Although presumptuous man will not stand to examine, judge, and pass sentence upon God and his words and works, yet shall no man be able to bear a blot upon God; but every conscience, when awake, shall be found to blame the man, and to justify God in all his words and proceedings, as David is forced to blame himself here; *that God may be justified when he speaketh, and clear when he judgeth.* 11. As original sin is common to all men by

natural propagation, so is it not abolished out of the most
holy in this life; and as it is found to show itself in the
children of God by actual transgressions, so must the evil
thereof be acknowledged by them, and that not to extenuate
but to aggravate their sin, as David showeth here, saying,
*behold, I was shapen in iniquity, and in sin did my mother
conceive me.*   12. No confession of sin, or any other part
of God's worship, giveth ease to the mind, or is acceptable
to God, except it be done in sincerity and truth, and when
it is done in spirit and truth, it is acceptable to God, and
giveth ease to the conscience; behold, saith David after his
deep confession, *thou desirest truth in the inward parts.*   13.
The last operation of God's grace in us, is worthy to be observed, acknowledged, and made use of, as an evidence that
God hath some work in us, wherein he taketh pleasure : behold, saith David to God, *thou desirest, or delightest in
truth in the inward parts.*   14. When a man hath found
some spark of grace in himself, he may expect to find yet
more grace from God, as David, after this experience of
grace given to him to make a sincere confession of his sin,
expecteth that God shall effectually teach him more wisdom,
or wise behaviour in his sight. *In the hidden parts thou wilt
make me to know wisdom ;* that is, thou wilt make my conscience judge yet more impartially of my native sinfulness,
and wilt teach me to walk more circumspectly before thee,
in the sense of my fulness.

7. *Purge me with hyssop, and I shall be clean;
wash me, and I shall be whiter than snow.*

8. *Make me to hear joy and gladness ;* that *the bones*
which *thou hast broken may rejoice.*

He prayeth for remission of sin the second time, with an
eye to the blood of the Messiah Christ, and joineth with it,
a petition for comfort to his afflicted spirit.   Whence learn,
1. No less loathsome than leprosy is the sight of sin, when
it is looked upon as unpardoned; and nothing less than the
blood of Christ signified by the blood of the clean bird slain
to cleanse the leper, can purge a man of it, for David looketh unto the manner of cleansing the leper, as it is set down,
Levit. xiv.   Where two birds were taken, and one of them
slain, the living bird, being dipped with hyssop in the blood
of the slain bird, was let fly away, to signify the leprous

sinner's deliverance from perdition by the blood of the pure sacrifice of Jesus Christ : *purge me with hyssop,* saith he. 2. Whatsoever application of Christ's blood in justification of his person, hath been made to a man, it hindereth not but rather openeth a way unto the renewed acts of application thereof, according as new sins draw on new guiltiness : for here justified David prayeth to be yet again purged with hyssop.　3. Renewed acts of remission of sin granted, by new application of the virtue of Christ's blood, cleanse the conscience of the guilt of sin, and clear the man before God's justice : *purge me with hyssop, and I shall be clean,* saith he.　4. Howsoever remission of guilt for Christ's sake be inseparable from the imputation of righteousness for Christ's sake, yet may these two be distinguished, and distinctly looked upon for the believer's comfort; for here David, looking on the removing of the guiltiness of sin by Christ's death, saith, *purge me with hyssop, and I shall be clean;* and looking upon the imputation of Christ's righteousness, or obedience even unto the death, he saith, *wash me and I shall be whiter than snow.* Now, that these two branches of mercy are distinguishable, may appear from this, that, as to be delivered from eternal torment is one benefit, (supposing that a man were annihilated in his escape from it,) and to be not only freed from eternal torment, but also made blessed by the gift of eternal life, is another and a greater benefit; so, deliverance from the guilt of sin, in relation to the removing of punishment, is one thing, and the assignation of Christ's righteousness, in relation to eternal life, is another thing; and both these two benefits are purchased by Christ's perfect obedience unto death, and are holden forth, Levit. xiv; for, after the delivery of the leper from death, figured and symbolized by the letting go of the living bird dipped in the blood of the slain bird, the clothing of the leper with righteousness is figured and symbolized, by the washing of the man and putting clean clothes upon him.　Now, it is not the man's inherent personal sanctification, (which, in every man, is joined with much pollution,) that maketh him clean, but the imputation of Christ's righteousness; this maketh him *whiter than snow.*　5. As we must not neglect the ordinances of God, but must use them carefully for obedience unto God, and for strengthening our faith; so we must not rest upon

them, but search for the signification, substance, and end of
them, which is Christ; as here David seeketh perfect pardon by Christ's blood, and perfect purging and cleansing
through him, under the terms of *purging with hyssop and
washing.*   6. The grief and torment which follow sin, and
are felt by a wounded spirit, are greater, even in the children of God, in the time of their repentance, than ever the
pleasure of sin was to them, as David showeth here, who
speaketh of his vexation and wounded spirit, as of the most
painful trouble which can befall the body; for, by *the bones
which thou hast broken*, he meaneth the chastisement of his
spirit inflicted by God.   7. Nothing can heal this wound of
the spirit save the hand that made it; nothing but God's
effectual application of his word of grace and pardon to the
guilty sinner can do it; for David will not rest with what
Nathan had spoken, till God speak the same effectually unto
him : *make me to hear joy and gladness.*   8. As there is
no sorrow so deep as the sense of God's displeasure, so there
is no joy so refreshing as the inward consolation of God's
Spirit; for David's broken bones will rejoice if God speak
peace to his soul: *make me to hear joy and gladness, that
the bones which thou hast broken may rejoice.*

9. *Hide thy face from my sins, and blot out mine
iniquities.*

10. *Create in me a clean heart, O God; and renew
a right spirit within me.*

11. *Cast me not away from thy presence; and take
not thy Holy Spirit from me.*

12. *Restore unto me the joy of thy salvation; and
uphold me with thy free Spirit:*

13. Then *will I teach transgressors thy ways; and
sinners shall be converted unto thee.*

He prayeth for remission of sin the third time, v. 9, and
joineth therewith a petition for rectifying his sad condition;
first, by renovation of that grace which was decayed, and,
as it were, lost, in his sense, v. 10; secondly, by preventing
his deserved and dreaded separation from God and from
communion with his Spirit, v. 11; thirdly, by repairing and
restoring his former gracious condition, and settling him
therein by the Spirit of adoption, v. 12; and then he promiseth to make good use thereof for the comfort and edifi-

cation of other sinners, v. 13.   Whence learn, 1. Sin is soon
committed, and guiltiness and misery soon drawn on, but
not soon and easily removed; many a cry to God may be
uttered, in the sense of the felt displeasure of God and fear
of more and more evil following it, before the soul feel freedom from it; as this frequently repeated petition for pardon,
and those expressions here set down make evident.   2. Earnestness of affection maketh frequent repetition not to be
babbling, and when that which most presseth us is most in-
sisted on by us in our prayer, it is no vain repetition or idle
multiplication of words, as may here be seen.   3. Sin, seen
in its own shape, is a loathsome sight to God, and horrible
to the sinner; which loathsome sight nothing can remove
save the Lord's voluntarily forgiving it, and his not setting
it before his own face to be punished in severe justice : *hide
thy face from my sins.*   4. As one sin wakeneth up the consciousness of many other sins, so nothing can quiet the conscience about any one sin, except both it and all other sins
be forgiven; therefore, saith he, *blot out all mine iniquities.*
5. A sincere penitent is no less desirous of renovation and
sanctification than he is of forgiveness of sin; for, with *blot
out mine iniquities*, he joineth, *create in me a clean heart,
and renew a right spirit within me.*   6. Albeit sin against
the conscience, in a renewed man, defileth it thoroughly,
and defaceth the work of the Holy Spirit, openeth the flood-
gate of natural corruption, to the pollution of the whole frame
of a holy heart, openeth the way unto, and strengtheneth
the work of, an evil and deluding spirit; yet no principle of
grace in the renewed man is able to remove this evil, but
the removing of it must be by the immediate work of God's
own omnipotent hand.   This work is no less than creation;
therefore, saith he, *create in me a clean heart, and renew a
right spirit within me ;* that is, it is not in my power to clear
my conscience and my polluted heart, or to set my perverted
spirit in a right frame again; but thy creating and renewing
power, which borroweth nothing from the creature, must
do it; *create in me*, importeth this.   7. Albeit a renewed
soul cannot be utterly cast off from God, nor bereft utterly
of saving grace once bestowed on him; yet, if he grieve the
Lord's Spirit by presumptuous sinning, his assurance of standing in God's favour may be mightily endangered, and he put
in fear of losing the possession of what is behind of the saving

work of God's Spirit in him, especially when he considereth
that his provocation deserveth no less at God's hand; therefore, saith he, *cast me not away from thy presence, and take
not away thy Holy Spirit from me.*   8. Nothing is so terrible to a renewed soul, which hath been sometimes sensible
of God's favour and sure of the presence of his Spirit, as
to be shut out from God's favour, and severed from the
communion of his Spirit, as this prayer testifieth : *cast me
not away, &c.*   9. As a believer may come to assurance of
his own salvation, and when he keepeth a good conscience,
may sweetly rejoice therein; so when he seeth that the pleasure of sin hath marred this joy unto him, he cannot rest
or be quiet till he recover the assurance he had, and his
wonted joy be joined therewith : *restore unto me the joy of
thy salvation.*   10. The godly, by their fall, should learn
sensibly to acknowledge their own weakness, and their need
of the supporting strength of God's Spirit, and to account
the bonds of his Spirit, keeping them in order and in obedience, to be their only freedom.   Therefore David, after
prayer to have the joy of God's salvation restored unto him,
fearing lest he should lose it again if he were left to himself,
addeth another prayer, *uphold me with thy free Spirit.*   11.
As the end of seeking mercy to ourselves should be this,
that we may be enabled to be instruments of glorifying God,
and saving others; so the sensible feeling of mercy which is
sought after greatly encourageth a man to the work : *then
will I teach transgressors thy ways.   Then,* that is, when
the joy of God's salvation is restored to me, and I confirmed
somewhat in the grace of God.   12. As the way which God
keepeth in manifesting his justice against transgressors, and
his mercy to self-condemned sinners flying to him in Christ,
is not known by nature to sinners, so long as they go on in
their evil course, or before they be effectually taught to
know both; so, none are so fit to teach and persuade them
of this mystery as those who, by frequent experience, are
acquainted with the ways of God : *then will I teach transgressors thy ways.*   13. The communicating the knowledge
and experience of God's justice and mercy, according to
every man's place and calling, is a good means of converting others who know no such thing : *I will teach others thy
ways, and sinners shall be converted unto thee.*

14. *Deliver me from blood-guil'iness, O God, thou*

God of my salvation; and my tongue shall sing aloud of thy righteousness.

He prayeth the fourth time for remission of sin, and particularly of that fearful and bloody transgression in the matter of Uriah, which now troubleth his conscience most. Whence learn, 1. As the conscience passeth to particulars, in the midst of confused challenges for multitudes of sins; so, it presseth some particulars more eagerly than others, according as it is set on work, as here the guiltiness in the matter of Bathsheba and Uriah presseth David : *deliver me from blood-guiltiness.* 2. Though sin seem pleasant at the beginning, yet at length it is found a devouring enemy, from which none can deliver a soul save God alone: *deliver me from blood-guiltiness, O God.* 3. Upon the general grounds of the covenant of grace made with us for salvation through Christ, must a soul seek to have particular mercies: *deliver me, thou God of my salvation.* 4. The righteousness of God, which standeth in the remission of sin and imputation of Christ's obedience unto us, through faith, according to God's promise, is the matter of our joy and song of praise to God : which song a soul being in thraldom by felt guiltiness can hardly sing, but after the intimation of pardon will sing it cheerfully : *deliver me from blood-guiltiness, then shall my tongue sing aloud of thy righteousness.*

15. *O Lord, open thou my lips; and my mouth shall shew forth thy praise.*

16. *For thou desirest not sacrifice, else would I give it ; thou delightest not in burnt-offering.*

17. *The sacrifices of God are a broken spirit: a broken and a contrite heart, O God, thou wilt not despise.*

He pursueth this fourth petition for remission of sin, with a request for enlarging his heart, and furnishing him with matter and ability for praising God; wherein he sincerely renounceth all confidence in external ceremonies of the law, or in any thing else which he could perform. Whence learn, 1. Howsoever proud spirits think that they can do any thing they please in God's service, yet a humbled soul under exercise, knoweth that it is God who giveth both to will and to do of his good pleasure; such a man knoweth that the habit of grace is a gift, and the bringing of the habit into exercise is another gift; he knoweth that when one hath gotten grace to will to praise God, he must have grace to put this will to act effectually: this the psalmist acknowledgeth and prayeth, *open thou my lips, and my tongue shall show forth thy praise.* 2. Whatsoever holy ordinances and outward services God prescribeth to his church, are not required for satisfaction of his justice, nor are they the main thing he is pleased with, but they are means only to lead men to himself in Christ, in whom only justice findeth satisfaction, and man findeth strength to go about the worship, that so God himself may have all the praise of our services: therefore David giveth it for a reason of his former petition, *for thou desirest not,* or thou hast not pleasure in, *sacrifice.* 3. That which God aimeth at we should most desire, and what he is well pleased with we should most endeavour after: *thou desirest not sacrifice, else would I give it.* 4. The main design of the sacrifices under the law was, that a man under the sense of sin and deserved judgment, and inability to satisfy for his faults, should come and empty himself before God, and rely only on the one propitiatory sacrifice, represented in those external sacrifices: *the sacrifices of God are a broken spirit;* that is, the right way of sacrificing is, that a man's spirit be emptied of its own self-confidence when it cometh to offer unto God the external sacrifices which otherwise God regardeth not. 5. The man who most renounceth his own works, worth, or merits, and despiseth all his own doings, as a broken earthen vessel, is most acceptable in his approaches to God's free grace in the Mediator: *a broken and a contrite heart, O God, thou wilt not despise;* and that not for any worth in the matter of contrition, but because by contrition is expelled all conceit of self-worth, and so the man is most fit for receiving grace and free pardon from God.

18. *Do good in thy good pleasure unto Zion: build thou the walls of Jerusalem.*

19. *Then shalt thou be pleased with the sacrifices of righteousness, with burnt-offering, and whole burnt-offering: then shall they offer bullocks upon thine altar.*

In the last verse David prayeth for the Lord's people; that what breach had been made in the walls of God's protection about them, by his sins and theirs, might be repaired; and God more holily and heartily worshipped, both by himself and by them, in time coming. Whence learn, 1. As every true member of the church should bear in heart the condition of the body, and offer it up to God, whatsoever be the man's own private condition; so in special he that hath by his sins provoked God to withdraw his protection from the incorporation wherein he is, should most earnestly intercede for the good of the body, as David doth here: *do good in thy good pleasure unto Zion, build thou the walls of Jerusalem.* 2. The rich grace of God, his free love and unchangeable good-will to his people, are the cause of all the welfare of the church: *do good in thy good pleasure unto Zion.* 3. Whosoever have been most instrumental in the building of God's church, must some way be emptied of the glory of this work, that it may be all ascribed unto God alone, who is the only builder of his own church; as David here emptieth himself of this honour and ascribeth it to God, saying, *build thou up the walls of Jerusalem.* 4. When God poureth out upon his people his Spirit of grace and supplication, and other proper effects of his good-will to them, then, and not till then, are they fit to do him service acceptably: *do good in thy good pleasure to Zion, then shalt thou be pleased with the sacrifices, &c.* 5. No sacrifice is acceptable to God save the sacrifices of righteousness; now the sacrifices of righteousness are, first, the propitiatory sacrifice of Christ, whereunto every believer must have respect, as offered in his name, when he cometh to God; and next, the sacrifices of thankfulness and new obedience, offered up by virtue of Christ's sacrifice, to be accepted. The first sort of sacrifice was represented most specially by burnt-offering, and whole burnt-offering; and the other sort by peace-offerings and other oblations: *then shalt thou be pleased with the sacrifices of righteousness, with burnt-offering, and whole burnt-offering; then shall they offer bullocks upon thine altar.*

PSALM LII.

To the chief musician, Maschil. A psalm of David, when Doeg the Edomite came and told Saul, and said unto him, David is come to the house of Ahimelech.

The scope of the psalmist is to show that Doeg, his enemy, had no reason to glory in the favour of the court, purchased by his false and cruel calumnies against him and the Lord's priests, which he proveth by four reasons; first, because God's kindness could not be taken away by Doeg's cruel calumnies, ver. 1; secondly, because God would root Doeg out of the world for his wicked calumnies, ver. 2—5; thirdly, because Doeg would be made a laughing-stock and matter of derision to the godly, ver. 6, 7; fourthly, because maugre his malice, David should be blessed as a believer in God, and a true worshipper of him, ver. 8; whereupon, he concludeth with praise to God, ver. 9.

From the inscription, learn, 1. It is no new policy of wicked men to seek to be great in court and in the favour of princes, by maligning the godly and fostering the displeasure of princes against them; for Doeg of old climbed into court this way. 2. Such practices are most suitable to false brethren; for this Doeg is an Edomite, of the posterity of Esau. 3. When the wicked come to be in power and credit with kings for their very enmity against God's people, it is a narrow trial, and a sore temptation to the godly, as here, in David's case with Doeg, is to be seen. 4. In this case there is nothing so needful as to go to God for direction and consolation; for so David did, and came back with a *maschil*, or psalm, for instruction to himself and others. 5. It is no advantage to a malicious calumniator, to pretend that he told nothing but the truth, and told no more than what he saw; for it is true that David came to the house of Ahimelech, but the telling of this to Saul imported much mischief in the matter, even all the evil which happened, and all this is laid on Doeg, presupposing he had said no more than is expressed here, that is, that he told Saul *David is come to the house of Ahimelech.*

1. *Why boastest thou thyself in mischief, O mighty man ? the goodness of God* endureth *continually.*

David chargeth Doeg with the vanity of his gloriation, that he was now made so mighty a man, for his ill service done against the Lord's servants, and refuteth his folly, because he could not take the kindness of God from the godly so easily as he might steal their good estimation from them among men. Whence learn, 1. Prosperity and success following upon a wicked course, hide the sin and mischief which is in it from the sinner; as we see here, how the favour which foolish Doeg found at court for his calumniating David and the Lord's priests, puffed him up. 2. There is small reason for a wicked man to glory in his wickedness, whatsoever profit or preferment it may bring to him, for, after examination he will not be able to give a reason of his vain boasting : *why boastest thou thyself of thy mischief, O thou mighty man?* 3. Albeit the wicked think that God forgetteth his simple and weak servants, yet it is not so; and albeit the Lord altereth the exercise of the godly, and changeth their prosperity into adversity, yet he changeth not his affection to them; this remaineth fast for ever, whatsoever may appear to the carnal spectator of the Lord's dealing with his people : *the goodness of God endureth continually.* 4. So long as God's unchangeable kindness endureth, the wicked have no cause to exult over the godly, nor have the godly cause to faint or be discouraged, for this goodness of God David opposeth, both to Doeg's boasting, and to his own temptation: *the kindness of the Lord endureth for ever.*

2. *Thy tongue deviseth mischiefs ; like a sharp razor, working deceitfully.*

3. *Thou lovest evil more than good,* and *lying rather than to speak righteousness.　Selah.*

4. *Thou lovest all devouring words,* O thou *deceitful tongue.*

The next argument for refuting Doeg's folly, is, because this cruel calumny would bring God's vengeance on Doeg, and root him out of all felicity; and here he first sets down his ditty in these three verses, before he sets down his doom, v. 5.　Whence learn, 1. The tongue, when it is abused, is a world of wickedness, setting the world on fire, as itself is set on fire from hell by Satan : for, whatsoever mischief the devil can suggest, or a wicked heart can devise, the tongue will serve to vent; therefore is the tongue charged with devising mischief: *thy tongue deviseth mischief.* 2. The smooth convey of a wicked device, hideth not the mischief of it from God's sight, nor extenuateth the man's fault, but rather helpeth on the mischief more cunningly and powerfully : *like a sharp razor, working deceitfully.* 3. When a man speaketh no more of a tale of his neighbour, but what may serve to the man's hurt and prejudice, and keepeth up the relation of that part of the tale which might clear the man's innocence, or might give a right construction of his actions; albeit that part of the tale told be true, if all the rest of the tale had been told with it, yet, being told alone as if it were the full history, *it is evil, it is false lying.*　It is a murdering and devouring speech, and full of deceit, and argueth the speaker to be such a one as Doeg was, in this particular at least, to whom David saith, *thou lovest evil more than good, and lying rather than to speak righteousness ; thou lovest all-devouring words, O thou deceitful tongue.* 4. The more design, deliberation, and affection there is in a sin; the heavier is the guilt, and the challenge for it more just. *Doeg's devising mischief, Doeg's choosing evil and not good ; choosing lying, and not righteousness ; loving these evil and all-devouring words,* make his ditty most fearful.

5. *God shall likewise destroy thee for ever : he shall take thee away, and pluck thee out of* thy *dwelling-place, and root thee out of the land of the living. Selah.*

Now followeth his doom : Whence learn, 1. As any wicked man is instrumental for bringing temporal destruction on the godly, so is he instrumental in drawing everlasting destruction upon himself from God's hand : *God shall likewise destroy thee for ever.* 2. He that seeketh to settle himself, to enlarge himself, to root himself in the earth, and to prolong his standing in the world, by wrong means; and in special, by hurting the godly, and their good name and cause, shall find the event quite contrary to his desire, design, and expectation, as Doeg did, whose doom was destruction, for his evil offences done at court against David and the Lord's ministers : *God shall take thee away, and pluck thee out of thy dwelling-place, and root thee out of the land of the living.*

6. *The righteous also shall see, and fear, and shall laugh at him :*

7. *Lo,* this is *the man* that *made not God his strength ; but trusted in the abundance of his riches,* and *strengthened himself in his wickedness.*

The third argument of refutation of Doeg's vain boasting, is, that his wisdom should appear ridiculous folly, and his boasting the matter of his shame and disgrace. Whence learn, 1. The notable enemies of God's children and servants may expect to be notably punished, and that they who saw their sin, shall see also God's vengeance on them : *the righteous shall see it.* 2. As the godly are the only wise observers of God's work, and the dispensation of his mercy and justice; so also are they the only persons who gain spiritual

advantage thereby : *the righteous shall see it, and fear.* 3.
As the good of godliness is seen and felt by the godly in their
own experience of God's blessing upon themselves, so is it
seen and observed also in the contrary evils which befall the
ungodly : *lo, this is the man that made not God his strength,*
say they, *but trusted in the abundance of his riches, and
strengthened himself in his wickedness.*

8. *But I* am *like a green olive-tree in the house of
God : I trust in the mercy of God for ever and ever.*

The fourth argument for refutation of Doeg's foolish
boasting, is because, I, saith David, shall flourish in God's
favour, in despite of Doeg. Whence learn, 1. Whatsoever
may befall the godly by the malice of their enemies, it shall
not diminish their felicity; when their enemies are running
to their own destruction, it shall be well with the godly, they
may be persuaded of it, for the psalmist's example encourageth to it : *but I am like a green olive-tree.* 2. As the
olive-tree, being planted in a fertile ground, draweth in moisture, whereby it is nourished and groweth up : so the believer, being planted in the church, draweth spirit and life
from God by holy ordinances, whereby he groweth up : *I am
like a green olive tree in the house of God.* 3. The wisdom
of the godly, and the ground of their true blessedness is this,
they make fast work of their everlasting felicity by faith
in God, and this maketh them like green olives all the days
of their life : *for I trust in the mercy of God for ever and
ever,* is given here for a reason of his happy growing in the
house of God.

9. *I will praise thee for ever, because thou hast done
it : and I will wait on thy name ; for it is good before
thy saints.*

He closeth the psalm comfortably, with resolution to
praise God, and to depend upon him. Whence learn, 1.
Victory over temptations obtained by faith, is very glorious;
for faith maketh a man as sure of what is to come, as if it
were perfected, and filleth him with praise for the certain
hope of the performance of promises : *I will praise thee for
ever,* saith David, *because thou hast done it.* 2. Faith being
solidly fixed, bringeth forth hope and quiet expectation of
what is promised : *I will wait on thy name.* 3. As the
Christian patience of one of the saints, is a matter of good

example and great encouragement unto all the rest that behold it : so the consideration of the good which may redound to others, who shall be witnesses of our patient attending upon God, should stir us up to this duty of patient hope in God : *I will wait on thee, for it is good before thy saints.*

PSALM LIII.

To the chief musician upon Mahalath, Maschil. A psalm of David.

As in the fourteenth psalm, so here David comforteth himself and the rest of the godly in their sad sufferings which they felt from godless men, lying in the miserable condition of nature, v. 1—3. The grounds of comfort are three ; the first, because God was engaged in the sufferings of his own, and would plead their controversy against the wicked, v. 4 ; the next, because God's judgments were to come on all the persecutors of the godly, v. 5 ; and the third, because there is hope of the full salvation of the godly in Christ, v. 6. Comparing this psalm with psalm xiv, wherein the enmity of the wicked against the godly, and the comfort of the godly in that case, are the same in this place, as those set down there, we learn, that as the godly men may fall oftener than once, in one case, under one and the same temptation, some sort of hard exercise and grief: so may they and should they make use of the same comforts, and bring to memory the same doctrines for that end, as the church is taught to do, psalm xiv, and here in this psalm.

1. *The fool hath said in his heart,* There is *no God. Corrupt are they, and have done abominable iniquity :* there is *none that doeth good.*

2. *God looked down from heaven upon the children of men, to see if there were* any *that did understand, that did seek God.*

3. *Every one of them is gone back ; they are altogether become filthy :* there is *none that doeth good, no, not one.*

From the description of the miserable condition wherein the world and every unrenewed man within the church visible lie, learn, 1. All the unrenewed persons are fools before God, how wise soever they may seem to men. 2. All unrenewed men are, inwardly in their affections and resolutions, atheists in effect, and such as do not regard God in any thing; whatsoever they may seem to themselves or others outwardly, *they say in their heart, There is no God.* 3. All unrenewed men are altogether rotten in their principles and motives of action : *they are corrupt.* 4. The actions of the unrenewed will be found abomination before God, and will prove them to be corrupt: *they have done abominable iniquity.* 5. Among all unrenewed men, whether without or within the visible church, not one man shall be found to have done so much as one good action, which can stand for good in God's account: *there is none that doeth good.* 6. The truth of this doctrine is put to trial and proof by God himself, and sentence is pronounced of all men's natural averseness from God, and impotency to do good: *God looked down from heaven upon the children of men, to see if there were any that did good, and he found none.* 7. As it is impossible that those can do any good, or be wise, who seek not God; so the proof and trial of this naughtiness of all men, so long as they lie in nature unrenewed, are found by their not *understanding, nor seeking of God: the Lord looked to see if there were any that did understand, that did seek God.* 8. Every man by nature is a revolter from God, and from the state wherein once God made man: *every one of them is gone back.* 9. There is nothing clear and unpolluted in soul or body of the unrenewed man, but the longer he liveth in nature, the viler is he: *they are altogether become filthy.* 10. Seeing all men by nature are concluded under sin, without exception, *and there is none that doeth good, no, not one;* it is no wonder that the image of God, appearing in his children, be ill entertained by natural men, and that God's children expect no good fruits from such ill trees as all men are by nature; for this doctrine is delivered to quiet the hearts of the godly, when they are molested by the men of this world. It should yield comfort to the godly to behold the miserable condition wherein all men are by nature, and themselves called forth from this miserable estate and converted; for this doctrine offereth ground for comparison, and for consolation.

4. *Have the workers of iniquity no knowledge? who eat up my people* as *they eat bread: they have not called upon God.*

The first direct argument for the comforting of the godly under their persecution by the wicked among whom they live, is, that God considereth their case, and will plead their cause. Whence learn, 1. The Lord observeth every point of enmity which the world carrieth against his people; he taketh their case to heart, and will plead their cause; and this is a solid ground of comfort to his people in all their sufferings : *have the workers of iniquity no knowledge ? that eat up,* &c. 2. The grounds of difference between the unrenewed and the renewed or reconciled, offered in this opposition of the one sort to the other, are these : first, the unrenewed, all of them are called *workers of iniquity ;* but they that are reconciled, although they are not free from sin, yet they are not counted by God to be the workers of iniquity. Again, the Lord acknowledgeth the regenerate, and calleth them *his own people ;* but disclaimeth the other, as in effect not his people, but his enemies. And lastly, the unregenerate *do not call upon God,* to wit, in earnest, or in truth; but the regenerate, by the opposition made, are presupposed here to call on God, and to depend upon him in truth. 3. Nothing maketh more evident the blindness and beastly besotting of the conscience of sinners, than the persecuting of the saints; it will not suffice the ungodly to live a godless life themselves, except they malign and most unreasonably oppose piety in others : *have the workers of iniquity no knowledge? that they eat up my people as they eat bread.* 4. To vex, bear down, and destroy the godly, is as great a pleasure to the wicked, as to eat their meat : *they eat up my people as they eat bread.*

5. *There were they in great fear,* where *no fear was : for God hath scattered the bones of him that encampeth* against *thee : thou hast put* them *to shame, because God hath despised them.*

The next ground of comfort to the godly against persecution, is, because God's judgments shall overtake the troublers of God's people, when they least fear it. Whence learn, 1. As persecution cauterizeth the conscience, and maketh it senseless of sin; so also it maketh the persecutors fearless of judgment, when they eat up the people of God as bread without fear : *for there,* saith he, *no fear was.* 2. The more secure a sinner is, and in special a persecutor of God's people, the more terrible shall his wakening be, when God's judgment cometh on him : *there were they in great fear, where no fear was.* 3. The enemies of God's church make it their study and main work to overthrow the godly, and to compass them, as it were, by way of laying siege about them, that they escape not : *they encamp against thee,* saith the psalmist, speaking as it were to every one of God's people. 4. Wrath pursueth the persecutor, both living and dead, and ceaseth not to follow him so long as there is any thing of him capable of punishment; for God not only raiseth the siege, and destroyeth the enemy, and consumeth his flesh, but also he hath *scattered the bones of him that encampeth against thee.* 5. When there is nothing left of the persecutor's substance unpunished in the world, the wrath of God pursueth his name and memorial; and the wrong done to the innocent is the persecutor's greatest disgrace: *thou hast put them to shame.* 6. As true honour, and the conferring of respect from men upon any, are the gifts of God, who honoureth them that honour him; so deserved shame and disgrace for sin committed, when poured out as the effect of God's justice, make them who dishonour him to be lightly esteemed : *thou hast put them to shame, because God hath despised them.*

6. *Oh that the salvation of Israel* were come *out of Zion ! When God bringeth back the captivity of his people, Jacob shall rejoice,* and *Israel shall be glad.*

The last ground of comfort to the persecuted godly, is the hope of complete salvation to the church of God, and of every true member thereof in Christ. Whence learn, 1. There is no solid consolation against persecution, or any other grievance, save in the salvation which is to be had in Christ : *he is the Saviour and salvation of Israel.* 2. As Christ's coming to accomplish salvation part by part, in his own order and time, is most certainly to be believed and hoped for : so is it most earnestly to be wished, longed after, and prayed for : as the example of the Lord's people here (longing for his coming to *Zion*, in his incarnation and manifestation of his grace; and then in the spreading forth of his grace and salvation out of *Zion* to Gentiles and Jews) teacheth us : *O that the salvation of Israel was come out of Zion.* 3. As the captivity of God's people remaineth in any degree and measure, which may make Christ's coming to be so much the more desirable, and to be the object of wishes and matter of prayer; so shall every sort and degree of captivity at last be removed from God's people, till redemption be completely fulfilled; God shall bring back the captivity of his people. 4. As of all people, who ever had

the name of God's people, the miseries and captivities of the
Israelites, because of their provocation against God, have
been the most conspicuous and signal: so of all the people
on the earth, and of all the nations which have been honoured
with the title of *God's people*; the deliverance of Israel from
captivity shall be most eminently and conspicuously com--
fortable; for, *when God shall bring back the captivity of his
people, then Jacob shall rejoice and Israel shall be glad.*

PSALM LIV.

*To the chief musician, on Neginóth, Maschil. A psalm of David,
when the Ziphim came and said to Saul, doth not David hide himself with us ?*

David being betrayed by the Ziphim; first, maketh his prayer to God
for delivery, v. 1, 2 ; secondly, he strengtheneth his faith by some reasons, v. 3 ; thirdly, he is confident of his own delivery, and of God's
judgment on the Ziphim, whereunto he subscribes, v. 4, 5 ; and, last
of all, he promiseth praise to God for his own assured deliverance,
v. 6, 7.

From the inscription, learn, 1. Particular straits and
particular deliveries should be particularly remarked: as
David here remembereth the danger he was in by the
treachery of the Ziphim.   2. Mighty men will find readily
more friends in an evil cause, than the godly find in a good
one : as Saul hath the Ziphim to offer their service to his
cruelty, when David was in straits.   3. The wicked are
very hearty to do an ill action, and glad to find occasion
for it : *doth not David,* say they, *hide himself with us ?* as
if this had been good and blessed news.

1. *Save me, O God, by thy name, and judge me by
thy strength.*

2. *Hear my prayer, O God ; give ear to the words
of my mouth.*

From David's prayer, learn, 1. The godly can never
be so surprised with trouble, but they may fly to God for
delivery, as David doth here; and it is a rare virtue not
to forget this relief in depth of distress.   2. When men
believe that God is all-sufficient and answerable for what is
spoken of him, they have great encouragement to go to
him in difficulty; *save me by thy name,* saith David. God's
name gave him ground to pray and hope for deliverance.

3. Albeit no man should rashly call God to give judgment, yet in a good cause, against a strong party, an upright man may call for and expect assistance from God : *judge me by thy strength*, saith he. 4. In fervent prayer, the very voice hath use; as with the supplicant to express his earnestness, and his faith in God, and to stir him up and hold him fixed to his supplication; so with God also, for it is an express invocation of him, and a sign of dependence upon him, and of expectation of a good answer from him; *hear my prayer, O God, give ear unto the words of my mouth.*

3. *For strangers are risen up against me ; and oppressors seek after my soul : they have not set God before them. Selah.*

The reasons supporting his faith in his prayer, are taken from the unkindness, unnaturalness and cruelty, not only of his countrymen, but also of his father-in-law and his old acquaintance, slippery courtiers, who some time professed friendship. Whence learn, 1. No strangers are more strange than they who cast off the bands of civility and nature, whereby they were bound : false countrymen, false brethren, false friends, false alliance, are those of whom men may expect least in their need, for David findeth such men to be his greatest enemies : *strangers are risen up against me,* saith he. 2. When they who should protect a man, do him most wrong, God will hear the plaints put up against such men : *oppressors seek after my soul,* or life. 3. When the fear of God is laid aside, there is nothing to be expected of the godless man but the worst of evils which he is able to do; there is no awband to restrain him : for *they have not set God before them.* 4. The less hope there be of man's mercy, the more hope is of God's help; the more unkind and cruel men be, who should be friends, the more may the Lord's kindness and comfort be expected for supply of inlacks, as here the drift of David's argument holdeth forth.

4. *Behold, God is mine helper : the Lord is with them that uphold my soul.*

5. *He shall reward evil unto mine enemies : cut them off in thy truth.*

In the third place, he is assured of help to himself and to his friends, and of vengeance to his enemies. Whence learn,

1. Fervent prayer hath readily a swift answer, and sometimes wonderfully swift, even before a man have ended speech, as here David findeth in experience : *behold,* saith he, *God is my helper.* 2. The sight of faith is very clear, and piercing through all clouds; when God holds forth the light of his Spirit to it, it can demonstrate God present in an instant, ready to help in greatest straits : *behold, God is my helper.* 3. There is more joy in God's felt presence, than grief in felt trouble; for, *behold, God is my helper,* is more comfort than his friends' unkindness, and strangers' malice were grievous. 4. Such as comfort and help a man in time of his temptation, are not only helpers unto him in the matter of his temporal life, but also instruments to save his soul, which by temptations is like to be drawn into sin, and so to destruction; for David saith of such men, *they uphold my soul.* 5. Such as take part with the persecuted saints, God will take part with : *the Lord is with them that uphold my soul.* 6. As God is a friend to the friends of his distressed children, so he is a foe to their foes; and their foes shall smart for their enmity in due time : *he shall reward evil to my enemies.* 7. The doom of the wicked enemies of God's children, is set down in God's word; his truth is the wicked man's terror, and the godly man's strength : *cut them off in thy truth.* 8. Albeit we may not without clear warrant pray against particular persons, yet we may subscribe to God's word set down in Scripture against his obstinate enemies, and our enemies for his cause : *cut them off in thy truth.*

6. *I will freely sacrifice unto thee ; I will praise thy name, O Lord, for* it *is good.*

7. *For he hath delivered me out of all trouble ; and mine eye hath seen* his desire *upon mine enemies.*

In the last place, he promiseth praise to God for the certainty he had of his deliverance, whereof he was no less assured than if he had seen it with his eyes. Whence learn, 1. Promised and hoped for deliverance is able to affect the heart, as a mercy present and already past, as here it doth David : *I will sacrifice to thee, and praise thee.* 2. Readiness of heart to glorify God, and liberty of spirit, with occasion granted to praise him for a benefit, are other new benefits superadded and greatly to be esteemed, as David accounteth it: *I will freely sacrifice unto thee, and praise thy name, for it is good ;* that is, not only is thy name good, but to have a heart sincerely to serve thee, and liberty to express thy praise before others, is good. 3. An action is good, when it is done because it is a good action, and is not gone about for by ends : *I will praise his name, for it is good,* saith he. 4. In experience of one delivery man may have a foresight of a full delivery out of every evil or trouble wherein he can fall, as here David speaketh of hopes for full delivery : *he hath delivered me out of all troubles.* 5. The same light of God's word, made lively by God's Spirit, is able to show a man, both the destruction of his wicked enemies, and his own deliverance from them; and as a man may rejoice, in God's mercy towards himself, so also may he rejoice in God's justice against his enemies, provided he be free of private revenge: *mine eye hath seen thy judgments upon mine enemies.*

PSALM LV.

To the chief musician on Neginoth, Maschil.   A psalm of David.

This psalm containeth this doctrine, That albeit Christ and his followers may be in great straits by the treachery of their pretended friends, yet through God's favour they shall be delivered, as David felt in experience.   The use of which doctrine is subjoined in the end of the psalm, which well agreeth with the psalmist's condition in the time of Absalom and Ahitophel's conspiracy.   The parts of the psalm we may make these three.   In the first is set down his sorrowful supplication, to v. 16 ; in the next, his comforting himself in the Lord for his deliverer, to v. 22 ; in the third, use of this experience, in the last two verses.
In his supplication he prayeth, in the first place, for a gracious hearing, because of the calumnies and cruelty of his enemies, v. 1—3.   In the next place, he setteth down his pitiful condition of mind, v. 4—5, making him to wish to be far from the company of those conspirators who were combined against him, v. 6—8.   In the third place, he prayeth to God to confound their counsels, because the whole city was in an uproar against him, seeking how to execute their mischievous plot, v. 9—11.   In the fourth place, he condescends upon a more particular reason of his prayer for confounding their counsels, because the plotter of the conspiracy had been most intimate in his familiarity, and deep upon his counsel, v. 12—14.   Whereupon, in the last place, by way of prayer he prophesieth of the curse of God to come upon them, v. 15. In the second part of the psalm he comforteth himself in God ; first, by his resolution constantly to depend upon God, and hopefully to pray, v. 16, 17; secondly, by his former experiences of deliverances granted to him before, v. 18; thirdly, because he was assured God would punish his enemies for their treacherous breach of covenant, and cloaking of their malicious designs with fair pretences and deep dissimulation,

v. 19—21. In the third part of the psalm are the uses of this experience, v. 22—23.

1. *Give ear to my prayer, O God ; and hide not thyself from my supplication.*

2. *Attend unto me, and hear me : I mourn in my complaint, and make a noise ;*

3. *Because of the voice of the enemy, because of the oppression of the wicked : for they cast iniquity upon me, and in wrath they hate me.*

From his address to God for relief in this, as in his other sad conditions, learn, 1. Many grievances are the godly subject unto, but in none of them all is there any ease for them, till they go to God and lay out their case before him : *give ear to my prayer, O God.* 2. As it is ease of heart to supplicants to have any sign of the acceptance of their supplication; so not to find access in prayer addeth much weight to their trouble : *hide not,* saith he, *thyself from my supplication.* 3. When a sad heart is fixed on God, and findeth what to say to him, it may expect that its words shall not be misregarded of God, but punctually taken knowledge of : *attend unto me and hear me.* 4. Though a child of God were ever so stout-hearted naturally, yet when God exerciseth his spirit with trouble, he shall be made to weep before God as a child, and must not be ashamed to be thus humbled before him : *I mourn in my complaint,* saith he, *and make a noise.* 5. A mourning supplicant shall neither lose his prayers nor his tears; for, *I mourn,* is brought as a reason of his hope that God shall *attend and hear him.* 6. When the godly fall into persecution and trouble from men, their lives, their estate, and their good name, readily come altogether to be in danger at once, as it befell David when the conspirators made head against him; they traduced his former government, as if he had been a wicked man, and sought to bear him down, and to have his life : *because of the voice of the enemy,* there is their railing; *because of the oppression of the wicked,* there is their violent robbing him of his estate; *they cast iniquity upon me,* there are their slanderous traducings of him, and charging him with faults falsely; *in wrath they hate me,* there is their cruel seeking to kill him.

4. *My heart is sore pained within me ; and the terrors of death are fallen upon me.*

5. *Fearfulness and trembling are come upon me, and horror hath overwhelmed me.*

In this pitiful condition of mind, learn, 1. It is not a thing inconsistent with godliness to be much moved with fear in time of danger; natural affections are not taken away in conversion, but sanctified and moderated : *my heart is ore pained within me.*   2. Natural sagacity and courage re not sufficient to bear a man out in a great stress, for they will fail him; and if a man have not stronger supporters than his natural parts, he is undone; for here *the terrors of death are fallen upon me, and horror hath overwhelmed me.*   3. The godly have an advantage above all natural men : for when natural strength and courage fail them, they have nothing behind; but the godly have faith in God, to open a fountain of fresh supply of wisdom, courage, and strength to them, when all natural parts fail them; for, David being now emptied of natural strength, hath wisdom and strength to go to God, and hope of heart to be helped by him.

6. *And I said, Oh that I had wings like a dove!* for then *would I fly away, and be at rest.*

7. *Lo,* then *would I wander far off,* and *remain in the wilderness.   Selah.*

8. *I would hasten my escape from the windy storm* and *tempest.*

Whereas he wished to have been out of the reach and society of such wicked enemies, learn, 1. When a man may escape a present hazard of life, with a good conscience, he may lawfully flee and eschew the danger, as David here wished he could have escaped : *O if I had wings, then would I fly away.*   2. A godly man may be in such peril as it seems to him he cannot without a miracle be delivered, as David saw no way to escape the conspiracy, save this way : *O that I had the wings of a dove*; and yet God may so dispose, as he may be delivered in an ordinary way, as here David was.   3. It is better to be in the wilderness in some cases, than to be in the company of the wicked : *lo, I would wander far off, and remain in the wilderness.*   4. The way to eschew the fury of a sudden insurrection of a tumultuous multitude, is not to come forth and appease them with words, but to decline their present fury by going out of the way, if God offer occasion : *I would hasten my escape from the windy storm and tempest.*

9. *Destroy, O Lord, and divide their tongues : for I have seen violence and strife in the city.*

10. *Day and night they go about it upon the walls thereof : mischief also and sorrow are in the midst of it.*

11. *Wickedness is in the midst thereof; deceit and guile depart not from her streets.*

In the third place, he prayeth to confound the counsel of his enemies, because they had put the whole city in confusion, and set the citizens upon a course of cruelty and violence. Whence learn, 1. A visible church may sometimes be in so sinful a condition, as a godly man shall not know what to do, or to whom he may have recourse, or where to hide himself; as here the condition of the holy city, the city of Jerusalem is described. 2. The prayers of the godly are more able to disappoint the plots of cruel enemies, than all human policy : *destroy, O Lord, and divide their tongues.* 3. The believer should make use of such courses as God hath taken before for disappointing wicked enterprises, for supporting his faith in his need, as here David maketh use of God's dissolving the conspiracy of Corah, Dathan, and Abiram, and of the proud enterprise of the wicked in building Babel: *destroy, O Lord, and divide their tongues.* 4. A man should be very sure, that such as he prayeth against, and complaineth of unto God, are in a wicked condition, and upon a mischievous course; for David giveth for a reason of his imprecation, that he had *seen violence and strife in the city,* the rulers of the city diligently watching for his life to do mischief ; *day and night going about the walls, mischief, sorrow, wickedness, deceit, guile in the midst of it,* and openly avowed in the streets.

12. *For* it was *not an enemy* that *reproached me ; then I could have borne* it : *neither* was it *he that hated me* that *did magnify* himself *against me ; then I would have hid myself from him :*

13. *But* it was *thou, a man mine equal, my guide, and mine acquaintance.*

14. *We took sweet counsel together,* and *walked unto the house of God in company.*

In the fourth place, he condescendeth upon a more special reason of his imprecation, because Ahitophel and other like traitors, (fit types of Judas) had treacherously abused their trust and familiarity which they had with him, whose ingratitude grieved him more than the injuries of others. Whence learn, 1. It is not a strange thing for the godly to find such as should be their friends become their greatest foes, especially in a good cause; this David's experience maketh evident. 2. The worst that a professed enemy can do against the godly in a good cause, is more tolerable than treachery against us, or the forsaking of us by a professed friend; for that importeth a reproach in the party forsaken, as having a bad cause, or being unworthy to be assisted : *it was not an enemy that reproached me, then I could have borne it.* 3. The injuries of a suspected enemy, are not so unavoidable before they be done, nor so piercing when they are done, as the injuries of one whom a man suspecteth not, or as the injuries done to us by a professed and trusted friend : *neither was it he that hated me, then I could have hid myself from him.* 4. The disappointing of us by a friend in a good cause, much more the open opposition, and most of all the treachery of a trusted friend against us in a good cause, carry with them a vilifying and despising of our person and cause, and import our ill deserving at his hand, our ill carriage in the cause, and our deserving to be forsaken; and say in effect, that the false friend or traitor hath reason to be avenged on us, and to oppose us in that cause; and what can be heavier to a godly persecuted person ? for this is a very exalting of the traitor against us : *neither was it he that hated me, that did magnify himself against me.* 5. Amongst many friendly neighbours, it has been the custom of godly and wise men, to choose out some to be their most intimate friends, whom they would use most familiarly and freely, whose counsel they would take, and most readily follow : *it was thou, O man, mine equal, my guide, and my acquaintance.* 6. To find a godly and wise man with whom we may be free in all cases of mind or conscience into which we may fall, to whom we may freely open our mind, and be strengthened by him in the service of God, is a notable refreshment, and part of happiness and contentment : *we took sweet counsel together, and walked unto the house of God in company.* 7. A godly and wise man may

be deceived in his choice by the close carriage of a hypocrite, who, because he hath no sound principles of steadfastness in a good cause, may both disappoint his friend, and deceive himself also, and so do that which he did not at first intend to do. This disappointment to the godly is a very heavy
affliction : *but it was thou, O man, mine equal, my guide.*

15. *Let death seize upon them,* and *let them go down
quick into hell : for wickedness* is *in their dwellings,*
and *among them.*

From his prophetical imprecation against his enemies,
such as Ahitophel was to David and Judas to Christ, and
such like, together with their followers and accomplices,
learn, 1. Swift destruction is the reward of the enemies of
God's servants, and specially of treacherous apostates from a
good cause, as Ahitophel's and Judas's latter end gave example : *let death seize upon them, and let them go down quick
into hell.* 2. Such as give entertainment and lodging unto
wickedness, shall have hell for their lodging, where wickedness lodgeth; for here it is given for a reason why the wicked
shall go down to hell : *because wickedness is in their dwellings, and among them.* 3. What the Lord hath revealed to
be his righteous decree, the godly may warrantably subscribe
unto it : *let death seize on them, &c.*

16. *As for me, I will call upon God; and the Lord
shall save me.*

17. *Evening, and morning, and at noon, will I pray,
and cry aloud ; and he shall hear my voice.*

In the second part of the psalm he comforteth himself in
his resolution constantly to depend on God, and his confidence
to find access in worship. Whence learn, 1. The right use
of God's judgments on the wicked for their wickedness is to
draw near to God, to worship him and depend upon him, as
David here resolved : *as for me, I will call upon God.* 2. A
man may be sure to be saved in drawing near to the Lord,
whatsoever shall befall the wicked : *I will call on God, and
the Lord shall save me.* 3. He who resolveth to live upon
God's good-will and bounty, and hopeth to be saved at last,
must resolve also to be constant, fervent, and importunate in
his daily worship and attendance on God : *evening and morning will I pray, and cry aloud.* 4. As it is needful upon
all occasions to watch unto prayer, and to entertain a frame

of spirit fit for supplication : so is it fit for giving ourselves more specially and fully to this work, to have (albeit not fixed canonic hours,) yet set times every day, at or about which we may follow religious worship, such as are *morning*, *evening and noon*, or any other time most fitting for the work, all circumstances being compared; as here David's resolution and example teach us.

18. *He hath delivered my soul in peace from the battle* that was *against me; for there were many with me.*

His next encouragement is taken from the experiences of former deliveries given to him by God.   Whence learn, 1. We make good use of experiences, when we stir up ourselves thereby, to believe the more in God, and to call on him in all conditions, as David here giveth this, *he hath delivered my soul*, as a reason of his former resolution.   2. In the midst of war, the Lord can keep a man as safe as in the time of peace, and in extreme perils preserve him from danger : *he hath delivered my soul in peace from the battle that was against me.*   3. He that depends upon God in the time of trouble, albeit he had a host against him, yet hath he more with him when God is with him, than can be against him : *he hath delivered my soul, for there are many with me.*

19. *God shall hear, and afflict them, even he that abideth of old.   Selah.   Because they have no changes, therefore they fear not God.*

20. *He hath put forth his hands against such as be at peace with him; he hath broken his covenant.*

21. The words *of his mouth were smoother than butter, but war* was *in his heart: his words were softer than oil, yet* were *they drawn swords.*

His third encouragement is taken from assurance, that God should punish his enemies for their godless security, breach of covenant, and deep dissimulation.   Whence learn, 1. Upon the complaint of the oppressed servants of God, not only are they delivered themselves, but also their enemies are punished : *God shall hear and afflict them.*   2. God's eternity and immutability is a sufficient ground of the manifestation of his mercy to his own people, and his justice against their enemies from generation to generation : *God shall hear me, and afflict them, even he that abideth of old.   Selah.*

3. The more gently the Lord deals with the wicked in not exercising them with so many crosses, outward and inward, as he doth his own, the more godless are they, the more secure are they; and the more godless and secure they are, the more certainly is their vexation coming : *he will afflict them sore ; because they have no changes, therefore they fear not God.* This is one reason of the Lord's pursuing the wicked. 4. Whoever he be that maketh a breach in the peace between himself and others, shall have God for his party, who shall not fail to afflict the peace-breaker; he shall afflict them, especially the chief ringleaders, *who have put forth their hands against such as be at peace with them :* and this is another reason of the Lord's punishing the enemies of his people. 5. The Lord will make a quarrel, and pursue for the breach of covenant in special, because this is a most solemn confirmation of peace, and one which God hath special interest to see performed, or the breach of it punished : *he has broken his covenant ;* and this is the third reason of God's punishing false brethren, pretended friends to God's people, but in effect most pernicious foes. 6. The bosom enemies of the church, and underminers of the Lord's people, and of his work in their hands, make fairest pretences; when their vilest plots are in hand, then they are at Hail Master, and offering kisses, then they are about to betray : *the words of his mouth were smoother than butter, but war was in his heart ; his words were softer than oil, yet were they drawn swords ;* and this vile dissimulation is the fourth reason of the Lord's avenging the persecution of false brethren.

22. *Cast thy burden upon the Lord, and he shall sustain thee : he shall never suffer the righteous to be moved.*

23. *But thou, O God, shalt bring them down into the pit of destruction : bloody and deceitful men shall not live out half their days ; but I will trust in thee.*

The use of this experience the psalmist setteth forth; first by giving counsel to the oppressed to cast their burden upon the Lord, when they are over-burdened, and by making promises for encouraging them thereto; secondly, by giving assurance of the perdition of the treacherous enemies of the church; thirdly, by setting forth his own resolution to keep confidence in God. Whence learn, 1. The use of the experience which godly persons have had, of comfort in and delivery out of trouble, is the encouragement of us to take the same course which the godly followed before us, by seeking our relief in God only : *cast thy burden on the Lord.*   2. Whosoever repose with confidence on God in their weighty troubles, shall never sink under them; *cast thy burden on the Lord, and he shall sustain thee.*   3. Though the godly be troubled and tossed, yet because they continue to seek God, and to walk in the way of righteousness, they shall never be driven from their anchor-hold, they shall not be loosed at the root; their building shall be found still in its own place, upon the rock : *he shall never suffer the righteous to be moved.*   4. As on the one hand the Lord shall uphold the believer, how low soever he shall be brought, that he perish not : so shall the Lord still bring down the wicked to perdition, how high soever, how fixed soever his state appear; believe this who will : *God will not suffer the righteous to be moved, but thou, O God, shalt bring them down into the pit of destruction.*   5. Treacherous and cruel adversaries of the Lord's people shall be cut off before they accomplish their bloody plots; they shall never die full of days, but wrath shall take them away when they would least : *bloody and deceitful men shall not live half their days.*   6. Whether such as trouble the godly live longer or shorter, they will cause trouble to the godly, so long as they live; and the only rest that godly hearts can have against all the trouble they feel or fear from their enemies, or otherwise, is to stay themselves on the Lord; for so resolveth the psalmist : *but I will trust in thee,* saith he, and so closeth.

PSALM LVI.

To the chief musician upon Jonath-Elem-Rechokim, Michtam of David, when the Philistines took him in Gath.

David flying from Saul to the country of the Philistines, (as we read, 1 Sam. xxi. 13.) is apprehended, prayeth to God, and is delivered. There are two parts of the psalm.   In the former part there are three conflicts of David's faith with his trouble and temptation, and three victories.   The first conflict is in prayer, laying forth his enemies' carriage against him, v. 1, 2; and his first victory by faith, v. 3, 4.   The second conflict in his complaint he maketh against his enemies, v. 5, 6; and his second victory by faith, v. 7.   His third conflict is by laying forth his mournful condition before God, with hope to be regarded, v. 8; and his third and greatest victory by faith, v. 9—11.   In the latter part of the psalm is David's obligation thankfully to acknowledge his merciful delivery, with a petition for grace to persevere in the course of obedience, under God's protection, v. 12, 13,

From the inscription, learn, 1. When once God's children are entered on their trials, they meet with new and unexpected difficulties, as David here flying from one enemy, falls into the hands of another. 2. Those means of safety which God's children devise themselves, readily prove snares; David flying out of the holy land, falleth into the hands of his adversaries : *the Philistines took him in Gath.*

1. *Be merciful unto me, O God; for man would swallow me up : he fighting daily oppresseth me.*

2. *Mine enemies would daily swallow me up ; for* they be *many that fight against me, O thou most High.*

His first wrestling in prayer is with the check of his conscience, whether for his daily sins, or in particular for casting himself in so apparent danger as to have ventured without probable security, to seek shelter among the enemies of the people of God, whose blood he himself had shed abundantly; for this rashness or other sins he beggeth mercy, and layeth out before God the pressing temptation from Saul and his countrymen's cruelty, which drove him to this poor shift. Whence learn, 1. There is no fence for challenges of conscience for by-gone sins meeting with trouble drawn on by our folly, but flying to the mercy and rich grace and pity of God, as David doth here: *be merciful to me, O God.* 2. When all men and means fail us, and we see none but wolves and lions ready to devour us, there is hope of help in God's mercy; *be merciful to me, O God, for man would swallow me up.* 3. Continued temptations, and renewed dangers, overset the strength of a frail man, till he go to God to have relief from the temptation, or new strength: *he fighting daily oppresseth me.* 4. Whatsoever inconveniences the godly fall into by flying from persecution, they are all charged justly upon the persecutor, and the chief authors of their trouble: *he fighting daily oppresseth me,* saith David of Saul, who drove him to these straits. 5. Bloody persecutors follow hard after the chase of God's servants, without intermission, as dogs or lions after their prey; with as great desire to have their blood, as hungry beasts have after their food; *mine enemies would daily swallow me up.* 6. One ringleader in the persecution of the godly, will find a multitude follow him; *many are they that fight against me.* 7. There is one above all, who can and will take order with all the enemies of his people, who only can ease their hearts when they complain of their foes : *many are they that fight against me, O thou most High.*

3. *What time I am afraid, I will trust in thee.*

4. *In God I will praise his word ; in God I have put my trust: I will not fear what flesh can do unto me.*

Here faith gets the victory, by setting God's word against all difficulties, within or without him, whereupon the psalmist defieth what man can do unto him. Whence learn, 1. Albeit the godly be not so stout in their trials, as not to feel their own infirmity, or not to be afraid, yet they are kept from fainting in their fear, by faith in God : *what time I am afraid, I will trust in thee.* 2. Albeit faith doth not always put forth itself, yet when fear assaulteth most, then faith in God most evidently manifesteth its force; for then especially by directing the man's eye towards God, it settleth a troubled mind, strengtheneth weak courage, and relieveth the oppressed heart: *what time I am afraid, I will trust in thee.* 3. The experience of the sweet fruit of faith endeareth the Lord to a soul, and strengtheneth a man to the employing of faith, come what can, as David's affectionate resolution here teacheth us : *what time I am afraid, I will trust in thee.* 4. Faith groweth valiant in fight; albeit it begin like a coward, and stagger in the first conflict, yet it groweth stout and triumphant and pulls its adversaries under foot: *in God I have put my trust, I will not fear what flesh can do unto me.* 5. When faith prevaileth fear ceaseth, and all opposition of enemies is despised : *I will not fear what flesh can do unto me.* 6. The best hold that faith can have of God, is to take him by his word : however his dispensation seem to be; this will give satisfaction at length; for, *in God I will praise his word,* is as much as, albeit he withhold comfort and deliverance from me, so that I cannot find what I would, yet let me have his word, and I will give him the glory of all his attributes.

5. *Every day they wrest my words: all their thoughts* are *against me for evil.*

6. *They gather themselves together, they hide themselves, they mark my steps, when they wait for my soul.*

His second conflict is with the malice of his crafty and cruel enemies; of whom he complained that they misconstrued his actions, words, and deeds, as smelling only of treason and rebellion, whether he remained in the country or fled out of it, and whatsoever expressions fell from him, at any time, for his own clearing, all was wrested to another meaning. 2. They devised, each of them, how to bring mischief upon him. 3. What they could not make out severally they sought to ripen by consulting. 4. They covered all their plots with fair pretences, and dissembled their intentions. 5. They observed narrowly every one of his steps, to make out something against him in their observations, for which it might seem justice to kill him. 6. They thought to double their course by more and more iniquity against him, for which he prayeth the Lord to execute justice against them. Whence learn, 1. Let the godly say or do whatsoever they can, how justly, how innocently soever they carry themselves, yet their adversaries will put another face upon their words and deeds than what is right: *every day they wrest my words.* 2. The persecutors of God's people spend their wits in devising some harm or other against them: *all their thoughts are against me for evil.* 3. What the wicked cannot make out against the godly by themselves severally, they labour to make out by mutual counsel and concurrence: *they gather themselves together.* 4. Though the wicked reveal themselves, one to another, in their plots and designs against the godly, yet before others they use to put a veil over their malice, and some fair pretence on what they intend to do: *they hide themselves.* 5. The wicked take occasion to forge their pretences from observation of some passage of the carriage of the godly, that they may make them odious and cut them off: *they mark my steps, they wait for my soul.*

7. *Shall they escape by iniquity? in* thine *anger cast down the people, O God.*

The second victory of faith is in the psalmist's foresight of the punishment of his enemies approaching, howsoever they feared no such thing.　Whence learn, 1. Sinners see no way to hide the mischief of their actions save by doing more mischief, and in special by colouring their injuries with calumnies against the persons they injure, and by pretending law for what they do : *they think to escape by iniquity.*　2. Howsoever the wicked may by false pretences deceive themselves and others like them, and so escape man's punishment, yet shall they not eschew the vengeance of God, but rather be so much the more liable to it, as they multiply iniquity to hide iniquity : *shall they escape by their iniquity ? cast them down.*　3. Neither high place, nor multitude of people following wicked men in an evil course against God's servants, shall save them from the wrath of God: *in thine anger cast down the people, O God.*

8. *Thou tellest my wanderings: put thou my tears into thy bottle:* are they *not in thy book?*

The third conflict, wherein he layeth out his mournful condition before God, with hope to find pity.　Whence learn, 1. When faith hath gotten victory, it will find new assaults; though faith overcome a temptation, the tempter will make head again; though faith overcome one temptation, another will enter the lists and set on, as conflict after conflict here maketh evident.　2. Many a tear may the godly shed before their trial be ended, when once it is begun, and many uncouth paths may they tread who are forced to fly the cruelty of persecutors, before they find rest ; multitude of *wanderings* had David, and large *measure of tears* shed he, before he was delivered.　3. The looking back upon many and long-continued troubles, laid together in a heap, or put in order one after another, musters terribly, and makes a great assault against a man's faith and patience, as here the multitude of David's wanderings and tears showed themselves together before him.　4. God hath so great compassion on his servants in trouble that he reckoneth even the steps of their wanderings and pilgrimage, and numbereth all their tears, and keepeth the count thereof, as it were in a register; and therefore every troubled servant of God, when he looks upon his sufferings, should look upon God also taking as particular notice of his troubles as he himself can do: *thou tellest my wanderings : put thou my tears into thy bottle : are they not in thy book?*

9. *When I cry* unto thee, *then shall mine enemies turn back : this I know ; for God* is *for me.*

10. *In God will I praise* his *word ; in the Lord will I praise* his *word.*

11. *In God have I put my trust : I will not be afraid what man can do unto me.*

In these verses we behold the third and complete victory of faith. Now the psalmist is confident to rout all his enemies by prayer, and to defy all mortals by faith in God's word. Whence learn, 1. Laying forth our cares and fears before God in prayer, is the way to get a satisfactory delivery by faith before the bodily delivery come : *when I cry unto thee, then shall mine enemies turn back.* 2. Faith goeth upon solid grounds, and is not a fallible conjecture but a sure knowledge : *this I know*, saith he. 3. A reconciled man, praying to God in a good cause for victory over his persecutors, may be assured that God will own his quarrel and give him the victory : *this I know, because God is for me.* 4. The special attribute of God wherewith faith meeteth, and whereby it attaineth unto, rest and contentment in God, is his truth and fidelity to his promises : *in God I will praise his word ;* albeit there be no appearance of performance, God's word is sure enough to fix upon. 5. The grounds of faith are the more sweet and satisfactory the more they are examined and compared with their effects ; for David is not content once to say, *in God will I praise his word ;* but with comfort and confidence he reneweth his commendation of God's word, and the benefit he hath by it : *I will not be afraid what man can do unto me.* 6. As it is necessary for our justification to believe in God, so is it necessary for our consolation to observe that we have believed ; for then may we promise to ourselves all the blessedness which belongs to the believer : *in God I have put my trust, I will not be afraid ;* for when we thus resolutely set our seal to God's truth, believing, and asserting our belief : then he setteth his seal to our faith, in comforting and relieving us.

12. *Thy vows* are *upon me, O God : I will render praises unto thee.*

13. *For thou hast delivered my soul from death :* wilt not thou deliver *my feet from falling, that I may walk before God in the light of the living?*

In the latter part of the psalm, having now obtained delivery in his spirit by faith, he obliges himself to thankfulness, wishing to be preserved and enabled of God for that end. Whence learn, 1. As God puts the duty of glorifying him upon the supplicant, when he promiseth delivery to him; so may the supplicant put the obligation of glorifying God upon himself, when he is praying for delivery out of his trouble, as David giveth us to understand he did, while he saith, *thy vows are upon me.* 2. An honest heart is no less desirous to perform the duty of praise to God after delivery, than he was ready to make his vow and promise before his delivery; yea, the consciousness of the twofold obligation is a burden upon his spirit, till he go about the payment of his twice due debt: *thy vows are upon me, O God, I will render praises to thee.* 3. As deep dangers serve to discover our weakness and our need of God's help; so a well-seen danger maketh clear the greatness of the delivery, and the greatness of the delivery deciphers the wisdom, power, and goodness of God to us, and our obligation to him: *I will render praises unto thee, for thou hast delivered my soul from death.* 4. The right use of bypast dangers and deliveries is to prepare for new dangers and difficulties, (for when one danger is past all perils are not past;) to renounce our own wisdom and strength, as insufficient to preserve us from ruin either of soul or body; to give up ourselves to God's guiding and preservation; and to depend upon God, and steadfastly hope to be directed and preserved by him: all this is imported in David's words, *thou hast delivered my soul from death, wilt thou not preserve my feet from falling?* 5. The end of our desires to have deliveries and benefits from God should be, that we may spend our life, and the gifts bestowed upon us, sincerely in the service of God, for the edification of his people: *wilt thou not preserve my feet from falling, that I may walk before God in the light of the living?*

PSALM LVII.

To the chief musician, Al-taschith, Michtam of David, when he fled from Saul in the cave.

This psalm of David, as many others of his psalms, representeth the condition of his spirit, both in the time of his trouble and after his delivery from it: what was his exercise in the cave, and what was his condition after he was delivered out of that danger, whereof we read 1 Sam. xxiv. There are two parts of this psalm: the first containeth his prayer for deliverance, which is pressed by six arguments, all serving to strengthen his faith. The first is, because he trusted in God, ver. 1; the second, because he resolved to insist in prayer till he was heard, ver. 2; the third, because he hoped certainly to find signal delivery from this extraordinary danger, ver. 3; the fourth, because his enemies were beastly cruel, ver. 4; the fifth, because this mercy might contribute much to the glorifying of God, ver. 5; the sixth is from the low condition whereunto his spirit is brought, by their crafty and cruel pursuit of him, ver. 6. In the rest of the psalm is his thanksgiving, consisting of five parts: the first is the acknowledgment of the mercy and delivery granted, ver. 6; the next is his fixed resolution to praise God for it, ver. 7; the third is the upstirring of tongue and hand, and the whole man, to praise God, ver. 8; the fourth is a promise to transmit the knowledge of God's mercy to other nations, ver. 9; the fifth is the acknowledgment of the glory of this mercy, with a wish that it might be more and more seen and acknowledged by giving new experience of it, ver. 10, 11.

From the inscription, learn, That the godly may be involved in a deadly danger, (as David was, when he fled from Saul in the cave,) and yet not perish. Now he was as a man ready to be buried quick; for the cave was as a grave, and the army of Saul at the mouth of the cave, was as the grave-stone: let, then, the army of Saul only know that he is there, and keep him in, and he is gone; yet God blinded them, brought David out, and so delivered him.

1. *Be merciful unto me, O God, be merciful unto me; for my soul trusteth in thee: yea, in the shadow of thy wings will I make my refuge, until* these *calamities be overpast.*

From the psalmist's prayer for deliverance, and first argument taken from his trusting in God, learn, 1. The only refuge of a man in trouble is the mercy of the Lord; be it sin, be it misery, be it peril, or pressing evil; in mercy only is the relief of one and all sad conditions: and in this case must a soul double its petition in the Lord's bosom: *be merciful unto me, O God, be merciful unto me.* 2. As it is not trouble simply which maketh prayer to be fervent, but solid faith pressed with trouble, which doubleth petitions unto God; so where faith in trouble fleeth unto God it cannot but speed: *be merciful, O God, for I trust in thee.* The force of the reason is, The Lord cannot forsake the soul which hath committed itself to him. 3. The Lord offereth relief and protection in Christ to miserable sinners, in as warm a manner as the similitude of a hen gathering her

chickens, or the type of stretching the wings of the cherubim about the mercy-seat could express; and faith clingeth
no less warmly to this offer in time of straits, than this similitude importeth : *yea, in the shadow of thy wings will I
make my refuge.* 4. The use of God's protection and warm
love is best known in time of trouble, and faith is also best
set on work, to make use of God's love and protection in
time of trouble : *in the shadow of thy wings will I make my
refuge, until these calamities be overpast.*

2. *I will cry unto God most High ; unto God that
performeth* all things *for me.*

From the second argument which he useth for strengthening his faith, learn, 1. Faith in God and invocation of his
name, are graces inseparable; and resolution to persevere
in believing is inseparable from resolution to persevere in
praying unto God : and he that findeth in his heart such
resolutions, may also be confident to speed in his requests
made to God; for as the psalmist resolved to believe in the
former verse, so here he addeth, *I will cry unto God,* and
hereby expecteth that God shall be merciful unto him. 2. It
is needful for the supplicant in his straits, to keep in sight
the Lord's supremacy and omnipotency, for encouraging
himself in hope to speed : *I will cry to God most High,*
saith he. 3. The consideration of the Lord's constant going on in the perfecting of the work of grace, which once
he beginneth graciously in us or for us, serveth much to
strengthen our faith in prayer : *I will cry to God, who performeth all things for me.*

3. *He shall send from heaven, and save me* from *the
reproach of him that would swallow me up. Selah. God
shall send forth his mercy and his truth.*

From the third argument and prop of his prayer, taken
from his hope to be helped, learn, 1. Albeit faith see no
help on earth, yet it looketh for help in heaven; and if ordinary means fail, it assureth itself of God's working wonders
for perfecting his promises : *he shall send from heaven and
save me.* 2. The godly man's making God his refuge, is a
matter of mocking to the wicked; which mocking God will
certainly refute, by making the godly find the fruit of their
flying to him : *he will save me from the reproach of him that
would swallow me up.* 3. The mercy and truth of God,

whereupon faith fixeth itself, remove all impediments, and set on work all the means of the salvation of the believer, and that effectually : *God shall send forth his mercy and his truth.*

4. *My soul* is *among lions ;* and *I lie* even among *them that are set on fire,* even *the sons of men, whose teeth* are *spears and arrows, and their tongue a sharp sword.*

From the fourth reason of his prayer, taken from the beastly cruelty of his enemies, learn, 1. The condition of the people of the Lord in this world may be ofttimes like sheep in peril of their lives, compassed about with ravenous beasts: *my soul is among lions.* 2. Yea, they may be so desolate, as having no assistance from without themselves to fly or fight, they shall be forced, like darned birds chased by the hawk, or like bound sheep, to clap close to the ground : *I lie,* saith he, *among them.* 3. The desolate condition of the godly moveth not their persecutors to pity: deadly malice is most ready then to break forth and devour : *I lie even among them that are set on fire.* 4. Graceless men, destitute of the fear of God, are fit enough instruments for the persecution of God's children and his dear servants, if they be no more, but in nature, *even the children of men.* 5. The slanders, mockings, lies, calumnies, reproaches, and aspersions, cast upon the godly by godless men, are no little part of their cruel persecution, of cutting and piercing the Lord's people very deeply : *whose teeth are spears and arrows, and their tongue a sharp sword.*

5. *Be thou exalted, O God, above the heavens ;* let *thy glory* be *above all the earth.*

From the fifth reason of his petition, learn, 1. When the godly are borne down, and the wicked carry all matters before them, the glory of the Lord is obscured and eclipsed in some sort among men; therefore saith he, *be thou exalted, O God.* 2. In what measure God's children are helped by him, and his enemies are borne down, in that measure is he gloriously manifested to be the Ruler of heaven and earth : *be thou exalted above the heavens, and thy glory above all the earth.* 3. However the wicked obscure the glory of the Lord, and how little evidence soever God's children see of his appearing for their relief; yet they ought to glorify him in their heart, and not only believe his sovereign power able to set all things in order, but also to profess their hope, that he shall manifest himself from heaven, to be Lord over all his enemies and adverse powers of the world : *be thou exalted above the heavens, and thy glory above all the earth.*

6. *They have prepared a net for my steps ; my soul is bowed down : they have digged a pit before me, into the midst whereof they are fallen* themselves. *Selah.*

From the last reason of his supplication, learn, 1. That the wicked use great sleight and subtilty to overtake the godly in some snare or other : *they have prepared a net for my steps.* 2. The godly man's strength will soon fail him in time of straits, if the Lord give not supply : yea, the Lord, for the clearer manifestation of his glory, both before the godly, and before the wicked, suffereth his children to come to so low a condition of spirit, that they are ready to succumb if he help not : *my soul is bowed down.* 3. When the enemies are at the highest of their plots, and the godly at the lowest step of their humiliation, then is the Lord's time to turn the chase, and to fall upon his enemies; and that ofttimes by the very same means whereby they were about to make all fast for their own power, and the oppression of the godly : *they have digged a pit before me, into the midst whereof they are fallen themselves.* And this last sentence is the first of his thanksgiving, in acknowledging the Lord's wonderful mercy and justice, in changing upside down the scales of his low condition, and the enemy's lofty persecution on a sudden.

7. *My heart is fixed, O God, my heart is fixed ; I will sing and give praise.*

In the rest of the psalm he prosecuteth his thanksgiving, and this is the second part of it, wherein he professed his fixed purpose to praise the Lord for his delivery. Whence learn, 1. Renewed sense of God's favour, and fresh experience of his mercy towards his children, and of his justice against his and their enemies, much refresheth, quieteth, and settleth the hearts of his people, and confirmeth their faith : *my heart is fixed.* 2. It is a part of our thanksgiving unto God, to acknowledge the fruit of his gracious working for us, felt upon our spirits, whensoever our hearts are cheered up by him after any sad exercise : *my heart is fixed, O God, my heart is fixed.* 3. As it is needful to labour on the heart, that it may be fitted and prepared, fixed and bended, for God's worship; so in special, for the work of praise, whereunto naturally we are most dull and indisposed; then shall the work go on more cheerfully : *my heart is fixed, I will sing and give praise.*

8. *Awake up, my glory ; awake, psaltery and harp : I* myself *will awake early.*

From the third part of his thanksgiving, wherein he stirs up himself, by all means, within and without himself, to set forth his sense of God's mercy, and glory in bestowing it, learn, 1. A well-employed tongue for praising God, and edifying others, is indeed a man's commendation and glory above other creatures; therefore David, directing his speech towards his tongue, after the manner of orators, affectionately speaking, saith, *awake, my glory.* 2. Albeit the abolition of the ceremonial law hath taken away the room which musical instruments once had in the stately, public, instituted worship of God in the congregation; yet neither is the natural private use thereof taken away, nor the signification of that typical ordinance to be forgotten, to wit, that we of ourselves are dull and unapt to holy things, and that the Lord's praises are above our power to reach or express; and that we should stir up all the faculties of our souls unto this holy service, as David here insinuateth to be the moral signification thereof; for, after he hath said, *awake, psaltery and harp*, he subjoineth, *I myself will awake.* 3. As he who in earnest is wakened up to glorify and praise God, will find himself short in abilities to discharge this work of praise; so will he find the choicest time of the day, when the body is best refreshed, most deservedly bestowed upon this exercise : *I myself will awake early.*

9. *I will praise thee, O Lord, among the people ; I will sing unto thee among the nations :*

From the fourth part of this thanksgiving, wherein he promiseth to let all the world know the mercy bestowed upon him, learn, 1. The Spirit of God, who inditeth this scripture, made his penman know that the Gentiles should have the use of his psalms : *I will praise thee among the people.* 2. David was a type of Christ in sufferings, spiritual exercises, and in receiving deliveries; for this promise is fulfilled in Christ, and this undertaking is applied unto Christ, Rom. xv. 9. 3. We seriously mind the praise of God when, according to our place, we labour to make others also know God, as we know him : *I will praise thee among the people.*

10. *For thy mercy* is *great unto the heavens, and thy truth unto the clouds.*

11. *Be thou exalted, O God, above the heavens :* let *thy glory* be *above all the earth.*

From the last part of his thanksgiving, wherein the psalmist confesseth that the excellency of the glory of God transcendeth his reach and capacity, and that he can follow it no further than by wishing the Lord to glorify himself, learn, 1. The matter of the joy of the saints, and of their sweetest songs, is the goodness of God, which appointed and promised such and such mercies unto them, and the faithfulness of God, which bringeth to pass his gracious purpose and promises made unto them : *for thy mercy is great, and thy truth,* saith he. 2. There is no possibility of taking up the greatness of God's mercy and truth; they reach so far as our sight cannot overtake them : *thy mercy is great unto the heavens,* where mortal eyes cannot come to see what is there, *and thy truth unto the clouds,* through which man's eye cannot pierce. 3. Seeing the Lord's glory is greater than heaven or earth can contain, and God himself only can manifest his own glory, it is our part when we have said all we can for glorifying God, to pray to him to glorify himself, and to make it appear to all, that his glory is greater than heaven or earth can comprehend : *be exalted above the heavens, and let thy glory be above all the earth.*

PSALM LVIII.

To the chief musician Al-taschith, Michtam of David.

The psalmist, being oppressed by the calumnies of the courtiers of king Saul, and by the senators of the courts of justice, who should have provided against the oppression of the subjects, chargeth them, in the first part of this psalm, as most guilty of injustice done to him, v. 1—5. In the second part, he prayeth against them, that God would execute judgment upon them, v. 6—8. And, in the third part, he pronounceth the sentence of their deserved destruction, v. 9—11. From this experience of the prophet, we may see what strong parties and hard opposition the godly may meet with in the defence of a good cause, and how necessary it is in such trials to exercise our faith, and to exalt God above all opposite powers, that we may be borne out, and get consolation and victory in the Lord.

1. *Do ye indeed speak righteousness, O congregation? do ye judge uprightly, O ye sons of men?*

2. *Yea, in heart ye work wickedness; ye weigh the violence of your hands in the earth.*

3. *The wicked are estranged from the womb; they go astray as soon as they be born, speaking lies.*

4. *Their poison* is *like the poison of a serpent:* they are *like the deaf adder,* that *stoppeth her ear;*

5. *Which will not hearken to the voice of charmers, charming never so wisely.*

In the last part David chargeth the council and senate, or congregation of the judges; first, with not giving out righteous decrees or sentences, v. 1; secondly, with their obstinate, violent, oppressing decrees, v. 2; thirdly, with their inveterate wickedness and falsehood from the womb, v. 3; fourthly, with their incorrigible wickedness, which they will not for any admonition or advice amend, v. 4, 5. Whence learn, 1. There is a congregation of rulers, whose office it is to administer justice to the people, who presuppose they are the supreme court, in authority and place above the body of the people; yet are they subject to God's challenge, which he sendeth unto them by the hand of his messengers when they do wrong, as here we see: *do ye indeed speak righteousness, O congregation?* 2. When the just cause of the righteous cometh before the Judge, whosoever be pursuer, were he as great a party as king Saul pursuing David, the Judge should defend the righteous, and absolve him, without fearing man's face; and if he do not he shall be called to a reckoning for it before God: *do ye judge uprightly, O ye sons of men?* 3. The Lord looketh to the affections, purposes, and conclusions of a man's heart, and what ill action a man is resolved to do; for that is a done work before God: and the man is so much the more guilty, as his sin is deliberate: *yea, in heart you work wickedness.* 4. A wicked judge hesitates not to give out a decree for as much oppression as he is able to put in execution: *you weigh the violence of your hands in the earth.* And when he is thus oppressing men, he will labour to seem to make his decree no less agreeable to the law, than the equal scales of the merchant's balance answer in a just weight, one to another: *you weigh the violence of your hands.* 5. An unrenewed man is a born stranger to

God, to good men, and all goodness: *the wicked are estranged from the womb.* 6. Men's wicked actions prove the wickedness of nature; or men's original sin augmenteth the ditty and condemnation of unrenewed men for their actual sins: *they are estranged from the womb,* is here made a part of their challenge. 7. Error and falsehood are kindly sins to men; they break out early, continue long, and draw on guiltiness the longer the more : *they go astray as soon as they be born, speaking lies.* 8. There is as great natural enmity in the wicked against the godly, as there is in serpents against mankind, and they are as ready to vent their deadly hatred against them, as serpents are to spue forth their deadly venom: *their poison is like the poison of a serpent.* 9. That which filleth up the measure of the sins of the wicked is this, they are obdured in their sins, incorrigible, and will not receive instruction, admonition, or correction from the word of God : *they are like the deaf adder that stoppeth her ear.* 10. Albeit Holy Scripture useth to compare the best things in some points with the worst things, for clearing the purpose in hand by a similitude; yet doth it not therefore justify the wicked thing by borrowing a similitude from it, as here the admonition and reproof of sinners are compared to the charming of an adder: and yet for that comparison the damnable sin of charming is not the less damnable, nor is the duty of reproof and admonition of sinners the worse or less laudable for the comparison: for it is a challenge : *they are like the deaf adder that stoppeth her ear, which will not hearken unto the charmer, charming never so wisely.*

6. *Break their teeth, O God, in their mouth ; break out the great teeth of the young lions, O Lord.*

7. *Let them melt away as waters* which *run continually :* when *he bendeth* his bow to shoot *his arrows, let them be as cut in pieces.*

8. *As a snail* which *melteth, let* every one of them *pass away ;* like *the untimely birth of a woman,* that *they may not see the sun.*

In the second part of this psalm David maketh imprecation against them, by special warrant of the Spirit of God, who indited this psalm to him, that judgment might be executed against them unto destruction. Whence learn, 1. The Lord shall in due time disable the wicked from doing the harm they intend to do against God's people; for this prayer is a prophecy and promise to the church's comfort : *break their teeth, O God, in their mouth.* 2. Were the wicked ever so potent and resolute to execute their cruelty, God shall break their power in pieces : *break out the great teeth of the young lions, O Lord.* 3. When once God entereth into judgment with the enemies of his people, he shall bring upon them a constant daily consumption and wasting of their power and abilities, till they be abolished : *let them melt away like mater that runs continually.* 4. The chief plots of the wicked shall miscarry in the very point of their putting them in execution : *when he bendeth his bow to shoot his arrows, let them be as cut in pieces.* 5. How strong soever the foundation of the enterprises of the wicked against the godly seem to themselves to be, yet the event shall prove them to be weak, feeble, and effectless devices : *as a snail which melteth, let them pass away, as the untimely birth of a woman, that they may not see the sun.*

9. *Before your pots can feel the thorns, he shall take them away as with a whirlwind, both living, and in* his *wrath.*

10. *The righteous shall rejoice when he seeth the vengeance; he shall wash his feet in the blood of the wicked.*

11. *So that a man shall say, Verily,* there is *a reward for the righteous : verily he is a God that judgeth in the earth.*

In the last part of the psalm, David pronounceth the sentence of deserved destruction upon the wicked and unrighteous potentates, oppressors of the godly, as an answer from God to the former imprecation against them, and that for the consolation of the godly, and clearing of God's justice among men. Whence learn, 1. Howsoever the ungodly hope to procure for themselves good cheer by their works of iniquity, and rejoice a while in their hopes, yet before they find any ripe satisfaction by their ill deeds, suddenly they are destroyed, and as it were swallowed up quickly, and taken away by the fierce wrath of God against them : *before your pots can feel the thorns, he shall take them away as with a whirlwind, both living and in his wrath.* 2. It is lawful for the godly to rejoice in God's justice against the obstinate enemies of his people, provided their joy be indeed in God's

justice; not in the destruction of the creature, but in the manifestation of God's just avenging hand: *the righteous shall
rejoice when he seeth the vengeance.*   3. The punishment of
the wicked should teach the Lord's people to be more holy
in all their ways, for this is one of the ends of God's punishing the wicked in their sight: *the righteous shall wash his
feet in the blood of the wicked.*   4. When the Lord executeth
judgment against the wicked, then men who knew not what
to think of God's providence, when they saw the godly oppressed and the wicked high in power, shall come to a right
judging of matters: *so that a man shall say, Verily there
is a reward for the righteous.*   5. No man serveth God for
nought; in following the course of friendship with God, and
walking in obedience unto him, fruit certainly will be found:
verily there is a reward for the righteous.   6. Albeit the
Lord setteth not down his court for executing justice so soon
as men would, yet he fails not to show himself ruler of the
affairs of men and a righteous judge, as to relieve the oppressed, so also to take order with oppressors: *verily he is a
God that judgeth in the earth.*

PSALM. LIX.

*To the chief musician, Al-taschith, Michtam of David, when Saul sent,
and they watched the house to kill him.*

David, in present danger of his life by Saul, (who having David inclosed
within the city and within his own house, thought surely to have killed
him, as we read, 1 Sam. xix. 11,) prayeth to God for deliverance, v. 1, 2;
and as a reason for his prayer, maketh a complaint against his enemies,
v. 3, 4.   In the next place, he prayeth the second time for delivery to
himself and judgment against his enemies, v. 5, and complaineth of
them the second time, v. 6, 7.   In the third place, he declareth his confidence of being delivered, v. 8—10.   In the fourth place, he maketh
imprecation against his enemies for their wickedness, v. 11—15.   And,
in the last place, he promiseth thanks to God for his delivery, whereof
he was assured before it came, v. 16, 17.

From the inscription, learn, 1. No common bands of nature or civil relations can secure the godly from the persecution of the wicked : for Saul, David's father-in-law, sendeth to kill David.   2. God's children cannot be in so great
straits, nor the vigilance of the wicked to overtake the godly
be so great in a strait, but God can deliver a supplicant;
they watched the house to kill him, yet he escaped, and wrote
this psalm : by what means he escaped he doth not tell here,

for he attributeth the delivery to God, from whom he sought it by prayer.

1. *Deliver me from mine enemies, O my God ; defend me from them that rise up against me.*

2. *Deliver me from the workers of iniquity, and save me from bloody men.*

From his prayer, learn, 1. Whatsoever means God shall offer for escaping out of a trouble, prayer is our best weapon against our enemies, the best of all means, and first of all to be used for a delivery : *deliver me from mine enemies.* 2. Time of trouble and difficulty compelleth believers to make use of the covenant of grace, and of God's friendship and power for their deliverance : *O my God, defend me from them that rise up against me.* 3. When wicked, powerful, and bloodthirsty men turn persecutors of the godly, no power but divine can be looked to for relief : *deliver me from the workers of iniquity, and save me from bloody men.*

3. *For, lo, they lie in wait for my soul : the mighty are gathered against me ; not for my transgression, nor for my sin, O Lord.*

4. *They run and prepare themselves without my fault : awake to help me, and behold.*

From his complaint against his enemies, and reason of his prayer, learn, 1. Desperate-like dangers, arising from the power and craftiness of enemies, must not discourage the godly, but sharpen their prayer to God, with whom are power and wisdom to deliver them : *for lo, they lie in wait for my soul.* 2. It is no new thing, to see them who are in greatest power, the chief in the persecution of God's children : *the mighty are gathered together against me.* 3. A good conscience, especially in the particular for which a man is pursued, giveth greatest comfort in the time of trouble : *not for my transgression nor my sin, O Lord.* 4. Albeit the persecutors of the godly cannot find a fault in them, for which they may pursue them; yet will they devise some challenge and make a great business to accomplish their design : *they run and prepare themselves not for my fault.* 5. The Lord will let the plot go on, and the danger of the godly grow, as if he minded not to take notice of it, that he may first put his children to prayer, and then appear in the fit time : *awake to help me, and behold.*

5. *Thou therefore, O Lord God of hosts, the God of Israel, awake to visit all the heathen : be not merciful to any wicked transgressors.   Selah.*

6. *They return at evening : they make a noise like a dog, and go round about the city.*

7. *Behold, they belch out with their mouth : swords are in their lips ; for who* (say they) *doth hear?*

For his repeated prayer and complaint presented the second time, learn, 1. In time of straits we should set our eyes most upon those providences of God, which most serve to strengthen our faith, especially such as hold forth his power, and good-will to employ his power for us: *thou therefore, O Lord God of hosts, the God of Israel, awake.*　2. Counterfeit professors and professed pagans are in effect all one before God, and the counterfeit professor will be as ready an instrument to persecute the godly as a professed enemy; for so are Saul and his followers named here : *awake to visit all the heathen.*　3. Although the Lord bear with the wicked a while, he will at last take order with hypocrites and obstinately malicious transgressors : *awake to visit all the heathen, be not merciful to any wicked transgressor.*　4. From the time that persecutors have once resolved cruelty, they cease not to pursue their purpose, but like bloody dogs, they run to and fro till they catch their prey; they are busy all the day, and set watches in the night to hurt the man they would have : *they return at evening, they make a noise like a dog, and go round about the city.*　5. Resolved obstinacy in sin taketh away all remorse of conscience, all fear of God and shame before men, and maketh men openly avow their wickedness; yea and their cruel hearts will vent their bloody purpose, when they think they are sure to accomplish their design : *behold, they belch out with their mouth, swords are in their lips ; for who, say they, will hear?*

8. *But thou, O Lord, shalt laugh at them ; thou shalt have all the heathen in derision.*

9. *Because of his strength will I wait upon thee : for God is my defence.*

10. *The God of my mercy shall prevent me : God shall let me see* my desire *upon mine enemies.*

In the third place, the psalmist declareth his confidence

to be delivered, and maketh use of his faith for keeping up his heart under his trouble. Whence learn, 1. The first fruit of an humble prayer, is a spiritual delivery of a man's oppressed spirit, granted unto him by faith and assurance of an outgate; as here and many times elsewhere appeareth. 2. When faith seeth God to be a friend, it scorneth all opposition of whatsoever enemies, few or many, all is one to the clear-sighted believer : *but thou, O Lord, shalt laugh at them, thou shalt have all the heathen in derision.* 3. How weak soever the believer may find himself, and how powerful soever he perceive his enemies to be, it is all one to him, he hath no more to do, but to put faith on work and wait till God work; because of his strength, that is, the enemies' strength; *I will wait upon thee,* saith he to the Lord, *for God is my defence.* 4. When faith gets up the head, it seeth its own deliverance and the overthrow of the enemy, both at once in the proper cause thereof, to wit, the fountain of over-running mercy, engaged unto it by covenant : *the God of my mercy.* There is the fountain of *everlasting mercy,* whereof God is called God, because he is the believer's God for ever, and therefore the Lord of all mercy, consolation, and salvation to the believer : *he,* saith he, *shall prevent me ;* that is, he shall give manifest deliverance before I succumb : it shall come sooner than I could set it a time. Then, for his enemies, he saith, *God shall let me see my desire upon mine enemies ;* to wit, what I could lawfully desire, or what should satisfy me.

11. *Slay them not, lest my people forget: scatter them by thy power ; and bring them down, O Lord our shield.*

12. For *the sin of their mouth,* and *the words of their lips, let them even be taken in their pride ; and for cursing and lying* which *they speak.*

13. *Consume* them *in wrath ; consume* them, *that they* may *not* be *; and let them know that God ruleth in Jacob unto the ends of the earth. Selah.*

14. *And at evening let them return ;* and *let them make a noise like a dog, and go round about the city.*

15. *Let them wander up and down for meat, and grudge if they be not satisfied.*

In the fourth place, David prayeth to God to glorify himself in the manner and measure of his just judgment on his obstinate enemies; which in effect is a prophecy of the punishment of the persecutors of the righteous, and of the wrath to come upon the enemies of Christ, of whom David in his trouble and unjust sufferings was a type. Whence learn, 1. Sometimes the Lord will delay cutting off wicked enemies of his people, for a curse to them and a benefit to his people: *slay them not, lest my people forget.* 2. The Lord's people are subject to forget the Lord's doing for them, and punishing their enemies, except he renew the evidence of the care he hath of them, by often renewed, or long-continued judgment on their enemies, whose misery is more to them, by lingering judgments in the sight of men, than if they were cut off suddenly: *slay them not, lest my people forget.* 3. In praying against our wicked enemies that persecute us, we must take heed that we be found pleading, not our own particular revenge, but the common cause of the church and the Lord's quarrel: *slay them not, lest my people forget; scatter and bring them down, O Lord, our shield.* It is the good of the Lord's people, and the glorifying of God which is in his eye. 4. Albeit the Lord cuts not off at first the troublers of his church, but suffers them to live for the exercise of his people; yet it is mercy worthy to be prayed for, if God disable them and break their power, that they prevail not over the righteous: *scatter them by thy power, and bring them down, O Lord our shield.* 5. Albeit the persecutors accomplish not their purpose against the righteous; yet their pride, their brags, their lies, their slanders, their curses against the godly, are a sufficient ditty for damnation and wrath to come upon them: *for the sin of their mouth, and the words of their lips, let them even be taken in their pride, and for cursing and lying which they speak.* 6. After the keeping alive of the wicked for a time, to the increasing of their misery, at length utter destruction cometh upon them: *consume them in wrath, consume them, that they may not be.* 7. By the judgments of God upon the adversaries of his people, the knowledge of his sovereignty over, and kingly care for, his church is made more known to the world, the increase of which glory of the Lord should be the scope of the prayers of the saints against their foes: *and let them know that God ruleth in Jacob unto the ends of the earth.* 8. It is suitable to God's justice and no strange thing to see such as have been messengers, servants, officers of persecuting powers, or searchers out of the godly, as beagles or blood-hounds, made beggars, vagabonds, and miserable spectacles of God's wrath before they die, roving to and fro like hungry and masterless dogs : *at evening let them return, and let them make a noise like a dog, and go round about the city ; let them wander up and down for meat, and grudge if they be not satisfied.*

16. *But I will sing of thy power ; yea, I will sing aloud of thy mercy in the morning : for thou hast been my defence and refuge in the day of my trouble.*

17. *Unto thee, O my strength, will I sing : for God is my defence, and the God of my mercy.*

In the last place, David promiseth thanksgiving for the mercy which he felt in the day of his trouble, and fixeth his faith on God, as his merciful protector and only strength, whereon he was to lean in every condition wherein he could fall. Whence learn, 1. Whatsoever mischief fall upon the wicked, the Lord's children, whom they malign, shall have reason to rejoice and praise God for supporting them in their trials, and delivering them out of troubles : *but I will sing of thy power.* 2. When the godly compare the Lord's putting difference between them and the rest of the wicked world, pitying them and pardoning their sins, when he justly punisheth the sins of others, they cannot but rejoice, and proclaim God's mercy with earnest affection : *yea I will sing aloud of thy mercy in the morning.* 3. The shining light of one late experience of God's care of a man, serveth to bring to remembrance, and to illuminate the whole course of God's by past care and kindness to him, and to raise a song of joy and praise to God for altogether : *for thou hast been my refuge and defence in the day of trouble.* 4. What God hath been unto us, being looked on rightly, may serve to certify what God is unto us, what he shall be to us, and what we may expect of him: for from *thou hast been my defence and my refuge,* he inferreth hope of joyful experience of the same mercy for time to come : *unto thee, O my strength, will I sing.* 5. When a man is sure of God's being engaged to him by good-will and covenant, and proof given for letting out to him protection and mercy, as his soul needeth, he cannot but have a heart full of joy, and a mouth full of joyful praises unto God: *unto thee, O my strength, will I sing, for God is my defence, and the God of my mercy.*

PSALM LX.

To the chief musician upon Shushan-eduth, Michtam of David, to teach; when he strove with Aram-naharaim, and with Aram-zobah, when Joab returned, and smote of Edom in the valley of Salt twelve thousand.

This psalm is a prayer for the victory of Israel over their enemies, indited unto the prophet when Israel was fighting with the Syrians and Edomites. It may be divided into three parts. In the first part the psalmist prayeth for help more largely, ver. 1—5; in the second, David is made confident of the victory, ver. 6—10; in the third, he repeateth his prayer more briefly, and his confidence of his having the victory, ver. 11, 12.

From the inscription learn, 1. The children of God must not think it strange to be put to wrestling, striving, and fighting for a promised kingdom, before they be settled in possession, as David was; yea, the church of Christ must expect such like exercises; for this psalm is given to the public ministers of the church for use in all ages. 2. The church must make use of her prayers as well when she is furnished with a regular army as when she wanteth bodily arms, as David teacheth the church here. 3. There is hope of victory, when God, by prayer, is more relied upon than the army in the field; for, with the psalmist the mention of the victory of the Lord's host is set down and the slaughter of the enemy recorded: *that Joab smote of Edom twelve thousand.*

1. *O God, thou hast cast us off, thou hast scattered us, thou hast been displeased; O turn thyself to us again.*

Of the larger prayer there are three branches. The first is for reconciliation with God, v. 1; the second for reparation of the decayed state of the kingdom, v. 2, 3; the third, for delivery and victory in the conflict with the enemy, v. 4, 5.

In the first branch of his prayer the psalmist acknowledgeth bygone judgments as the fruit of God's displeasure, and of the people's provocation of God to wrath, and so he prayeth that God would turn again and be reconciled to his people. Whence learn, 1. Terrible evils may befall the Lord's people, or the visible church, when they, by their sin, provoke him to wrath, as was seen in the time of the Judges and in Saul's time: *O God, thou hast cast us off, hou hast scattered us.* 2. When God plagueth a whole kingdom, or the body of the visible church, it is not a matter of simple exercise or trial, (as when he bringeth trouble on some of his dear servants in the time of their upright carriage,) but it is for their sins and provocation of the eyes of his glory : *thou hast been displeased.* 3. Such as would have plagues removed must acknowledge their sin, and seek to be reconciled with God; and in this way may they expect to find favour : *O turn thyself to us again.* 4. Whatsoever sins the visible church and incorporation of professors have committed against God, or whatsoever injuries they have done against the godly, in assisting persecuting powers against them; yet the godly must not only not separate from them, but must also be ready to receive them into favour, be reconciled to them, forgive their former injuries, join in church-and camp-fellowship with them, being reconciled, by compassion share with them in calamities, intercede with God for them as for themselves, as being all of one incorporation; as David, the type of Christ's moderate and merciful governing, and a pattern to all the godly, forgave those that persecuted him, fought against him under king Saul, and stood longest out against him when Saul was dead : for David here saith with and for the people, *O God, thou hast scattered us; O turn thyself again to us.*

2. *Thou hast made the earth to tremble; thou hast broken it: heal the breaches thereof; for it shaketh.*

3. *Thou hast shewed thy people hard things: thou hast made us to drink the wine of astonishment.*

When Saul reigned, all things went wrong; the wicked abounded, vile men were exalted, and God plagued the land; therefore, in the second branch of his prayer, he prayeth for restoration of the dejected state of the kingdom : the calamities whereof he layeth forth, both before and after the petition. Whence learn, 1. When people will not stand in awe of God and fear him, he will strike them with the fear of his wrath and sense of sore judgments : *thou hast made the earth to tremble.* 2. War, and in special civil and intestine war, is most able to ruin a kingdom, and, like an earthquake, to make ruptures and breaches in it to the renting of it in pieces : *thou hast made the earth to tremble, thou hast broken it.* 3. It is a Christian and royal virtue to seek the union of the subjects among themselves, and to remove divisions of the kingdom, without the removing whereof the state can never be settled; but it is a divine power to work this union effectually, therefore David prayeth to God for it: *heal the breaches thereof, for it shaketh.* 4. When people will not see nor take knowledge of their sins against God, and their bounden duties to him, he will let them see sa spectacles of bloody wars, foreign and intestine: *thou hast shewed thy people hard things.* 5. When people have be-sotted themselves in their sin, and have not believed what God hath threatened against them, no wonder they know not what hand to turn them to, and be stricken with asto-nishment in the execution of his judgments, which, when they fall upon a people, either suddenly or more heavily than they could have expected, put men's minds in confusion, as if they were drunk; for sudden, sore, and lasting judg-ments confound the thoughts of secure sinners, so as they can make little use of the word of God, or of their wit, or any other means of relief, more than a drunken man over-charged with wine: *thou hast made us to drink the wine of astonishment.*

4. *Thou hast given a banner to them that fear thee, that it may be displayed because of the truth. Selah.*

5. *That thy beloved may be delivered, save* with *thy right hand, and hear me.*

In the third branch of his prayer, David seeketh delivery and victory over the enemy, and that because God had begun to give some hope of changing the face of affairs, by raising a banner in David's hand for the Lord's cause and people. Whence learn, 1. When the godly are oppressed, the truth of religion and of God's promises is prostrated, like a fallen standard; and when God raiseth up instruments for their protection and comfort, as here he did in bringing David to the kingdom, it is like the lifting up of an ensign in the hand of a valiant standard-bearer: *thou hast given a banner to them that fear thee.* 2. It is on the godly's account that mercy is shown to a whole land: *thou hast given a banner to them that fear thee.* 3. When the godly get up their head, all their endeavour, according to the utmost of their power, should be to advance true religion and the practice of it: *thou hast given a banner, that it may be displayed, because*

13

of the truth. 4. As nothing is respected by God in a land so much as his elect that fear him; so, nothing can encourage us to seek and hope for mercy to a land, so much as the Lord's love to them that fear him it: *that thy beloved may be delivered, save.* 5. When God hath begun to appear for his church, then in special should we follow a begun blessing, with prayer that God would work out the benefit: *thou hast given a banner to them that fear thee; that thy beloved may be delivered, save.* 6. Whatsover difficulties appear in the way of the church's delivery, we must oppose the omnipotency of God to them all, and sustain our faith in prayer by looking to his love towards his church and power to do for her: *that thy beloved may be delivered, save with thy right hand, and hear me.*

6. *God hath spoken in his holiness; I will rejoice: I will divide Shechem, and mete out the valley of Succoth.*

7. *Gilead* is *mine, and Manasseh* is *mine; Ephraim also* is *the strength of mine head; Judah* is *my lawgiver;*

In the second part of the psalm is set down David's confidence to have the victory over his enemies, and to have his kingdom both settled at home, v. 6, 7, and enlarged abroad, v. 8—10.

By David's prayer, the word of promise, that he should be established king, is made evident to him, whereupon he is comforted and made confident of the accomplishment thereof in all points. Whence learn, 1. As faith helpeth up prayer, so by prayer faith is settled and strengthened, as here is evidenced. 2. The word of promise is a more sure evidence than begun possession, for David was not so sure of his kingdom now, because he had begun to reign, as *because God had spoken.* 3. The word of God is rested on and rejoiced in, when it is received as his word, when his holiness is taken as a pledge of performance: *God hath spoken in his holiness; I will rejoice.* 4. Whatsoever resteth unperfected, of what is promised to us by God, shall be fully put in our possession, as David here assureth himself to exercise the supreme government in those parts of his kingdom, on the one or other side of Jordan, which yet were not brought into subjection or settled under him: *I will divide Shechem, and mete out the valley of Succoth, &c.* 5. What-

soever strength or increase of number the kingdom of Israel
was to have from the plurality of tribes and their strength,
yet the union of the sons of Abraham and stability of the
kingdom of Israel, consisted in their joint subjection to the
lawgiver and government of Judah, out of which tribe Christ
came, who is the true lawgiver and king of Israel, towards
whom the church of old was to direct its eye through its
typical governors: *Judah is my lawgiver.*

8. *Moab is my wash-pot; over Edom will I cast out
my shoe : Philistia, triumph thou because of me.*

9. *Who will bring me into the strong city? who will
lead me into Edom?*

10. Wilt *not thou, O God,* which *hadst cast us off?
and* thou, *O God,* which *didst not go out with our
armies?*

Here David is assured by the Lord's word, not only of
the establishment of his kingdom at home, but also of the
enlarging of it abroad, by the subduing of such as had been
enemies to Israel before. Whence learn, 1. When the Lord
uniteth his people under the government of Judah, and
giveth them grace to take the true ruler of the tribe of
Judah for their lawgiver, then shall the enemies of Israel
be brought low, and either used contemptibly, as they sometimes used the Lord's people, or else shall profess themselves
happy in their subjection to the King of Israel; for, after
David, as the type of Christ, had indited a song to the church,
wherein they should acknowledge Judah their lawgiver, then
he, as the type of Christ, giveth them to sing this also:
Moab is my wash-pot; that is, the Moabites shall serve me
in the basest service I shall put them to: *over Edom will I cast
out my shoe;* that is, I shall subdue them and trample them
under my feet as I pass through them: *Philistia, triumph
thou because of me;* that is, instead of thy triumphing over
my people, thou shalt be made to profess thy joy to be under
my government. 2. The believer, when he promiseth to
himself great things, must neither be senseless of the difficulties of opposition which he is to meet with, nor of his
own inability to overcome difficulties; but, being sensible of
both, must look to God for assistance and strength to overcome; for, when David considered the strength of the fenced
royal cities of the enemy, he saith, *who will bring me into*

*the strong city? who will lead me into Edom? wilt not thou,
O God?* 3. It is God's absence from, or gracious presence
with, a people, which maketh the success of the wars of his
people against their enemies worse or better, and their bad
success in former time, or bypast judgment on them; for
sin must be so far from marring the confidence of a people
turning home to God, and seeking to find help from him,
that, on the contrary, the judgments inflicted upon them
in their impenitency, serving for confirmation of the threatenings of God's word, and evidence of his justice, must be
made arguments of confirmation of faith in God's promises
of merciful assistance, when they are turned towards God;
for so reasoneth David: *who will bring me into Edom? wilt
not thou, O God, which hadst cast us off? and thou, O God,
which didst not go out with our armies?*

11. *Give us help from trouble: for vain is the help
of man.*

12. *Through God we shall do valiantly: for he* it is
that *shall tread down our enemies.*

In the last place, he briefly resumeth his prayer and
confidence to be heard. Whence learn. 1. The certainty
of hope should not make us the more slack, but rather the
more earnest and fervent in prayer ; for, after this professed assurance, David insisteth in prayer : *give us help from
trouble.* 2. Seeing God only is the strength and furniture
of his people, and he cannot endure that they should rely
upon any means which they may and must use, but upon
himself only; therefore the less confidence we put in the
creature, the more may we be confident of help from God :
give us help from trouble, for vain is the help of man. 3.
A self-denying and humbled believer may go with courage
and hope of success to the use of the means, and may encounter with whatsoever opposition of enemies : *through God
we shall do valiantly.* 4. Praise of the valour and gallan-
try of victorious soldiers must not separate betwixt God and
the victor: but whatsoever God doth in us or by us, must
be no less wholly ascribed unto God, than if he had done
all the work without us; for, both the valour of the instrument, and the victory, are the works of the Lord. The
motions of the body and soul of the victor are the work
and upstirring of God within him; and the operation and

effects wrought by the instrument, are the works of God, without the victor: *for he it is that shall tread down our enemies.*

PSALM LXI.

To the chief musician upon Neginah. A psalm of David.

David now in his exile maketh his address to God in a sad condition, v. 1—3; is comforted in the Lord, and persuaded of his present and future happiness, v. 4, 5; and of the perpetuity of the kingdom of Christ, represented by him, to the comfort of all Christ's subjects in all ages, v. 6—8.

1. *Hear my cry, O God; attend unto my prayer.*

2. *From the end of the earth will I cry unto thee, when my heart is overwhelmed: lead me to the Rock* that *is higher than I.*

3. *For thou hast been a shelter for me,* and *a strong tower from the enemy.*

In his sad supplication David prayeth for a comfortable receiving of his request, and a comfortable rest of his soul on God himself through Christ, hoping to be heard because he was resolved to look toward God and to continue praying, whatsoever condition of spirit he should be in, and in whatsoever part he should be; and also because he had experience of God's help in his straits in former times. Whence learn, 1. The best expedient for a sad soul, is to run to God by prayer for comfort, and to insist earnestly, albeit God should seem not to attend: *hear my cry, O God, attend unto my prayer.* 2. When the godly are driven from their country and fellowship with the saints, and from exercise of public ordinances, no wonder they fall into perplexity of spirit; for David, forced to flee to *the ends of the land,* finds his heart *overwhelmed within him.* 3. It is exile indeed to be secluded from the liberty of public ordinances, and it is our home to be where God is publicly worshipped; for David counteth himself cast out *unto the ends of the earth,* when he is debarred from the temple of the Lord. 4. Albeit a man were ever so far banished from the free society of the church, and communion with God's people in ordinances, yet he is still within cry unto God : *from the ends of the earth will I cry unto thee.* 5. There is a rock of refuge for safety and comfort to the exiled and perplexed

saint, which is able to supply all wants, and to sweeten all
sorrows; and this is the rock of God's felt friendship in
Christ from heaven, represented by the visible rock of *Zion,*
where the tabernacle and mercy-seat were situate, the appointed trysting place, where God received the prayers of
his people, and answered them from heaven; when David
could not come to the typical mount or rock, he prayeth to
have access to the thing signified : *lead me to the rock that
is higher than I.* 6. Sensible and comfortable communion
with God, is a mystery spiritual, which man's wisdom or
power cannot discover, nor bring unto him: but God himself must reveal, and must renew the revealing of himself
to a soul in trouble, and must make a man's soul apply
itself to him powerfully, else a man cannot feel this comfortable fellowship with God, more than a blind man can
find out what is removed from him, or a weak child can go
not being led, or a man can reach up to a steep high place,
not being lifted up unto it. Therefore must the Lord himself draw us near to himself, and lift us up to himself : *lead
me to the rock that is higher than I.* 7. This spiritual felt
communion with God is able to put a man far from the reach
of any enemy, and maketh a soul quietly to rest itself from fear
of trouble, how great soever the external danger can be, as
David many times felt by experience : *for thou hast been a
shelter unto me, and a strong tower from the enemy.* 8. A
believer's resolution for depending on God and praying to him
in hardest conditions, and his present use-making of former
experiences, as they serve much for strengthening his faith
in prayer; so they are the nearest means that can be for
coming by a renewed sensible comfort, as here we see: for
David resolveth, *from the ends of the earth I will cry;*
and prayeth, *lead me to the rock;* and saith, *thou hast been
a strong tower to me ;* and so comfort followeth quickly after this preparation, as the next verse showeth.

4. *I will abide in thy tabernacle for ever ; I will trust
in the covert of thy wings. Selah.*

5. *For thou, O God, hast heard my vows : thou hast
given* me *the heritage of those that fear thy name.*

Here he is comforted in his exile, and made to be at home
in his spirit, by reason of the present sense of God's favour
to him, and of his confirmed hope in the performance of the

promises made unto him. Whence learn, 1. The Lord can give such satisfaction to a sad heart in the time of its trouble, that the trouble may turn to be no trouble, even while it lieth on still, as here is to be seen in David's comfort, who speaketh as if he were restored, while he is yet in exile. 2. Spiritual consolations in temporal troubles, give satisfaction to a soul both for the present and for time to come, for everlasting happiness: *I will abide in thy tabernacle for ever:* his hope is, that not only shall he be restored to the fellowship of the saints, at the tabernacle in Jerusalem, but also that he shall be in God's company in heaven, represented by the tabernacle, and that for ever. 3. True consolation standeth not in earthly things, but in things heavenly, and things having nearest relation thereto; for David's comfort was not so much that he should be brought to the kingdom, as that he should be brought to the tabernacle, and to heaven by that means: *I will abide in thy tabernacle.* 4. Sincerity setteth no term-day to God's service, or to the seeking of communion with him: *I will abide in thy tabernacle for ever.* 5. The ground of all spiritual consolations is in the mercy and grace of God offered to us in Christ, represented by the wings of the cherubim stretched out over the mercy-seat; there faith findeth a rest and solid ground able to furnish comfort abundantly: *I will trust in the covert of thy wings.* 6. Access to God in prayer, and approbation of the conscience, and the sincere pouring forth of the heart melting with present felt sense of God's love, strengthen greatly the assurance of everlasting communion with God: *for thou, O God, hast heard my voice.* 7. As spiritual comfort in time of trouble granted to a believer, is indeed the earnest of everlasting life, so should they, to whomsoever the earnest is given, make reckoning that by this earnest the inheritance is confirmed to them by way of possession begun: *thou hast given me the heritage of those that fear thy name.* 8. The inheritance of the chief of God's servants, and of the meanest and weakest of them, is one; the right of every believer is alike good, albeit the hold laid upon the right by all is not alike strong: and what the strongest of the godly believe for their own consolation and salvation, the weakest may believe the same to belong to every believer that feareth God, as David doth here: *thou hast given me the heritage of those that fear thy name.*

6. *Thou wilt prolong the king's life;* and *his years as many generations.*

7. *He shall abide before God for ever : O prepare mercy and truth,* which *may preserve him.*

8. *So will I sing praise unto thy name for ever, that I may daily perform my vows.*

In the third place, the psalmist prophesieth, not simply of the stability of the kingdom in his own person and posterity, but under the type; namely, he speaketh of the perpetuity of the kingdom of Christ the true king of Israel; for which end he prayeth that mercy and truth may be forthcoming to subjects of Christ, that his kingdom may be prolonged; and so David in his time, and all the saints in their time, may joyfully praise God continually.   Whence learn, 1. It is not unusual with God, together with present consolation and the light of future salvation in Christ, to reveal also and give assurance of great things concerning Christ's kingdom, as here and elsewhere in the Scripture is to be seen : *thou wilt prolong the king's life, and his years as many generations.* 2. The glory of Christ, and the perpetuity of his kingdom are every subject's good and comfort; for this is comfort to David, that Christ shall live for ever : *that he shall abide before God for ever.*   3. The kingdom of Christ, and government of his subjects in his church, shall be allowed of God, and be protected of God, and blessed of God for ever, however it be opposed by men in the world : *he shall abide before God for ever.*   4. The perpetuity of Christ's kingdom, and preservation of his subjects in this life, till they be possessed of heaven, is by the merciful remedying of the misery and removing of the sin which they are subject unto, and by performing what he hath promised and prepared through Christ to bestow upon them : *O prepare mercy and truth, which may preserve him.*   5. The best retreat that can be made, after wrestling and victory over troubles, are prayer and praises; as here David after his exercises prayeth, *O prepare mercy and truth ;* and then saith, *unto thee will I sing.* 6. As the main matter of our vows is the moral duty of rejoicing in God and hearty praising him; so renewed experience of God's mercy and truth towards his people in Christ, is the main matter of our joy in him, and praise unto him : *O prepare mercy and truth, &c. so will I sing praise unto thy name, that I may daily perform my vows.*

PSALM LXII.

To the chief musician, to Jeduthun.   A psalm of David.

This psalm is the issue of a sore conflict and inward combat, which David felt from the strong opposition of his irreconcileable adversaries, and from the lasting troubles which he sustained by their persecution, and by his friends forsaking him, whereby he was puzzled what to think or what to do: at length faith in God giveth him victory, and maketh him first to break forth in avowing his faith and hope in God, v. 1, 2; next, to insult over his enemies as dead men, because of their sinful course, v. 3, 4; thirdly, to strengthen himself in his faith and hope, v. 5—7; fourthly, to exhort all men to trust in God, and to depend on him, for reasons set down, v. 8, 9; and not to trust in oppression and robbery, for reasons set down, v. 10—12.

1. *Truly my soul waiteth upon God: from him com-*eth *my salvation.*

2. *He only is my rock and my salvation; he is my defence ; I shall not be greatly moved.*

From this abrupt beginning of the psalm, declaring that David hath had a sore disputation and wrestling with temptations within him, and out of which this is the first coming forth, learn, 1. Albeit strong faith be put to a conflict when trouble and temptations abound, yet when it looketh on God and his promises, it gets the victory, and putteth the soul to a submissive attendance on God, and a quiet hope of complete deliverance : *truly my soul waiteth upon God; from him cometh my salvation.*   2. Then is faith well tried and approved, when, being stript of all supporters except God, it contenteth itself with him alone, as all-sufficient : *he only is my rock and my salvation.*   3. Faith findeth as many answers in God's sufficiency, as temptations can make objections against it : *he is my rock and my salvation: he is my defence.*   4. As a man resolveth to believe and follow the course of sound faith, so he may assure himself of establishment and victory over all temptations, notwithstanding his own weakness: *I shall not be greatly moved,* David concludeth, from his resolution to rest on God.

3. *How long will ye imagine mischief against a man ? ye shall be slain, all of you : as a bowing wall* shall ye be, and as *a tottering fence.*

4. *They only consult to cast* him *down from his excellency ; they delight in lies : they bless with their mouth, but they curse inwardly.   Selah.*

In the second place, David insulteth over his enemies, and

layeth before them the danger of their wicked ways. Whence learn, 1. So soon as a man hath fastened himself on God, he may reckon with all adverse powers, and insult over them; for the seeing of God's help discovers to the believer the vanity of all opposition : *how long will ye imagine mischief against a man ?* 2. As the godly, when they fall under persecution, may lie long under it, and must resolve patience all the while on the one hand; so, on the other hand, persecutors are unreasonably carried on in the course of persecution, like mad men, who cannot give over the pursuit, albeit they see God against themselves and with the godly whom they pursue : *how long will ye imagine mischief against a man ?* 3. Persecutors shall not have their will against the godly, but by their persecution shall draw upon themselves complete, sudden, and irrecoverable destruction : *ye shall be slain, all of you, as a bowing wall, and a tottering fence ;* that is, you shall perish suddenly, as when a bowing wall and tottering fence rush to the ground in a moment. 4. As standing fast in the faith and service of God in a good cause, is the excellency of the believer; so is it the eye-sore of his adversaries, which they of all things can least endure in the godly; and therefore chiefly bend all their wit and forces, to break them off their holy carriage and course : *they only consult to cast him down from his excellency.* 5. Not truth and light, but darkness, error, falsehood, and deceit, are the pleasure of the wicked : *they delight in lies.* 6. When the wicked intend their worst against the godly, then will they speak fairest words to them, to see whether by falsehood or force they can prevail most, to draw them off their good course : *they bless with their mouth, but they curse inwardly.*

5. *My soul, wait thou only upon God ; for my expectation* is *from him.*

6. *He only* is *my rock and my salvation :* he is *my defence ; I shall not be moved.*

7. *In God* is *my salvation and my glory : the rock of my strength,* and *my refuge,* is *in God.*

In the third place, David strengtheneth his faith and his hope, that he may be able to endure trouble till the sin of the wicked be ripe, and their judgment be executed. Whence learn, 1. Our resolution patiently to keep silence in waiting on God, and our putting the resolution to practice, differ :

our practising is so short of our resolution, that we had need to be stirred up, and to stir up ourselves to our duty. And as Satan is still moving new perturbations; so have we need of, and must study to have, new confirmations : *my soul, wait thou only upon God.*   2. They that expect their help from God, must not expect help from any other airth, no not when they shall use all means lawful for their delivery; but the success must be, without haste-making, patiently waited for from God alone : *wait thou only on God, for my expectation is from him.*   3. The grounds of confidence are able to abide new assaults, and must be brought forth and averred, so oft as they are opposed : for here unto the new stirrings of the same temptations, he opposeth this over again : *he only is my rock : he is my defence and my salvation.*   And whereas he said before, I shall not be greatly moved; now he saith more confidently, *I shall not be moved :* and yet more he triumphs in the Lord : *he is my salvation and glory;* which he speaketh in regard of hope to have all good which he needed.   And lastly, in regard of supply, in whatsoever wants, and delivery from all evil, he saith, *he is the rock of my strength, and my refuge is in God :* and so his faith settleth itself, and temptations are overcome.

8. *Trust in him at all times ; ye people, pour out your heart before him : God* is *a refuge for us. Selah.*

9. *Surely men of low degree* are *vanity,* and *men of high degree* are *a lie : to be laid in the balance, they* are *altogether* lighter *than vanity.*

In the fourth place, the psalmist exhorteth all men to place confidence upon God, partly because God is able to give deliverance, as a place of refuge, and partly because men, whether great or small, few or many, cannot but deceive and disappoint the man that trusteth in them. Whence learn, 1. The duty of comforted and victorious believers, is to communicate the fruit of their experience, for strengthening their brethren, and edification of others, as their calling permitteth them, as David doth here : *trust in him at all times, ye people.*   2. Whatsoever condition, how hard soever, we fall into, the grace of God and grounds of confidence in God must not be lost, but always made use of : *trust in him at all times.*   3. As a guilty conscience, heavy trouble, misbelief and suspicion of God's good-will, lock up the heart in sorrow; so any measure of faith in God, going to him by prayer, easeth the heart and layeth the burden of grief down before the Lord : *ye people pour out your heart before him : God is a refuge to us.* 4. The way to place our confidence in God, is to lift our confidence off all creatures, and in special off men of superior or inferior ranks : and the way to lift our confidence off the creature, is to consider the inability of men to help us, except God make them do it; and that, without God, they are nothing worth to us : *men of low degree are vanity.* 5. Whosoever trust on men, higher or lower, are sure to be disappointed in their expectation, and of whatsoever man's help can promise : and, if we will not be deceived, the voice of God and experience of his saints may give us certainty of the truth of the doctrine; for out of experience David saith, *surely men of low degree are vanity, &c.* 6. Carnal confidence is not only unable to help a man, when he hath most need, but also bringeth damage unto him, and makes him to find God in his jealousy an adversary and just judge to plague and curse him; and so if the matter be well weighed, creature-help, and creature-comfort, when it is relied upon, is worse than no help : *being laid in the balance, they are altogether lighter than vanity.*

10. *Trust not in oppression, and become not vain in robbery : if riches increase, set not your heart* upon them.

11. *God hath spoken once ; twice have I heard this, that power* belongeth *unto God.*

12. *Also unto thee, O Lord,* belongeth *mercy : for thou renderest to every man according to his work.*

The other part of the exhortation forbiddeth trust in oppression, or riches, or power, or greatness of place, because God disposeth of all things as he pleaseth, showing mercy to such as trust in him, and rendering to every man according to his work. Whence learn, 1. There are many more idols than one to draw away a man's heart from God; for, when trusting in men of high degree and low degree is cast down, then oppression, robbery, and riches stand up, and take God's room in the heart, as here we see. 2. It is more hard to divert a man from confidence in himself, and what is in his own power, then to draw him from confidence in men of higher or lower degree. Therefore, after casting down carnal confidence in men, high or low; he dischargeth confidence in whatsoever a man is able to do of himself, as might, and riches, and authority of high place: *trust not in oppression; if riches increase, &c.* 3. Whosoever is confident, by his own strength and might, to debate his business against any man, and to do his adversaries two wrongs for one, shall find himself to have disobeyed God, and to have been proud in a matter of nothing : *trust not in oppression, become not vain in robbery.* 4. It may stand with godliness and trusting in God, to be rich; but not to have our heart set upon riches, either to gather or keep them, either to rejoice in them, or be proud because of them : *if riches increase, set not thy heart thereon.* 5. Nothing is able to settle man's confidence in God, and to keep his heart from idols, or carnal confidence in creatures, or to bear in upon others this twofold duty, save the powerful impression of the unchangeable word of God; therefore saith he, *God hath spoken once.* 6. Albeit one testimony of Scripture for a ground of faith, or rule of life, rightly considered, be abundantly sufficient to settle our faith in that point, and to warrant our obedience; yet God will inculcate that truth oftener, and have us receive it oftener, and more firmly; and as it is the Lord's kindness to us and care of us, to cause his once spoken word to be often repeated to us, oftener cleared and confirmed unto us by repeated experimental evidence of the certainty thereof : so it is our duty, to receive it more and more heartily, so oft as it is repeated and inculcated, to meditate on and consider it, and to take a deeper and a deeper impression from it: *God hath spoken once, twice have I heard it.* 7. The possession of authority and power to do all and every thing, is the Lord's only : and as for the power of the creature, it is but lent and derived to it, at God's pleasure. The creature can neither hurt us, nor help itself or us, but as God is pleased to use it as an instrument: *twice have I heard this, that power belongeth to God.* 8. To induce a soul to trust in God only, it is necessary, that it so look to his power, as it looks to his mercy, and lay hold on both : faith hath need of both, as of two wings, to carry it up to God above all vain enticements, and terrors, and temptations, and as props whereon to settle and fix itself jointly : *also unto thee, O Lord, belongeth mercy.* 9. As the man that puts his trust in God, and studieth to obey his word, shall find God's mercy to pardon his transgression, and God's power to sustain him in all his difficulties, and to perform all the promises made to his servants: so the man that trusts not in God, but in himself, or in some creature without himself, thinking to work his own happiness by his own ways, shall find the fruit of his wicked course according as God hath forewarned : *for thou renderest to every man according to his works.*

PSALM LXIII.

A psalm of David, when he was in the wilderness of Judah.

We have in this psalm David's exercise in his banishment, when he was hiding himself from Saul in the wilderness of Judah ; wherein are set down his lingering and prayer after the benefit of public ordinances, v. 1, 2; and the fruits of a gracious and comfortable answer given to his prayer, in number four. The first is a resolution to follow spiritual duties, and in special to praise God, v. 3 ; to be a constant supplicant depending on God, v. 4; to take his contentment in God and in his praises, v. 5, 6 ; and joyfully to trust in God's mercy, v. 7. The second fruit is the acknowledgment of God's power, sustaining him in his adherence unto God, practised by him for time past, and purposed for time to come, v. 8. The third fruit is confidence of the destruction of his enemies, v. 9, 10. The fourth is assurance that he shall receive the kingdom promised unto him, to the confusion of all such as slandered him as a traitor.

From the inscription, learn, 1. Such of God's children as dwell most stately and commodiously among their neighbours, may be driven sometimes to hide themselves in a wilderness, as David was. 2. Banishment from among friends cannot banish a man from God, but may serve rather to drive him toward God. 3. Troubles are grievous when they are present, but may prove a matter of a joyful song, when called to remembrance : *a psalm of David, when he was in the wilderness of Judah.*

1. *O God, thou art my God ; early will I seek thee : my soul thirsteth for thee, my flesh longeth for thee in a dry and thirsty land, where no water is ;*

2. *To see thy power and thy glory, so as I have seen thee in the sanctuary.*

From this prayer learn, 1. The Lord is the only ease of a distressed mind, and there is no speedier relief than to

go to God in prayer, as the psalmist did, saying, *O God.*
2. When we would speak unto God to purpose, we should
fasten our hold on the covenant : *O God, thou art my God.*
3. Troubles will sharpen a man in the use of the means,
and rouse him out of sluggish security : *early will I seek
thee.* 4. It is good to fasten duties on ourselves by resolution, and to strengthen our resolution by showing it to the
Lord : *early will I seek thee.* 5. A lively soul will be no
less desirous of spiritual comfort from God than the body
for natural food after long fasting ; *my soul thirsteth for thee.*
6. Spiritual affections, when they are strong, will affect the
body with impressions answerable thereto; *my flesh longeth
after thee.* 7. It is a barren place to a godly soul, where
the public exercises of religion cannot be had; for this cause
mainly David called the wilderness *a dry and thirsty land,
where no water is.* 8. Because the power and glory of God
are nowhere so clearly seen as in public ordinances, therefore should the ordinances be loved and earnestly sought
after; that we may find communion with God in them: *my
soul thirsteth to see thy power and thy glory.* 9. The more
good a man hath found in the public exercises of religion,
the more will he esteem them, and, in special, when he is
deprived of them: *my soul thirsts to see thy power and glory,
so as I have seen thee in thy sanctuary.*

3. *Because thy loving-kindness* is *better than life, my
lips shall praise thee.*

4. *Thus will I bless thee while I live : I will lift up
my hands in thy name.*

5. *My soul shall be satisfied as* with *marrow and
fatness ; and my mouth shall praise* thee *with joyful
lips ;*

6. *When I remember thee upon my bed,* and *meditate
on thee in the* night-*watches.*

7. *Because thou hast been my help, therefore in the
shadow of thy wings will I rejoice.*

Here the Lord giveth to his servant a gracious answer,
and sweeteneth his condition in the wilderness, making him
no less glad than ever he was in the public exercise of religion, by granting him the comfort of his Holy Spirit, as
the fruits of the answer to his prayer make manifest. The
first whereof is shown in sundry holy resolutions to praise

the kindness of God, to bless God, to call on his name in
all conditions, to possess contentment in God, and to trust
in him. Whence learn, 1. When a man who loveth the
public ordinances is debarred from them, and maketh use
of private exercises of religion, God can and will supply unto
him what he wanteth, and be a little sanctuary unto him,
as here appeareth. 2. The felt kindness of God, and shed-
ding abroad of his love in the heart of a believer, is joy
unspeakable and glorious, able to supply all wants unto
him, and to sweeten all troubles unto him, and to give him
more comfort than what is most comfortable in this world;
yea, to make life itself, without the feeling, or hope of feeling, this love, to be little worth to him: *thy loving-kindness
is better than life.* 3. Rich experiences of the felt love of
God, in the use of means, deserve to be brought forth to
the praise of God when it may glorify him: *because thy
loving-kindness is better than life, my lips shall praise thee.*
4. One proof of God's loving-kindness towards us is reason
abundant for us to bless God for ever thereafter, and to
acknowledge him the fountain of blessings, even to ourselves, whatsoever change of dispensations we shall meet
with: *thus will I bless thee while I live.* 5. As our assurance of God's love unto us, and of his purpose to bless us,
serveth to prepare us for straits and difficulties hereafter;
so also it helpeth us to pray to God with confidence of being
helped, into whatsoever change of condition we may afterwards fall: *thus will I bless thee while I live, I will lift up
my hands in thy name;* to wit, as a man engaged to depend
upon thee, to call upon thee as my need requireth, and a
man particularly encouraged by thee, and confirmed by experience from thy former helping of me, that I shall have
a good answer from thee, who hast manifested thyself unto
me by thy word and works. 6. The spiritual life of the
soul hath its own food as well as the bodily life of nature;
and the life of the godly is not so barren, so sad and uncomfortable, as the world believeth. They have their hidden
manna and the water of life, solid and satisfactory consolations and joy in the Holy Spirit, wherewith strangers inter-
meddle not, of which joys the sweetest morsel of delicate
banquets is but a shadow: *my soul shall be satisfied as with
marrow and fatness.* 7. Such as hunger and thirst after
communion with God in Christ, and resolve to spend their

life in God's service, may promise to themselves that they shall feel sweet satisfaction in this course, and with David say, *my soul shall be satisfied as with marrow.* 8. Spiritual joys are not like carnal joys, which end in sadness, but they terminate in glorifying, and make the very outward man partaker of the benefit; therefore the psalmist addeth, *and my mouth shall praise thee with joyful lips.* 9. The way to find spiritual refreshment, is, beside public ordinances, to give ourselves to spiritual exercises in secret, at such times as our necessities, civil and natural, may best spare, and then and there to recall to mind what we have heard, seen, or felt of God's word or working, and to keep up our thoughts upon this holy subject by prayer, soliloquy, and meditation, as David showeth to us the example : *when I remember thee upon my bed, and meditate on thee in the night-watches.* 10. As one experience should call another to remembrance, so the calling of experiences to our memory should lead and encourage us, in all conditions, joyfully to make use, by faith, of God's standing offer of grace for us in Christ, shadowed forth by the wings of the cherubim stretched out always over the mercy-seat : *because thou hast been my helper, therefore in the shadow of thy wings will I rejoice;* for here, and here only, is the remedy of all sin and misery.

8. *My soul followeth hard after thee : thy right hand upholdeth me.*

From the second fruit of the gracious answer given to David's prayer; that is, from his giving the glory of the acts of grace which he did, unto God the furnisher thereof, learn, 1. The Lord useth to exercise the souls of his own children with a sense of desertion, and withdrawing of his presence one way or other. This is presupposed in David's *following after the Lord,* when he felt him withdrawing himself, as it were. 2. A believer in God cannot endure a thought of separation from God, nor forbear to seek after God, when he misseth his presence, but will use all means to recover the sense of his presence which he hath felt before : *my soul followeth hard after thee.* 3. It is our wisdom to reflect upon and acknowledge the grace of God in us, and review the acts of our faith and love toward God, for our own strengthening, as David doth here, saying, *my soul followeth hard after thee.* 4. Although the exercise of gracious habits be our act, yet the enabling us to bring our acts forth is the Lord's work, who giveth us both to will and to do of his own good pleasure; and as it is our duty to acknowledge this, so it is the fruit of our feelings of God's help to profess it : *my soul followeth hard after thee;* but by what power, strength, and furniture doth he this? *thy right hand upholdeth me.*

9. *But those* that *seek my soul, to destroy* it, *shall go into the lower parts of the earth.*

10. *They shall fall by the sword; they shall be a portion for foxes.*

The third fruit of the answer to David's prayer, is assurance given that his enemies shall be destroyed, for it is revealed to him that Saul would be slain by the sword; he knew by revelation that his carcass would lie in the fields, a prey for foxes and wild beasts. Whence learn, 1. The deadly and irreconcilable enemies of God's people, hating them for a good cause, draw destruction on themselves : *those that seek my soul to destroy it, shall go down to the lower parts of the earth.* 2. It is agreeable to God's justice that bloody enemies of God's people be punished by their bloody enemies; God can stir up the wicked against the wicked, to avenge the wrongs done to his children : *they shall fall by the sword, they shall be a portion for the foxes.* 3. The Lord, to ease the hearts of his oppressed children, sometimes maketh them foresee beforehand the destruction of his adversaries, whether by teaching them in an ordinary way to apply the general sentences of the Scripture unto them, or in a more special way revealing his mind, as he seeth fit, as here : *they shall fall by the sword, &c.*

11. *But the king shall rejoice in God; every one that sweareth by him shall glory : but the mouth of them that speak lies shall be stopped.*

The last fruit of David's prayer is assurance that he shall be king, that all the godly shall be comforted by this means, and that his righteousness shall be cleared against all the calumnies of the wicked. Whence learn, 1. Howsoever it may go hard with the righteous, and their enemies may prosper for a time, yet their lot shall be changed to the better at length; and when their enemies are borne down, their head shall be lifted up; and whatsoever is promised unto them, they may be as sure of it as if they had possession of it, yea they may style themselves by the title which God's word hath given unto them, as David doth in this particular, calling himself king now when he was a banished man in the wilderness of Judah : *the king shall rejoice*, saith he. 2. The true ground of a believer's joy is not the gift he receiveth from God, how great soever it may be, but the good-will of the giver, even God himself : *the king shall rejoice in God.* 3. Every true worshipper of God (whose property truly it is to fear the true God, and the cognizance of whose sincerity is his conscience-making of an oath,) shall have matter of gloriation, after a while's patient suffering in time of trial : *every one that sweareth by him shall glory.* 4. The borne-down righteousness of the godly, and of their cause, by the lies, slanders, and calumnies of the wicked, shall be brought to light in due time, and the wicked made ashamed of their lies : *the mouth of them that speak lies shall be stopped.*

PSALM LXIV.
To the chief musician. A psalm of David.

This psalm hath two parts. In the former is David's heavy complaint unto God against his deadly enemies, laid forth before God in sundry particular evidences of their malice, v. 1—6 ; and in the latter part is the Lord's comfortable answer unto him, by giving him assurance of God's judgment coming on them, to their own and others astonishment, and to the comfort of the godly, v. 7—10.

1. *Hear my voice, O God, in my prayer : preserve my life from fear of the enemy.*

2. *Hide me from the secret counsel of the wicked ; from the insurrection of the workers of iniquity :*

In his prayer David requested first in general, delivery of his life from the secret plotting and often practising of his enemies against him. Whence learn, 1. Present danger is able to force out cries to God, and such earnest prayers, poured out in extreme necessity, shall not want an answer : *hear my voice, O God, in my prayer.* 2. The danger cannot be so great, wherein help may not be had from God; he is so near to a supplicant, so powerful, and so ready to save the man who hath made God his refuge : *preserve my life from fear of the enemy.* 3. God can so overrule and outwit the devices of our enemies, that they shall either not light upon the mean whereby they might overtake us, or shall miss their intent in case their device be probable : *hide me from the secret counsel of the wicked.* 4. What the wicked cannot do against the righteous by craft, they will pursue with open violence; but God, as he is wiser in counsel, and able to befool them, so is he stronger in power and able to break them : *hide me from their insurrection.* 5. That we may have the greater confidence to be delivered from our enemies, we had need to be sure that we are in a good cause, and that our adversaries have a wrong cause : *hide me from the workers of iniquity.*

3. *Who whet their tongue like a sword,* and *bend* their bows to shoot *their arrows,* even *bitter words ;*

4. *That they may shoot in secret at the perfect : suddenly do they shoot at him, and fear not.*

5. *They encourage themselves in an evil matter : they commune of laying snares privily ; they say, Who shall see them ?*

6. *They search out iniquities ; they accomplish a diligent search : both the inward* thought *of every one* of them, *and the heart,* is *deep.*

Here David complaineth of his enemies, and layeth forth several degrees of their desperate wickedness before God, as so many arguments to strengthen his faith and hope for delivery from them. Whence learn, 1. The benefit of a good cause, and of a good conscience appeareth best in a strait, when nothing can help a man against his enemies save God alone, as here appeareth in David's case. 2. Calumnies and slanders against the godly are very cruel weapons; for not only hurt they the estimation of their good cause, and personal good behaviour, but they also stir up all men to take their lives : *they whet their tongue as a sword, and bend their bows to shoot their arrows, bitter words.* 3. There is no dread of a privy slander; a man is wounded ere he is aware, and no man's innocency or integrity of life can be a guard against the shot of a calumniator's tongue : *they shoot in secret at the perfect, suddenly do they shoot at him.* 4. Because God only can heal the wound of a slander, and sustain the man in the consciousness of his good cause and carriage, till he clear him; the righteous man must content

himself to refer the matter to God, as David doth here. 5.
Godless men are dangerous enemies; *for they fear not God,*
and so have no powerful restraint within them from doing
any mischief, and the more they sin, they acquire the greater
boldness to sin more : *they encourage themselves in an evil
matter.* 6. The wit and wickedness which is within themselves, will not suffice their devilish intention, therefore they
seek all help they can find from without: *they commune of
laying snares privily.* 7. They seek how they may overtake the man's person, after they have killed his good name
and cause with calumnies and bitter aspersions. Yea, Satan so blindeth them, that they neither look to God, the
avenger of such plots and practices, nor do they consider that
God seeth them, and they think their pretences before men
are so thick a covering, that no man can see through them:
they say, Who shall see them? 8. If there hath been any
slander of the upright man's misdemeanour in any former
time, which for the falsehood of it is evanished, they make
search after it, to waken it up again; and if there be any
possibility to devise new inventions, with any probability, they
go about it busily, yea they search hell itself to find out how
to bring a mischief upon the upright : *they search out iniquities, they accomplish a diligent search.* 9. Last of all,
their wickedness is unsearchable, the uncontrolled bent of
their wicked wit and will, assisted with what Satan can suggest, furnish, and stir up—all is employed—and it is hard
to say whether their wit or will be most wicked, or draw
nearest to hell; but of both it may be truly affirmed, that
both the thoughts of every one of them, and the heart is deep.

7. *But God shall shoot at them* with *an arrow ;
suddenly shall they be wounded.*

8. *So they shall make their own tongue to fall upon
themselves : all that see them shall flee away.*

9. *And all men shall fear, and shall declare the work
of God ; for they shall wisely consider of his doing.*

10. *The righteous shall be glad in the Lord, and
shall trust in him ; and all the upright in heart shall
glory.*

In the latter part of the psalm is set down David's prayer
and confidence of justice to be executed against his enemies, and mercy to be shown to him, and to all the godly.

Whence learn, 1. The godly want not a friend to avenge their quarrel : God will shoot against wicked archers and not miss the mark : *but God shall shoot at them ; with an arrow shall they be wounded.* 2. Where desperate malice is seen, there sudden mischief may be foreseen; it shall light upon the malicious : *suddenly shall they be wounded.* 3. The wicked adversaries of God's people are destroyers of themselves by their opposition unto them; for as they thought to do unto God's children, God doth to them : *so they shall make their own tongue fall upon themselves.* 4. Sometimes God will make the wicked spectacles of his judgment to the affrightment of all that know them and see their plague : *all that see them shall flee away.* 5. The judgment of the wicked should be all men's lesson; and all sorts of people shall learn, by their plagues, to know God's justice and terror : *and all men shall fear and declare the works of God.* 6. Not every spectator of God's work giveth glory to God, but they only who compare his word with his works, and through the veil of means and instruments look to God the righteous judge of the world : *they shall declare the work of God, for they shall consider wisely of his doing.* 7. When woe and wrack come upon the wicked, then joy and comfort come to the godly, not so much for the damage of the wicked, as for the manifestation of the glory of God : *the righteous shall be glad in the Lord.* 8. As the Lord's mercies confirm the faith of the righteous, so also do the works of his justice : *they shall be glad in the Lord, and shall trust in him.* 9. The delivery of one of the godly, is a pledge of the like delivery to all in the like case: and as one, so all and every one of the righteous and upright in heart shall triumph at length over all enemies, and make their boast of God : *all the upright in heart shall glory.*

PSALM LXV.

To the chief musician.   A psalm and song of David.

This psalm is all of God's praises. The proposition that he is to be praised, is set down, v. 1. The reasons of his praise unto the end, are nine. The first whereof is, because he heareth prayer, v. 2 ; the second, because he mercifully pardoneth sins, v. 3 ; the third, because of his gracious purpose and powerful prosecution of the decree of election of his own redeemed ones, v. 4 ; the fourth, because of his defending his church in all places, v. 5; the fifth, from the strength manifested in framing and settling the mountains, v. 6; the sixth, from the wise and powerful overruling of all unruly and raging creatures, v. 7; the seventh, from his preventing troubles, which are coming to his church, by terrifying all nations at beholding the tokens of his displeasure against the enemies of his people, v. 8; the eighth argument is taken from the joyful peace, granted sometimes to his people, v. 8; the ninth argument of God's praise, is from the rich plenty of all necessary food from year to year, which God provideth for maintenance of man and beast, and specially of his people Israel in their land, v. 9—13.

1. *Praise waiteth for thee, O God, in Zion : and unto thee shall the vow be performed.*

From the proposition concerning his purpose to spend this psalm only in praising God, learn, 1. Although prayer and praises always agree well, yet some time may call for praises and the work of praise only, and may take up the whole man for a time, as here. 2. How mournful soever a condition the Lord's people may be in, yet God is preparing matter thereby for his own glory; *praise waiteth for thee.* And whatsoever matter of praise be seen, or whatsoever measure of praise be given unto God by his people, more is due to him, and more is making ready for him : *praise waiteth for thee.* 3. Although the rest of the world be senseless of God's benefits, yet his church must set about the work of his praise, and shall be enabled to give him praise: *praise waiteth for thee, O God, in Zion.* 4. As it is the duty of every man, who seeketh deliverance from trouble, or any other benefit from God, to oblige himself to praise God for it: so it is the Lord's manner to gain to himself praise by granting prayers, and to purchase the performance of promised praises unto him: *unto thee shall the vow be performed.*

2. *O thou that hearest prayer, unto thee shall all flesh come.*

From the first reason of the Lord's praise, learn, 1. The hearing and granting of prayer are the Lord's property, and his usual practice, and his pleasure, and his nature, and his glory : *O thou that hearest prayer !* 2. The readiness of the Lord to hear prayer, openeth the door of access to all sorts of people, who are sensible of their own frailty and necessities, and know his readiness to relieve them : Gentiles as well as Jews shall come unto him; *O thou that hearest prayer ! all flesh shall come unto thee.*

3. *Iniquities prevail against me :* as for *our trans-gressions, thou shalt purge them away.*

From the second reason of the Lord's praise, learn, 1. Sin is a sore adversary, and many times prevails over us, and draws troubles on us, which make us know the ill of it better than we knew before committing it: *iniquities prevail against me.* 2. Whatsoever be the sins of the people we live amongst, let us make special account of our own guiltiness in the point of confession, as David doth here, when he saith, *iniquities prevail against me.* 3. Our sins should be looked upon, not to chase us from God, but to humble us, and drive us to seek pardon and purgation from the Lord, whose free grace only can take sins away; *iniquity prevails over me : but as for our transgressions, thou shalt purge them away.* 4. The holy prophets and penmen of Scripture have no grounds of hope for pardon of sin, save those which are common to the meanest of God's people; for David in his confession cometh in by himself alone, aggravating his own sins most : *iniquities prevail against me,* saith he; but, in hope of pardon, he joineth with the rest of God's people, saying, *as for our transgressions, thou shalt purge them away.*

4. *Blessed* is the man whom *thou choosest, and causest to approach* unto thee, that *he may dwell in thy courts : we shall be satisfied with the goodness of thy house,* even *of thy holy temple.*

From the third reason of the Lord's praise, learn, 1. God hath made election of some out of the rest of mankind, on whom he effectually bestoweth blessedness : *blessed is the man whom thou choosest.* 2. All those whom God effectually calleth, and reconcileth and draweth into communion and society with himself, are elected and blessed persons : *blessed is the man whom thou choosest, and causest to approach unto thee.* 3. It is the free good-will of God which putteth the difference among men, and maketh some to be partakers of blessedness, and not others : *blessed is the man whom thou choosest.* 4. The power and glory of the work of conversion, reconciliation, and drawing near to God, for communion with him, of so many as are converted, are the Lord's power and glory no less than election is his free choice and glory : *blessed is the man whom thou choosest,*

and whom *thou causest to approach unto thee.* 5. The mar.
elected, effectually called, reconciled and drawn into society
with God, is a true member of his church, a constant member thereof in this life, and one who shall be a member of
the church triumphant, in the life to come, and so effectually blessed; *he shall dwell in thy courts,* saith the text in
the original. 6. Whatsoever is sufficient for begetting
and entertaining the life of grace and of true blessedness in
God's elect, is to be found by means of public ordinances
in the church of God : *we shall be satisfied with the goodness of thy house, even of thy holy temple.* 7. Whosoever
find in themselves the proper effects or consequents of election in special, a powerful drawing of them to the covenant
with God, and to a nearer and nearer approach unto God,
in the way of obedience to the public ordinances of his
house; may be assured of their election, of their effectual
calling, of their blessedness, and of their interest in all the
goodness of God's house, to their full contentment; for, after the general doctrine, he applieth, *we shall be satisfied
with the goodness of thy house, even of thy holy temple.*

5. By *terrible things in righteousness wilt thou
answer us, O God of our salvation;* who art *the confidence of all the ends of the earth, and of them* that
are *afar off* upon *the sea.*

The fourth reason of the Lord's praise is taken from the
defending of his church in all ages and places, and saving
of his people, by giving terrible answers to their prayers
against their enemies, for the performance of his own word,
and confirmation of the faith of his own people, in whatsoever part of the earth, unto the end of the world. Whence
learn, 1. As the love of God to his people exempteth not
them from the molestation of enemies, because the Lord
will have the faith of his people by this means exercised, and
them put to pray unto him, and complain of the injuries
done unto them; so his love to them will not suffer their
prayers to want an answer in their troubles, to the amaze-
ment of their adversaries : *by terrible things wilt thou answer us.* 2. In the Lord's relieving his people and destroying their enemies, he will have the work looked upon as
the performance of his word, wherein he hath promised to
be a friend to the friends of his people, and a foe to their

foes : *by terrible things in righteousness wilt thou answer us.* 3. The reason of particular deliveries of God's people from their enemies, is, because these deliveries are appendices of the covenant of grace, established for giving to them everlasting life: *thou wilt answer us, O God of our salvation.* 4. What the Lord hath promised and done to his church of old, is a sufficient ground of confidence to the people of God, in all times and places, to expect and find the like mercy unto that which they of old expected and found; *O God of our salvation, the confidence of all the ends of the earth, and of them that are afar off upon the sea ;* that is, thy people, whether dwelling on the continent, or in isles, or sailing on the sea.

6. *Which by his strength setteth fast the mountains; being girded with power :*

The fifth reason of the Lord's praise is his strong power, whereby he is able to do all things, as appeareth by his framing and settling the mountains. Whence learn, 1. The power of God manifested in the work of creation, is a prop to the faith of his people to believe the promises, and a pledge of the performance thereof unto them : *by his strength he setteth fast the mountains.* 2. Whatsoever great work the Lord hath done, he is able and ready to do a greater work, if need be, for his people: *he is girded with power.*

7. *Which stilleth the noise of the seas, the noise of their waves, and the tumult of the people.*

From the sixth reason, taken from his wise and powerful overruling all commotions of unruly creatures of whatsoever sorts, learn, 1. There is nothing so turbulent, and raging, and reasonless in the whole world, which God doth not rule and bridle, and make quiet as he pleaseth : *he stilleth the noise of the seas, the noise of their waters.* 2. As the commotions of people, their seditions, their insurrections and conspiracies against God's people within and without the visible church, are no less raging and reasonless than are the commotions of the sea; so God hath the ruling of them as well as of the seas, and by his *stilling the noise of the seas, the noise of the waters thereof,* he giveth an evidence of his power and purpose to bridle the fury and rage of reasonless men who threaten trouble and destruction to his people : *he stilleth their waves, and the tumult of the people.*

8. *They also that dwell in the uttermost parts are afraid at thy tokens: thou makest the outgoings of the morning and evening to rejoice.*

From the seventh reason of God's praise, taken from the affrighting of all the world by his judgments against the enemies of the people, lest they should attempt the like, learn, 1. As the Lord can still the tumults of the people, when they rage most; so he can by his terror prevent their commotions against his church, by showing them his terrible judgments executed on others, which are the tokens of the power of his displeasure against all who shall dare to be adversaries to his people : *they also that dwell in the uttermost parts, are afraid at thy tokens.*

The eigthth reason of God's praise, is from the joyful tranquillity and peace, which he, when he pleaseth, giveth to his people, after he has settled their enemies' rage and power against them. Whence learn, as the Lord sometimes exerciseth his people with trouble and persecution from their enemies; so also he can, and doth give them some breathing times, some comfortable seasons, as it were fair days, from morning to evening; yea, sundry full fair days, one after another, so that his people are made to rejoice before him from day to day; *thou makest the outgoings of the morning and evening to rejoice.*

9. *Thou visitest the earth, and waterest it: thou greatly enrichest it with the river of God, which is full of water : thou preparest them corn, when thou hast so provided for it.*

10. *Thou waterest the ridges thereof abundantly; thou settlest the furrows thereof ; thou makest it soft with showers ; thou blessest the springing thereof:*

11. *Thou crownest the year with thy goodness ; and thy paths drop fatness.*

12. *They drop upon the pastures of the wilderness , and the little hills rejoice on every side.*

13. *The pastures are clothed with flocks ; the val-*

*leys also are covered over with corn; they shout for
joy, they also sing.*

The ninth reason of the Lord's praise, is from his plentiful furnishing of food yearly for man and beast, but in
special for his making the promised land fruitful unto his
people Israel, when he shall give them rest from their enemies, and peace therein, after their being exercised with
troubles.   What may be prophetical, in this whole psalm,
as touching the Israelites, we will not here inquire; nor
how far the prophet looked beyond his own and Solomon's
time, when he said, *praise waiteth for thee in Zion, &c.*
Only, hence learn general doctrines, 1. The Lord's blessing the ground, and making it fruitful, is his coming as it
were to visit: *thou visitest the earth, and waterest it.* 2.
God's providence is then best seen, when particular parts
are looked upon, one after another; *thou waterest it, thou
enrichest it, thou preparest them corn, &c.* 3. The sending
of timely rain and plenty of it, and after that abundance of
victual, should not be slightly passed over, but well and
carefully marked: for the husbandry is all the Lord's: *thou
preparest them corn, when thou hast so provided for it.* 4.
Second causes, and the natural course of conveying benefits
unto us, are not rightly seen, except when God, the first
and prime cause, is seen to be nearest unto the actual disposing of them for producing the effect: *thou waterest the
ridges thereof abundantly, &c., thou blessest the springing
thereof.* 5. From the one end of the year to the other
God hath continual work about the bringing forth of the
fruits of the ground, and gloriously perfecteth it once a-
year : *thou crownest the year with thy goodness.* 6. Every
one of the footsteps of God's providence, for the provision
of his people's food, hath its own blessing, as appeareth
in the profitable use of the straw and stubble and chaff, and
multiplication of the seed : *thy paths drop fatness.* 7. The
Lord hath a care to provide food, not only for man, but also for beasts; and not only for tame beasts, which are most
useful for man, but also for wild beasts in the wilderness;
making his rain fall on all parts of the ground : *they drop
upon the pastures of the wilderness, and the little hills rejoice on every side.* 8. Albeit temporal benefits be inferior
to spiritual, yet because unto God's children they be appen-

dices of the spiritual, they are worthy to be taken notice
of, and God should be praised for them; as here the psalmist showeth, praising God for spiritual blessings, in the beginning of the psalm, and here, in the end, for temporal
benefits.   9. The plurality of God's creatures, and the comparison of God's benefits set before our eyes, are the scale,
music book, and noted lessons of the harmony and melody
which we ought to have in our hearts, in praising him : yea,
these benefits begin and take up the song in their own kind,
that we may follow them in our kind: *the pastures are
clothed with flocks, the valleys also are covered over with
corn, they shout for joy, they also sing.*

PSALM LXVI.
To the chief musician.   A song or psalm.

This psalm being all of praises, may be divided into three parts. In the
first, the psalmist exhorteth all the earth to praise God, v. 1—4, and
that because of the works which God did of old for his people, v. 5, 6,
and because he is able to do the like when he pleaseth, v. 7. In the
second part, he exhorts the church of Israel living with him in that
age, to praise God for the late experience of God's goodness towards
them, in the delivery granted to them out of their late trials, troubles,
and sore vexations, v. 8—12. In the third place, the prophet expresseth
his own purpose of thankfulness unto God for the large experience which
he had in particular of God's mercies to himself, from v. 13, to the end.

1. *Make a joyful noise unto God, all ye lands :*
2. *Sing forth the honour of his name ; make his
praise glorious.*

From this urgent exhortation to praise God, learn, 1. As
the duty of praise is most necessary, and most spiritual, so
are we more dull and indisposed thereto than to any other
spiritual exercise, and had need to be stirred up thereunto;
therefore, saith he, *make a noise, sing forth, &c.* 2. The
prophets of old had it revealed to them, that the Gentiles
should be brought to the knowledge of God, and made to
worship him, as, *make a joyful noise unto God, all ye lands,*
importeth.   3. The praise of the Lord is a task for all the
world to be employed about, and a duty whereunto all are
bound; for all see his works, and hold what they have of
him, but specially those that hear of him by his word, to
whom most specially the word speaketh : *make a joyful noise,
all ye lands.*   4. Men ought to go about the work of praising God so cheerfully, so wisely, and so avowedly, that they

who hear his praise spoken of, may understand his majesty, magnificence, goodness, power, and mercy : *make a noise unto God, sing forth the honour of his name, make his praise glorious.*

3. *Say unto God, How terrible art thou in thy works! through the greatness of thy power shall thine enemies submit themselves unto thee.*

4. *All the earth shall worship thee, and shall sing unto thee ; they shall sing to thy name. Selah.*

Here the psalmist, as the Lord's penman, furnisheth to the hearers matter and words for praising God, and prophesieth that the fulness of the Gentiles shall concur in his worship, and take part in the song of his praise. Whence learn, 1. Because we can do nothing of ourselves in this work of the Lord's praise, God must furnish to us matter and words: *say unto God, How terrible, &c.* 2. As the work of the praise of God should be done in love, confidence, sincerity, and in his own strength, so may it be directed to him immediately, and that without flattery; (otherwise than men are praised) for praise properly is due to God only, and no man can speak of him, except in his own audience : *say unto God, How terrible art thou in thy works!* 3. The works of the Lord, every one of them being rightly studied, are able to affright us by discovering the incomparable, dreadful, and omnipotent majesty of the worker thereof : *how terrible art thou in thy works!* 4. When the Lord is pleased to let forth his judgments on his adversaries, and to let them see what he can do, none of them dare stand out against him; and, if they be not converted, yet will they be forced to feign submission unto him : *through the greatness of thy power shall thine enemies submit themselves to thee.* 5. Over and above what is already accomplished of this prophecy concerning the conversion of the Gentiles, a higher measure is yet to be expected in the bringing in of that number of them which the Scripture calleth the "fullness of the Gentiles," and the making all the kingdoms of the earth to become the Lord's, and his Son Christ's; for this word must be fulfilled in a greater measure than yet is come to pass : *all the earth shall worship thee ; they shall sing unto thee ; they shall sing unto thy name.* Which word importeth the revealing of the glad tidings of Jesus Christ unto them, their joyful acceptation of the gospel, and glorifying of God for it. 6. As it is the Lord's glory to have many praising him, so should it be the joy of all that love him, now to foresee the success of Christ's kingdom, as well as it was of old, when it was the church's song : *all the earth shall worship thee.*

5. *Come and see the works of God :* he is *terrible* in his *doing toward the children of men.*

6. *He turned the sea into dry*-land : *they went through the flood on foot ; there did we rejoice in him.*

7. *He ruleth by his power for ever ; his eyes behold the nations : let not the rebellious exalt themselves. Selah.*

He pointeth out in special the Lord's works, already wrought for his people. Whence learn, 1. Albeit the Lord worketh for the delivery of the church and his own glory, yet men are so careless to observe his works, that they can neither make use thereof for their own profit, nor for God's praise; so that there is much need to stir up our dullness to observe them and make right use thereof : *come and see the works of God.* 2. Whosoever observes the works of God, which he hath wrought for his people, shall be forced to fear and admire his wonderful acts for them, and his respect unto them : *he is terrible in his doings toward the children of men.* 3. The work of redemption of his church out of Egypt, is a work, one for all, worthy to be made use of to the end of the world, and sufficient to show that, if need be, God will invert the course of nature for the good of his people, and for their delivery out of difficulties : *he turned the sea into dry land.* 4. As the Lord will work wonders for the delivery of his people out of misery, so will he work wonders for performing promises to them, and for bringing them to the possession of what he hath given them right unto; for the drying of the river Jordan, that his people might go in to possess the promised land, was a pledge and evidence of this his purpose for all time coming : *they went through the flood on foot.* 5. As all the people of God are one body, and that which is done in one age to one generation concerneth all and every one to make use of it in their generation; so every one in after ages should reckon themselves one body with the Lord's people in former ages, and make use of God's dealing with them, as if they had been present then with them; as here the church, in the psalmist's time, joineth itself with the church in Joshua's time, rejoicing in God with them at their entering into Canaan : *there did we rejoice in him*, say they. 6. Whatsoever the Lord hath done for his people in any time bypast, he is able and ready to do the like for his people in any time to come : *he ruleth by his power for ever*, and for this cause his former acts are perpetual evidences and pledges of like acts to be done hereafter, as need is. 7. Nothing is done in any place, which the Lord is not witness unto, no plot or motion against his people which he seeth not : *his eyes behold the nations.* 8. Albeit there will be, from time to time, a generation who will not submit to this sovereign Ruler, but will stand out against him, and malign his church, yet shall they not long prosper, nor have cause of gloriation in their rebellion : *let not the rebellious exalt themselves.*

8. *O bless our God, ye people, and make the voice of his praise to be heard;*

9. *Which holdeth our soul in life, and suffereth not our feet to be moved.*

10. *For thou, O God, hast proved us : thou hast tried us, as silver is tried.*

11. *Thou broughtest us into the net; thou laidst affliction upon our loins.*

12. *Thou hast caused men to ride over our heads : we went through fire and through water; but thou broughtest us out into a wealthy* place.

In the second part of the psalm, the psalmist exhorts the church in his time to praise God for preserving them from extirpation in the time of their fiery trial and sore affliction under the tyranny and oppression of their enemies. Whence learn, 1. The Lord's people in every age, besides all the reasons they have to praise God for his former works, want not their own particular reasons for his care, providence, and kindness to themselves in their own time, to stir up one another to bless his majesty : *O bless our God, ye people.* 2. It is the church's proper privilege, and her glory above all other incorporations and societies beside, to have special interest in God as her own : *O bless our God.* 3. It is not sufficient that the Lord's people acknowledge inwardly the

mercies of God to themselves; but it is their duty in an orderly way to bring others on to the knowledge of God, and
show how praiseworthy he is: *make the voice of his praise
to be heard.* 4. Albeit the Lord takes many things away
from his people, when he is pleased to exercise them, yet he
keeps life in their soul, some sweet communion of spirit between himself and them, and suffereth not all his people to
be extirpated from the earth : *which holdeth our soul in life.*
5. It is a great mercy to be kept from desperate courses in
the time of sad calamities, and to be supported under bur-
dens, that we sink not: and to be prevented from denying
God or his truth in time of persecution : *he suffereth not
our feet to be moved.* 6. One end of the troubles of the
church, among others, is, the trial of the graces of his people, and purging them from their corruptions; for which
cause the Lord useth to bring on one trouble after another,
as metal is put in the fire oftener than once : *for thou, O
God, hast proved us, thou hast tried us, as silver is tried.*
7. When God bringeth his church into trial there is no escaping; we must look for affliction, and not dream of declining it by our own judgment or skill : *thou broughtest us
into the net, thou laidst affliction upon our loins.* 8. It is
wisdom, and justice, and goodness in God, to make his people know sometimes, whether his service or men's service
be most easy : *thou hast caused men to ride over our heads.*
9. When God's service and men's service are compared, the
service of man is a beastly bondage in comparison; for the
enemies of the church will abuse God's people like beasts,
when they fall under their power : *thou hast made men ride
over our heads.* 10. There is no sort of affliction, or extremity of affliction, from which the godly may secure themselves, after the time of entering into their trials, till God's
time come wherein their trial is to end : *we went through
fire, and through water.* 11. After troubles and trials, the
Lord giveth ever an event, and a gracious delivery to his
own, which bringeth as much comfort with it as their trial
had grief in it : *but thou broughtest us out into a wealthy
place.*

13. *I will go into thy house with burnt-offerings ; I
will pay thee my vows,*

14. *Which my lips have uttered, and my mouth hath
spoken, when I was in trouble.*

14

15. *I will offer unto thee burnt-sacrifices of fatlings,
with the incense of rams : I will offer bullocks with
goats.   Selah.*

In the third and last part of the psalm, the psalmist showeth forth his thankfulness for the favours showed to himself
in particular; and first, he promiseth to acknowledge his obligation to God in the place of public worship, as the Lord
had required in the ceremonial law, v. 13—15.   Secondly,
he declareth his particular experience of God's mercy, tes-
tifying his hearing of his prayer, by his acceptance of it,
v. 18, 19.   And, last of all, he blesseth the Lord for the
gracious answer of his prayer, v. 20.

From the promise which he maketh of public acknowledgment of the mercy, according to the prescription of the
Lord's appointment, learn, 1. In common favours and deliveries granted to the visible church, each true member has
his own special mercies bestowed upon him, besides the
common, for which in particular, and for the common mercies also, he ought publicly to be thankful, as the psalmist
is here, saying, *I will go into thy house with burnt-offerings.*
2. As it is a token of lively faith in desperate troubles to
trust in God, and to hope for his deliverance, and to promise him praise before the delivery come : so it is a token of
an upright heart, to be as willing to perform promises after
the benefit received, as it was ready to make promises, before the benefit received : *I will pay thee my vows which my
lips have uttered, and my mouth hath spoken when I was in
trouble.*   3. As our persons and best services are polluted,
except they be cleansed by the sacrifice of Christ : so in our
approaches unto God, we should acknowledge the sinfulness
of our persons and performances, and the need we stand in
of Christ's mediation, and the riches of grace bestowed upon us through him, who perfumeth our persons, and prayers,
and praises, as was shadowed forth in the ceremonies of the
law; for this was the prophet's meaning, when he said, *I will
offer unto thee burnt sacrifices of fatlings, with the incense of
rams : I will offer bullocks with goats,* which were appointed in the law to be offered, partly for sin, and partly by way
of thanksgiving.

16. *Come* and *hear, all ye that fear God, and I will
declare what he hath done for my soul.*

17. *I cried unto him with my mouth, and he was extolled with my tongue.*

From his declaration of his lately felt experience of God's mercy to him: learn, 1. As a spiritual man will not neglect outward rites of commanded public worship: so will he not rest on them, but will go about the real glorifying of God before others, as the psalmist doth here : *come and hear what the Lord hath done for my soul.* 2. The true disciples of God's grace who can best discern God's works, and the experience of others, and who will be most ready to praise God with us, are those that fear God : *come and hear, all ye that fear God, I will declare what he hath done for my soul.* 3. It is no less needful for glorifying God, and the edification of others, to make the way of our coming by a benefit manifest to others—that it was by the use of holy ordinances—than to make mention of the benefit itself; *I cried unto him,* saith he; that is, I was instant in prayer for the benefit. 4. There are cases wherein the uttering of words in prayer serveth much, not only for our own upstirring, and fixing our minds, and for others' edification; but also concerneth God's glory, on whom we profess dependence, and in whom we acknowledge power and goodness to dwell : *and he was extolled with my tongue.*

18. *If I regard iniquity in my heart, the Lord will not hear* me :

19. But *verily God hath heard* me; *he hath attended to the voice of my prayer.*

From the clearing of David's sincerity in prayer, learn, 1. Sincerity of heart should be joined with the supplication of the mouth, and with self-examination, that we may be sure we pray sincerely : for, *if I regard iniquity in my heart,* imports so much in the psalmist's practice. 2. He is an upright man in God's account, who entertaineth not affection to any known sin, but opposeth it sincerely in God's sight; for this the psalmist bringeth for the proof of his sincerity, that he did not *regard sin in his heart.* 3. Those only are sinners, whose prayer God will not hear, who live in the love of known sins, and pray for having satisfaction to their corrupt lusts : *if I regard iniquity in my heart, the Lord will not hear me.* 4. The lawful prayer of the upright heart shall be granted in substance, and it may be just as it was

desired: which, as it is no small mercy, should be well marked, as the return of our prayer : *but verily God hath heard
me, he hath attended to the voice of my supplication.*

20. *Blessed* be *God, which hath not turned away my
prayer, nor his mercy from me.*

David closeth with thanksgiving for this particular experience, as an evidence of the running of the fountain of
God's mercy toward him.   Whence learn, 1. As it is no
small mercy that our prayers are not rejected of God, albeit
he should delay to answer us for a long time; so when he delayeth not to answer us, the mercy is the greater, and ought
to be acknowledged in both respects : *blessed be God, which
hath not turned away my prayer.*   2. The gracious answer
of an upright supplication, evidenceth ready access prepared
yet more for the supplicant, to the fountain of God's mercy;
and this is more mercy still : *he hath not turned away my
prayer, nor his mercy from me.*

PSALM LXVII.

To the chief musician on Neginoth.   A psalm or song.

This psalm is a prophetical prayer for a blessing upon the church of the
Jews, for the good of the Gentiles and the enlargement of the kingdom of Christ among them.   The petition is propounded, v. 1, 2.   In
the next place, is an acclamation with the Gentiles, glorifying God at
their inbringing, now foreseen that it should come most certainly, v. 3, 4.
In the third place, the church of the Jews applaud the second time the
conversion of the Gentiles, and their praising God, promising to themselves, that by that means the increase of God's blessing on them shall
follow, and the enlarging of the kingdom of God through all the world,
v. 5—7.

1. *God be merciful unto us, and bless us ; and cause
his face to shine upon us.   Selah.*

2. *That thy way may be known upon earth, thy saving health among all nations.*

This is the blessing which the Lord commanded the children of Aaron to pronounce upon the people of Israel,
Numb. vi. 22, 23, which here the people turn into a prayer,
for the drawing in of the Gentiles unto God's service.
Whence learn, 1. It is safe to turn God's offers, promises,
and forms of blessing his people into prayers; we are sure
so to pray according to God's will, as the church doth here.

2. It is the duty of all citizens of the church, as lively members of that body, to' pray for the blessing of God upon all his people : *God be merciful unto us, and cause his face to shine upon us.* 3. Then are the Lord's people blessed, when God maketh them instrumental to enlarge his kingdom and to propagate the true religion, that is, the doctrine of man's salvation and God's service : and this should be the aim we shoot at in seeking any blessing to his people : *that the Lord may be known upon earth, his saving health among all nations.* 4. The world is ignorant of true religion, till God by his own instruments reveal it; and no way of religion will please God, or profit men, save God's way only, wherein he will have men to walk in the course of faith and obedience, and wherein he revealeth how he will deal with us, and how we must behave ourselves towards him; therefore say the godly, *that thy way may be known upon earth, thy saving health among all nations.*

3. *Let the people praise thee, O God ; let all the people praise thee.*

4. *O let the nations be glad, and sing for joy : for thou shalt judge the people righteously, and govern the nations upon earth. Selah.*

The psalmist foreseeth by the revelation of God's Spirit, that the Gentiles shall be converted, and shall rejoice in God and praise him, and therefore will have the church of the Jews to welcome them, and to join with them in acclamation of praise to God, because of Christ's reigning among them and ruling them by his most holy laws. Whence learn, 1. The manifestation of God's freely gifted salvation in Christ, and the revealing of his manner of dealing with people, and how he will have people to deal with him, and one with another, are matters of unspeakable praise to God and joy to men, to whom this grace is revealed : *that thy saving health may be known among all nations; let the people praise thee, O God.* 2. True converts unto Christ, besides the joy they have of their own salvation, have also daily new accession of joy at the conversion of others, as they come in; and ought to bless and praise God heartily with them, when they behold their conversion; *let all the people praise thee,* do they say twice, and hereafter also the third time. 3. The conversion of the Gentiles was a thing not only wished for by the church of the Jews, but also prophesied of unto them clearly : *O let the nations be glad, and sing for joy : for thou shalt judge the people righteously, &c.* 4. The Spirit which indited the psalms, did not degrade the promised Messiah Jesus Christ from his Godhead, for his future incarnation; but speaketh of him, and to him, as " God blessed for ever;" that is, the true God to the Jewish church before his coming : and true God to the converted Gentiles after his coming in the flesh, one with the Father and holy Spirit; for six times in this psalm he is called God, and acknowledged here to be the fountain of mercy, and blessing to men, and of manifested reconciliation with men; the object of all divine honour and praise, God the Lord and lawgiver of the converted Gentiles : *thou shalt judge the people righteously, and govern the nations upon earth.* 5. The doctrine and discipline of Christ, whereby he judgeth and governeth his church, is most holy and righteous, and in as far as particular churches and Christians submit themselves to his laws, doctrine, and government, they are his true subjects, and shall find the fruit of his governing and judging : *for these shall he judge righteously,* unto these shall he do the part of a governor, even on earth : *he shall govern the nations upon earth.*

5. *Let the people praise thee, O God ; let all the people praise thee.*

6. Then *shall the earth yield her increase ;* and *God,* even *our own God, shall bless us.*

7. *God shall bless us ; and all the ends of the earth shall fear him.*

In the last place, the Jewish church giveth a second acclamation to the incoming of the Gentiles, and promise to themselves by that means God's blessing more abundantly upon themselves, as now being one body with the Gentiles, in the same covenant of grace with them. Whence learn, 1. As the conversion of the Gentiles was esteemed by the Jews, a matter worthy to be oftener presented to God, and prayed for, and earnestly pursued by all that loved God; so was it foreseen to be a matter of growing and lasting joy to men, and growing and lasting praise to God, and to Christ, who is God, the converter of them, and the governor and teacher of them effectually, to know his name and salvation : *let all the people praise thee, O God, let all the people praise thee.* 2. The Spirit of God gave the church of the Jews to understand, that the conversion of the Gentiles, especially the conversion of the fulness of the Gentiles, (which here is prayed for, when he saith, *let all the people praise thee,)* was to be a means or a mercy antecedent unto, or nearly joined with, the bringing in and blessing of the Jewish church, and possibly in their own land : *then shall the earth yield her increase, and God even our own God shall bless us :* for, by the earth he meaneth the promised land of Canaan, which has been, and is accursed, during the time of their ejection out of it. 3. When God shall be gracious to the Jews, after the conversion and bringing in of the Gentiles, and shall renew the covenant with them in Christ, it shall fare the better with true religion, and with the Christian churches among the Gentiles; it shall be to them as a resurrection from the dead, in regard both of the purity of doctrine and worship, and the multiplication of persons converted unto Christ in all places; *God shall bless us,* saith he then; and what more? *And all the ends of the earth shall fear him.*

PSALM LXVIII.

To the chief musician.   A psalm or song of David.

This psalm is very suitable to that time when David, having gotten the victory over his enemies round about, assembled all Israel, and carried the ark of God, now returned from the land of the Philistines, triumphantly out of the house of Obed-Edom into the city of David, as a type of Christ's ascension after the work of redemption in the world. In which psalm, after the manner that Moses prayed to God, or to Christ who was to be incarnate, when the ark marched, David prayeth here, first, against the Lord's enemies, ver. 1, 2, and then for the Lord's people, ver. 3. In the next place, he exhorteth all the Lord's people to praise God, ver. 4, and giveth twelve or thirteen reasons for it ; first, because of his mercy to the desolate and afflicted, ver. 5, 6; secondly, because of his wonderfulness and terribleness in delivering his people out of bondage, as appeared in his bringing his people out of Egypt and through the wilderness, ver. 7, 8; thirdly, because of his fatherly care to entertain his redeemed people, as appeared in his nourishing his church in Canaan, ver. 9, 10; fourthly, because of the victories which he giveth usually to his people when their enemies invade them, ver. 11, 12; fifthly, because of the delivery which he will give to his people out of their most sad calamities, as he hath oftentimes given proof, ver. 13, 14 ; sixthly, because his church is the most glorious kingdom in the world, being compared therewith, ver. 15, 16; seventhly, because Christ, the king of the church, hath all the angels at his command to serve him ; and, having ended the work of redemption, was to ascend gloriously, for sending down gifts to his church and ruling it, ver. 17, 18;

eighthly, because of God's bounty to his people, in daily renewed mercies, till he perfect the work of their salvation, ver. 19, 20; ninthly, because of his avenging himself on all his enemies, ver. 21; tenthly, because God hath undertaken to work over again in effect, as need shall require, what he hath done in bringing his people out of Egypt, and in giving them victory over the Canaanites, ver. 22, 23, whereof the experience of his power, already manifested for Israel, was a proof and pledge sufficient, ver. 24—27; eleventhly, because it was decreed by God to establish his church and to make her strong by making kings become converts, ver. 28, 29; and that, partly by treading down some of her enemies, ver. 30, and partly by making others, even some of her greatest enemies, seek reconciliation with God, even her od, ver. 31: twelfthly, he exhorteth to praise God, because of his omnipotent power, in conversion of kingdoms, ready to be let forth for the defence of his people, ver. 31—34, and ready to overthrow their enemies, and all for the strengthening of his church; for all which he exhorteth all to bless the Lord, ver. 35.

1. *Let God arise, let his enemies be scattered: let them also that hate him flee before him.*

2. *As smoke is driven away,* so *drive* them *away: as wax melteth before the fire,* so *let the wicked perish at the presence of God.*

3. *But let the righteous be glad: let them rejoice before God; yea, let them exceedingly rejoice.*

In David's prayer against his enemies and for God's people, learn, 1. Such prayers as the Spirit hath indited unto the saints in Scripture, it is lawful and expedient, for strengthening our faith, to use the same or the like words in the like case; for David prayeth here, as Moses prayed at the marching of the ark, Numb. x. 35, *let God arise, &c.* 2. As the ark was amongst the Israelites, so is Christ amongst his people; and what ground of confidence the church had, because of that pledge of God's presence at the ark, we have the same, and a more sure ground of confidence in Christ's incarnation, represented thereby; that, upon every appearance of his beginning to stir against the enemies of his work, we may say, *let God arise.* 3. The enemies of the church are the enemies of God, and esteemed haters of him because they are haters of his people; with whom, albeit the Lord doth bear for a while, yet will he take order when he pleaseth; it will not cost him much labour: only *let God arise, and let his enemies be scattered.* 4. Although all the enemies of God make head against his people, yet will they not prevail; when God appeareth, they will turn back: *let them also that hate him flee before him.* 5. Whatsoever strength of forces or number the enemies of God's people have in appearance, it is nothing before God but like smoke before the wind and wax before the fire: *as smoke is driven away, as wax melteth before the fire, so let the wicked perish at the presence of God.*   6. Albeit the Lord exercise his people with affliction and with grief for a while, yet he alloweth unto them comfort and joy, whatsoever become of their enemies: *but let the righteous be glad.*   7. The only true matter of the saint's joy are God himself and his manifested presence, and he will not be pleased except his children lift up their hearts, and comfort themselves in him above and against all grief and sense of whatsoever enemies' opposition: *let them rejoice before God; yea, let them exceedingly rejoice.*

4. *Sing unto God, sing praises to his name: extol him that rideth upon the heavens by his name JAH, and rejoice before him.*

From his exhortation of the church to praise God with the joyful voice of singing, learn, 1. Vocal singing of praises unto God is a moral duty, and a part of his holy worship, frequently called for in Scripture: *sing unto God, sing praises to his name.*   2. Our thoughts of God should not be base, but high and heavenly, lifting his name up above the most glorious creatures, all they being but his servants, as he pleaseth to make use of them; *extol him that rideth upon the heavens.*   3. The Lord is only and properly worthy of praise, because he only hath his being of himself, and giveth being to all things which are beside himself: *his name is JAH.*   4. The Lord's praises are his people's advantage, and the true matter of their confidence and joy: *sing praises unto him, and rejoice before him.*

5. *A father of the fatherless, and a judge of the widows, is God in his holy habitation.*

6. *God setteth the solitary in families: he bringeth out those which are bound with chains; but the rebellious dwell in a dry* land.

From the first reason of the exhortation to praise God, learn, 1. The Lord's highness above the heavens hindereth him not from taking notice of the lowest of his poor people: yea, the most helpless and desolate among men are the first objects of his warmest love: *a father of the fatherless, and a judge of the widows, is God.*   2. Albeit the Lord be infinite and incomprehensible by any place, yet he hath appointed a trysting-place where his people shall find him by his own ordinance; to wit, the assembly of his saints, his holy temple, shadowing forth Christ to be incarnate, who now is in heaven, now is incarnate, and sitting at the right hand of God, in whom dwells the Godhead; here, here is God to be found: *God is in his holy habitation.* 3. It is the Lord's nature, pleasure, and ordinary practice, to make up the wants, and to change to the better the disconsolate condition of his own humbled and emptied children : *God setteth the solitary in families.* 4. The souls that are most sensible of bonds and bondage lie nearest the seeking of the fruit of his redemption; yea, none in bonds have made, or shall make, use of God the Redeemer, but his bonds and fetters, hindering him from freedom of God's service, and from attaining felicity, have been, and shall be, loosed off : *he bringeth out those which are bound in chains.* 5. Such as will not be ruled by his word, according as they are disloyal rebels to him, so shall they be dealt with as rebels; that is, they shall neither have God's blessing joined with any benefit which they seem to possess, nor any spiritual comfort in their afflictions when their calamity cometh upon them : *but the rebellious dwell in a dry land.*

7. *O God, when thou wentest forth before thy people, when thou didst march through the wilderness; Selah:*

8. *The earth shook, the heavens also dropped at the presence of God: even Sinai itself was moved at the presence of God, the God of Israel.*

From the second reason of praising God, learn, 1. It is expedient for our upstirring unto thankfulness, to cast our eye upon some particulars wherein the Lord's goodness to us, and our obligation to his love, may appear, as here the psalmist leadeth us by the hand unto the Lord's particular work of redemption of Israel out of Egypt. 2. That one work of the church's delivery out of Egypt, representing the redemption of his people from the misery of sin and Satan's bondage, is a sufficient proof for ever of the Lord's love, care, power, and faithfulness, to deliver his own out of all their misery; which the church, and every member thereof, should always make use of unto the end of the world : whether we look upon that work in the type singly, or as it is a representation or pledge of the spiritual delivery of his people, this work we should often look upon, and still hold it up unto God: *O God, when thou wentest forth before thy people, when thou didst march through the wilderness.* 3. In the works of the Lord it is needful not only to look upon that which may foster faith in God and love toward him, but also to set before us what may serve to keep our hearts in fear and awe of his dreadful majesty : *the earth shook, the heavens dropped at the presence of God; even Sinai itself was moved at the presence of God, the God of Israel.*

9. *Thou, O God, didst send a plentiful rain, whereby thou didst confirm thine inheritance, when it was weary.*

10. *Thy congregation hath dwelt therein : thou, O God, hast prepared of thy goodness for the poor.*

From the third reason of God's praise, learn, 1. The ordinary sustaining of God's people bodily and spiritually, in the possession of any benefit, temporal or spiritual, given unto them, should be observed, as well as the bestowing of any benefit in an extraordinary way, as here the ordinary sustaining of Israel in Canaan, is made a part of the song of praise, no less than their miraculous delivery out of Egypt: *thou, O Lord, didst send a plentiful rain, whereby thou didst confirm thine inheritance when it was weary.* 2. The people who are in covenant with God externally, are the Lord's own peculiar, more nearly and properly than any society in the world: therefore Israel here is called by the prophet speaking to God, *thy congregation.* 3. It is for the church's cause, that the land wherein his people dwelleth, is blessed at any time by God : *thy congregation hath dwelt in it.* 4. The blessing bestowed upon the church or the place wherein they dwell, is not given for any goodness in his people, but for the goodness, grace, and good-will of God to them : *thou, O God, hast prepared of thy goodness for the poor.*

11. *The Lord gave the word; great was the company of those that published* it.

12. *Kings of armies did flee apace ; and she that tarried at home divided the spoil.*

From the fourth reason of praise, learn, 1. The Lord

will sometimes exercise his church with wars, afflictions, and trials, when he intendeth not to punish them, but to give them the victory over their enemies, and that for his own glory, as in Joshua's time and David's, whereunto the text relateth. The matter of joyful news, or the word of the church's victory over her foes, whensoever it is, proceeds from the Lord, who furnisheth matter for, and words and utterance of, joy to his people and praise to himself : *the Lord gave the word.* 2. When God will glorify himself by comforting his church, he shall not want heralds of his praise : *great was the company of those that published it.* 3. Were the enemies of the church ever so powerful, and God's people ever so far inferior unto the enemies in power, yet shall the enemy not be able to stand, when God begins to fight for his people : *kings of armies did flee apace.* 4. It is easy for the Lord to make them a prey to the weakest of his people, who set themselves to make havoc of the church, yea and to enrich his people with the spoil of such adversaries : *she that tarried at home divided the spoil.*

13. *Though ye have lien among the pots,* yet shall ye be as *the wings of a dove covered with silver, and her feathers with yellow gold.*

14. *When the Almighty scattered kings in it, it was* white *as snow in Salmon.*

From the fifth reason of praise, learn, 1. As the Lord sometimes adorneth his people with victories and wealth : so also at other times for just reasons, he will darken all their outward glory, and make them look as blacked scullions in the kitchen : *though ye have lien among the pots, &c.* 2. The Lord after the trial and hard exercises of his people for a time, will give them so glorious an event and delivery, as shall take off all the ignominy of their former affliction, and make up all their losses; yea he will cause their formerly deforming afflictions, to serve for washing balls of soap, to make them so much the more beautiful : *though ye have lien among the pots, ye shall be as the wings of a dove covered with silver, and her feathers with yellow gold.* 3. Experiences of mercies shown to the Lord's people, are pledges and evidences of like mercies in time to come, as here, *when the Almighty scattered kings in the land, it was made white,* is made a proof of the promise made, v. 13.

4. As a dark, dusky mountain, whereupon groweth no green thing but black heath, is made white, when covered with snow : so is a disgraced, shamed, impoverished, enslaved land made glorious again by a merciful manner of delivery manifesting the Lord's kind respects unto it : *when the Almighty scattered kings in Judah, it was white as snow in Salmon.*

15. *The hill of God* is as *the hill of Bashan; an high hill,* as *the hill of Bashan.*

16. *Why leap ye, ye high hills?* this is *the hill* which *God desireth to dwell in ; yea, the Lord will dwell in it for ever.*

From the sixth reason of praise, learn, 1. The kingdoms of this world, especially some of more eminent sort, seem very rich and glorious in comparison of the outward appearance of the kingdom of Christ in his church, as the great, high, and fruitful hill of Bashan seemed to be more glorious, than the hill of Zion; yet, all things being compared, in special the spiritual privileges of the one, with the temporal privileges of the other, the church of God will outreach the most glorious kingdom on the earth : *the hill of God is as the hill of Bashan, an high hill as the hill of Bashan.* 2. Although the kingdoms of the world rejoice in their prerogatives, and despise the kingdom of Christ in his church, yet they have no cause to exalt themselves: *why leap ye, ye high hills?* 3. This is one privilege of the church, that it is the place of God's residence, wherein he will manifest himself familiarly and comfortably to his own, and may oversway all the excellency of all the kingdoms of the world : no kingdom which hath not God's church in it can say the like : *this is the hill which God desireth to dwell in, yea the Lord will dwell in it for ever.*

17. *The chariots of God are* twenty thousand, *even* thousands of angels: the Lord *is* among them, *as in Sinai, in the holy* place.

18. *Thou hast ascended on high, thou hast led captivity captive : thou hast received gifts for men ; yea, for the rebellious also, that the Lord God might dwell among them.*

From the seventh reason of praise, learn, 1. No king-

dom hath such defence, so potent and so numerous armies
to fight their battles, as the church hath : *the chariots of
God are twenty thousand, even thousands of angels.* 2. The
defence of angels is made fast to his church, and their power
made sure to be for her, because God is in his church, even
the Lord whom all angels serve and attend upon, is in his
church, as appeared at his giving of the law upon mount
Sinai : *the Lord is among them as in Sinai.* 3. The
Lord is no less terrible against his foes in Zion, than in Sinai; and whatsoever terror the Lord showed to his church
in Sinai against the violators of his law, he will manifest it
for the comfort and defence of his people, who heartily embrace his gospel : *the Lord is among them,* to wit, these
chariots and angels, *as in Sinai, so in the holy place.* 4.
The ark was not more gloriously conveyed from the house
of Obed-edom unto the city of David, than God,—that is,
Christ, who is God, who descended to assume human nature, that he might therein perfect the work of redemption,—
ascended gloriously into heaven, after the price of redemption was paid by him : *thou hast ascended on high,* Ephes. iv.
8—10. 5. The praises of God and joy of the church are perfected in Christ; no satisfaction in the shadows, till Christ the
substance be looked unto; therefore here the Lord's Spirit led
his people to look through the shadow of the ascending
of the ark toward the city of David, unto the ascending of
God incarnate, represented by the ark into heaven : *thou
hast ascended on high.* 6. Christ did not enter into his
glory without a battle going before, and that with strong
and many enemies : and in his fighting he carried the victory, and after his victory he triumphed, first in the cross
and then in his ascension, over sin, Satan, the world, hell,
grave, and all : *he led captivity captive.* 7. Christ as
mediator and king of his church, was fully furnished with
all things needful, for gathering his church, for edifying,
governing, and perfecting it : *thou hast received gifts for
men ;* even those gifts which the apostle speaketh of, for the
gathering and edifying of the body of the saints, Ephes. iv.
11, 13. 8. The gifts which Christ hath received and
given forth, are not for the Jews only, or Gentiles only,
for the poor only, or rich only; but for men indefinitely :
thou hast received gifts for men. 9. As he hath received
gifts for bringing on to life those that are reconciled; so al-

so to conquer, subdue, and bring in rebels, and to reconcile enemies : *thou hast received gifts for men, yea and for the rebellious also.* 10. The end of Christ's ascension, and receiving and sending down gifts among men, is to gather and preserve and establish unto God a church in the world, wherein he may make himself manifest, and dwell and rule in the midst of his enemies : *thou hast received gifts for men, that the Lord might dwell among them.* 11. Yea, whatsoever gifts are bestowed upon unregenerate men within the visible church, or without it, which may any way be serviceable to the church, they are all bestowed on them in favour of the church, that God may dwell in his visible church, which by those gifts is edified : *thou hast received gifts for men, yea for the rebellious also, that the Lord God might dwell among them.*

19. *Blessed* be *the Lord,* who *daily loadeth us* with benefits, *even the God of our salvation. Selah.*

20. He that is *our God* is *the God of salvation; and unto God the Lord* belong *the issues from death.*

From the eighth reason of praise, learn, 1. Where the Lord will be merciful, he will be merciful, and not weary in doing good to his people in a current course of bounty; the observation whereof should stir up our hearts to thankfulness : *blessed be the Lord, who daily loadeth us with benefits.* 2. The favours and benefits which God bestoweth upon his people, come in greater number and measure unto them, than they are able to acknowledge, make use of, or be thankful for; and so, in a sort, burden the feelings of the truly godly : *blessed be God, who daily loadeth us with benefits.* 3. As all benefits flow unto God's children from the covenanted kindness of God, for giving unto them eternal salvation; so should all benefits confirm their faith in the covenant, and lead them to the hope of receiving after all other benefits, salvation also : *blessed be the Lord, who daily loadeth us with benefits, even the God of our salvation.* 4. Albeit the covenant of salvation be sure and solid in itself, yet are we slow to believe it, and weak in our laying hold of it; and have need to have the stamp and impression of it set deep upon our hearts, as here the psalmist teacheth the church by inculcating this point : *he that is our God, is the God of salvation.* 5. Temporal things which men idolize, may serve a man in this life; but at death, in death, and after death, he can have no good by them. It is God only who can deliver from death, and give an issue out of it : *unto God the Lord belong the issues from death.* 6. Let a man be once settled in the faith of his salvation, then he shall be comforted against all the troubles and dangers wherein he can fall, yea even against death itself ; if he can say, *he that is our God, is the God of salvation,* he may also say with confidence, and application to himself, and comfort, *unto God the Lord belong the issues from death.*

21. *But God shall wound the head of his enemies, and the hairy scalp of such an one as goeth on still in his trespasses.*

From the ninth reason of God's praise, learn, 1. How great soever be the majesty of God, and the riches of bounty and grace offered in Christ, yet will men be found even within the visible church, who will wickedly refuse his grace, and oppose his kingdom, but all to their own shame and damage : *but God shall wound the head of his enemies.* 2. The character of God's irreconcilable enemies is, that they cease not to follow the course of sin : *he goeth on still in his trespasses.* 3. Though God spare his enemies long, and suffer them to grow old in the course of enmity against him, yet shall shameful, sudden, and irrecoverable judgments overtake them in their old days : *but God shall wound the hoary scalp of such a one as goeth on still in his trespasses.*

22. *The Lord said, I will bring again from Bashan; I will bring* my people *again from the depths of the sea :*

23. *That thy foot may be dipped in the blood of thine enemies,* and *the tongue of thy dogs in the same.*

From the tenth reason of praise, wherein the prophet promiseth in the Lord's name, that God shall work over again such works of delivery to his people, and such works of victory over their enemies as he had wrought before, learn, 1. The Lord's word is certainly sufficient for performance of his promises, and ground of comfort, and confidence, and thanksgiving, and praise to God even before the work be wrought : *the Lord said, I will bring again, &c.* 2. As the Lord will have the memory of former dangers and deliveries of his church kept in remembrance for his

own glory; so will he have former dangers for his people's
good to be looked upon as advertisements of what straits his
church may be cast into, and his former merciful deliveries
looked upon as pledges of the promises of like mercies in
time to come, as need shall require : *I will bring again from
Bashan, I will bring my people again from the depths of the
sea,* importeth thus much.   3. As the Lord will give as
great deliverances to his church when they are in straits, as
ever he did before; so will he give as terrible blows to the
adversaries as ever he did, according as the church's need
or good shall require : *I will bring again from Bashan, &c.,
that thy foot may be dipped in the blood of thine enemies.* 4. Albeit neither the Lord nor his people delight in bloodshed, yet
will he let his people and all men see, in the bloodshed of
their enemies, how terrible he is in justice, especially against
the enemies of his church, and how dear his people are to
him, and that, rather than they should be overthrown, he
will destroy nations for their safety, and give unto his people, in their own defence against their oppressors, notable
victories : *so that thy foot may be dipped in the blood of thine
enemies.*   5. When the Lord thinks it fit not to make his
own people instrumental in their own delivery, then can he
yoke the enemies among themselves, or raise up profane
dogs like themselves, to avenge the quarrel of the Lord's
people upon their enemies : *that the tongue of thy dogs may
be dipped in the same ;* that is, in the blood of thine enemies.

24. *They have seen thy goings, O God ;* even *the
goings of my God, my King, in the sanctuary.*

25. *The singers went before, the players on instruments* followed *after ; among* them were *the damsels
playing with timbrels.*

To confirm what is promised, he bringeth forth old experiences acknowledged by the enemies, registered in the
word of the Lord, and read in the temple.   Whence learn,
1. The Lord useth to work so evidently for his people, and
against his enemies, that both his people and their enemies
are made witnesses, and are forced to acknowledge the Lord's
work : *they have seen thy goings, O God.* 2. It is the glory
of a people, when God so worketh, as he is seen to be their
God, their leader, their defender, and all as in covenant with
them : *they have seen thy goings, O God, even the goings of*

my God, saith he. 3. That God's honour may be seen, man's honour should be laid down at his feet: and supposing a man were the greatest king, yet is it greater glory and matter of contentment to have God for his king, than to be a king without God : *they have seen thy goings, O my God, my King,* saith David, now settled in the kingdom. 4. The most clear, sure, and profitable sight of the Lord's work and ways, is to be had in the use of public ordinances, where his name, nature, covenant, and course he keepeth with all men, together with the causes, use, and ends of his works, are to be seen : *they have seen the goings of my God in the sanctuary.* 5. Where all the people receive a benefit, it becometh all the people publicly and solemnly, and with their best expression of affection, as God appointeth, to praise God, and in his worship to see that all things may be done orderly, as Israel did, when they came through the Red Sea, and at other times as the Lord gave occasion : *the singers went before, the players on instruments followed after; amongst them,* in the middle ward, *the damsels playing with timbrels.* 6. All the powers of our souls and bodies should concur, each of them in its own order, with the best harmony of knowledge, affections, and expressions which can be attained, for setting forth the Lord's praises, and our obligation to him for his goodness to his people: and so should we march on all the days of our pilgrimage and warfare, till we come to the promised rest; for this the external ceremonies used under the pedagogy of the law, taught; which ceremonies, although they be abolished now, yet the substance and intended duties pointed at in them, being moral, still remain : *the singers went before, players on instruments followed after, &c.*

26. *Bless ye God in the congregations,* even *the Lord, from the fountain of Israel.*

27. *There* is *little Benjamin* with *their ruler, the princes of Judah* and *their council, the princes of Zebulun,* and *the princes of Naphtali.*

As the psalmist cleared the doctrine of God's dealing for his church, and against their enemies, by experiences of old; so he points here at experience later, as was to be seen by all, at the glorious triumphing of Israel over all their enemies, when they were now assembled in their several tribes,

the least as well as the greatest, the most remote tribes, as
well as those that were nearest hand; all of them conveying
the ark of God unto the city of David, which was the type
of Christ, God incarnate, ascending after his victories into
heaven. Whence learn, 1. The mercies of God to his people, in special the great work of redemption, and victory
over all enemies obtained by Christ in favour of his people,
are abundant matter and cause to praise God, and to bless
him in all the assemblies of the church: for here it is a commanded duty : *bless ye God in the congregation.* 2. Whatsoever be the part of others in discharging this duty, it is
expected most at the hands of every kindly Israelite, who
draws his original from the fountain of Israel, whether he
be of the natural stock of Jacob, descended of him, as water
out of a fountain, or have his descent of the same Spirit of
regeneration with him : *bless ye God, even the Lord, from
the fountain of Israel.* 3. Examples and practices of God's
children at any time, are the encouragements of his people
at all times thereafter : *there is little Benjamin with their
ruler, &c.,* set forth here for example. 4. The piety of governors, and their precedency before, or joining with, others
in the Lord's service, are more honourable unto them than
their places of dignity, or their gifts of wisdom and power :
*there were the princes of Judah with their council, the
princes of Zebulun, and the princes of Naphtali.* 5. In the
exercise of God's worship, and in spiritual privileges, the
Lord joineth the smallest with the greatest, the lowest with
the highest, that the lowest may glory in their exaltation,
and the highest in their humiliation : *there was little Benjamin with Judah, the people with their princes and rulers.*

28. *Thy God hath commanded thy strength: strength-
en, O God, that which thou hast wrought for us.*

29. *Because of thy temple at Jerusalem shall kings
bring presents unto thee.*

From the eleventh reason of God's praise, learn, 1. Not
in kings, or rulers, or any thing else, but in the Lord, and
from the Lord, is the strength of his church, which she may
expect always to be furnished with by virtue of the covenant : *thy God hath commanded thy strength,* said David to
the church. 2. As the Lord hath decreed to establish his
church, so hath he means and instruments in every age and

place prepared for this purpose, and hath given out order by actual providence, which is always going about the work in all ages : *thy God hath commanded thy strength.* 3. The Lord's decree, and the order given forth to accomplish it, consist well with the church's using all lawful means to further that end, and in special should be joined with thankful acknowledging of what the Lord hath begun to do, or done already for it, and with earnest prayer for accomplishing what is to be further done; so teach David's example and prayer here : *strengthen, O God, that which thou hast wrought for us.* 4. The Lord's known presence in his church, maintaining and blessing his public ordinances, shall move kings at last to do homage to God incarnate, that is, to Christ represented by his dwelling in the temple of Jerusalem : *because of thy temple at Jerusalem shall kings bring presents unto thee.*

30. *Rebuke the company of spearmen, the multitude of the bulls, with the calves of the people,* till every one *submit himself with pieces of silver : scatter thou the people* that *delight in war.*

31. *Princes shall come out of Egypt ; Ethiopia shall soon stretch out her hands unto God.*

How this shall come to pass he showeth; to wit, partly by breaking the power of some of them, when they make opposition, and partly by the powerful conversion of others. Whence learn, 1. It is not against the precept of love to pray against public enemies of the church, when private spleen is not the motive, but zeal for the glory of God : *rebuke the company of spearmen.* 2. The leaders of armies, parties, and factions against God's church and cause, and the followers of such leaders, are all of them a company of beasts: *rebuke the multitude of the bulls, with the calves of the people.* 3. God is adversary to all who oppose his people and his cause in their hand, and can as easily repulse them really and overturn them, as reprove them verbally : *rebuke the spearmen, &c.* 4. The end of the church's prayer against her enemies, is, that God may be glorified, and people at least brought to outward obedience unto God, which may be a means to real conversion in God's time : *rebuke them, &c., till every one submit himself with pieces of silver ;* that is, till they offer to contribute to God's service. 5. The punishing of some of God's enemies may be a means to move others to offer obedience and submit to God, when people that delight in war are scattered: *for princes shall come out of Egypt.* 6. God will draw into subjection unto himself some of his most open and inveterate enemies : *princes shall come out of Egypt, Ethiopia shall soon stretch out her hands unto thee.*

32. *Sing unto God, ye kingdoms of the earth; O sing praises unto the Lord; Selah:*

33. *To him that rideth upon the heavens of heavens,* which were *of old; lo, he doth send out his voice, and* that *a mighty voice.*

34. *Ascribe ye strength unto God: his excellency* is *over Israel, and his strength* is *in the clouds.*

35. *O God,* thou art *terrible out of thy holy places: the God of Israel* is *he that giveth strength and power unto* his *people.   Blessed* be *God.*

From the last reason of praising God, taken from his almighty power in the conversion of kingdoms of Gentiles, ready to be put forth for the preservation of his church gathered and for the overthrow of his enemies, learn, 1. The time shall come when the kingdoms of the earth shall turn Christians in profession, in a greater measure than yet hath been seen; for, *sing unto God, ye kingdoms of the earth,* is not a simple telling of their duty, but a prophecy of their joyful joining in the worship of God, and that they shall have cause of joy within themselves to praise him: *O sing praises unto the Lord.* 2. True converts will renounce idols and false gods, and reverently worship the omnipotent Creator and Governor of heaven, the eternal God: *sing praises to God that rideth upon the heavens of heavens, that were of old.* 3. As the glorious government of heaven showeth the Lord's power; so the thunder also showeth his power and terror, the consideration whereof is needful to dispose our stupid minds to praise him: *lo, he doth send out his voice, even a mighty voice.* 4. The right use of God's great, and sensible, and daily seen works, is to cause us to glorify the power of God, who is able to work whatsoever he pleaseth: *ascribe strength unto the Lord.* 5. The Lord's glory in his church is more excellent than all that is to be seen in the works of creation: *his excellency is over Israel.* 6. The true worshipper must study the power and all other properties of God, both by what he hears in the society of the church, and by what he seeth in his visible works; as well daily transient works, such as the clouds are, as constantly enduring works, such as the heavens are: *his excellency is over Israel, and his strength is in the clouds.* And surely it is no small power which beareth up such weight of mountains of snow and seas of water, and maketh them sail, as it were, and fly with wings in the air, God dissolving them by little and little, as we daily behold. 7. Wheresoever God showeth his presence, whether in heaven, or in his church, in any place of the earth, there and from thence he showeth himself a dreadful God to such as fear him not : *O God, thou art terrible out of thy holy places.* 8. Albeit there were no man to hear us glorify God, or no man to take his praise off our hand, we should acknowledge his greatness in our heart, and before himself, who will take true worship off our hand; for David here turneth his speech to God in the end of the psalm, saying to him, *O God, thou art terrible out of thy holy places.* 9. The Lord hath an everlasting interest in the people of Israel, and they in him, for the election's cause ; and every true Israelite hath an everlasting interest in God : he is *the God of Israel.* 10. What the Lord hath is forthcoming to his people's support, as they have need : *the God of Israel is he that giveth power and strength to his people.* 11. It is reason that at all the several remembrances of God's mercy to us, we should acknowledge his blessedness and his blessing of us, and this is all we can do, and that also we cannot do, except he strengthen and enable us for praise; for, *blessed be God,* saith the prophet, for this very reason, after he hath spoken of his giving *power to his people.*

PSALM LXIX.

To the chief musician upon Shoshannim. A psalm of David.

David, as a type of Christ, earnestly dealeth with God for a delivery from his perplexed condition, and from the malice of his adversaries, and findeth a comfortable event. There are three parts of the psalm. In the first part is his prayer, six times presented, and strengthened with new reasons, to ver. 22; in the second, is his imprecation of ten plagues against his enemies, with some reasons added, showing the justice of inflicting the plagues, mentioned ver. 29; in the third, are four evidences of his victory, from ver. 29 to the end. In all which, whatsoever is proper to the type, is to be referred to the type only ; and whatsoever

is fit also to be applied unto Christ, the antitype, must be referred to
him only in that sense which is suitable to his majesty.
His prayer, at first, is propounded in few words: *save me.* The reasons
are four. The first is, from the danger he was in, ver. 1, 2; the next,
from his long and patient waiting for an answer to his prayer, ver. 3;
the third, from the multitude, and malice, and iniquity of his enemies,
ver. 4; the fourth is by way of attestation of God, that he was innocent
of that whereof he was charged by his enemies, joined in with his humble
acknowledging of whatsoever other sins justice could charge upon him
in any other respect, ver. 5.

1. *Save me, O God; for the waters are come in unto*
my *soul.*

2. *I sink in deep mire, where* there is *no standing ;*
I am come into deep waters, where the floods overflow
me.

His first petition is to be saved, and the first reason of it
is because of the danger he was in. Whence learn, 1. A
child of God may, in his own sense, be very near to perishing, and yet must not, in the most desperate condition, cease
to pray, nor cease to hope for delivery prayed for : *save me,*
O God. 2. With danger of bodily death a child of God may
have in his spirit a sore conflict with the sense of wrath, like
to swallow up his soul, as deep waters do a drowning man : *the*
waters are come in unto my soul. 3. The condition of a soul
exercised with the sense of wrath threateneth no less than perdition, certain, inevitable, without any outgate, and endless,
whereof the bodily danger of a drowning man is but a shadow: *I sink in deep mire, where there is no standing: I*
am come into deep waters, where the floods overflow me.

3. *I am weary of my crying; my throat is dried:*
mine eyes fail while I wait for my God.

The second reason of the first petition is, because he had
long and patiently waited on God. Whence learn, 1. Faith
in hard exercises ceaseth not for appearances of perdition,
knowing that what is impossible in man's sight, is not impossible to God; for David, as a believer and a type of Christ,
prayeth still for all this, although he find no delivery : *I am*
weary of my crying. 2. Prayer put up in faith to God
keepeth in life, and is like a man's drawing breath in the
water, when the head is lifted up above the floods; for here,
although the floods overflowed the psalmist, yet he is able
to show this to God, and to cry till he be *weary of crying.*
3. For exercising faith and making patience to have her

perfect work, it is no strange thing for God to delay relief
unto an earnest supplicant till he be like to give over, till
his case seem desperate and his relief hopeless : *mine eyes
fail while I wait for my God.*   4. Though the flesh of the
regenerate man be weak, yet the spirit is ready, and will
never give over calling on God, depending on him, holding
fast the covenant and the hope of deliverance; for the spirit
will make this a new ground of speech unto God that it is
not able to speak any thing, and a new ground of laying
hold on God and hoping for help from him, because its hope
is failing, as here: *I am weary of my crying, my throat is
dried ; mine eyes fail while I wait for my God.*

4. *They that hate me without a cause are more than
the hairs of mine head: they that would destroy me,*
being *mine enemies wrongfully, are mighty; then I restored* that *which I took not away.*

The third reason of the first petition is, because his enemies were many, mighty, and malicious.   Whence learn, 1.
Holiness and integrity cannot ward off the enmity of a wicked
world; for the enemies of David, who was a well-deserving
man, and Christ, (whose type he was,) much more beneficial
to men, had foes innumerable : *they that hate me without
cause are more than the hairs of my head.*   2. Albeit many
aggravate their own grief foolishly, when they suffer hurt
of them whom they did not injure or provoke; yet the conscience of harmless men toward such as wish harm to them,
is a great support of their confidence when they are inju-
riously dealt with : *they hate me without a cause.*   3. It is
no strange matter to see truly godly men to be out of credit
and affection with men who are in power and authority in
the world: *they that would destroy me, being mine enemies
wrongfully, are mighty.*   4. He that is most just may be
troubled and hated without a cause, and may be dealt with
as a thief, being verily an honest man : *then I restored that
which I took not away.*

5. *O God, thou knowest my foolishness ; and my sins
are not hid from thee.*

The fourth reason of the first petition is, because God
was witness to his disposition and carriage.   Whence learn,
When we are condemned of men unjustly we have God to
appeal to; and although there may be sins upon us in our

private reckoning with God, yet, being free of what men lay to our charge, we may appeal to God in the controversy betwixt our enemies and us, and when we have acknowledged what sins are in reckoning betwixt God and us, our supplication to God shall not be cast back for our sins; for this is the force of the psalmist's reasoning, for the strengthening of his own faith in prayer, saying, *O God, thou knowest my foolishness, and my sins are not hid from thee;* that is, whether I be so foolish and injurious to my persecutors as they say or not, thou, Lord, knowest; and, whatsoever other sins may be imputed unto me upon any other score, I refuse not to reckon for them, but I am free, thou knowest, of what I am charged with. This is applicable also in some sort unto Christ, who was most free of what men laid to his charge, although in another reckoning all the iniquities of the elect were charged upon him by imputation, according to his transaction with the Father about our debt.

6. *Let not them that wait on thee, O Lord God of hosts, be ashamed for my sake; let not those that seek thee be confounded for my sake, O God of Israel.*

The second petition is, that the godly may not be hurt by his manner of exercise, which he strengthens by four reasons. First, because his sufferings were for God's cause, v. 7; secondly, because he was cast off by his friends, v. 8; thirdly, because he laid God's honour deeply to heart, v. 9; fourthly, because his holy and religious carriage was mocked, and, both by high and low, by honourable and base rascals, he was opposed and persecuted, v. 10—12.

From the second petition, learn, 1. The property of the godly is to seek communion with God, and patiently to attend his answer for the time, manner, and measure of it; for they are here described: *they that wait on thee, O Lord, those that seek thee.* 2. When one of God's children is persecuted for righteousness, all the rest are waiting to see the event, and it cannot but be a great dash to them to see the righteous lie under, or a good cause lie long oppressed; which inconvenience we should request the Lord to prevent: *let not them that wait on thee be ashamed; let not those that seek thee be confounded.* 3. It is a kindly mark and property of a godly person to be a lover of the good of all God's children, and to be careful that no cause or occasion of stumbling be furnished unto them by him : *let them not be ashamed for my sake ; let them not be confounded for my sake.* 4. Faith sets its eyes in prayer upon those titles of God which serve most for its purpose, as here the psalmist hath to do with enemies—*O Lord God of hosts* will do his turn against them: he is praying for the good of God's children, and, *O God of Israel,* speaketh to that point.

7. *Because for thy sake I have borne reproach; shame hath covered my face.*

The first reason of the second petition is, because his sufferings were for God's cause. Whence learn, 1. Though suffering for God's cause in maintenance of his truth, be a glorious sort of suffering, wherein a man may go unto God confidently; yet it may be accompanied with shame from men of this world, and the godly for a time may be so delayed in point of relief, that they know not what to say to their scorners, but may be forced to hang the head for a while : *for thy cause I have borne reproach.* 2. He that suffers shame for God's cause, shall neither have cause at length to be ashamed of his suffering, nor shall any other have cause to be ashamed for him : *let them not be confounded for my sake, because for thy sake I have borne reproach.*

8. *I am become a stranger unto my brethren, and an alien unto my mother's children.*

The second reason of the second petition is, because his friends had cast him off. Whence learn, 1. In affliction for God's cause friends will more readily forsake a sufferer, than in his affliction for a civil cause : *I am become a stranger to my brethren.* 2. The power of religion in the godly, is stronger than the bonds of blood with their kinsmen, and it will make them cleave to God, when their kindred cast them off : *I am an alien unto my mother's children.*

9. *For the zeal of thine house hath eaten me up ; and the reproaches of them that reproached thee are fallen upon me.*

The third reason of the second petition is, because he was deeply affected with the dishonour done to God. Whence learn, 1. It is not enough to love God, and his ordinances and kingdom, and his people's good; but it is required also that we be zealous here : *the zeal of thine house hath eaten me up.* 2. Spiritual affections and passions will no less affect

and trouble the body, than natural affections and passions : *the zeal of thine house hath eaten me up.* 3. Injuries done to God and religion, and to the godly, should affect us no less nearly, and be laid to heart, than injuries personally concerning us : *the reproaches of them that reproached thee, have fallen upon me.*

10. *When I wept,* and chastened *my soul with fasting, that was to my reproach.*

11. *I made sackcloth also my garment ; and I became a proverb to them.*

12. *They that sit in the gate speak against me ; and I* was *the song of the drunkards.*

The fourth reason of the second petition, is, because he was greatly mocked of all sorts for his holy carriage. Whence learn, 1. True zeal is ruled by knowledge, joined with humility in the man's self, and tempered with love to men, even toward persecutors; such was David's zeal: but Christ's zeal was perfectly such : *I wept and chastened my soul.* 2. Fasting in earnest is not so much the abstinence from meat, as it is the afflicting of the soul : *when I chastened my soul with fasting.* 3. The godly behaviour of the righteous is subject to horrible misconstruction; yet must they not desist from duties for all this : *fasting was to my reproach ; I made sackcloth also my garment, and I became a proverb to them.* 4. It is a sore affliction to the godly to be condemned by magistrates and judges, and yet the truly religious, even Christ and his followers, were, and are, subject to this exercise : *they that sit in the gate* (or in the courts of justice, which were erected at the entry of the parts of cities) *do speak against me.* 5. Righteousness and truth are not the worse for their being condemned by civil judges; God will not disclaim his own cause for that, but will hear such complaints as this is in this case : *they that sit in the gate speak against me.* 6. When magistrates discountenance true religion, then it becometh a matter of derision to rascals, and to every base villain without controlment, and a table-talk to every tippler : *I was a song of the drunkards.* 7. The shame of the cross is more grievous than the rest of the trouble of it. This is the fourth time that the shame of the cross is presented unto God, in these last four verses ; *I was a song of the drunkards* after complaining of his being reproached, and *being made a proverb.*

13. *But as for me, my prayer is unto thee, O Lord, in an acceptable time: O God, in the multitude of thy mercy hear me, in the truth of thy salvation.*

This is the third petition for deliverance, or for granting his prayer, or the third time he presenteth it; whereunto he addeth reasons taken from the time of presenting it, the multitude of God's mercies, and the truth of his promises, or covenant of salvation. Whence learn, 1. The best way to bear out the persecution of the mighty and the mockery of the base multitude, is to be frequent in prayer to God for our part: *but as for me, my prayer is unto thee, O Lord.* 2. So long as God offereth a gracious ear to supplicants, a man may be confident that petitions of grace shall have ready access and answer: *my prayer is unto thee in an acceptable time.* 3. The largeness of God's mercy is a sufficient encouragement for the afflicted to come and take the benefit thereof: *in the multitude of thy mercies hear thou me.* 4. When, besides the mercifulness of God, we have also his covenant and promise of salvation, we may upon these two pillars lean and roll over, and rest our faith: *hear me in the truth of thy salvation.*

14. *Deliver me out of the mire, and let me not sink: let me be delivered from them that hate me, and out of the deep waters.*

15. *Let not the water-flood overflow me, neither let the deep swallow me up, and let not the pit shut her mouth upon me.*

The fourth petition for delivery, or fourth time he presenteth it, whereunto he addeth reasons taken from the danger he was in. Whence learn, 1. Faith useth to correct the expressions of sense; and as faith gathereth strength, a man's condition groweth clearer: it was the expression of sense, v. 2, *I sink in deep mire*, and here the fear is something lessened, because faith is something more cleared: *deliver me out of the mire, let me not sink.* 2. The man that loveth truth better than worldly prosperity, and maketh the Lord his refuge, shall not faint under persecution, but shall be borne through all troubles, and delivered: *let me be delivered from them that hate me, and out of the deep waters.* 3. Faith in God giveth hope to be helped, and is half a delivery, before the full delivery come; for the psalmist is now with his head above the water, and not so afraid as when he began the psalm; for here he saith, *let not the water-floods overflow me, neither let the deep swallow me up.* 4. As the sense of danger sharpens prayer, so the greatness of it is a ground of hope, that the evil which is feared shall not prevail over us; for albeit the Lord suffer the danger to be great, yet will he not leave us in a case desperate : *let not the pit shut her mouth upon me.*

16. *Hear me, O Lord ; for thy loving-kindness is good : turn unto me according to the multitude of thy tender mercies.*

17. *And hide not thy face from thy servant ; for I am in trouble : hear me speedily.*

The fifth petition for delivery, or fifth time he presenteth it, whereunto he addeth reasons taken from the multitude of God's mercies, consciousness of his uprightness, and the greatness of his trouble. Whence learn, 1. Albeit God should give no answer for a time, faith will still press for an answer, for it knoweth it hath to do with the hearer of prayer : *hear me,* said he before and here over again, *hear me, O Lord.* 2. Faith seeth what is in God's heart, whatsoever it findeth or misseth in his hand; it fastens on love, and draweth hope and love from that : *hear me, for thy loving-kindness is good.* 3. Though a believing soul find itself deserted of God in some respects; yet, while it holds fast on his merciful nature, it may be sure to meet with a change of dispensation more comfortable : *turn unto me according to the multitude of thy tender mercies.* 4. When a believer is persecuted by man for righteousness, and friends and families turn their backs upon him; it is not strange that God, for the man's trial, should seem to hide his countenance from him also; which trial the believer counteth more heavy than all the rest, and can be content to want all the creature's kindness so he may find the Lord's kindness; for he cannot endure long to want God's presence : *hide not thy face from thy servant.* 5. The conscience of endeavour to serve God, giveth hope of comfort in time of trouble, and not so much the sooner, if the trouble be great, and perdition apparently near : *hide not thy face from thy servant, for I am in trouble, hear me speedily.* 6. An upright servant, albeit he be troubled for God's cause, and miss comfort from God, yet will he not change his master, nor despair of his favour :

hide not thy face from thy servant, for I am in trouble. 7. It is no limitation of God, to press his hasting to help, when trouble presseth us so sore, as we seem near to perish, if he speedily prevent not : *hear me speedily.*

18. *Draw nigh unto my soul,* and *redeem it : deliver me, because of mine enemies.*

19. *Thou hast known my reproach, and my shame, and my dishonour : mine adversaries* are *all before thee.*

20. *Reproach hath broken my heart, and I am full of heaviness : and I looked* for some *to take pity, but* there was *none ; and for comforters, but I found none.*

21. *They gave me also gall for my meat ; and in my thirst they gave me vinegar to drink.*

In the sixth petition, or sixth time, he prayeth for obtaining delivery, whereunto he addeth reasons taken from the inhumanity and cruelty of his enemies, and desertion of his friends, and want of comfort from all men. Whence learn, 1. As straits serve to drive the godly nearer and nearer to God ; so they serve to prepare men for a renewed sense of communion with God, or for God's sensible drawing nearer to them : *draw nigh unto my soul,* saith he. 2. A new manifestation of God's love to a soul, is present relief and delivery, whatsoever be the trouble : *draw nigh to my soul, and redeem me.* 3. In the delivery of God's children from the hand of persecutors, the Lord looketh, not only to the necessity of his children, but also to the insolent pride of the enemies, in case they should prevail : *deliver me, because of mine enemies.* 4. The consideration of God's being witness to all the sufferings of the saints, is a ground of patience under trouble, and of hope to be delivered : *thou hast known my reproach, and my shame, and my dishonour : mine adversaries are all before thee.* 5. Before a believer once entered into sufferings, and put upon his trials, be delivered, he shall be made very sensible of the weight of trouble, especially of reproaches, and of his own weakness to bear the burden of the cross alone : *reproach hath broken my heart, and I am full of heaviness.* 6. As a persecuted saint may possibly be deprived of all common comfort, pity, and help from men ; so the less his comfort is on earth, he may look for the more and readier comfort from God : *I looked for some to take pity, and there was none ; and for comforters, but I found none.*　7. As the wicked are ready to add affliction to affliction unto the godly, so must the godly ever look for it : yea, they must not think it strange to find the means of natural life, and ordinary refreshments of the body, made bitter to them by persecution : *they gave me gall for my meat ;* that is, they made my natural refreshments tasteless, yea and bitter to me : they gave me cause of grief, instead of comforting me.　8. As all the sufferings of the saints are but shadows of the sufferings of Christ : so are they all mitigated and sanctified in the sufferings of Christ, upon whom all the sufferings mentioned in this psalm, it was foretold, should fall, for expiation of the sin, and sanctifying the crosses of all his followers : *in my thirst they gave me vinegar to drink,* was a prophecy of Christ's suffering on the cross.

22. *Let their table become a snare before them : and* that which should have been *for* their *welfare,* let it become *a trap.*

23. *Let their eyes be darkened, that they see not ; and make their loins continually to shake.*

24. *Pour out thine indignation upon them, and let thy wrathful anger take hold of them.*

25. *Let their habitation be desolate,* and *let none dwell in their tents.*

This is the second part of the psalm; wherein the prophet, as a type of Christ, by way of imprecation against his malicious enemies, prophesieth of the vengeance of God against all obstinate adversaries, and malicious persecutors of him, whether in his own person or in his members; and denounceth ten plagues, or effects of God's wrath, to come upon them for their wickedness.　The first whereof is this, God shall curse all the comforts of this life unto the obstinate adversaries of Christ, and of his followers : all these comforts shall serve to harden their hearts in sin, and lengthen their life therein, till they fill up the measure of their iniquities : *let their table become a snare before them.*　The second plague is, all the means appointed for men's conversion and salvation shall turn for the aggravating of their sin and just damnation : and as all things work together for the good of those that love God, so shall all things work for the woe and torment of God's enemies : *that which should have*

been for their welfare, let it become a trap. The third plague
is, they shall not perceive the true intent of God's work,
nor consider the day of their visitation : *let their eyes be
darkened, that they see not.* The fourth plague is, there
shall be no peace to the wicked, but as even in laughter
their heart shall be sorrowful; so also their conscience for
fear shall never dare to abide the light of the Lord's word,
to be examined by it; and even in their greatest prosperity
they shall have perpetual secret fear, smother it as they
will : *make their loins continually to shake.* The fifth
plague is, the threatened wrath of God shall be fully executed against them, and never depart from them when it is
once poured out : *pour out thy indignation on them, and
let thy wrathful anger take hold of them.* The sixth plague
is, the curse of God shall be on their houses and posterity,
and the place they have dwelt in shall be abhorred : *let their
habitation be desolate, and let none dwell in their tents.*

26. *For they persecute* him *whom thou hast smitten ;
and they talk to the grief of those whom thou hast
wounded.*

He giveth a reason of those fearful imprecations on
Christ's adversaries, because they were cruel in their persecution of him and of the godly, even in the time of their
affliction, otherwise sent by God. Whence learn, 1. It
consisteth well with the love of God to his children, (even
his only begotten Son Jesus Christ not being excepted,) to
exercise them with sad calamities, for bringing to pass the
work of man's redemption by Christ, and for perfecting the
sanctification and salvation of the redeemed by Christ; of
all of whom now and then it may be said to God, *thou hast
smitten him, and they are those whom thou hast wounded.*
2. Whatsoever may be the reason of the Lord's smiting and
wounding his own children, yet their wicked enemies have
no just reason to malign them, or to trouble them, and
therefore their troubling of God's children is persecution :
they persecute him whom thou hast smitten. 3. The very
talking and venting of ill speeches, to the prejudice of
Christ's cause and truth, and true holiness in his saints, especially when they are under sufferings and afflictions whatsoever, is a high provocation of God's wrath : *they talk to
the grief of those whom thou hast wounded.* 4. The persecution of God's children for righteousness, is a sufficient

ditty for all the forenamed damnation in the preceding verses: this is the reason of the justice of the imprecation : *for they persecute him whom thou hast smitten.* 5. Without breach of duty to men, the church may sing and rejoice in these fearful imprecations against the malicious enemies of Christ and his church; first, as lovers of God more than of men : secondly, as followers, not of their own quarrel, but of the controversy of the Lord of hosts, whose soldiers they are against all his enemies whatsoever : thirdly, as subscribers to the justice of God, who will not suffer malicious cruelty to be unpunished : and fourthly, as rejoicers in God's love to his people, who owns the wrongs done to his church and servants therein, as done to himself, and will be avenged upon their adversaries; and having decreed doom against the adversaries of his church, will have his children to be ministers under the great Judge, to pronounce the sentence against his and their enemies, and, as it were, to give out order for execution of the sentence, saying, *let their table, let their eyes, let their habitation be so and so disposed of.*

27. *Add iniquity unto their iniquity ; and let them not come into thy righteousness.*

28. *Let them be blotted out of the book of the living, and not be written with the righteous.*

The seventh plague of the enemies of Christ and his church, is this : howsoever ignorant zealots, some of them may find mercy; yet malicious persecutors of truth and piety grow worse and worse, and, being entered into the course of persecution, cannot go off, but draw deeper and deeper in guiltiness, and that in God's righteous judgment, punishing sin by sin : they *add iniquity unto their iniquity.* The eighth plague is, they are given over to a reprobate mind, so as they cannot lay their own sins to heart, and cannot therefore see the necessity of the remission of sin, nor put a price upon the purchase of justification unto sinners by Christ the redeemer, nor be found among the persons justified by faith in him : *let them not come into thy righteousness.* The ninth plague is this : albeit the enemies of Christ and his people may pretend to be among the number of his friends, and to have their names written in great letters, in the catalogue of the visible church, yet God shall disclaim them one day as none of his, and thrust them

15

from him as workers of iniquity : *let them be blotted out of the book of the living.* The tenth plague is this: as the visible church hath an open book, wherein all within the external covenant are written, as saints by calling, and co-venanters with God for life and salvation, out of which book God dashes the names of his wicked enemies; so God hath a secret book and roll, as it were, wherein he enrolleth all the regenerate, all the justified; and among the names of this sort or among the names of the true members of the invisible church of the regenerate, none of the names of Christ's malicious enemies shall be written : *let them not be written with the righteous.*

29. *But I* am *poor and sorrowful: let thy salvation, O God, set me up on high.*

The third and last part of the psalm, wherein is set down the glorious event of this sad exercise in four evidences of victory of his faith over this assault. The first whereof is in his confident prayer, not only to be delivered, but also to be exalted, v. 29. The second evidence is, in his hearty promise of thanksgiving, v. 30, 31. The third evidence is in a prophecy of the fruit of this exercise which the believers shall have by it, v. 32, 33. . The fourth is a thanksgiving for mercies foreseen, which shall come to the church, and in special to the church of Israel, v. 34—36. All which, in as far as they concern David the type, are but little in comparison of Christ the antitype. From the first evidence of the victory of his faith, appearing in his confident prayer, learn, 1. It is no strange thing to see poverty of spirit and sad afflictions joined, the one to help and season the other : *but I am poor and sorrowful.* 2. There is as sure ground of hope of deliverance out of every trouble wherein the children of God can fall, as there is ground of hope of the overturning of the most settled worldly prosperity of their enemies; for the forenamed curses shall come on the enemies of the godly, but the child of God in the mean time may expect salvation, and to be set on high, which he confidently prayeth for : *but I am poor and sorrowful, let thy salvation, O God, set me up.* 3. The conscience of humiliation under God's hand, is a great evidence of delivery out of whatsoever trouble; if a man in a righteous cause be emptied of self-conceit and carnal confidence,

and brought down to poverty of spirit, and affected with
the sense of sin and misery following upon it, and withal
go to God in this condition, he may be sure to be helped;
the poor in spirit are freed from the curse : *but I am poor
and sorrowful*, saith the psalmist here, *let thy salvation set
me up on high.* 4. The man afflicted and persecuted for
righteousness, humbled in himself, and drawn to God for
relief, shall not only be delivered, but also shall be as much
exalted after his delivery, as ever he was cast down : *let thy
salvation, O God, set me up on high.* 5. The kindly sufferer of righteousness, will have no deliverance, but such
as God will allow him, as God shall bring unto him; and as
he looketh not for delivery another way, so he looketh for
a glorious delivery this way; *let thy salvation, O God, set
me up on high.*

30. *I will praise the name of God with a song, and
will magnify him with thanksgiving.*

31. This *also shall please the Lord better than an
ox* or *bullock that hath horns and hoofs.*

From the second evidence of the victory of David's faith
in his promised thanksgiving learn, 1. When the Lord
comforts the heart of a sufferer for his cause, he can make
him glad before the delivery come, by giving him the assurance that it shall come; and can engage his heart to solemn
thanksgiving in the midst of trouble; for poverty of spirit
will esteem the far foresight of delivery at last, as a rich
mercy, and matter of a song : *I will praise the name of
God, with a song.* 2. The Lord in the delivering of his
children out of their troubles, will give evidence of his
greatness, as well as of his goodness, of his power as well as
of his mercy to them, that he may have the more glory and
thanks for his work : *I will magnify him with thanksgiving.* 3. Moral worship offered in spirit and truth, in the
meanest degree of sincerity, is more acceptable to God than
the most pompous ceremonial service, which can be done to
him without spirit and truth : *this also shall please the Lord
better than an ox or bullock, that hath horns and hoofs :*
that is, which is perfect and wanteth nothing in the external part of commanded service. 4. What we know shall
be most acceptable to God, we ought to study and follow
most, that we may walk before God unto all well-pleasing,

in special to praise him in affliction, and to praise him from a contrite spirit : *this also shall please the Lord better than, &c.*

32. *The humble shall see* this, and *be glad: and your heart shall live that seek God.*

33. *For the Lord heareth the poor, and despiseth not his prisoners.*

From the third evidence of the victory of David's faith, in the prophecy of the fruits of his sufferings, mainly, as he was a type of Christ, who here is most intended, learn, 1. The trial of the saints set down in Scripture, also the trial of David and of Christ represented by him, were foretold, that they would be of great use to the church of God in after-times, as now we see in effect : *the humble shall see this, and be glad.* 2. The humble soul is most capable of divine knowledge and comfort : *the humble shall see this.* 3. The escape of our Lord Jesus out of his sufferings for us, and the escape of his afflicted children out of their sufferings through faith in him, is a matter of instruction, comfort, and joy to every humbled believer : *the humble shall see this, and be glad.* 4. As those who are pure in spirit and truly humbled, live upon God's alms, and are daily at his doors for relief of their necessities, and for communion with his gracious goodness ; so shall they thrive well in this trade : *your heart shall live that seek God.* 5. The Lord's children have a life beyond the children of men, which is able to quicken them in their deepest troubles, and to make them blessed in their delivery out of troubles; a life moral and spiritual, whereby their conscience is comforted : *your heart shall live that seek God.* 6. The right way for the godly afflicted to have the benefit of the troubles and events which Christ and his followers have had experience of, is to comfort themselves in hope of the like event and success in seeking God as they did : *the humble shall see this and be glad, and your heart shall live that seek God.* 7. As the Lord's poor men are much in prayer, so shall they be rich in good answers : *for the Lord heareth the poor.* 8. Whoever, in defence of any point of God's truth, are put to trouble, either in body or mind, by men, or Satan, or both, are all sufferers for God; they are all prisoners who, howsoever they may be misregarded by men, shall be of much price in God's eyes : *he despiseth not his prisoners.*

34. *Let the heaven and earth praise him, the seas, and every thing that moveth therein :*

35. *For God will save Zion, and will build the cities of Judah; that they may dwell there, and have it in possession.*

36. *The seed also of his servants shall inherit it ; and they that love his name shall dwell therein.*

From the last evidence of the victory of faith, set down in a prophetical thanksgiving for the foreseen mercies which were to come to the church by Christ's procurement, and specially to the Jews, learn, 1. Large sense of troubles maketh way for large observation, and a corresponding sense of mercies. The evil of the deepest afflictions the Lord can recompense with highest consolation, as the beginning and ending of this psalm giveth evidence. 2. The soul that seeth the mercy of God toward itself, seeth also the mercy of God upon the same grounds to all others his people in Zion, his church in every place and time; seeth the benefits of Christ's sufferings to be matter of praise unto God, able to fill the whole world; seeth its own insufficiency for praising God also, and that all the creatures are few enough, when they all concur in this song : *let the heaven and the earth praise him, and the seas and every thing that moveth therein.* 3. Whatsoever condition of God's people can be represented by the various condition, motion, settlement, or commotion of heaven, earth, and seas, and things therein, cannot but furnish matter of joyful praise to God, and come up to contribute to God's praises : *let the heaven and earth, the seas, and every thing that moveth therein, praise him.* 4. Every delivery of every believer, and above all the delivery of Christ as man from his expiatory sufferings, are earnests and pledges of the delivery of the church militant out of all its troubles : *for God will save Zion,* saith the psalmist, being now delivered out of his trouble. 5. As the Lord will ever maintain his church, his Zion and his Judah, so hath he a purpose to give a special evidence of this his care among the Jews, how far soever they may sometimes be from all appearance of his respect to them; for in the promise he keepeth expressly the name of Judah : *he will build the cities of Judah.* 6. What outward testimonies of God's respect to the Jews for Christ's sake shall be given unto them, after the destruction of their cities here presupposed, we must leave to God, to be in due time by his own works interpreted, and to be made out according to what here is said : *that the cities of Judah shall be builded, that they may dwell there and have it* (to wit, the promised land) *in possession, the seed also of his servants shall inherit it, and they that love his name shall dwell therein.* Only let us observe, that the duty of the true citizens of the church is, to transmit true religion to their posterity, and that this is the best and only way to transmit also the blessing of God, and the constant possession thereof unto them : *the seed also of his servants shall inherit it, and they that love his name. &c.*

PSALM LXX.

To the chief musician. A psalm of David, to bring to remembrance.

This psalm is almost one in words with the latter end of psalm xl. wherein David, being in present danger of his life by his enemies, prayeth, first, for speedy delivery, v. 1 ; next, for shameful disappointment to his enemies, v. 2, 3 ; and thirdly, for a comfortable life to all the godly, v. 4 ; from which condition albeit he himself was very far for the present, yet he professeth he relieth on God by faith, and prayeth for a timous delivery, v. 5.

From the inscription, learn, 1. Our most notable dangers and deliveries should most carefully be observed and remembered, and made use of : *this is a psalm to bring to remembrance.* 2. What hard condition we have been in before, we may fall into the like again; and the same gracious means we have used before, in seeking our relief of God, we should use again; and what words of prayer we have used before, we may use again, without any either needless affectation of other words, or superstitious tying of ourselves to the same words, as the example of David teacheth us, when we compare the end of the xl. psalm with this psalm.

1. Make haste, *O God, to deliver me ; make haste to help me, O Lord.*

From the first petition, learn, 1. Though death, or danger of it, were never so near, God can come quickly and prevent it; and prayer is a swift messenger, which in the twinkling of an eye can go and return with an answer from heaven, as this abrupt beginning of his prayer teacheth us : *O Lord, to deliver me.* These words, *make haste,* are not expressed in the original: for the haste was so great as he could not express it till he drew his breath. 2. As we have need of help, God will make haste unto our help: *make haste to help me, O Lord.*

2. *Let them be ashamed and confounded that seek after my soul: let them be turned backward, and put to confusion, that desire my hurt.*
3. *Let them be turned back for a reward of their shame that say, Aha, aha!*

From the second petition, learn, 1. The more that the enemies of God's people promise to themselves certainly to destroy such of the saints as they pitch upon, when their plot shall be ripe and fixed, when God disappointeth them they are the more confounded and ashamed: *let them be ashamed and confounded that seek after my soul*, or my life. 2. All the enemies of God's children, shall at last think shame of their injuries done to them, and evils which they have wished to them: to wit, when they shall know whose children they are, and what interest God hath in them; then at last shall they flee and hide themselves for shame: *let them be turned backward, and put to confusion, that desire my hurt.* 3. The damage of the godly is the delight of the wicked; and an enemy to the godly, is he that laughs and scorns at the misery of the godly: *they say*, when they see them in trouble, *Aha, aha.* 4. Albeit what shame the wicked put upon the godly for righteousness, or for their sufferings for righteousness, is not the shame of the godly, but the shame of the enemies, who do what they can to expose the godly to shame; yet shall the enemies have shame still more for their pains, and the terrible wrath of God shall chase them out of God's presence: *let them be turned back for a reward of their shame that say, Aha, aha!*

4. *Let all those that seek thee rejoice and be glad in thee: and let such as love thy salvation say continually, Let God be magnified.*

From the third petition, learn, 1. Whatsoever be our own hard condition at any time, we should seek the welfare and prosperity of the rest of God's children, and it is the property of each of the godly in their trouble, to wish all the rest to be partakers of the blessedness which their own souls seek after, but not to be like to them in trouble or bonds : *let all those that seek thee rejoice and be glad in thee.* 2. If one of the godly be delivered out of his troubles, all the rest, who prayed for the delivery should rejoice in God also as for a benefit given to themselves : *let all those that seek thee, rejoice and be glad in thee.* 3. The godly do not desire deliverance to themselves or their fellows except in God's way, in a cleanly and holy way : and the more of God that is seen in the delivery of his servants, the more are they glad in the Lord : *they are those that love God's salvation.* 4. It is a most suitable service for the saints, to be always praising God : *let those that love thy salvation, say continually, The Lord be magnified.*

5. *But I* am *poor and needy ; make haste unto me, O God : thou* art *my help and my deliverer : O Lord make no tarrying.*

From the fifth petition, learn, 1. Albeit we be not in such a condition, as we wish all the godly men were in, yet let us lay out that condition before a pitiful God, and submit ourselves to him in the condition wherein we are : *but I am poor and needy.* 2. The sense of a hard condition, is a preparation and a ground of hope to be brought out of it to a better : *I am poor and needy, make haste unto me, O God.* 3. Whatsoever dispensation we shall meet with, we should hold fast the claim of faith, and of our interest in God : *thou art my help, and my deliverer.* 4. Having settled our dependence upon God, we may, without being mistaken by God, speak all our desires to him; and, having done so, should leave our supplication and case at his feet with confidence : *O Lord, make no tarrying.*

PSALM LXXI.

This psalm is a prayer of David in his old age, requesting delivery from the conspiracy of Absalom, wherein he wrestleth with the Lord by fervent supplication, in seven petitions, all tending to this purpose, that he may be delivered, to v. 14; and, from v. 14 to the end, we have his confidence to be delivered set forth in four evidences thereof. Absalom is not named here, nor is the particular case set down, otherwise than in general expressions, that so it may serve the better for the larger use of the church of God, and of the particular members thereof in their afflictions.

1. *In thee, O Lord, do I put my trust ; let me never be put to confusion.*

The first petition is general, wherein he professeth his

confidence in God, and prayeth that he be not put to confusion. Whence learn, 1. As long as a child of God liveth
in the world, he must look for new afflictions, as here the
experience of the psalmist tossed in his old age, warneth us.
2. Look how many new troubles befall God's servants; so
many new messengers are sent of God to call them to him:
so many new errands are furnished unto them; so many new
petitions are put into their mouth; and so many pressing necessities are sent to make them earnest in their supplication, and frugal in making use of their interest in God by
faith, as here and elsewhere appeareth. 3. He that cometh
to God must believe in him, and fasten his faith on God,
and avow it, how weak soever he find it to be: *in thee, O
Lord, do I put my trust.* 4. Albeit such as believe in God,
may have many temptations to mistrust God, and great
fears that they shall be disappointed of their hopes, and for
a time may seem to be disappointed and put to confusion, yet
it shall not be for ever; if they do not take shame unto them
by distrust, they shall never have cause to be ashamed : *let
me never be put to confusion.*

2. *Deliver me in thy righteousness, and cause me to
escape ; incline thine ear unto me, and save me.*

The second petition is more special for safety and delivery
from his enemies. Whence learn, 1. The righteousness of
God is a pledge to the godly that their lawful petitions shall
be granted, and especially when they seek delivery from their
ungodly adversaries : *deliver me in thy righteousness, and
cause me to escape.* 2. When the Lord giveth a heart to a
believer to pray, he will also grant him audience and a good
answer: *incline thine ear unto me, and save me.*

3. *Be thou my strong habitation, whereunto I may
continually resort : thou hast given commandment to save
me ; for thou* art *my rock and my fortress.*

The third petition is, that the Lord would show himself
to him in effect, what he hath engaged himself to be unto
believers according to the covenant. Whence learn, 1.
What the Lord is to his people by covenant, he will be to
them the same effectually and in deed, as their need shall
require, and as they shall employ him : *be thou my strong
habitation.* 2. The goodness of God covenanted to his
people, is not for one good turn, but for every good which

they need; not for one day, but for daily use-making, and constant enjoying of it : *be thou my strong habitation, whereunto continually I may resort.* 3. As the Lord hath all second causes, all creatures at his command, being Lord of hosts, to execute whatever he giveth order to be done; so hath he really set his active providence on work, to accomplish what he hath covenanted to every believer : *thou hast given commandment to save me, for thou art my rock nd fortress :* he giveth his believing in God who is his rock, as a reason of his saying, that God was about to save him.

4. *Deliver me, O my God, out of the hand of the wicked ; out of the hand of the unrighteous and cruel man.*

5. *For thou art my hope, O Lord God :* thou art *my trust from my youth.*

6. *By thee have I been holden up from the womb : thou art he that took me out of my mother's bowels : my praise* shall be *continually of thee.*

The fourth petition for delivery is strengthened by reasons taken from the wickedness of the enemy, v. 4 ; from his own confidence in God, v. 5; and from his own experience of God's kindness unto him in time past, v. 6. Whence learn, 1. It is a great advantage to be a confederate with God, when we have to deal with his enemies and ours in any debate : *deliver me O God*, saith he, *out of the hand of the wicked.* 2. The integrity of the believer in a good cause, and the iniquity of his adversaries in their ill cause, are good tokens of the believer's victory over them : *deliver me out of the hand of the unrighteous and cruel man.* 3. Confidence in God avowed against all temptations in God's presence, and specially when it is of long standing, is so strong an argument of being heard in a lawful petition, that it may persuade the believer he shall speed : *deliver me, for thou art my hope, O Lord God, thou art my trust from my youth.* 4. True thankfulness will not pass by common benefits, and true faith will read special love in common and ordinary favours, and make use thereof among other experiences for strengthening faith : *by thee have I been holden up from the womb, thou art he that took me out of my mother's bowels.* 5. The forming of us in the belly, and the common benefit of birth and bringing forth quick into the world, is a smothered wonder, and so glorious a work of God, that he deserveth perpetual praise from us for that one work : *thou art he that took me out of my mother's belly.*

7. *I am as a wonder unto many : but thou* art *my strong refuge.*

8. *Let my mouth be filled* with *thy praise* and with *thy honour all the day.*

The fifth petition is strengthened by reasons taken from his hard condition, and from the opportunity of God's having glory by his delivery out of it. Whence learn, 1. The exercise of the Lord's children is sometimes so strange to the beholder, as the world wondereth at them : *I am as a wonder unto many.* 2. Knowledge of God's word and ways, and faith in his name, make a believer not think strange, whatsoever fiery trial come upon him, but to rest on God's will, whatsoever befall him; *I am as a wonder unto many, but thou art my strong refuge ;* for faith judgeth not of itself, as the world judgeth, but as God hath judged and spoken of it in his word. 3. The more strange the exercise of the godly be, the more glorious is the Lord's upholding of them in it, and delivering of them out of it; and, for the hope of the glory which shall redound to God by such exercises, the hardship should be the more patiently borne, and the delivery sought and expected more confidently, that it shall come when it may be most for God's praise : *I am a wonder unto many, let my mouth be filled with thy praise, and with thy honour all the day.*

9. *Cast me not off in the time of old age : forsake me not when my strength faileth.*

10. *For mine enemies speak against me ; and they that lay wait for my soul take counsel together,*

11. *Saying, God hath forsaken him : persecute and take him ; for* there is *none to deliver* him.

The sixth petition is strengthened with reasons taken from his own old age and weakness, and from his enemies' malice. Whence learn, 1. Such as have been the Lord's servants in their youth, may be sure to find God a good and kind master to them in their old age : *cast me not off in the time of old age.* 2. Infirmities in God's children shall not move loathing and casting off, but pitying and cherishing them, that they may be supported in their weakness : *forsake me not when my strength faileth.*   3. The world conceiveth that God casteth off his children, when he bringeth them under any sad calamity, and by this means think that they have not to do with God's children when they persecute his dearest servants; yea and they encourage themselves to persecute them the more that God afflicteth them : *mine enemies speak against me, and they that lay wait for my soul take counsel together, saying, God hath forsaken him, persecute and take him, for there is none to deliver him.*   4. The misconstructions of the world, their plots and conspiracies against the godly, their evil speeches of them, their resolved cruelty to undo them, are so many arguments of good hope that God shall deliver them : *forsake me not, for mine enemies speak against me, &c.*

12. *O God, be not far from me : O my God, make haste for my help.*

13. *Let them be confounded* and *consumed that are adversaries to my soul ; let them be covered* with *reproach and dishonour that seek my hurt.*

The seventh petition for delivery and disappointing of his enemies, is strengthened by reasons taken from the covenant between God and him, and from the glory which God shall have by shaming his enemies.   Whence learn, 1. When temptations are most, dangers greatest, and the assault is strongest, then the believer draweth nearest unto God, and holdeth him most closely : *O God be not far from me, &c.* 2. Relying upon and avowing of the covenant between God and the soul of a believer is able to bear the greatest stress whereunto temptations and troubles can drive him : *O my God, make haste for my help.*   3. God, for the glory of his justice against the wicked, and the glory of his grace to his own, shall pour confusion, consumption, reproach, and dishonour upon persecutors of righteousness, and adversaries of his suffering servants : *let them be confounded and consumed, that are adversaries to my soul ; let them be covered with reproach and dishonour that seek my hurt.*

14. *But I will hope continually, and will yet praise thee more and more.*

15. *My mouth shall shew forth thy righteousness* and

thy salvation all the day; for I know not the numbers
thereof.

16. *I will go in the strength of the Lord God : I will*
make mention of thy righteousness, even *of thine only.*

In the latter part of the psalm is the psalmist's confidence
to be delivered set forth in four evidences thereof.   The first
is his resolution to persevere in hope to be helped, and in
praising God and relying only on the Lord's power and
righteousness, and not on his own strength.   Whence learn,
1. He that is resolved to persevere in hope, may be sure of
a gracious deliverance out of his trouble : *but I will hope*
continually.   2. Resolute hope comforteth, enlargeth, and
stirreth up the heart unto more and more praising and
thanksgiving: *I will hope continually, and I will yet praise*
thee more and more.   3. The matter of the continual praise
of God, is partly his righteousness, whereby he keepeth his
promise, not only according to, but also above condition, and
giveth also remission of sins, which deserved wrath; and
partly his deliverances, which he giveth to his children, out
of danger of body and soul : *my mouth shall show forth thy*
righteousness, and thy salvatior all the day ; for I know not
the numbers thereof.   4. Because in troubles a man's own
strength will fail him, and fail him also in commanded duties, therefore the believer must renounce confidence in his
own ability in both cases, and lean on the support of God :
I will go in the strength of the Lord God.   5. Because the
conscience of sins and sinfulness still stareth the believer in
the face, and all to discourage him; the believer must renounce all confidence in his own holiness, and rely upor the
imputed righteousness of Christ only, which is called the
righteousness of God by faith, being witnessed unto both by
the law and the prophets, Rom. iii. 21.   *I will make mention*
of thy righteousness, even of thine only ; for, in the point
of justification and absolving of us from sin, this righteousness of God only hath place.

17. *O God, thou hast taught me from my youth : and*
hitherto have I declared thy wondrous works.

18. *Now also, when I am old and gray-headed, O*
God, forsake me not, until I have shewed thy strength
unto this *generation,* and *thy power to every one* that is
to come.

The second evidence of the prophet's confidence to be delivered, is the experience of God's kindness for time past,
making him, with comfortable assurance of being heard, to
pray for the continuance of that same kindness for time
to come. Whence learn, 1. We are all of us ignorant of
God and his ways, till he teach us by his word, and by his
Spirit, and by his giving to us experimental knowledge
thereof : *O God, thou hast taught me from my youth.* 2. The
consciousness of sincere endeavour to make use of God's
gifts to us for the glory of God, and edification of others,
according to our place, is very sweet and comfortable in the
day of trouble, and giveth much encouragement in approaching to God : *hitherto have I declared thy wondrous works.*
3. He that hath had long experience of God's mercy to himself, and thankfully acknowledgeth the same, may assure
himself that the course of God's kindness to him shall not be
broken off : *O God, thou hast taught me from my youth, now
also when I am old and gray-headed, forsake me not, O Lord.*
4. It is a noble design for a man who hath received gifts,
whereby he may glorify God and edify his people, to destin-
ate all the days he hath to live, to serve his own generation
and their posterity, in communicating to them what he
knoweth of the Lord's all-sufficiency, and not to love to live
in this world, except for this end : *forsake me not until I have
shewed thy strength to this generation, and thy power to every
one that is to come.*

19. *Thy righteousness also, O God, is very high,
who hast done great things : O God, who is like unto
thee ?*

20. Thou, *which hast shewed me great and sore
troubles, shalt quicken me again, and shalt bring me up
again from the depths of the earth.*

21. *Thou shalt increase my greatness, and comfort
me on every side.*

The third evidence of his confidence to be delivered, is his
looking to the unsearchable fountain of God's wisdom, faithfulness, and omnipotency, and his expecting from this well-
spring, that as large consolation shall come forth to him, as
he hath had a large measure of troubles. Whence learn,
1. Albeit the effects of God's wisdom, faithfulness, and omnipotence, be near to us and fall under our sense in his daily

operations; yet the fountain thereof, which is God's own perfection, is unsearchable, incomprehensible, and incomparably great : *thy righteousness, O God, is very high, who hast done great things : O God, who is like unto thee?* 2. That which we see of the Lord's works, may lead us up to know what is not seen in relation to difficulties and power of men, and to see what he is able to do; and when we see the invisible God, we cannot but admire his majesty, and exalt him as sovereign over all; and then, and not till then, that we give him the honour of omnipotence and faithfulness, can the heart rest and be quiet: *thy righteousness, O God, is very high, who hast done great things : who is like to thee?* 3. He that acknowledgeth God's justice and wisdom in his troubles, may look to see God's power and grace no less evident in his delivery and consolation : and he who in trouble hath seen his own infirmity, emptiness, and death, may look to see God's power and life in raising him out of the grave of his trouble : *thou which hast showed me great and sore troubles, shalt quicken me again ; and shalt bring me up again from the depths of the earth.* 4. As trouble humbleth and abaseth a man before the world : so the Lord's delivering of him, and showing his respect to him, honour the man again, and exalt him before men : *thou shalt increase my greatness.* 5. As no trouble cometh alone, but multitudes of troubles joined together, when the Lord will humble and try a man; so no comfort cometh single or alone, when the Lord will change the man's exercise, but a multitude of comforts joined together : *thou wilt comfort me on every side.* 6. Losses are made lighter, and comforts weightier, when God is seen and acknowledged in them : *thou which hast showed me sore troubles,* (it is but a view of trouble what we have felt, when troubles are seen to come from God's hand,) *thou shalt increase my greatness, and comfort me on every side.*

22. *I will also praise thee with the psaltery,* even *thy truth, O my God : unto thee will I sing with the harp, O thou Holy One of Israel.*

23. *My lips shall greatly rejoice when I sing unto thee ; and my soul, which thou hast redeemed.*

24. *My tongue also shall talk of thy righteousness*

all the day long : for they are confounded, for they are brought unto shame, that seek my hurt.

The fourth and last evidence of his confidence, is his promise of joyful thanksgiving, by way of a begun song, and that for the foresight of his own delivery, and of his enemies' overthrow. Whence learn, 1. Faith is so satisfied with God's promise, that it can praise heartily for what is promised, before it find performance ? *I will praise thee with the psaltery, even thy truth.* 2. It is our interest in the covenant, which makes us have interest in particular promises : *I will praise thy truth, O my God.* 3. A soul sensible of God's kindness, and by faith sure of the performance of his faithful promises, cannot satisfy itself in praising God, it hath so high estimation of his fidelity, power, and love : therefore, after he hath said, *I will praise thee,* he addeth, *unto thee will I sing with the harp.* 4. How hardly soever a soul hath been exercised with troubles for a while, so soon as it seeth by faith the Lord's prepared event, it will regard all the passages of God's providence, as just and wise and good, and in a word, as holy in all respects : *to thee will I sing, O holy One of Israel.* 5. Singing with our voice unto the Lord, is a part of moral worship, as well as prayer with the voice, when his honour, and our upstirring, and others' edifying call for it : *my lips shall greatly rejoice when I sing unto thee.* 6. As the work of praising God requireth sincerity, earnestness, and cheerfulness; so the work thus done, becometh not only honourable to God, but also refreshful to the worshipper: *my lips shall greatly rejoice when I sing unto thee.* 7. Dangers and distresses, how grievous soever they be for the time, yet furnish matter of praise to God, and joy to the party troubled afterward when the delivery cometh : *my lips shall rejoice, and my soul which thou hast redeemed.* 8. Beside, singing of psalms unto God, speaking of his praise in all companies and upon all occasions, are parts of our bounden duty of thankfulness for making his word good to us in the overthrow of our enemies and delivering us : *my tongue also shall talk of thy righteousness all the day long.* 9. The overthrow of the enemies of the godly is as certain to come, as if we saw it with our eyes already come to pass. The same word of God, the same light and persuasion of spirit, manifest the delivery of the godly, and the destruction of their enemies : *for they are confounded, for they are brought to shame, that seek my hurt.*

PSALM LXXII.

A psalm for Solomon.

In this psalm, under the shadow of king Solomon's reign, Christ's gracious government is praised. And, first, the church is taught to pray for a blessing on king David and his son's government, including Christ's, v. 1. Next, the answer is given by the Spirit of the Lord in a prophecy of the blessedness of the reign and kingdom of Christ the Son of David, from v. 2 to v. 18. Thirdly, the use hereof is set down in thanksgiving unto God, v. 18, 19; and herein is the accomplishment of all the desires of David, obtained by this satisfactory answer, v. 20.

From the inscription and prayer, learn, A king may command within his kingdom many things, but he cannot command a blessing on his own government; he must make suit for this to God. He may leave a kingdom to his child; but because a kingdom is nothing without God's blessing, he must pray for this blessing, and seek the assistance of the prayers of the church for this intent: and this duty kings may crave of the church, and God's people should not refuse it; *a psalm for Solomon.*

1. *Give the king thy judgments, O God, and thy righteousness unto the king's son.*

From the prayer of the church, learn, 1. Gifts from God are necessary to fit a man for an office; and it is not every gift which maketh fit for a particular office, but such gifts specially as are for the discharge of the place a man hath, and those must be asked from, and granted by God, and by this means sanctified: *give the king thy judgments, O God.* 2. Nothing is more conducible to make a king's government prosperous and blessed than equity and justice, according to the revealed will of God : *give the king thy judgments, and thy righteousness unto the king's son.*

2. *He shall judge thy people with righteousness, and thy poor with judgment.*

3. *The mountains shall bring peace to the people, and the little hills, by righteousness.*

4. *He shall judge the poor of the people, he shall save the children of the needy, and shall break in pieces the oppressor.*

5. *They shall fear thee as long as the sun and moon endure, throughout all generations.*

6. *He shall come down like rain upon the mown grass; as showers that water the earth.*

7. *In his days shall the righteous flourish; and abundance of peace so long as the moon endureth.*

8. *He shall have dominion also from sea to sea, and from the river unto the ends of the earth.*

9. *They that dwell in the wilderness shall bow before him; and his enemies shall lick the dust.*

10. *The kings of Tarshish and of the isles shall bring presents: the kings of Sheba and Seba shall offer gifts.*

11. *Yea, all kings shall fall down before him; all nations shall serve him.*

12. *For he shall deliver the needy when he crieth; the poor also, and* him *that hath no helper.*

13. *He shall spare the poor and needy, and shall save the souls of the needy.*

14. *He shall redeem their soul from deceit and violence: and precious shall their blood be in his sight.*

15. *And he shall live, and to him shall be given of the gold of Sheba: prayer also shall be made for him continually; and daily shall he be praised.*

16. *There shall be an handful of corn in the earth upon the top of the mountains; the fruit thereof shall shake like Lebanon: and* they *of the city shall flourish like grass of the earth.*

17. *His name shall endure for ever: his name shall be continued as long as the sun; and* men *shall be blessed in him: all nations shall call him blessed.*

The prophetical answer given here to the church's prayer promiseth above twenty benefits of Christ's government, all of them tending to the glory of the king and good of the subjects; the shadow whereof was to be seen in David and Solomon's reigns, joined with many imperfections, but the real accomplishment is only in Christ. The first is, Christ's subjects shall have good rules how to carry themselves in all duties, how to behave themselves righteously, and how to be made righteous, by his direction and conduct: *he shall judge thy people with righteousness.* The second benefit of commendation is, Christ will see the necessities of his subjects, his humble ones, his afflicted ones, to be supplied most discreetly, and the wrongs done unto them repaired : *he shall judge thy poor with judgment,* v. 3. The third benefit is, Christ is not to take away civil governors' or potentates' places, nor the several orders and ranks of greatness of superior and inferior powers, rulers, and judges; all these are to be fixed rather by him for the good of the people : the superior as *mountains,* and the inferior as *little hills,* shall stand in their places for him. The fourth benefit is, Christ shall make such magistrates as embrace him for their Lord and Governor, a blessing to the people under them; for, by their righteous government the people shall live quiet and safe in God's service under them : *the mountains shall bring peace to the people, and the little hills;* but how shall the mountains and little hills do this ? *by righteousness,* v. 4. The fifth benefit is, albeit Christ suffer his subjects to be brought low, in the sense of their own weakness, and in danger of being swallowed up by their persecutors, yet shall he take their controversy to his cognition, and deliver his people out of the hands of their adversaries : *he shall judge the poor of the people; he shall save the children of the needy; he shall break in pieces the oppressors,* v. 5. The sixth benefit is, Christ, the true king of Israel, shall never want a kingdom, he shall never want subjects, but shall always have a church of such as shall worship and fear him, and do homage unto him, so long as the world standeth, amidst all changes and revolutions that can come : *they shall fear thee as long as the sun and moon endure, throughout all generations,* v. 6. The seventh benefit is, whatsoever sad condition his people, shall be in, how far soever spoiled of their lustre and glory in the world, or in any other respects whatsoever, they shall be made as a mown down meadow possibly, yet Christ, by his word, Spirit, and effectual blessing, shall revive and recover them; as grass cut down, being watered by rain, is made to grow again : *he shall come down like rain upon the mown grass, as showers that water the earth,* v. 7. The eighth benefit is, all the true subjects of Christ are justified persons, and devoted in their hearts to righteousness, in the obedience of God's will, and such as endeavour to abound in the fruits of righteousness : *the righteous shall flourish in*

his day. The ninth benefit is, Christ's justified subjects **and**
students of holiness shall have peace with God, peace abounding and passing all understanding, *lasting peace,* without
end, in all his revolution of conditions : *the righteous shall
flourish, and have abundant peace, so long as the world endureth,* v. 8. The tenth benefit of Christ's government is,
the enlargement of the church and the number of his subjects, according to the length and breadth of God's promises
made to his people Israel, whether Israel in the letter or in
the spirit : *he shall have dominion also from sea to sea, and
from the river unto the ends of the earth,* v. 9. The eleventh
benefit of Christ's government is more special: whomsoever
he pleaseth to make subject unto himself, how wild and savage soever they be, yea, how great enemies soever they
have been to his kingdom, he shall tame them, bring them
in subjection to himself, and to most humble submission unto
his commands : *they that dwell in the dust shall bow before
him, and his enemies shall lick the dust,* v. 10. The twelfth
benefit is yet more special: the kings and rulers of the Gentiles shall find it a blessing to themselves and to their domi-
nions to be under Christ's government, and shall effectually
contribute their riches, power, and authority, to advance
the kingdom of Christ, their sovereign Lord and protector :
*the kings of Tarshish and of the isles shall bring presents;
the kings of Sheba and Seba shall offer gifts,* v. 11. The
thirteenth benefit of Christ's government, is so great an
enlargement of his kingdom, by bringing all kingdoms and
nations some way under his sceptre, that the prophecy of
John the Divine, Rev. xi. 15, shall be acknowledged to be
fulfilled: *all the kingdoms of the earth are become the Lord's
and his Son Christ's,* how improbable soever this may seem;
for answerably hereunto is it said here, *yea, all kings shall
fall down before him, all nations shall serve him,* v. 12. The
fourteenth benefit serving for the commendation of his government, is, by way of giving a reason of the marvellous
enlargement of his kingdom, from his care of the meanest
of his subjects, from his effectual pity toward them, love and
estimation of them. The care Christ hath of his subjects
is such, that there is not one so mean in all his kingdom, of
whom, and whose necessities, and of whose particular petitions, he taketh not most particular and exact knowledge,
whose petitions, being presented in the sense of their need,

he granteth not : *he shall deliver the needy when he crieth.*
There needeth no mediator between him and his subjects :
he heareth the needy when they cry. The man that hath
nothing within him or without him to commend him to
Christ, to assist, help, relieve, or comfort him, in heaven
or earth, is not despised by Christ, but delivered from that
which he feareth : *he shall deliver the poor, and him also
that hath no helper;* and this he doth by teaching his subjects to bear troubles, by strengthening them for the burden,
by comforting them in their grief, by giving a delivery to
their spirits by faith, and a full delivery at last, v. 13. The
fifteenth benefit and commendation of Christ's government
is, he exacteth from his subjects but that which he offereth
to furnish and enable them to discharge : he lets none be
tempted above his strength; he taketh small beginnings in
good part, he spareth the rod in a great measure, mitigates
the correction, and, in midst of wrath, he remembereth
mercy : *he shall spare the poor and needy;* whatsoever hard
exercise he put them to, he will give them their soul for a
prey : they shall not perish, who, in the sense of their need,
depend upon him : *he shall save the souls of the needy,* v. 14.
The sixteenth benefit and commendation of Christ's kingdom is, albeit the Lord suffer his subjects to be tried with
heresies and seducers, by oppressors and persecutors, yet
he will assist them in the trial and bring them out of it : *he
shall redeem their soul from deceit and violence ;* and if, for
his own glory, he put any of them to lay down their life for
his cause, it shall be a point of special honouring of them,
as of precious sons whom he esteemeth much, both living
and dead : *precious shall their blood be in his sight,* v. 15.
The seventeenth benefit and commendation of Christ's government is from its everlasting endurance ; albeit other
kings die and leave their kingdoms to their successors, yet
it is not so with Christ; he endureth for ever : his death,
for paying the ransom of our sins, did not interrupt his reign,
but made way for his more glorious reigning, after his resurrection : he hath life in himself, as in the fountain : *he
shall live,* he shall live conquering and bringing in more
subjects, who shall pay tribute unto him : *to him shall be
given of the gold of Sheba.* The eighteenth benefit and
commendation of Christ's kingdom is, Christ shall be well-
beloved of all his subjects, whose exercise it shall be to wish

and pray for the prosperity of his kingdom, church, **and** mystical body, and who shall commend and praise his glorious and lovely majesty : *prayer also shall be made for him continually, and daily shall he be praised*, v. 16. The nineteenth benefit and commendation of Christ's government **is**, that a little seed of his precious word sown among men, **of** whose conversion there might be least hope, like a handful of corn sown upon the mountains or most barren ground, shall have a glorious increase in the conversion of many notable saints, like as corn in a barren place should grow up like cedar-trees : *there shall be an handful of corn in the earth, on the top of the mountains, the fruit thereof shall shake like Lebanon :* and this blessing of the gospel he can make to be without prejudice of the manured land of churches already planted, which are as cities inhabited; those he can bless, and will bless at his pleasure, with the abundant growth of grace amongst them: *and they of the city shall flourish as the grass of the earth*, v. 17.   The last commendation and benefit of Christ's government summeth up all that can be said in these four generals : 1. That Christ's name, fame, and honour, shall be perpetuated from one generation to another, for the running of his benefits to his subjects, and for the course of his judgments on his enemies : *his name shall endure for ever ; his name shall be continued as long as the sun.*   2. His gospel shall spread further and further among men, to deliver his own from the curse due for sin, to make them partakers of the blessing of full felicity : *men shall be blessed in him.*   3. It shall be in vain to seek blessedness any where, except in him only who is the procurer, applier, and maintainer of true blessedness, the way whereunto is, to come to God in and through Christ : *in him men shall be blessed.*   And, 4. Such a fulness of converted Gentiles at length shall be brought in, that the blessedness of the gospel of Christ and of spiritual communion with him, and the riches of his goodness and grace shall generally be acknowledged in all the world : *all nations shall call him blessed.*

18. *Blessed* be *the Lord God, the God of Israel, who only doeth wondrous things.*

19. *And blessed* be *his glorious name for ever : and let the whole earth be filled* with *his glory. Amen, and Amen.*

After this gracious answer of the church's prayer in so glorious a prophecy of Christ, thanksgiving and praise are indited unto the church, to be offered up to God for this mercy. Whence learn, 1. When the heart hath believed what the ear hath heard of the blessedness to be found in Christ, the mouth should be opened to praise and bless God: *blessed be the Lord God, the God of Israel.* 2. As the keeping of the race of David till the coming of Christ, distinct from other families, in so many revolutions of affairs, as were between David's reign and Christ's coming, is very wonderful: so the enlarging of the kingdom of Christ, since he came, is full of wonder also, whether we look to the King, or to the subjects converted, or the way of converting them, by the preaching of his word, or the preservation or continuing of Christ's kingdom in the world amongst so many devils and wicked adversaries, all his subjects being so weak and sinful as they are; it is a matter of great wonder indeed. *Blessed be the God of Israel, who only doeth wondrous things.* There are no wonders like the wonders done in the redemption of men by Christ, yea there is no other who can work any wonders, but by Christ alone. 3. As the blessings of Christ are everlasting, so should the thanksgiving for them be; and no less can content the heart of a true believer, who, the more he thinks of Christ, the more glory he seeth in him : *and blessed be his glorious name for ever,* saith he. 4. Before Christ puts an end to his work, and gives up the kingdom to the Father, his glory shall shine in all parts of the world, for the prayers indited to the church are not vanishing wishes, but real promises and certain prophecies : *let the whole earth be filled with his glory.* 5. As faith sets to its seal unto the truth of God's word, in special what concerneth the salvation of men and the glory of God in Christ; so love, both to the glory of God, and salvation of souls, sets to its seal also; or both faith and love subscribe the same truth of God in both respects, again and again : *amen, and amen.*

20. *The prayers of David the son of Jesse are ended.*

This closure of the psalm is added by the psalmist David himself, and is a part of the text; serving, first, to show, that

this was the last of the psalms, indited by the Spirit to him
a little before his death, when Solomon was now reigning:
howsoever in the order of providence it be not in the hind-
most place of this book of the psalms.   And next, it serveth to show, that in this answer made to his prayer set down
in this psalm, all his desires were granted, both concerning
himself and his house; for he could wish no more.   And,
thirdly, it serveth to show his mean estimation of himself, notwithstanding the Lord's lifting of him up so high, that so
the grace of God in him may be the more conspicuous; for
which causes he calleth himself, *the son of Jesse.*   Whence
learn, 1. As a man liveth, so readily he dieth.   David was
a worshipper of God all his life, and now when he hath
given over the kingdom to his son, and is going on his
way, he is upon the same work of praying and singing
psalms, for God's glory and the edification of his church.
2. Meditation on Christ, contemplation of his glory, seeking after and foreseeing the enlargement of his kingdom,
from a noble and comfortable closing of a man's life, as here
we see.   3. It is the mark of true humility and sincere love
to God, to abase ourselves, and acknowledge our low
condition, wherein God found us when he let forth his love
to us, that thereby we may commend the riches of God's
goodness and grace unto us, as appeareth here in David.

PSALM LXXIII.

A psalm of Asaph.

The psalmist setteth down here the doctrine of God's goodness to the
faithful, however he seem to deal with them, v. 1, and cleareth it by
his own experience.   Wherein, first, after he had stumbled to see the
wicked prosper in the world, comparing his own calamities with their
prosperity, v. 2—12; he was like to be overcome with the temptation,
and to forsake the course of godliness, v. 13, 14; next with this temptation he wrestles, v. 15, 16; and, thirdly, he getteth the victory, consulting the word of God, v. 17—20; in the last place, he maketh a
fourfold use of this experience; the first whereof is, the acknowledging
of his own weakness under the temptation, v. 21, 22; the next, the
confessing of God's kindness to him in the time of temptation, v. 23;
the third, the confirming of his own faith for time to come, v. 24—26;
the fourth, his resolution to draw more near to God hereafter, v. 27,
28.

1. *Truly God is good to Israel,* even *to such as are
of a clean heart.*

The doctrine set down in this verse, is the result of Asaph's sad trial after he had gotten the victory of the temptation which called in question the blessedness of believers, whensoever their outward condition should be found more miserable than the condition of the wicked. Whence learn, 1. As the temptations of Satan aim at the weakening of our believing of saving doctrine, so our trials, our experiences of conflicts against temptation, and our victories over it, should strengthen our faith so much the more, to hold fast that truth which the temptation opposed. After this experience, the prophet not only holds forth this doctrine, *that God is good*, but also prefixeth unto it, *truly, yet, or notwithstanding.* 2. However the Lord seem to deal more hardly with humble believers and worshippers of him, than with the wicked, yet is his dispensation toward them always for their welfare: *truly, God is good to Israel.* 3. Those persons are true Israelites, who not only cleanse their conscience by the blood of the Lamb of God, but also study to be holy in soul and body in the sincerity of their heart. This is the cleanness of heart which the Scripture teacheth. *God is good to Israel, even to such as are of a clean heart.*

2. *But as for me, my feet were almost gone ; my steps had well nigh slipped.*

3. *For I was envious at the foolish, when I saw the prosperity of the wicked.*

The psalmist compareth his late carriage under a temptation with the rule of this doctrine, and acknowledgeth that he did not hold it so firmly as he should have done, but was almost driven from maintaining it. Whence learn, 1. In the time of adversity, a believer may prove weak in the faith of that truth which was not questioned by him in prosperity, and be near hand unto the quitting and renouncing of it : *but as for me my feet were almost gone, my steps had well nigh slipped.* 2. Albeit the Lord so far decypher the weakness of his own children, as to let them be brought to the very brink of misbelieving a necessary and saving truth, yet he preventeth their quitting it altogether; they may be very near the fall, and not fall altogether : *my feet were almost gone, my steps had well nigh slipped.* 3. The godly will not hesitate to confess to their own shame their own weakness, when it may serve to strengthen others and give warning to prevent the fall of others, or any way prove profitable to others, as in this example we see. 4. The measure of our faith or love to God and religion, the measure of our faith to obey known truth, is best known in time of temptation, when the object is in our eye, and the tempter is making use of it to insnare us : *I was envious at the foolish, when I saw the prosperity of the wicked.* 5. If the prosperity of the wicked, and trouble of the godly be looked upon, in respect of their outward worldly estate only; it cannot but trouble a man's thoughts : *I was envious at the foolish, when I saw the prosperity of the wicked.*

4. *For* there are *no bands in their death ; but their strength* is *firm.*

5. *They* are *not in trouble* as other *men ; neither are they plagued like* other *men.*

6. *Therefore pride compasseth them about as a chain; violence covereth them* as *a garment.*

7. *Their eyes stand out with fatness : they have more than heart could wish.*

8. *They are corrupt, and speak wickedly* concerning *oppression : they speak loftily.*

9. *They set their mouth against the heavens ; and their tongue walketh through the earth.*

10. *Therefore his people return hither ; and waters of a full* cup *are wrung out to them :*

What was the prosperity of the wicked, which stumbled the psalmist, he setteth down in particular in these verses. Whence learn, 1. Albeit the great multitude of the wicked are subject to such outward miseries as others are; yet to some of them, yea and to some of the worst of them, God for his own holy ends useth to give health of body, long life, little sickness, and a quiet death, when the time of it is come, and in their death to keep them from many troubles which others are subject unto : yet God doth not love them, nor approve any whit more of them for this: *there are no bands in their death, but their strength is firm ; they are not in trouble as other men, &c.* 2. The more liberally the Lord deals with the wicked, they are the more insolent, and

proud, and vain-glorious; they are the more unjust and
violent oppressors of others : their prosperity blindeth them,
and serveth to increase their wickedness : *therefore pride
compasseth them as a chain ; violence covereth them as a
garment.* They glory in their oppression. 3. Albeit God
bestow riches on the wicked, and more than they could
reasonably wish, and give them health of body to make use
of their riches as they please, so that they swell for fatness,
(which abundance should oblige a man to serve the Lord
more heartily :) yet the recompense they render to God is,
that they become more and more vicious in their own persons, and threaten more and more injuries to their neighbours : *they are corrupt, and speak wickedly concerning oppression.* They stand in awe neither of God nor man, but
openly in their speeches they despise all authority over them.
they speak loftily : they scoff and mock religion, and speak
blasphemously of God and his providence. *They set their
mouth against the heavens :* they speak as they please of
all things, and all men, not caring against whom they speak,
or what they speak to any man's prejudice. *Their tongue
walketh through the earth :* not caring whom it tread upon,
or whom it abuse. 4. The prosperity of the wicked, and
their thriving in an ill course, insnare many inconsiderate
people, even members of the visible church, and move them
to follow the evil ways of the openly wicked, and to make
defection from their own professed duties : *therefore his
people return hither,* saith he. 5. When men stumble at
righteousness because of trouble, and follow the course of
the wicked for love of worldly advantage; it is righteousness with God to give both the bait for a while to such
changelings, and the hook also, for hardening them in their
own wicked choice; *and waters of a full cup,* saith he, *are
wrung out unto them :* that is, they find some worldly commodity by their defection. 6. There is a threefold temptation to draw a man from the course of holiness unto looseness and profanity; one, when the wicked are observed to
prosper in the world; another, when multitudes turn off a
good course and follow the example of the wicked : and a
third, when those backsliders also seem to prosper after
their defection, as here. 1. The wicked calumniate every
good course, and they prosper. 2. God's people return
hither for love of prosperity. 3. *Then waters of a full*

cup are wrung out unto them.   All these things may concur, and the way meantime be most damnable notwithstanding.

11. *And they say, How doth God know? and is
there knowledge in the most High?*

12. *Behold, these are the ungodly, who prosper in the
world: they increase in riches.*

Here Asaph bringeth in the poor deluded people defending their defection, and their following the example of the
ungodly, and hardening themselves in their evil course: saying in substance, that if God disliked the ungodly, he would
not let them prosper so in the world, and heap riches upon
them as he doth; and this is in substance to blaspheme God
as an ignorant Governor of the world, or a misregarder how
men carry themselves.   Whence learn, 1. When men are
once insnared in an ill course, they will seek reasons to justify themselves; those thoughts which insnared them also
hold them; for they to whom *waters of a full cup are wrung
out do say, How doth God know?*   2. Men are ready to
reproach the Lord if he do not guide the world to their
fancy, yea, and to blaspheme God rather than blame themselves for their faults, as these words import : *how doth God
know?* that is, how can it be that God taketh notice of such
men's ways as wrong, seeing he prospereth them?   3. To
think that God is well pleased with the way of the wicked,
because they prosper, and that he respects not his saints,
because he afflicteth them more than the wicked, is as much
as in effect to say, The Lord is not wise that doeth so well
to his foes, and dealeth so hardly with his friends; for so
here is it interpreted by the world: *is there knowledge in the
most High?*   4. It seemeth very reasonable to carnal reason, that if God hate ungodliness, he should not suffer the
ungodly to prosper in the world; and if he suffer them to
prosper, then he doth not hate ungodliness; and therefore
when it is clear to all men that the ungodly prosper, they
conclude, *that God knoweth not ;* taketh no notice of ungodliness, or is not displeased with it: for here is their proof:
behold, say they, *these are the ungodly who prosper in the
world, they increase in riches.*   5. The thing that deceiveth
the ungodly and the misbelieving world about God's dispensations is, that they look only to that which is done by God

in this world; no punishment after death, or felicity after death do they think upon : *these are the ungodly, say they, who prosper in the world.*   6. In the very temptation whereby the wicked are ensnared, the worm of their gourd, and the stain of their felicity are discovered; their felicity is but in their riches, and their prosperity is but in this present world : *they prosper in the world*, say they.

13. *Verily I have cleansed my heart* in *vain, and washed my hands in innocency.*

14. *For all the day long have I been plagued, and chastened every morning.*

Here is the well near slipping of the psalmist's feet, set down in his begun yielding unto the devil's temptation, forcibly borne in upon him, and repeated over by him, after the manner of a resolute conclusion, condemning all his former course of godliness upon this one poor pretence, because he seemed to himself more miserable than the wicked were. Whence learn, 1. A temptation sometimes may be so powerfully borne in upon the spirit of a child of God, as it may seem to be admitted, yielded unto, and subscribed unto as truth, as here we see : *verily I have cleansed in vain, &c.* 2. The true course of sanctification consists in the study of cleansing a man from all pollution, both of soul and body, or *in cleansing the heart and the hands*, as here is set down. The heart is cleansed by the blood of the expiatory sacrifice laid hold on by faith, and by the begun works of the Lord's Spirit manifested in the hearty resolution, purpose, and study of holiness; the hands are cleansed by a blameless and harmless conversation or course of life and actions : *I have cleansed my heart and hands in innocency.*   3. When a man is under a temptation, or in a fleshly temper of spirit, for the present he putteth a high price upon any good he hath done, and forgetteth by what strength he did it; he forgetteth God's part, and his glory in it; for the psalmist's part was the consenter's part, the instrument's part, and he was in the point of action only a subordinate agent, and co-worker at the best by a borrowed strength; and yet as if all the work had been his work alone, *in vain*, saith he, *have I cleansed my heart, and washed my hands in innocency.* 4. That which is the break-neck of the wicked, may readily be a stumbling-stone for a time to the godly; that which is the irrecoverable deadly sickness of the wicked, may be the hot fever or distemper of the godly for a season. In special, as the wicked man at all times looketh only to this present world, and to what may make him prosperous or miserable in this present life, so it may befall the godly man also in a fit, at a time, to look only upon temporal prosperity and trouble, as here we see the psalmist looketh only to his present troubles : *for all the day long I have been plagued ;* never a word here of his sweet consolations and manifold benefits bestowed on him. 5. To find some new cross daily, either from God immediately, or from the world, or from Satan, or from our own corruption, is no strange thing to the godly : *all the day long I have been plagued, and chastened every morning*, saith the psalmist, even when he was daily cleansing his heart and washing his hands; so doth divine wisdom see it fit for the good of his children and glorifying of his own name.

15. *If I say, I will speak thus ; behold, I should offend* against *the generation of thy children.*

Thus have we seen the psalmist's temptation. In the next place, we have his wrestling with it, by bringing the conclusion suggested by Satan to a further examination; and first, of human reason, whereby he perceiveth that if this conclusion should be maintained, then the church of God in all ages, and all the godly from the beginning of the world would be condemned as miserable souls; which consequence he thinketh to be a rash condemning of the constant resolution of the godly wise in all ages past. Whence learn, 1. Temptations driving at the subversion of faith in Christ and holiness of life, find resistance in the heart of a renewed man, how far soever they seem to prevail at first. The seed of God remaineth in him, the principles of spiritual life, the infused habits of saving grace, the new creature by God's upstirring, make opposition, as in this example we see. 2. The way to take up and decipher Satan's temptations, is to consider what they aim at, tend unto, drive at, what may be the consequence thereof : *if I say, I will speak thus,* then such a thing will follow. 3. So long as a temptation remaineth under dispute, and is not come to a settled decree and resolved practice, it hath not obtained full victory; it is with the psalmist here, for all that was suggested and seemingly yielded, no more yet, but, *if I say, I will speak thus.* 4. Whosoever condemneth piety and holy conversa-tion, because the world doth so, or because trouble followeth such a course, he doth a high injury to all the saints from the beginning of the world, and to God the author of all holiness: *if I should speak thus, behold, I should offend against the generation of thy children.* 5. The godly are not the authors of their own spiritual being, the making them new creatures is the work of God, they are the children of God, begotten of him by his word and Spirit, and re-semble their father in wisdom and righteousness; so the psalmist styleth them in the time of his hard trial here, *the generation of God's children.* 6. In our disputing with temptations by the weapons of reason, we shall do well to make God moderator of the disputants, and to look to God in our reasoning, that we may, by his testimonies, rectify every thing, lest we reason amiss, as here the psalmist doth : *I should offend against the generation of thy children.* We ought to reverence the judgment of the godly; and the more universally their judgment is one, and agreeing in a point of controversy, the more fear should we have to dissent from them, as the psalmist's example teacheth us.

16. *When I thought to know this, it* was *too painful for me.*

17. *Until I went into the sanctuary of God ;* then *understood I their end.*

18. *Surely thou didst set them in slippery places, thou castedst them down into destruction.*

19. *How are they* brought *into desolation, as in a moment ! they are utterly consumed with terrors.*

20. *As a dream when one awaketh ;* so, O Lord, *when thou awakest, thou shalt despise their image.*

In the third place, finding himself not yet satisfied, the psalmist consulteth the oracle of God, revealed in his Scrip-ture, and the ordinances of his house, and so he findeth his doubt resolved, and victory over his bitter temptation granted unto him. Whence learn, 1. When a man seeth himself in a mist, and out of the Lord's way, he is not able by himself to find it again; for the strongest of human testimonies will not settle him and make him quiet : *when I thought to know this, it was too painful.* 2. The last refuge of brangled

faith, is God himself manifesting his will in his word and
ordinances; no settling or satisfaction of doubts in divinity
but by the Scriptures : *it was too painful for me until I
went unto the sanctuary of God ;* that is, till I consulted the
Scriptures, and considered what God had revealed in his
church by his ordinances : this satisfied and settled him.
3. The Lord hath revealed in Scripture what shall be the
end and close of men's course, who study not to walk according to his direction, how prosperous soever they may
seem to be; and because the felicity of men is not to be
known by God's outward dispensation of worldly comforts
or crosses, therefore man's end must determine the difference : *then understood I their end.*   4. Whatsoever alterations and changes the godly man be subject unto in his temporal condition, bodily or spiritual, yet his felicity is settled
unto him on the rock; but the felicity of the wicked is built
on the sand; the higher they are lifted up in that earthly
felicity, which alone they affect, the nearer are they to a
fall and fearful ruin : *thou hast set them upon slippery places.*
5. Whatsoever may seem to the wicked themselves, or to the
world, or to the godly who look upon the wicked, how little
appearance soever there be of their fall; yet it is decreed it
shall be : for, notwithstanding all appearances, it is said,
surely thou hast set them in slippery places.   6. As the
wicked do not rise unto any greatness or power in the world
by themselves, but the Lord is he that setteth them up for his
own glory; so they do not fall of their own accord, but the
Lord casteth them down; beside their own weight, they have
the throw of the right hand of the Lord, who showeth his
power in the overthrow, and driveth them to more deaths than
one : *thou castedst them down into destruction.*   7. The wicked
perish suddenly, when neither they themselves nor others are
looking for their ruin, in a way much more wonderful than
their lifting up was: *they are destroyed ; how are they brought
into desolation as in a moment ?*   8. The destruction of the
wicked is full of terror, how senselessly soever some of them
go away; all their riches, honour, and prosperity are pulled
from them, and in great wrath they are sent out of the world,
never to see any token of favour again; they are adjudged
to irrecoverable perdition of soul and body for ever : *they
are utterly consumed with terrors.*   9. When the wicked are
flourishing in wealth, ease, and honour, men think that God

is, as it were, sleeping; but the truth is, both the wicked themselves, and all who look upon them, and judge them to be happy, are in a dream, as they shall see when the Lord's time is come to execute judgment on them; for then all their riches, honour, pleasure, and contentment shall be found nothing but a despicable picture of these things : *as a dream when one awaketh; so, O Lord, when thou awakest, thou shalt despise their image.*

21. *Thus my heart was grieved, and I was pricked in my reins.*

22. *So foolish* was *I, and ignorant : I was* as *a beast before thee.*

In the fourth place, the psalmist makes a sixfold use of this experience. The first is this, that by it he is taught how weak and foolish he is in himself, and how unable to stand in time of trial and temptation. Whence learn, 1. Hardly will a man discern a powerful temptation, when he is under it. The best sight to be had of the danger of a temptation is, when it is overcome and gone; and look how well pleased a man is, when the temptation is beautified with specious colours of carnal reason, so much will he be displeased with it when it is seen, and discerned by spiritual light, as here we see in the psalmist's experience. 2. Much trouble do we bring to our own spirits, when we examine God's dispensations by carnal reason, and not by the Scriptures; and we may thank ourselves for the misery which we draw upon ourselves, as here the psalmist doth : *thus my heart was grieved, and I was pricked in my reins.* 3. So soon as the godly can perceive their own error, they will no longer maintain it, and no man will more sharply censure them for their fault than they will do themselves. This is a part of their uprightness and ingenuous honesty of heart : *so foolish was I and ignorant.* 4. The sin of envy and malcontent with God's afflicting us and sparing the wicked, hath its own judgment bound upon the back of it : for as a sour-leavened vessel turneth all things put into it unto sourness, so envy of the prosperity of others maketh all the good that the Lord doeth to ourselves, uncomfortable and unpleasant to us : for the phrase, *my heart was grieved,* is in the force of the original, *my heart was imbittered, made sour, and leavened.* 5. Perplexity of mind, arising from the mistaking of God's providence, is like the pain of the gravel in the reins, very troublesome till we be rid of it : *I was pricked in my reins*, is a similitude borrowed from the bodily pain of the gravel. 6. Carnal reason not corrected by God's word, is beastly ignorance : it may bear some show of reason among foolish men, but indeed it is nothing before God, but brutish folly : *I was as a beast before thee.*

23. *Nevertheless I* am *continually with thee ; thou hast holden* me *by my right hand.*

The second use of this exercise, is the acknowledgment that his standing in grace and God's obedience, depended only upon the Lord, by whose powerful sustaining of him he was kept from being utterly overcome by the temptations of Satan, and falling from the way of God by the temptation. Whence learn, 1. The perseverance of the saints, is not of themselves, but of the Lord, who forsaketh them not, when they of themselves are ready to forsake him, but by his power secretly upholdeth them, and keepeth them fast to himself. This the psalmist here acknowledgeth : *nevertheless I am continually with thee.* 2. When we have gotten proof of our own folly and weakness, and ill-deserving, then we most clearly see and confess God's grace and power in preserving us : *thou hast holden me by my right hand.*

24. *Thou shalt guide me with thy counsel, and afterward receive me to glory.*

The third use is the confirmation of his faith and hope in God for time to come. Whence learn, 1. The believer, how sensible soever he be of his own weakness, may be persuaded of his own perseverance, by looking on God's constancy, and felt experience of his work of grace in him in time past : *thou wilt guide me with thy counsel, &c.* 2. There is an inseparable connexion between walking by God's direction in the time of this life, and our reception into heaven after this life : and he who is resolved to walk by the rule of God's direction, may promise to himself to be received into glory immediately after his journey in this life is ended : *thou shalt guide me with thy counsel, and afterward receive me to glory.* 3. Albeit the believer may meet with many doubts and difficulties in his way, yet hath he a guide to direct him, and a rule to walk by, to wit, the word of God revealed in the church or sanctuary; whereby he may be advised effectually how to walk on his way to heaven : *thou wilt guide me with thy counsel.*

25. *Whom have I in heaven* but thee ? *and* there is *none upon earth* that *I desire besides thee.*

26. *My flesh and my heart faileth :* but *God* is *the strength of my heart, and my portion for ever.*

The fourth use of this exercise is, the settling of his affection and confidence on God, as the matter of his satisfactory contentment and upholding, when all creatures failed him. Whence learn, 1. As nothing can give true contentment, except God : so God will have us to loose our heart from all creatures, and expect no contentment in any of them, but in himself : *whom have I in heaven but thee? and there is none upon earth that I desire besides thee.* 2. He that seeth God's sufficiency, seeth also the emptiness of the creatures, and nothing to be in them, but what they have of God. A believer may see that he needeth nothing in heaven or earth, but communion with God, to make him fully blessed : *whom have I in heaven but thee? and there is none upon earth that I desire besides thee.* 3. As to find all things to fail us, except God, in the time of trial, serveth to loose our affections and confidence off them : so to find help in God when all things fail, serveth to tie the heart of a believer strongly to the Lord : *my heart and my flesh fail me, but God is the strength of my heart.* 4. When the believer hath seen his own strength fail him, and yet believeth not the less in God, he shall find his failing heart and fainting courage upholden, and his own exhausted strength supplied with a greater strength from God : *my heart and my flesh fail me, but God is the strength of my heart.* 5. Every man seeketh something for his portion; some one thing in the creature, some another, but the believer's portion is the Lord himself, and no less will content him: *the Lord is the strength of my heart, and my portion.* 6. This is the believer's advantage above all that seek their blessedness in the creature; for his person is the eternal God, and he is made an everlasting enjoyer of him : *God is my portion for ever.*

27. *For, lo, they that are far from thee shall perish : thou hast destroyed all them that go a-whoring from thee.*

The fifth use is the psalmist's resolution to draw nearer unto God. The reasons of which resolution are two; the one, because they perish who draw not near to God v. 27;

the other, because great advantage is to be had by drawing
near to him, v. 28. Whence learn, 1. The Lord's child
profiteth by hardest exercises, and his temptations, being resisted by faith, leave him in better case than they found him:
his knowledge of God's ways, his faith, his love to God and
hatred of wicked courses are augmented, as in this example
is to be seen.   2. They whose confidence, affections, course
of life and actions run toward and cleave unto the creature
depart from God more and more; for here they are said to
be far from God : and they that depart from God draw near
to eternal perdition : *they that are far from thee shall perish.*
And howsoever this truth be not believed, yet it is as sure
and certain, as if it were seen with our eyes : *for lo, they
that are far from thee shall perish.*   3. A chaste soul hath
no choice, no love to delight itself in contentedly, except
God : no confidence to rest itself upon, but God. And whosoever seek their delight and satisfaction in the creature, especially if they be members of the visible church, in covenant with God, are adulterers : *they go a-whoring from
God :* and they shall not find felicity in the creatures, but
perdition, no less certainly, than if it were already past : *thou
hast destroyed all them that go a-whoring from thee.*

28. *But* it is *good for me to draw near to God : I
have put my trust in the Lord God, that I may declare
all thy works.*

In this verse, the psalmist giveth the other reason of his
adherence unto God, from the advantage he findeth by so
doing, and closeth the psalm with the sixth use of his experience, which is the fixing of his faith on God, that his experiences may be more and more frequent, and he may be a
fitter instrument to glorify God. Whence learn, 1. The
right use of the perishing of the wicked, is to be more holy,
and to seek nearer communion with God, as our only blessedness, how many soever depart from him : *they shall perish who are far from thee ; but it is good for me to draw
near to God.*   2. No man is so near in communion with God
in this life, but there is a further degree to be aimed at, and
possibly to be found; as there are degrees of departing from
God; so also are there degrees of coming near unto him; and
the better for us, the nearer we draw : *it is good for me to draw
near to God.*   3. The use of all assaults against our faith,

is more and more to fix our faith and confidence on God; for this is the use the psalmist maketh of the assault spoken of in this psalm : *I have put my trust in the Lord God.* 4. None but a deliverer can discern the Lord's working; it is only faith that giveth a right construction unto all the Lord's works ; faith alone makes men fit instruments to glorify God : *I put my trust in the Lord God, that I may declare all thy works.* 5. As the believer is the best observer of God's works, and fittest to set them forth before others; so he is the man of greatest experience; and he of all men is filled with most matter of God's praise : for the Lord never disappoints the believer, but makes him have new proofs of his wonderful wisdom, power, and goodness; so doth the psalmist lay his reckoning : *I have put my trust in the Lord God, that I may declare all thy works.*

PSALM LXXIV.

Maschil of Asaph.

Of this psalm there are three parts. In the first part is the pitiful lamentation of the church presented unto God, because of the destruction of Jerusalem, and burning of the temple by the Chaldeans, to v. 11. In the next is the strengthening of the faith and hope of God's people, that God would send a delivery, to v. 18. In the third, there are sundry petitions for relief of his people, restitution of his own work, and suppression of his enemies, to the end of the psalm.

1. *O God, why hast thou cast* us *off for ever ?* why *doth thine anger smoke against the sheep of thy pasture ?*

2. *Remember thy congregation,* which *thou hast purchased of old ; the rod of thine inheritance,* which *thou hast redeemed ; this mount Zion, wherein thou hast dwelt.*

In the first part of the psalm there are a lamentation and prayer for relief in general, v. 1, 2 ; secondly, a complaint against the enemy, laying forth before God the desolation which the Chaldeans had made, especially in destroying the temple, v. 3—9; and, thirdly, a prayer unto God for vengeance upon them for their pains, v. 10, 11.

From the lamentation and prayer for relief in general, learn, 1. In all judgments, inflicted by whatsoever instruments, the Lord's people must look first to God; and albeit wrath, and fear of utter wrath stare them in the face, as hardly it can be otherwise when God putteth hand in his own temple, and taketh away all the tokens of his presence from among a people, and seemeth to cast them utterly off; yet must they make their address to God, how angry soever he seem to be; as here the church under this sad judgment doth, saying, *O God, why hast thou cast us off?* 2. In the point of casting off, and fear of casting off for ever, the Lord craveth no yielding and submission to the pressing thoughts thereof, but will allow us to call in question every appearance of any such purpose of God, and to debate that point with him, and not to endure utter casting off, yea and to say, *Why hast thou cast us off for ever?* whether it be our own particular case, or the case of the visible church, ours and others' case with us, we cannot endure to be separate from God. 3. When the wrath of the Lord is kindled against his people, all that they see seemeth to be but the beginning of more wrath, as smoke is but the beginning of burning : *why doth thine anger smoke against thy sheep?* 4. Albeit we by our sins have provoked the Lord to fall upon us, as his enemies; yet must we not quit the least relation, no, not of the external covenant between God and us, but make use of it for supporting our faith in him, as here : *why doth thine anger smoke against the sheep of thy pasture?* that is, thy church and people, the care of whom thou hast taken, as a shepherd over his flock. 5. The believer's asking *why?* is no quarrelling: nor is any speech of the saints unto God a quarrelling, which endeth or resolveth in petition and supplication, as this doth: wherein after their asking *why?* they turn themselves to supplication, and pray, *remember thy congregation.* 6. Let the Lord do to his people what he pleaseth, they must pray unto him, and make use of all the bonds between him and them, as here the church doth; pleading, 1. That they are by outward covenant his church, consecrated unto him : *remember thy congregation.* And, 2. That they are his purchase by paying price, and conquest: *thy congregation which thou hast purchased.* And, 3. That they have been in his possession for a long time : *which thou hast purchased of old.* And, 4. That the Lord had taken them into cultivation, as a piece of land measured out by line or rod, and his inheritance, not to dispose or put away : *the rod of thine inheritance.* And, 5. That he had granted deliverances out of straits before : *the inheritance which thou hast redeemed.*   And, 6. That he had taken up house amongst them in his public ordinances: *this mount Zion, wherein thou hast dwelt.*

3. *Lift up thy feet unto the perpetual desolations,* even *all* that *the enemy hath done wickedly in the sanctuary.*

4. *Thine enemies roar in the midst of thy congregations; they set up their ensigns* for *signs.*

5. A man *was famous according as he had lifted up axes upon the thick trees.*

6. *But now they break down the carved work thereof at once with axes and hammers.*

7. *They have cast fire into thy sanctuary; they have defiled* by casting down *the dwelling-place of thy name to the ground.*

8. *They said in their hearts, Let us destroy them together: they have burnt up all the synagogues of God in the land.*

9. *We see not our signs:* there is *no more any prophet: neither* is there *among us any that knoweth how long.*

In the complaint, the psalmist desireth the Lord to come and see, and to take order with the desolation made by the enemies in his land, and specially in the temple, v. 3; what insolent domineering of them was over his people, yea, over God himself, so far as their lifted up banner against him could do, v. 4; each of them thinking it as great matter of commendation to him to throw down the temple, as ever it was for any man to build it, or prepare materials for it, v. 5, 6: how they had burned and demolished the Lord's house, v. 7, with a resolution to root out his people, according as they had burned all their synagogues in the land, v. 8; and how there was no appearance of comfort or delivery from this calamity, v. 9.   Whence learn, 1. All the evils which the enemy doth unto God's church, proceed from the Lord's desertion of, and departing from his people, who have provoked him to wrath; for this prayer, *Lift up thy feet*, or come and see, importeth his departure, and leaving his people naked without his protection. 2. Albeit the Lord seemeth to turn his back, and depart far away from his own

people, when they provoke him to anger, and to let their
enemies do unto them what they please; yet will he be entreated by his people to come again, and see, and pity the
desolation brought upon them, and punish the instruments
of it : *lift up thy feet unto the perpetual desolations ;* that
is, Lord, come speedily, and see what desolations thy enemies have made amongst us, and pity and relieve us by thy
manifested presence. 3. Amongst all the calamities of God's
people, nothing afflicteth them so much as the insolent pro-
fanation of the worship and name of God among them; for
here, in the first petition, they lament the abusing of the
temple : *even all that the enemies have done wickedly in the
sanctuary*—and then insist most upon this. 4. When the
wicked are let loose upon God's people, they are most insolent, cruel, and savage in their carriage toward them :
thy enemies roar in the midst of thy congregations. 5. It will
not suffice the enemies of the church to insult over God's
people, but they will insult over their way of religion, and
over God whom they worship : *they set up their ensigns for
signs ;* they display their banner upon the ruins of the temple, as signs of their victory over that religion which is professed there, and over God's worship there. 6. When God's
people abuse religion, and mock God in their profession of
worship, and dishonour him by their carriage and conversation, it is justice with God to give over his people, and all
the means of religion, into the hands of his enemies, to be
abused by them, rather than to suffer his own people to
mock him continually, as in this example is to be seen. 7.
It is matter of a man's commendation to contribute any way
to the setting up of God's worship and ordinances in a land :
*a man was famous according as he had lifted up axes upon
the thick trees ;* that is, as he had cut down timber out of
Lebanon, wood to build the Lord's temple withal. 8. When
the Lord is provoked by his people's evil carriage towards
him, no wonder he let the work of edification or reformation of religion go as fast down amongst them as ever it rose
up, as the church of the Jews felt by experience, when *now
the enemies did break down the carved work of the temple at
once, with axes and hammers,* much more speedily than it
was built : *they have cast fire into the sanctuary, they have
defiled by casting down the dwelling-place of thy name to the
ground.* This the Lord chose to permit, rather than suffer

his people still to mock religion, and still to abuse the temple, and make it a shelter for them to trust in against all God's threatenings, so long as it stood. 9. Albeit the Lord's mind be only to correct his people, by letting them see their provocation in the judgments brought upon them; yet the enemies whom he useth as instruments in their correction, intend their utter destruction, and the rooting them out of the world: *they say in their hearts, Let us destroy them.* 10. When the enemies of religion cannot kill all the worshippers of God, yet will they labour to mar the means of their assembling for public worship so far as they can: for, after they have said, *Let us destroy them together*, it is subjoined, *they have burnt up all the synagogues of God in the land ;* that is, all the houses built for the weekly assembling of the people unto public worship in their several divisions through the land. 11. Houses built for meetings of the Lord's people to public worship, albeit they be not typically holy, as the temple at Jerusalem was, yet they belong to God, as means dedicated for maintaining his service, and when they are marred, it is a wrong done to God, and a cause of complaint to God against the sacrilegious spoilers thereof, as here we see. 12. External troubles are much lighter when the public ordinances and signs of God's presence in a land may be had for spiritual comfort; but when those are removed, every trouble is the more heavy: *we see not our signs, there is no more any prophet, neither any among us that knoweth how long ;* that is, public means, ordinary and extraordinary, which may give us comfort, now cease. If it be asked, how can this be applied unto the time of the captivity, seeing Jeremiah, Ezekiel, Daniel, and the prophet who wrote this psalm by inspiration, were living at the beginning of the captivity, and after the burning of the temple? it may be answered, that Jeremiah was carried away to Egypt, and the people could not have use of his ministry; Ezekiel and Daniel were carried away to Babylon, and the poor which remained in the land had none of the prophets to comfort them; yea Ezekiel and Daniel were but now and then employed of God to utter their prophecies, and the multitude of the captives, who were to make use of this psalm, were scattered in sundry places, and could not have the benefit of their or of any others' ministry, as they were wont to have. And this in special maketh the lamentation to have a ground, that the table was drawn from the children; the people had not that access which they enjoyed before, unto means either extraordinary or ordinary; they had not their former allowance; and howsoever in the copies of Jeremiah's prophecy, seventy years were determined for the people's captivity, yet none of the prophets, at the time of writing this, told, or could tell them, how long time would pass before their desolation would be repaired; how long it would be ere the temple would be rebuilt; and the prophet, by whom this psalm was indited, had no further commission than he speaketh of ; and so these foresaid expressions may stand with the time of the beginning of the captivity of Babylon.

10. *O God, how long shall the adversary reproach? shall the enemy blaspheme thy name for ever?*

11. *Why withdrawest thou thy hand, even thy right hand? pluck it out of thy bosom.*

After the lamentation is subjoined an imprecation against the enemies, that God would not defer to punish them. Whence learn, 1. Men's patience is much short of God's long-suffering and forbearance: for here it is the speech of a suffering people : *O God, how long shall the adversary reproach?* when with God it is not yet time to fall upon them. 2. The Lord's long-suffering patience greatly hardeneth the adversaries in their insolent mocking of God's people; for, instead of saying, Lord, how long wilt thou bear with them ? he saith, *O God, how long shall the adversaries reproach?* 3. The truly godly can endure their own troubles better than they can bear the open dishonouring and blaspheming of God, by occasion of their trouble : therefore this expression, from the deepest sense of his heart, breaketh forth : *shall the enemy blaspheme thy name for ever?* 4. Albeit temptations from carnal sense represent God as if he were idle when he suffers his enemies to trample on his people, and on his glorious name; yet faith will not admit of such a thought, but dealeth with God by prayer, to let his strength and power be so manifest, that the world may not think his hand is in his bosom : *why withdrawest thou thy hand, even thy right hand? pluck it out of thy bosom.* This he believeth the Lord shall do, and giveth reasons for his hope in what followeth.

12. *For God* is *my King of old, working salvation in the midst of the earth.*

13. *Thou didst divide the sea by thy strength :* thou *brakest the heads of the dragons in the waters.*

14. *Thou brakest the heads of leviathan in pieces,* and *gavest him* to be *meat to the people inhabiting the wilderness.*

15. *Thou didst cleave the fountain and the flood:* thou *driedst up mighty rivers.*

16. *The day* is *thine, the night also* is *thine :* thou *hast prepared the light and the sun.*

17. *Thou hast set all the borders of the earth :* thou *hast made summer and winter.*

In the second part of the psalm, the psalmist confirmeth his own and other believers' faith that God would undoubtedly deliver his people, and take order with their enemies; first, from the interest they have in God, and God in them; secondly, from the experience of sensible deliveries past of his people, v. 12; thirdly, from the great work of redemption of his people from Pharoah's tyranny, v. 13, 14; fourthly, from the Lord's feeding his people in the wilderness, v. 15; fifthly, from the Lord's sovereignty and disposing of all creatures in the world, v. 16, 17. Whence learn, 1. Relations between God and his church, and in special this, that he hath made himself King thereof, are pledges of God's defending his kingdom and injured subjects, and punishing his enemies; for here the church giveth it for a reason of her hope of delivery : *God is my King.* 2. The more that is past since God avowed himself King of his church, the more confident may later generations of the church be, to find new evidences of his royal actions for them, and against their enemies : *God is my King of old.* 3. New troubles must not make us forget old mercies, but rather call them to memory, to be made use of afresh, as pledges that what he hath done before, he will do the like again; *God is my King of old, working salvation in the earth :* that is, such deliverances of his church as all the earth was witness of. 4. The delivery of Israel out of Egypt, and the destruction of the Egyptians, is a pledge unto the church in every age after, that God will destroy their enemies, how strong and terrible soever they be, and will deliver his church : *thou didst divide the sea by thy strength, thou brakest the heads of the dragons in the waters.*   5. As all the enemies of the church are no less cruel and savage against the Lord's people, than unreasonable sea-beasts and sea-monsters; so can he make their carcases a prey to unreasonable beasts, as he made Pharaoh and his captains become food to the beasts of the wilderness, when the sea did cast up their carcases on the shore, like sea wreck : *thou brakest the heads of leviathan in pieces, and gavest him to be meat to the people inhabiting the wilderness.*   6. The Lord will not fail to provide consolation to his church in her necessity, though no probable means appear, as he furnished his people with drink from the flinty rock in the wilderness: *thou didst cleave the fountain.*   7. The Lord can and will remove all impediments out of the way of his people which may hinder them from the possession of promises, as he did to Israel : *thou didst cleave the fountain and the flood, thou driedst up mighty rivers.*   8. Faith is so thrifty as not to let the works of creation and common providence pass by, without use-making thereof : *the day is thine, the night also is thine, &c.*   9. As God hath appointed vicissitudes of day and night, light and darkness, summer and winter; so hath he no less resolvedly, wisely, and graciously appointed vicissitudes of dangers and deliverances, of grief and consolation to his people, for their good : *the day is thine, the night also is thine : thou hast prepared the light and the sun.*   10. As the Lord hath set bounds to the sea, bounds and borders to every kingdom, to summer's heat and to winter's cold: so can he do, and so hath he done, and so will he do unto all the troubles of his own, to all the rage, power, plots, and purposes of their enemies : *thou hast set all the borders of the earth, thou hast made summer and winter.*

18. *Remember this,* that *the enemy hath reproached, O Lord, and* that *the foolish people have blasphemed thy name.*

19. *O deliver not the soul of thy turtle-dove unto the multitude* of the wicked: *forget not the congregation of thy poor for ever.*

20. *Have respect unto the covenant : for the dark places of the earth are full of the habitations of cruelty.*

21. *O let not the oppressed return ashamed : let the poor and needy praise thy name.*

22. *Arise, O God, plead thine own cause: remember how the foolish man reproacheth thee daily.*

23. *Forget not the voice of thine enemies : the tumult of those that rise up against thee increaseth continually.*

In the third part of the psalm, the psalmist returneth to prayer, and redoubleth his requests for delivery to the church; taking arguments, first, from the injuries done to God by the enemy, v. 18; secondly, from the danger and weakness of God's people, v. 19; thirdly, from covenanted help in time of need, v. 20, 21; fourthly, from the Lord's interest in his own quarrel against the growing insolency of his despiteful enemies, v. 22, 23. Whence learn, 1. Although sins, especially persecution of God's people, and blasphemy against God, be not presently punished, yet shall they not be forgiven: *remember this, that the enemy hath reproached, O Lord.* 2. All sins, but in special blasphemy of God's name, are aggravated by the naughtiness of the sinner, and excellency of God : *the foolish people have blasphemed thy name.* 3. The church of God, in comparison of her many and strong enemies, is like a solitary, weak, desolate turtle dove, harmless, meek, lowly, patient in desolation, easing her grief by sighing, and exposed to a multitude of ravenous birds: *O deliver not the soul of thy turtle dove.* 4. How weak soever the church be, and how many and strong soever the enemies be, yet cannot they all devour the church, except the Lord should deliver his church over into their hands, against which evil the church hath ground of confidence to pray, *O deliver not the soul of thy turtle dove, unto the multitude of the wicked ;* for he hath given his church wings, and a hiding-place too, as the comparison importeth, if he please to give her the use thereof also. 5. The church is the Lord's hospital, where his poor ones are sustained upon his provision and furniture, and he will not neglect them : *O forget not the congregation of thy poor for ever.* 6. Albeit the Lord's people deserve to be secluded many times from the covenant of grace, yet the Lord will never debar them from their right unto it, when they in their need draw near to him, and plead for the benefit of it : *have respect,* saith he, *to the covenant.* 7. Such places as want the light of the Lord's presence in his ordinances, are but dark and uncomfortable places, where there is no less hazard for the people of God to remain, than for sheep to be in the midst of the dens of cruel lions and ravenous beasts. And when it pleaseth God to cast his people by captivity or exile into such places, there is much need to make use of God's covenant for preservation : *have respect unto the covenant ; for the dark places of the earth are full of the habitations of cruelty.* 8. The emptied supplicant coming to God, especially when overloaden with troubles, shall find comfort, and shall not be disappointed of his hope : *O let not the oppressed return ashamed.* 9. The sense of need and emptiness, is the best disposition for prayer, and best preparation for praises also : and such as are poor in their prayers, shall be rich in their praises : *let the poor and needy praise thy name.* 10. The church's cause is the Lord's cause; for the wicked do not malign the godly for their sins, but for righteousness, and so the quarrel is the Lord's, which he will and must maintain, though he seem to sit still a while : *arise, O Lord, plead thine own cause.* 11. The Lord's enemies are all foolish men; for they beat out their brains upon the church's bulwark : because the Lord forbeareth for a time, they go on to blaspheme him daily to his face, but shall find at length, that God hath all their reproaches upon record : *remember how the foolish man reproacheth thee daily.* 12. Every sin, and in special enmity against God and his church, is fearful; but open gloriation therein is worse, which God will take knowledge of, and punish : for so much is imported in this prayer, *forget not the voice of thine enemies.* 13. Sin, and in special persecution, gloried in, groweth daily more and more; and the growing of sin, and in special of persecution, hasteneth the delivery of the godly, and the destruction of the enemies : *the tumult of those that arise against thee increaseth continually.*

PSALM LXXV.
To the chief musician, Altaschith. A psalm or song of Asaph.

This psalm well agreeth with the time of David's entry into the kingdom after Saul's death, before he was established king over all the tribes; wherein he, with the church, first thanketh God for bringing him wonderfully to a begun possession of a part of the kingdom, ver. 1; secondly, he promiseth that when the Lord shall give him the rest of the kingdom in possession, to employ his power for righteously governing and settling it, after it shall be put once in a right frame, ver. 2, 3; thirdly, he begins to triumph over the wicked that followed Saul, bringing to their mind the advertisement he had given them not to be proud in their places, ver. 4, 5; partly because God had the disposing of preferments in his own hand, ver. 6, 7, and partly because albeit God gave to all his own children a taste of troubles as he saw fit, yet the dregs of wrath were reserved for the wicked, ver. 8; fourthly, he promiseth to praise God continually, for casting down the wicked and exalting the godly, ver. 9, 10.

1. *Unto thee, O God, do we give thanks,* unto thee *do we give thanks : for* that *thy name* is *near thy wondrous works declare.*

From his thanksgiving, learn, 1. The church of God should take out of his hand every beginning of mercies and deliverances with affectionate and frequent thanksgiving : *unto thee, O Lord, do we give thanks, unto thee do we give thanks.* 2. As the Lord is described in his word, so will he be found in his works; to wit, near at hand and ready to help his people as they stand in need : *we do give thanks, because thy name is near;* for this is the nearness of God's name, when his powerful, gracious, felt presence is answerable to what is said of him in his word. 3. Whensoever the Lord showeth himself for his church's comfort, he doth it by some wonderful means, in one respect or other; that is, a far other way than any could have expected : *that thy name is near thy wondrous works declare.*

2. *When I shall receive the congregation I will judge uprightly.*

3. *The earth and all the inhabitants thereof are dissolved : I bear up the pillars of it. Selah.*

From David's undertaking to govern the kingdom well when it came all into his power, learn, 1. Possession in part of promises made to us, giveth good hope to have the whole of what is promised in possession also; for, *when I shall receive the congregation,* presupposeth his certain hope and expectation to have it. 2. He that is advanced to a civil kingdom consisting of people in covenant with God, hath gotten charge to nourish the church, and to procure whatsoever a king civilly can procure to a church, that his subjects may be all of them God's church : therefore David saith not, *when I receive the kingdom, but when I receive the congregation,* or the church. 3. Foresight of a charge whereunto a man is likely to be called should make him prepare himself, and resolve beforehand on doing the duties of that calling, as David did before he was possessed of the kingdom : *when I shall receive the congregation I will judge uprightly.* 4. When a land is destitute of godly and gracious governors, the whole country is left loose, both in the matter of religion and civil justice, as was seen in Saul's time before David was settled : *the earth and all the inhabitants thereof are dissolved.* 5. Kingdoms and commonwealths have their pillars whereupon they should stand, to wit, religious and righteous government : for, *I will judge uprightly,* in the second verse, is as good as, *I will bear up the pillars thereof,* in the third verse. 6. Those that mind the reformation of a land should be sensible of the desolation of it, and have not only will, but also skill and place of power, to set matters in a right frame, as here the psalmist, after saying, *the land and all the inhabitants thereof are dissolved,* addeth, *I bear up, or shall bear up the pillars of it.* And here, whatsoever David speaketh, or could say, was but a shadow of what is to be found in Christ, of whom he is a type: for the kingdom and country is ill guided where Christ reigneth not; but when people subject themselves to him, he sets the kingdom or country upon true pillars, and sustaineth all by his power.

4. *I said unto the fools, Deal not foolishly ; and to the wicked, Lift not up the horn :*

5. *Lift not up your horn on high : speak not with a stiff neck.*

In the third place, he calleth to mind his own prophecy of the change of affairs, and advertisement given by him before to his adversaries not to behave so insolently as they did. Whence learn, 1. Even in time of trouble the godly, by the light of God's word, may be enabled to foresee and prophesy of the overturning of the wicked from the top of their preferment : *I said unto the fools, Deal not so foolishly,* saith the psalmist. 2. When the prophecy, uttered according to God's word, is like to take effect, it is no small comfort for believers to call to remembrance acts of their believing beforehand, what they saw in their own time : *I said to the foolish, Deal not so foolishly,* is a sort of triumph over his enemies here. 3. Such as are acquainted with true wis-

dom justly account all wicked men to be fools, forsakers of
God's teaching, and followers of their own wit and will, to
the ruin of their own bodies, souls, houses, and fame : *I said
unto the fools.*   4. The fruits of a wicked man's prosperity
are pride, vain-glory, audacious boasting against the godly,
wherein they grow more and more insolent against all warn-
ings of God's word, as this reproof importeth: *deal not
foolishly, lift not up the horn : lift it not on high, speak not
with a stiff neck.*

6. *For promotion* cometh *neither from the east, nor
from the west, nor from the south.*

7. *But God* is *the judge : he putteth down one and
setteth up another.*

From the first reason of his admonition unto the wicked,
learn, 1. As the cause of men's pride in a wicked course is
the forgetting of God and of his government in the world,
on the one hand, and a strong conceit of their own ability to
compass their designs by their own wit, power, and indus-
try, on the other hand; so the way of wisdom to remedy the
evil, is to consider that God governeth the world, and that
men are nothing but what he pleaseth to make them: *promotion cometh neither from the east, nor from the west, nor
from the south;* that is, howsoever, or from whence soever,
preferment to places of power in the world seemeth to come,
yet the disposing of places is from a higher hand.   2. Places
of power and preferment are disposed of only by the wise
and righteous pleasure, and determination of the supreme
Ruler of the world : *but God is judge.*   He opposeth God
the judge's determination to all appearances from second
causes.   3. As God hath a mind, for the glory of his grace,
to try, or to correct, or to comfort and employ some men in
his service, so he putteth them down or setteth them up; and
as he hath a mind to have the glory of his justice displayed
on others, so he setteth them up or putteth them down: *God
is judge ; he putteth down one, and setteth up another.*

8. *For in the hand of the Lord* there is *a cup, and
the wine is red ; it is full of mixture ; and he poureth
out of the same : but the dregs thereof, all the wicked of
the earth shall wring* them *out,* and *drink* them.

From the second reason of the admonition given to the
wicked, learn, 1. As the Lord wisely distributeth his benefits

and temporal comforts among men, to testify his goodness
to his creatures; so also afflictions and calamities are measured out by him unto men, to testify his justice and indignation against sin : *for in the hand of the Lord is a cup ;* that
is, a measure of affliction proportioned unto them for whom
it is prepared.   2. This measure of affliction ordained for
each man, is prepared for the time appointed, like drink,
ready for the mouth of him to whose head the cup shall be
put : it is a cup with *wine* in it, *in God's hand*, ready to be
set to any man's head he pleaseth.   3. The affliction is like
strong wine, quickly piercing through all the man's veins
who drinketh it, and cleaving fast unto him : *the wine is red.*
4. The Lord hath, as it were, both hot and cooling waters,
whereby he mitigateth the cup of calamities to some, and
increaseth the sense of his fiery indignation to others : *it is
full of mixture ;* or it is perfectly mixed as the case requireth.   5. What is each man's measure of calamities, however
mixed when it is executed, all is in God's dispensation : *he
poureth forth of the same* into the mouth and belly of every
person as he pleaseth.   6. The calamities of the wicked follow ofttimes after the godly have drunk the first draughts
of the Lord's cup.   It is toward the bottom and dregs when
the wicked drink; the hottest wrath and heaviest indignation
is reserved for them, and none of them shall escape, how
long soever their judgment shall be delayed : *but the dregs
thereof all the wicked of the earth shall drink.*   7. The
wicked shall be no less accessory to the drawing on of their
own calamities, than he that wringeth the dregs to draw
out more liquor for himself to drink is accessory to his own
drunkenness and damage : *the dregs thereof all the wicked
of the earth shall wring them out, and drink them ;* their
vanity, pride, greediness, lust, ambition, envy, and pleasant
courses of sinning, wherein they delight themselves whilst
they are drinking in iniquity as an ox doth water, shall be
their destruction, as in point of merit, so also in point of
the means of their own overthrow.

9. *But I will declare for ever ; I will sing praises to
the God of Jacob.*

10. *All the horns of the wicked also will I cut off;*
but *the horns of the righteous shall be exalted.*

In the last place, David promiseth to make this holy and

wise dispensation of justice upon the wicked and mercy toward the godly, the matter of his song in God's praise. Whence learn, 1. However matters seem to go, how deep soever the godly drink of the cup of calamities, yet the believers in God shall ever have matter of joy in God and of praising him: *but I will declare for ever*, saith the psalmist, *I will sing praises to the God of Jacob;* yea, sanctified affliction shall be a part of their joy and praising of God. 2. It delighteth the godly to be in the same covenant, and of the same faith, with those that are commended by God in the Scriptures: *I will sing praises*, saith he, *to the God of Jacob.* 3. As a sincere heart resolveth never to be weary in God's service, so may it be assured never to want matter of great joy; for, after he hath said, *I will declare for ever*, he then addeth, *I will sing praises to the God of Jacob.* 4. It is the magistrates' part, as they have authority in their supreme or subordinate places, to cut short the power of wicked men: *all the horns of the wicked also will I cut off*, saith David; which promise he did not cease to execute, by turning every man, indifferently, whom he did not judge to be regenerated, out of his place, and by taking course how every man whom he found in place, should be bound to apply his power for the good of religion and justice, as the history of the Scripture showeth; and by this means especially David reformed the church of Israel, and this was the way of his true policy, to cut off *all the horns of the wicked:* not to kill, or banish, or forfeit, or put from all place of power and trust, all those leading men who opposed and maligned him under king Saul; but by causing them all to concur with him to set up true religion, and bring up the ark to mount Zion, and to administer justice to the subjects in their several places. Thus, by binding all men to religion and justice, and ordaining that wickedness should have no horn or power for it, but all bound to be against it, *he cut off all the horns of the wicked.* And because the civil magistrate or ecclesiastical governors are able to do in their courts externally not so much as were needful, the real effecting of what here is undertaken by David belongeth to the antitype, Christ; for he only can say, and make his words good: *all the horns of the wicked will I cut off.* 5. The godly shall be victorious over all their wicked opposers, and righteousness shall bear them better out, and shall purchase more help and power

unto them, than any course the wicked take to have their
power established against them: *the horns of the righteous
shall be exalted.*

PSALM LXXVI.

To the chief musician on Neginoth.   A psalm or song of Asaph.

This psalm of praise was given forth upon occasion of some great deliverance of the church, such as that was when Sennacherib's host was destroyed, or some other like overthrow given to the enemy.
The sum of the psalm is this: The Lord is glorious in his church, and
greatly to be praised by his people, set down ver. 1, 2.   The reasons
given for this are six: the first, ver. 3; the second, ver. 4; the third,
ver. 5, 6; the fourth, ver. 7; the fifth, ver. 8, 9; the sixth, ver. 10;
the use whereof, with a reason for it, is set down ver. 11, 12.

From the inscription, learn, 1. The visible church hath
need to be stirred up to the work of thanksgiving unto, and
praising of God, no less than to any other duty; for this
duty is no less needful, no less spiritual, no less difficult and
disagreeable to our carnal and corrupt natural inclination
than any other duty; and usually is more neglected and more
slighted than any point of worship, although frequent occasion and cause be given unto it; therefore it is oftenest called
for of any.   If we compare this title with others, this is *a
song, a psalm,* taught to the church, to stir her up to the
praising of God.   2. God had more psalmists, more sweet
singers in Israel, than one; David's name is not prefixed
here, and the matter is more suitable to a later time than
his.   3. We are not to be curious about the penmen of
canonical Scripture.   The first author is he to whom we
must look most, and on whom we must rest; for, concerning all the Hebrew Bible, we are taught by Christ and his
apostles that it was all given by inspiration, and that the
holy writers spake as they were moved by the Holy Spirit;
for here it is not certain whether Asaph was the name of
the writer of it, or whether Asaph be the name of the order
of such of Aaron's posterity as were precentors to the church,
and had the charge of the music, to whom this psalm was
committed for the church's use, as many more psalms in
David's time, and after it also, were.   *A psalm or song of
Asaph,* or *to Asaph;* the words may bear both alike.

1. *In Judah* is *God known; his name* is *great in
Israel.*

2. *In Salem also is his tabernacle, and his dwelling-place in Zion.*

From the sum and scope of the psalm set down here, learn, 1. Albeit God be in some sort known in all the world, because of the works of creation, manifesting some way the invisible excellencies of God, yet is he most of all made manifest to his visible church, where his word soundeth, and his works are best interpreted: *in Judah God is known.* 2. Where the knowledge of God's name is most revealed, there should he of duty be most glorified; for albeit Israel many times did not understand, did not acknowledge him, but were more ignorant and neglective of him than the ox or ass were of their owner and master's crib, yet daily among them he manifested his great majesty, and sometimes he made them all acknowledge it, and of duty always they should have magnified his majesty, and so *his name is great in Israel.* 3. The Lord provideth always a place where his church may visibly profess his name and worship him : he will not want a place where he hath a people in covenant bond unto him : *in Salem is his tabernacle.* 4. It is a great glory to the place where God is worshipped, for there also he maketh his residence : *in Salem also, or Jerusalem, is his tabernacle, and his dwelling-place in Zion.* 5. It is not for the worthiness of any people or place, that the Lord is among them, or manifested there; but it is his own free choice, among whom, and where he will reside. The place where the vile Canaanite had been, and the place longest possessed and abused by the Canaanite, will he choose for his chief dwellings; he will turn the Canaanite's Salem to be Jerusalem: and the stronghold of the Jebusites to be the place of his temple; therefore, saith he, *in Salem* rather than *Jerusalem is his tabernacle, and his dwelling-place in Zion.*

3. *There brake he the arrows of the bow, the shield, and the sword, and the battle. Selah.*

The first reason of God's praise is taken from the Lord's fighting at Jerusalem against the enemies of the church, and discomfiting them. Whence learn, 1. The greatest overthrow given to armies will be found in their fighting against God's church : there in special manner *brake he the arrows of the bow, &c.* 2. In the deliverance of the church the Lord will be seen to do all the work : *there brake he the arrows.*   3. As there are no means or instruments fit to destroy men which the enemy will not make use of against the church : so there is no weapon formed against her which shall prosper when she relieth on her Lord : *there brake he the arrows of the bow, the shield, and the sword, and the battle.*

4. *Thou* art *more glorious* and *excellent than the mountains of prey.*

The second reason of God's praise is, because he is more glorious then all the kings and kingdoms of the world, wherein the cruel and beastly raging enemies of his church have their strength and strongholds. Whence learn, 1. Those kingdoms and powers which do not subject themselves to God or Christ the king of saints, are to be esteemed as mountains where wild and ravenous beasts lie, all of them according as they are more mighty, oppressing the weaker; for they are called here, mountains of prey, or powers maintaining all oppression, as mountains give shelter to ravenous beasts, which live upon prey.   2. Whatsoever excellency is to be found in the kingdoms of the world, wherein men glory, as wisdom, riches, strength, multitude, courage, or what else can be imagined, is all nothing to the matter of gloriation which the church hath in God : *thou,* saith the psalmist unto God, *art more glorious than the mountains of prey.*

5. *The stout-hearted are spoiled, they have slept their sleep ; and none of the men of might have found their hands.*

6. *At thy rebuke, O God of Jacob, both the chariot and horse are cast into a dead sleep.*

The third reason of God's praise is, because he evacuated, and made of no use unto the enemy, whatsoever they put their confidence in.   Whence learn, 1. Whatsoever strength, courage, wit, or any other point of perfection any man hath, God who gave it, can take it away when he pleaseth; yea, can make it a means of hardening his heart in carnal confidence, to engage him in a business for a mischief to him, that he may lose all whereunto he leaned : *the stout-hearted are spoiled, they have slept their sleep, and none of the men of might have found their hands ;* that is, God hath made the courageous and strong to be found feeble and weak, and unable to save their own goods or lives. 2. Albeit the church hath no strength in herself, yet the Lord can with a word of his mouth do all her work, and defeat her enemies : *at thy rebuke, O God of Jacob, they are cast into a dead sleep.* 3. The more powerful, wise, and stout the enemies of God's church be, the more should the church rely upon God, and the more glory doth the Lord get in overthrowing them : therefore *the stout-hearted men of might, chariots and horse* are here mentioned.

7. *Thou,* even *thou,* art *to be feared ; and who may stand in thy sight when once thou art angry?*

The fourth reason of God's praise is, because he is so terrible that none can stand before him when he is angry. Whence learn, 1. When the Lord smiteth the wicked, he warneth his own people to stand in awe; therefore the church maketh use of what is set down before : *thou, even thou art to be feared.* 2. Only God is to be feared lest we offend him, and no man's anger is to be feared in comparison of provoking God to anger : *thou, even thou art to be feared ;* and no regard is to be paid to, nor mention made of, any other to be feared in comparison of him. 3. Man against man may stand, and wicked men in the time of God's patience may stand : but when the time cometh of God's judging and letting forth his wrath upon his enemies, none can escape his hand: *who may stand in thy sight, when once thou art angry?* 4. The terror of the Lord against his foes, is the comfort of his people, and the matter as of his praise, so of their singing and rejoicing, as here is to be seen.

8. *Thou didst cause judgment to be heard from heaven ; the earth feared, and was still,*

9. *When God arose to judgment, to save all the meek of the earth. Selah.*

The fifth reason of God's praise is, from the experience of fearful judgments on God's enemies, when he was about to deliver his people from their oppression. Whence learn, 1. Late mercies and deliverances given to the church, should renew the thankful memory of old deliveries, as here is done. 2. When ordinary means and advertisements do not make the persecutors of the church cease, God hath extraordinary judgments from heaven, whereby he will speak unto his ad-

versaries : *thou didst cause judgments to be heard from
heaven.* 3. If by one sort of more mild advertisement or rebuke men cannot be brought into order, by another and
more terrible rebuke they shall be made quiet : *thou didst
cause judgment to be heard from heaven ; the earth feared
and was still.* 4. The property of the Lord's people is to
be so acquainted with afflictions, and so sensible of their own
sinfulness, that they do not impatiently fret at God's dispensation, even when they are oppressed by men; but study
submission unto God, and commit their cause to him : therefore are they called *the meek of the earth.* 5. When the
Lord's meek ones are in danger to be swallowed up and destroyed by their oppressors, the Lord, who is the sovereign
judge to decide controversies, and to determine who is in the
wrong, albeit he be silent for a while, yet will arise in due
time, and speak from heaven by judgments, to the terrifying and silencing of proud oppressors : *the earth feared and
was still, when God arose to judgment, to save all the meek
of the earth.* 6. When the Lord ariseth to save the meek in
one place and of one generation, it is an evidence and earnest that he shall arise to save at length all and every one of
the meek in every place, in all times after; because his arising for his people, which was now past, is said here to be
to save all the meek of the earth.

10. *Surely the wrath of man shall praise thee ; the
remainder of wrath shalt thou restrain.*

The sixth reason of God's praise is, that he shall make the
malice of the adversaries of his people contribute to his glory.
Whence learn, 1. Albeit the rage and cruelty of men against
the Lord's meek ones, may seem for the present to obscure
God's glory, and to tend to his dishonour; yet, when he hath
humbled, tried, purified his own, and done his work in mount
Zion, all the rage of persecutors shall turn to God's glory
undoubtedly: *surely the wrath of man shall praise thee.*
2. When God hath glorified himself in purging his saints and
punishing their persecutors, yet the enmity of the wicked
world against God's people will not cease; there will be still,
as here is presupposed, a remainder of wrath. 3. Let the
wrath of the wicked against the godly be ever so great, inveterate, lasting, and unquenchable, yet it shall vent itself
only as the Lord sees fitting : he shall moderate the outlet-

ting of it, as he seeth expedient for his people's good; it shall not break out to the destruction of the people : *the remainder of wrath shalt thou restrain.*

11. *Vow, and pay unto the Lord your God : let all that be round about him bring presents unto him that ought to be feared.*

12. *He shall cut off the spirit of princes :* he is *terrible to the kings of the earth.*

The use of the former doctrine is, to teach God's people to give unto God that respect and praise which are due to him from them, and to exhort all nations without the compass of the visible church to submit themselves unto him, lest he cut off fearfully the chiefest of them. Whence learn, 1. The use of the Lord's deliverances of his church, which the people of God should make, is to call on God in their troubles, engage themselves to glorify him in word and deed for his mercies, and to entertain the consciousness of their obligation : *vow and pay unto the Lord.* 2. It is not enough to discharge a promised duty to God in outward formality, as the Philistines made their offering to the ark of God, but the godly must do what service they do to God, as to their God, reconciled unto them, and in covenant with them : *vow and pay unto the Lord your God.* 3. The Lord is to be feared and honoured of all that are near to him in covenant or profession, yea or in vicinity of place unto his people and church, where the Lord manifested himself in his ordinances : *let all that be round about him, bring presents to him that ought to be feared.* 4. How terrible soever the power of princes and great men seem unto the Lord's people, when they engage themselves and their subjects against the church; yet, ere they bring forth the ripe grapes of their designs and plots against God's people, God can and will cut off their wisdom, courage, and life, as easily as the branches of a vine tree : *he shall cut off the spirit of princes.* 5. There is greater cause why princes should be afraid of God, than why God's people should be afraid of princes : princes cannot do so much to any one of God's people, as God can do to the highest princes on earth; God can make their fall great according to the height of their place; he can root them out and their posterity, not only from all places of power, but also from all being on the earth; he can make them a terror to themselves; he can destroy them, soul and body; yea, he useth to do this to his adversaries : *he is terrible to the kings of the earth.*

PSALM LXXVII.

To the chief musician, to Jeduthun. A psalm of Asaph.

This psalm expresseth the deep exercise of the psalmist, troubled with the sense of God's displeasure, and how he wrestled under this condition, and had deliverance from it, which is summarily propounded, v. 1, and made plain more particularly in the rest of the psalm. For, first, he setteth down his trouble of mind, v. 2—4; secondly, his wrestling with the sense of felt wrath, v. 5—9; thirdly, his begun victory by faith, v. 10—12; fourthly, the settling of his mind by consideration of God's manner of dealing with his church of old, to the end of the psalm.

1. *I cried unto God with my voice, even unto God with my voice ; and he gave ear unto me.*

In this summary proposition of the psalmist's sad exercise of spirit, and of his delivery out of that condition, learn, That as there are many troubles whereunto God's children are subject (whereof this is one of the most heavy, to be under the sense of the wrath of God, and fear of final cutting off) ; so God hath set down examples of this exercise in some of his dear children, for preparation of those who have not yet been acquainted with the like, and to teach patience and furnish consolation to those who are under such exercises; for here is one of the saints telling us, 1. That his own trouble in this kind was so pressing, as it made him cry. 2. Showing the course he took—*he cried to God,* and put the whole powers of soul and body to a bensal, in seeking God : *I cried to God with my voice.* 3. That he saw there was no remedy for this evil, save from God above, to whom he made his address with resolution to hold unto God only : *even unto God with my voice I cried.* 4. That at length he prevailed and received his request, graciously granted unto him : *and he gave ear to me;* and so he was relieved.

2. *In the day of my trouble I sought the Lord : my sore ran in the night, and ceased not : my soul refused to be comforted.*

3. *I remembered God, and was troubled : I complained, and my spirit was overwhelmed. Selah.*

4. *Thou holdest mine eyes waking : I am so troubled that I cannot speak.*

Asaph declareth this his sad exercise more specially; and, first, how great his trouble was. Whence learn, 1. The fearing and feeling the sense of God's wrath and displeasure, are of all troubles the chief; and challenge to themselves most deservedly the name of trouble, or straitening affliction, as if the psalmist had never known any trouble in comparison of them. 2. Albeit the sense of God's wrath and displeasure, while it lasteth, seemeth a sort of eternity, as, *shall I never be remembered?* and such like expressions declare; yet, when the trouble is gone, it is counted but a short time, but a day : *in the day of my trouble,* saith he, now being relieved. 3. As in this trouble most of God's face or comfortable presence is withdrawn; so nothing in this case can content a godly soul, till he find the Lord reconciled, and his gracious face shining again toward him : *in the day of my trouble I sought the Lord.* The wicked, in such a case, will, either not seek God at all, but some earthly comfort, or but take an essay what they can have by calling on God : they will not make it their work to seek him. 4. The sense of wrath giveth a sore wound unto a man's spirit, like to a wound in the body, which is like to bleed unto death : *my sore ran in the night.* 5. Trouble of conscience, as it is like a deadly wound; so is it also like a filthy boil, venting rotten issue : for many are the sins which the conscience casteth up in this case, which to look upon, causeth pain and loathing : *my sore,* or my plague, my stroke by thy hand, *ran in the night.* 6. There is no healing of this wound, no easing of this sore, no cleansing of the conscience, no quieting of a man's spirit, till God whom the soul seeketh, show himself physician; the evil continueth still and groweth : *my sore ran in the night, and ceased not.* 7. Where misery seemeth remediless, there the sad soul fitteth itself to endless sorrow : and as it is hopeless of relief, so it is heartless to seek comfort, yea what earthly comforts are offered for the relief of a spiritual wound, are but a burden to a broken spirit : *my soul refused to be comforted.* Nothing can satisfy a soul which is sensible of God's displeasure, save the sense of God's favour. 8. A troubled spirit hath many thoughts; for it runs out in meditation, calleth for the records of the memory, but can find nothing to fix upon, save God himself : *I remembered God.* 9. It is possible that the matter of

most comfort at some time may give no ease; the sweet
promises of grace, when a soul is not able to apply them,
yea, the thought of God himself and his goodness, may augment grief, when the conscience presenteth his abused favours as the cause of God's present felt wrath : *I remembered God and was troubled.*   10. Lamentation and complaints, when vented and not eased with following comfort,
but double the grief : *I complained, and my spirit was overwhelmed.*   11. Redoubled thoughts of a perplexed soul, cast
it over into confusion, and a sort of wound : *I complained,
and my spirit was overwhelmed.*   12. A wounded spirit is
able to bereave a man of the night's rest, and affect the
body with a share of its miserable condition : *thou holdest
mine eyes waking.*   13. When a soul could possibly desire
to ease its grief with a little forgetting of it, and seek a
sleep when the body is now weary; it may fall out, that
even thus much ease may be refused to a saint for a time,
which must be looked on as God's hand, for the further exercise of the Lord's sick child : *thou holdest mine eyes waking.*   14. Trouble not lenified nor mitigated, groweth to
such a height, that it stops the use of natural powers : *I am
so troubled, that I cannot speak.*   The sorrows of a soul
sensible of God's wrath, are unspeakable, neither can the
tongue utter them, nor the mind indite to the tongue what
it feeleth.

5. *I have considered the days of old, the years of
ancient times.*

6. *I call to remembrance my song in the night: I
commune with mine own heart ; and my spirit made
diligent search.*

7. *Will the Lord cast off for ever ? and will he be
favourable no more ?*

8. *Is his mercy clean gone for ever ? doth* his *promise fail for evermore ?*

9. *Hath God forgotten to be gracious? hath he in
anger shut up his tender mercies? Selah.*

In the second place, the psalmist setteth down his wrestling, and how, after he was overwhelmed, he fell again about
the using of all means to be relieved, considering the Lord's
work of old with others of his children, and his own exper-

ience, and what could be the cause of the change, v. 6, and how the Lord's unchangeableness in his loving-kindness towards his own, might help him, v. 7—9. Whence learn, 1. Were our cause ever so desperate, yet must we not give over, but gather strength after swounding, and use all means of relief, as the psalmist here doth. 2. To cast an eye upon the Lord's manner of dealing with his saints, mentioned in Scripture, as the psalmist did, who had the books of Moses and Job at least to make use of, is one chief means of comforting a troubled sinner, and of strengthening the faith of a weak wrestler: *I have considered the days of old, and the years of ancient times.* 3. To call to mind its own experiences of deliveries and consolations received after trouble, and its own observations made upon its own experiences, is also a good means for gathering strength and comfort for a soul under the sense of wrath: *I call to remembrance my song in the night.* 4. To search our ways, and to seek out diligently what cause in us we can find, which might procure such desertion and sense of wrath that we lie under, is a third holy means for deliverance from the straits of a troubled conscience; *I communed with my own heart, and my spirit made diligent search.* 5. Albeit it be possible, when all the former means are used, and diligent search is made by our conscience, what may be the reason of our hard exercise, that for all that we find no consolation, no ease, nor relief; yet the use of these means will witness for our wise and upright dealing, and be evidences of our endeavour and diligence in duties, as here we see the prophet making mention of his diligence for this end. 6. Albeit it be no strange thing for a wounded spirit to have suggestions cast in for the overthrow of faith, yea to have a sense of wrath speaking no less than what the temptation unto desperation allegeth; yet the nature of faith is such, that it cannot yield, but must fight against the temptation, as a thing which cannot be true, cannot be admitted, as this disputation of the psalmist giveth evidence: *will the Lord cast off for ever? and will he be favourable no more?* 7. The Lord may seem to cast a man off, and to stop the course of his wonted favour toward him, but this exercise is only for a time. It is not possible that God should cast off for ever the soul that cannot endure to be thrust from him: it is not possible that God should not be favourable to such as have had experience of his favour, and long to have new proofs thereof : *will the Lord cast off for ever? will he be favourable no more?* Which question, *will he do so and so,* is this much in effect, as if he had said, it is not possible that the Lord should do so, albeit it seem he will do so.   8. When the consciousness of sin maketh objection against faith, then faith makes its defence in God's mercy, and the constancy of the course of mercy, where grace is begun to run; yea faith will not yield to a contrary thought : *is his mercy clean gone for ever?*   9. The troubled conscience hungering after the sense of mercy, hath not only God's merciful nature and God's constancy in his good-will, but also his promises to lean to, for supporting itself.   Therefore after mention made of God's favour and mercy, he mentioneth here his promise also.   10. It is possible that for a time no promise may occur to a wounded spirit, which is fit for its present condition; at least no promise which it dare or is able to apply; yea it is possible that the conditional frame of the promises being made to such as are so and so qualified, may seem to pertain nothing to the troubled conscience, yet faith will not quit its interest in the promise, but will expect good according to the promise at last : *doth his promise fail for evermore?* 11. As it is the Lord's nature to be gracious to such as come to him in the sense of their unworthiness; so faith layeth hold on him as gracious, and will never admit a suggestion of any change in him, whatsoever seem to be in his dispensation : *hath God forgotten to be gracious?* this is to faith an absurdity and impossibility.   12. The compassions of God toward the miserable when they come before him are like a running fountain, that cannot restrain itself; yet may it seem to be shut up, and wrath and displeasure to run in the place thereof, when God is pleased to exercise his child with the sense of wrath against sin; but faith will not admit this seeming for a certainty : *hath he in anger shut up his tender mercies?*   This is a saying which a believer must abhor to give way unto, and yet may be assaulted with, and brangled, and weakened by the temptation of it.

10. *And I said, This* is *my infirmity :* but I will remember *the years of the right hand of the most* **High.**

11. *I will remember the works of the Lord: surely I will remember thy wonders of old.*

12. *I will meditate also of all thy work, and talk of thy doings.*

In the third place is set down the begun victory of faith, wherein the believer checketh himself for hearkening so much unto sense, for admitting the suggestions of misbelief into a disputation, and resolveth to make use of the grounds of faith and of his former comfortable experiences, v. 10, and of the wonderful dealing of God with others of his saints before, v. 11, and to settle his faith on God's word, confirmed by his works, and to set himself to give glory unto God, v. 12. Whence learn, 1. In the inward exercise of God's children, after a while's darkness cometh light; after grief, comfort; and after wrestling, cometh victory, as here we see. 2. The trouble and disquietness which arise from fear of utter rejection by God, are from the root of natural unbelief and inlack of the strength of faith : *this is my infirmity*, saith he, as being now assured that matters were not as they seemed to him, concerning God's merciful affection to him. 3. Weakness of faith, and fear of utter wrath, are sicknesses whereunto God's children are subject, but whereof they will certainly recover : sicknesses not unto death : *this is my infirmity*. 4. Our outgate from inward trouble, and our victory over it, begin at the right side of our own weakness, of our own faults, and of a right judging of ourselves for them : *and, I said this is my infirmity*. 5. The remembrance of the experiences of former changes which we have found wrought by God's great power, serveth to make us both patient under a sad condition, and hopeful to come out of it: *I will remember the years of the right hand of God.* 6. Albeit we do not see how our comfort, delivery, and outgate from trouble shall come, yet may we find solid ground to expect that it shall come, if we consider aright God's sovereignty over all creatures, that he is *most high*, and the omnipotency of his right hand, and his continuance, being the eternal, unchangeable one, and the same from year to year, from age to age : *I will remember the years of the right hand of the most High.* From this ground he expecteth that he shall yet have experience of the omnipotency of a sovereign and

constant God, working for his consolation.   7. When faith
beginneth to recover after its infirmity or sickness, it will
make use of memory, meditation, judgment, and speech,
which were all bound up before : *I will remember, meditate,
and talk.*   8. We must not think to come out of perplexity, out of sense of wrath, out of trouble of conscience, out
of hard exercises of faith by having great consolations, high
and ravishing joys of the Spirit at the first hand; but must
be content to come creeping out of trouble by little and little: for here the psalmist under the deepest sense of God's
displeasure, must use all ordinary means, and wrestle with
bitter temptations, till he come to such height as is expressed, v. 7—9, and, for an outgate, must begin and reprove
his own misbelief, dispute for the help of his faith, taking
argument from his experience of God's power and good-
will, and God's dealing with others before him.   9. The
works of God, when they are looked on cursorily, or lightly past by, cannot be discerned, but when they are well considered, they will be found wonderful : *I will remember the
works of the Lord, surely I will remember thy wonders of
old.*   10. It is good for a soul in a hard exercise, to raise
itself from thinking of God and of his works, speaking unto
God directly; no ease or relief will be found, till address be
made unto himself, till we turn our face toward him, and
direct our speech unto him, as here the psalmist doth, from
the midst of the eleventh verse to the end of the psalm.
11. Estimation of any of God's works, and good gotten by
meditation on some of his works, are able to engage the
heart to a deeper consideration of all his works : *I will meditate also of all thy works,* saith he.   12. He that would
have profit by God's works, must bridle the levity of his
own mind, which cannot stay fixed in the consideration, till
it be tied in meditation: *I will meditate of all thy works.*
13. When we have fed our own souls upon God's works,
we should study to make use of what we have learned
thereby, to the good of others and the glory of God : *I will
meditate of all thy works, and talk of all thy doings.*

   13. *Thy way, O God, is in the sanctuary ; who* is
so *great a God as* our *God?*

   14. *Thou* art *the God that doest wonders ; thou
hast declared thy strength among the people.*

In the last place, the psalmist confirmeth his faith, and settleth his mind, by consideration of the Lord's dealing with his people, recorded in holy Scripture, whereof he speaketh; first, in general, v. 13, 14, then more specially, of the bringing of his people out of Egypt through the wilderness, terribly discomfiting their enemies, and tenderly leading them, as his own flock, by weak and few instruments. Whence learn, 1. When the heart of a man is turned toward the Lord, then the veil of darkness, confusion, and misbelief is removed; he can justify the Lord in all that he doeth, as most holy and just; as here we see in the psalmist, who, since he began to direct himself toward God, can now say to him, *thy way, O God, is in the sanctuary.* 2. There is no understanding of God's dealing with us, nor can any right construction be made of his exercising us, except we come to the Lord's ordinances, where his word, his oracles of Scripture, expound his works perfectly: *thy way, O God, is in the sanctuary.* 3. When the works and ways of God are looked upon by the light of the word, in his sanctuary or church, and God is looked to through his works and word, then is a soul forced to admire his holiness, wisdom, justice, power, and goodness, above all comparison : *who is so great a God as our God?* 4. The trial of the believer's conscience with fears and suspicions of God's affection unto him, endeth in admiration and exaltation of God, in believing more firmly in him, in magnifying the grace of his being in covenant with him, in acknowledging his own blessedness and the blessedness of all other believers, for having him for their God : *who is so great a God as our God?* 5. So much in general may be seen of God's dealing with his people, as may quiet a man in his own particular case, who is troubled about God's dispensation toward him : for when Israel in Egypt was put to such straits, that they saw nothing but rooting of them out with cruelty and oppression, God wrought so well, so wisely, so powerfully, and so graciously for them, that all their hard exercise was turned to their great comfort, and God's greater glory. This, in general, is the use that the psalmist maketh of God's dealing with his people, and he findeth it applicable to his own condition: *thou art the God that doest wonders.* 6. When we cannot see how it is likely or possible that we can be extricated out of the difficulties we are cast into, especially in our spiritual condition, we are obliged to give unto God the glory of doing above all things we can conceive, for the good of those that desire to be his subjects: *thou art the God that doest wonders.*   7. What God hath convinced the world of already, concerning what he can do for his people, may satisfy every particular soul of his wisdom, power, and goodness toward itself, when it draweth toward him, as one of his people; for this use the psalmist maketh of God's doing for his people: *thou hast declared thy strength among thy people.*

15. *Thou hast with* thine *arm redeemed thy people, the sons of Jacob and Joseph.*   *Selah.*
16. *The waters saw thee, O God, the waters saw thee ; they were afraid : the depths also were troubled.*
17. *The clouds poured out water ; the skies sent out a sound : thine arrows also went abroad.*
18. *The voice of thy thunder* was *in the heaven : the lightnings lightened the world : the earth trembled and shook.*

The psalmist descendeth more specially to the consideration of the redemption of Israel out of Egypt, (which is a representation of the spiritual redemption of his people,) whom, at the time when they were in the deepest misery, and least able to help themselves, were most oppressed by the enemies, and, for their own disposition, were in a most sinful condition, and in a desperate mood against the means and instruments of their delivery ; God delivered : he removed all the difficulties which might hinder their outgate and escape from misery ; whence he might strongly reason for his own comfort, that God would not fail to deal graciously with his soul, who was seeking favour from God, and a renewed sense of reconciliation with him.   Hence learn, 1. That no soul can be under such sense of wrath and desolation, but he may draw comfort from the great work of the redemption of lost sinners : for, if, when we were enemies, we were reconciled to God by the death of his Son, much more being reconciled, we shall be saved from wrath by his life.   And this spiritual redemption was figured by the bodily delivery of Israel out of Egypt : *thou hast with thine arm redeemed thy people, the sons of Jacob and Joseph.*

2. It is by reason of the covenant that people receive deliverances, and consolations, and proofs of God's power working for them : therefore doth he style them sons of Jacob from their interest in God, and God's interest in them by covenant : *thou hast redeemed thy people.* 3. No obstacle, how great soever, can stand in the way of the delivery and comfort of God's people, but God can and will remove it; were it as the Red sea, so soon as he manifests himself, it will get out of the way as affrighted at his majesty : *the waters saw thee, O God, the waters saw thee; they were afraid : the depths also were troubled.* 4. The commotions which God hath made in heaven by rain, hailstone, thunder, fire, and lightning, when he would show himself for his people and against their enemies, testify sufficiently what God can and will do for his own children, who draw near unto him ; and how he will rebuke every adverse power which is against them : *the clouds poured out water, the skies sent out a sound ; thine arrows went abroad, the voice of thy thunder was in heaven ; the lightnings lightened the world, the earth trembled and shook.* Whether we refer these words to what God did in plaguing Egypt, before he brought out his people ; or after, when he showed his anger in pursuing the Egyptians in their flight, when they were seeking to escape out of the Red sea ; or to what the Lord did in fighting for his people against the Canaanites, they teach the same doctrine to us.

19. *Thy way is in the sea, and thy path in the great waters, and thy footsteps are not known.*

20. *Thou leddest thy people like a flock by the hand of Moses and Aaron.*

He closeth his meditation with two observations. One is, that the Lord's ways are past finding out, which he indicateth by *making a way through the Red sea,* where never one went before, and never one could follow after ; the other observation is, that God can save his people by how few and weak instruments he pleaseth. Whence learn, 1. The Lord draweth deep in the working out the delivery and salvation of his own people, bringing them first unto extremity of danger, and then making a plain and clear escape from all their straits : *thy way is in the sea,* where no man can wade, except God be before him, and where any man may

walk, if God take him by the hand, and lead him through.
2. What God is in working, when he engages his children
in dangers, and which way he is going when he leads them
into overflowing troubles and deep waters, they cannot understand, till he hath done his work : *thy path is in the great
waters.* 3. A particular reason of every thing that God
doeth, can no man find out : for the which cause the Lord
craveth submission of all his children in their exercises, as
he did of Job: *thy footsteps are not known.* 4. Whether
men see the reasons of God's dealing with them or not, the
Lord hath a care of his weak and witless people, as a shepherd hath of his flock, and is a gracious leader of his people
that follow him : *thou leadest thy people like a flock.* 5. The
Lord hath his means and instruments, of whose ministry he
maketh use : and those, albeit they be few and weak, yet
shall he do his greatest works by them, according as he doth
employ them : *thou leddest thy people as a flock, by the
hand of Moses and Aaron.*

END OF FIRST VOLUME.

OTHER FINE VOLUMES AVAILABLE

1979 - 80

0201	Murphy, James G.	COMMENTARY ON THE BOOK OF EXODUS	11.50
1901	Dickson, David	A COMMENTARY ON THE PSALMS (2 vol.)	26.50
2301	Kelly, William	AN EXPOSITION OF THE BOOK OF ISAIAH	11.95
2601	Fairbairn, Patrick	AN EXPOSITION OF EZEKIEL	14.95
3801	Wright, Charles H.H.	ZECHARIAH AND HIS PROPHECIES	19.95
4101	Alexander, Joseph	COMMENTARY ON THE GOSPEL OF MARK	13.95
4401	Alexander, Joseph	COMMENTARY ON THE ACTS OF THE APOSTLES (2 Vol.)	24.95
4402	Gloag, Paton J.	A CRITICAL AND EXEGETICAL COMMENTARY ON THE ACTS OF THE APOSTLES	24.95
4602	Edwards, Thomas C.	A COMMENTARY ON THE FIRST EPISTLE TO THE CORINTHIANS	14.75
5601	Taylor, Thomas	AN EXPOSITION OF TITUS	15.95
5802	Bruce, Alexander B.	THE EPISTLE TO THE HEBREWS	13.75
7002	Alford, Dean Henry	THE BOOK OF GENESIS AND PART OF THE BOOK OF EXODUS	10.25
7003	Marbury, Edward	OBADIAH AND HABAKKUK	19.50
7103	Hort, F.J.A.	EXPOSITORY AND EXEGETICAL STUDIES	18.95
7104	Milligan, George	ST. PAUL'S EPISTLES TO THE THESSALONIANS	9.50
8601	Shedd, W.G.T.	DOGMATIC THEOLOGY (4 Vol.)	44.95
8703	Kurtz, John Henry	SACRIFICIAL WORSHIP OF THE OLD TESTAMENT	13.75
8901	Fawcett, John	CHRIST PRECIOUS TO THOSE THAT BELIEVE	8.50
9401	Neal, Daniel	HISTORY OF THE PURITANS (3 Vol.)	49.95
9802	Pink, Arthur W.	THE ANTICHRIST	9.50
9803	Shedd, W.G.T.	THE DOCTRINE OF ENDLESS PUNISHMENT	7.50

TITLES CURRENTLY AVAILABLE

0101	Delitzsch, Franz	A NEW COMMENTARY ON GENESIS (2 Vol.)	24.25
0301	Kellogg, Samuel H.	THE BOOK OF LEVITICUS	17.25
0601	Blaikie, William G.	THE BOOK OF JOSHUA	12.75
0901	Blaikie, William G.	THE FIRST BOOK OF SAMUEL	12.25
1001	Blaikie, William G.	THE SECOND BOOK OF SAMUEL	12.25
1801	Gibson, Edgar	THE BOOK OF JOB	8.75
1802	Green, William H.	THE ARGUMENT OF THE BOOK OF JOB UNFOLDED	9.75
2401	Orelli, Hans C. von	THE PROPHECIES OF JEREMIAH	12.25
2701	Pusey, Edward B.	DANIEL THE PROPHET	18.25
4301	Brown, John	THE INTERCESSORY PRAYER OF OUR LORD JESUS CHRIST	9.50
4501	Shedd, W.G.T.	CRITICAL AND DOCTRINAL COMMENTARY ON ROMANS	14.25
4601	Brown, John	THE RESURRECTION OF LIFE	11.95
4801	Ramsay, William	HISTORICAL COMMENTARY ON THE EPISTLE TO THE GALATIANS	14.25
4901	Westcott, Brooke F.	ST. PAUL'S EPISTLE TO THE EPHESIANS	8.75
5001	Johnstone, Robert	LECTURES ON THE BOOK OF PHILIPPIANS	14.95
5401	Liddon, Henry P.	THE FIRST EPISTLE TO TIMOTHY	5.50
5801	Delitzsch, Franz	COMMENTARY ON THE EPISTLE TO THE HEBREWS (2 Vol.)	27.50
5901	Johnstone, Robert	LECTURES ON THE EPISTLE OF JAMES	12.75
5902	Mayor, Joseph B.	THE EPISTLE OF ST. JAMES	17.50
6501	Manton, Thomas	AN EXPOSITION OF THE EPISTLE OF JUDE	10.95
6601	Trench, Richard C.	COMMENTARY ON THE EPSITLES TO THE SEVEN CHURCHES	7.75
7001	Orelli, Hans C. von	THE TWELVE MINOR PROPHETS	12.25
7101	Mayor, Joseph B.	THE EPISTLE OF ST. JUDE & THE SECOND EPISTLE OF PETER	13.75
7102	Lillie, John	LECTURES ON THE FIRST AND SECOND EPISTLES OF PETER	16.50
8001	Fairweather, William	BACKGROUND OF THE GOSPELS	13.75
8002	Fairweather, William	BACKGROUND OF THE EPISTLES	12.75
8003	Zahn, Theodor	INTRODUCTION TO THE NEW TESTAMENT (3 Vol.)	43.95
8004	Bernard, Thomas	THE PROGRESS OF DOCTRINE IN THE NEW TESTAMENT	8.25
8701	Shedd, W.G.T.	HISTORY OF CHRISTIAN DOCTRINE (2 Vol.)	27.50
8702	Oehler, Gustave	THEOLOGY OF THE OLD TESTAMENT	18.25
9501	Shilder, Klass	THE TRILOGY (3 Vol.)	13.95
9801	Liddon, Henry P.	THE DIVINITY OF OUR LORD	18.50